Organizational Performance and Results

Satisfying Customer
Needs
in
Industry, Government,
and
Other Types of Organizations

MANAGEMENT

MANAGEMENT

ROBERT L. TREWATHA

Head, Department of Management
and Marketing
Southwest Missouri State University

M. GENE NEWPORT

Dean, School of Business
The University of Alabama
in Birmingham

1982 Third Edition

BUSINESS PUBLICATIONS, INC. Plano, Texas 75075

This book was previously published under the title of
Management: Functions and Behavior.

ISBN 0-256-02713-7

Library of Congress Catalog Card No. 81–68090

Printed in the United States of America

1 2 3 4 5 6 7 8 9 0 K 9 8 7 6 5 4 3 2

PREFACE

The first two editions of this book, which were entitled *Management: Functions and Behavior,* attempted to create an awareness of the fact that *any* organization's ability to succeed in an environment of change rests with its management. In this respect, we showed that decisions in most successfully managed organizations depend upon environmental conditions and managerial judgment relating to a particular situation. Accordingly, a contingency view of management theory and practice remains as a significant feature of this edition.

Based on favorable responses from persons adopting earlier editions of the book, this revision also retains the approach which integrates the functions of management with behavioral concepts and appropriate quantitative methods. In particular, operations management techniques and quantitative tools are discussed as they relate to decision making, planning, and controlling. The focus of these discussions, however, remains on the particular management function or process under consideration, and the quantitative materials are presented in a descriptive manner to emphasize substance in addition to technique. For those who wish to pursue these materials in more depth, a detailed coverage of various operations management models and quantitative techniques is included in Appendixes B and C at the end of the book.

Revisions throughout this edition are numerous. A statement of purpose precedes the learning objectives set forth at the beginning of each chapter and serves to introduce chapter materials in a brief and concise manner. Key terms have been added at the end of all chapters to provide a review of major concepts presented in each chapter. New and revised review questions and problems have been added throughout the book, and some 20 percent of the case materials are new. Of major importance, a Student Study Guide has been developed to accompany this edition. By integrating text and study guide materials, a reinforcement of major concepts is assured on a chapter-by-chapter basis.

Although discussed throughout the text, the decision-making chapter now comes at the beginning of Part II, "Planning for Performance and Results," to emphasize the importance of the decision-making process in the planning function and in strategic management. Materials related to strategy planning have also been expanded, and updated examples are used to stress the important relationships between organizational strategies, objectives, and policies.

In Part III, characteristics of formal organizations and organizational design are preceded by a discussion of the nature of organizations and their objectives. Later, in Part IV, the characteristics of informal organizations are detailed prior to examining the behavioral dimensions of management through discussions of communication, individual behavior, interpersonal relations, motivation, and leadership. To provide better continuity in discussing the management functions, Part V, on Control, is placed after the chapters on organizational actuation. The result reflects a completion of a cycle of planning, organizing, actuating, and controlling.

Part VI concludes the book by reiterating the need for perception and adaptability in managing organizational growth and change. And, since most organizations now function within an international environment, the unique problems and challenges of managing transnational operations are cited as further evidence of the need for a contingency-based practice of management, both now and in the future.

Finally, many people have contributed advice, support, and time to the preparation of this edition. Our wives, Carolyn and Sandy, and our children deserve special recognition for their continued encouragement and support of our efforts. Thomas K. Hearn, Jr., Vice President, University College, The University of Alabama in Birmingham, and Ralph W. Williams, Dean of the School of Business, Southwest Missouri State University, also deserve thanks, as do various professors who have made invaluable suggestions for change since this book was first published in 1976. Among them, we wish to note the contributions of John Mee, Indiana University; Bruce McSparrin, Memphis State University; David Van Fleet, Texas A & M University; Thomas Carey, Western Michigan University; and La Rue Hubbard, Glendale Community College.

The formidable task of typing revisions and reviewing final manuscript copy was shared by Carolyn Trewatha, Lois Ayres, Becky Roy, and Linda Wilson. We thank them for their patience and professional skills which brought order out of chaos.

Robert L. Trewatha
M. Gene Newport

CONTENTS

The study of management. The management process. Importance of the management functions. Early applications of management. Foundations of modern management thought: *Management competence versus technical competence. Scientific nature of management. Universality of management.* Approaches to the study of management. The art and science of management.

The changing U.S. environment. Management's changing role and scope. Challenges of the future: *Social responsibility and ethics. Energy crisis. Underutilization of human resources. Technology. Productivity. Computers. Management science. Multinational corporations. Government regulation.*

CASES FOR PART ONE

Meaning of decision making. Importance of management decision making. Objectives and decision making. The decision-making process: *Determining the problem. Identifying alternative solutions. Analyzing alternatives. Selecting an alternative for implementation.* Minimizing the complexity of the decision process. Environmental constraints. Behavioral considerations. Measurement and quantification of alternatives. Scientific approach to decision making. The application of systems and science to decision making. Use of models in the decisional process: *Deterministic versus probabilistic models. Elements of model use.*

Planning—the fundamental function: *Planning and objectives. Role of the future in planning. Relationship of planning to decision making. Elements of planning.* Planning at all levels of management. Separating planning and doing: *A problem in providing coordination. Behavioral considerations.* Forecasting and planning. Balancing quantitative approaches and judgment. Time series analysis.

Gantt charts: *Description of Gantt charts. Advantages of using Gantt charts. The growth of network models.* Program evaluation and review technique: *Application of PERT network. Initial steps in setting up a PERT time network. Planning value of PERT. Advantages of PERT systems.* Budgets: *Role of budgets. Overcoming budget failures. Zero-base budgeting. Behavioral considerations in budgeting.*

The rising importance of strategy planning. Advantages of strategy planning. Managing strategy planning. Strategy planning as a process. Specific steps in strategy planning. Effectively performing the steps in strategic planning. National Cash Register's new strategy: *Product substrategy. Manufacturing substrategy. Marketing substrategy.* Environmental considerations for strategy planning: *General economic assumptions. Industry assumptions. Individual company assumptions. Sociological assumptions. Public attitude assumptions. Technological assumptions. Political assumptions. Assumptions concerning foreign competition and labor unions.*

Evolutionary role of facilitators. Policies aid in achieving objectives: *Role and importance of policy. Broad policies versus narrow rules. Managerial problems with policies. Exceptions to policies. Determining exceptional situations. Policy areas.* Procedures: *The scope of procedures. Application of procedures. Generalizations about good procedures.* Methods: *Standard methods. Studying standard work methods. Motion study. Work simplification. Work measurement. Impact of time standards on incentive wages.* Management standards: *Types of standards—ideal, engineered, and managerial. Quantitative and qualitative standards. Standardization.*

CASES FOR PART TWO

X

and Schmidt. Ohio State leadership studies. Managerial Grid—Blake and Mouton. The 3-D theory—Reddin. Comparison of the various leader behavior models. Situational models in predicting leadership effectiveness: *Path-Goal Theory of leadership. Fiedler Contingency Model of leadership. The Vroom-Yetton Decision Model.*

An overview of control. The need for control. The scope of control: *Precontrols. Concurrent controls. Postcontrols.* Steps and problems in the control process: *Standards as the basis for control. Measuring actual performance. Comparing actual performance to standards. Evaluating differences between actual performance and standards. Taking corrective action.* Cost justification and control. Additional control considerations.

Marketing controls: *Sales control. Marketing cost controls.* Production control: *Production scheduling. Job order control. Quality control.* Inventory control: *Types of inventory costs. Economic order quantity.* Overall cost controls: *Break-even analysis. Variable budgeting.* Overall financial controls: *Comparative statements. Financial ratio analysis. Du Pont system of return on investment.* Controlling human resources.

Management philosophies and the controlling function. Problems resulting from an overreliance on controls: *Higher costs due to lower output and quality. Defensive behavior. Ineffective achievement of goals. Unreliable performance information. Low motivation and personal dissatisfaction.* Reasons why dysfunctional consequences occur: *Direct hierarchical pressure. Negative feedback. Decline in trust and confidence in management. Overreliance on quantitative measures of performance.* Guidelines for avoiding dysfunctional controls: *Focus on the future. Strive for flexibility. Avoid obsolescence. Gain employee commitment. Seek rapid feedback. Recognize the human element.*

PART
ONE

MANAGEMENT
PERSPECTIVES
AND PRACTICES

1

MANAGEMENT
FUNDAMENTALS

PURPOSE

Writing to congratulate the Society for the Advancement of Management on its golden anniversary in 1963, President John F. Kennedy stated: "Much of the Free World's success in using its human resources fully and with dignity can be laid to enlightened and progressive management. . . . It is to managers who grow with the needs and resources of their time that we must continue to look for the new ideas and their implementation to meet the challenges of the future."

Today, we see or hear the word *management* almost daily. Some of our friends are managers, and we read of well-run and poorly managed organizations. When one stops to think about management, however, various questions come to mind. What is management? Why is it so important today? Has it always been important? Is there a body of knowledge about management? If so, can the practice of management be improved through a study of such knowledge?

Questions such as these cannot be answered in a single chapter. As an introduction, therefore, this chapter surveys only those fundamental issues that will provide a foundation for an in-depth study of the management concepts and theories presented in all other chapters.

OBJECTIVES

1. To portray management as a dynamic process that is essential in coordinating the human and material resources of all organizations.

2. To introduce and discuss the importance of planning, organizing, actuating, and controlling as the functions of management.

3. To outline various concepts and issues that are found in current management thought.

4. To present approaches that have been followed in the study and practice of management.

5. To show that the art of management cannot be separated from the science of management.

The goals of organizations are reached through the use of human and material resources. These resources, however, are incomplete without the presence of management. Within any organization, management is the essential element in performing work efficiently and effectively. *Organizations, being social and technical systems of consciously coordinated activities of two or more persons,* must be managed if they are to reach objectives for any extended period of time.[1]

Although management is not always apparent to the casual observer, it is a central activity in all organizations throughout our society. Henri Fayol, one of the early scholars and writers in management, suggested that the nervous system in animals bears a close comparison to the managerial activities in a social organization.[2] Thus, management branches into all phases of an organization and is essential in achieving a coordination of effort whenever people join together to seek a common goal.

THE STUDY OF MANAGEMENT

Management is practiced in businesses, hospitals, universities, churches, and governmental agencies as well as in all other types of organized activities. While the practice of management is as old as civilization, systematic study of the field is fairly young. In fact, only a limited formal study of management took place until larger and more complex business organizations appeared at the turn of the present century. Despite this 20th century interest, however, management has been an important element through the ages in the growth and progress of all societies.

Although scholars and practicing managers have now produced an impressive body of knowledge, a comprehensive understanding of management is still limited. Yet, through a continuous refinement of managerial theories, techniques, and practices that have proven useful in a variety of organizations, a broader understanding of management is being developed. By studying this growing body of knowledge, one can better understand how management contributes to the general welfare of our society. At the same time, a systematic study of the field helps us to recognize the essential management skills needed in all organizations. Finally, a concerted effort in studying, understanding, and applying management theories is required if we are to deal effectively with the increasingly complex societal problems of today and tomorrow. Managers of the future cannot merely adapt to environ-

---

[1] Chester I. Barnard, *The Functions of the Executive* (Cambridge, Mass.: Harvard University Press, 1938), p. 73.

[2] Henri Fayol, *General and Industrial Management* (London: Sir Isaac Pitman and Sons, 1949), p. 59.

mental changes but must be able to shape the environment so that it will sustain the internal momentum of their organizations.[3]

THE MANAGEMENT PROCESS

Various definitions of management exist, most of which point out the nature and importance of the management process. Similarly, this book defines management as the *process of planning, organizing, actuating, and controlling an organization's operations in order to achieve a coordination of the human and material resources essential in the effective and efficient attainment of objectives.*[4] The activities in this process (planning, organizing, actuating, and controlling) are called the *functions of management.* These functions must be performed by all persons in managerial positions, whether administrators, directors, generals, department heads, or first-line supervisors. In addition, it should be recognized that the management process is best described by these functions, rather than by the status or rank held by certain managers in an organization. Management is neither the privilege nor the responsibility of only a few members of an organization—it is the work of all individuals whose jobs are involved with reaching objectives through the coordination of available resources.

Applications of the management functions must be considered within the confines of a given organizational setting. The functions are clearly not part of a fixed mechanical process that produces equal degrees of success for all managers. Since we live in a world where change is constant, managers must deal with all kinds of uncertainties as they seek to accomplish organizational goals. As a result, planning, organizing, actuating, and controlling must be blended and appropriately applied as they relate to the situation. Therefore, managers must be knowledgeable of the management process and situationally informed if they expect to be successful in meeting the challenges found in their respective organizations.

IMPORTANCE OF THE MANAGEMENT FUNCTIONS

Certain inputs are required before any organization can create desired outputs. Figure 1–1 illustrates the role of the management process in acquiring and utilizing these inputs to produce various goods or services. When a new organization is being developed, the perfor-

---

[3] See *The Changing Expectations of Society in the Next Thirty Years* (St. Louis: American Assembly of Collegiate Schools of Business and the European Foundation for Management Development, 1979).

[4] There are various listings of the management functions, but most differ only in name, rather than in meaning. For example, see John B. Miner, *The Management Process: Theory, Research, and Practice* (New York: Macmillan, 1978), pp. 51–57. While use of the terms *direction* or *leadership* is more common than *actuating*, we prefer the comprehensive meaning of the latter as defined in George R. Terry, *Principles of Management* (Homewood, Ill.: Richard D. Irwin, 1977).

FIGURE 1–1
The management process and organizational effort

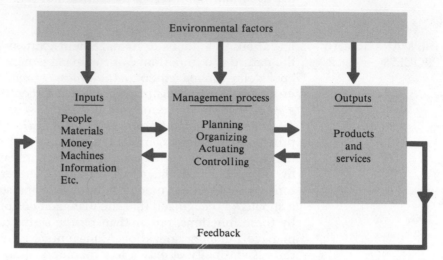

mance of the management functions might follow the order of planning, organizing, actuating, and controlling. Within established organizations, however, it may be difficult to determine which of these functions a manager is performing at any given time since the functions do not have to be performed in any specific order and may, at times, be combined.

The actual impact of the management process on an organization is influenced by numerous factors, including (1) the quantity and quality of inputs; (2) the knowledge, experience, and authority of managers; (3) the stage of development of the organization; and (4) environmental factors, such as governmental regulations, economic conditions, actions of competitors, and the desires of consumers. Keep in mind, also, that consumers may be students, patients, clients, or any other group that an organization seeks to attract and serve.

Although specific definitions of the management functions vary, their basic characteristics include the following:

Planning results in the selection of courses of action (plans) that will direct an organization's human and material resources for future time spans. Plans establish the boundaries within which people make decisions and carry out assigned activities. As such, plans must anticipate future events, problems, and causal relationships. In this sense, planning refers to deciding what to do and how to do it before action is taken. Because of the great uncertainties in most organizational situations, managers must also provide for contingencies by developing a series of alternative plans in guiding actions. Thus, as a formal process, planning implies a rational approach that looks into the future, develops alternative courses of action, examines the possible results of each alternative, and selects the best course of action (plan).

Organizing combines various human and material resources into a meaningful whole. This is accomplished by dividing the work to be done into specialities, grouping similar activities (departmentalizing), identifying desired authority relationships between individuals and groups, delegating authority, and considering the social and economic consequences associated with various organizational forms. By combining people, work to be done, and physical factors into a meaningful structure, goals can be achieved more effectively. In addition to these formally established relationships, various informal groups are created by employees. The informal relationships that result influence behavior within an organization as much as formally established positions of authority.

Actuating includes motivation, leadership, communication, training, and other forms of personal influence. This function is also discussed as initiating and directing the work to be done in an organization. Accordingly, actuating must be closely interrelated with the other functions of planning, organizing, and controlling if organizational goals are to be met in a desired manner.

Controlling involves checking and comparing performance to established standards. If performance deviates from standards, corrective action is required to get things back on path. Such action might take the form of repairing faulty equipment, changing the behavior of employees, reorganizing a department, or revising an original plan.

Through the performance of these functions, managers seek to achieve a coordination of effort throughout the organization. Although coordination is not considered as one of the management functions, it results from planning, organizing, actuating, and controlling. Through planning, for example, managers outline courses of action that assist in coordinating the efforts of organizational members. The organizing function identifies duties and authority relationships as another step toward coordinating individual efforts. Actuating involves the initiation and guidance of those actions as spelled out in policies, plans, systems, procedures, and rules. Finally, managerial control seeks to prevent performance that detracts from an overall coordination of effort.

The content of the management process discussed above is summarized in Figure 1–2. When examining the figure, remember that a successful performance of the management functions requires adaptation to specific situational factors. Thus, having to be contingency oriented to achieve results successfully, managers must analyze objectives, resources, structure, and environmental influences in determining the particular combination of functions to be performed in a given organizational situation.

FIGURE 1–2
The content of management

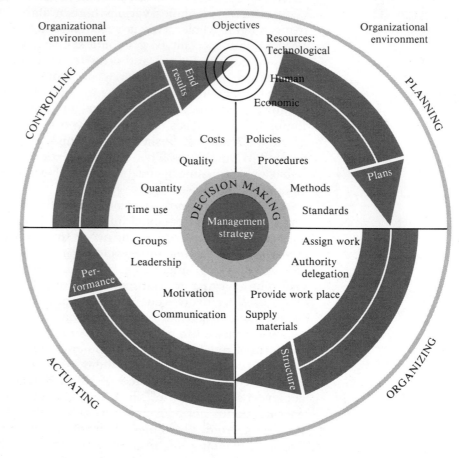

EARLY APPLICATIONS OF MANAGEMENT

Applications of management go back as far as early primitive tribes. For example, anthropologists relate that the concept of authority was very apparent in many early societies and that survival depended to a great extent upon established authority structures. In later civilizations, management planning, organizing, and control became more evident, particularly in the construction of pyramids in ancient Egypt.[5]

One of the earliest and most interesting applications of management is seen in the Biblical story of Moses and the exodus of the Israelites from Egypt.[6] In this story, Jethro—Moses' father-in-law—advised him that he should choose able men as rulers over thousands, hundreds, fifties, and tens since he (Moses) did not have the time and strength

---

[5] Daniel A. Wren, *The Evolution of Management Thought* (New York: John Wiley & Sons, 1979), chap. 2; and James D. Mooney and Alan C. Reiley, *Onward Industry* (New York: Harper & Row, 1931).

[6] Exod. 18:13–26.

to judge all of the people personally. Here, an important management concept is shown in Moses' acceptance of the staff advice and counsel given by Jethro. Also, the organizing ability of Moses is illustrated through his delegation of authority to others in order to create a hierarchy of authority. The statement that every great matter should be brought to Moses, but every small matter should be judged by the people themselves, is an example of management by exception. In addition, the selection of "able men out of all Israel" illustrates the importance of the actuating function.

In early Greece, management concepts were recognized by Plato, particularly the importance of a specialization of labor as a means for increasing productivity. Socrates noted that a good manager in one organization could, in the right situation, be equally successful in another. Furthermore, descriptions of the ancient Greek city-states indicate that the functions of government were highly organized and managed.[7]

Other applications of management can be seen in the early Greek and Roman military organizations. From Alexander the Great to Caesar, the functions of planning, organizing, actuating, and controlling were extremely important in winning battles and wars. In advance of a battle, for example, Caesar used the intelligent and loyal commanders of his legions for assistance in planning and then delegated authority to these commanders to provide a coordinated and effective fighting force.[8] The vast domains of Rome were held together by an elaborate set of roads and by a hierarchical (scalar) structure of authority. Rulers of the empire's territories, dioceses, and divisions were delegated appropriate authority to make decisions applicable to each unit.[9] Thus, coordination achieved by planning, organizing, and actuating was largely responsible for Rome's success in ruling vast domains.

Not unlike the Roman Empire, the early Roman Catholic Church was also faced with organizing a large group of people spread over a wide geographical area. The organizational efforts of the early church, however, were quite different. Through the pope, the church retained a great deal of authority by developing only a few administrative levels. In turn, a fairly large number of people reported to superiors at each level. Particularly important in this respect was the extensive use of staff personnel who advised the pope.

Many of today's managerial concepts can also be found in an interesting historical description of the building of Venetian ships during the Renaissance period of the 15th and 16th centuries.[10] The Arsenal of

---

[7] James D. Mooney, *The Principles of Organization* (New York: Harper & Row, 1947), pp. 57–64.

[8] John Warrington, *Caesar's War Commentaries* (New York: E. P. Dutton, 1958).

[9] Mooney, *Principles of Organization*, pp. 62–72.

[10] Frederick C. Lane, *Venetian Ships and Shipbuilders of the Renaissance* (Baltimore: Johns Hopkins Press, 1934).

Venice, a government facility that produced military ships on an assembly-line basis, practiced advanced management techniques in warehousing; personnel management; standardization; and control over inventory, costs, and other financial matters.

The use of carpenters, oarmakers, fasteners of timbers and planks, mastmakers, and caulkers emphasized the importance of a division of labor. The building of ships was divided into three stages: (1) framing by the carpenters, (2) fastening the plankings and building the cabins and superstructures by carpenters and caulkers, and (3) the final assembly.

All equipment and parts such as rudders, gun carriages, rigging, oars, and arms were manufactured in separate craft shops under the watchful eyes of supervisors who directed the technical work, provided needed materials and supplies, and inspected completed work. The production of these items was arranged along a canal so that a ship could be launched and then fitted with all of its equipment and arms in the final assembly process. For this purpose, the ship was towed along a canal and the equipment and arms were placed on the craft through the windows of warehouses along the canal. These achievements were also possible because the Lords of the Arsenal performed the management functions as a full-time activity, while technical experts and skilled craftsmen carried out the various steps of the assembly process. As a result, the Arsenal was highly efficient in producing the ships that made Venice a mighty naval power.

FOUNDATIONS OF MODERN MANAGEMENT THOUGHT

Henri Fayol developed one of the earliest comprehensive theories of general management.[11] As managing director of the Commentary-Fourchambault Mining Company in France from 1888 to 1918, Fayol moved the company from a declining business to one of France's greatest combines. This success was largely due to Fayol's development and application of various management concepts. Many of his writings are still relevant and have contributed greatly to modern management thought. In recognition of his work, Fayol is often called the father of the management process point of view. His major book, however, was not translated from French into English until 1925 and received little attention in the United States until 1949. Thus, applications of his earlier work were delayed for more than 20 years, thereby slowing the advancement of management thought in the United States.

Since several of Fayol's ideas assist in explaining the nature and content of management, they deserve added consideration. Three of these concepts concern (1) management competence versus technical competence, (2) the scientific nature of management, and (3) the uni-

---

[11] Fayol's concepts were first published in France in 1916 in *Administration Industrielle et Generale*. See Fayol, *General and Industrial Management*.

versality of management. These and other issues are discussed in the following sections.

Management competence vers technical competence

Fayol suggested that managerial competence should be distinguished from the technical competencies found in engineering, production, marketing, and finance. Without question, managers cannot completely remove themselves from the performance of certain specialized types of work, such as production or sales. Likewise, the director of nursing in a hospital may work closely with floor nurses. A major difference between managers and nonmanagers stems from the fact that managers plan, organize, actuate, and exercise control over the various technical operations of an organization. Thus, managers must have a working knowledge of certain technical operations, even though they are not directly responsible for performing such duties themselves.

To expand, we see that top-management positions do not normally include the narrow technical responsibilities found in middle- or lower-level management jobs. This is especially true in large organizations where decision making at higher management levels is less likely to focus on a single technical operation. Increasingly, however, managerial advancement will require an ability to deal with a variety of technical and social functions of organizations not as compartmentalized, but as interrelated, portions of the total management process.[12] Efforts to achieve this coordination of specialities in organizations operating within complex and changing environments may lead to renewed interest in the "Office of the President" where two or more top-level executives operate as a management team to develop and to implement policies at the presidential level.[13]

Scientific nature of management

To advance the development of a general theory, Fayol suggested that management should be studied from a scientific approach. In this sense, scientific inquiry would follow the guidelines identified by René Descartes in his *Discourse on Method* (1637) and would be used to determine:

What exists in the real world, as shown by observation and experience.

Why a given phenomenon behaves as it does.

How to classify data related to a real world phenomenon.

Through scientific inquiry, a body of knowledge can be developed that helps explain relationships among various factors in given situations. Thus, the goal of scientific inquiry is to provide an understanding

---

[12] *Changing Expectations of Society,* p. 35.

[13] As an example, see "A Management Leapfrog at DuPont," *Business Week,* December 15, 1973, pp. 47–51.

of certain events in nature so as to better predict their possible impact on future courses of action.

With some changes, the steps of the scientific method have been employed in managerial problem solving and are generally expressed in the following manner:

1. Define, outline, and state the problem that is to be solved.
2. Review the literature on the problem area and discuss it with informed persons so as to investigate thoroughly all facts that have a bearing on the problem.
3. Develop a statement of hypothesis or a tentative solution to the problem.
4. Collect, organize, and classify all relevant data.
5. Analyze the data as related to the problem and hypothesis.
6. Set forth the findings, conclusions, and recommendations that flow from the analysis of data.
7. Implement recommendations and evaluate results to determine the success of the solution.

Because of the human element in organizations, management practitioners and scholars have found it difficult to apply the steps of the scientific method as precisely as researchers in the physical and life sciences. It is hoped, however, that this difficulty will not retard the use of a scientific approach to the study and practice of management. As stated by Koontz, O'Donnell, and Weihrich, "A scientific approach to management cannot wait until an exact science of management is developed."[14] These and other scholars note that a considerable body of management knowledge has been derived from experience and observation. It would be unfortunate, therefore, to curtail the advancement and refinement of management theory by waiting until the guidelines included in this body of knowledge could be validated scientifically.

The evolving applications of science in management Since history points out many important managerial contributions through the ages, it is strange that serious efforts to study management were so long in coming. For example, major scientific discoveries were made in the life and physical sciences 100 to 400 years before Fayol's writings. But, it was about the time of Fayol and F. W. Taylor (who was working on a scientific approach to management in the United States) before management was considered more than just good common sense combined with some degree of technical competence. Apparently, it took a research-oriented manager like Fayol with a background in mining, engineering, and geology to recognize the importance of science in developing a better understanding of management.

---

[14] Harold Koontz, Cyril O'Donnell, and Heinz Weihrich, *Management* (New York: McGraw-Hill, 1980), p. 12.

Management principles One way to classify portions of current management knowledge is through the use of principles. Regarded as general statements of truth concerning management, principles identify cause and effect relationships that can assist in predicting the result(s) of particular actions. By suggesting possible results of alternative courses of action, principles also provide guides to thought and action. Consequently, through an application of principles, managers can avoid many of the costly mistakes associated with management by trial and error.

Many of the principles of management included in Appendix A have been followed by practicing managers in all types of organizations. Yet, groups of both practitioners and scholars still disagree on the validity of principles.[15] Others note that the diverse environments within which management is practiced have become too complex for principles to be used in the development of a general theory of management.[16] As much as anything, these differing opinions may point out the benefits of a contingency approach to management where environmental conditions and managerial judgment are of utmost importance in determining the applicability of principles to given situations.

To summarize, rigorous investigation is required to develop valid principles. We know that a principle in the physical sciences is meaningful only when developed through the steps of conceptualizing, hypothesizing, and theorizing. For an inexact science such as management, however, the starting point may well be that of developing principles based on observation and experience. Through scientific investigation, one can then seek to prove or disprove them. Although such procedures lack the accurate predictability of those in the physical sciences, the lessons learned from experience, experimentation, and observation are still superior to using only a trial-and-error approach to the practice of management.

Universality of management

The universality of management is an important concept to consider in modern management thought. When describing management as universal, we refer to the widespread practice of management in all types of organizations. As noted before, one cannot bring a group of people together, regardless of the nature of the endeavor, and expect them to accomplish objectives unless their efforts are coordinated. Among other things, plans must be outlined, tasks identified, authority relationships specified, lines of communication established, and leadership exercised. Management, therefore, is required before any organization can expect to be effective.

---

[15] For a critical examination, see Herbert A. Simon, *Administrative Behavior, A Study of Decision-Making Processes in Administrative Organization* (New York: Free Press, 1966), pp. 20–35.

[16] See George S. Odiorne, "The Management Theory Jungle and the Existential Manager," *Academy of Management Journal,* June 1966, pp. 109–16.

Although management is universal, we should not assume that all managers are the same; if, for no other reason, differences exist because no two individuals are alike. However, all managers perform broad groups of duties that are similar. These groups of duties are the functions of planning, organizing, actuating, and controlling. Although the responsibilities associated with performing the functions vary among levels of authority, managers at all levels accomplish objectives through the use of various human and material resources. Since the management functions must be performed to some degree in order to achieve desired goals, we can say that there is, indeed, a universality of management.

The universal nature of management also implies that managerial skills are transferable from one type of organization to another. If this is the case, a manager should expect to experience few problems in moving from one industry to another, from the military to business, from business to government, from education to business, or from one department to another within the same organization. There are certainly persons who have been successful in making such moves.[17] Others, however, have failed. For example, Laurence J. Peter cites numerous cases that show promotions in an organization often accomplish little beyond pointing out the incompetencies of those persons who have been promoted.[18]

Although proven performance in one management position is no guarantee of success in another, various issues should still be explored. First, managerial success depends on how well managers do their jobs— that is, how well they perform the management functions in meeting their responsibilities. Remember that the manager is not a narrow technical specialist, but a person who must plan, organize, actuate, and control. Again, this does not overlook the need for technical information in the decision-making process. Technological, social, political, and economic factors must be considered in most decisions. At the same time, managers must recognize the importance of balancing the needs and goals of various organizational members. This, in turn, requires an ability to understand the overall nature of an organization's operations.

A second factor to consider concerns the need for flexibility when adjusting to a new organizational environment. All organizations have unique differences. Thus, for managers to be successful in moving from one organization to another, they must be capable of adapting to change. In addition, initiative, motivation to achieve, and the courage to accept and overcome setbacks are important personal characteristics. When moving from large to smaller organizations, these latter

---

[17] For some success stories, see "Opportunists," *MBA*, July–August 1977, pp. 24–25.

[18] Laurence J. Peter and Raymond Hull, *The Peter Principle* (New York: Bantam Books, 1970).

characteristics appear to be especially critical. Perhaps this is due to the fact that smaller organizations do not have the technical specialists and staff support groups found in their larger counterparts. In any event, career movements from small organizations to larger ones seem to present fewer problems.[19]

APPROACHES TO THE STUDY OF MANAGEMENT

During the past 50 years, major social, political, economic, and technical changes have had a tremendous impact on the practice of management. Simultaneously, this time period produced a growing interest in the study of management. Of course, earlier steps in this direction had been taken by Frederick W. Taylor (1856–1917).[20] Taylor and his associates searched for better ways to cut costs, improve productivity, measure performance, and select and train workers. Through his experimentation and writing, Taylor became known as the father of the movement called scientific management.

In the 1920s and 1930s, the focus of management study shifted to a more detailed examination of the human element in organizations. The study of interrelationships between people and work environments resulted in a new field of management called human relations. Pioneers, such as Elton Mayo and F. J. Roethlisberger, were among the first to be involved in extensive research directed toward providing a better understanding of human behavior in work situations. Since the 1930s, contributions from the areas of psychology, sociology, and anthropology have added significantly to the behavioral knowledge available to modern managers.

During the 1950s, other approaches to the study of management started to develop. The proliferation of these approaches was quite rapid and continues even today. Writing in 1961, for example, Harold Koontz discussed six schools of management thought and referred to them as the "management theory jungle."[21] Almost 20 years later, Koontz revisited the jungle, and identified 11 approaches to management theory and science, as outlined below:[22]

1. *Empirical or case*—seeks to advance the understanding of management through a study of past experience, usually through cases, and a transfer of the lessons of such experience to practitioners and students.
2. *Interpersonal behavior*—studies management by concentrating on interpersonal relations in organizations, with a focus on individuals and their motivations.

---

[19] "Choosing a Second Career," *Business Week,* September 19, 1977, pp. 119–24.

[20] Frederick W. Taylor, *Scientific Management* (New York: Harper & Row, 1947).

[21] See Harold Koontz, "The Management Theory Jungle," *Journal of the Academy of Management,* December 1961, pp. 174–88.

[22] Harold Koontz, "The Management Theory Jungle Revisited," *The Academy of Management Review,* April 1980, pp. 177–83.

3. *Group behavior*—concentrates on the study of group behavior patterns in organizations rather than on interpersonal relations.

4. *Cooperative social systems*—modifies the interpersonal and group behavior approaches by studying human relations as cooperative social systems that link two or more persons together in the pursuit of common purposes.

5. *Sociotechnical systems*—emphasizes the need for considering social and technical systems simultaneously in the practice of management since technical systems have a great influence on the social system(s) of organizations.

6. *Decision theory*—stresses decision making as a major responsibility of all managers and focuses on the development of management thought around the decision-making process.

7. *Systems*—studies the interdependent parts of organizations as they interact with, and are influenced by, their environments.

8. *Mathematical or "management science"*—considers management as a process that can be studied through mathematical models that express the basic elements of a problem, while providing a means for identifying and evaluating alternative solutions to the problem.

9. *Contingency or situational*—examines managerial behavior as a response to a given set of circumstances in order to suggest management practices that appear most suitable for dealing with a particular situation.

10. *Managerial roles*—observes what managers do in an attempt to identify and classify those roles common to all managers.

11. *Operational*—attempts to tie together the concepts, principles, theory, and techniques that underpin the practice of management by relating them to the functions of managers.

While each of these approaches presents a somewhat different avenue to the study of management, all have the potential to contribute something to the advancement of management knowledge. Similarly, they can contribute to improving the practice of management. Since managers must deal with a variety of environmental influences and organizational inputs, they often find that a combination of approaches is useful in the practice of management. For example, the operational approach can be used as a framework for guiding some managerial actions, while an understanding of systems and human behavior in the work environment can be of benefit in other situations; or, quantitative methods and mathematical models might contribute to improving managerial decision making. In this sense, management theory does not include approaches that represent the "one best way" for dealing with all situations. Instead, it is a body of interrelated concepts, principles, and techniques that provides useful guides to managerial thought and action.

THE ART AND SCIENCE OF MANAGEMENT

To bring about desired results in organizations, R. L. Katz suggests that we give more consideration to those managerial skills and abilities that can be developed and improved in applying management knowledge.[23] He classifies these skills as (1) technical—the vocational skills obtained through a specialization of labor, (2) human—the ability to work with people versus the technical skill of working with things and processes, and (3) conceptual—the ability to recognize the interrelationships between the parts of an organization and overall organizational goals. Basically, then, the successful practice of management goes beyond the scientific method of problem solving. How management knowledge is applied depends on the skills and abilities of individual managers and may be referred to as the art of management. As such, an artful practice of management depends upon the technical, human, and conceptual abilities of managers and is just as essential in the achievement of objectives as the science of management.

Upon reflection, there is no doubt that the science and art of management must go hand in hand. One without the other is certainly of little value to managers of today and tomorrow. Another way to look at this point is to think of the surgeon who performs delicate operations skillfully (the art). This person's skill, however, depends on a vast amount of knowledge provided by the study of chemistry, biology, anatomy, and physics (the science).

SUMMARY

Management is a process that includes the functions of planning, organizing, actuating, and controlling. These functions must be performed in all organizations if goals are to be achieved satisfactorily through the use of human and material resources. In the performance of these functions, management is normally viewed as both an art and a science. To become more effective in blending the art and science of management, managers can draw upon the vast body of knowledge that has been produced through various approaches to the study of management. At the same time, successful managers must demonstrate technical, human relations, and conceptual skills in the performance of their duties.

KEY TERMS

Actuating: The management function that includes motivation, leadership, communication, training, and other forms of personal influence.

Contingency approach to management: An approach to management which states that there is no one best way to perform the management functions, but that organizational decisions depend upon

---

[23] Robert L. Katz, "Skills of an Effective Administrator," *Harvard Business Review,* January–February 1955, pp. 33–42.

environmental conditions and managerial judgment relating to the particular situation.

Controlling: The management function that involves checking and comparing performance to established standards and initiates corrective action(s) if necessary.

Coordination: The harmonious combination of efforts and resources resulting from a performance of the management functions.

Management: The process of planning, organizing, actuating, and controlling an organization's operations in order to achieve a coordination of the human and material resources essential in the effective and efficient attainment of objectives.

Management functions: The activities of planning, organizing, actuating, and controlling included in the management process.

Management principles: General statements of truth that identify possible cause and effect relationships and provide guides to managerial thought and action.

Organizing: The management function that involves combining human and material resources into a meaningful whole (organization).

Planning: The management function that involves the selection of courses of action (plans) that will direct an organization's human and material resources for future time spans.

Scientific management: An approach to solving problems and improving the practice of management through an application of methods of scientific inquiry.

Universality of management: The concept that refers to the need for the practice of management in all organizations.

QUESTIONS

1. Define management in your own words. Based on your definition, do you practice management when *(a)* writing a term paper, *(b)* studying for final examinations, *(c)* participating as an officer in a campus organization? Why or why not?

2. You and two friends stop on the street to help a motorist change a flat tire. Will you need to practice management to get the job done? Justify your answer.

3. What are the management functions? Is the performance of these functions required in some organizations but not in others?

4. What is meant by the statement, "coordination results from a satisfactory performance of the management functions"?

5. Does the importance of management in an intensive care unit of a hospital differ from that in a hospital cafeteria?

6. If an organization does not accomplish its stated objectives, can we say that management has not been practiced?

7. How can changing environmental factors serve to draw more, or less, attention to planning as a management function?

8. Distinguish between management competence and technical competence.

9. Is management really required in all organizations? Cite two examples to justify your answer.

10. Although management is an inexact science, is there value in considering it as having scientific dimensions?

11. Since there are so many different approaches to the study of management, should we assume that researchers in this area are merely wasting their time? Why?

12. Distinguish among the empirical, decision theory, sociotechnical systems, and operational approaches to the study of management.

13. Why should all managers be interested in learning more about the various approaches being used to study management?

14. Why is it reasonable to view management as both an art and a science?

PROBLEMS

1. In June 1979, 55 young alligators were moved from the swamps of southwest Louisiana to the Tennessee River in the Wheeler National Wildlife Refuge in northern Alabama. After being relocated, the gators were supposed to help curb a rapidly increasing beaver population in the refuge. Following statements of public concern, however, a U.S. Fish and Wildlife representative stated that the agency was merely moving surplus alligators from one area to another that was once a part of the alligators' range.

Residents of the area argued that the alligators could not survive the winters in northern Alabama. U.S. Representative Ronnie Flippo of Florence, Alabama, objected to the move of this endangered species and complained that conservation personnel acted without holding public hearings on the matter. He further demanded the gators be rounded up and hauled back to Louisiana.

Unfortunately, the "Great Gator Roundup" of northern Alabama has been a failure to date. Only two alligators were caught during five nights of hunting in June 1980. Even worse, direct costs of the recovery operation have already amounted to over $5,000. Thus, each alligator apprehended so far is worth over $2,000 of the taxpayers' money.

a. Cite examples from this incident that show a lack of coordination as one possible cause of the problems encountered.

b. How could a proper execution of the functions of planning, organizing, actuating, and controlling have led to a better coordination of effort and resources in this situation?

2. We often think of the practice of management in terms of today's organizations, both large and small. As discussed in this chapter, however, management has been practiced through the ages. It is not something unique to General Motors, United Airlines, Texas Instruments, or Al's Stop and Shop at the corner of Fifth and Main.

Discuss why management had to be practiced in the following examples:

a. Construction of the Great Wall of China that covers a distance equal to that between New York City and Omaha, Nebraska. Built of a brick and granite shell filled with earth, the wall was completed entirely by hand

and required the labor of tens of thousands of laborers over a period of hundreds of years.

b. Organization and operation of the Pony Express between Sacramento, California, and St. Joseph, Missouri, a distance of almost 2,000 miles. Eighty men and over 400 horses were involved, and 190 relay stations were necessary so that riders could change horses every 10 miles.

c. Battling the Chicago fire of 1871 that resulted in property losses of $196 million and 250 deaths; or, rebuilding San Francisco after the earthquake of 1906 that destroyed property valued at $350 million and resulted in over 400 deaths.

3. Government experts compute that the United States will need 4 to 5 billion more board feet of lumber per year by 1985 to meet national demands at relatively stable prices. In an attempt to provide this amount of lumber, while at the same time desiring to moderate the inflationary spiral of housing costs, some governmental officials recommend that timber production be significantly increased in national forests.

This alternative solution raises ecological issues in terms of environmental, recreational, and agricultural restraints. There are also economic questions regarding an increase of timber quotas on public lands. For example, every additional billion board feet of lumber sold from the national forests may require an additional 2,000 new administrative personnel positions. Other expenses generated include road building and reforestation. In relation to home building costs, a 50 percent annual increase in the current national sales of 10 billion board feet would result in less than a 1 percent drop in housing costs. The reason for this is that only 25 percent of the timber used for home construction originates from national forests and only 14 percent of an average residence is made of wood.

a. In providing additional timber for the U.S. economy and developing programs to hold housing costs down, indicate how the management process is relevant in governmental organizations.

b. Discuss the role of each of the management functions in working toward a solution to the problem.

c. How can the art and science of management be applied to this situation?

4. After a major reorganization several years ago, 11 of the 15 top-ranking officers of the Cudahy Packing Company were not only new to the company but new to the meat packing industry as well. In 1948 Dwight D. Eisenhower completed a distinguished military career, became president of Columbia University, and later became the 34th president of the United States. More recently, former astronaut Frank Borman became chief executive officer and president of Eastern Airlines, Inc.

a. What do examples such as these show about the transferability of management skills?

b. Cite three other examples that show individuals who seem to have been successful in transferring their management skills from one type of organization to another. Also, cite three examples that show individuals who seem to have been unsuccessful in making such moves.

c. What factors seem to account for the success or failure of the persons cited in your examples given above?

5. Refer to the principles of management included in Appendix A. Does there appear to be a major theme around which all of the principles were developed? Of what value are these principles to managers in the 1980s?

SUGGESTED READINGS

Boettinger, H. M. "Is Management Really an Art?" *Harvard Business Review,* January–February 1975, pp. 56–64.

Drucker, P. F. *Management: Tasks, Responsibilities, Practices.* New York: Harper & Row, 1974.

————. *People and Performance: The Best of Peter Drucker on Management.* New York: Harper & Row, 1977.

Fry, L. W. "The Maligned F. W. Taylor: A Reply to His Many Critics." *Academy of Management Review,* July 1976, pp. 124–29.

Koontz, H. "The Management Theory Jungle Revisited." *Academy of Management Review,* April 1980, pp. 177–83.

Lilienthal, D. E. *Management: A Humanist Art.* Pittsburgh: Carnegie Institute of Technology, 1967.

Luthans, F., and T. I. Stewart. "A General Contingency Theory of Management." *The Academy of Management Review,* April 1977, pp. 181–95.

McGregor, D. M. *The Professional Manager.* New York: McGraw-Hill, 1967.

Mintzberg, H. *The Nature of Managerial Work.* New York: Harper & Row, 1973.

Newman, W. H., and H. W. Wallender, III. "Managing Not-for-Profit Enterprises." *The Academy of Management Review,* January 1978, pp. 24–31.

Sheldon, O. *Philosophy of Management.* New York: Pitman Publishing, 1935.

Stewart, R. *Managers and Their Jobs.* London: Macmillan, 1967.

————. "To Understand the Manager's Job: Consider Demands, Constraints, Choices." *Organizational Dynamics,* Spring 1976, pp. 22–32.

Webber, R. "Career Problems of Young Managers." *California Management Review,* Summer 1976, pp. 19–33.

Wren, D. A. *The Evolution of Management Thought.* New York: John Wiley & Sons, 1979.

2

MANAGEMENT'S CHALLENGING FUTURE

PURPOSE

A grim picture is painted for the world in the year 2000. If current trends continue, population will increase by some 50 percent to a total of over 6 billion persons. At the same time, however, food output may increase by less than 15 percent per capita. Hunger and starvation may be a natural result. In addition, the quality of our air and water may continue to worsen, farm lands may erode, and many large forests may disappear.

If the possibilities noted above are not enough, managers will be called upon to be more socially responsible, while demands for new technology and increased productivity will continue. Likewise, continuing energy shortages will be a part of the future, as will the need to use all human resources to their maximum potential.

This chapter examines various environmental changes that will have an impact on managers of the future. Rather than looking at these changes as problems, however, we prefer to discuss them as challenges. After all, problems are often only challenges in disguise.

OBJECTIVES

1. To outline the challenging future being produced by the different environments within which management is practiced.

2. To examine the interrelationships between management and its external environments.

3. To show how the role and scope of management have changed to keep pace with various environmental changes.

4. To discuss several of the more important issues that will provide continuing challenges for future managers.

5. To indicate that management must be future oriented.

Management contributes greatly to any nation's standard of living. As an example, consider the role of management while comparing the wide differences in national income among nations. In the less economically developed countries, few managers have had opportunities to work in large-scale business organizations. Also, these countries have underdeveloped business services, financial institutions, and marketing channels. Due to a lack of skilled workers, engineers, and trained managers, production is often based on obsolete methods. The problem is compounded by a lack of universities, research institutions, and scientists who can adapt new methods to local conditions. In contrast, western Europe and Japan rebuilt rapidly after World War II because of their technical know-how, managerial abilities, and established social institutions.

Obviously, then, management is an important part of the total environment in which we live. It is not only influenced by environmental factors but is also a force in changing them. As shown in Figure 2–1, social, political, scientific/technological, and economic systems make up these external environments. All of them have had major impacts on the growth and development of management. By examining each, it is possible to gain a greater awareness of those variables that interact with management to influence organizational behavior.

THE CHANGING U.S. ENVIRONMENT

The United States has changed significantly during this century. In 1900, about 60 percent of the nation's population lived in rural areas, with some 38 percent of the labor force employed in agriculture. By 1970, just over 26 percent of the population lived in rural areas, with less than 4 percent of the work force employed in agriculture; and even today, the rapid decline in farm population continues.

Service industries and government now make up our largest employment categories with one out of every five employed persons receiving a paycheck from some government body. It is also interesting to note that increased employee mobility contributes to frequent shifts among employment categories. Between 1965 and 1970, one employee in three moved from a job in one occupational category to a different job in the same category, or to a job in another occupational category. Such attitudes toward job mobility continue at the present time.

Other changes are also having a deep-felt impact on both management and its environments. Specifically, national interests have caused private institutions to work at meeting our needs to control pollution, develop new energy sources, improve health care, support disadvantaged groups, and protect consumers. Similarly, federal and local governments have played major roles in advancing these areas. Of course, government actions also affect management decisions in such areas as employment, working conditions, prices, wages, ecology, collective bargaining, product standards, and advertising.

FIGURE 2–1
Interrelationships between management and its external environments

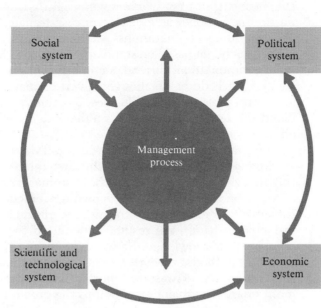

What has been called the postindustrial society is producing other dramatic environmental changes.[1] These changes can be seen in the mass production of standardized products as well as in the technological advancements being made in computerization, communication, and other areas. As this postindustrial era continues, society becomes more concerned with services, research, science, and education than with manufacturing. Consequently, more managerial leadership in the future must be provided by those with backgrounds in the sciences, mathematics, and computer technology. It is also important to note that today's students are the stock from which future managers will come. In this sense, the year 2000 is already here in terms of the managers and leaders who are now in offices and classrooms throughout the nation.

MANAGEMENT'S CHANGING ROLE AND SCOPE

Due to various environmental changes, management theory and practice have also changed during the past 100 years. The first part of this period saw mechanization and automation advance with industrial growth. Growth in industry, however, created problems between management and labor. As noted in Chapter 1, management practice

---

[1] See Daniel Bell, *The Coming of the Post-Industrial Society: A Venture in Social Forecasting* (New York: Basic Books, 1973).

was little more than a day-to-day, fire-fighting operation at the beginning of this century. Managers saw their duties as those of getting the most output from workers with as little labor cost as possible. Only passing attention was given to any systematic planning, organizing, or controlling of operations. Manufacturing activities, for example, were usually not based on standards developed from scientific research or experimentation. Instead, standards were often established subjectively with little or no thought given to matching the demands of a job with employee skills. Guesses, hunches, and past experiences provided the bases for most management decisions and employee alienation was quite common.

The practice of management changed dramatically when *scientific management* emerged during the first quarter of the 20th century. Initially, the term referred to the systematic study and measurement of work in order to achieve maximum efficiency in production. Although these early efforts to improve productivity were carried out in factory settings, the results contributed to an overall expansion of management knowledge. New insights were provided into the analysis of work methods, authority relationships, production planning, and the elimination of wasteful efforts. Unfortunately, scientific management often gave major attention to the creation of the ideal organization, and if performance failed to meet standards, it was assumed to be the fault of either unqualified workers or improper engineering methods. In either case, employee social needs were considered to be far less important than organizational goals.

By the early 1930s, more attention was given to the role of both individuals and groups within organizations. This changed the focus of management thought from an impersonal view of employees to one that considered their feelings, attitudes, beliefs, perceptions, and ideas.[2] The latter view was based on a belief that employees could be motivated to work more productively when provided with opportunities to satisfy certain social and psychological needs. Consequently, the human element was given major consideration while other environmental factors were pushed out of the mainstream of management thought for a decade or so. Since 1950, however, management theorists have been concerned with both external and internal environments as they influence, and are influenced by, the human element.

The need to view management in a broader context will be increasingly important in years to come. Managers will soon be affected by even more pressures from different groups within our society. Decision-making techniques will need to be improved, and current research must be used to provide a better understanding of the total management process. In this respect, a knowledge of how environmental

---

[2] This stage of management is classified as the human relations era. See F. J. Roethlisberger and W. J. Dickson, *Management and the Worker* (Cambridge, Mass.: Harvard University Press, 1939).

changes affect managers as they seek to balance employee needs and organizational goals will be especially critical.

Managers of the future will also find that they cannot respond to a changing world by merely following procedures or techniques that have worked in the past. Responding to a greater number of pressures and needs will require an understanding of relationships within and among organizations, the complex nature of organizational life, and the critical factors in an organization's external environment.[3] Thus, the demands on all managers will continue to increase as more individuals and groups turn to organizations for help in preventing or solving a variety of social problems.

CHALLENGES OF THE FUTURE

Prior to the growth of industrialization, environmental forces were less numerous and complex than they are today. Changes in wealth, power, and prestige were basically determined by those who had the best-trained and best-equipped armies to wage war and plunder the countryside. Other leadership positions were filled by priests who often used various religious myths to gain power. With the introduction of mechanization, however, leadership positions were to be filled by the risk takers, engineers, and professional managers who created and directed a growing industrial complex.

Current interest in the challenging future of management is based on many of the same problems and issues that concern the average citizen. The energy crisis has touched all of our lives and will continue to do so for years to come. Technology, productivity, and the economy present new challenges almost daily. At the same time, government bureaucracy continues to control many of the actions of organizations and individuals throughout society. For managers to meet these and other challenges, they must realize that the future has already arrived. Time, as stated by Saint Augustine, is a threefold present: the present as we experience it, the past as a present memory, and the future as a present expectation. Thus, the future begins with the present and is influenced by decisions that managers make today.

Gazing into the future is important because it provides managers with some information about the possible results of their present actions. By anticipating the future, problems are not as likely to appear as surprises. With some advance notice, managers can begin looking for contingent solutions to future problems, thus providing their organizations with more options to consider in adapting to changing environmental conditions.

The following sections will not attempt to make precise predictions concerning management's future since there is no forecasting method

[3] See Paul R. Lawrence and Jay W. Lorsch, *Organization and Environment* (Homewood, Ill.: Richard D. Irwin, 1969); and R. Hall, *Organizations: Structure and Process* (Englewood Cliffs, N.J.: Prentice-Hall, 1972).

that can be so exact. Therefore, the "world tomorrow" will be left to the philosophers, theologians, and futurologists.[4] Our discussion will be limited to a brief review of current trends that appear likely to influence the future.

Social responsibility and ethics

If organizations are to survive, they must make meaningful contributions to the societies in which they operate. In the United States, organizations are generally free to satisfy the needs of society by producing goods and services of their own choosing. Yet, social values and norms still serve to limit the alternatives available to all organizations.

Accepting changes in social and ethical values is a slow process. Managers are now, however, recognizing the importance of adapting to dynamic, changing social requirements. They are beginning to develop a more complete understanding of their role in society and what society expects from its organizational partners. To a considerable degree, this expectation is becoming more clearly defined as that of overcoming values and attitudes that disregard human rights. As such, the expectation is also close to Dr. Albert Schweitzer's definition that states, "Ethics is the name we give to our concern for good behavior. We feel an obligation to consider not only our own personal well-being, but also that of others and of human society as a whole."[5]

To understand the present level of socially and ethically responsible actions of managers, it is necessary to examine two major points. First, many organizations see their role as that of being an efficient supplier of goods and services demanded by the public.[6] In this sense, they feel that the best way to solve social problems is to continue their contributions to economic growth.

A second point is that some organizations feel they lack both the wealth and skill to accept a heavy social responsibility. This belief implies that a major social burden might result in lower profits. Deciding where profits end and social responsibility begins, however, may be impossible. In fact, it can be argued that profit, ethical behavior, and social responsibility must go together. By providing a proper balance among goals in each area, one is reached through an achievement of the others.

Just as managers consider themselves to be ethical, they also view their organizations as socially responsible entities. Consequently, it is not unusual to find them actively supporting educational programs or working to expand employment opportunities for minority groups. In so doing, these managers have found that people who are given a

---

[4] See James Traub, "Futurology: The Rise of the Predicting Profession," *Saturday Review*, December, 1979, pp. 24–32.

[5] *Common Sense and Everyday Ethics* (Washington, D.C.: American Viewpoint, 1980), p. 5.

[6] Gilbert Burck, "The Hazards of 'Corporate Responsibility,'" *Fortune*, June 1973, pp. 144ff.

chance to succeed often make better neighbors, employees, and customers than those who are poor, ignorant, and neglected. Thus, their actions can have a favorable long-run impact on both the organizations and communities involved.

As concerns ecological problems, the future demands of stockholders are more likely to be met by organizations that work to eliminate pollution. Where ways to control air, water, and noise pollution are not at hand, new technology must be developed. Companies that are able to meet such challenges may find that future profits will increase as long-run social needs are balanced with short-run economic considerations. Perhaps the *social audit* that attempts to measure the impact of an organization's actions on society will be of value in seeking to maintain this difficult balance.[7]

Energy crisis

In earlier years, about the only resource problem facing many organizations was that of managing surplus supplies.[8] Today, however, the problem of scarce resources is more common. For most nonrenewable energy resources, the usage rate is growing faster than the population. Not only are more people consuming resources, but the average consumption per person also increases each year. What are the consequences of this and other related problems? According to one study, pollution, the present growth rate of world population, and a depletion of resources will severely limit the world's industrial growth during the next 100 years.[9]

Energy is one of the most important resources linked to productivity and the standard of living. Oil and gas now account for a major proportion of the total world energy supply as noted in Figure 2–2. Some forecasts indicate that the annual increase in petroleum usage of 7 percent could double by 1985 unless other fuel supplies are found. Thus, with a continued depletion of supplies, the world is being forced to start major programs directed toward finding alternative energy sources. These programs, as noted in Figure 2–3, must include not only the technology needed to find new energy sources, but also an approach for creating political and economic environments that will encourage conservation.[10] To this extent, business and government relationships will become more important, requiring a high degree of cooperation. Managers of U.S. businesses, for instance, are being asked to support government programs designed to solve national energy problems. However, if these programs are to work, they must

---

[7] For a good discussion of the social audit, see Patrick E. Murphy and E. James Burton, "Accountants Assess the Social Audit," *Business*, September–October 1980.

[8] "The Scramble for Resources," *Business Week*, June 30, 1973, p. 56.

[9] Donella H. Meadows et al., *The Limits to Growth* (New York: Universe Books, 1972).

[10] Maurice F. Granville, *Balancing Regulation and Energy*, Texaco, September 18, 1973.

FIGURE 2–2
World energy supply*

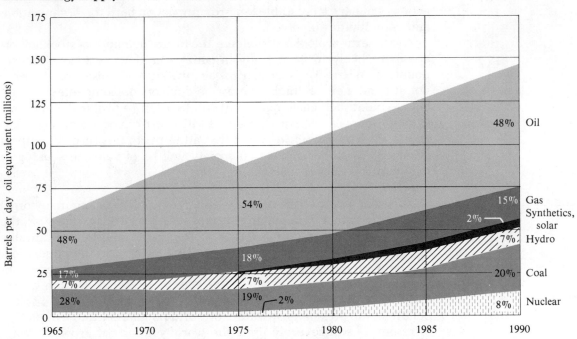

* Excluding communist areas.
Source: *World Energy Outlook*, Exxon Corporation, New York, April 1978, p. 13.

also provide incentives that will encourage the continued search for expanded energy resources.

While the energy crisis will be a major problem for years to come, a national commitment to develop alternative energy sources could provide numerous opportunities for those organizations prepared to meet the challenges of change. Already, Exxon and other major oil companies have expanded their activities in the areas of exploration for uranium and research into the development of synthetic fuels. Large corporations will undoubtedly lead the way in these and related areas. However, spin-off opportunities will be available for smaller organizations capable of adjusting to changing environmental conditions.

Underutilization of human resources

Although the United States is faced with a rapid depletion of some resources, others are not being used to their full potential. Of these, an underutilization of certain human resources is most apparent. Statistics show that the unemployment rates for women, blacks, and youths are above the national average. While some of these persons may be jobless due to employment discrimination, other reasons can be found in the changing composition of the work force.

Current data indicate that there will continue to be a youth boom

FIGURE 2–3
New sources of energy

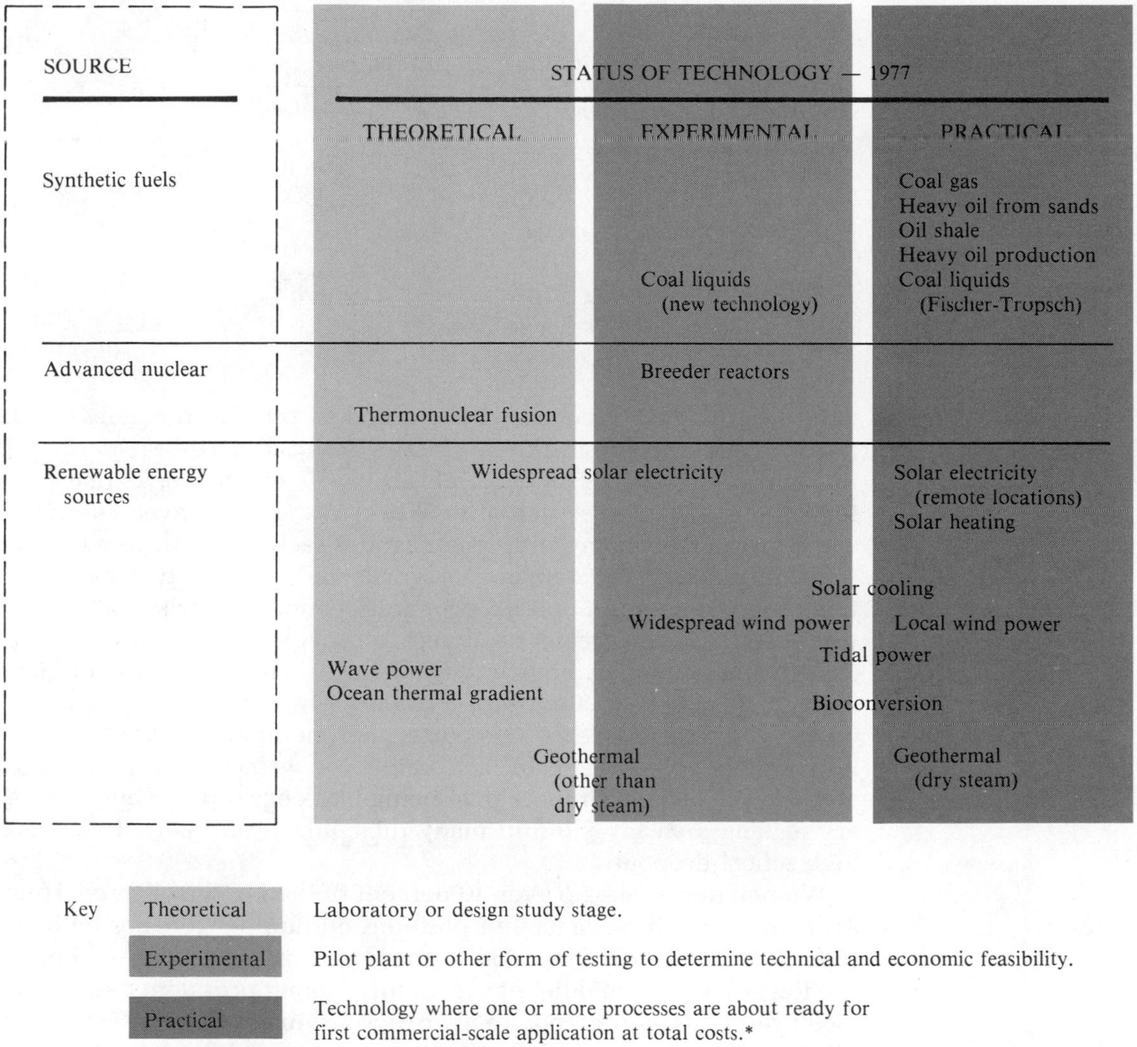

SOURCE	STATUS OF TECHNOLOGY — 1977		
	THEORETICAL	EXPERIMENTAL	PRACTICAL
Synthetic fuels		Coal liquids (new technology)	Coal gas Heavy oil from sands Oil shale Heavy oil production Coal liquids (Fischer-Tropsch)
Advanced nuclear	Thermonuclear fusion	Breeder reactors	
Renewable energy sources	Widespread solar electricity		Solar electricity (remote locations) Solar heating
			Solar cooling
		Widespread wind power	Local wind power
			Tidal power
	Wave power Ocean thermal gradient		
			Bioconversion
		Geothermal (other than dry steam)	Geothermal (dry steam)

Key		
	Theoretical	Laboratory or design study stage.
	Experimental	Pilot plant or other form of testing to determine technical and economic feasibility.
	Practical	Technology where one or more processes are about ready for first commercial-scale application at total costs.*

* This includes capital charges, taxes, and royalties. Technology is considered economically practical at twice the present real price level of world oil.

Note: There is overlap among stages of theoretical, experimental, and practical technologies since several processes or experiments are at different points in their development.

Source: *World Energy Outlook,* Exxon Corporation, New York, April 1978, p. 29.

in the labor force. While the 15–29 age group will decline during the next 20 years, it is still expected to include 20 percent of the U.S. population in the year 2000. At the same time, Figure 2–4 shows dramatic increases in the 30–39 age group until 1985. The challenge to provide jobs for persons in this age group will be great. Never

FIGURE 2–4
Age group trends—1976–1985

1976 age group	1976 total population (in millions)	Percent increase or decrease	
		To 1980	To 1985
30–34	13.8	+26	+42
35–39	11.6	+20	+49
40–44	11.1	+ 4	+23
45–49	11.8	− 8	− 3
50–54	11.8	− 3	−10
55–59	10.6	+ 6	+ 3

Source: U.S. Bureau of Labor Statistics.

before has the U.S. economy been asked to provide new jobs for 42 percent more people in the 30–34 age group in a 10-year period, or for 49 percent more 35–39-year-olds by 1985. Of course, a great need for job opportunities existed after World War II. However, there was also a growing economy with organizations seeking employees to assist them in meeting the demand for goods and services that existed at the time. Quite the opposite economic conditions exist today, thus presenting an even greater challenge to provide jobs for these persons.

Although unemployment among all blacks is high, the rate for black teenagers is even greater, with a range between 24 and 34 percent during the past few years. Of course, the unemployment rate among all young people is high. In fact, being young increases the chances of remaining jobless far more than being black or female. Thus, teenagers seeking a steady job find many difficulties, especially if they are high school dropouts.

Women now make up over 40 percent of the U.S. labor force. However, males in all management positions outnumber females by more than 5 to 1. In addition, most women are still found at, or below, the lower levels of middle management. Among presidents, executive vice presidents, and corporate chairpersons, males exceed females by a ratio of some 50 to 1. As might be expected, salary data also show wide differences between men and women in management positions. Just over five years ago, fewer than 6,000 women were in jobs paying over $30,000, while more than 190,000 males received such salaries.[11]

Beyond a changing composition of the labor force, management groups of the future will also have to deal with employees who are more highly educated. Consequently, new approaches to leadership, communication, and motivation will be required. Only when such approaches are combined with an elimination of employment practices

---

[11] See: "Up the Ladder, Finally," *Business Week*, November 24, 1975, pp. 58–68.

that have discriminated on the basis of race, sex, and age, will we move closer to a maximum utilization of our nation's human resources.

Technology

The state of technology is an important factor in the environment of management. Overall, the United States has been very successful in pushing back limits to economic growth through continued technological advancements. We can observe the results in new attitudes toward leisure and recreation, improved communications, the development of a broad-based educational system, improved health care, and many other areas. At the same time, technological advancements have caused various problems; for example, technology has contributed to the development of more complex organizations, increases in pollution, and a complex, urbanized industrial society. These and other changes have caused more rapid managerial obsolescence, uncertainty in decision making, overcrowding of highways and cities, and less clean air and water. Thus, technology has both positive and negative results.

Technological advancements come from many sources, and it is impossible to group them into one single category. The Wankel engine, birth control pills, computers, high-yield grains, television, and off-shore oil drilling rigs are all technological developments; but each plays a distinct role and has its own impact on the environment of management. In a broader sense, the question facing management of the future is whether modern technology can continue to provide economic growth for all nations. The answer depends clearly upon management's ability to advance technology in the areas of (1) additional food production, (2) new energy sources, (3) recyclable resources, (4) reduced pollution, (5) population control, and (6) medical advancements.[12]

Casual observation should make it clear that technological advancement requires good management. Above all, this means that future managers must be flexible and adaptive to change. With each new technological development, managers must determine the physical and social effects of the development as well as the managerial changes that will be necessary before it can be implemented properly.[13] More research will have to be conducted to find out what turns employees on to their jobs and how to get the most out of their efforts. A greater investment in equipment will also be required, and thus, a closer coordination between human and material resources. In general, then, challenges of the future will require that managers improve their skills in perceiving, analyzing, and adapting to the barriers and opportunities produced by technological changes.

---

[12] For a revealing look at the possible impact of today's decisions on tomorrow's environment see *Perspectives for the 70s and 80s: Tomorrow's Problems Confronting Today's Management* (New York: National Industrial Conference Board, 1970).

[13] See "The Speedup in Automation" and "Changing 45 Million Jobs," *Business Week,* August 3, 1981, pp. 58–67.

Productivity

Productivity has various meanings. It can be used as a measure of a system's total output of goods and services. More often, however, it refers to the relationship between the output of a system and its inputs. Here, productivity is the ratio of wanted output to scarce input. In this ratio, output represents the products and services of a system, while inputs are measured in terms of labor-hours worked and materials used.

As a ratio of output to input, productivity provides an indication of a system's efficiency. Productivity gains reflect increased output per unit of input, while declines in productivity show decreased output per unit of input. In technologically advanced nations, productivity is usually high, while the reverse is true in less-developed countries.

The United States has always been known for its high levels of productivity, but smaller increases and declines have been of concern for the last several years. As recently as 1980, for example, productivity growth in the United States was the lowest among all major industrial nations of the world.[14] If this trend is not reversed, we can expect continued periods of *stagflation* where conditions of inflation and recession exist simultaneously in the economy.[15]

When declines in productivity are discussed, it should also be noted that fingers of blame are pointed in several directions. The government is blamed for failing to provide a tax structure that stimulates capital formation and investment. Various laws and regulations are attacked as being only costly masses of red tape. Unions are seen as culprits that push labor costs too high while providing workers with so much security that they are no longer motivated to increase their productivity. Employees are blamed for poor attitudes toward the quantity and quality of their work. Finally, management groups are blamed for a number of things ranging from failure to replace obsolete industrial equipment soon enough to that of passing on too many costs to customers.

The task for future managers is that of moving beyond discussions of who is to blame for declines in productivity to viable programs of advancing productivity. Action, not blame, will be required to meet this challenge. While such action will require the cooperation of various groups, managers must provide the leadership that will pull these groups together.

Computers

Looking into the future of management certainly requires an examination of the role of computers. Their usefulness in classifying, storing, and speeding up the flow of information in an organization has been apparent for many years. For example, a daily classification and summary of sales information is helpful in maintaining desired inventory

---

[14] "Opportunity in a Polluted Economic Environment," in *From the Podium* (St. Louis: Beta Gamma Sigma, 1980), p. 2.

[15] Jules Backman, ed., *Business Problems of the Eighties* (Indianapolis: Bobbs-Merrill, 1980), p. 23.

levels and in assigning sales personnel. Other common computer applications are found in the implementation of automatic control systems; the manipulation of mathematical models; and the processing of accounts receivables, payroll data, and other accounting information.

A continuing question facing managers is how the computer will affect the number of people required to staff management positions in the years to come. One view holds that some middle- and lower-level managers may be replaced by new computers that can "think" on their own. We normally consider computers as doing only what they are programmed to do, such as calculate salaries and payroll deductions. However, new hardware being developed may soon enable computers to solve problems far more complex than those for which they are now used. If these possibilities become realities, computer programs may include such a high degree of artificial intelligence that there will be less need for some middle managers, particularly in larger organizations.

While one can forecast that computers will replace some managers in the future, an increase in the number of managers can also be projected. For example, an early study of a large utility company showed an overall growth of management employees, although fewer managers were found in clerical departments after computerization.[16] Thus, the future impact of computers on the number of managers or their jobs is not certain. It is very likely, however, that computers will continue to influence authority relationships within many organizations. As the number and size of computer installations continue to grow, authority relationships within the organizations that house them will certainly differ according to whether computer personnel are seen as expensive "number crunchers," or important members of the management team.

Management science

The field of management science uses various quantitative techniques and mathematical models to provide a more scientific approach to decision making. In many respects, however, the application of such techniques is not new. During World War II, mathematical models were used by decision makers in business, government, and the military. Other uses of such models date back as far as the 18th century.[17]

Today, changes throughout our society and the world have made decision making a much more complex task in even the smallest of organizations. As a result, many problems facing managers are too vast to be solved through mental models alone. The human mind is remarkable but can keep track of only a limited number of relationships among the numerous variables involved in many decisions. Consequently, managers must often rely on mathematical models when ana-

---

[16] Walter A. Hill, "The Impact of EDP Systems on Office Employees: Some Empirical Questions," *Academy of Management Journal,* March 1966, pp. 13–14.

[17] See Daniel A. Wren, *The Evolution of Management Thought* (New York: John Wiley & Sons, 1979), chap. 21.

lyzing the tremendous amount of information required in identifying and evaluating alternative solutions to complex problems.

Managers who fail to acquire an understanding of management science techniques will probably hurt their organizations as well as themselves. Competitors, for example, can often move into new market areas, introduce new products or services, and obtain a strong market position before managers who rely on nonquantitative techniques are fully aware of the opportunities they are missing. An alternative is to know the value of management science techniques, how they can be used, and how to interpret their results. Such knowledge is increasingly important not only in business but also among managers in government, education, the military, and health care delivery systems.

Multinational corporations

The future of management will be influenced greatly by the continued growth of transnational, transideological, or multinational corporations.[18] For some time, managers in international organizations have been faced with the problems of learning to work with people in foreign countries. These problems include training, motivation, communication, and leadership as they relate to workers and managers from different cultures. Studies of management in various countries also show that changes in an organization's external environment have a direct influence on the way managers carry out the functions of management.[19] It is obvious, therefore, that managers in one country will always have to manage somewhat differently from those in another.

Regardless of the countries where multinational corporations will be operating in the future, two factors will continue to affect the success of their managers. One will be the ability to adjust rapidly to the new problems and challenges produced by different cultures. An important requirement here will be that of developing the human resources of host countries, especially the development of qualified managers at the local level.

A second factor concerns the ability of managers to recognize the most important environmental constraints existing in different cultures. By knowing these constraints, managers will be better prepared to identify those practices which seem to have the greatest chance of success. An understanding of a given culture, for example, can assist managers in recognizing leadership styles that best fit the needs of employees within that culture. As a result, these managers are less likely to be resented as "outsiders" who are trying to force their own cultural values on others.

---

[18] Sotirios G. Mousouris, "The Impact of Transnational Corporations on the Development of International Relations," *The Changing Environment for Industrial Enterprise*, vol. 2 Sperry Rand, Corporation, March 1977, pp. 34–38.

[19] J. L. Mussie, J. Tuytzes, and N. W. Hazen, eds., *Management in the International Context* (New York: Harper & Row, 1972); and Endel-Jakob Kolde, *The Environment of International Business* (Boston: Kent Publishing Company, 1982).

**Government
regulation**

Like it or not, we live in a regulated society. Our homes, apartments, and condominiums are built according to code. Automobiles, airplanes, and boats must conform to a variety of governmental standards. The production and sale of food, cosmetics, and drugs are, likewise, subjected to numerous regulations.

At first glance, one might argue that regulations established by local, state, or national governments exist to provide an orderly society that protects the rights and well-being of all citizens. Regulations, however, are not self-enforcing but depend on regulatory agencies created for this purpose. Unfortunately, these agencies tend to increase in number and scope while perpetuating themselves through time.[20] The result is a bureaucratic maze whose disadvantages now seem to outweigh its benefits.

During 1978, the accounting firm of Arthur Andersen & Company was hired to study the incremental costs incurred by 48 Business Roundtable member companies to comply with the regulations of just six federal government agencies and programs. This study found that the 48 participating companies experienced incremental costs of $2.6 *billion* in 1977 to comply with regulations of just the six agencies involved.[21] Beyond the costs of compliance with government regulations, other impacts must also be noted. For example, innovation and technology can be slowed down by too much regulation. Productivity declines are partially the result of numerous and often conflicting regulations. With productivity declines and increased costs, prices increase and the inflation spiral continues.

This discussion serves to point out some results of the continuing trend of more involvement of government in practically all organizations. Although the objectives of many regulations may be worthy, we seem to be approaching a situation of regulatory overkill. To reverse this trend, attitudes toward regulation will have to change significantly, both in the private and public sectors. This will require much time and effort, and managers of the future must provide the leadership to accomplish the task.

SUMMARY

By looking at some of the challenges now facing management, we become more aware of the important role that managers must play in solving future problems. Throughout this chapter we have seen that management is influenced by many environmental forces. Some of these are (1) organizations and the jobs they provide; (2) society at large (including economic conditions, education, technology, government, religion, human values); and (3) the individual worker. All of

---

[20] Lee Loevinger, "The Sociology of Bureaucracy," *Business Lawyer,* November 1968, p. 7.

[21] *Government in Business* (Columbus, Ohio: College of Administrative Science, The Ohio State University, 1979), pp. 10–11.

these forces are changing, but at different rates of speed. Therefore, a part of management's job is that of balancing an organization's needs with those of employees and society at large.

Meeting challenges of the future will also require a full understanding of management functions and their applications. Such understanding is needed if managers are to be prepared to give adequate attention to the tasks of designing jobs, setting goals, establishing budgets, and a host of other responsibilities.

KEY TERMS

Postindustrial society: A society that has moved through a period of advanced industrialization to one where there is greater concern for services, research, science, and education than for manufacturing.

Futurologists: The name given to individuals who specialize in forecasting future conditions by analyzing numerous social, political, and economic trends and their effects on one another.

Social audit: A systematic attempt to measure the total impact of corporate activities on society in order to document an organization's social responsibility.

Productivity: A measure of efficiency that refers to the relationship between the output (goods and services) of a system and its inputs (labor-hours worked and materials used).

Social responsibility: The obligations or responsibilities of an organization to the society that it serves.

Stagflation: A set of circumstances where conditions of inflation and recession exist simultaneously in the economy.

Management science: That portion of the field of management that uses various quantitative techniques and mathematical models to provide a more scientific approach to decision making.

Multinational corporation: Large corporations based in one country with operations in foreign countries around the world. Also called transnational or transideological corporations.

Bureaucratic maze: The term used to describe the numerous agencies and regulations that exist to carry out the intent of various laws or executive orders.

QUESTIONS

1. How can a study of management history help managers prepare for the future?
2. Describe some of the major changes that have taken place within the United States during the last 20 years and discuss how each has affected the practice of management.

3. How has the scope of management changed since the end of the 19th century?

4. Can a company be socially responsible and maximize profits at the same time?

5. Why are productivity gains and technological advancements important to continued economic growth?

6. Can a company that has been successful in one country expect to be equally successful as it moves into multinational operations?

7. Some critics say that productivity declines are being caused by lazy workers. What do you think?

8. The government estimates that white-collar theft, fraud, and so forth, is now costing the U.S. economy as much as $44 billion a year. Since managers at all organizational levels commit such crimes, can we ever expect ethical behavior to be widespread in business?

PROBLEMS

1. In recent years, several major waterway projects have been halted due to the possible threat of further construction activities on the preservation of certain rare forms of marine life. The Tellico Dam was held up from 1973 to 1979 when a small fish called the Snail Darter was discovered in the Little Tennessee River. Arguments that this fish would be pushed into extinction persisted until Congress passed a special act permitting a lake to be formed to preserve the fish.

Commercial development along the Cahaba River in Alabama was delayed when the federal Office of Endangered Species proposed that further construction would lead to pollution that would destroy the habitats of the Cahaba Shiner and the Goldline Darter. At maturity, neither of these fish grows to a length of more than three inches.

A stumbling block in the way of the Tennessee-Tombigbee Waterway was presented by a mussel no bigger than a silver dollar. As in the cases noted above, various groups argued that continued construction of the waterway would destroy the habitat of the mussels and drive them into extinction.

Although these species of marine life appear to be rare, some persons argue that they are merely hard to locate and catch. For example, only a dozen or so Goldline Darters have been collected with a seine after four hours of work. In addition, even if they are rare, others agree that their value to society is not as great as the construction projects that their protectors have tried to stop.

a. What environmental relationships exist in these situations?

b. Would these issues have been debated 100 years ago? Is it likely that they will be debated 100 years from now?

c. Are the persons seeking to protect these forms of marine life acting in a socially responsible manner? How about those parties who are pushing for continued construction and commercial development?

d. How can future managers prevent problems of this type?

2. The National Association of Manufacturers has reported the following:

The number of patents issued to U.S. inventors has declined since 1971.
In 1977, foreigners received 35 percent of all U.S. patents issued.

The rate of formation of small companies has fallen sharply. In 1968, there were 300 small, high-technology companies formed; in 1977, none.

From 1953 to 1966, U.S. investment in research grew at a rate of 10 percent annually in inflation-adjusted dollars. For the last 10 years, investment in research has shown no real growth.

a. What conditions have existed during the last several years to cause this decline in innovation and technology?

b. What current and long-term results may be expected from a continued decline in technological advancements?

3. Government regulations often impact on the consumer. For example, various estimates indicate that safety devices required by the National Highway Traffic Safety Administration have added from $250 to $600 to the price of each new automobile.

Regulations governing other manufacturers are not only numerous but often conflict with one another. The federal Meat Inspection Service ordered a packing company to put an opening in a sausage conveyor line so samples could be taken out for testing. After this was done, the Occupational Safety and Health Administration (OSHA) ordered the company to close the opening because it was a safety hazard. Both agencies then threatened to close the plant if their respective orders were not followed.

a. In view of situations like these, can we say that government regulations have no place in our modern, complex society?

b. What can managers do to deal with regulations that impact negatively on their organizations?

c. Can consumers do anything to limit the growing burden of government regulations?

4. The movement of workers from goods producing industries into services such as finance, health care, and government has been very obvious for several years. This trend is expected to continue, so that by the year 2000 estimates indicate that 75 percent of the labor force will work in the service sector. At the same time, other shifts taking place in American social patterns will continue.

In 1960, the average American home consisted of 3.3 persons. Today, the average is less than 2.5 persons. In addition, only three out of every five homes now include traditional family units—father, mother, children. Among a majority of nontraditional households, the head of the household is female, with the largest number being over age 35.

a. Do changes such as these have any impact on our nation's productivity? If so, can the impact be measured?

b. As concerns the utilization of human resources, why should managers of the future be aware of these and other changes that will continue to affect the labor force?

5. Many retail stores, manufacturers, hospitals, and other organizations have added new departments to deal with consumer complaints about their products or services.

a. What external pressures have motivated organizations to add departments of this type?

b. Is it likely that such departments would have been created without external pressures?

c. Since some of the costs of these departments may be passed on in the form of higher prices, do they really provide benefits for consumers?

6. In 1971, President Nixon asked Congress to guarantee $250 million in loans to the nearly bankrupt Lockheed Aircraft Corporation. Many business leaders and government officials were against the request fearing that it would set a dangerous precedent. After lengthy debate, however, a bill authorizing the guarantee was passed by a very narrow margin.

As of October 1977, the books for this case were closed when Lockheed and the government's Emergency Loan Guarantee Board agreed to terminate the loan because of the company's improved financial situation. The ending was a happy one for U.S. taxpayers. The board did not have to advance a penny under the loan guarantee and earned $31 million in fees from Lockheed's bankers during the six-year life of the loan.

More recently, the government assisted Chrysler Corporation in developing a financial package to help the company stay in business. To date, Chrysler's comeback has been hampered by negative economic conditions. Even with improvements in the economy, however, it does not appear that the ending of this case will be as happy as that in the Lockheed situation.

a. In view of the complex environments within which businesses now function, is it reasonable to expect the government to play a greater role in cases such as the ones described above?

b. Are there dangers from too much government involvement in the management of business organizations? Are there advantages?

7. The licensing agency for the three major networks—NBC, CBS, and ABC—is the Federal Communications Commission. In March of each year, the communications subcommittee of the Senate Commerce Committee reviews the yearly broadcasting record of the networks. By law, however, the government can neither regulate programming nor act in a censorship capacity. Senatorial subcommittee hearings have no authoritative power; however, they can possibly arouse public opinion that can be important when broadcast licenses come up for renewal.

Over the past few years, public opinion and senatorial concern have developed over television's new permissiveness toward sex. Since television is a highly competitive field, it is evident that producers are becoming bolder, as previous ideas and approaches become shopworn.

What environmental forces are acting as constraints on managerial decisions within the television industry?

8. Errors involving computers are often in the headlines. We read of the retired person who received a social security check for over $1 million due to a computer error. Or, how about the near collision of two commercial aircraft that was attributed to a computer failure? Of more concern, the USSR was very upset when a computer error led to the launching of several of our NORAD interceptors. Finally, bankers across the country were shocked when they learned of a teller who used a bank's computer to embezzle $1.4 million.

Each year, $200 million in computer-related losses are reported to law enforcement agencies. However, the FBI estimates that this represents only 1 percent of the number of actual losses. Consequently, if the actual total of all computer-related losses could be isolated, the dollar figure would be staggering.

a. Since computer errors can have serious consequences for an organization, is it possible that the disadvantages of computers now outweigh their advantages? Why or why not?

b. What can managers of the future do to prevent computer-related errors and losses?

SUGGESTED READINGS

Bachman, Jules, ed. *Business Problems of the Eighties.* Indianapolis: Bobbs-Merrill, 1980.

Boyes, M., and P. M. Newton. "Women in Authority: A Sociopsychological Analysis." *The Journal of Applied Behavioral Science,* January–February–March 1978, pp. 7–20.

Cassell, F. H. "The Corporation and Community: Realities and Myths." *MSU Business Topics,* Autumn 1970, pp. 11–20.

Galbraith, J. K. "The Defense of the Multinational Company." *Harvard Business Review,* March–April 1978, pp. 83–93.

Glaser, E. M. "State-of-the-Art Questions about Quality of Worklife." *Personnel,* May–June 1976, pp. 39–47.

Gordon, F. E., and M. H. Strober, eds. *Bringing Women into Management.* New York: McGraw-Hill, 1975.

Jones, T. E. *Options for the Future: A Comparative Analysis of Policy-Oriented Forecasts.* New York: Praeger Publishers, 1980.

Kuehner, C. D., ed. *Capital and Job Formation: Our Nation's 3d-Century Challenge.* Homewood, Ill.: Dow Jones-Irwin, 1978.

McGuire, J. W., ed. *Contemporary Management: Issues and Viewpoints.* Englewood Cliffs, N.J.: Prentice-Hall, 1974.

Miner, J. B. *The Human Constraint: The Coming Shortage of Managerial Talent.* Washington, D.C.: BNA Books, 1974.

Seashore, S. E. "The Future of Work: How It May Change and What It May Mean." *Industrial and Labor Relations Report,* Fall 1975.

Tavernier, G. "Changing Climate for Future Managers." *International Management,* August 1976, pp. 10–13.

U.S.A.'s Energy Outlook 1980–2000. Houston: Exxon Corporation, Public Affairs Department, December 1979.

Viola, R. H. *Organizations in a Changing Society: Administration and Human Values.* Philadelphia: W. B. Saunders, 1977.

Walton, C. *The Ethics of Corporate Conduct.* Englewood Cliffs, N.J.: Prentice-Hall, 1977, pp. 1–30.

R. H. Macy & Company

Within the $890-billion-a-year retail industry, R. H. Macy & Company owns and operates 83 stores with sales close to $2 billion, almost double its volume of 10 years ago. During 1970, sales were $901 million, but earnings declined to $20.6 million (from $24.3 million a year earlier). The philosophy of the company is summarized in statements made by Jesse Straus, president from 1919 to 1933. For example, he once stated that persons going into the retail business should be merchants because everything depends on the successful buying and selling of goods.

When the company's president and chief executive officer, Earnest L. Molloy, retired, one of the individuals being considered for the top position was Donald B. Smiley. Mr. Smiley was an experienced lawyer and served as chairman of the board of directors and treasurer of the company.

The success of large retail chains requires not only expert merchandising, but also knowledge of governmental regulations, labor unions, consumerism, real estate, taxes, and stockholder relations. Mr. Smiley's support came from other managers and stockholders who said that retailing was undergoing some vast changes and, therefore, demanded a far more interdisciplinary management approach. In addition, these supporters claimed that many management problems could only be solved by a financially oriented and managerially experienced person.

In spite of his support, there were serious questions concerning whether Mr. Smiley could manage a business where past success had been so dependent on consumer-oriented merchants. In fact, a general feeling within the industry indicated that declining customer service was retailing's biggest problem and that it could best be handled by experienced retailers.

Questions

1. How would you support Mr. Smiley if you were a member of the board of directors and favored his selection?

2. If you were a member of the board and opposed to Mr. Smiley, what reasons would you present for not selecting him?

3. Does Mr. Smiley have a chance of being selected for the top post? What are the important factors influencing your decision?

Midville Ambulance Service

Midville Ambulance, a privately owned and operated company, is engaged in a running debate with city council members. The debate revolves around the company's policy of refusing to provide ambulance service to persons who are indigent or unable to pay. For instance, the dispatcher might refuse to send an ambulance if it is assumed that the person living at a given address is without visible means of support.

The latest incident involving the company's refusal to provide ambulance service took place when a call came from an out-of-state woman living in a local hotel. After learning that an ambulance was not available, the hotel manager called the police for help, informing them that the woman was pregnant and needed hospital attention. Police officers arriving on the scene felt that the woman was too ill to be taken to the hospital by car, and therefore, recalled Midville Ambulance. After being refused ambulance service for a second time, the police officers took the woman to the hospital in their patrol car. The woman subsequently lost her baby.

In response to the incident, the city council proposed a new city ordinance requiring any licensed ambulance service to respond to all emergency calls. Violations of the ordinance will carry a fine and license revocation. Midville Ambulance is the only company providing service in the community and is now arguing about the constitutionality of the proposed ordinance. Citizens hope that the company will not test the ordinance by refusing to answer an emergency call, thereby endangering someone's life.

Questions

1. Disregarding the proposed ordinance, does Midville Ambulance have a social responsibility to citizens of the community?
2. Do you feel that the first objective of Midville Ambulance is to make a profit? If so, is such an objective consistent with providing a service for the sick or injured?
3. Does this problem differ from situations where a new telephone or utility customer is refused service until a deposit is made?

ADCO Lead Chemicals Plant

The ADCO Lead Chemicals plant turns lead and zinc into refined products for other manufacturers. Products manufactured include (1) zinc and lead paint pigments, (2) zinc and lead chemicals for crystal and glass to give clarity and sparkle, and (3) zinc and lead chemicals for lubricants to prevent breakdown of oil and grease. The facility is located in the western part of the United States and is one of the largest such plants in the country.

ADCO workers have now been striking for over two months. Some of the strikers recall how a one-month strike three years ago seemed to ease their fatigue and muscle pains, symptoms they attributed to lead poisoning. Since lead and zinc can be toxic, the industry is generally considered one of the most hazardous to employees' health.

At the present time two versions—one by the company and one by the union—exist as to why the strike is in progress. Company officials say the strike results from an unreasonable request by the local United Rubber Workers Union for additional pay and fringe benefits. Presently receiving $5.27 to $5.77 an hour, union workers now desire a one-year contract with a 25 percent across-the-board pay raise. The company has offered a three-year contract with first year raises of about 7.5 percent.

The union's version for the strike goes beyond just money. Specifically, it hopes to obtain greater contractual protection from the problems of lead and zinc health hazards at the plant and better company awareness of the health complaints of employees.

Company position as to employee health

In a speech to employees prior to the strike, C. J. Batson, the manager of two ADCO chemical and fiber plants, noted that the company's medical program had existed for more than 60 years. He stated that ADCO Industries knows more about treating lead intoxication than does either the National Institute for Occupational Safety and Health or the United Rubber Workers. Furthermore, he related that the company will take whatever action is medically prudent to protect workers. A press release quoted Batson as saying, "Don't think for a moment that ADCO is less interested in the health and safety of workers than the government and union. Of course, not everyone has the same sensitivity to lead toxins, and people respond differently to treatment."

Throughout the history of the organization, employees have been taken off the job and hospitalized until the amount of lead in their body returns to an acceptable level. The plant's medical program director is Dr. Dee d'Meek. During a negotiation meeting, Dr. d'Meek noted there had been a number of people over the years with lead colic (severe abdominal pain). However, he stated, he did not consider lead colic a serious problem since it subsides with being off the job.

The company has a large infirmary. A portion of the unit is set up for dental care. A dentist comes regularly to the plant to extract teeth. Dr. d'Meek does not feel that there is sufficient proof that dental problems experienced by workers are connected to lead exposure. More specifically, the doctor believes the loss of teeth is due to poor personal hygiene on the part of the employees and people living in the community. Several people in the area, as observed by the doctor, are missing their original teeth.

Union-employee position

Larry Mercer, an ADCO employee for 10 years and division chairman for the local union, related to the news media that he has had five teeth pulled because they came loose. He did not say for sure that lead caused the problem, but his local physician advised him to leave the company. Mercer stated that ADCO officials refuse to acknowledge the effects of lead poisoning. Furthermore, he said that most employees do not have any confidence in Dr. d'Meek, particularly since he is unwilling to discuss medical problems with them. This point is substantiated by the statement made by Dr. d'Meek, "You can't give the employees a medical education every time they come and see you since most patients are better off not knowing the fine details."

OSHA position

A report prepared six months ago by a medical consultant of the Occupation Safety and Health Administration (OSHA) faulted the company for not acting quickly when faced with the possibility of lead intoxication of workers. Specifically the report stated:

> Not enough consideration is given to the potential long-term effects of lead exposure. As a general rule, only overtly symptomatic lead poisoning with lead colic was recognized by the medical department as lead intoxication. When a worker developed colic, he was treated symptomatically, held off work for a few days, and then returned to work. Most workers have had at least two episodes of lead colic and several workers returned many times for treatment.
>
> No comprehensive evaluation of any of the other potential or actual lead related illnesses were considered, no workup instituted, no consistent follow-up planned, and no prevention advised.

Negotiations are continuing at this time. The general impression of union members is that they are not making any significant progress with the company in achieving improved health care. Management representatives are basing their position on Dr. d'Meek's opinions.

Questions

1. Are the positions as proposed by the union and employees rational and logical?
2. What is management's responsibility in overcoming employee objections and what strategy should be followed?
3. What environmental forces does the company face?
4. Based on the OSHA report, what functional areas of management have not been performed, consequently resulting in this problem?
5. What more can the union do to force management to improve health conditions at the plant?

PART TWO

PLANNING FOR PERFORMANCE AND RESULTS

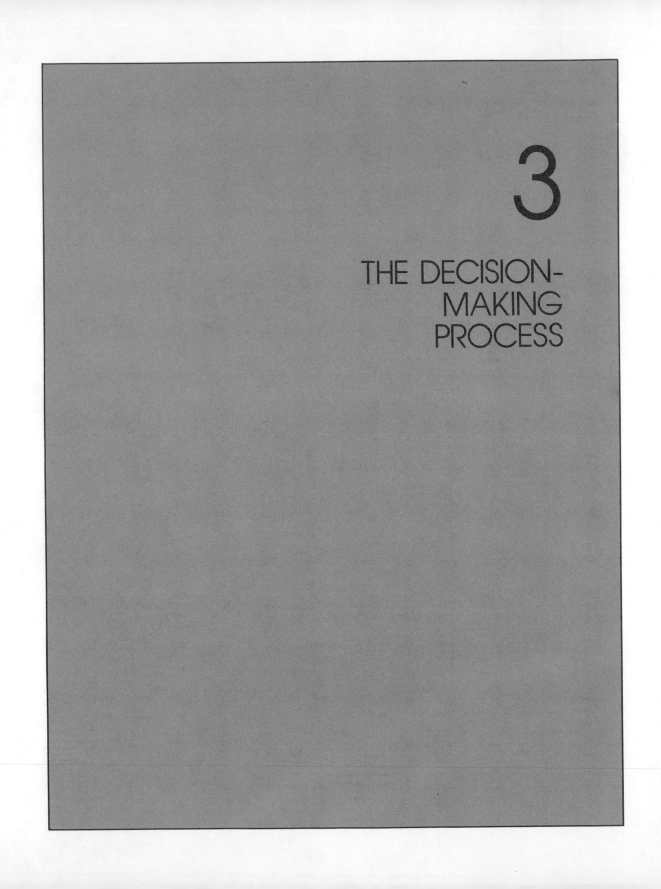

3

THE DECISION-MAKING PROCESS

PURPOSE

The forced resignation of Mary Cunningham, vice president for strategic planning at Bendix Corporation, was based in part on either an imagined or real romantic relationship between her and the company's chairman and chief executive officer (CEO), William M. Agee. Although Agee denied any romantic affair, Cunningham's meteoric rise in 15 months from executive assistant—to Agee—to vice president for corporate and public affairs, and then to her last position in the company seemed to be influenced by many other decisions. Specifically, just prior to Cunningham's promotion, Agee suddenly ousted Bendix's president and chief operating officer, William P. Panny. Simultaneously, Jerome Jacobson resigned as executive vice president for strategic planning. This opened the position for Cunningham. A week later, the company announced two major decisions: to sell its forest-products operation for $435 million and to put up for grabs its 20 percent stake in Asarco, the nonferrous-metals producer. During the same week, a major reorganization led to the eventual termination or transfer of about 250 of the 800 employees working at company headquarters in Southfield, Michigan. Without regard to the correctness of these decisions, it is important to recognize that decision making is complex.

At Bendix, as well as any other organization, decision making is critical to success. Therefore, this chapter looks at the meaning and nature of decision making within organizational settings. The decision-making process is examined, along with the impact of behavioral considerations on the process. Finally, the role of models in decision making is discussed.

OBJECTIVES

1. To develop an understanding of decision making as a process that influences all organizational activity.

2. To relate decision making to the functions of planning, organizing, actuating, and controlling.

3. To discuss the steps of the decision-making process.

4. To examine the impact of environmental constraints and behavioral considerations upon decision making.

5. To introduce the use of models as basic to decision making.

All individuals are forced to make choices, such as selecting a college to attend, choosing an occupation, or deciding upon a specific employer. Unfortunately, it is not obvious which decision in each situation will provide the greatest pleasure, avoid the most pain, or lead to a better world in the future. Goals to be achieved, environmental factors, and personal values must all be considered before a final choice can be made. For many decisions facing managers, therefore, specific solutions are not well defined.

Decision making is also a continuous process that pervades all organizational activity. To this extent, understanding what makes an organization successful depends upon our knowledge of how people make effective decisions. Within any organization, virtually every person is a decision maker. The worker who shuts down the lathe to smoke a cigarette is as much a part of an organization's decision-making system as the CEO who decides to build a new plant costing millions of dollars. The consequences of these decisions vary in their influence on the achievement of objectives, and the perceived risks of decision making cause many people to view it as a difficult and unrewarding task.

Some of the difficulties associated with decision making stem from the biological makeup of decision makers. People are usually dependent on others for the education and experience required in making meaningful choices. For example, members of primitive social groups (cultures) received advice on possible actions to take in a variety of situations from their leaders. To some degree this led to programmed decisions since the same choice could be used in basically similar situations. In our complex society, however, it is impossible to specify the most appropriate course of action for every problem. In fact, the critical issue may not be the particular choice selected, but how the manager goes about identifying the true problem requiring a decision.

MEANING OF DECISION MAKING

Decision making implies a choice from among two or more alternative courses of action. If a choice does not have to be made to solve a problem, an individual is not actually involved in a decision-making situation. For example, consider the manager who wants to determine when the office secretary left for lunch. This would not necessarily be a decision-making situation since a choice may not be involved. Instead, the problem might be only a matter of obtaining the correct information. Decision making, however, could appear if the manager had to decide how to obtain the desired information. Basically, then, decision making and problem solving are not necessarily identical. As defined here, *decision making is the process of choosing a course of action from among two or more possible alternatives in order to arrive at a solution for a given problem.* As implied, decision making involves an evaluation of alternatives prior to the act of choosing the one to be implemented in response to a certain problem situation.

FIGURE 3–1
Decision making and the management functions

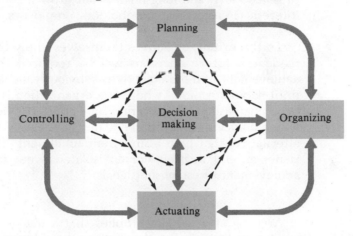

IMPORTANCE OF MANAGEMENT DECISION MAKING

Decision making is so basic that no management function can be performed without it. For management purposes, decisions are obviously required in planning, organizing, actuating, and controlling. As shown in Figure 3–1, the decision-making process is considered to be an activity inherent in all management functions. For this reason, the process is not regarded as a function by itself nor is it synonymous with the process of managing.

As already noted, managers at all organizational levels make decisions, although they differ in type and scope. At the top levels of an organization, decisions establishing overall objectives and strategies are included among the most important to be made. Decisions of this type are not routine, and choices do not exist within a programmed format. Middle managers are generally more involved with decision making constrained by overall operating policies and plans. First-line supervisors, in turn, are concerned with short-range decisions that relate to specific activities to be carried out within the framework of policies and procedures established at middle management levels. Due to this integration of authority levels, the decision-making process involves all managers in an organization and must be viewed as a total system of utmost importance to organizational success.

OBJECTIVES AND DECISION MAKING

Objectives are the targets managers seek to achieve over various time periods. Generally, they are broad statements that serve as guides for action in determining the direction organizations will go and the activities they will follow.[1] For example, the primary objective of Ral-

---

[1] Some authors make a distinction between objectives and goals, indicating that objectives are long range while goals are short-range targets. We use the terms *objectives* and *goals* synonymously throughout the chapters. See Chapter 8 for further discussion.

ston Purina Company is to optimize the use of its resources and to produce short- and long-term profit growth consistent with balanced interests of customers, shareholders, employees, suppliers, and society at large.

To this extent, objectives themselves imply that a choice has been made and future decisions will be required that contribute to the achievement of those objectives. Obviously, decisions cannot be made until it is determined where the organization is going and what is to be accomplished. To reiterate, objectives provide the focal point on which all decisions are based. They are the guides to the selection of alternatives that help assure their fulfillment. Thus, decision making is not an end in itself nor an isolated event but the means to the achievement of established goals.

THE DECISION-MAKING PROCESS

Arriving at a decision implies that a manger has gone through a series of systematically related steps. Basically, the steps of the decision-making process include (1) determining the problem as related to objectives being sought, (2) identifying alternative solutions, (3) analyzing the possible outcomes of each alternative, and (4) selecting an alternative for subsequent implementation. Pictorially, this process is shown in Figure 3–2. The process is, however, more complex than the steps suggest since each step itself involves the decision-making process. In essence, then, the decision maker does not go through the steps so systematically that decision making becomes a clearly defined, logical procedure. Managers are involved in a continuous flow of problems, many of which cannot be classified. At the same time, their attitudes toward risk may lead to choices that will be safe but not accomplish objectives as effectively as others. Thus, the importance of understanding the decision process is not to justify results, but to be aware of the steps involved while recognizing the need to develop a healthy way of thinking about the numerous decisions that must be made in the day-to-day life of an organization.[2]

Determining the problem

Determining the precise problem to be solved is the first and possibly most important step in the decisional process. The difficulty of this step can be seen in the fact that problems are subjective and relative to the decision maker. For example, managers may view differently the problem (gap) between the goal to be attained (terminal state) and the current situation (existing state). One manager may be aware that a gap or problem exists, while another manager may feel that current activities are right on target.

---

[2] For further insight into the processes of decision making, see Herbert A. Simon, *The New Science of Management Decision* (Englewood Cliffs, N.J.: Prentice-Hall, 1977), pp. 39–81.

FIGURE 3–2
The decision-making process

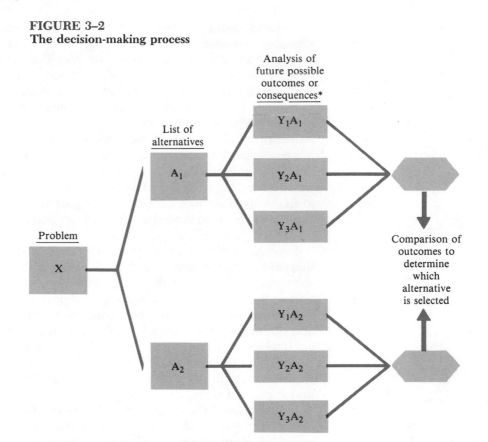

* Different alternatives will lead to different possible outcomes or consequences. This can be expressed symbolically as Y^1A^1; thus, the outcome, Y^1 if alternative A^1 is followed.

At this stage, time and effort should be expended only in gathering data and information that are relevant to identification of the real problem. The problem should be defined precisely and its magnitude understood. Otherwise, managers may concentrate on symptoms related to the problem rather than on the actual problem itself.

Of course, if only symptoms are considered, the basic problem will continue to come up over and over again. One way of zeroing in on the correct problem is to ask, "What is to be achieved?" For example, analyzing the gap between the objective of achieving $5 million sales this year while current sales are only $1 million is a good way of determining the true problem to be solved.

Identifying alternative solutions

The second step of the decision-making process involves the preparation of a detailed listing of alternative courses of action that could be used to solve the problem at hand. To be most meaningful, only viable and realistic alternatives should be included in the listing. For example, consider the manager who has the problem of determining how additional deliveries are to be met due to a large, temporary increase in sales. It would be meaningless to consider the alternative of purchasing a new truck if it would not be utilized after sales returned to normal. Obviously, the potential benefits and consequences of each alternative must be considered.

There are also time and cost constraints that will restrict the number of reasonable alternatives to be selected. Since these constraints are finite, the search for alternatives must eventually terminate. Time constraints can be exemplified by the student who did not include all available persons in a list of possible partners for a school dance. By the time such a list could have been completed, the date of the dance would surely have passed.

Psychological barriers may also restrict the number of alternatives that will be developed by a given manager. This is illustrated by the store manager who felt that a particular brand of cosmetics could not be handled because of certain unethical practices of the manufacturer.

Finally, various laws and regulations, as well as corporate objectives and policies, act as additional constraints on the number of alternatives applicable to any given problem. If, for example, the manufacturer of welding equipment holds down cost increases by introducing new technology, then an increase in prices would not be a viable alternative under present policy guidelines.

Creativity and the search for alternatives   Good managers are innovators who depend heavily on ingenuity and on the ability to think creatively. Innovation is referred to here as an idea, practice, or object perceived as new by the decision maker.[3] New ideas and ways of doing things often have to take precedence over more traditional alternatives that have proven successful in the past, and solutions to some problems may have to go beyond alternatives that are readily identifiable.[4] A situation that illustrates this point is that of a relatively young man who went into the apple-growing and packing business. The man knew almost nothing about growing apples, but he was willing to learn. Solutions to some of the problems he encountered were considered radical. In fact, many apple growers in the area felt that it would be just a matter of time before this "youngster" with his new ideas would learn a lesson and be out of business. Yet, due to a creative and innovative spirit, the operation prospered and grew to one of the largest in the state.

One point cited by many writers on creativity and innovation is

---

[3] See Gerald Zaltman et al., *Innovations and Organizations* (New York: Wiley-Interscience, 1973).

[4] See E. F. Harrison, *The Management Decision-Making Process* (Boston: Houghton Mifflin, 1975).

that these skills can be developed.[5] Individual company programs, such as those at General Electric and Minnesota Mining and Manufacturing, operate on this premise. Thus, all present and potential managers should delve into the mental and procedural aspects of creativity. This is especially true for supervisors and middle-management personnel since creativity is often one of the most important elements in promotion and advancement at these levels within an organization.

Without question, the application of creative ideas to managerial operations is often difficult. There seem to be three reasons for this difficulty:

1. The formal organization with its multiple levels of administrative authority may act as a barrier.
2. The desire for security on the part of some managers may hinder the approval and implementation of new ideas.
3. When it appears that an organization is operating successfully, managers may not be willing to rock the boat.

While the first of these reasons refers to structural barriers, the other two roadblocks are caused by resistance to change. As might be expected, this resistance is greatest when new ideas are not understood by those managers who will be affected by a change in operations.

Brainstorming alternatives   One creative technique used in indentifying alternative courses of action is referred to as brainstorming. There are many examples depicting successful applications of brainstorming, such as the development of the GL-70 slogan for Gleem toothpaste. Basically, the approach seeks to elicit ideas by pooling the efforts of several people who either meet as a cohesive group or work on a problem by themselves.[6]

In group participation, criticisms and an analysis of suggestions are postponed so as neither to stifle nor to restrict creative thinking. Without such interruptions, participants are encouraged to come up with new ideas by building on previous comments or suggestions. Possibly the key to the success of group brainstorming may be the length of

---

[5] For interesting materials on creativity and innovation, see Irvin Summers and David E. White, "Creativity Techniques: Toward Improvement of the Decision Process," in *Intercom: Readings in Organizational Communication,* ed. S. Ferguson and S. D. Ferguson, (Rochella Park, N.J.: Hayden Book, 1980), pp. 338–48; E. M. Rogers and R. A. Rogers, *Communication in Organizations* (New York: Free Press, 1976), chap. 6; Waino W. Suojanen and Stephen Brooke, "The Management of Creativity," *California Management Review,* Fall 1971, pp. 17–23.

[6] Alex F. Osborn, *Applied Imagination* (New York: Charles Scribner's Sons, 1953), emphasizes group participation to gain the greatest number of ideas, while Marvin Dunnette, John Campbell, and Kay Jaastad, "The Effect of Group Participation on Brainstorming Effectiveness for Two Industrial Samples," *Journal of Applied Psychology,* 1963, pp. 30–37 feel that group participation has an inhibiting influence on creative thinking during brainstorming. The latter reference indicates that individuals may produce more ideas without sacrificing quality when working alone; however, group participation may be useful in warming up for individual sessions.

the work period. With an extended period, a greater number of ideas tend to be produced.[7] Finally, before utilizing brainstorming, the technique should be researched thoroughly. Potential problems exist and should be understood by those who may wish to apply the technique.[8]

Analyzing alternatives

The third step in decision making is that of analyzing and evaluating each alternative in terms of its possible consequences and impact on goal attainment. Generally, managers can never be sure of the actual outcome of each alternative. Consequently, evaluating alternatives requires managers to call on present knowledge, past experience, foresight, and scientific acumen. A discussion of the probability decision model that considers the three relationships of certainty, risk, and uncertainty between alternatives and outcomes is presented in Appendix A.

Seeking strategic factors The astute decision maker must recognize the strategic or limiting factors creating a problem. *Strategic factors refer to those that are most important in determining the action to be taken in solving a given problem.* Identifying such factors in the right form, place, and time is, therefore, crucial in decision making.

In situations where a sequence of subdecisions is required to reach an overall goal, a determination of new strategic factors is necessary for each decision. Thus, several strategic factors may be present in making complex decisions, and the role of the manager is to recognize such limiting factors. When they are not considered, the chances of selecting an optimum course of action diminish rapidly.

To illustrate the role of strategic factors, we can consider the case of a computer that suddenly fails to operate. Several alternative courses of action could be followed to get the equipment working. These might include checking various electronic systems, reevaluating the program, or checking the sequence of inputs. Only when the decision makers discover that a circuit breaker is open (the strategic factor) will they be able to determine the course of action to be taken—reactivating the breaker to restore power. Thus, if strategic factors cannot be properly isolated, an analysis of alternatives will be faulty and may result in the selection of an inappropriate course of action.

Organizing strategic factors is also important in analyzing alternative courses of action. For example, a problem may lend itself to an organization of strategic factors under the classification of quality, quantity, time, and cost. Or, the who, what, why, where, when, and how approach might be appropriate. Regardless of how the factors are organized, a systematic approach must be followed in the analysis of alterna-

---

[7] M. E. Shaw, *Group Dynamics: The Psychology of Small Group Behavior* (New York: McGraw-Hill, 1971).

[8] Like many other management techniques—time study, work sampling, and sensitivity training—brainstorming is often performed or conducted by poorly trained persons who have not researched the area well enough to understand the benefits and problems associated with the technique.

tives. In this way, the probability of making a more rational selection from among alternative courses of action is increased.

Irrelevance of past decisions Without a consideration of present and future conditions, past decisions are quite irrelevant in the decision-making process. For example, the original cost of an asset may have little significance on present or future decisions. Consider the manager who plans to sell an old truck for its current market value of $5,000. Since the truck is no longer needed, the fact that it originally cost $25,000 may be interesting but not relevant to the present decision. Picture an investor who purchased XYZ Corporation stock for $100 a share and now holds it at $25 a share due to a general decline in the stock market. If the price of this stock will take longer to recover than other issues in the market, it may be logical to sell and invest the funds in a more active issue. Under these conditions, the fact that XYZ stock cost $100 is only one of several factors to consider in deciding to sell the stock.

The concept of utilizing past decisions appropriately is referred to as the principle of sunk cost which emphasizes that the past is only an uncertain approximation of the present. Therefore, managers should not rely on past decisions except as they can be of value in estimating the future. For any organization, the important costs are those that have not been incurred since decision making is concerned with the future, rather than with the past.

Selecting an alternative for implementation

The last step in decision making is selecting an alternative that seems to solve the problem. The key is to go through the process so that the best course of action is identified and selected to achieve a goal or to solve the problem at hand.

The selection of an alternative also requires that it be communicated to other members of the organization. The ultimate success of an alternative depends as much on how it is introduced into an organization as it does on how the decision was made. Acceptance of the decision by group members so that it has an impact on their performance is always essential to effective implementation.

To review, the decision-making process is composed of four distinct steps: (1) defining the problem, (2) arriving at a set of alternative solutions, (3) analyzing each alternative in terms of its possible consequences, and (4) selecting a satisfactory course of action. There are difficulties, however, that prevent the process from being performed in a rational manner. The deceiving simplicity of decision making is overshadowed by a series of complex problems and barriers.

MINIMIZING THE COMPLEXITY OF THE DECISION PROCESS

One way of simplifying the decision process is to establish objectives, policies, and procedures that will provide guidelines for managers to follow when making routine and repetitive decisions. Professional codes, rules, and policy manuals are steps in this direction, since they guide decision making by outlining acceptable behavior. Thus, problems that are well structured and not complex can be solved with programmed decisions. For example, consider the supervisor who needs to specify the wage rate for a new employee. Basically, this is a routine and repetitive decision that allows the supervisor to use the company's job specification to classify and determine the wage rate for the employee. If the job was new and ill-defined, then the decisional problem would be unprogrammed, requiring greater innovative responses. As will be noted later in this chapter, mathematical models along with the use of computers have made programmed decisions more available for routine problem-solving situations. Also, it is fortunate that the capacity to make better decisions can be developed through training, experience, and an expanded knowledge of the total decision-making process.

Although the decisional process implies a rational way of thinking about making a choice, Herbert A. Simon states that human beings are not always rational in making decisions.[9] He suggests that it is impossible for the behavior of an individual, regarding personal or organizational decisions, to reach a high degree of rationality. Four basic reasons for such a lack of rationality are listed below:

1. Individuals have incomplete knowledge of the facts surrounding a problem and are limited in their ability to foresee future events. At any given time, limited human and material resources restrict the amount of information that can be obtained about a given situation. Thus, for any situation, knowledge is fragmented, particularly that related to the possible consequences of various courses of action. As a result, it may be useless to search for the optimum (best possible) decision.[10]

2. Identifying all alternative solutions for a problem is normally impossible. As noted earlier, time and cost constraints require that only the most viable alternatives be considered. By eliminating alternatives that are not feasible, the list of possible courses of action can be narrowed. Since the number of alternatives must be limited, it is extremely important that the true problem be identified. The more accurate the statement of the problem, the more likely the selected alternative will produce a satisfactory solution.

3. The anticipated consequences of various alternatives often differ from those that are actually realized. Such differences result from changes in factors beyond a manager's sphere of influence.

---

[9] See Herbert A. Simon, *Administrative Behavior: A Study of Decision-Making Processes in Organization* (New York: Free Press, 1965), pp. 1–11, 61–109, and 220–47. Copyright © 1965 Macmillan Publishing Co.

[10] Realizing that perfectly rational decision making is not possible, Simon has suggested that a satisfactory rather than an optimum course of action is reasonable to seek. See H. A. Simon, "Theories of Decision Making in Economics and Behavioral Science," *American Economic Review*, June 1959, pp. 262–65.

Assume that the loan officer of a bank is considering a $7,500 loan to a customer who wants to purchase a new sailboat with complete rigging. Since the banker is not certain about changing conditions, it is impossible to determine the actual consequences that may occur if the loan is made. Some perceived consequences might include *(a)* the loan could overextend the customer's financial status and possibly result in a repossession of the boat; *(b)* a repossession could be viewed by top management as an exercise of poor judgment by the officer who granted the loan; or *(c)* loan payments might be late and, therefore, require additional time and money to collect them. In any event, the banker is not certain that the loan will be repaid. Yet, regardless of the difficulty associated with determining possible outcomes, predictions must be made and evaluated according to some scale of desirability. In terms of evaluating the effects of each alternative, there is no simple approach that is acceptable in all situations. In some cases, the alternatives could be evaluated in terms of profit. In others where there are multiple evaluation criteria, the process is much more complicated. This is particularly true when the problem involves uncertain or risky elements.

4. A decision by one manager may have an adverse effect on objectives in another area of the organization. Specifically, organizations have multiple goals, and decisions that optimize results in one department can cause lower levels of achievement (suboptimization) in other departments. For example, a production efficiency objective to mass produce high-volume goods would conflict with a marketing goal to sell distinctive quality products with high profit margins. As a result, an optimization of both goals may not be realistically possible. Also, since knowledge of the future is limited, a decision that produces optimal results in the short run may be suboptimal at a later date. Remember that the automobile was first viewed as preserving the environment since horses would not have to be on city streets. Air pollution today, however, is a major concern surrounding automobile emissions.

The effects of suboptimization can be lessened by following a systems approach for every decision. This allows each alternative to be evaluated in conjunction with decisions in other departments. Considering the impact of each decision on every phase of the organization, however, is complicated and time consuming. Regardless of this difficulty, the decision maker must make an attempt to specify how various alternatives will actually affect the system. Possibly, future advancements in computerized decision making will allow managers to evaluate systematically the impact of each alternative on the entire organization.[11] Even then, the degree of rationality found in the decision-making process will still be influenced by the quantity of information available,

---

[11] Efraim Turban and J. R. Meredith, *Fundamentals of Management Science* (Plano, Tex: Business Publications, 1977), pp. 30–31.

the number of alternatives that can be examined, and the pressures exerted by internal and external environments. An organization must, therefore, be concerned with the limits of rationality, how the limits can be overcome, and the impact of organizational structure on the decision maker.[12]

ENVIRONMENTAL CONSTRAINTS

Significant contributions to decision theory were made by Chester I. Barnard, a successful business executive in the telephone industry.[13] Barnard introduced the concept of the social environment as a constraint influencing the final outcome of a decision. He stated that nature, legal regulations, social responsiveness, competitors, and customer needs are all environmental constraints that affect the final outcome of a decision. To Barnard, the decision maker must have an understanding of the environment so that the effects of alternative solutions can be predicted. Environmental factors, he felt, become more distinct and exacting as objectives are redefined and made more explicit. He noted, as well, that objectives have no meaning except in an environment with a set of restrictions or limitations.

BEHAVIORAL CONSIDERATIONS

The previous two sections of this chapter should dispel the belief that managers rationally proceed step by step to define a problem, identify a wide range of alternatives with their consequences and risks, collect and analyze all data thoroughly, and select a specific alternative that is totally acceptable to all persons involved. With the problems of rationality and environmental constraints, the role of human behavior also restricts the decision-making process. This is particularly significant when we recognize that actions by dominant individuals or coalitions influence organizational decisions through negotiation and compromise.

Seldom does a manager make a decision that is supported by all organizational units. Some decisions will be bitterly opposed, some well supported, while others will fall within a zone of comparative indifference. Thus, from a behavioral viewpoint, managers must be sensitive to the power structures within an organization in order to predict which decisions will gain the greatest support in the pursuit of goals. Moreover, goal achievement depends upon how well managers influence the decisions of those personnel who are involved in perform-

---

[12] It would seem that a basis for much of the poor decision making in organizations is due to the barriers that are inherent in particular organizational structures and decision-making systems.

[13] Barnard's major book, *The Functions of the Executive,* was derived from eight of his lectures given at Lowell Institute in Boston in 1937.

ing tasks and implementing programs at lower levels of authority.[14]

Some of the behavioral elements that influence the decisional process are given below:

Group (peer) pressures, both supportive and nonsupportive, that are exerted on the decision maker.

The decision maker's stated position within various groups (managerial and nonmanagerial).

Personal attitudes about what and how others will think if a particular decision is made.

Feelings about the expectations of others and the weight of public opinion.

Ability to use the reactions of key individuals and groups to assess the impact of a decision on the organization.

The stress to which the decision maker is exposed.[15]

Personal knowledge and skill can also affect a decision, especially the amount of knowledge one has about a problem and its alternatives. Clearly, the manager must have the ability and resources if a decisional problem is to be meaningful.[16] For instance, if a manager knows very little about production but is very knowledgeable about computers, a decision concerning capital expenditures might be to purchase a new computer. A decision is also influenced by the personal values of the decision maker at the time each alternative action is being considered. Thus, the motivation to develop a strong work force may be sufficient to influence the manager to see the importance of creating a personnel department. However, this would not be likely unless it was felt that the department would better fulfill the company's overall objectives than some other available alternative. Unfortunately, in many organizations, managers perceive that problems of this type exist but are not sufficiently motivated to try to solve them.

MEASUREMENT AND QUANTIFICATION OF ALTERNATIVES

If alternatives are to provide the best payoff in a given situation, they should be quantifiable and measurable. Also, if several objectives are being sought, measurement is vitally important in establishing priorities among them. Realistically, when objectives cannot be stated

---

[14] See George Kelley, "Seducing the Elites: The Politics of Decision Making and Innovation in Organizational Networks," *The Academy of Management Review*, July 1976, pp. 66–74.

[15] For a discussion of additional factors, see B. Ripley, W. B. Moreland, and R. H. Sinnreich, "Policy-Making: A Conceptual Scheme," *American Political Quarterly*, 1973, pp. 3–42.

[16] A discussion of the preconditions for problem solving may be found in K. R. MacCrimmon and R. N. Taylor, "Decision Making and Problem Solving," *Handbook of Industrial and Organizational Psychology*, ed. Marvin D. Dunnette (Chicago: Rand McNally, 1976) pp. 1399–1400.

in quantifiable terms, alternative courses of action cannot be measured as effectively. Even if alternatives are quantifiable, of course, each one has a different degree of utility or desirability associated with it.[17] This explains why three managers may arrive at different conclusions to the same problem. The perceived utility of each alternative differs among them.

Since subjective utility values cannot be compared, some type of natural measure is needed for evaluating various outcomes. For cash transactions, one such measure utilizes monetary values. For example, in deciding how you will return from work in the evening, the cost of each method of transportation can be considered. Money, however, cannot provide an exact measurement for comparing alternatives since more dollars do not always imply greater utility. Time, convenience, peace of mind, and other considerations may be involved and cannot always be converted to a monetary scale. Consequently, it is best to treat the amount of money as a substitute for utility in a particular decision only when the amount of funds is relatively small compared to the total assets of an organization or individual.

In general, overcoming difficulties in measurement requires the manager to state problems so that progress toward their solution can be observed, measured, and evaluated. Here, again, the importance of quantification cannot be overemphasized. This is not to imply that all decisional problems can be quantified, but managers often make better decisions when quantitative measures can be applied in the evaluation of alternatives.

SCIENTIFIC APPROACH TO DECISION MAKING

As organizations grow in size and number, managers recognize that they cannot make all necessary decisions. Consequently, some authority to make decisions must be delegated to others. A proper utilization of this authority, in turn, requires that decision making be considered from a scientific approach.

Another reason for moving toward a scientific analysis of decisions is the desire to achieve greater productivity. At first, managers generally focus their decisional efforts on specific areas within businesses, especially manufacturing processes and techniques, job design, equipment layout, and production incentive systems. Later this interest expands to include virtually all organizational problems.

Prior to the 19th century, the practice of management included little systematic or scientific decision making. One of the earliest instances of a systematic approach being applied to solve planning problems took place in 1800 at the Soho Foundry in Great Britain where the Watt's steam engine was manufactured. In the United States, seeds

---

[17] Utility is defined as the ability of a decision to satisfy objectives or to overcome problems.

for the development and application of scientific decision making were sown by Eli Whitney, particularly in the manufacturing of standardized muskets for the federal government.

In retrospect, two distinct periods have witnessed extensive applications of scientific methodology to managerial decision making. The first period includes the "scientific management" movement that began around 1900. Fundamental to this movement were the attempts to identify principles that would assist managers in the decisional process. Beginning during the 1940s, the second period is known for applications of various scientific techniques to the practice of management.

Much of the scientific work that has been done in this second period is referred to as operations research. In operations research, the scientific method is applied to the solution of managerial problems. Starting in about 1970, scholars coined the phrases management science and mathematical model building to characterize this approach. Management science, however, tends to be broader than operations research. It has reference not only to applied decision theory requiring scientific, mathematical, and logical means to solve decisional problems but also to computerized information systems and environmental concerns. Figure 3–3 outlines a simple, systematic structure of the management science decision-making system. Inputs of the system are shown as problems and possible alternatives related to labor, materials, capital, energy, and communications. These inputs are then transformed into outputs or solutions to given problems.

FIGURE 3–3
Management science decision-making system

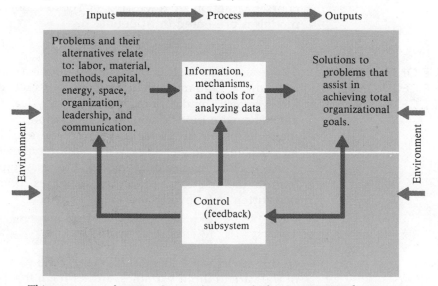

This system may be viewed as a subsystem of a larger aggregated system.

THE APPLICATION OF SYSTEMS AND SCIENCE TO DECISION MAKING

The importance of effective decision making is now more essential to good management than at any other time in the past. This is exemplified by the fact that the success of small business firms in the United States depends on how decisions are made and the quality of those decisions. Poor and improper decisions not only extend present crises but can ultimately threaten the basic survival of our economic system.

By combining the scientific method, research, systems analysis, and mathematical models to solve complex problems, managers are better prepared to evaluate alternative solutions from the standpoint of both efficiency and effectiveness. As a result, managers are less likely to be caught in the classic situation of building a better mousetrap only to find that no one is interested in buying the product.

Situations in which management science can be applied vary from determining the minimum cost of transporting finished goods from factories to warehouses, to the scheduling of passenger reservations for airlines. Most of these kinds of problems occur continuously—that is, they are repetitive and routine. By developing realistic models of these and other situations, output results can be expressed in quantitative terms. The development of such models, however, requires managers to define the exact problem and to establish ways to measures progress toward solving the problem; identify the most important variables; determine possible outcomes of the various alternatives; select the alternative that provides the most effective solution to the problem; and verify the model through experimentation and testing.

In summary, the application of science to decision making can be characterized as an approach to diagnose problems and predict their solutions by analyzing possible consequences of various alternative courses of action. A discussion of specific quantitative management models is presented in Appendix B.

USE OF MODELS IN THE DECISIONAL PROCESS

The use of models is basic to the decision-making process. Models are, however, no more than symbolic, abstract representations of real-life systems. For decisional purposes, physical models (scale models) and schematic models such as organization charts are useful, but the major emphasis in discussing operational decision-making systems is on mathematic models. These models are typically in the form of equations or mathematical statements. For example, a general model to express the relationships among expenses, revenues, and profit can be written as follows:

$$P \text{ (profit)} = R \text{ (revenues)} - E \text{ (expenses)}$$

In this model, the relationships among the parts, as well as the impact of the various input variables, are set forth in a precise, symbolic manner. Although the model is precise, it is simplified due to the complexity of reality and the irrelevancy of some variables. As a result, the decision maker can manipulate variables in the model to determine possible outcomes from various alternative courses of action.

Deterministic versus probabilistic models

Managers are basically interested in two types of mathematical decision-making models: (1) deterministic and (2) probabilistic (stochastic). *In deterministic models, all of the parts and units are determinately stated with nothing left to chance.* All of the variables are precise and their exact behaviors are known, such that for a particular input there·is a precise, determinable outcome. In a profit model, for instance, total profit equals profit per unit multiplied by the number of units sold. The one big drawback to a broad application of deterministic models is that the variables, although they are determined, are constantly changing in most organizational environments. Thus, the same decision developed from the model when repeated over and over for a particular problem will seldom give the same results. Consequently, the dynamics of change in management can restrict the use of deterministic models.

In probabilistic models, there is a consideration of the impact of change on the behavior of the variables. In this instance, a manager makes assumptions regarding conditions and determines the probability that these conditions will occur. The use of probability, or chance, makes these models fairly functional since most decisions do not involve constant truths and relationships.

Deciding whether to use deterministic or probabilistic models is based on the purpose of the decision maker and the accuracy of information available. If the purpose is to determine what should be done in order to achieve some objective and the variables are known precisely, a deterministic type model can be used. On the other hand, in circumstances of lesser information where variables are subject to change, a probabilistic model would have to be used even though the function of the model is still to select an alternative that will best achieve an objective.

Due to changing conditions, we can never be completely confident that models will provide the best possible decision. The validity and usefulness of management science always depend on the skill with which models are developed to accomplish a specific objective.[18] The seriousness of reaching quantitative solutions by using the wrong model is equivalent to solving the wrong problem.

Elements of model use

The *computer* is basic to a utilization of complex models in the decision-making process. In this sense, it is not necessarily the complexity of a model that demands computer time, but rather the monotonous

---

[18] See Paul C. Nutt, "Models for Decision Making in Organizations and Some Contextual Variables Which Stimulate Optimal Use," *The Academy of Management Review,* April 1976, pp. 84–98.

pencil and paper routines that can be handled more speedily by computers. Thus, solving a managerial problem involving a large number of variables may be too time consuming for human calculations but may require only seconds using a computer. Of course, not all computer-aided decisions are economical. With the availability of more computers, however, the cost of solving problems should decrease in the future. The final benefits depend on the cost of computer operations, the significance of the problem to be solved, and the competency of computer personnel.

A requirement in the use of models is that they *closely represent real world systems*. As an abstraction, models help decision makers develop a clearer understanding of the system under study. Yet, since models are expressed in mathematical symbols, *all variables must be stated clearly and accurately*. In addition, models must be able to *accommodate a large number of variables* without becoming too complex. Basically, models are made to be manipulated and must *be simpler than their complex environment*. At the same time, they must *be sufficiently complete to represent multiple conditions*.

In order for managers to test the outcome of various alternative courses of action, models must also *provide predictive capabilities*. Managers must be able to determine alternative outcomes by making changes in the variables and their interrelationships. Of course, no model can be built that will accurately represent all elements of a system. As an illustration, no organization chart can reflect the actual reality of all authority relationships among employees. Nevertheless, some degree of predictability must be provided.

At the present time, variables related to behavioral considerations and human values cannot be built into a model. Since subjective variables must be considered, managerial judgment remains important in arriving at a final decision. This point alone should clearly indicate why organizations are not being run by management science models. Human judgment is still an intricate element in the decision-making process.

Some of the models that are useful to managers are linear programming, economic lot size, break-even analysis, and probability decision theory. The probability decision model, linear programming, and simulation models are presented in Appendix B. Economic lot size and break-even analysis will be considered later in conjunction with the control function.

SUMMARY

Decision making is important in all management activities. In fact, the management functions could not be performed if decisions were not made. As a process, decision making refers to the selection of one action from a number of alternatives available for solving a problem.

The decision-making process is composed of four basic steps: (1) defining the problem, (2) determining alternatives, (3) analyzing alternatives in terms of their perceived consequences, and (4) selecting a course of action. Some definitive statements about decisions include the following:

There is no decisional problem until two or more alternative courses of action are available.

Only one course of action can be selected. However, any combination of actions can be considered as a single action.

A course of action is selected either to solve or to alleviate a problem. In order to choose an action that will lead to a desirable solution, the problem must be specified as clearly as possible.

A satisfactory decision implies that the decision maker has analyzed the alternatives and judged a particular action to have the greatest probability of solving the problem in a desirable manner.

The problem of measuring desirability has not been solved, particularly when there are several possible outcomes associated with each alternative.

For some managerial problems, the monetary scale can be used to measure the values in a problem. However, this scale is not completely satisfactory and should be used with care.

Logical and rational decision making requires the process to be systematic. When considering the infinite number of decisions to be made in an organization, decision models become important to those managers who seek to identify and to follow the most effective courses of action. Selecting the decision model to use, however, depends upon many variables since no one model is applicable to all organizational decision-making tasks. The complexity of the technological functions involved, the managerial level on which specific decisions are made, the dynamics of the environment, behavioral relationships of organizational members, and the complexity of decisional problems all influence the decision model to be used.

Academicians and practitioners in the areas of operations research and management science have contributed significantly to decision theory. Their emphasis has been on quantifying the decision-making process through the use of mathematical formulas. Although quantitative applications are required, most decisional models do not require an in-depth background in mathematics. In fact, the level of simplicity allows certain models to be applied to many personal situations in daily life: playing golf, betting on the horses, or purchasing a new home. For our purposes, the material in this chapter provides a framework within which the decision-making process can be better understood and improved.

KEY TERMS

Brainstorming: A technique used to arrive at alternative courses of action by pooling the efforts of several people who either meet as a cohesive group or work on the problem by themselves.

Decision: A choice selected from among alternatives to achieve a desired state in response to a problem.

Decision making: A process of selecting a course of action from among two or more possible alternatives in order to arrive at a solution for a given problem.

Decision-making process: The series of systematically related steps that are performed to arrive at a decision: determine the problem, identify alternatives, analyze consequences, and select an alternative for implementation.

Deterministic models: Symbolic, abstract representations of real life systems in which the exact behavior of each part is precise and nothing is left to chance.

Innovation: An idea, practice, or subject perceived as new by the decision maker.

Nonprogrammed decision: Unstructured decisions that are nonrepetitive either because the problem is complex or has not occurred previously in the same manner.

Objectives: Targets managers seek to achieve over various time periods.

Probability models: Symbolic, abstract representation of real life systems in which the values of the variables are not known precisely and the outcome is probabilistic rather than determinable.

Programmed decisions: Structured decisions made by following specific procedures established for dealing with problems that are repetitive and not complex.

Strategic factors: The most important factors that relate to the problem.

Suboptimization: With multiple objectives, decisions that optimize results in one department can cause lower levels of achievement (suboptimization) in other departments or in total achievement of objectives.

Sunk cost: The concept of recognizing that past decisions should not have any impact on current decisions unless they can be of value in estimating the future.

QUESTIONS

1. Does every problem require a decision? Explain.
2. Discuss the meaning of decision making in management.
3. What is the distinction between symptoms and problems?
4. What role does creativity play in the decisional process?

5. Describe the importance of identifying the strategic factors in a problem situation.

6. What is the role of the "principle of sunk cost" in decision making?

7. What factors tend to restrict rationality in the decisional process?

8. What behavioral factors should managers consider in the decision-making process?

9. Why are measurement and quantification of alternatives important? Can all decisions be quantified?

10. Describe the changes in society that require a more systematic way of approaching decision making.

11. Why are models important in decision making? What are the essential requirements in developing models?

12. Discuss the two types of mathematical models that managers are concerned with in decision making.

PROBLEMS

1. The approach to problem solving discussed in this chapter may be considered by some scholars as an oversimplification. Their criticism is that the computer, mathematics, statistical analysis, and model building have changed the decision-making process. Discuss the rationale of these scholars and include justifications for the approach presented.

2. When practicing managers are asked how they make decisions, they are often at a loss in stating just what they do. Why do you think this is true?

3. Although decision theory suggests a systematic way of selecting a course of action to accomplish some designated purpose, do we have a choice in many of the decisions in which we are involved?

4. In Herbert A. Simon's "Models of Man," he states that due to the time and effort involved, people do not know all of the possible alternative courses of action. Thus, they do not try to optimize—find the best course of action—but rather try to seek a satisfactory course of action that will be good enough. When a satisfactory alternative is selected, people adopt it and look no further. Do you feel that an optimizing approach, rather than seeking a satisfactory solution, provides the best framework for management science? Why? Which of the two procedures would a trust investment officer and a department store buyer be more likely to follow?

5. Referring to Problem 4 above, is it possible to reconcile the two models? (Consider the fact that possibly a satisfactory decision could be viewed in terms of maximization if the cost of searching for alternatives is compared to the utility of a feasible aspiration level based on costs and expectations.)

6. When the required state of technology became available, it was discovered that no one could build dams or design boats using the physics of Aristotle. Similarly, the weather could not be predicted on the basis of ancient Greek

meteorology. If the science of the Greeks was based on logic and reason, why do their findings fail to work today? (Assume that the mechanism of reason in arriving at a decision was sound.)

7. In the Matrix Production Company, the parts manager noticed an unusually large number of out-of-stock items in finished goods inventory. In discussing this problem with the production manager, the parts manager felt that the problem dealt with the company's inventory policy. The production manager, however, feels this approach overlooks the real problem of production scheduling. What aspect does this situation relate to in the decision-making process?

8. It seems natural for a decision maker to maximize expected values by selecting the alternative with the greatest expected utility. Although the maximization mode may not be possible from the standpoint of rationality, could the following axioms be useful to managers as guides for decisions?

a. Transversity—circular judgments should not be made.
b. Do not engage in wishful thinking.
c. Dominance—the preferred choice will always give at least as much utility as any other action.
d. Irrelevance of identical factors—consider only those factors that help to discriminate among alternatives.

SUGGESTED READINGS

American Accounting Association. "Report of the Committee on Managerial Decision Models." *The Accounting Review,* Supplement 1969, pp. 42–76.

Eilon, S. "What Is a Decision?" *Management Science,* December 1969, pp. 117–89.

Ford, C. H. "Manage by Decisions, Not by Objectives." *Business Horizons,* February 1980, pp. 7–18.

————. "The Elite Decision Makers: What Makes Them Tick?" *Human Resource Management,* Winter 1977, pp. 14–20.

Gaither, N. "The Adoption of Operations Research Techniques by Manufacturing Organizations." *Decision Sciences,* October 1975, pp. 797–813.

Hellriegel, D., and J. W. Slocum, Jr. "Managerial Problem-Solving Styles." *Business Horizons,* December 1975, pp. 29–37.

Holder, J. J., Jr. "Decision Making by Consensus." *Business Horizons,* April 1972, pp. 47–54.

Lapin, L. L. *Management Science for Business Decisions.* New York: Harcourt Brace Jovanovich, 1980.

Larson, S., and D. M. Merz. "Operations Research at Boise Cascade." *Management Accounting,* February 1978, 33 ff.

Tobin, N. R.; K. Rapley; and W. Teather. "The Changing Role of O.R." *The Journal of the Operational Research Society,* April 1980, pp. 279–88.

White, S. E.; J. E. Dittrich; and J. R. Lang. "The Effects of Group Decision-Making Process and Problem-Situation Complexity on Implementation Attempts." *Administrative Science Quarterly,* September 1980, pp. 428–40.

4

THE PLANNING FUNCTION

PURPOSE

The emphasis placed upon planning varies between organizations and the levels of authority within each. For this reason, the completeness of the planning function may be viewed as a continuum ranging from virtually no planning to a very involved, sophisticated process.

From a managerial perspective, students and practitioners may shudder to think that some organizations would dare operate without planning. *Business Week, Fortune, The Wall Street Journal, Industry Week* (to name just a few publications) include vivid reports on organizations that have achieved objectives of growth, record earnings, and high returns on equity through careful and meticulous planning. On the other hand, some organizational success stories seem unrelated either to short-run or overall strategy planning. What, then, are we saying to managers? Possibly, it does not make any difference if they do or do not plan. Or, does performance depend on who is doing the planning? Perhaps the key to the planning puzzle is to recognize the relationship between economic performance and the complexity/volatility of various environmental dimensions. To provide answers to these questions, some theoretical insights about planning are needed. Regardless of the situation—a star rock singing group, a crack bicycle racing team, or the best social organization on campus—theory exists before practice starts. In this chapter some of the secrets to the planning puzzle are examined as we develop a way of thinking about the planning function.

OBJECTIVES

1. To discuss planning as fundamental to the performance of all other management functions.

2. To examine planning as a process for determining future actions.

3. To identify the essential elements of planning.

4. To point out that all managers have some role in planning.

5. To create an awareness of the conditions of certainty, risk, or uncertainty under which planning must take place.

Planning is the mental and intellectual work required before physical effort takes place. It allows managers to bring together resources effectively in accomplishing objectives. When planning does not precede action, an organization deliberately limits its success—that is, unforeseen forces are allowed to control the organization and diminish its ability to cope effectively with crises.

Early leaders in the management field, such as Henri Fayol and Frederick W. Taylor, recognized the overall importance of planning in attaining goals.[1] Taylor stressed the need for planning in the selection, training, and development of workers. He believed that managers should be responsible for planning, rather than allowing workers to devise their own individual plans. Fayol stated that if foresight (planning) is not the whole of management, at least it is an essential element.[2] Henry Dennison, an industrialist during the 1920s who applied many of Fayol's and Taylor's concepts, summarized his thoughts on planning in the statement, "in complicated and changing situations . . . there must be the laying of the lines" (planning).[3] Thus, to these management pioneers, planning was the essential first step for effectively achieving goals.

PLANNING—THE
FUNDAMENTAL
FUNCTION

As suggested above, planning is a fundamental and primary management function—the foundation for performance of a manager's job. Managers must clearly plan before they can rationally perform the functions of organizing, actuating, and controlling. Organizing and the effective utilization of resources can only be performed in light of established plans. Likewise, controlling takes place in relationship to the activities and people required to achieve objectives contained in plans.

Without question, some organizational objectives have been achieved with relatively little planning. For example, some research studies suggest that there is no basis for believing that formal corporate planning is generally associated with high financial performance.[4] Other studies, however, note that planners significantly outperform nonplanners on most economic criteria. Although current research into the effects of planning on the economic performance of organizations is mixed, our view is that there is a positive relationship between

[1] Reference was made to Fayol in Chapter 1. Frederick W. Taylor was an engineer whose work was done in the production shops of manufacturing plants. His ideas were revolutionary, philosophical, and applicable to all social activities.

[2] Henri H. Fayol, *General and Industrial Management* (London: Sir Isaac Pitman and Sons, 1949), p. 43.

[3] Henry Dennison, *Organization Engineering.* Copyright 1931, McGraw-Hill Book Company. Used with permission of McGraw-Hill Book Company.

[4] For a good summarization article see Ronald J. Kudlar, "The Effect of Strategic Planning on Common Stock Returns," *Academy of Management Journal,* March 1980, pp. 5–20.

performance and planning. Achieving objectives effectively without planning is the exception rather than the rule. Effective managers do not, and cannot, depend on fate nor the words of oracles as substitutes for planning. By planning, decision making is set in a proper framework to reduce the likelihood of suboptimal choices. Consider the Apollo 13 spaceship that was on its way to the moon when it had to be called back due to an accident in space. Plans were outlined and practiced in simulators before flight procedures were transmitted to the astronauts. Reentry procedures for bringing the spacemen back safely were not left to chance. Planning permitted the reduction of uncertainty by anticipating future events with probable limits.

The mental work of planning must precede actual performance. The lack of forward thinking is well illustrated in the April 1980 attempt to rescue American hostages from Iran. As noted by a military review group, the attempt failed because of planning errors, leaving eight U.S. servicemen dead amid a tangle of flaming aircraft in an Iranian desert.[5] The planning errors most noted were the lack of a full-scale dress rehearsal, failure to brief pilots on weather conditions that could be encountered, uncertainty of command (authority) relationships that resulted in misunderstanding under pressure, and the poor selection of a rendezvous site that was near a road.

Because of constant changes in the environment, continuous planning is essential. This is illustrated in both the Apollo 13 flight and the Iranian rescue mission. Change forces managers to plan in an attempt to reveal in advance opportunities for, and threats to, the program. In most cases, success or failure depends on a capacity to adapt plans both to new information and to changing environmental conditions. Thus, planning is a process by which managers visualize and determine future actions that will lead to a realization of desired objectives. Specifically, *planning may be defined as the process of using related facts and future assumptions to arrive at courses of action to be followed in seeking specific goals.*

Planning and objectives

Certain organizational decisions cannot be made until it is determined where the organization is going and what is to be accomplished. For a business organization, objectives describe the nature of the business and the services provided to customers and society. Thus, objectives provide the basis for planning as well as the focal point for all other management functions. They serve as guides to the development of future actions to assure their fulfillment. In providing direction to individual and group effort, we noted in Chapter 3 that *objectives may be defined as the targets people seek to achieve over various time periods.*

---

[5] "Why Hostage Rescue Failed: Official Word," *U.S. News and World Report,* September 1, 1980, p. 7.

FIGURE 4–1
Environmental and internal factors influencing objectives

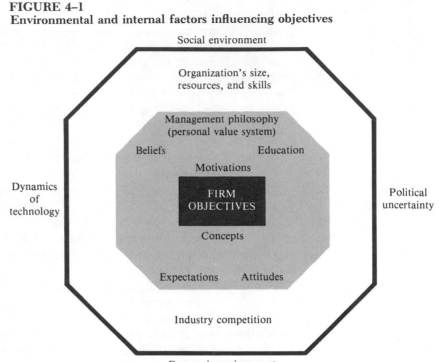

Environmental factors must always be recognized in the development of objectives since they influence overall performance and results. Equally influential are the philosophies (personal value systems) of managers, the nature of the industry, the size of the organization, and internal resources. (See Figure 4–1). Objectives, however, also influence the moral and ethical considerations of managers and have an effect on the environment in which an organization operates. Because of this two-way influence, very few objectives remain the same over a long period of time.

Role of the future in planning

Henry Dennison wrote that almost all work must be planned so that it can be done, even if this means planning it informally just a few minutes before the work begins.[6] Planning starts with the future and works to the present. The problem is to determine how far in advance and in what detail it is profitable for each manager to plan. Time is undoubtedly one of the important elements of planning. Plans have typically been somewhat simplistically characterized as short, medium, and long term. At this point, however, the designation of

[6] Henry Dennison, *Organization Engineering* (New York: McGraw-Hill, 1931), p. 150.

time frames is not as important to our understanding of planning as to its determination. The time period covered by planning is dependent upon the nature of objectives and the time it takes to complete them. Some objectives will require a longer period of time to attain than others. Consequently, the planning time dimensions associated with them will be longer than for shorter range objectives. Possibly the best way to view the time frame covered by planning is to recognize the amount of time related to the fulfillment of decisions involved in achieving committed objectives. In this sense, if decisions are made that are not related to organizational objectives, they are not part of the planning time period.

In planning what is to be done, managers are required to foresee events before they actually happen. In order to do this, information must be gathered that will provide some insight into the future. The importance of the future can be seen in the Xerox Corporation's entry into the computer business. At approximately the same time, IBM Corporation introduced its first copying machine. The plans of both corporations required significant long range planning since they were each competing in a field where the other was dominant. Each had to ask questions about itself, such as: Have we adequately predicted future opportunities? Do we have the managerial advantages and skills to turn projected opportunities into successful operations?

The importance of systematically considering the future is also illustrated by savings and loan associations in offering checking accounts, lines of credit, automatic bill-paying plans, credit cards, consumer loans, and trust arrangements in addition to traditional mortgage loans and savings. With the 1980 congressional approval to expand the role of savings and loans, systematic consideration of future services was essential in the battle with banks for consumer dollars. Above all, the survival of savings and loans in the 1980s means that they cannot operate as they have in the past but must be evaluating continuously future changes in the financial environment.

The risks of improperly assessing the future in planning are illustrated by viewing early planning premises used by analysts of the wristwatch industry. When the first solid state digital watch was introduced at the retail level in 1972, analysts were claiming that the market for traditional sweep-hand (analogue) watches would be quickly destroyed and that many jewelers would be driven out of the wristwatch business. Instead, many of the makers of mass-produced digital watches were driven out of the market completely, as they managed to capture only 20 to 40 percent of the estimated watches sold in 1980 and 1981. The industry now projects that its real future lies in the quartz sweep-hand timepiece that may perform a variety of functions.[7]

---

[7] Walter Galling and Robert Ball, "How Omega and Tissot Got Ticking Again," *Fortune*, January 14, 1980, pp. 68–70.

To review, the dynamics of our socioeconomic system clearly indicate that given conditions will not necessarily remain the same in the future. For management, the future ranges from conditions of certainty to those of uncertainty, as noted in Figure 4–2. By recognizing the degree of risk and uncertainty involved, managers are better able to establish levels of confidence about the possible occurrence of future events.

FIGURE 4–2
Types of planning models

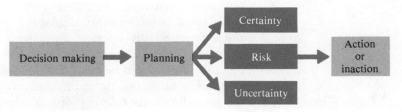

Planning under the various kinds of models noted in the figure can be characterized as:

Certainty—The manager is fully aware of the consequences of alternative strategies. Assumptions (environmental conditions) are perfectly understood and predictable.

Risk—The alternatives are recognized, but the selection is more complex. The states of nature, such as economic conditions, are predictable as to only their probabilistic outcome.

Uncertainty—The selection of alternative strategies is even more complex than under risk. The occurrence of environmental states is not known. Decision making is highly unsettled, and much more effort must be placed on forecasting by all managers.

Relationship of planning to decision making

While it is evident that decisions permeate all planning, all decision making is not necessarily planning. Decisions may be made without planning; however, one cannot conceive of planning without decision making. To clarify the distinction between decisions without planning and decisions based on planning, consider the examples of (1) firing an employee and (2) developing a long-range employment goal. The activity of firing a particular employee may not necessarily involve planning. On the other hand, the development of a long-range employment goal is definitely planning. Decisions, however, are necessary in both examples.

The Lockheed case also illustrates the distinction between planning and decision making. When Lockheed was in serious financial difficulty during the early 1970s, Daniel Houghton dominated most decisional situations, down to the smallest detail.[8] One unfortunate decision he

---

[8] Louis Kraar, "How Lockheed Got Back Its Wings," *Fortune*, October 1977, pp. 199–210.

made without the benefit of planning was to create a covert organization within the company to buy political influence abroad to help obtain sales. The payoff scandal that toppled a Japanese premier and embarrassed officials from Holland to the Philippines is now recognized as a decision that lost sight of the importance of proper planning and forward thinking.

Professor R. L. Ackoff emphasizes the distinction between planning and decision making by pointing out that planning implies anticipatory decision making, the interrelationship of decisions, and the creation of organizational goals.[9] Planning is anticipatory since it precedes action. At the same time, a plan often leads to additional, but related, decisions that must all be linked to overall goals of the organization.

Elements of planning

The planning process includes four essential elements. While these elements may seem separate and distinct, two or more must often be considered somewhat simultaneously. Therefore, they are separated here for purposes of discussion while, in practice, distinctions between them are quite blurred.

1. **Determining objectives** All planning is centered around objectives to be achieved, and these objectives are a result of the planning process. Consequently, the need to establish priorities among them within any organization requires that planning take place. By centering planning around objectives, direction is given to the planning process. Organizational objectives specify long-range growth, the products and markets to be emphasized, and the profit returns expected. These guides do not have to be expressed precisely nor be immutable, but without them, plans developed by various managers are likely to be inconsistent and out of phase with organizational intent.

2. **Forecasting the future** Looking ahead to anticipate opportunities and barriers is essential to planning. In forecasting, managers utilize appropriate information to arrive at external and internal assumptions (premises) about what will happen in the future. Assumptions provide the basis for planning, and their validity depends upon the accuracy of the forecasts. Effective decisions cannot be made without forecasts of sales, environmental considerations, production levels, personnel requirements, and all of the other resources required for operation of the organization.

In planning, the future includes degrees of uncertainty. The complexity and rapidity of change leave managers with few situations where the probable occurrence of a particular event will be known with certainty. As planning activity extends further into the future, it is natural that the degree of relative uncertainty increases. Thus, it is difficult to predict future events accurately. Nevertheless, assump-

---

[9] R. L. Ackoff, *A Concept of Corporate Planning* (New York: Wiley-Interscience, 1970), pp. 2–5.

tions must be made about the future, and the effectiveness of plans is related to the accuracy of such assumptions. Finally, since the future is uncertain, good plans must incorporate alternatives so that flexibility is built into their application. In fact, every step of the plan should allow for contingencies (unforeseen developments and barriers).

3. Making decisions Without decision making, the planning process would have no meaning. Managers must choose objectives to pursue, select assumptions about future conditions that will be used in implementing goals, and determine the specific policies that are necessary for goal achievement. Without managerial decisions about actions to be taken, the organization would exist in a state of confusion. Yet, while decision making is an integral and necessary part of the planning process, it is not synonymous with planning; but through planning, a decisional framework is provided for the entire organization.

4. Using an acceptable approach Effective planning requires that one use an acceptable approach to assemble, interpret, and evaluate information and assumptions related to a particular planning situation. In fact, many past planning failures may be due more to the approaches used in planning rather than to a lack of information.[10] Information may be from external and internal sources. External sources provide environmental information about economic, social, political, and competitive conditions. This kind of information is difficult to interpret and evaluate since only a portion of it is relevant to organizational objectives. Identifying an organization's strengths and weaknesses requires internal information about personnel changes, financial data, sales, marketing expenses, production, inventories, and changes in organizational policies and structure. Managers, consequently, need an acceptable approach in assembling, interpreting, and evaluating information to obtain meaningful inputs for planning the accomplishment of objectives.

While planning approaches vary from organization to organization, most still follow rather precise techniques.[11] Many of these are built around determining the best answers to the following questions:

What actions are required to accomplish the objectives?
Why must these actions be taken?
Who will be responsible for the actions?
When must the actions be taken?
Where will the actions be taken?
How will the actions take place?

---

[10] Fred H. Mitchell and Cherly C. Mitchell, "Development, Application, and Evaluation of an 'Action-Reaction' Planning Method," *The Academy of Management Review,* January 1980, p. 83.

[11] See George A. Steiner, *Top Management Planning* (New York: Macmillan, 1969).

The priority of these questions is extremely important in the planning process. Answers must first be found for *what* actions are required. Then, in a like manner, the why, who, when, where, and how must be answered. Determining *how* actions will take place should be delayed until all relevant information and assumptions have been obtained as they relate to the other questions. In this way, planning errors are minimized.

The questioning approach outlined above should be applied to all aspects of the planning process. These include:[12]

Specification of objectives to be achieved.

Selection of policies, programs, procedures, and practices by which objectives are to be pursued.

Determination of resources required and how they are to be acquired and allocated to activities.

Designation of decision-making systems along with their proper organization and implementation.

Designation of a control system to detect errors in plans and to determine how to get activities back on the desired path.

Follow-up to see if results are consistent with plans.

Following up results is essential for routine, as well as for long-range, strategic plans. If variances from a plan are exceptional, corrective action may be necessary. This may include a revision of plans, changes in operations, or both.

PLANNING AT ALL LEVELS OF MANAGEMENT

Every manager within an organization must plan. The involvement of managers in planning is based on the idea that the success of a plan depends on commitment to the plan by those responsible for performance. As noted in Figure 4–3, top-level managers spend a larger proportion of their time in planning activities than is true for middle managers or first-line supervisors. Generally, high-level executives are involved in establishing overall objectives and policies that provide guidelines for carrying out specific actions at lower levels of authority.

To do this, executives spend a large portion of their time surveying the economic, technical, political, and social environments to identify new opportunities and relationships that others have not seen. For top-level management planning, managers must develop various courses of action for making needed strategic changes during the life of an organization. This, in turn, requires an assessment and review of outcomes of past strategic actions. This type of planning is broad, long range, and quite creative in nature. Although the ultimate respon-

---

[12] Reprinted by permission of New York University Press from *Management Thought in a Dynamic Economy* by John F. Mee, © 1963 by New York University, p. 6.

FIGURE 4–3
Planning performed by levels of management

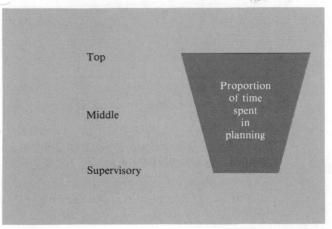

sibility for all planning rests with top executives, the authority to conduct certain types of planning is delegated to lower-level managers.

For middle and supervisory positions, planning is much more routine, specialized, and for short periods into the future. Some of the detailed plans developed by these managers are more closely related to standards, procedures, methods, schedules, and rules. In any event, planning cannot be successful unless top executives support the function and provide clear objectives on which plans can be based.

SEPARATING PLANNING AND DOING

Since Frederick W. Taylor there have been advocates who feel that the planning function should be separated from managers who are directly responsible for operations. As related to a manufacturing plant, Taylor's concept was to place the planning department in an office close to the center of the shops where it could act as a clearinghouse. The drafting room manager, superintendent, and their associates were to be close to the planning department, thereby bringing "all of the planning and purely brain work of the establishment close together." [13]

The rationale behind separating planning and performance implies that operating managers do not have the time, training, talent, or information needed to analyze situations and arrive at effective plans. Specialists in planning, therefore, can be (1) more creative by not being tied down to specific interests and (2) more objective in arriving at plans that must consider the future consequences of all current decisions.

---

[13] Frederick W. Taylor, "Shop Management," in *Scientific Management* (New York: Harper & Row, 1947), pp. 109–21.

There are still many organizations that reflect the Taylor concept. To a large extent, the NASA space program delegates the major responsibility for planning to specialists. This is true even though the crew of a spaceship may be required to perform certain planning activities with judgment, initiative, and analytical ability. To give greater emphasis to planning by specialists, planning departments have been established in large organizations. In colleges and universities, planning departments are often referred to as campus development offices and are concerned with long-range institutional planning. Furthermore, most collegiates are familiar with the innumerable campus committees that are charged with planning in the areas of curriculum design, registration, budgeting, student union programs, and so forth. Although such committees have specific purposes, they must plan in order to develop recommended courses of action.

A problem in providing coordination

The use of various planning specialists in an organization can create a problem of coordination. Plans proposed by one group must be linked at some point in time with those developed by other planning specialists. Likewise, the planning activities of managers within the functional departments of production, marketing, and finance must be coordinated.

One approach for establishing a more effective coordination of effort is to have a centralized planning department. As an illustration, the General Systems Division of IBM is organized with a centralized planning department. The various functional aspects of the business planning unit are shown in Figure 4–4. The finance/planning staff exists to coordinate business planning activities among the various departments.

An interesting corollary to the problem of providing coordination is to decide how far the role of the professional planner should extend. Should it go all the way to designing the planning systems that will be used by operating managers? There is the danger that these managers will resist a system that they have not been influential in developing. Consequently, planning specialists should build and maintain systems according to specifications provided through the participation of operating managers.

Behavioral considerations

The idea of totally separating planning from doing is not generally accepted from a behavioral viewpoint. The feeling here is that employees should have additional authority to do more of their own planning. Behaviorally oriented managers believe that productivity and worker satisfaction can be improved through such actions. At Texas Instruments, for example, executives have found that employee turnover has been significantly lowered and output moderately increased by allowing assembly-line workers to participate in setting their own goals

FIGURE 4–4
Organization design of the business planning function—IBM's General Systems Division

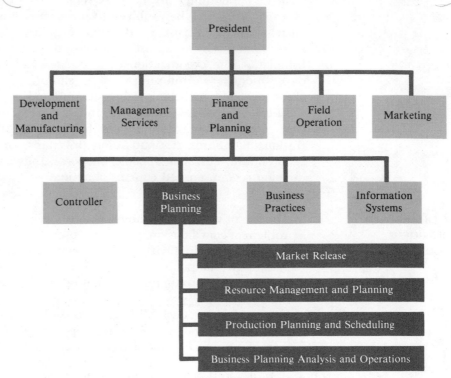

(performing the planning function). In another effort to involve production employees in a departmental reorganization, workers in a Detroit parts plant were asked to reevaluate the entire manufacturing operation of the plant. The plans developed by employees called for redesigning the work flow in one department, eliminating seven jobs, and reassigning displaced personnel elsewhere in the plant.

An interesting aspect of group involvement in planning is that a number of experiments have suggested that groups make riskier decisions than individuals. The shift toward risk may be explained by the mutual influences of (1) diffusion of responsibility through the group, (2) the social value of being perceived as a risk taker, and (3) the group's involvement in discussion of the problem and alternative choices.[14]

From an international perspective, companies in western Europe and Japan have realized benefits from involving employees in the plan-

---

[14] See A. Vinokur, "Review and Theoretical Analysis of the Effects of Group Decisions Involving Risk," *Psychological Bulletin*, 1971, pp. 231–50.

ning process. At the Kockums shipyards in Sweden, employees are asked for their suggestions in solving various problems and in scheduling the construction of tankers. Management's opinion is that people like to work when they know why and how they fit into future organizational plans.

By not separating planning from doing, people frequently feel more inclined to accept a plan since they have participated in its development. For the past several years, the Tavistock Institute in Britain has emphasized the importance of "self-managed" work groups in which employees define their roles and create their own methods for getting tasks done. The idea here is that people in organizations like to try to achieve the objectives they help set for the organization. To bring about this type of positive commitment to organizational goals, however, requires the managers brief employees on their products, their jobs, and their contributions to company profits.

At this point it is apparent that there are no definite conclusions concerning the extent to which employees, planning specialists, and managers should be involved in planning. Consequently, for any specific activity, the manager's role in planning is best perceived in terms of a triad, as seen in Figure 4–5. No organization operates exclusively with only one element of the triad since planning is performed by operating managers, workers, and staff specialists. Managers depend on certain advice and assistance from all organizational members. Since no person can be an expert in all areas, effective managers find that many groups must be involved to some extent in the planning function. In the future, possibly even the public will participate more in planning. In England, public participation is now required by statute in

FIGURE 4–5
The planning triad

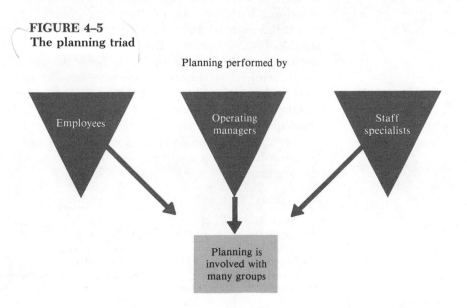

Planning performed by

Employees

Operating managers

Staff specialists

Planning is involved with many groups

specific types of strategic planning.[15] One point, however, should be reemphasized—that is, all managers must plan since it is inherent in the work of management. They cannot totally delegate the planning function to staff planners, to subordinates, or to other organizational members.

FORECASTING AND PLANNING

Almost all planning involves forecasts, and managers depend upon these forecasts in determining courses of action. Even now, some forecasters suggest that many of the problems organizations face in the United States are worse than they might otherwise have been because of past failures to forecast or to acknowledge trends.[16] The message is that effective forecasting assists in preventing (1) ad hoc decisions, (2) random decisions, and (3) decisions that unnecessarily and expensively narrow future choices.

The art of forecasting is by no means a simple matter and is intrinsically difficult. The approaches used by managers vary from unscientific hunches to elaborate statistical and quantitative techniques, such as simulation models. Some of the more common forecasts include information about general economic conditions, industry demand and growth, company sales, governmental actions, market share, consumer behavior, and product profit. Of course, other forecasts can be made concerning such factors as population, the stock market, energy, and technology. Forecasts, however, must result in significant impacts upon an organization's activities; otherwise, they may not be considered in the planning process. More specifically, forecasts must also be used to predict the behavior of future systems and the impact of various programs. Information provided by a forecast is of limited value unless used as a basis for such predictions.

At this point no attempt is made to discuss approaches to forecasting in detail since to do so is beyond the scope of this chapter.[17] Managers, however, have a large number of forecasts available to them on quarterly, semiannual, or annual bases. Many current publications provide forecasts of various types that include the considered opinions of knowledgeable people. These, of course, have an important place in any manager's planning activities. Thus, by reading trade journals, business publications, and professional journals, managers can keep abreast of what is happening and can develop some insights on which to base future plans.

---

[15] See Mary Benwell, "Public Participation in Planning—A Research Report," *Long Range Planning*, August 1980, pp. 71–79.

[16] See William Ascher, *Forecasting: An Appraisal for Policy-Makers and Planners* (Baltimore, Johns Hopkins University Press, 1979).

[17] Appendix C at the end of the text presents some of the more common forecasting techniques in current usage.

**BALANCING
QUANTITATIVE
APPROACHES AND
JUDGMENT**

As noted earlier, forecasts can be based upon elaborate statistical and quantitative techniques.[18] Two such techniques that are often used in predicting future changes are (1) extrapolation—that is, the extension of present trends incorporating modifications for future changes—and (2) analytical forecasting, which measures the impact of variables on one another. These approaches to forecasting, however, are only starting points and can by no means solve problems by themselves.

Forecasting must always balance quantitative data with judgment and wisdom. In developing quantitative forecasts, the past is involved. Yet, changes in environmental pressures exerted by consumers, governmental agencies, suppliers, financial institutions, labor unions, and so forth may require modifications of a quantitative forecast to make it viable for future activities. Consequently, there is no assurance that a specific quantitative forecast will be satisfactory, and the more scientific the forecast becomes, the more possible it is for the forecast to drift from reality. Such deviations may result because of the following:

The role of human relationships may be overlooked in highly quantitative forecasts.

If all people involved in making a forecast possess similar backgrounds and attitudes, they may study a situation from only one point of view and fail to consider different perspectives. The idea here is that no one person or homogeneous group is likely to arrive at an accurate forecast. Instead, the diverse efforts of several people are required to assay the relevant aspects of all factors influencing future conditions.

If a forecast is made by managers who are accustomed to making only routine decisions in somewhat static situations, unusual circumstances requiring imagination, ingenuity, resolution, and drive may result in incorrect strategy formulation. For example, past strategies useful in a seller's market are of little value to the organization faced with a recessionary situation.

A fairly new predictive approach that utilizes a variety of viewpoints is called the Delphi technique.[19] It is a popular way of measuring and forecasting the potential impact of various factors on changing societal values. Simply stated, the Delphi approach establishes a panel of experts on a specific subject. Members are asked independently about their forecasts and the reasons for them. All forecasts are collected and returned to each of the panelists who, in turn, makes another

---

[18] Some of these techniques are least squares regression, moving average, exponential smoothing, lead-lag analysis, various cyclical techniques, and Monte Carlo simulation.

[19] Andrew H. VanDeVen and Andre L. Delbecq, "The Effectiveness of Nominal, Delphi, and Interacting Group Decision Making Processes," *Academy of Management Journal*, December 1974, pp. 605–21; and Richard J. Tersine and Walter E. Riggs, "The Delphi Technique: A Long-Range Planning Tool," *Intercom*, ed. S. Ferguson and S. D. Ferguson (Rochelle Park, N.J.: Hayden Books, 1980), pp. 366–73.

individual forecast. The process is repeated until an acceptable consensus or convergence of opinion emerges.

Some individuals distrust quantitative data to such a degree that they place a greater emphasis on intuition and hunch in forecasting. For example, Eliot Janeway, the flamboyant economist, author, and advisor, shuns the use of econometrics, models, computer inputs, statistics, and economic values, such as the gross national product accounts. Most managers, however, do not have an uncanny feel for economic conditions and must depend on more systematic approaches in forecasting. For most managers, forecasting future events and relationships usually results from several approaches or sources. These may range from a single instinct to complex mathematical and statistical techniques, all of which must be considered in a proper balance.

One of the most interesting examples of the balance required between scientific forecasting and judgment was seen in the 1979–80 downturn of the U.S. economy. In an attempt to hold down double digit inflation, the government increased the interest rate to slow down industry and consumer spending. The projection was that savings would increase, inflation lessen, and a mild downturn would occur. The intent was to achieve greater future prosperity. Unfortunately, savings continued to decrease, inflation remained high, and the worst economic recession since the 1930s resulted. Similarly, the scientific forecasting of the 1981 recovery was again as perplexing as a Chinese puzzle.

Today, it is recognized that consumer buying decisions depend as much on social and psychological factors as they do on economic conditions or on the actual desirability of a given product. Therefore, understanding shifts in consumer behavior and spending priorities depends upon both the use of specific forecasting techniques and good judgment.

TIME SERIES ANALYSIS

Forecasting is the primary source in devising assumptions on which to base plans. Data related to three sets of these assumptions—economic, industry, and firm—lend themselves to more quantitative analysis than do the political climate, social norms, technological developments, and demographic characteristics. When data can be reliably collected over a period of time, time series analysis can be beneficial.

The longer the planning period, the more important it is to understand the implications and meaning of using data in various ways. Short-term analysis operates on the assumption that the future will not differ much from the present. Consequently, what we have today may be an indicator of what tomorrow will be like. As the time span increases, an analysis of past data becomes more critical. Long-term analyses of past data are referred to as trends. Past data may also show fluctuations that occur frequently but without regularity in terms of specific periods of time.

FIGURE 4–6
Time Series Components of Business Data

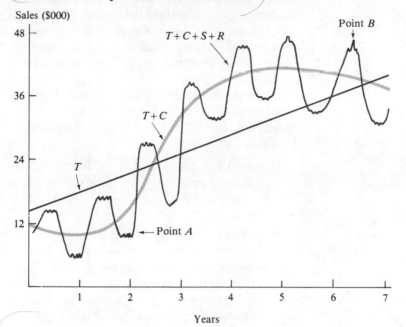

The factors making up observable data are *T*—Trend, *C*—Business Cycle, *S*—Seasonal Variation, and *R*—Residual Variation including all other factors that cannot be accounted for by *T*, *S*, and *C*. Points *A* and *B* represent the actual, observable data along the curve that is referred to as *Y*.

The most important component in time series analysis is the trend. This is true because it is the foundational factor used in understanding the behavior of all other data. Referring to Point *A* in Figure 4–6, we see that sales are approximately $10,500 for the second month in year two. This is considerably below trend (line *T*) that shows company sales of $20,500. The difference can be explained in part by the fact that the business cycle (line *T* + *C*) is below trend, indicating a period of recession or depression. In addition, the seasonal variation (line *T* + *C* + *S* + *R*) is at a low point, causing sales to be even slower. Point *B* is much higher than trend because of more prosperous times (even though the business cycle is starting a downward movement) and because of various seasonal factors. For a more complete discussion of time series analysis, see Appendix C at the end of the text.

In forecasting it should be recognized that no statistical or mathematical technique is sufficient by itself since assumptions based on the past may not be true in the future. Also, random events may occur that can turn a mathematical forecast into meaningless paper. Changes in the motivation and attitudes of employees can also be important in determining the ultimate realism of a given forecast.

SUMMARY

Managers find that an effective achievement of objectives requires planning. In fact, the basic nature of planning points out the role of the future as well as the relationship between organizational objectives and specific courses of action. Since planning is future oriented, the importance of forecasting is also obvious with assumptions about the future being essential in the development and implementation of all plans.

Some general characteristics about the planning process can be derived from the material presented in this chapter. Given specific organizational objectives, the following provide useful guides to managers in planning:

Essentiality—All managers and organizations need to plan for tomorrow. By considering the future, planning brings to light opportunities and organizational weaknesses that might otherwise not be observed.

Relatedness—The planning process has as its foundation the basic objectives of the organization. In fact, objectives constitute the framework in which planning takes place.

Flexibility—Each plan should be so devised that it becomes adaptable to changes in the external environment and internal operations. As the planning horizon is expanded, greater awareness of flexibility is essential since the environment is constantly shifting and plans must be modified appropriately in response to these changes.

Consistency—All types of plans and the various functional areas involved in them must be consistently integrated for the attainment of established objectives. If plans are not consistent with organizational goals, time and energy are wasted.

While all managers can rely on past experiences and proven guides in meeting their planning responsibilities, the special characteristics of each organization make a standardization of the planning process impossible. Resources, time, heritage, and pressures from the external environment make the planning problems of one organization different from those of others. Thus, while broad guidelines can be of value, managers must seek to develop and utilize those special techniques that hold the greatest potential for overcoming the planning barriers with which they are confronted. To assume that the techniques that have worked for one organization will be equally successful to all others is a very dangerous assumption to follow.

KEY TERMS

Delphi technique: A technique for improving forecasts and decisions by comparing independent judgments that are summarized and returned to the experts who then provide another judgment on the topic.

Environment: The forces or elements external to a specific system that have an impact on the operational effectiveness of that system.

Forecasting: The process of looking ahead and making judgments about various factors that will influence the attainment of goals and the use of this information in developing plans.

Objectives: The targets people seek to achieve over various time periods, providing direction to individual and group effort.

Planning: The primary management function involving the selection of courses of action (plans) that direct an organization's human and material resources in attaining specific objectives.

Planning elements: The essential elements of the planning process that include determining goals, forecasting the future, making decisions, and using an acceptable approach to analyze facts and assumptions.

Planning triad: Planning that involves employees, planning specialists, and managers, although the extent to which each participates varies depending upon the situation.

Time series components: Economic data expressed in quantitative terms over several time periods, shown as trend, business cycle, seasonal variation, and residual variation.

QUESTIONS

1. Why is planning considered to be the fundamental and primary management function?
2. Define planning.
3. Why is decision making not necessarily planning?
4. Discuss the four elements of planning.
5. How does the responsibility for planning vary among the different levels of management?
6. What three groups can be involved in the planning process?
7. What kinds of problems are likely to evolve when planning is separated completely from the operating manager's job?
8. How does the future relate to planning?
9. What is the importance of forecasting in managerial planning?
10. Is a balance between quantitative approaches and judgment essential to good forecasting? Discuss.
11. In time series analysis, which assumptions can be treated more completely on a quantitative basis?

PROBLEMS

1. Today there is considerable discussion that the disadvantages of planning outweigh the advantages. One argument hinges on the fact that plans often fail because environmental factors change rapidly and assumptions cannot be forecasted accurately. Another criticism is that crisis situations are not adequately met since managerial actions are delayed by planning.

Although such arguments are true, do you feel they outweigh the rationale for engaging in planning?

2. The "principle of commitment" suggests that the time period covered by planning should encompass enough time to fulfill the commitment of resources made by management. Viewed from the basis of decision making, what factors would determine the length of the planning period?

3. At a recent management development workshop, one manager stated that three "one-year" plans added together composed the company's three-year plan. Do you agree with this planning attitude?

4. In the Japanese management system, planning is conducted on a consensus basis. Most major decisional matters do not start at the top but rather begin in the administrative unit that will initiate the plan. Part of the rationale for this approach is that when consensus can first be obtained on the need for a plan, the specific plan developed is much more agreeable to the persons involved.

In the United States, top-level managers reserve major long-range planning decisions for their attention rather than dispersing the decision-making process to lower managerial levels. Consequently, major planning decisions are made at the top of these organizations.

List the advantages of both systems. Which one best fits your thinking about management? Could some combination of both approaches be viable?

5. From the standpoint of planning, what implications does the following statement have?

One should never fail to recognize the impact that shifts in public sentiment, governmental actions, and social goals can have on a secure position in the market.

6. What factors make it difficult to develop detailed plans for periods beyond three years into the future?

7. Should the role of the staff planners be expanded to include more of the total planning process, such as the responsibility for formal planning and approval of all plans within the organization?

SUGGESTED READINGS

Bierman, H., Jr.; C. P. Bonini; and W. H. Hausman. *Quantitative Analysis for Business Decisions.* 5th ed. Homewood, Ill. Richard D. Irwin, 1977.

Greiner, L. E.; D. P. Leitch; and L. B. Barnes. "Putting Judgment Back into Decisions." *Management Science,* March 1968, pp. 416–28.

Halter, A. N., and G. W. Dean. *Decisions under Uncertainty.* Cincinnati: South-Western Publishing, 1971.

Imhoff, E. A., Jr. "A Closer Look at Management Forecasts." *Management Accounting,* May 1980, pp. 18–23.

Lau, A. W., and C. M. Pavett. "The Nature of Managerial Work: A Comparison of Public- and Private-Sector Managers." *Group and Organization Studies,* December 1980, pp. 453–66.

Leontiades, M. "Perspectives on Planners and Planning." *Business,* September–October 1980, pp. 20–24.

Leven, R. I., and C. A. Kirkpatrick. *Quantitative Approaches to Management.* New York: McGraw-Hill, 1978, chap. 4.

Most, K. S. "Wanted: A Planning Model for the Firm." *Managerial Planning,* July–August 1973, pp. 1–6.

Rue, L. W., and L. L. Byars. *Management Theory and Application.* Homewood, Ill.: Richard D. Irwin, 1977, chap. 5.

Tersine, R. J., and W. E. Riggs. "The Delphi Technique: A Long-Range Planning Tool." *Business Horizons,* April 1976, pp. 51–56.

Turban, E., and J. R. Meredith. *Fundamentals of Management Science.* Revised ed. Plano, Tex.: Business Publications, Inc., 1981.

Turner, R. C. "Should You Take Business Forecasting Seriously?" *Business Horizons,* April 1978, pp. 65–72.

5

PLANNING TOOLS AND TECHNIQUES

PURPOSE

The year was 1917 and the United States was fighting World War I. Government experts, financial wizards, and top military leaders in Washington, D.C., were at a loss in planning and running the war effort in terms of coordinating the production of ordnance by private and government plants scattered all over the country. Scheduling of activities was ineffective due to the lack of information to plan and coordinate the efforts of private contractors with those of government agencies. Likewise, at the Navy shipyards, shipbuilding was off schedule and the operation of the fleet was losing tonnage. Apparently, everything was too complicated to be efficiently planned.

Out of the maze of confusion, people, and reams of paper, one person stood alone in trying to unravel this mess. That person was Henry L. Gantt, who gave up a lucrative consulting practice to aid the war effort. After spending three months on the project, Gantt rushed out of his office on F Street shouting, "I have the whole world by the tail!" He excitedly explained, "We have all been wrong in scheduling on the basis of quantities. The essential element in the situation is time, and this should be the basis of laying out any program." Gantt had come up with the idea of straight-line charts that would measure any activity by the amount of time needed to perform it. For the first time, it was possible to compare visually actual performance against an original plan and to balance the record daily and weekly as the work progressed and the schedule changed. With the application of this new management tool, Washington's shipping and production problems all but vanished and Gantt's name was carried around the world. Materials flowed more smoothly, shipbuilding blossomed, and the productivity of the United States revealed its tremendous ability to produce goods for the world.

This chapter attempts to develop an appreciation for the fact that organizational effectiveness depends upon management planning and that the use of appropriate tools can allow an organization to move from the backwaters to the mainstream of modern management practice.

OBJECTIVES

1. To illustrate that planning is carried out through the use of various tools and techniques.

2. To discuss Gantt Charts as they relate to planning.

3. To show how the Program Evaluation and Review Technique (PERT) can be useful in planning.

4. To examine budgeting as a systematic process that aids managers in planning and controlling resources.

5.. To outline behavioral considerations important to successful budgeting.

The concern expressed in the past three chapters has been the idea that to affect the future something must be done in the present. Hence, preparing for the future requires managers to determine in advance what is to be done and what decisions are needed today for action tomorrow.

Changes are occurring within today's organizations that require managers to place more importance on planning than at any other time in the past. For example, the effect of the economic environment has a dramatic influence on planning requirements. Often it is so great that soon after a forecast is completed, economic planning premises about the future are superseded in the news by such events as new tax changes, inflationary conditions, or changes in the prime interest rate. In anticipating the future in a dynamic environment, attention, therefore, must be focused on the character of the period as a whole, rather than on an isolated time period.

Technology also has its impact on the requirements for planning. The complexity of tasks, new production processes, and new sophisticated products require an increasing span of time from the planning phase to the completion of the job. Thus, the task of planning becomes more critical in recognizing potential events that may occur in the future and in devising contingency actions to be able to stay on track.

Three management tools that are extremely useful in the planning function include Gantt Charts, Program Evaluation and Review Technique, and budgeting. They aid by interrelating the various functional aspects of marketing, production, finance, personnel, engineering, and other activities. This chapter presents an insight into Gantt Charts, Program Evaluation and Review Technique, and budgeting as important planning tools.

GANTT CHARTS

In terms of planning for the severity of the future, decisions such as buying insurance or entering into hedging operations can reduce certain types of risks. Although these types of decisions can help reduce specified risks, the risk of overall error in the allocation and utilization of resources remains. In order to plan for minimizing this risk, managers must be able to evaluate past performance as a basis for making deterministic assumptions about the future. Henry L. Gantt in the early 1900s showed managers how this could be done in chart form. His charts related types of activities to the amount of time required for their completion by showing work planned and work completed in relationship to time.[1] This charting technique was one of the first

---

[1] Other than the many works by Gantt, two books written about him are classics in the literature: L. P. Alford, *Henry Lawrence Gantt* (New York: Harper & Row, 1934); and Wallace Clark, *The Gantt Chart* (New York: Ronald Press, 1922). Writing in 1922, Clark stated that the Gantt Chart represented "the most valuable contribution to the art of management made in this generation." To some degree this statement is still true today.

to facilitate the advanced planning of work loads, and it has provided the foundation for the development of other scheduling charts and planning tools. A pioneer in management history, Gantt also emphasized a philosophical and psychological approach to the problems of training workers in industry.

FIGURE 5–1
Gantt Chart for a manufacturing firm

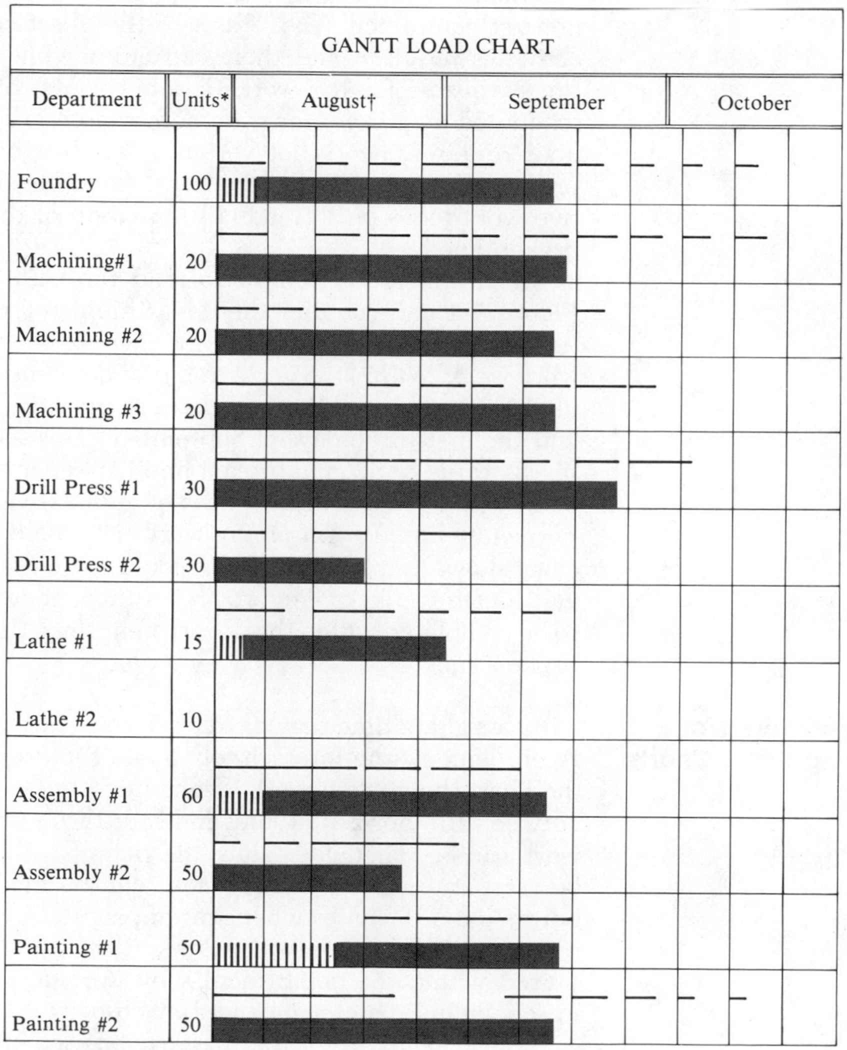

GANTT LOAD CHART				
Department	Units*	August†	September	October
Foundry	100			
Machining#1	20			
Machining #2	20			
Machining #3	20			
Drill Press #1	30			
Drill Press #2	30			
Lathe #1	15			
Lathe #2	10			
Assembly #1	60			
Assembly #2	50			
Painting #1	50			
Painting #2	50			

* Weekly capacity in units.

† Each block represents one work week beginning with Monday and ending with Friday.

Description of Gantt Charts

Gantt developed several types of charts. Two important charts are the machine-record chart and the progress chart. With each, emphasis is placed on comparing desired quantity output to time in the allocation of various resource capacities. With the assistance of charts, this allocation is accomplished by assigning the time required for performing given tasks within the boundaries of available resources. Allocations can be shifted to reflect newly acquired information as conditions change.

As shown in Figure 5–1, the variables used in the Gantt Chart include (1) determining and sequencing the work steps or activities and (2) scheduling the work by periods, cumulative work ahead, and work not yet completed. The Y axis of the chart represents the kinds of activities required and their capacities while the X axis represents time available for the work. The horizontal broken line shows work scheduled by periods for each department. The short vertical broken lines represent work not yet completed or work carried over from previous periods. Finally, the heavy solid bar line represents cumulative work to be performed (a summation of the individual horizontal broken lines).

As an illustration of how to read the Gantt Chart, refer again to Figure 5–1 and consider the department referred to as Drill Press 2. In the chart, time is divided into weeks that represent days of the work week. Within the department under consideration, work is scheduled for the first and third weeks in August; the last two days of August; and the first three days of September. This scheduled work is shown by the three horizontal broken lines. When added together these broken lines represent three weeks of cumulative work—the heavy solid horizontal line. By examining work scheduled in the department, the chart shows that additional jobs could be scheduled during the second and fourth weeks of August. In addition, there is no backlog of work to be completed within the department since there are no short vertical broken lines.

Advantages of using Gantt Charts

By assigning time periods to work activities, it is possible to schedule a completion time for each job. Since the horizontal broken lines on the chart show when work is scheduled to begin and end, the breaks between the horizontal lines indicate those time periods where new work can be scheduled. Thus, the planned utilization of facilities can be seen at a glance, and revisions can be made in order to obtain a better use of facilities whenever appropriate. Simultaneously, the cumulative work line aids managers in calculating total work hours required within the department while providing valuable information in scheduling maintenance and machinery overhaul.

As an evaluative tool, the chart can be used in analyzing performance for control purposes. Variations between planned work and actual performance can be isolated early and necessary reallocations made to keep work flowing as smoothly as possible. In fact, applications of this technique are almost unlimited since it can be adapted to many kinds of scheduling problems.

As might be expected, the overall benefits of Gantt Charts to planning are more sophisticated than merely facilitating the planning of work loads for future time periods. For example, the charts provide empirical evidence required in (1) establishing realistic standards for worker output, (2) obtaining data for employee training records, (3) developing bonus compensation systems, and (4) scheduling of activities.

According to Gantt, methods associated with determining tasks and promoting worker motivation can also be refined and facilitated by using the charts. In this regard, Gantt felt that the charts should indicate the wages and production goals of workers. If incorporated in the charts, these data would show the results of, or need for, management planning.

In summary, the Gantt Chart represents one of the first systematic tools to planning. From an international perspective, Russian central planners completely designed their first "five-year plan" on Gantt Charts. By using Gantt's method, the modern manager can (1) work toward the establishment of long-range objectives; (2) determine times for the completion of events; (3) make changes in standards, or performance, when necessary; and (4) identify the jobs that must be completed along with the capacities of available resources.

The growth of network models

In project planning, the Gantt Chart emphasizes the importance of a systematic arrangement of all work to be performed. However, the vertical arrangement of activities on the Gantt Chart gives no indication of the tasks to be completed before others can begin. To provide for this aspect in planning, network models have been developed. As noted in Figure 5–2, lines in the network represent the work

FIGURE 5–2
Network of activities showing sequential dependencies

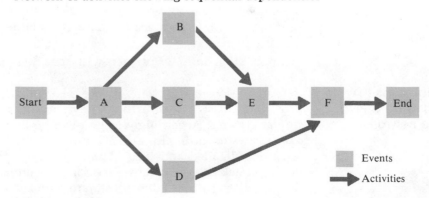

activity required to complete particular events. Represented by boxes (nodes), events are designated by the words *start* and *end,* as well as letters *A* through *F.* Within the network, each preceding event must be completed before the following one connected by the arrow line (activity) can begin. Consequently, no event can be accomplished until all work leading to it has been completed. Within the sequential series of activities, parallel arrangements of specific tasks may take place in the network. For example, activities AB, AC, and AD may be carried on concurrently.

PROGRAM EVALUATION AND REVIEW TECHNIQUE

The increased use of network models has resulted in some rather sophisticated managerial planning and control techniques. One of these is called Program Evaluation and Review Technique that forms the acronym PERT. In conjunction with other team members, the PERT technique was developed in 1958 by the special projects officer of the U.S. Navy. Specifically, the technique was designed for use in planning and controlling the Polaris fleet ballistic missile program. Without question, the project was one of vast engineering uncertainty and complexity. Yet, the successful application of PERT was shown by saving two years' time in the completion of the naval missile program.

Application of PERT network

The goal of PERT is to determine the optimum (best) way to attain objectives within a particular period of time. Application of the technique is especially beneficial when a project is extremely complex, such as with the Polaris program. Of course, the computer becomes an essential part of the total package in such cases. Regardless of the scope, however, PERT networks are valuable tools to assist managers in planning such activities as:

Research and development programs.

Development of new processes and production methods.

Construction of new plant and building facilities.

Maintenance of computer installations.

Complex projects with many interdependent activities.

Projects with large money outlays and a large number of personnel involved.

Completion dates for projects with specified time and/or cost limits.

Initial steps in setting up a PERT time network

Our mission at this point is to explain the nature of PERT while providing a basis for its further study and the understanding of other similar systems. Accordingly, each of the following steps is discussed as it relates to setting up a PERT time network.

Listing detailed activities The first step is to prepare a detailed list of all activities and jobs necessary to complete the project. This listing is often the most difficult step to perform. Consequently, managers must be familiar with all aspects of the total plan in order to identify the specific activities and events to be completed.

To illustrate this step, consider the activities required in marketing a new product. Among others, they would include:[2]

1. Receive initial approval to consider the product.
2. Determine product feasibility through market research.
3. Select and train sales force in test market area.
4. Determine brand name, price, and selling qualities.
5. Select advertising agency.
6. Determine package design.
7. Make production arrangements.
8. Produce product and ship to test market area.
9. Launch advertising program.
10. Introduce product in test market.

Determining sequencing dependencies Once an analytical and objective determination of the activities and jobs is completed, the second step in PERT analysis is to arrange the required activities according to the order in which they should be performed. Any logical sequencing of activities must be based on both technological and administrative dependencies. This step can be facilitated by considering the following questions:

1. What activities can be started without dependence on other activities?

2. What activities must start or finish at each particular event?

The PERT network shown in Figure 5–3 illustrates the relationship, flows, and interdependencies among the activities cited above for introducing a new product into a test market. Since each activity leads to the completion of an event, all aspects of the total system must be considered. In sequencing activities and events, ample time must be given to determining alternative network configurations. This requires creative and imaginative thinking since the viewpoint of the planner always affects the number of paths and events in the final network.

As suggested earlier, PERT is representative of a fully constrained type of plan where each element in the total system is completely known and understood. Of course, this does not mean that changes in assumptions cannot be made. However, if changes occur, activities in the network must be reconsidered and/or resequenced.

Estimating times The third step in developing a PERT network involves an estimation of the time required for completing each activity

---

[2] Since the example is given for illustrative purposes, many of the subactivities essential to the introduction of a new product are not included.

FIGURE 5–3
PERT/time network for test marketing a newly developed product

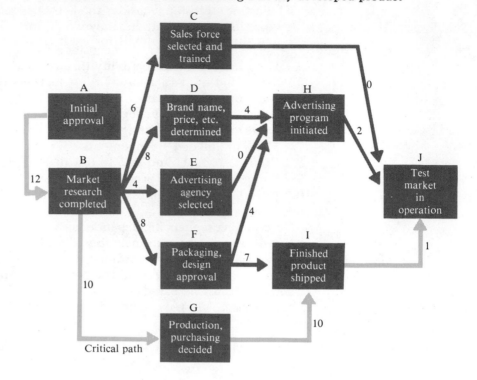

in the network. Three time estimates are generally noted on the activity line. For example:

These time estimates are referred to as follows:

    a—Optimistic time where everything goes according to plan with no major obstacles.

    m—Most likely time required to complete the activity.

    b—Pessimistic time where everything might go wrong.

The three estimates are used in computing the expected time (t_e) for completing a network activity. The t_e is much more realistic when based on three estimates, rather than on only one estimate.

In computing the t_e for each activity, the three times are weighted and averaged as shown in the following equation:

$$\frac{\text{Optimistic} + 4\ (\text{Most likely}) + \text{Pessimistic}}{6} = t_e$$

Using the assigned symbols for each time estimate, the equation becomes:

$$\frac{1\ (a) + 4\ (m) + 1\ (b)}{6} = t_e$$

By substituting the time estimates cited above for each symbol, a t_e can be calculated as follows:

$$\frac{12 + 4(15) + 24}{6} = 16 \quad \text{[expected time } (t_e) \text{ for the completion of the activity]}$$

Now, refer again to Figure 5–3 where the expected times (t_e) are shown for each activity. Keep in mind that each t_e was calculated by using the formula cited above.

Planning value of PERT

At this point, the planning value of PERT becomes more obvious. Specifically, PERT aids managers in answering the following questions:

What is the best way to direct effort toward the completion of a given project?

What is the completion time for the entire project—that is, what is the summation of times for the individual activities (t_e) on the longest network path?

What is the earliest expected time (T_E) in which the various events and paths of the program can be completed?

What are the chances of completing the project within the calculated time constraints?

The answer to question one is normally determined through the network that has been established. If a manager is under either time or cost pressures, however, a better plan (composite network) may go unnoticed. If so, the end result may take the form of an opportunity cost penalty. Consequently, ample time must be devoted to determining contingency network configurations. In this way, network adjustments can be made as environmental factors change.

As concerns the search for answers to the second and third questions in the foregoing list, other PERT concepts are of value—critical path and slack time.

Critical path   The critical path in a network is that sequence of activities and events requiring the longest period of time to complete. This path is considered "critical" since a delay in completing any of

FIGURE 5–4
Earliest expected time and slack time for each path in the network (in weeks)

Paths	Total $t_{es} = T_E$	Slack time†
A,B,C,J	18	15
A,B,D,H,J	26	7
A,B,E,H,J	18	15
A,B,F,H,J	26	7
A,B,F,I,J	28	5
A,B,G,I,J*	33	0

* The critical path since it is the longest path in the network.

† Slack time is found by subtracting T_E from the latest allowable time (T_L) on which an event or path can occur—thus, $T_L - T_E =$ Slack Time. The time of 33 weeks is designated as T_L, which is the time in which the project must be completed.

Source: Figure 5–3.

the events on it will result in a delay for the entire project. Remember that each path in a network is considered independent of every other path even though they are interrelated.

Since the critical path requires the longest period of time to complete, it also represents the shortest time in which the entire project can be accomplished. For example, in Figure 5–4, the critical path is designated as *A, B, G, I,* and *J*—requiring 33 weeks to complete. Since all activities must be performed, the entire project cannot be finished in less than 33 weeks. In addition, as noted earlier, any delay on the critical path extends the completion time of the total project by an amount of time equal to the delay.

Slack time The slack time in a network represents the amount of extra time that can be spent without delaying the entire project. Keep in mind that if the time on the critical path is the same as the latest allowable time to complete the project, there is no leeway or slack time available on the critical path. Slack time for each of the branches in a network can be found by subtracting the total amount of time (T_E) from the latest allowable time (T_L). Such calculations are shown in Figure 5–4.

Even more valuable for management planning is the determination of slack time for each of the individual events in a network. To arrive at the slack time for each event, two time periods must be determined: (1) the earliest expected time and (2) the latest allowable time. The earliest expected time for the completion of each event is represented by T_E in Figure 5–5 and is found by adding all activity times (t_e) between the beginning event and the particular event under consideration. Sometimes two or more activities lead into an event (such as *H, I,* and *J* in Figure 5–3). When this occurs, add the longest of the path time estimates in determining T_E.

To arrive at the latest allowable time (T_L) for completing each indi-

FIGURE 5–5
Earliest expected time, latest allowable time, and
slack time for each event in network (in weeks)

Event	T_E	T_L	Slack time $(T_L - T_E)$
A	0	0	0
B	12	12	0
C	18	33	15
D	20	27	7
E	16	31	15
F	20	25	5
G	22	22	0
H	24	31	7
I	32	32	0
J	33	33	0

Source: Figure 5–3.

vidual event without delaying the total project, one must start at the end of the network and work backwards. For instance, to compute the T_L for event H, we subtract 2 weeks from 33 weeks. Recall that our example requires 33 weeks to complete the critical path. The 2 weeks represent the time necessary for completing the activity between H and J. Thus, the latest allowable time for completing H is 31 weeks. If event H started on week 32, and 2 weeks are required to get from H to J, the project would take 34 weeks. Thus, a delay of 1 week for the entire project.

When tracing backwards through the network branches, two or more activities sometimes converge at one event. This is shown in Figure 5–3 where J—H and J—I come together at event F. In such cases we must calculate the shortest T_L for the particular event under consideration. For event F in Figure 5–3, the calculation would be as follows:

$$J\text{-}H\text{-}F = 33 - 2 - 4 = 27$$
$$\text{or}$$
$$J\text{-}I\text{-}F = 33 - 1 - 7 = 25$$

Therefore, the T_L for event F is 25 since it is the shortest of the two computed times.

Chances of completing project on time We can now determine the chances of completing our project within the latest allowable time of 33 weeks. Since the PERT network assumes a normal distribution, the answer can be stated in probabilistic terms. Without going into detail of a commonly used statistical measure, assume that the standard deviation (a measure of dispersion) for all items on the critical path is equal to 2 weeks. Based on the normal curve, we know that the

T_E of 33 weeks is accurate 95 percent of the time within plus or minus 1.96 standard deviations.[3] Therefore, we can assume a 95 percent chance that the actual completion time of the project will fall within the following range:

$$33 \text{ weeks} \pm (1.96)\ 2.0 = 33 \text{ weeks} - 3.92 \text{ and } 33 + 3.92$$
$$= 29.08 \text{ weeks to } 36.92 \text{ weeks}$$

Advantages of PERT systems

Various advantages accrue from a determination of the critical path in a PERT network. For instance, managers can focus attention on preventing delays along the paths. Concurrently, efforts can be made to reduce the time required for performing activities on the critical path. In addition, certain events in branch networks may be completed earlier, or later, to assist in a more rapid accomplishment of critical path events.

It may also be possible to divert resources from branch paths with high slack times to assist in completing activities on the critical path. In doing so, however, it should be realized that a transfer of resources can sometimes make branch paths become critical paths. On the other hand, a reallocation of resources does not change the overall network design of the path: only the time values or costs associated with the paths are changed. Even though there are limits to the interchange of resources, PERT provides managers with a planning tool to use in determining where reallocations of resources could possibly take place.

As a communication tool, PERT has still other advantages. The system provides a way of communicating and coordinating the roles and relationships of all people involved in a project. As a result, all participants better understand the total system of which they are a part.

Up to this point, very little has been said of the evaluative advantages of PERT. It should be recognized that PERT is as important in the control function as it is in planning. With PERT, managers are able

---

[3] The normal distribution is represented by the following curve that shows that ±1.965 standard deviations includes 95.0 percent of all items within a specific range.

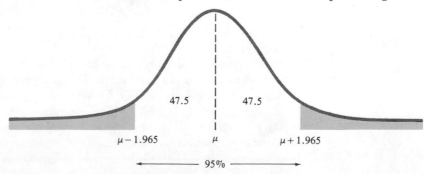

to evaluate progress as compared to predetermined time standards for a given project. If there are deviations from the plan, PERT assists the manager in determining when and where corrective action should be taken. While PERT cannot prevent delays, changes, or unforeseen events, it does allow for improvement to be made through corrective action.

BUDGETS

Budgeting is a systematic process that aids managers in planning and controlling the resources required in the achievement of objectives. The preparation of a budget can be thought of as an essential part of the planning process. Yet, control is also involved since managers compare actual results with budgeted figures and take corrective action when necessary. Figure 5–6 shows a budget report where budgeted amounts for a given period and actual expenditures to date are compared so that managers can analyze performance and take steps to correct deviations where necessary.

At this point it should be noted that budgets are not restricted to financial (dollar) data. They may be expressions of personnel requirements, units of production, or any other important factor within an organization. Some examples of budgets include the following:

FIGURE 5–6
Budget of expense items in relationship to actual expenses

Budget Report

Department _____   Date _____
Supervisor _____

Description	Budget	Actual	Better or worse (−) than budget
Materials	$ 60,000	$ 64,300	$−4,300
Direct labor	47,000	50,660	−3,660
Supervision	4,000	4,100	− 100
Clerical	900	790	110
Indirect labor:			
Vacation pay	3,000	3,750	− 750
Social security	2,000	2,170	− 170
Pensions	2,200	2,400	− 200
Overtime premium	—	100	− 100
Unemployment tax	1,500	1,050	450
Miscellaneous	2,000	2,230	− 230
Repairs	500	310	190
Factory supplies	400	—	400
Overhead (heat, lights, depreciation, etc.)	5,400	4,930	470
Total expenses	$128,900	$136,790	$−7,890

Projected income statements and balance sheets for future operating periods.

Budgeted sales of major products for a 12-month period.

Budgeted cash to pay for certain expenditures incurred during a year.

Budgeted personnel requirements and capital expenditures incurred during a year.

Budgeted personnel requirements and capital expenditures, by department, for the next five years.

Role of budgets

Consider the situation of Alex, who is responsible for developing initial budgeted revenues, expenses, and net profit figures for 25 stores in a discount chain operation. This assignment has always been a hectic one for Alex since a considerable amount of time, both on and off the job, must be spent preparing the budget. To some degree, Alex feels working on these budgets is a waste of time since figures cannot dictate what sales, profit margins, or expenses will be for a given period. As he has said on many occasions, "sales will be what they are going to be, and all of the budgets in the country cannot affect them."

As his superior, what would you say to Alex to change his viewpoint? Or, is Alex justified in his thinking? To some extent Alex may be quite correct. However, the superior may have failed to explain the role of budgeting thoroughly to Alex. In this respect, some of the benefits that could be expressed are:

1. Budgets are plans of action that force managers to anticipate those future opportunities and barriers that might confront an organization. They require managers to take a systematic look at the future in order to outline the plans that will provide the organization with the best advantages and payoffs.
2. Most people like to have a goal or plan that lets them know where they are going. In this sense, budgets provide performance goals that give direction and meaning to the efforts of employees.
3. By comparing actual results with budgeted amounts, corrective action can be taken before a plan gets completely out of control. As such, corrective action can take the form of revising original budget figures or changing actual performance so that it more nearly falls into line with the budget.
4. Budgets are coordinative devices that bring together various functions within an organization. For example, the sales budget is of prime importance in business organizations since all other budgets depend on forecasted sales. Production requirements in the form of inventory levels, material purchases, and labor indicate items that must support the sales budget. Similarly, cash and capital requirements, advertising, distribution, sales effort, and marketing

research depend on projected sales. Thus, as a coordinating force, budgets bring various organizational elements together in an integrative manner.

Overcoming budget failures

Although budgets have many advantages, problems do exist. One of the biggest is that of adjusting budgets to changing levels of output or revenue. The budgeting process often fails to achieve its full potential because appropriations are made on only one projected revenue base. No single revenue projection is realistic since forecasts are only estimations of the future and do not include the precise data required for the development of a fixed budget.

One way of increasing budget flexibility is to have periodic revisions. This technique has resulted in the development of *moving budgets.* By having periodic revisions, managers follow a scheduled format in revising budgets for the next operating period. If the budget is for a one-year period, managers might revise budgeted figures for the next 11 months at the end of each month. They would then add an additional month to maintain a complete 12-month moving budget. In this manner the most current information is used to keep the budget up to date while adjusting it to changing conditions.

For most business organizations, certain costs are a function of the volume of production, sales, or some other measure of activity. A budget that reflects the costs associated with various volumes of activity can be described as an *incremental* or *step budget* (see Figure 5–7). Basically, an incremental budget can be applied to any type of organization since the steps could represent hours, revenue, or even patients in a hospital. In this sense incremental budgets are more realistic than

FIGURE 5–7
Annual incremental budget of expenditures in units

Expenses	100,000 to 199,999	200,000 to 299,999	300,000 to 399,999
Shipping	$ 30,000	$ 50,000	$ 70,000
Materials	150,000	250,000	350,000
Labor:			
Direct	180,000	300,000	420,000
Supervisory and indirect	27,000	35,000	43,000
Overhead:			
Administration	42,000	50,000	58,000
Utilities	3,000	5,000	7,000
Repair and maintenance	18,500	27,500	36,500
Depreciation	20,000	20,000	20,000
Selling expenses	71,000	95,000	119,000
Total	$541,500	$832,500	$1,123,500

fixed budgets since they show that total costs vary with different output levels.

By using the output column of 200,000 to 299,999 units from Figure 5–7, a more precise budget of projected expenses can be developed for levels of operations falling within this range. This more precise approach is called a *variable budget* and is illustrated in Figure 5–8. It is often more useful than the incremental budget since changes in various expenditures can be directly related to small changes in the number of units produced. Consequently, the basis for comparing actual results to budgeted amounts is more accurate.

Another major problem in budgeting deals with budgetary surpluses. Consider the manager who, in being efficient, has a budgetary surplus at the end of an operating period. Yet, since the surplus exists, the proposed budget for a future period may be reduced because of it. There is no easy solution to this problem. Managers do not deserve to have their budgets cut just because they strive for greater efficiency. At the same time there is no justification in a budget being larger than necessary. Unfortunately, most managers solve this dichotomous situation by exhausting the budget even though all expenditures are not needed. This intent is to prove that budget allocations for the next period must be at least as large as for the last period.

Viewed from a systems approach, budgets must be integrated with all other organizational plans. In this way total budgetary needs are recognized throughout the entire organization, and allocations are made as they relate to overall objectives. From a managerial perspective, a good budget environment is based on:

FIGURE 5–8
Annual variable budget of expenditures in units

Expenses	250,000 units	Fixed portion	Variable portion	Variable rate per unit
Shipping	$ 50,000	$ 0	$ 50,000	$0.20
Material	250,000	0	250,000	1.00
Labor:				
Direct	300,000	0	300,000	1.20
Supervisory and indirect	35,000	15,000	20,000	0.08
Overhead:				
Administrative	50,000	45,000	5,000	0.02
Utilities	5,000	2,000	3,000	0.01
Repair and maintenance	27,500	5,000	22,500	0.09
Depreciation	20,000	20,000	0	—
Selling expense	95,000	35,000	60,000	0.24
Total expense	$832,500	$122,000	$710,500	$2.84

1. Meaningful budgets related to the advantages and limitations of the organization.
2. A clear statement of the objectives and plans that can be integrated with organizational budgets.
3. Clear lines of authority and responsibility relating to budgetary development and control.
4. A viable cost structure.
5. An adequate basis for measuring actual performance against budgeted results.
6. An ability to take corrective action, such as revising budgets or performance, when necessary.

Zero-base budgeting

The previous section indicated many of the problems associated with budgets. A relatively new management planning and budgeting tool called zero-base budgeting has been considered by its proponents as a way to overcome many of these problems.

Only a few organizations, both public and private, have made extensive use of zero-base budgeting. One of the early users was the state of Georgia under Governor Jimmy Carter. Basically, the concept advocates rejustifying budget programs annually. Most traditional budget systems are based on the assumption that last year's programs are probably sufficient for the following year and that the budgetary effort should concentrate on incremental changes (additions and reductions) to the previous budget. Zero-base budgeting, however, requires each budgetary unit to identify the functions it performs and the personnel and costs for performing those functions. Thus, all activities and priorities are evaluated anew, so as to obtain a better set of allocations for the upcoming budget year. By following this technique, managers must be able to justify each activity's total projected level of expenditures and no level is taken for granted.

According to Peter A. Pyhrr, the process has three steps.[4] These are:

1. Describe each discrete organizational activity (decision package) that competes for limited resources.
2. Evaluate and rank all these packages using a cost-benefit approach.
3. Allocate resources accordingly.

In summary, the concept is based on analyzing the inputs and outputs for specific programs, rather than on emphasizing the traditional line-items or expenditure approach.

As with any management planning tool, there are advantages and

---

[4] Peter Pyhrr in 1970 introduced and popularized the term *zero-base budgeting*. As with most management techniques, the concept was not entirely new since it had been referred to at earlier times. See Peter A. Pyhrr, "Zero-Base Budgeting," *Harvard Business Review*, November–December 1970. Copyright © 1970 by the President and Fellows of Harvard College; all rights reserved.

disadvantages of its use. Zero-base budgeting does not work equally well in all organizations. Consequently, the astute manager must learn how to apply the technique selectively to those areas that offer the greatest potential payoff. Clearly, it requires top-management support and sensitivity and a knowledge of whether the behavioral environment of the organization would be receptive to this type of program.

Behavioral considerations in budgeting

The success or failure of a budgetary plan depends on the attitudes of both managerial and nonmanagerial employees. The key point here is that acceptance is based on how employees see the budget, not how managers feel that the employees should perceive it. For example, when budgets are imposed on organizational members without consideration of their needs and attitudes, the result may be a sense of frustration, rather than one of higher productivity.

Chris Argyris reports that lower-level managers dislike budgets because they (1) tend to report only results, not reasons, (2) emphasize the past and not the present, (3) are too rigid, (4) apply pressure for an ever-changing goal, and (5) tend to create failure for the supervisor.[5]

In terms of gaining employee acceptance of budgets, managers can take several positive actions. One of the most important is to prepare employees intellectually and emotionally prior to the development and implementation of budgets. In this sense, preparation is facilitated by explaining the purposes of budgets and the results that can be achieved through their use. Also, employee participation in the formulation of budgets is important in preventing and overcoming problems of acceptance. Likewise, budgetary flexibility is important. From a behavioral viewpoint, the acceptance of budgets would certainly be enhanced if managers would modify them to meet changing conditions, rather than holding them constant while requiring organizational and human modifications.

SUMMARY

Three techniques to assist managers in deciding on an allocation of resources were examined in this chapter. The first two were Gantt Charts and network models. Both are extremely useful in considering combinations of resources. Similarly, they are valuable as control devices. As a network model, PERT is useful in preventing unnecessary conflicts and delays by focusing on an optimum utilization of resources for nonrepetitive programs. The third technique—budgeting—is an excellent tool in providing the means by which objectives are converted into action and in unifying and coordinating many diverse operational activities.

---

[5] Chris Argyris, *Personality and Organization* (New York: Harper & Row, Publishers, © 1957), p. 136. See also Chris Argyris, "Human Problems with Budgets," *Harvard Business Review,* January–February 1953, that emphasizes the impact budgets have on people in creating pressure and frustration for the supervisory-level manager.

As planning tools and techniques, managers should overcome any fear or hesitancy in using Gantt Charts, PERT, and budgets. Each can be as simple or complex as required by the situation. The key point to recognize is that these tools can help tie together the various diverse operations of an organization and point them in a direction consistent with organizational objectives.

KEY TERMS

Budgets: Plans of action that coordinate the allocation of funds and resources necessary for the achievement of specific objectives in a future time period.

Critical path: A sequence of activities and events within a network that requires the longest period of time to complete.

Gantt charts: A technique presented in chart form to compare desired quantity output to time in the allocation of various resource capacities.

Moving budgets: Budgets that are periodically reviewed such that at the review time budget figures are revised for the remaining period and a new period of time is added to replace the expired period.

Network models: A group of activities oriented toward a strategic objective.

PERT: A series of activities and events that have been designed to achieve a particular objective providing for the evaluation and review of their completion within designated time periods. PERT is an acronym for Program Evaluation Review Technique.

Slack time: Within a particular network, the amount of extra time that can be spent without delaying the entire project.

Variable budgets: Budgets designed to show the various expenditures that are directly related to small changes in the number of units produced.

Zero-base budgeting: A bottom-up budget planning approach that focuses on tasks that each operating line unit is to perform in justifying annual budget programs.

QUESTIONS

1. How do Gantt Charts and PERT relate to planning?
2. What advantages would Gantt Charts have for a manufacturing enterprise?
3. Describe the relationship between "events" and "activities" in network models.
4. Why are network models, such as PERT, valuable management techniques?
5. List the initial steps in setting up a PERT time network.

6. How is the t_e for each activity determined?

7. If the required time to complete a project is equal to the longest path through the network, why is slack time on the critical path always equal to zero? (Define your terms.)

8. What is the meaning of T_E and T_L? Do they have reference to the various events in a network?

9. What are the advantages of using PERT? What are some problems that managers may encounter in using it?

10. Is budgeting more closely related to planning or to controlling?

11. What are the advantages of budgets?

12. What is a fixed budget? How does it differ from incremental and variable budgets?

13. Note actions that managers can take in preventing or overcoming human problems in budgeting.

PROBLEMS

1. Henry L. Gantt (1861–1919) receives credit for creating a systematic approach (in chart form) that specifies the work required in a project; the time necessary for completing the tasks; and the order in which these tasks are to be performed. If this is true, how would you account for the successful completion of the Great Wall of China, the Taj Mahal, and the Pyramids of Egypt since there were no Gantt Charts?

2. The design of a PERT network system begins by listing the activities and events necessary to complete a given project. Would you develop this listing as the best (optimal) or as a feasible beginning design?

3. Refer back to Figure 5–3 in this chapter that shows the t_e for each activity. Redraw the network and show (a) the T_E and (b) the T_L for each event. (Hint: Remember that the difference between the earliest expected event time and the latest time is equal to slack time for each event.)

4. On New Year's Eve, four wrecked cars were hauled into Joe's Body and Paint Shop. When the business opened on January 2, the shop manager had to schedule the work to be performed on each of the cars. Basically, each car must go through two departments or stations; namely, the body shop (the first department) and the paint shop (the second department). The shop supervisor estimated the time required for body work and painting. Expressed in hours, these times are as follows:

| | Cars | | | | Total |
	1	2	3	4	(hours)
Body work	9	4	8	2	23
Painting	4	9	4	6	23

Assume:

a. There is no backlog of work in the shop nor any jobs in process.

b. In order to minimize the time interval for working on the cars, sequencing can be based on the following schedule rule: Select the shortest times for cars in both departments. Then schedule first the car requiring the least amount of body repair time. Schedule last the car requiring the least amount of painting time. Repeat this rule for each sequence until all cars are scheduled.

Required:
a. Develop a Gantt Chart for the four cars. By sequencing, move each car from one department to the next while minimizing the total time required to complete all of the work.
b. Determine how long it will take to complete the work on all four cars.

5. The t_e for each activity is shown below on the PERT/time network system.

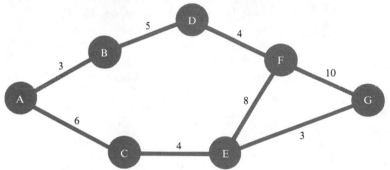

Required:
a. What are the various paths in the PERT network?
b. Determine which path is the critical path.
c. Determine the T_E for each event.
d. If the T_L for event G is equal to its T_E, what is the T_L for each event?
e. What does the difference between T_E and T_L represent?

6. At the Aron Company, the assistant quality control manager is interested in attending a three-day quality control conference in San Francisco. Without question, this is one of the best conferences of its kind in the country. The assistant manager has submitted a travel requisition to attend the meeting, and it has been approved by the quality control manager. The controller, however, has denied the requisition on the grounds that all of the funds budgeted for travel have been spent by the quality control division.

The company has had a profitable year. Cash reserves are available, and the conference would have a high payoff in terms of information obtained that could be utilized by the company.

Discuss the budget implications in this situation. What should the assistant quality control manager do since the conference would be extremely beneficial?

SUGGESTED READINGS

Adams, E. E., Jr., and R. J. Eber. *Production and Operations Management.* Englewood Cliffs, N.J.: Prentice-Hall, 1978, chap. 13.

Cowen, S. S.; B. V. Dean; and A. Lohrasbi. "Zero-Base Budgeting as a Management Tool." *MSU Business Topics,* Spring 1978, pp. 27–39.

Evans, H. E. *Introduction to PERT.* Boston: Allyn and Bacon. 1974.

Kostolansky, J. C. "Budgeting Control at Corning Glass Works." *Management Accounting,* November 1977, pp. 21 ff.

Levy, F. K.; G. L. Thompson; and J. D. Wiest. "The ABC's of the Critical Path Method." *Harvard Business Review,* September–October 1963, pp. 98–108.

Pattillo, J. W. *Zero-Base Budgeting: A Planning, Resource Allocation and Control Tool.* New York: National Association of Accountants, 1977.

Schlissel, M. R. "Budget Planning Approaches." *Arkansas Business and Economic Review,* Fall 1979, pp. 21–28.

Schonberger, R. J. "Custom-Tailored PERT/CPM Systems. *Business Horizons,* December 1972, pp. 64–66.

Verma, H. L., and C. W. Gross. *Introduction to Quantitative Methods: A Managerial Emphasis.* Santa Barbara, Calif.: John Wiley & Sons, 1978, chap. 12.

Wright, N. H. "Zero-Base Planning and Budgeting—The Ranking Process." *Management World,* February 1977, pp. 31–33.

6

STRATEGY PLANNING AND STRATEGIC MANAGEMENT

PURPOSE

In 1888, the best-selling book, *Looking Backward,* by Edward Bellamy, noted, "If we could have devised an arrangement for providing everybody with music in their homes, perfect in quality, unlimited in quantity, suited to every mood, and beginning and ceasing at will, we should have considered the limit of human felicity already attained."

Before the days of the automobile, Otto Bettman in his book, *The Good Old Days—They Were Terrible,* related that adulterated food was commonplace, sweatshops crushed the lives of those who worked in them, and pigs walked the streets of New York making it a "nasal disaster."

During the time of Thomas Jefferson, the European tables of mortality showed that of the adults living at any moment of time, the majority would be dead in about 19 years.

These scenarios illustrate that advancements in technology, business practices, urban development, and medical knowledge are not achieved overnight but require a long gestation period. Likewise, they are not events of happenstance but the results of long-range strategy planning. Planning of this type changes crises of fearful proportions to manageable situations and leadership into unique events and innovations within the environment.

If the issues of technology, productivity, and organizational design are to lead the way in solving human problems, they cannot be dealt with in the short run. They involve the development of strategies based on knowledge, organized efforts, appropriate evaluation of results against expectations, and the exercise of managerial judgment and leadership. This chapter provides an understanding about why strategy planning involves more than second-guessing or good intentions. In the process, it focuses on strategic planning as a systematic process that is crucial to the success of all organizations.

OBJECTIVES

1. To contribute to an understanding of the nature and content of strategic planning.

2. To illustrate the importance of strategic planning to modern organizations.

3. To outline the steps in strategy planning.

4. To show the use of strategy planning in a specific organization.

5. To summarize environmental considerations important in strategy planning.

From a military standpoint there are wars and battles—wars are won through strategy planning, while battles are guided by tactical plans. The battle is a short-term achievement whose success may result from luck, astute decision making, initiative, intuitive leadership, and/or opportunism. Victory in war, however, depends on strategy planning.

For definitional purposes, *strategy planning involves the long-range planning activities of managers that consider environmental factors in setting forth organizational character, purpose, and direction.* In abbreviated form, the strategy-planning process involves (1) establishing overall goals, (2) determining long-range actions to be taken by anticipating the impact of future environmental forces, (3) identifying resources and the methods used to allocate them in carrying out decisions, and (4) evaluating performance in relationship to established goals.

In business organizations, both large and small, strategy planning and tactical plans have the same meaning as in military operations. For example, planning for the week's activities would normally be regarded as tactical, but when the planning time frame involves three years or longer, it can be considered strategic. Of course, the strategy-planning horizon varies with different industries. A manufacturing firm, such as Scripto, utilizes a 3-year time frame, while a utility company generally plans on a 20-year basis. Since strategy planning involves longer planning horizons, it must include all activities that relate to an accomplishment of organizational goals. In this chapter we will look specifically at the nature and content of strategic planning, the forecasting assumptions involved in developing a plan, and an example of how a company changed its strategy to improve its market position.

THE RISING IMPORTANCE OF STRATEGY PLANNING

Strategic planning has been around for a long time. What is not so obvious is the shifting of managerial attention from the technicalities of the planning process to the substantive issues affecting long-term performance.[1] This is a result of rapidly changing economic, social, and political environments, all of which affect every organization whether it be a small grocery store, an international conglomerate, or a social welfare agency.

Prior to 1940 most business firms concentrated on a single product or group of related products or services. Planning was informal and basically concerned with producing a product and having it available to meet demand profitably. Thus, many business managers were preoccupied with day-to-day problems, rather than with appraising current performance and assessing long-term needs and prospects of the busi-

---

[1] S. W. Glueck, S. P. Kaufman, and A. S. Walleck, "Strategic Management for Competitive Advantage," *Harvard Business Review*, July–August 1980, pp. 154–61.

ness. If any long-range planning was undertaken, it generally dealt with expanding the product line or the geographical sales area.

With World War II, business firms had to make massive operational and managerial changes. Since the 1950s, new markets have appeared, competitors no longer follow traditional lines of business, stockholders view investments in firms with long-range profit growth, technology has accelerated at an even greater pace, and social values have changed to fit new lifestyles. With these types of changes, traditional planning is inadequate. Top-level managers must shift their concerns from short-term problems to long-range opportunities by constantly analyzing various courses of action. This type of analysis involves recognition of changing environments and strengths and weaknesses of organizational resources.

To illustrate this point, Eagle-Picher Industries was principally a lead and zinc mining and processing company prior to 1950. In the 1970s, the company decided to expand into a balanced diversity of manufacturing operations. This decision required managers to define the company's business philosophy and overall directional purpose. Social, political, and economic trends affecting the business had to be assessed to determine if each diversification decision was internally consistent with overall goals. Also, the new strategy required an evaluation of management capabilities and skills so that these resources could be focused on products and markets with similar characteristics to those in which the company already excelled. Such a strategic change increased managerial complexity of the organization and forced management to replace sporadic diagnoses of cyclical swings in metal prices and the nonferrous metal market with continuous market surveillance.

ADVANTAGES OF STRATEGY PLANNING

Not all managers believe that strategy planning is useful or even possible. Some suggest that the future is too complex and difficult to anticipate. Of course, perfect accuracy in forecasting is impossible since the future holds many uncertainties. But, what is likely to happen to an organization that does not try to understand those basic marketplace phenomena that both lead and force change? More than likely it will be blighted with troubles affecting survival and growth. Changes in society, the future impact of current decisions, the complexity of governmental regulations, and the increased pressures of competition can hinder survival unless managers make strategic decisions. Surely, strategy planning can assist management in anticipating unfavorable factors and changing environments in which organizations must survive and grow.

In terms of management decisions, strategy planning asks the questions: What is the company's business? Is it the right business? Are product lines obsolete and/or markets eroding? If an organization does not know where it is going, it surely cannot get there. By focusing on the future, as well as on present constraints and policies, managers become better equipped to direct resources toward a successful achievement of goals.

By anticipating the future there is less temptation to focus on short-run results while sacrificing long-run gains, and this is more likely to happen when performance is evaluated on the basis of adherence to strategy plans, rather than on short-term results. Since strategy planning involves long-run considerations, managers can actually capitalize on anticipated changes for the benefit and growth of their organizations. As an example, consider the case of General Electric where "strategic business planning" is used to analyze various product lines systematically in an effort to decide which ventures deserve the most investment capital and which should be sold. Specifically, the concept involves a continuing in-depth analysis of the market share, growth prospects, profitability, and cash-generating power of each venture. In order to continue on a path of growth, General Electric's strategic-planning techniques also put old-line businesses, such as toasters and turbines, under the same analysis as new ventures. In this way, management isolates product lines that are not particularly attractive, either now or in the future. Consequently, strategy planning allows GE to predict the profitability of product lines in as little as one year, as opposed to two or three years as had been normal under its previous planning process.

While other examples could be cited, two major advantages of strategy planning can be seen in the General Electric example. First, more effective plans can be developed, especially those requiring long periods of time to formulate. Managers become involved in shaping the destiny of their organizations and are not content to depend on fortuitous events. To this extent, important contingency plans are taken into account to meet the realities of extreme risks. As a continuous challenge that is never complete, strategy planning requires managers to look at their organizations in a different way from the way they did the previous year.

Second, motivation and cohesiveness are enhanced since all individuals in the organization have an opportunity to know what is going on, where the organization is headed, and what is expected of them in achieving objectives. Of course, if a strategy is to have this value, it must be communicated and understood at all levels within the organization. Planning of this type also requires exceptional leadership by top-level management if given strategies are to be implemented successfully.

MANAGING STRATEGY PLANNING

Strategy-planning systems are not managed the same in all organizations; however, there seems to be a logical evolutionary progression of the process. The four phases noted in Figure 6–1 suggest that strategy planning in Phase 1 is basically forecasting financial data. With these data, financial performance can be evaluated in terms of budgetary targets. Recognizing environmental complexities requires forecasts of economic, social, political, and technological trends, causing Phase II to emerge. Even though the effectiveness of decisions is improved by using forecasting models, major environmental changes may not be predicted accurately enough to deal meaningfully with long-range capital investment, foreign competition, and shifts in customer demand. Since market forecasts can become obsolete quickly, externally oriented planning (Phase III) becomes essential. In this phase the intent is to understand the phenomena that cause changes in the marketplace and in marketshare. From the standpoint of organization structure, strategic business units may be set up around group-related activities or distinct business interests. These organizational entities make decisions that affect their performance and offer alternative strategy plans to top-level managers. However, the need to have top management

FIGURE 6–1
Four phases of the evolution of formal strategic planning

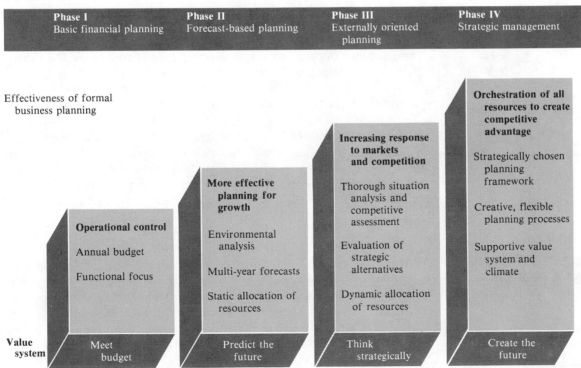

Source: S. W. Glueck, S. P. Kaufman, and A. S. Walleck, "Strategic Management for Competitive Advantage," *Harvard Business Review,* July–August 1980, p. 157. Adapted by permission. © 1980 by the President and Fellows of Harvard College; all rights reserved.

124

FIGURE 6–2
Interrelationship of forecasting and types of plans

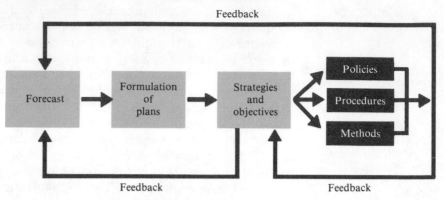

more heavily involved sets the stage for Phase IV. Here the object is to link strategy planning to operational decisions creatively by developing a planning framework that cuts across organizational boundaries. Managers and corporate planning staffs are encouraged to become aware of gaps in their thinking, overcome organizational inflexibility, open up communications, and begin viewing the organization as capable of determining its own destiny, rather than being directed by the winds of environmental change.

Similar to a blueprint, strategy planning helps prepare for the future and helps develop the type of future desired. Yet, if strategy is to influence the future, it must be preceded by forecasts. In turn, strategy provides the basis for policies, procedures, and methods as they relate to an organization's growth, size, and products. (See Figure 6–2.)

Although the long-term intent of strategy is unlikely to change rapidly, this is not to suggest that strategies are unchanging. More specifically, while strategies provide stability, their nature does not preclude short-run changes. To be truly effective, however, strategy must be formulated and implemented for the long run if organizational efforts are to be given meaningful direction.

STRATEGY PLANNING AS A PROCESS

Without question, there are situations where an achievement of goals seems to occur without any conscious definition of strategy. On the other hand, there are many examples showing that the successful achievement of goals depends on systematically established strategies. By planning strategically, management moves away from spending too much time on immediate problems and focuses on long-range goals that, in fact, may be the best way to solve day-to-day problems.

Strategy planning is formalized in the sense that there is an established process involved in devising strategic plans. Yet, the process should not be treated as a highly structured approach but rather as an organized process by which managers coordinate their planning efforts. For our purposes, how the process actually works is probably less important than knowing the issues, who will be involved, and the steps to be considered. In the final analysis, a given strategic-planning process should be tailored to a specific organization, its behavioral styles, and the preferences of its managers. Although it may be apparent, strategy planning must be thoroughly integrated with various management control and information systems.

SPECIFIC STEPS IN STRATEGY PLANNING

For the organization seeking long-term growth, profitability, and continuity, specific steps in developing a sound strategy must be followed. In the time that elapses between these steps, there is a great deal of interaction among managers at various levels in the organization hierarchy.

The first step is to identify the specific objectives to be sought. Paramount in this respect is an analysis of the markets to be penetrated along with a consideration of the organization's desired position in the total market, levels of revenue, debt structure, and profit margins. For planning to be effective, however, objectives must be operationally defined so that their attainment can be measured. They must provide for a proper match between environmental opportunities and organizational resources.

Second, a product and/or service line must be developed that will carry the organization toward its established objectives. An illustration of this point can be seen in the early operations of Litton Industries, Inc. In 1953, Charles Thornton set forth the objective of becoming a major company in military, industrial, and commercial electronics. The accompanying product strategy was that of entering the new advanced electronics industry. Emphasis was placed on (1) creating change through research and development accomplishments, (2) entering those fields that were the most difficult in terms of technology and management, and (3) satisfying markets that other companies did not perceive as being profitable. Of course, the product strategy of Litton Industries is no longer as clear as it was earlier. In fact, its current diversity of programs has led to a conglomerate form of organization that almost defies outside analysis.

The third step in strategy planning involves the development of an organization structure. Without question, an organization structure must provide for the performance of all necessary activities while promoting the style of management required in achieving established goals. For Litton Industries, this step is illustrated by a horizontal management system of delegating authority, free-wheeling entrepreneurial and creative managers, and divisional centers that participate in key decisions that will affect them. To a large extent, Litton's type of organizational design has provided top executives with the time required for strategic planning. In addition, top management is able to make more rapid decisions on acquisitions and product development as required in implementing its strategy.

As a fourth step, strategy planning requires an acquisition of personnel possessing the abilities and skills essential in achieving organizational objectives. People make an organization—not buildings, machines, dollars, or stacks of books. Again, referring to the Litton story, it was important for Litton to acquire the type of managers who could make entrepreneurial types of decisions while constantly developing new ideas within the organization.

A fifth step in strategy planning involves spending time on strategic matters rather than on only day-to-day operational or technical activities. Frequently, top-level managers spend too much of their time handling matters that could, or should, be delegated. Of course, such actions limit the time available for planning. Consequently, managers often find that they are not involved in strategy planning. Instead, they are devoting their time and energy to fighting brush fires or solving daily crises. This is not to infer that daily emergencies should not be handled in an expeditious manner. But, if top-level managers focus on these tasks, they will not have ample time for strategy planning—that is, planning concerned with determining what the organization should be doing, channeling resources in that direction, and motivating team members.

The final step in strategy planning involves an evaluation of given strategies in order to make changes where necessary. By having an adequate control system, the organization's plan can become more responsive to unforeseeable changes in the environment, such as international affairs, new technology, or new governmental regulations. Within IBM, the quarterly review process of tracking, measuring, and analyzing performance is an essential step in the strategic-planning process. Questions to ask in judging the attributes of a strategy are noted in Figure 6–3. Basically, these questions indicate that managers are more likely to succeed when strategies are developed systematically and changed when necessary.

EFFECTIVELY PERFORMING THE STEPS IN STRATEGIC PLANNING

Any strategy involves various substrategies and sub-substrategies. Systems theory emphasizes the importance of coordinating all substrategies so that the total is integrative, yet flexible in nature. As conditions change, strategies must not be so rigid that they cannot incorporate new information and thereby avoid those areas of greatest risk and uncertainty. Specifically, the effective performance of the steps in strategy planning is based on an ability to:

Recognize the environmental factors affecting the organization's success as related to its capabilities.

FIGURE 6–3
Questions to ask in evaluating a strategy

1. Can the strategy be identified in word or practice?
2. Does the strategy fit the character of the organization?
3. Does the strategy of the firm capitalize upon opportunities in its environment?
4. Is the firm competent within the areas of the strategy so that it can build upon its strengths?
5. Are policies of the organization consistent with the strategy?
6. Is the strategy consistent with the moral and personal values of key executives?
7. Is the strategy consistent with the social responsibility of the firm?
8. Can the results of the strategy be properly measured so that they can be weighed against the risks?

Source: Seymour Tilles, "How to Evaluate Corporate Strategy," *Harvard Business Review*, July–August 1963, Copyright © 1963 by the President and Fellows of Harvard College; all right reserved.

Analyze the organization to identify (1) strengths and opportunities that can be capitalized and (2) limitations that must be recognized and overcome. Some of the questions that can be asked here are: Can personnel be properly trained to shift to possibly a radically different type of business? Are funds available for new ventures? Will new or different facilities, machinery, or materials be needed?

Adjust quickly to changing environmental conditions.

Recognize that attempts to motivate others to changing strategies are influenced by an organizational climate composed of the attitudes and personal values of all managers.

Balance organizational goals as they relate to owners, customers, employees, and the public.

An example of foresight in developing new strategy is found in the operations of the Boeing Aircraft Company. During the late 1940s, Boeing executives felt that future demand for passenger and cargo transportation would depend on speed. As a result, their strategy was changed from the production of propeller-driven to four-engine jet airplanes. Other manufacturers in the industry were less flexible and experienced varying degrees of financial difficulty due to their more rigid strategies.

In some cases, an entire industry has proven reluctant to change strategy. A classic example of such rigidity is found among U.S. automobile manufacturers. While foreign compacts were carving out a major niche in the auto market, American manufacturers continued to fill dealers' showrooms with large-size automobiles. This fixation was highlighted by Ford's desire to manufacture and sell the Edsel as a luxury model. Coupled with a lack of consumer acceptance, this inflexibility resulted in an estimated loss of several hundred million dollars for Ford; and, even today, American automotive manufacturers are playing catch-up in the small car market.

One way to emphasize the value and impact of strategy planning is to consider the case of National Cash Register Corporation (NCR). In the following discussion, note how strategy planning facilitates the management process and how the plan is drafted by the managers who must carry it out. Also observe that no single statement of strategy is sufficient for guidance of all elements in a large, complex organization. In fact, each level within the organization requires another strategic statement, more specific than the previous one, to guide the next level of corporate managers. To this extent, the entire organization is a part of the strategy. No segment or group is left out; and consequently, each must be integrated within the plan.

NATIONAL CASH REGISTER'S NEW STRATEGY

From its beginning until 1970, NCR had been parochial and tradition bound in terms of its products, manufacturing, marketing, and organizational management. The company's success and reputation had been based on turning out electromechanical (key-driven) cash registers and accounting machines. By the middle 1960s, however, electronic computers, computer terminals, and electronic data-processing equipment had entered the scene. With NCR's apparent rigidities, questions arose about the company's capability to survive, particularly in its basic markets of retail systems and banking.

While NCR was developing its Century series computers (an attempt to match IBM's System/360), it made no attempt to modernize its cash register and accounting machines. Meanwhile, Burroughs was busily converting its accounting machine line from mechanical to electronic and taking big market shares from NCR. Furthermore, Singer's Business Machines Division had leaped ahead of NCR in new electronic point-of-sale systems in retailing.

During this critical time period, the board of directors reassessed its current disastrous strategy and began planning for a new strategy. This type of planning involved considering opportunities within the organization's environment and analyzing corporate resources and strengths. One of the first steps in developing and implementing a new strategy was to select a new president, William S. Anderson (now chairman), who had previously run the company's profitable Japanese operation. Anderson's role was to instill a new spirit in the company by (1) deciding on the company's objectives and goals, (2) recovering the basic markets that had been lost, (3) reallocating resources among the different functional divisions of the business, and (4) improving the decision-making process among managers.

Within this spirit, NCR developed a new strategy: to focus on electronic data-processing equipment in the banking and retail fields—

the two areas where NCR had its traditional strengths. The strategy was also built around the idea of encouraging NCR customers to start small in data processing and then upgrade to more sophisticated equipment.

To implement this strategy, managers in the corporate hierarchy developed additional strategies. These included revamping the management structure in order to speed up company reaction to needs of the market, decentralizing manufacturing, restructuring the marketing operation, and reorganizing the international divisions. Within each of these areas, strategies had to be framed in progressively more detailed terms; and later, more managers at the lower levels were involved where final choices and specific budgets were established for each cost center.

Product substrategy

To support the new strategy, NCR decided to become a full-line supplier of electronic data-processing systems and terminals and of specialized electronic products for bankers and retailers. Although terminals arc a kcy part of NCR's business, the core of the product substrategy was a low-priced, entry-level computer and a large multimillion-dollar computer. With these two models, the intent was to roundout a full line of compatible computers.

Manufacturing substrategy

For production, the new strategy in moving from "key-driven," electromechanical equipment to electronic products meant a change to smaller manufacturing plants chartered for a limited line or group of products. Prior to the switch to electronic products, about 80 percent of NCR's production had been in Dayton where now only 30 percent is located. This phase of the strategy also implied decentralization of engineering and development, thus allowing each plant to have its own resident engineer and, consequently, more product-line responsibility. By working in smaller plants, personnel in purchasing, engineering, and manufacturing areas had to work more closely as a team, as compared to the large vertically integrated Dayton plant where the company had even made its own screws. The transition from metalworking to electronic production also resulted in lower costs, as a large number of skilled machinists were replaced by lower-paid electronics assemblers.

Marketing substrategy

Prior to the new strategy, NCR's marketing organization centered on branch offices that followed political boundaries. Under this system salespeople emphasized the most profitable products, and each product was sold by a different representative. The resulting lack of marketing coordination was further intensified by field service personnel working independently of the marketing organization. In order to promote communication between product designers and the sales operation, the new marketing strategy divided sales into three groups—retail, financial, and commercial-industrial. This allowed each salesperson to be responsible for selling all NCR products to customers in a particular vocational area. Sales personnel are regarded as consultants to their customers, being trained to listen to customer needs, rather than telling them what they need.

The NCR strategy plan and the system for its implementation is not static but changes continually. One reason for this is that changes are constantly taking place in the external environment, for example, competition from IBM, Burroughs, and Singer Business Machines. These competitors have a major impact on daily decisions and quarterly budget projections. In addition, changes in the organizational structure and management ranks require each aspect of the organization to be finely tuned continuously. From an integrative viewpoint, it is not meaningful to refer to an overall strategy for NCR but rather to a collection of strategies that link managers, divisions, and departments within the entire organization.

ENVIRONMENTAL CONSIDERATIONS FOR STRATEGY PLANNING

Strategic planning involves choosing the more desirable future alternatives in order to obtain better current decisions. As noted above, long-term decisions easily become obsolete because assumptions about environmental trends can change very quickly. Regardless of this difficulty, some attempt must be made to consider economic, social, political, and technological assumptions, as well as other environmental factors.

This chapter concludes with a discussion of the various kinds of environmental assumptions that managers must consider, whether they are employed by a hospital, a multinational corporation, or a small firm selling imported gift items.

General economic assumptions

Assumptions about general economic conditions are extremely important in strategy planning. In fact, it is difficult to understand how managers could possibly plan effectively without making assumptions about future economic conditions.

An economic forecast is not a substitute for good planning. Instead, it is the way managers use general economic assumptions that is important in arriving at meaningful plans. For example, assume that an economic forecast indicates that business activity will not be as vigorous for the next 12 months when compared to the past year. Armed with the specific information inherent in such a forecast, managers can plan to continue the production of certain products while identifying lines that should be discontinued.

An effective strategy must be based on meaningful and correct economic assumptions. In this respect, there is a great deal of economic data that can be used in developing economic forecasts. Some of these data included retail sales, employment figures, industrial production, interest rates, wholesale prices, inventory levels, capital expenditures by business, freight car loadings, and bank loans. One popular approach to forecasting the state of the economy combines changes in general business conditions to arrive at a value known as the gross national product (GNP—the market value of the final goods and services produced in a specified year). There are various statistical techniques used in projecting GNP. All of them, however, attempt to analyze quantitative data over a period of time so as to arrive at a measured forecast for some future period. In general, GNP forecasts reflect a long-term trend projected into the future, as well as short-term cyclical fluctuations that move up and down on the path of the trend.

Long-term projections   Long-term projections of GNP are vital to the development of strategy planning. For example, if a company projects that the U.S. economy will continue to grow for the next 20 years, plans can be established for plant expansion and product diversification that will take advantage of such growth conditions. Without question, long-term projections are not completely reliable since environmental conditions change over time, even though some changes are evolutionary in nature. However, without some knowledge of economic trends, strategy planning is likely to be much less viable.

Short-term projections   Short-term forecasts of GNP (usually referred to as stages of the business cycle) can be regarded as the summation of a wide variety of short-run changes that are taking place within the economy. Managers are anxious to know if general business conditions will be above or below the forecasted trend. Consequently, projections of this type are important not only to short-range planning, but also to long-range planning as well. If a forecast indicates that a downturn in the economy is right around the corner, top management may delay building a new plant, particularly when interest rates are high and money is relatively tight. For short-range planning, a similar forecast would suggest reductions in raw materials and finished goods inventories with a review of advertising and promotional plans.

The case of Montgomery Ward provides one of the classic examples of an economic forecast that resulted in serious error. Under the direction of Sewell Avery, the top management of Wards waited for the big recession that was expected after World War II. The company maintained large cash reserves so that new stores could be built at lower recessionary costs. Rather than a postwar recession, as had been expected, the country experienced a sustained period of inflation. Thus, the longer Wards waited, the more expensive it became to build new stores. The plans that seemed realistic a few years earlier were based on the wrong economic assumptions. As a result, Wards fell 10 to 15 years behind Sears Roebuck and Company, its biggest competitor, which had forecasted inflationary conditions and had expanded in anticipation of a growing economy.

Industry assumptions

General economic forecasts are more applicable to specific organizational plans when they are balanced with overall industry forecasts. Basically, industry assumptions relate to the demand for products or services of the industry or industries in which a firm is involved. To develop these assumptions, it is important for managers to follow trade association publications and assess (1) the state of the industry and the growth of consumer demand for its products or services, (2) the capacity of the industry to supply the demand, (3) projected changes in operating costs, (4) technological advancements in the industry, and (5) present and future competition from all sources. Another good source of information to use in developing industry assumptions is found in the data, by industrial classification, published by the U.S. Department of Commerce.

In arriving at industry assumptions, it is important to observe changes in demand from one period to the next. For example, there is a much greater cyclical variability in the demand for automobiles than for kilowatt hours of electric power over a sustained period of time. This is due primarily to the differing degrees of durability between the two products. Electrical power cannot be stored by consumers, but the replacement date of an automobile can be shifted by consumers since it is a durable good. An analysis of this type helps managers forecast fluctuations in sales volume in order to achieve a better balance among goods subject to cyclical demand patterns.

Obviously, managers must recognize the importance of appraising the outlook of the industry in which they are involved. In this respect, most people are familiar with stories of various industries that have been replaced by others.[2] Similarly, we have seen new industries appear when present ones failed to recognize and/or satisfy changing consumer demands.[3] One of the most exciting stories concerning the recognition of an industry's potential is that of Arthur Ash and Roy Thornton. These men left Hughes Aircraft in 1956 and started manufacturing miniature electronic products at a time when most companies in the industry did not foresee the emergence of this vast new field. From the foresight and planning of Ash and Thornton, the impressive Litton organization was created.

Individual company assumptions

After considering general economy and industry forecasts, the forecast of company sales is a logical step. One way of arriving at company assumptions is to consider the organization's position within the total

---

[2] The disappearance of the neighborhood grocery store and the small local butcher shop came about with the emergence of supermarkets. Also, when diesel engines were introduced for train locomotive power, steam engine locomotive manufacturers went out of business.

[3] On more than one occasion, the railroad industry has failed to see that it is in the transportation industry, rather than in the industry of moving goods and people only on rails. Of course, many companies have gone out of business because they defined their business improperly. An example is that of a wooden container manufacturer who saw his product as wood and went out of business when shippers turned to paperboard containers.

industry. Some of the factors that are essential in making these assumptions are:

Penetration of the market—company sales as a percentage of industry sales.

Public and consumer image of company products and services.

Location of operations   requires consideration of the economic development and growth of the area(s).

Financial and profit positions.

Internal and external risks and how they are covered by the company.

Planning and control of labor and material requirements necessary for operations.

Changes in asset requirements and their effects on costs and productivity.

The general nature of these factors indicate the specific data that are helpful to managers in doing a better job of forecasting company sales.

Also implicit in making individual company assumptions is the importance of coupling the requirements of the market with the company's technical ability. For example, Hewlett-Packard Company balanced its technical strength in building electronic testing and measuring instrumentation to the sophistication demanded by the market. Equally important to Hewlett-Packard in making appropriate market assumptions is that the company does not design a fantastic piece of equipment that is not demanded.

Sociological assumptions

In terms of various cultures, education, age, sex, race, population, and social institutions are becoming more important in the formulation of strategic plans. Generally, vast social changes do not occur in the short run, but they occur often enough to influence long-range plans.

Many examples of social forces at work can be seen in the changes taking place in the organization and curriculum structures of elementary and secondary schools, as well as in colleges and universities. Likewise, book publishers are being prompted by pressure groups, including the back-to-basics movement, women's organizations, fundamentalists, and racial and ethnic minorities, to rewrite American textbooks. Publishers who are not willing to recognize these types of trends are not likely to be selling many books in the $650 million elementary and secondary school market.

Today, managers recognize that markets for clothing, hair styling needs, cosmetics, and other products differ among races and cultures. Health-conscious Americans have supported the move banning cigarette advertising on television and have contributed to the growth of organic food stores. The insistent problem of heart disease will, no doubt, bring about major changes in food processing to provide foods that are low in cholesterol and high in polyunsaturates. Again, these illustrations indicate that meaningful planning considers various sociological assumptions.

Public attitude assumptions

Many public sentiments are difficult to recognize and measure, although some very basic attitudes come through loud and clear. Through Congress, for example, Douglas Aircraft Corporation was given a resounding NO by the public concerning the use of government funds for building the supersonic transport plane (SST). Other managers now recognize that plans having a potential for polluting the air or water cannot be successfully implemented since the public attitude is one of cleaning up the environment.

The importance of utilizing assumptions based on public attitudes is also clearly highlighted in the automobile industry. When considering the future demand for automobiles, researchers in one auto company used such variables as population, income, and demand for transportation to project sales of 13 million to 14 million units in 1982. However, by considering such other factors as (1) customer attraction to small U.S. cars compared to foreign imports, (2) the increased cost of cars due to technical equipment, (3) the growing congestion in urban areas, (4) an apparent move of people back to apartments and town houses in the central city, (5) governmental action to change the design of cars to discourage their use, and (6) the energy crisis, auto sales might be different from those projected for 1982. By recognizing public attitudes, therefore, auto makers can more astutely plan their strategy regarding plant capacity and capital investment.

Technological assumptions

Probably no field of endeavor has ever experienced the impact of technological advancements more than that of the computer. The importance of new technology in the computer field as it relates to individual business, government, multinational organizations, and the military has few precedents throughout history. Arriving at technological assumptions in this field, as in others where the state of the art is advancing rapidly, depends on an understanding of the problems encountered in making improvements, the means of resolving such problems, and the probable limits to their solution.

During the past decade managers have recognized the need to incorporate technological issues within strategy planning. The need for such integration can be observed if we think of technology as more than just nuts and bolts and include its impact on an organization's total planning and delivery system. This broader combination of technology and strategy planning (knowing the business the company is in, identifying goals, and formulating long-term policies and other plans to meet them) suggests that the two are inseparable. Specifically, research studies note that a main key to the success of new innovations and products is a proper match of technical possibilities with market needs and user requirements.[4] By including the importance of good communications, purposeful allocation of resources, and top-level management support to assure success of innovations, the importance of technological assumptions in defining and implementing corporate strategy is quite apparent.

Political assumptions

Few assumptions have a greater impact on managerial planning than those related to the political arena. In most organizations, pricing, employment practices, accounting methods, production, competitive practices, and other decisions are influenced by governmental actions. Major conflicts, however, often exist between stated policies, the means to implement them, and relationships among governmental agencies. For example, state legislatures and the U.S. Congress pass bills that become laws, while the specific interpretation of these laws is left to other groups. Often, regulatory agencies charged with enforcing specific legislation are not certain about what constitutes compliance. Due to this fact, some agencies, such as the FTC, have their own interpretations that exceed the intent of the enabling legislation.

Another difficulty in properly assessing political assumptions arises when government standards conflict. As one example, reducing oxides of nitrogen from tail pipes of automobiles increases the amount of carbon monoxide emitted. Consequently, automobile manufacturers will soon be required to install two-way catalytic converters on cars to reduce both pollutants.

Monetary and fiscal actions by the government also have a great influence on strategy planning. Monetary policies are reflected in the prime rate of interest and the supply of money that consists mainly of demand deposits in commercial banks. Capital investment and expenditure plans of business are generally based on assumptions about the rate of interest in the market. Consider the owner of a trucking company who believes that the purchase of a new truck could earn 17 percent on the original investment. If a loan for purchasing the truck carried an interest rate of 18 percent per annum, it would not be profitable to buy the truck. On the other hand, if a loan could be acquired for something less than 17 percent, consideration may be given to purchasing the truck. The timing of such decisions clearly depends on assumptions concerning future shifts in the rate of interest.

Fiscal policy refers to the taxation and spending programs of the government, both of which should be considered in strategy planning. Since managers are interested in how taxes can be reduced, it is extremely important for them to understand various tax reform acts and

---

[4] Christopher Freeman, *The Economics of Industrial Innovation* (Baltimore: Penguin, 1974), pp. 173–90. Also see Alan M. Kantrow, "The Strategy-Technology Connection," *Harvard Business Review,* July–August 1980, pp. 6–21; and Alfred A. Marcus, "Policy Uncertainty and Technological Innovation," *The Academy of Management Review,* July 1981, pp. 443–48.

tax regulations. In making real estate investments, for example, syndicated plans become quite appealing when they can reduce the taxes and risks associated with various projects.

In summary, governmental actions now touch almost all organizations, large and small. Thus, managers must assess the potential impact of government policies and regulations as they formulate strategic plans. Some organizations, such as Hewlett-Packard Company, feel that doing business with the government results in red tape and unwarranted restrictions. Consequently, Hewlett-Packard limits its government sales to approximately 15 percent of its current business. To illustrate further, U.S. oil refineries have had to make fairly accurate assumptions about the impact of the standards decreed by the Department of Health, Education, and Welfare (now the Department of Health and Human Services) for removing tetraethyl lead from gasoline. It has been estimated that the industry will probably invest over $6 billion to comply with these standards. From a financial standpoint, small refineries are finding it difficult to meet their share of these costs. They, as well as some larger petroleum companies, may find that the only answer to this problem lies in acquisition or merger with other refineries unless there are substantial changes in the federal standards.

Assumptions concerning foreign competition and labor unions

More than ever before, foreign competition must be a consideration in establishing planning premises. American companies no longer hold a monopoly on managerial and technical competence that can lead to industrial superiority. Japanese and European steel makers now hold a $4 billion share of the $30 billion U.S. steel market by having low prices and by building a network of steel warehouses and finishing plants in the United States. Based on its technology, Nippon Steel Corporation, Japan's largest steel company, obtained U.S. steel contracts from transformer manufacturers by developing a steel with special electrical properties. Consequently, American steel companies are now paying license fees to Nippon for its technology.

Labor unions also play an impressive role in determining the direction of the U.S. economy. Union goals and actions must, therefore, be considered in the formation of all organizational plans. The interaction between management and labor is not something that is decided by either group. Instead, such interaction is influenced by state and federal legislation, legal decisions, public attitudes, and the power of specific labor and management groups. Union power has clearly limited managerial prerogatives in some areas. However, this has not been reflected in an extensive encroachment on management's authority to run an organization, but rather in a monitoring of the management decisions affecting employees. Yet, increased union and worker influences on decision making and strategy cannot be overlooked. Realistically, then, managers must always make assumptions about future relationships between labor and management if they are to develop sound strategic plans.

SUMMARY

Every organization must distinguish between short-range tactical planning and longer-range strategy planning. The longer the time period covered by planning, the more strategic it becomes. Strategy is not involved with asking questions about what activities and schedules will be followed in the near term, but with defining the purposes for an organization's existence. For example, the strategy planning of McDonald's Restaurants deals not only with what to sell customers, but also with what the company can do for its customers in terms of quality, service, and convenience. Such strategy planning emphasizes the establishment of objectives to guide an organization for years to come.

Strategy planning also involves forecasts of anticipated events as they relate to organizational objectives. In making forecasts, many different types of information about the environment are required such as assumptions about the economy, society, political developments, technological advancements, foreign competition, and labor unions.

KEY TERMS

Economic assumptions: Forecasts of GNP and stages of the business cycle reflecting employment, personal income, retail sales, price levels, and other economic data.

Environmental factors: Elements external to an organization that are in constant change, thus requiring managers to make assumptions about their future impact.

Gross national product: The market value of the final goods and services produced in a specific year. The acronym for this term is GNP.

Sociological assumptions: Cultural factors of education, race, population, social institutions, and other demographic variables that must be considered in formulating strategic plans.

Strategic planning process: The specific steps followed by managers in developing a sound strategy. These include: (1) identifying the specific objectives to be sought, (2) developing product/service lines that will carry the organization toward established objectives, (3) developing an effective organization structure, (4) acquiring personnel who are skilled and able to achieve objectives, (5) spending time on strategic issues while delegating operational activities, and (6) evaluating how well the strategy is working and making changes where necessary.

Strategy planning: The long-range planning activities of managers that consider environmental factors in setting forth organizational character, purpose, and direction.

Substrategies: Established strategies of various functional areas, such as marketing, production, and finance that are tightly integrated and coordinated to achieve an organization's overall strategy effectively.

Technological assumptions: Predictions about the current and future skills and capabilities of the organization in the planning and production of goods and services.

QUESTIONS

1. What is the meaning of strategy planning?
2. Note the factors that have brought about the rising importance of strategy planning.
3. What impact does the "future" have in strategy planning?
4. What questions are generally asked by managers in strategy planning?
5. List the advantages of strategy planning.
6. What are the steps that a manager should follow in developing sound strategy?
7. What kinds of assumptions are necessary in making a forecast?
8. Which types of assumptions can be treated more completely on a quantitative basis?

PROBLEMS

1. What factors make it difficult to develop detailed plans for periods beyond three years into the future?

2. What can managers do to overcome the constraining factors noted in question 1 above while still obtaining the benefits of strategy planning?

3. Give examples to show why forecasts concerning governmental taxation and spending programs are important to *(a)* a farmer and *(b)* the management group of an oil refinery.

4. ETC Incorporated produces tubes for sale to radio manufacturers. With the growing use of transistors, the president foresees a continued decline in demand for electronic radio tubes. Consequently, it is felt that long-range planning is essential for the continued survival of the company. Outline the specific steps that the president should follow relative to strategy planning.

5. "Managers must realize the determining influence of major managerial decisions that were made 10 to 20 years ago to produce today's products and opportunities." Comment on this statement by a GE executive.

6. In strategic planning, an essential element is to be aware of environmental forces, such as economic changes. Unfortunately, most organizations are

not attuned to unique events nor to the reasons and underlying factors of change. By "listening" only to particular information to which the organization is attuned, the type of strategy that will best take advantage of the situation cannot be developed. How effective will an organization's strategy be if it is not in harmony with the external environment?

7. One of the classical examples of successful strategy development is a situation at General Motors under the direction of Alfred Sloan. In spite of the depression of the 1930s, sales of all low-priced cars in the industry had grown from 52 percent in 1926 to 73 percent in 1933. For GM, the sales of Pontiac, Oldsmobile, Buick, and Cadillac were down drastically. In an attempt to reduce operating costs, Donaldson Brown, GM's chief financial officer, proposed the elimination of two divisions in the high-price group. Sloan, however, decided not to drop any, but to increase the product line variety within the high-price group to overlap with Chevrolet.

a. Does Sloan's strategy seem to be a radical alternative at a time when the economy was in the depth of a depression?
b. Do you feel that with today's advancements in mathematical forecasting models and computer-based analyses more support would have been given to Brown or Sloan?
c. How does your answer in (b) relate to the relationship between scientific forecasts and reality?

SUGGESTED READINGS

Ansoff, H. I.; R. P. Declerch; and R. L. Hayes. *From Strategic Planning to Strategic Management.* New York: John Wiley & Sons, 1976.

Bales, C. F. "Strategic Control: The President's Paradox." *Business Horizons,* August 1977, pp. 17–28.

Bracker, J. "The Historical Development of the Strategic Management Concept." *Academy of Management Review,* April 1980, pp. 219–24.

Fahey, L., and W. R. King. "Environmental Scanning for Corporate Planning." *Business Horizons,* August 1977, pp. 61–71.

Fischer, William A. "Follow-up Strategies for Technological Growth." *California Management Review,* Fall 1978, pp. 10–19.

Gerstner, L. V., Jr. "Can Strategic Planning Pay Off?" *Marketing Management—Perspective and Applications.* Homewood, Ill.: Richard D. Irwin, 1976, p. 174.

Khtaian, G. A. "Strategic and Financial Models for a Utility." *Management Accounting,* June 1977, pp. 44–51.

King, W. R., and D. I. Cleland. "Decision and Information Systems for Strategic Planning." *Business Horizons,* April 1973, pp. 29–36.

"Market Strategy at Phillip Morris Involves More than Spending Money." *Management Accounting,* January 1980, pp. 12–16.

Paul, R. N.; N. B. Conovan; and J. W. Taylor. "The Reality Gap in Strategic Planning." *Harvard Business Review,* May–June 1978, pp. 124–30.

Schendel, D. E., and C. W. Hofer. *Strategic Management: A New View of Business Policy and Planning.* Boston: Little Brown, 1979.

Seed, A. H. III. "Strategic Planning: The Cutting Edge of Management Accounting." *Management Accounting,* May 1980, pp. 10–16.

Smith, L. " 'Equal Opportunity' Rules Are Getting Tougher." *Fortune,* June 19, 1978, pp. 152–156.

"A Surprise NCR Leap into the Chip Market." *Business Week,* July 13, 1981, p. 22.

"Technologies for the 80's." *Business Week,* July 6, 1981, pp. 48–56.

Wheelwright, S. C. "Reflecting Corporate Strategy in Manufacturing Decisions." *Business Horizons,* February 1978, pp. 57–66.

Woodward, H. N. "Management Strategies for Small Companies." *Harvard Business Review,* January–February 1976, pp. 113–21.

7

THE IMPLEMENTATION
OF PLANS

PURPOSE

The board of directors of a medium-sized manufacturing plant in California recently hired a new chief executive officer. The CEO noticed that the company did not have a formal policies and procedures manual guiding routine operational activities. Several departmental managers made decisions without guidance from earlier policy statements since many were now stored in dusty filing cabinets. The issue of not having established policies and procedures available for a rather routine type of problem came to light recently. Several manufactured items were moved from the warehouse to the production department to be repackaged in smaller quantities. The warehouse manager was on vacation and no one else in the department knew the accounting procedures to follow in tracking the flow of items and recording their costs. Also, no one knew how to inform officially the production and inventory control managers about the repackaging decision. Likewise, the production department was confused, since the production manager was at a regional seminar and the production schedule for that day did not include the repackaging order.

The loss of time and the frustrations encountered in this situation would not have occurred if subordinates' actions had been guided by well-established policies and procedures. In all organizations, policies, procedures, methods, and standards are essential for integrating managerial decisions. Without an understanding of the nature and importance of such facilitators in the management process, the problem illustrated above becomes a common experience rather than a rare occurrence.

In this chapter, we will look at how policies, operating procedures, methods, and standards guide resources toward the accomplishment of objectives.

OBJECTIVES

1. To illustrate how policies, procedures, methods, and standards are essential in the implementation of plans.

2. To discuss policies as broad guidelines to decisions and action.

3. To identify some of the problems accompanying the development and application of policies.

4. To provide an understanding of methods, procedures, and standards.

5. To show how methods, procedures, and standards are developed within the framework of policies.

If an organization is to function effectively, it must satisfy a number of conditions. Three of these are concerned with the selection of objectives, the implementation of means to achieve goals, and the coordination of human and material resources. Objectives and strategic plans, however, are not self-effectuating. A facilitating mechanism in the form of policies, procedures, methods, and standards is necessary to guide future thought and action in implementing plans.

EVOLUTIONARY ROLE OF FACILITATORS

The search to achieve objectives with the least cost has led to the development of many planning approaches. Each approach, however, has relied on the use of policies, procedures, methods, and standards in the planning process. During the 1930s and 1940s, for example, emphasis was placed on motion and time studies in an effort to increase productivity by finding better ways to perform work activities. Methods and standards were two significant elements in these studies.

As an adjunct to motion study, human engineering (designing equipment to suit and serve workers better) became popular in the 1940s. Placing machines at eye level, improving lighting, and making equipment safer to operate all depended on the development and implementation of appropriate policies and standards.

In the 1950s, the advance of automation and the advent of electronic controls freed the human element from many routine activities and caused managers to place a greater reliance on standard operating procedures and product standardization. Management by objectives was introduced to many organizations in the early 1960s. This approach stresses the need for clearly defined objectives throughout the hierarchy and the necessity of policies for achieving them.

During the 1970s, employees continued expressing the desire for more meaningful work. The desire to use their skills more fully while accepting greater degrees of responsibility resulted in various programs such as job enrichment. Enriching routine jobs to make them more productive and self-satisfying depends, in part, on analyzing work methods and work procedures in arriving at final job designs. In addition, policies must be established to provide workers with decision-making control. Although job enrichment is contingent upon a variety of other organizational variables, policies, procedures, and methods are extremely important in designing jobs so they relate to a desired quality of work life.

In summary, managers use various approaches in seeking efficiency. Yet, policies, procedures, methods, and standards are essential elements of all approaches and they are inevitable in guiding resources toward the accomplishment of objectives.

POLICIES AID IN ACHIEVING OBJECTIVES

If a particular plan, such as changing the design of a product or implementing a new wage incentive program is to be carried out successfully, appropriate direction must be provided to the plan. One way of providing direction is through policy statements with regard to organizational values, ideas, and overall goals. Policies guide thoughts and actions by identifying the boundaries of acceptable behavior. In turn, such boundaries are essential in coordinating all of the decisions and actions related to the accomplishment of objectives.

As part of the framework in which planning takes place, *policies may be defined as broad guidelines to decisions and actions required in attaining organizational objectives.* Thus, policies focus attention on various future alternatives, consequences, and risks that must be considered in making decisions. The relationships among objectives, policies, and organizational decisions are shown in Figure 7–1. As indicated, policy formulation is based on the strategies and objectives that determine the directional thrust of an organization. Remember, however, that environmental factors affecting organizational objectives also influence policies. Stockholders, government, cultural influences, labor unions, and the general public all have an impact on policy determination.

Role and importance of policy   Policies fulfill many roles in an organization. Since they serve to direct future action, they are important in (1) achieving coordination, (2) gaining efficiency, (3) developing future managers, and (4) establishing an organizational image.

Achieving coordination   Coordination implies that the elements of an organization are related and linked together so that all persons perform the right actions at the right time in seeking to accomplish goals. Within any organization the amount of coordination needed may vary between units, but a certain degree is always essential since no unit functions in a purely self-contained and autonomous manner. An example of achieving coordination is seen in the organizational design of duPont where all divisions are related through a finance committee. Since financial decisions affect all divisions, they are interrelated and linked together through financial policies.

As a coordinating technique, policies guide the general direction of activities and decisions. The efforts of organizational members can, thereby, be interrelated so that they work together and do not pull in opposite directions. In a manufacturing company, for example, policies in the areas of production, marketing, finance, personnel, and

FIGURE 7–1
Relationship of objectives, policies, and organizational decisions

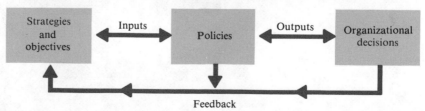

purchasing help guide each unit in a coordinated manner. This point is illustrated in Figure 7–2.

In most business organizations, specific types of decisions occur rather frequently. That is, decisions in pricing, product selection, credit, and merchandise return are common types of decisions that are usually made on a daily basis. To help ensure consistency in dealing with recurring decisional problems, policies are essential. Guiding decision making, however, implies that policies should be sufficiently broad to allow managers room for interpretation. In this way discretion and flexibility are provided in the decision-making process. If managers have some discretion in the decisions they make, they are more motivated to pull as team members toward overall goal accomplishment. In this sense, policies promote cooperation as well as coordination. Of course, teamwork should also be extended to policy formulation. If policies evolve from team thinking and planning, coordination is more likely to result.

Gaining efficiency Policies save time for managers by guiding decision making. For many operating decisions, policy guidelines permit decisions to be made with minimum delay. If a policy statement clearly sets out the guidelines to follow, there is little need to seek assistance from superiors or others. At the same time, policies enable managers

FIGURE 7–2
Policies coordinate organizational activities

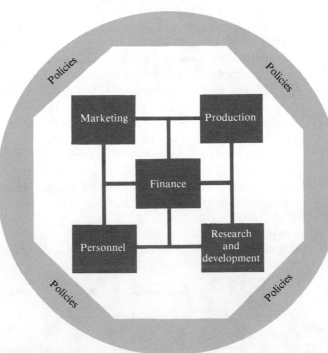

to delegate authority while maintaining reasonable assurance that decisions will be made within acceptable boundaries. Thus, managers do not have to be directly involved in the decisions of subordinates, except in unusual or exceptional cases.

Developing future managers   In developing future managers, top executives must be willing to delegate certain decision-making responsibilities to subordinates. Policies play an important role in this process since they provide guidelines outlining the parameters within which decisions should be made. Policies should also provide subordinates with enough leeway to be creative and innovative in solving problems but yet provide some assurance to superiors that decisions are being made within established guidelines.

Establishing an organizational image   Since policies reflect the basic thinking and attitudes of management, they portray an organizational image to the public. Stated policies inform customers, owners, employees, government, suppliers, and the general public about an organization's attitudes and intentions. Through policy statements, for example, the Ford Motor Company sets forth its desire to be a responsible citizen within the communities where it operates. Yet, in the final analysis, how organizational participants perceive such policy statements determines the actual image of an organization.

Broad policies versus narrow rules

Polices must be broad enough to permit discretionary action. If a policy is interpreted so narrowly that there is no leeway for decision making, the implication is that the statement is a rule, rather than a policy. Figure 7–3 shows that policies and rules are polarized when it comes to room for interpretation and discretion. For example, the policy statement "promotions to management positions will be made from within the organization" leaves room for interpretation. It does not suggest who should be promoted or what other factors to consider. It does, however, give the general direction to be taken in filling a managerial position.

If a statement reads, "promote the person with the longest seniority," there is no room for interpretation since a decision is clearly specified. This statement is a rule since there is only one alternative that could possibly be followed and no decision needs to be made. The distinction between policies and rules does not suggest that one

FIGURE 7–3
Policy-rule continuum

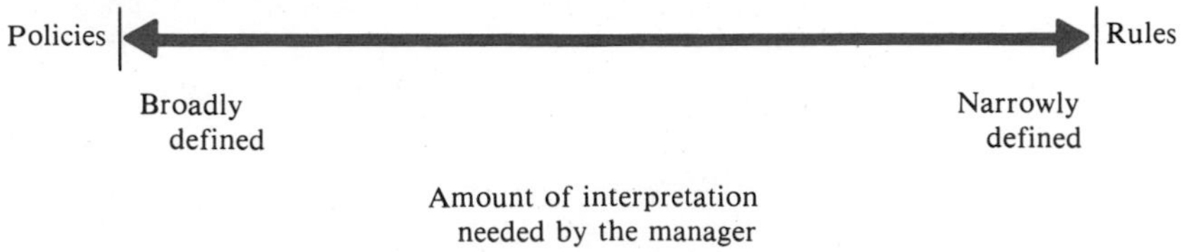

Policies | ⬅————————————————————➤ | Rules

Broadly   Narrowly
defined   defined

Amount of interpretation
needed by the manager

is bad and the other is good. Rules, however, should be established within the framework of policies and evaluated as to their contribution in transforming plans into operational realities.

Managerial problems with policies   Although policies have definite benefits, they are not without their limitations. As an illustration, policies do not always contribute to a coordination of effort, and employee actions are often sidetracked rather than guided by policies. Some of the causes underlying problems such as these can be classified under the headings of (1) policy formulation and implementation, (2) overdefined policies, and (3) policy administration.

Policy formulation and implementation   Environmental conditions affect policies and all internal resources of any organization. With a constant change in an organization's environment, policies must remain current and dynamic. In the broadest sense, then, policies are actually concerned with the achievement of established goals within the framework of a given organizational environment. In the formulation of policies to satisfy this purpose, two classifications emerge—stated and implied.

Stated policies   Policies that are formally established and approved by top management are referred to as stated policies. If only top-level managers are involved in the formulation process, however, private deliberations and personal interests are quite likely to lead to interpretations that differ from the real intent. For this reason, committees or staff groups are quite important to help draft policy statements for management approval. Otherwise, the needs and goals of all groups in the organization may not be considered in the development of policies.

The extent to which stated policies originate below top management depends upon the delegation of policy-making authority. Referred to as decentralization of authority, top management partially steps out of the operating picture by delegating a wider range of authority to lower-level managers.

Organizational size often forces the responsibility for policy formulation further down the management hierarchy. In addition, technology and computerization have reduced the need for stringent, centralized policies. Computers, for instance, have streamlined reporting systems, thus providing more rapid feedback on actual performance.

Another pressure working against a centralized development and statement of policies is the decline of paternalistic management styles. More organizations are moving toward participative management where self-expression and joint deliberation are encouraged.

Implied policies   Many policies are not consciously established by management. These are referred to as implied policies since they are unstated and may be developed without official sanction. Yet, while implied policies do not necessarily have official approval, they are often enforced by those in positions of authority.

Implied policies often become accepted guidelines when (1) managers do not want to make their true intentions known in a stated policy (for example, an unwillingness to hire women for particular jobs would not be stated), or (2) guidelines to action are required but are not officially formulated or stated. In this respect, implied policies are often developed by informal leaders or specific work groups.

At this point it should be obvious that policies exist even though they may not be stated. When a policy vacuum occurs, the void will be filled by implied policies. In such cases an implied policy may be quite sufficient for dealing with specialized situations. On the other hand, complete dependence on implied policies is dangerous. If implied policies are contributing to coordination and an achievement of goals, they should be considered for formal endorsement by management. Where implied policies are not in line with organizational efforts, they should be eliminated or replaced by stated policies that express the intentions of management more clearly.

How managers can best implement formulated policies has received increased attention for the last several years. This has resulted in more empirical research on implementation.[1] Some findings from this research suggest that one major incentive to encourage managers to implement official policies is to tie effective implementation to a manager's performance appraisal and rewards. Also, how managers perceive the need for policies and their impact on organizational behavior determines how receptive they will be in implementing them. The variables influencing the implementation of policy are still complex and unclear. No doubt, more research and study are needed in this area to develop models that will be useful to all practicing managers.

Overdefined policies   The implication of overdefined policies is that the intent and meaning of some policy statements are in direct opposition to others.[2] This problem can be explained by examining the policies of a branch store selling and servicing electric razors. The branch manager supervises three other employees in the store. The layout includes a counter displaying new razors, parts, and a line of toiletry items promoted by the parent company. In addition, there is a small workshop for repairing razors. The regional office of the company recently sent two new policies to the manager. One states that selling and overhead expenses must be reduced by 20 percent. The other states that customer service must be expanded to improve branch sales.

---

[1] J. M. Stevens, J. M. Beyer, and H. M. Trice, "Management Receptivity and Implementation of Policies," *Journal of Management*, Spring 1980, pp. 33–54.

[2] The concept of overdefined conditions is attributed to a Joseph A. Litterer. See *The Analysis of Organizations* (New York: John Wiley & Sons, 1973), p. 328.

The two new policies place the manager in a difficult position. If selling costs are cut by 20 percent, the manager may have to (1) shorten the hours that the shop is open, (2) reduce the number of sales and repair personnel, and/or (3) reduce inventory levels. Any of these actions could possibly result in less customer satisfaction. But, if customer service is expanded it would be difficult to reduce costs by 20 percent. To follow either policy requires that the other be disregarded. Yet, a decision must be made, even though both policies cannot possibly be implemented simultaneously. The only remaining alternatives for the manager are (1) to disregard both policies or (2) to try to develop a new approach that would operate satisfactorily under both policies.

This example makes it apparent that newly developed policies become overdefined when their relationships to existing policies are not determined prior to implementation. Executives may become so busy that they do not provide adequate time for policy review and overlook the importance of seeing that policies are internally consistent. In any event, overdefined policies are not uncommon in organizations and often result in frustrating situations for managers who are held responsible for following all established policies.

Policy administration   One way of assessing how well a policy is working is to determine if it is achieving desired results. When policies are not influencing behavior and decision making in the right direction, the problem could be one of improper administration.

If employees see a policy applied unfairly and inconsistently, they may seek ways of getting around it. In such cases, poor administration destroys the true intent of sound policies and causes employees to lose faith in the judgment and wisdom of management.

Briefly, poor administration of policies is generally a result of (1) a failure to consider alternative policies systematically, (2) an inability to challenge existing policies effectively due to resistance to change, (3) too little criticism of false assumptions underlying policies, and (4) tradition-bound methods of policy making.[3] From these problems, we see that improving policy administration is very dependent on an ability to exercise good judgment while being fair and consistent. In addition, the writing and continuous review of policies can contribute significantly to good policy administration.

Written policies   Some managers disagree with the idea that policies should be in writing. These managers feel unwritten policies promote flexibility in administration and increase the understanding of policies that are difficult to express in writing. Written policies, however, reduce confusion and misinterpretation by providing employees with an accessible statement as to what is actually intended. They also provide a reference whereby controversial phrases can be dis-

[3] I. I. Mitroff and J. R. Emshoff, "On Strategic Assumption-Making: A Dialectical Approach to Policy and Planning," *The Academy of Management Review*, January 1979, pp. 1–12.

cussed. By having access to written policies, people see them in the same form and they generate a feeling of consistency in policy interpretation and administration.

Policy review A policy that remains in existence when it is no longer needed can reduce effectiveness in goal achievement. Thus, in order to be effective, managers may find that they must violate stated policies rather than operate by the book. In addition, policies that are not applicable to present conditions are seldom viewed as being fair and consistent. To overcome such attitudes, policy reviews are essential and are generally more successful when they are conducted by a task force of managers appointed by top management.[4]

When managers do not review policies, they can also become insensitive to the role of policies in responding to changing environmental conditions. For example, one major movie studio had a policy stating that all of its picture and sound equipment would be owned by the company. As the movie industry fell on hard times, the policy became meaningless and a costly burden to the company. If a periodic review of policies had been undertaken, company executives could have changed this policy to permit the sale of equipment while authorizing the rental of new equipment when needed.

Exceptions to policies

Policies are not expected to cover every eventuality, and some situations occur that are beyond the boundaries of a particular policy statement. When these exceptional situations occur, they must be referred to a higher level of authority. This approach—*the exception principle*—denotes that management is only interested in those items that are exceptional in nature. Possibly a more descriptive term to use here is *management by exception.*

When an exception to a policy arises, the superior is consulted and asked to make a decision. If the immediate superior is unable to solve the problem, it must be referred upward until it reaches an individual who has the authority to make a decision on the matter. At times, the authority to deviate from policy may be delegated to lower-level managers who will then deal with exceptions when they arise.

The repetitiveness of similar situations is a controlling factor in determining the extent and use of management by exception. Some organizations find that the variables affecting their operations are so erratic that it is impossible to think in terms of repetitive situations. As an illustration, consider a wholesale fruit and vegetable company where the pricing structure is highly variable. Since there is no one policy that could be applied continuously, top management must make all pricing decisions. As a result, there may be fewer policies and less management by exception.

---

[4] For a thorough discussion of policy review, see Dale Zand, "Reviewing the Policy Process," *California Management Review,* Fall 1978, pp. 35–46.

**Determining
exceptional
situations**

What is considered an exception? For illustrative purposes, consider a management report showing production falling three days behind target. Is this an exceptional situation? The answer depends on an evaluation of consequences. If the cost of the deviation is less than the cost associated with corrective action, there is no exception. However, if the cost of the deviation is greater than that for corrective action, an exception exists and the matter requires managerial attention.

When management by exception is practiced, there is no guarantee that the judgment exercised by a manager will result in the best possible decision. The manager may be far removed from the conditions surrounding a given problem; thus, if the manager is pressed for a decision, a lack of time and an inadequate evaluation of the problem may result in a solution that is far from optimal.

Quantitative models have been developed to help determine the amount (percentage) of management by exception that should be practiced in any particular case. For example, a computer can be programmed to accept a series of decision rules and to process a series of instructions. An exceptional situation would then be referred automatically to the appropriate manager.

Policy areas

Two policy classification schemes exist that are useful in understanding policy areas. They include those that differentiate between basic activities of an organization and the basic management functions. As related to the management functions, the policy areas are divided into planning, organizing, actuating, and controlling. Examples of these are shown in Figure 7–4. The classification scheme that is related to business functions, as shown in Figure 7–5, permits managers to view areas that should be considered in developing supporting policies for a designated strategy.

One way of examining interrelationships among key policy areas and to reemphasize the points made earlier is to consider the role of policies in the success of the K mart discount department store chain. Much of the success of K mart (which will be discussed further in Chapter 19) is due to Harry B. Cunningham past president of Kresge. In 1957, as general vice president of the company, Cunningham conducted a marketing study that included an investigation of the competitive environment for discount department stores throughout the United States. The first step of the study was to calculate the strengths and weaknesses of all discount stores in order to develop sound and viable policies to guide the chain. Merchandise and service policies of offering low-priced, top-quality merchandise to customers were developed before the first K mart store was opened in 1962.[5]

All of K mart's policies are coordinated and integrated to contribute

---

[5] "Keeping Up with Kresge," *Business Week*, October 19, 1974, pp. 70–84.

FIGURE 7–4
Policies classified by the management functions

Planning policies
1. Extent and use of forecasting.
2. Amount of long-range and short-range planning undertaken.
3. Emphasis placed upon management science in formulating and implementing plans.
4. Recognition and formulation of a social responsibility along with other objectives.

Organizing policies
1. Securing human, material, and capital resources.
2. The degree of the division of work and departmentation.
3. Extent of delegation of authority and responsibility and the span of supervision.
4. Style of organization structure: decentralization versus centralization.

Actuating policies
1. Importance of executive development and training.
2. Recognition of satisfying human needs.
3. Style of leadership utilized.
4. Importance of communication and information systems.

Controlling policies
1. Use made of budgetary control.
2. Development of inventory control models.
3. Extent of controlling taking place at the point of activity.
4. Development of an integrated control system throughout the organization.

---

to the success of the entire operation. No policy stands alone but is considered in terms of how it affects and relates to the entire system of policies. If a strict enforcement of specific policies by top management is a key to determining the most important policy, the one on *competitive pricing* would probably be selected. This policy states that K mart's prices must be as low as, or lower than, any competitor's within the trading area of a K mart store. Prices are set by a team of marketing officials in the Detroit home office; however, they may be lowered by the store manager to remain competitive. A parameter of the policy is that a store manager is never permitted to raise recommended prices for any reason.

As a *product policy*, fair trade items that must be sold at manufacturers' stated prices are replaced as quickly as possible with other items of equal or superior value and selling merit. In these instances, the approach has been to put K mart labels on products normally sold under fair trade laws so that the pricing policy can be blended with product policies. *Product-line policies* are centered around making K mart a one-stop center where customers can park and shop for all

FIGURE 7–5
Policies classified by business functions

Marketing policies

1. Product—type, depth of product line, sizes, and quality of product or service.
2. Place—channels of distribution, types of outlets, and transportation methods desired.
3. Price—methods of pricing, trade and quantity discounts, markups, and markdowns.
4. Promotion—advertising, personal sales effort, and sales promotion as related to product classification, seasonality, and slow-moving merchandise.
5. Customer services provided.

Production policies

1. Determining factory layout.
2. Maintaining minimum movement of materials and work-in-process.
3. Production control and scheduling.
4. Machine utilization and inventory control.

Purchasing policies

1. Deciding if established suppliers will be used exclusively, or if orders will be placed with any available vendor.
2. Determining how much should be bought on each order.
3. Determining the minimum inventory size of each item in computing the reorder point.
4. Utilizing purchase discounts.

Financial policies

1. Establishing fixed and variable expense relationships.
2. Determining the degrees of risks involved and cost of capital in capitalizing potential earnings.
3. Utilizing financial ratios and control techniques in analyzing sources of funds.
4. Implementing an accounting and management information system.
5. Determining the methods used in valuing inventories and in depreciating fixed assests.

Credit policies

1. Deciding upon the total amount of credit that can be granted by the company.
2. Establishing the type of credit terms and accounts to be offered to customers.
3. Handling of overdue accounts.
4. Use of credit cards.
5. Steps to be followed in determining if a customer should be granted credit.

Personnel policies

1. Developing job descriptions.
2. Recruiting employees.
3. Use of testing programs in establishing applicant capabilities.
4. Using application forms and interview sessions.
5. Implementing training programs.
6. Developing fair compensation and fringe benefit programs.

---

goods including groceries. As concerns *procurement policies*, all non-leased departmental buying is centralized and highly standardized. After the buying is completed, store managers receive a "list book" of goods and prices from which they order the items that are best suited to their particular markets.

Laboratory testing policies have been instituted to assure that new products are competitive with nationally advertised brands. These policies are related to the profitability of each product line by the volume it produces, the selling expense incurred, and the number of times a product line turns over annually. For the total organizational system, *personnel policies* are established to maintain consistently high standards for department heads and sales personnel. All of these policies provide the means by which the company can achieve its objectives: (1) satisfaction guaranteed to its customers and (2) a satisfactory rate of return on investment.

The successful formulation, implementation, and systematic review of K mart policies by top-level managers is considered the basic reason why K mart has been one of the most successfully operated discount chains in the United States, Canada, and Puerto Rico. All levels of managers not only recognize the need for policies to make a discount chain operate successfully, but also establish policies that put direction and meaning into the strategy of the company.

In closing this section, we see that policies are best thought of as broad guidelines to action. This formulation results from the planning process and must take into consideration changing environmental and internal factors. Characteristics of good policies can be summarized as follows:

1. Policies are based on objectives in order to fit total organizational needs.
2. If a policy is not absolutely essential in maintaining broad direction within the organization, it should not be established.
3. Policies need to be flexible if they are to encourage managerial judgment in meeting special situations.
4. Policies are not rules and must leave room for judgment and interpretation as required by specific conditions. Policies that are narrowly defined result in inflexible organizations.
5. A policy should be definite, positive, clearly understandable, and provide reasons for its existence. If there is a statement indicating why a policy is in force, misunderstanding is minimized and acceptance is encouraged.
6. Written policy statements help reduce confusion and misinterpretation among organizational members.
7. By constantly reviewing policies, there is a better chance that they will be improved, when necessary.
8. Policy formulation can take place at any level within an organiza-

tion. In modern organizations, computer science and technology permit policy formulation and control to take place at lower managerial levels.

PROCEDURES

Procedures refer to a series of sequentially related steps that are followed to accomplish a given purpose. As such, procedures are prescriptive in nature since they help promote coordination by providing employees with guides to action in repetitive situations. In this sense, procedures are viewed as routine or programmed responses to problem situations that are rather common and well structured. In both public and business organizations, these types of organizational responses are generally referred to as standard operating procedures (SOP). By using such procedures, organizational members have some degree of assurance that others will behave in a fairly predictable manner in relationship to their responsibilities.[6] As a facilitating mechanism for the implementation of plans, therefore, procedures guide the flow of information and outline ways in which managerial and operating activities are related.

The scope of procedures

Procedures are much more specific and narrow in scope than policies. As a reflection of policy intent, they provide prescribed ways as to how and where plans will be carried out within the organization. Consequently, new employees often spend considerable time learning proper procedures in order to perform their duties.

The formulation of procedures must take place within the framework of policies. Therefore, it is important that central policies be sufficiently broad and clear to guide the formulation of meaningful procedures. In the final analysis, both policies and procedures should reinforce one another so that they provide maximum contribution to goal accomplishment.

Application of procedures

Considering the large number of activities taking place within an organization, a myriad of procedures are essential if coordination is to be achieved. For a business enterprise, procedures are required for handling grievances, ordering raw materials, controlling inventories, delivering finished goods, filling customer orders, granting credit, maintaining customer accounts, and so forth.

Most students are quite familiar with the registration procedures in a college or university. Even though they are a source of complaint, a large number of students could end up without seats in classrooms, with more than one class at the same hour, or with credit hours not

---

[6] For a discussion of the efficiency of standard operating procedures see R. M. Cyert and J. G. Marsh, *A Behavioral Theory of the Firm,* (Englewood Cliffs, N.J.: Prentice Hall, 1963), pp. 458–67.

being properly recorded for graduation if such procedures did not exist.

The specific steps outlined in a procedure depend upon an organization's structure, size, leadership, and environment. In large companies, for example, the steps involved and the forms to be completed when hiring a new employee are generally much more complex than in an operation involving two or three individuals. Organizations operating in highly dynamic environments, however, may find that elaborate and constrictive steps in procedures are detrimental to goal achievement. The space program, for instance, is structured around a series of partially constrained procedures that have built-in contingencies so that adjustments can be made to meet changing variables. Astronauts cannot be tied down to fully constrained procedures if they are to remain open to various alternative actions.

By reducing the details in a procedure, work can often be made more meaningful. Fewer steps increase the scope of a job and place less emphasis on specialization of labor. Thus, rather than have one individual perform a separate, specialized step of a job, several steps might be combined and subsequently performed by the same employee.

Generalizations about good procedures

As is true with policies, procedures can be systematically formulated or they can develop through common usage. The assumption in this section is that the systematic development of procedures leads to more efficient and effective planning than is true when their development is left to chance.

Some general points to consider in a systematic formulation of procedures are listed below:

1. A procedure should be consistent with policy statements and established objectives. Directly or indirectly, it must clearly assist in the achievement of overall goals.
2. Since environmental factors vary and internal variables are inherently different among organizations, a standard operating procedure for one organization may not be viable in another.
3. All procedures within an organization should be completely integrated and coordinated through adequate information systems.
4. People required to follow procedures should have ready access to them. Thus, procedures may be written in job descriptions, employee handbooks, or procedural manuals. Additionally, when procedures are changed or applicable only during a specific time period, they should be properly communicated to those employees responsible for their implementation. By having standardized forms, essential information can also be recorded, processed, and stored more efficiently than when information is communicated by some nonstandardized method.

5. To meet environmental changes, procedures must be sufficiently flexible. In fact, managers should constantly review procedures so that they can be changed as new developments occur. Frequent adjustments in procedures, however, may be sufficient reason to question if they are even needed in the first place.

6. Procedures should reflect alternative courses of action and not be so constrained that flexibility is lost. Options should be made available to incorporate the idea of contingency planning when risks are high.

7. Like policies, good procedures are important coordinating techniques. Coordination, however, depends on procedures that ensure clarity, understanding, adequate records, and internal control.

Although our discussion of procedures implies their necessity, we should realize that many organizations are not administering them adequately. In fact, many seemingly well-managed companies do not have a clear knowledge of the procedures being used. Departmental managers may have procedures formally typed, or some may be found on the back of used envelopes and on bulletin boards, while others may be misplaced in filing cabinets. Our point here is that procedures as a planning element are often not handled well and require a great deal more managerial attention if the behavior of organizational members is to be consistent in achieving organizational goals.

METHODS

Even though policies and methods are closely related, there is a difference. Policy sets the intent, while *methods refer to the prescribed manner or way (technology) in which a particular activity or task is to be performed.* The major difference is found in how completely people are guided and structured in performing prescribed duties. Methods are also governed by procedures; thus, they represent the steps that make up a procedure. The relationship between planning, objectives, policies, procedures, and methods is shown in Figure 7–6.

Standard methods

The word *standard* implies that a method has been systematically and deliberately planned and that a common behavior pattern is acceptable to management. One of the major uses of standard methods is to seek increased efficiency of operations.

Frank B. Gilbreth, and later Frederick W. Taylor, were pioneers in the study and development of standard methods. Their concern was with the particular motions involved in a job and with standardizing the internal work environment. Work conditions that were studied included raw materials handling, layout of the work place, maintenance, equipment design, heating, ventilation, and so forth. Both Gilbreth and Taylor emphasized the standardization and specialization of working conditions and the methods of doing a job as ways to increase productivity.

FIGURE 7–6
Relationships among various management plans

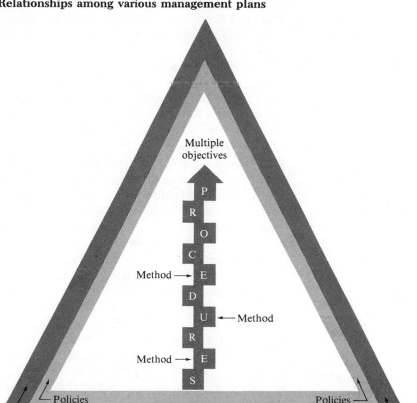

At present, the application of standardized methods has moved from the production line to almost every aspect of an organization. Assembly-line operations, restaurant kitchens, and church worship services are observable examples. Of course, standard methods also have general reference to a wide variety of human activities such as computer programming, the skilled use of a surgeon's hands in a medical operation, office routines, and improving the reading level of a child. On a more personal basis, reconciling a bank statement can be done more efficiently by following a standardized method.

Studying standard work methods

The prototype of the present-day standardization of work methods began with studies conducted by Frank B. Gilbreth in the late 1800s and the early 1900s.[7] Prior to this time, managers left the responsibility for work methods up to employees. The methods followed were often

---

[7] A compilation of part of Gilbreth's work is found in Frank B. Gilbreth, *Bricklaying System* (New York: Marion C. Clark, Publishing Co., 1909).

based on how fellow workers did a job (which may or may not have been the best way) or on personal adaptations consistent with skills and past experience. Managerial concern was not with job efficiency, but with obtaining a rate of work that was acceptable in relationship to wages paid.

Both Gilbreth and Taylor encouraged managers to plan and accept more responsibility in determining exactly how, when, and what workers should do. Originally, the study of work methods was mainly concerned with the analysis of hand and body motions involved in performing a specific job. Today designing work methods includes not only hand and body motions but also the study of detailed movements of materials and the layout of the work place. In a furniture manufacturing plant, the components must be properly placed on the line so that the workers performing various operations have short and easy moves. Decisions must also be made as to the number of machines a person can effectively operate. As we will see later, a standard method is not the only dimension of a worker's performance on the job. Sociological and psychological factors also play an important part in understanding an employee's actions and behavior. Problems of monotony and boredom caused by the way a job is performed can create fatigue, absenteeism, and high labor turnover.

More than anything else, competition is probably the main reason for studying work methods. Producing and marketing goods and services at lower costs require a systematic analysis of how waste and inefficiency can be eliminated. In addition to cost reduction, method study has resulted in improved working environments and in jobs being performed more easily and simply. Within the United States, the application of standard methods has brought about astonishing results in all types of organizations.

Motion study

By designing work and arranging work methods in the best possible sequence, motion study has been useful in facilitating the planning process. *Motion study is the systematic analysis of a worker's movements in order to reduce the number of wasteful, time-consuming motions involved in performing a job.* Theoretically, if each part of an operation is studied in detail, small improvements in each can add up to major improvements in the overall operation. By describing in detail exactly what a person does, managers become cognizant of ineffective motions while planning work for future operations. Of course, in order to improve work methods, each activity must be viewed as if it can be improved. Spotting ineffective motions can be facilitated by asking whether some elements can be eliminated, combined, or simplified; if the materials and the sequence of operations can be rearranged; and if product, work place, and working conditions can be changed.

Motion study is applied to two major groups—product analysis and

FIGURE 7–7
Process chart symbols

Symbols	Name	Definition
●	Operations	When something is done to a part of a product in a location in which there may be labor expenditures or other costs.
➤	Transportation	Change in location from one work place to another.
◗	Delay or waiting	A temporary storage situation in the progress of the work.
▼	Storage	A controlled and planned delay in the overall process of the work in which removal must be authorized.
■	Inspection	Verification or checking by comparing the product with a quality and/or quantity standard.
○	Combined activity	Activities are performed concurrently by the same operator at the same work station.

worker analysis. Products are studied generally by direct observation, while worker analysis is conducted by direct observation only when the task is relatively simple. If the task involves many complex movements, a movie camera and microchronometer (a large clock that records time in 1/2000 of a minute) are often used.[8] With such equipment, each movement of a person can be traced and analyzed while the time it takes to complete each motion can be determined.

In order to analyze and plan work as a series of activities, details of work being done can be presented in chart form. Several types of charts are available to managers. One of the most useful is the flow chart that shows the basic parts or steps in a process. By using various symbols, some of which are shown in Figure 7–7, complete and detailed information can be determined for a given work operation. For example, if the number of delays and transports that occur for each operation are found to be relatively large, their reduction could result in lowering expenses associated with the operation. Also by properly planning work methods, wasted motions and idle labor time can be reduced to improve efficiency. Thus, charts facilitate the analysis, interpretation, and modification of specified work systems.

At present, computers have brought about a resurging interest in process charts, particularly where data processing is an integral link

---

[8] The microchronometer was developed by Frank Gilbreth. At the time of his work, such an instrument was necessary because movie cameras were turned by hand and the frames per second varied.

in the flow of forms and information systems used in an organization. Flow diagrams, a type of process chart, are used in developing computerized systems of inventory control and accounts receivable.

Managers are finding that work improvement must also be based on human factors. Equipment, work place, location of tools, and the methods followed are only meaningful in improving productivity when they fit the attributes of people involved in the job. Thus, sociological, psychological, and anthropological factors must be taken into account when seeking to get people to do their jobs in a better way.

In summary, the purpose of work design and analysis is to find more simplified and less costly ways of performing a job. The idea here is that better methods can reduce worker fatigue, improve morale, and offer a more objective basis for studying plant layout and material handling.

Work simplification

Work simplification is very closely related to motion study. Basically it is a simplified, common-sense approach of motion study that any individual can apply in order to find a better way of doing a job. The criteria for finding a better way include the cost, time, and ease of human effort.

Work simplification programs can be successfully applied by managers if they encourage employees to become involved in the process. Where such encouragement has been combined with managerial support, there have been substantial increases in productivity and significant reductions in human effort. One aspect of managerial support in encouraging work simplification is to provide proper rewards to those employees who have improved their jobs. Arguments exist, however, as to whether or not rewards should be reflected in wage rates when employees increase their productivity due to work simplification. The manager should, therefore, act cautiously in this area by basing decisions on careful assessments of all relevant information.

Work measurement

Once a "better way" of doing a job has been found, work measurement may be applied to determine how long an operation should take. This process allows managers to set a time standard for a series of activities whether performed by an individual or group. After time standards are set, they can be used for determining how many people or machines are needed for a desired output level, scheduling production, measuring performance, determining standard output for incentive systems, and estimating the cost of goods sold.

Several techniques are available to managers in determining time standards. They range from guess and past experience to systematic estimation. The more common systematic techniques are (1) time studies with the use of a stopwatch, (2) predetermined time standards, and (3) work sampling.

Stopwatch time studies were developed by F. W. Taylor and are especially viable in repetitive processing type operations. In time study, the work of an employee is divided into elements and each element is timed systematically. By providing for appropriate allowances (time for personal needs and irregular activities), the times for each element are then added together to compute a standard time for the total job. Although the stopwatch technique is an excellent way of obtaining the time required to perform the work, it has acquired a poor reputation since its use has not always been properly applied.

Predetermined time standards for a job are developed by utilizing past stopwatch calculations. Averages are determined by studying a large number of workers performing tasks over a long period of time. Predetermined time values are then assigned to certain basic manual motions required in performing certain jobs. Tables of manual times have been developed for several activities used by workers, including reaching, grasping, turning, and bending. Synthetic timetables are also available to compute times for machining operations.

One of the most widely used systems involving predetermined times is Method-Time-Measurement (MTM). As an illustration, consider the operation in which a worker solders a single wire to a television chassis. By adding together all of the time values of the work activities while providing for various allowances, such as fatigue, a standard time for positioning the wire and applying the soldering iron can be determined. A general feeling among managers is that the establishment of standards in this manner is quite accurate and acceptable to workers.

Another viable way of setting time standards is a technique called *work sampling*, which includes the following steps:

1. Determining the major elements in a job. For a secretary these might include typing, dictation, answering the telephone, and so forth.
2. Setting up a periodic, chronological listing of times for several days or weeks for the person performing the job.
3. Determining the number of observations needed.[9]
4. Randomly observing what is being done at a particular designated moment.
5. Developing a percentage distribution of recorded activities that reflects the proportion of time a worker spends in performing various designated elements.

The applications of work sampling are virtually unlimited. For example, managers at various levels within an organization can determine the time spent in performing various duties. With such information, managers can determine those adjustments in their activities that will lead to a better utilization of available time.

---

[9] Statistically, the number of observations can be determined to give a level of confidence as to the degree of certainty of the results.

Impact of time standards on incentive wages

Time standards are essential in the operation of incentive wage plans. Incentive systems can range from very simple piece-rate systems to rather complicated ones that adjust the wage rate according to the output of an individual or a group of workers. In most systems, the established standards allow workers more time to do a job than should actually be required. This provides employees with an opportunity to turn out more than is required during a normal working day and thereby earn a premium. When standards are too low, however, workers may hold down production levels in fear that the work will be retimed and higher standards established. In any event, it is generally believed that the simpler the system, the better. The current trend is toward using the simpler, more readily calculated types of incentive systems.

Changes in environmental factors may result in less frequent use of incentive systems based on time standards. Rapid changes in technology can easily cause time standards to become obsolete. As production lines become more automated, machine-paced operations make incentive plans less useful. In the assembly of automobiles, for instance, the flow of production lines and equipment is preset. In this situation, workers can do little by working harder or faster to increase output.

MANAGEMENT STANDARDS

In today's changing environment, managers can no longer rely strictly upon judgment and past experience to evaluate performance. However, few operations remain sufficiently stable to gain the necessary experience with which to set standards. Consequently, useful standards for judging performance must be flexible so that adjustments can be made to recognize crises and to take advantage of unforeseen opportunities. A standard, therefore, reflects the present state of development of a particular entity, but not the ultimate state of an art and/or science.

Types of standards—ideal, engineered, and managerial

Managers deal with three basic types of standards—ideal, engineered (technical), and managerial. An ideal standard is like the perfect circle that is a vision in one's mind and cannot be found in real life. Thus, we can strive to achieve such standards only to the extent that humans can envision them.

Engineered standards apply to the production function and are useful in the areas of materials, parts, products, supplies, production processes, inspection, design, and drafting. An application of engineered standards is seen in the manufacturing of Chrysler's K-Cars. A central programmable logic computer evaluates information received from the different manufacturing assembly and testing operations. If a boring machine produces several successive bores below a specific standard, a 54-step test is made on a Hot Test Stand during which various checks must meet established standards. All information on rejected engines is stored in the computer and can be displayed on a screen or printout when the engine goes into a repair area. Through this process, the computer advises what to look for and suggests what repairs to make.

Since it is unlikely that most manufacturing processes will meet standards without deviation, we must have a range of acceptable variances (tolerances). These tolerances cannot be so great that they impair the functional utility of a product, nor so small that the price is increased beyond the limits customers are willing to pay. For example, the use of a machine to fill jars with instant coffee results in differing amounts of coffee in each jar. If the standard is 1.75 ounces per jar, some jars will weigh more and some less. Thus, managers must strike a proper balance between variations in quantity that are acceptable to the public and the cost of reducing the variations so that 1.75 ounces of coffee are placed in each jar.

Managerial standards are concerned with all of the forces, factors, effects, and relationships that face individuals responsible for performing the managerial functions. They apply specifically to such areas as personnel, accounting, and financial systems; performance evaluation; cost controls; safety practices; and security regulations. These standards may be established internally or imposed by external forces. For example, profit before taxes as a percentage of sales is an internal standard, while air quality standards are imposed externally.

Quantitative and qualitative standards

Even though applicable at all levels within an organization, standards cannot always be expressed with the same degree of preciseness. In some areas of an organization, the units of measurement can be expressed quantitatively. In others, however, standards are much more qualitative since the output itself may be quite intangible. For example, consider the following areas for which managerial standards would be required in a large manufacturing concern:

Market position in terms of industry performance.

Performance in terms of productivity and return on investment.

Policies and procedures to be followed in executing strategy.

Personnel administration, including individual and group satisfaction on the job.

The plans to be used in implementing a selected strategy.

Service and product leadership.

Executive development.

Social responsibility.

Within each of these areas, standards are necessary to evaluate performance; however, the unit of measure in some can be more quantitatively expressed than in others.[10] Market position, for instance, can

---

[10] For an in-depth discussion of the importance of measuring, see Richard O. Mason and E. Burton Swanson, "Measurement for Management Decision: A Perspective," *California Management Review*, Spring 1979, pp. 70–81.

FIGURE 7–8
Objectives and standard measuring criteria for corporate recruiting and training director

Objectives to be achieved	Standard measuring criteria
1. Reduce college recruiting cost by $5,000, while maintaining number and quality of job applicants.	1. *a.* Compare total recruiting expenses to budget. *b.* Measure the effectiveness and quality of recruiting efforts in relation to corporate personnel needs.
2. Reduce inventory of recruiting literature by 25 percent and increase the number of contacts made at each college.	2. *a.* Outdated and inappropriate recruiting literature should be discarded. *b.* Inventory level of literature should not be larger than amount required for a one-year recruiting period.
3. Plan management training program for the next 12 months, hire an assistant training director, and maintain departmental expenses within 5 percent of budget.	3. *a.* Complete proposed training schedule by December 31. *b.* Hire new assistant training director by October 1. *c.* Compare monthly training expenses to budget figures.
4. Expand and improve management training program for the next fiscal period.	4. *a.* Increase the management training program to include first-line supervisory personnel. *b.* Offer management training to middle and top-level managers who have not participated in a training program for the past three years.

be reflected in quantitative units of measurement, such as 10 percent of industry sales, or a 5 percent increase in sales over the last fiscal period. To some extent, policies, procedures, and personnel standards can also be expressed quantitatively, as noted in Figure 7–8.

Recent efforts have been made to quantify service and product leadership standards. Some consumer affairs groups are helping to obtain quantitative product and service standards for consumers. As a result, some standardization of products has been achieved in the form of unit pricing, open dating, and a listing of specific ingredients and nutritional content.

As shown in Figure 7–9, qualitative standards could be incorporated for many products used by consumers although very little progress

FIGURE 7–9
Product standards for barbecue cookout set—metal tongs and spatula

Characteristics	*Description*	*Rating**
Product design	Barbecue cooking utensils—2-piece set (tongs and spatula).	2
Materials	Chromium coated steel tongs and spatula. Spatula has a varnished hard oak handle.	4
Heat resistance	The thicker and more even the plating process, the greater the resistance to deterioration by heat.	4
	Handle is flammable.	1
Durability	Durability is related to the quality of plating, which in turn, depends upon properly preparing parts for barrel tumbling and acid dipping.	4
Ease in handling	Serrated teeth on end of tongs to facilitate grasping. Tight tension spring is formed of a one-piece, quarter-inch rod.	3

* Rating scale for product line:
1. Lowest rating
2. Moderate to fair.
3. Average (adequate).
4. Excellent.
5. Insurpassable in product line.

has been made in this direction. Some groups guarantee or certify certain products. Two familiar groups offering seals of approval are *Good Housekeeping* and The Underwriters' Laboratories, Inc. In addition, independent testing laboratories evaluate safety standards for various manufacturers' associations, such as the Bicycle Manufacturers' Association of America. Yet, the standards set by some of these groups are subjective in nature and not open to rigorous, objective evaluation by consumers.

Performance standards for measuring the benefits of executive development programs are also without the benefit of quantitative standards. Various approaches to executive development, such as testing programs and sensitivity training, are seriously questioned by some managers since their success cannot be effectively judged. In addition, the lack of quantitative standards for judging the fulfillment of social responsibilities to employees, customers, and other groups is also quite apparent.

Standardization

At this point, it should be obvious that standards are applicable to many goods and services. For example, a shoe size of 9–C will fit a person with a 9–C size foot any place within the United States. Similarly, a 3/8-inch American standard screw thread bolt will fit the same size and type of thread tap whether on the West Coast or on the East Coast.

The process of establishing a standard is referred to as standardization. Through this process an organization or association establishes a standard while obtaining agreement and consent from others who will use the standard. Standardization can be traced to early civilizations. The ancient pyramids provide early examples of standard block forms and sizes. It was not until the Industrial Revolution, however, that standardization was found to be extremely important in manufacturing processes. The work of Eli Whitney in standardizing gun parts resulted in the concept of an interchangeability of parts and led to our modern assembly-line type of operation.

In the production of industrial and consumer goods, managers concentrate on specific sizes and styles in order to manufacture and market such goods at lower costs. For example, lower setup costs and longer equipment runs in manufacturing an item imply that the product can be sold at lower prices than would be the case if a larger number of sizes and shapes were produced. As a further example, consider the manager of a retail shoe store who is faced with reducing the number of shoe styles in stock from 100 to 75. If, on the average, there are 80 pairs of shoes per style, such a reduction would lower the inventory level by 2,000 pairs of shoes. If the average cost of a pair of shoes is $12, the working capital tied up in inventory could be reduced by $24,000 a year. In addition, inventory carrying costs could be reduced and the required storage space for shoes would be less. Thus, the manager would find this standardization resulting in many operating economies.

At present, the automobile industry is doing more to standardize its products. Ford, for example, has established a policy of reducing its parts list by 20 percent within the next few years while also reducing the number of options available on its models.

In terms of standardizing models, U.S. automobile manufacturers are also trying to lengthen the time between major model design changes from three to four or five years. The aim is to reduce the fixed costs of each car by reducing tooling (new equipment) costs, the costs of training workers for new assignments, layoff benefits, and overtime costs required in building up an inventory of new models when plants are reopened after retooling. By standardizing models and parts, it is also anticipated that labor costs can be reduced in the total assembly process.

SUMMARY

As noted throughout this chapter, the achievement of objectives depends upon the proper implementation of plans. In this respect, policies, operating procedures, methods, and standards are especially important. These planning facilitators not only provide the means by which objectives are converted into action, but also unite and coordinate many diverse activities.

While policies, procedures, methods, and standards can be beneficial in the achievement of organizational goals, they may also become stumbling blocks. Their impact depends on how they are established, implemented, and reviewed by various organizational members. Without question, few organizations can achieve objectives without utilizing these facilitators. Yet, without a consideration of human needs and behavioral characteristics, they can become a source of anger, discontent, and employee dissatisfaction. People like to have a voice in matters that influence and direct their actions within an organization. Therefore, it becomes management's job to determine how this desire to participate can be utilized most effectively in implementing plans.

KEY TERMS

Efficiency: The concept of an organization's ability to produce outputs with the minimum use of inputs that may be measured in terms of the ratios output/cost and output/time.

Implied policies: Policies that are *not* formally established and approved by top-level managers but are accepted as guidelines in making decisions.

Management by exception: When exceptional situations occur that are not covered by a particular policy statement, they are referred to a higher level of management for action.

Method: The prescribed manner or way in which a particular activity or task is performed.

Motion study: The process of analyzing work to determine the preferred motions to be used in completing a task.

Overdefined policies: Policies with specific intents that are in conflict with other stated policies.

Policies: Broad guidelines to assist organizational members in making decisions and in directing their behavior toward the efficient achievement of goals.

Procedure: A series of sequentially related steps that are followed by organizational members to accomplish a specific purpose.

Rules: Guides that leave no room for interpretation or discretion, thereby minimizing a person's freedom of thought or action.

Standard: Targets or benchmarks that are used in comparing actual performance to desired results.

Time study: The process of determining the appropriate elapsed time for each element of a job in computing a standard time for the completion of a task.

QUESTIONS

1. Define the meaning of policy.
2. What are the specific roles or advantages of policies?
3. How do policies differ from rules?
4. Distinguish between stated and implied policies.
5. What is the meaning of "overdefined" policies?
6. What managerial practices contribute to effective policy administration?
7. Discuss the meaning of "management by exception."
8. How do operating procedures differ from policies?
9. Why are procedures essential in large organizations? What suggestions can be made to improve their formulation and use?
10. How are methods and policies closely related? How are they different?
11. Could the same statement be viewed as a method by one manager and as a policy by another? Explain.
12. Is the use of standard methods more applicable in production than in other functional areas? What are some reasons for studying standard work methods?
13. Discuss work measurement and the approaches that can be used in determining time standards. In what ways are time standards important in management?
14. What is the meaning of work simplification?
15. What are three basic types of standards with which managers deal? Are all standards quantitative in nature? Discuss.
16. What advantages does standardization have for management?

PROBLEMS

1. Identify the characteristics of a good policy. Then use these characteristics to evaluate the following statement: "As a matter of policy, Chrysler Corporation will change the design of its automobiles less frequently and less extensively."

2. Assume that the top management of United Pencil Company is considering the purchase of a computer for maintaining its accounting, payroll, inventory, and sales records. Is this a policy decision? Why or why not? Would such a change influence the company's present organizational structure? If so, in what ways would the structure be changed?

3. Policies are sometimes criticized because they are developed to deal with repetitive conditions. In the real world, however, all environments are unique and changing. Therefore, is it logical to think that policies can be formulated in a scientific manner?

4. It is often stated that policies stifle initiative and creativity in organizations. Describe the conditions under which such a situation would be true.

5. The one-person shoe repair shop at the end of a shopping mall is quite different from a shoe store at the other end of the mall that employs 10 sales personnel and 2 managers. In addition, the shoe store is one of four in a

chain located around the city. To what extent are policies likely to be used by the shoe repair shop? The shoe store?

6. Gather several policy statement from organizations with which you are familiar. From among those collected, choose two or three that are more like rules than policies. Contrast those chosen with others that you feel exhibit the characteristics of good policies.

7. The merchandising manager of a department store with three suburban branches was concerned about the high percentage of goods returned by customers. In an attempt to reduce the returns, she issued a very detailed and restrictive procedure that was to be followed in handling returned goods. Within three months each of the suburban stores reported significantly lower net sales figures. The three branch managers felt that the detailed steps that customers had to follow in returning goods resulted in their shopping elsewhere. Why are such restrictive procedures created? What might be done to rectify the above situation?

8. Deere and Company developed a standard on "O" rings that made it possible to reduce the number of different rings by 43 percent. The resulting savings were estimated at $90,000 per year. This standard was clearly an aid to design engineers. What other departments (areas) within the organization would benefit from such standardization?

9. At the Sony color-television plant in San Diego, the operations chief holds frequent meetings with supervisors to develop new policies and to suggest how to implement formulated policies. The chief constantly emphasizes that, if workers do not understand changes in policies, the supervisors must explain them to subordinates. An unacceptable statement by supervisors is "I don't understand the policy, but I have to enforce it." Why is the latter statement generally considered a management cop-out?

10. Assume that you are president of a manufacturing company that makes small hand tools such as screw drivers, hammers, chisels, and so forth. For the past several years, most of your products have been manufactured under the private brand labels of two large discount chain stores. The products are of fairly high quality in relationship to their price. However, they are not the best product on the market. You have been asked by your best chain store customer to increase the quality of the products sold to him by improving both the functional design and the finish of the product. In addition, he wants a wider range of styles and sizes for all of the products.

a. What problems do you see facing your company?
b. What role would standards play in this situation?
c. What courses of action are available to you for responding to this customer's request?

11. Tom Shunpert, who owns a tobacco shop, cut lengthwise a cigar with a factory-made hole in it. The shredded cigar contained bits of paper filler in the middle. After cutting a premium cigar without a hole, the filler was

readily indentifiable as tobacco leaf. "Years ago," he said, all cigars were all tobacco and handmade. I don't see how there could have been such a thing as a cheap cigar." What type of standard do you think Tom is referencing? What is the connotation of the word *cheap?*

12. One Ford Motor Co. executive has recently stated that Japanese cars are the standard of the automobile world today. Detroit's increasing imitation of Japanese cars, both in styling and engineering, proves that the Japanese have set the international standard. As far back as 1971, Chrysler made a deal with Mitsubishi for the production of its subcompacts, the Colt and the Champ. However, it was not until 1979 that it advertised blantantly that "one of Japan's most technologically advanced cars is a Dodge."

In what sense is the automobile executive using the word *standard?*

SUGGESTED READINGS

Adams, C. H.   "The Improvement Curve Technique." *Purchasing Systems and Procedures,* November 1980.

Adams, E. E., Jr., and R. J. Ebert.   *Production and Operations Management.* Englewood Cliffs, N.J.: Prentice-Hall, 1978, chaps. 4 and 9.

Buffa, E. S.   *Modern Production/Operations Management.*   New York: John Wiley & Sons, 1980.

Chase, R. B., and N. J. Aquilano.   *Production and Operations Management: A Life Cycle Approach.*   Homewood, Ill.: Richard D. Irwin, Inc., 1981.

Hemenway, D.   *Industrywide Voluntary Standards.* Cambridge: Ballinger, 1975.

Higginson, M. V.   *Management Policies I: Their Development as Corporate Guides.* New York: American Management Association, 1966.

Morse, W. J.   "Reporting Production Costs that Follow the Learning Curve Phenomenon." In *Contemporary Issues in Cost and Managerial Accounting,* edited by H. R. Anton, P. A. Firmin, and H. D. Grove. Boston: Houghton Mifflin, 1978, pp. 447–66.

Papathanasis, T.   "Standards and the Firm." *Regional Business Review,* June 1980, pp. 34–38.

Schroeder, R. G.   *Operations Management: Decision Making in the Operations Function.*   New York: McGraw-Hill Book Company, 1981.

Van Meter, D. S., and C. E. Van Horn.   "The Policy Implementation Process: A Conceptual Framework." *Administration and Society,* February 1975, pp. 445–87.

Emerson Converters

The growth of Emerson Converters has been phenomenal for a firm that has been in business for only three years. Employment has grown from 2 people to over 40 employees, and sales reached the $1 million mark during the last year. The company converts factory shell vans to plush family vehicles that are used for traveling, camping, and general in-town use. The van is designed as both an RV (recreational vechicle) and a family van.

Marvin Emerson, owner and chief executive officer of the company, has had little experience with a manufacturing, assembly-line type of operation. He has, however, worked in automobile sales and has knowledge of shop and body work. The company's sales manager worked previously for a large van converter in advertising and sales.

Van conversion is quite different from what is known as van customization. Generally, the customized van is not a family type of vehicle. For instance, it may have a fireplace in one corner and a water bed in another. At Emerson, the family van conversion includes two captain chairs in front; two independent swivel seats directly behind the two front seats; a couch running the width of the van at the rear; center console; matching carpet and interior upholstery; separate rear controlled air conditioning and heating; load leveler air shocks; "moon-roof;" individualized side windows; reading lights; side storage compartments; mini-refrigerator/stove combination; Sony eight-inch color TV set; and an AM-FM stereo cassette.

New, unconverted vans are purchased from Chevrolet, Ford, and Dodge dealers at their invoice price plus a nominal markup. Finished vans are marketed both to wholesale and retail automobile dealers, with Emerson's profits being derived primarily from the conversion of the basic van.

The market areas for Emerson include the West Coast and the southwestern regions of the United States. Emerson offers high quality, reliability, and dealer integrity. All work performed by Emerson is warranted for 12 months or 12,000 miles, whichever comes first. The manufacturer of the van honors the factory warranty on components supplied with the basic van.

Emerson maintains a close relationship with its dealers. This is essential for profitability and for reducing the need to search constantly for new markets. The present sales strategy is to drive demonstrator models to dealers to familiarize them with Emerson's design.

Marketing

Vans are purchased from dealers at $75 over invoice price. They are financed through the company's banker with monthly interest charges running about $100 per van. In repurchasing converted vans, dealers pay the original price of the van plus conversion costs that run approximately $4,000 to $5,000 per van. Even though dealers may sell the unconverted vans to Emerson, they are not obligated to repurchase converted vehicles.

Dealers who handle finished vans from several converters are highly conscious of quality and design. Consequently, even though price competition is vigorous, small changes in price are not the major variable that dealers consider in deciding which vans to buy. In addition to selling to dealers, Emerson has a state license to sell new vehicles. Thus, Emerson is allowed to pass on manufacturers' warranties and earn the profits associated with the sale of vans to final customers.

Currently, the primary competition to all van converters is from pooling companies that mass-produce converted vans. The advantages that pooling companies have over independent converters include higher volume, lower material costs due to quantity purchases, and the ability to deal directly with manufacturers. In addition, poolers do not have to take ownership of vans for conversion. This eliminates finance and interest charges on vans and leaves them free from the problems associated with reselling converted vans to dealers.

When dealers receive several converted vans directly from manufacturers, Emerson's chances for making a sale to them are severely reduced. Many dealers, however, prefer to buy from Emerson and other independent converters because of their high quality and individualized conversion. For this reason, Emerson employs three full-time salespeople who are assigned geographical regions. They work primarily on commissions plus expenses.

Production

The production shop is capable of producing 50 vans per month, with a break-even point of 20 per month. The average current monthly production rate is 45 vans. The shop is divided into five basic areas—construction, painting, upholstery, interior installation, and parts.

The shop has 32 employees, of which 5 are lead supervisors. The interior installation department has 16 employees and is the largest department. The production shop has one foreman, Dennis Allen. He not only supervises the lead people, but also assists in various operational phases of the work, including daily interactions with workers on matters related to their job performance. At the same time, Allen is responsible for a large number of other complex jobs, varying from job scheduling, engineering design, inspection of vans at various stages of production, inventory control, and evaluation of manufacturing costs.

Lead supervisors do not possess the authority to hire and fire workers. Although supervisors are paid more than other workers, their supervisory authority is limited to routine order giving. In fact, production employees generally feel that work is not necessarily assigned but is accomplished "when there is a need to do it." This highly unstructured arrangement causes employees to feel that they work for two people—the lead supervisor and the shop foreman.

The survey

With an extension to his line of credit from $250,000 to $500,000, Mr. Emerson felt he could increase production and take quantity discounts on materials and parts. After approaching his banker with this request, it was noted that the company's collateral and assets did not justify the extension of an additional $250,000 liability. The banker, however, suggested that some consideration would be given to the request if the business made an extensive analysis of how to increase productivity and reduce costs.

Realizing that such an effort would require the help of a consultant, Mr. Emerson contacted Management Associates to conduct the study. In brief, a questionnaire was administered to 30 of the shop employees to obtain information about employee attitudes toward performance evaluation, organizational elements, management practices, and job productivity.

The survey provided the following information:

Performance evaluation The employees felt that the major factors most often used in evaluating their performance were (1) the time involved in doing the job and (2) the quality and expense of the work performed.

Exhibit 1 indicates the factors respondents felt were fair to consider in evaluating employee performance. The rankings of first, second, and third—craftsmanship, dependability, and knowledge of the job—relate quite closely to the factors of time, quality, and experience that the respondents suggested were used in evaluating their general performance on the job.

Peer evaluation Utilizing the factors they considered fair to use in evalutation, the employees rated the work performance of fellow workers in their own department as well as all other shop employees. In general, the respondents who rated other employees as "very good" or "good" based their comments on:

1. Work habits allow people to produce at a quality level and within specified times.
2. People know what they are doing.
3. People work well together and get along well. (A group of "good-ole-boys.")
4. Pride of work, enthusiasm, ability to meet production goals.

EXHIBIT 1
Rank ordering of factors considered to be fair in evaluating performance

Factor	Rank as determined by respondents
Craftsmanship, quality, and minimizing waste	1*
Utilization of work time during day (working at full potential)	5
Dependability in carrying out job assignment	2
Ability to adapt and adjust to job	4
Attendance (days absent/tardy)	5
Attitude, cooperation, and effort to improve performance	6
Knowledge of job performed	3
Initiative (original thinking and solving problems)	4

* The number represents the relative importance of each factor. Thus, one (1) represents the highest level of importance, two (2) the next highest level of importance, and so on.

Respondents who rated other employees as "fair" or "poor," based their ratings on these factors:

1. Constant rush that hampers quality.
2. Bad attitude by some employees
3. Unwillingness of some employees to work continuously, resulting in loafing and too much "playing around."

Self evaluation In a self evaluation of their own productivity and performance, the respondents suggested the following ratings:

Level of rating	Percentage response
High	42
Acceptable	54
Low	4
	100

The major reasons noted for choosing the "high" and "acceptable" ratings were (1) the quality of work performed and (2) the intent to stay busy on the job.

Some negative comments made by the respondents who indicated an "acceptable" rating were:

When production mistakes are made (things go wrong), one gets into a slump.

Scheduling of vans could be better—personally have too much slack time.

Lack managerial support to improve effectiveness.

With a smoother flow of work, individual productivity could be increased.

Improving productivity The suggested changes to be followed to improve worker productivity are listed below:

1. Better scheduling of work. Unfortunately the flow of work often comes in batches. Also, the flow is interrupted by designated re-work priorities and special remodifications of specific vans. Better communication between salespeople and shop employees would help eliminate the problem.
2. Better supervision to overcome favoritism, stop people from gold-bricking, and encourage people to report to work on time. Also, there is a need for more direction from lead supervisors, better communications, less talking during work, and responsibility assigned for quality control.
3. Better availability of parts to provide a more even distribution of van production throughout the month.
4. Other comments included better work areas, more equitable pay scale, and more people to help during rush periods.

For their own specific jobs, the respondents suggested that the following changes could be implemented (in order of those most often mentioned) to improve job performance:

1. Better scheduling of production to achieve a smoother flow of work. Related to this recommendation were comments such as set time standard for each job (van), schedule three vans at a time for interior work, divide shop into stalls where work can be done, and vans should be systematically moved through the shop even though one area cannot completely finish all of its work in a specific time.
2. Better availability of material when needed.
3. Better supervision, which includes improved communications, firing inefficient workers, and more discipline.
4. Additional comments included more experienced workers, improve morale, reduce/eliminate special modifications for completed vans, and more assistance in specific departments.

Evaluation of supervisors and other personnel The employees rated the attributes important for a supervisor. The factor receiving the highest level of importance was the need to be able to communicate work plans and schedules. Fairness, understanding, honesty, ability to relate to others, and knowledge of work to be done all received about the same number of responses. Interestingly, helping others in their job was ranked last. Apparently, the employees were sufficiently comfortable with their own levels of skill and competence that the need of the supervisors to help others perform the job was not extremely important to them. In general, respondents noted a need for the supervisor to plan, organize, and control the operational tasks of the work effectively. They saw this being done on a supportive and understanding basis to the extent the supervisor knows what is going on and is able to relate this knowledge to subordinates. Next, the respondents realized that the planning of work is not adequate in itself unless the supervisor is able to evaluate subordinates effectively in terms of their work performance.

Questions

1. Based on the responses by employees, has the planning function as performed by management kept pace with the growth of the firm?
2. As viewed by employees, what management practices need to be improved?
3. Do you feel that the shop foreman's job is properly defined? If not, what changes could be made to improve his productivity?
4. Draw an organization chart showing how you perceive the organization to exist now, and another chart to show what changes you would implement.
5. What types of production planning techniques could be implemented to overcome the objections expressed by employees?

National Paper and Bag Company

The National Paper and Bag Company was formed by two brothers in 1918 and was once ranked among the top 10 paper-producing companies in the United States. Six months ago, Robert Harris was selected as the company's new president. At the time, the company was experiencing its worst financial loss since the Great Depression. In fact, the company's current financial position is considered by some company officials to be hopeless, if not fatal. (See Exhibit 2.)

Since Harris became president, he has been confronted with (1) a major business recession; (2) company mills that are considered obsolete by current standards, thereby accounting for a high level of fixed costs; (3) the possibility of bankruptcy due to a shortage of current assets; and (4) a cash drain due to losses incurred in 8 out of the last 10 years. Thus, there is little doubt in Harris' mind that raising capital from the usual sources is unlikely.

At present, the union is demanding an $1.50 increase in hourly wages over the next three years, thereby adding another dimension to National's financial problems. The board of directors feels that the

EXHIBIT 2

NATIONAL PAPER AND BAG COMPANY
Balance Sheet
December 31, 198–

Assets

Current assets:

Cash	$ 100,000	
Accounts receivable	500,000	
Inventories	750,000	
Total current assets		$1,350,000

Fixed assets:

Land	$ 125,000	
Building	175,000	
Machinery equipment	1,150,000	
Total fixed assets		1,450,000
Deferred charges		5,000
Total assets		$2,805,000

Liabilities and Stockholders' Equity

Current liabilities:

Notes payable	$ 50,000	
Accounts payable	585,000	
Total current liabilities		$ 635,000
Funded debt		400,000

Stockholders' equity:

Common stock	1,800,000	
Surplus	(30,000)	
Total stockholders' equity		1,770,000
Total liabilities and equity		$2,805,000

union is asking for an unrealistic wage increase, particularly during a period of recession. Yet, there is a very good chance that there will be an extended strike unless the new contract demands are met by management.

Prior to Harris' selection as president, the company did very little long-range planning due to its unstable financial position. In addition, most planning activities were centralized in the president's office. No arrangements were made for either planning committees or staff personnel who could assist in the planning process.

One of the items being considered by the board is the possibility of moving into the corrugated box business by either building or buying a few plants in New England and the Middle West. However, Harris points out that the most successful paper companies are located in the Carolinas, Florida, Georgia, Alabama, Louisiana, and Arkansas.

These mills generally have lower production costs than northern plants since they are closer to the pulpwood supply. In addition, many of the successful companies own timberlands. Consequently, they are able to control the source of their raw materials.

1. What are the major problems facing the management of National Paper and Bag?
2. Can the planning process be used to identify future opportunities that might be available to the company? How?
3. Based on these limited data, what should management do now? Be specific.

Instant Furniture

The retail furniture industry in the United States has an annual volume of $20 billion and includes more than 25,000 furniture stores. Furniture retailing has always been a highly fragmented enterprise, marked by scores of local "mom and pop" stores and regional chains.

The conventional furniture store is a service-oriented operation that offers furniture and accessories for the home, interior decorating ideas, delivery, merchandise on approval, and liberal credit arrangements. However, customers must often wait for delivery of a particular piece of furniture since conventional stores do not usually stock merchandise in quantity. Thus, it is not uncommon for customers to wait six weeks or longer for an item.

Rudy Nesbit of Detroit, Michigan, now operates a traditional furniture store but has an idea that he could imitate the carryout convenience of supermarket shopping. Basically, he envisions a single store that combines a giant warehouse and showroom. The strategy would be to offer a wide selection of medium-priced, brand-name furniture at discount prices for instant delivery. The long-range objectives of Nesbit are shown in Exhibit 3. As indicated, he feels that his strategy will generate an average sales growth of more than 60 percent a year for at least a 15-year period.

EXHIBIT 3
Proposed growth plans for a 15-year period

Item	Current period	In 5 years	In 8 years	In 10 years	In 15 years
Number of stores	1	5	27	49	75
Sales ($ millions)	3.00	24.0	175.0	350.0	550.0
Profit ($ millions)	0.13	1.0	8.3	15.7	20.5
Profit margin	—	—	—	4.5%	4.5%

Buildings

Nesbit feels that all buildings must be owned by someone other than the Nesbit Corporation since he does not want to tie up needed capital in real estate. The larger stores will range from 155,000 to 200,000 square feet and will be located in population centers of at least 750,000. Smaller stores are to range from 70,000 to 130,000 square feet and will be located in cities of 200,000 to 700,000 population. The objective is to have most of the stores in the larger category.

Stores are to be situated on expressways where land is cheaper and railroad sidings are available. As customers enter the building, they will be shown the warehouse first to emphasize the availability of stock. Exhibit 4 shows the total store layout that will include a showroom with 250 model room vignettes separated by wide aisles. Only the merchandise shown on the floor will be kept in stock and available for purchase by customers.

Inventory

One of the biggest problems facing Nesbit deals with inventory. Since each store will have approximately 30,000 furniture items in inventory plus 25,000 accessory items, over $1 million will be tied up in the inventory of each store. Inventory financing, Nesbit feels, must come from retained earnings and public stock issues if the required inventory levels are to be achieved. Inventory control will consist of daily sales being recorded on punched cards with results being sent to corporate headquarters.

EXHIBIT 4
Proposed warehouse-showroom furniture store layout

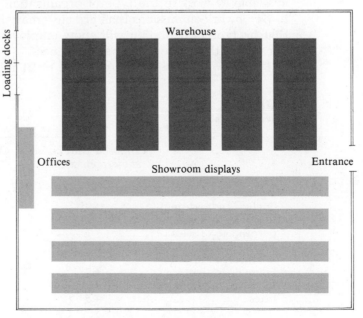

It is planned that the stores will never be out of stock of any particular item more than 10 percent of the time. To keep merchandise flowing to the stores, manufacturers will be forced to do more warehousing than for conventional furniture retailers so that backup furniture will be available between production runs of the various items. Merchandise is to be neatly stacked on seven-tiered cantilevered warehouse racks. Special equipment will be used to unload trucks and box cars and to stack items in the warehouse. The merchandise will not be classified as the most expensive, and there will be a limited assortment of fabrics. No carpeting or appliances will be sold.

Marketing

The customer appeal will be to the young, mobile group that does not want to be tied down with expensive items; to both low- and middle-income families; and to retirees who do not want to put expensive furnishings in a retirement home or condominium.

Each item on the floor is to be ticketed with two prices: (1) a deluxe, full-service price comparable to that of a local dealer and (2) a special discount price if the item is picked up at the warehouse by the customer. Prices between these ranges vary depending on the services to be provided. If furniture is delivered by the store, for example, there is a 4 percent increase in the price as well as an additional 4 percent charge if the item is set up for the customer. For items that are picked up by the customer, prices will run 15 to 25 percent lower than those in conventional furniture stores.

Personnel and store operations

Nesbit feels that there are a lot of good, experienced employees available to work in the type of organization he envisions. He plans to pay lower commissions than are customary in the industry but feels that his type of operation will allow employees to earn more money because of the higher volume of business.

Plans also include a training team of 21 members who will travel

EXHIBIT 5
Operating statistics

	Proposed warehouse-showroom strategy	Current conventional selling method
Operating expenses as a percentage of sales (includes advertising)	29%	41%
Advertising as a percentage of sales	7	3
Percentage of personnel involved in warehouse operations	65	90
Profit margin before taxes	4.5	8 to 10

among the stores. Through a concentrated program, it is expected that people can be trained to open a new store in as little as three weeks. Additional operating statistics developed by Nesbit that distinguish his proposed outlets from conventional operations are noted in Exhibit 5.

Questions

1. Evaluate Nesbit's strategy for marketing furniture. Does this strategy fit into the overall outlook of marketing within the United States?
2. Based on the facts of the case, do you feel that Nesbit has considered all necessary factors for going into the new marketing venture?
3. If cost of goods sold represents 50 percent of the retail price in conventional furniture store operations, is Nesbit's anticipated profit margin realistic for the warehouse-showroom type store?
4. Do you recommend that Nesbit switch from his conventional operation to the warehouse-showroom concept? Why?

The Custom Automotive Company

As Louis Forani and his father, Marcello, walked from the design shop of the Custom Automotive Company, Marcello said, "It is imperative that you uphold the company's good name. It has taken me 22 years to build this company, and it is respected by fine car lovers all over the world." Being forced into retirement at age 73 due to poor health, Marcello plans to turn the business over to Louis. Marcello continued, "And I want you to leave my old friend Pragetti alone; he has worked long and hard by my side since we started." Louis Forani nodded his head affirmatively and walked with his father in silence, having learned long ago that arguments with him were fruitless.

Forani and Pragetti started the company with the idea of custom building cars in the sporting tradition of the old country. They succeeded in developing some distinctive designs and normally had work scheduled up to six months in advance. In the late 1950s, however, European sports cars invaded the American market. These cars not only featured distinctive styling but sold for prices much below what Forani had to charge to custom build an American model.

Pragetti, a former race car mechanic, has designed industrial equipment as well as automobiles. In fact, his industrial designs were the basis for starting two new divisions of the company; namely, the tractor and equipment design division headed by Pragetti and the small construction equipment sales division directed by Louis Forani.

Currently, Marcello is totally responsible for cost control throughout the entire organization. Louis and Pragetti have complete authority over pricing and marketing policies within their own divisions; however, production policies are centralized with Marcello Forani.

During the past year, profits from the construction equipment division were reinvested in the automotive custom shop in an effort to improve its sales. To achieve this goal, Pragetti and Louis have also been forced to assume more of the day-to-day duties required in running the corporation. Although Louis Forani's division is the most profitable in the company, he has not been involved in major decision-making activities and is not a member of the board of directors.

Company outlook

Automotive shop   The market for well-designed custom-built cars has expanded with the increased affluence of American consumers. However, increasing labor and developmental costs have caused the automotive shop to run in the red. Marcello Forani wants the company to remain a small, family-owned organization. Consequently, he refuses to listen to any ideas on either selling the business or entering into an aggressive nationwide advertising campaign.

Tractor and equipment design division   Pragetti has not been able to give sufficient time to managing this division, since he has taken over some of the corporate decisions formerly made by Forani. In addition, the demand for industrial design services has decreased as business activity has declined in the surrounding area. Yet, the quality of the division's design work is acclaimed by experts as the best in the industry.

Construction equipment sales division   Traditionally, industry sales of small construction equipment have reflected an irratic pattern. By following an aggressive but selective marketing policy, Louis has managed to increase sales by an average of almost 10 percent per year. He is happy about the growth in sales and is optimistic about the future. However, he would like to diversify into other product lines that would offset current sales fluctuations.

Questions

1. What are the major factors that have affected this company's growth? Have changes in the organization been adaptive to a dynamic environment?

2. Assume that Marcello Forani succumbs to a heart attack, leaving Louis Forani 60 percent of the stock of the company with 25 percent being held by his mother, 10 percent by Pragetti, and 5 percent by various other relatives. In order of priority, list the actions that Louis should take as president of the company.

3. Should the operating policies established by Marcello be continued even though economic and industry conditions have changed?

PART THREE

ORGANIZING RESOURCES

8

ORGANIZATIONS
AND THEIR
OBJECTIVES

PURPOSE

Life today means living in a society of organizations. Institutions, ranging from school systems, government agencies, and business enterprises to medical care facilities, surround most of our daily activities. Even in thinking about a trip abroad or to Mexico, we become quite aware of the innumerable organizations that have an impact on our plans before the journey can commence.

In all organizations, managers are required. They are the people to whom organizations are entrusted and who are responsible for the practice of management. Managing an organization, however, is somewhat different from managing our own personal affairs. What, then, is an organization, and why is management required for its successful performance? What can managers do to assure that organizations are not destined for obsolescence in a dynamic society? This chapter is the first of four that provides answers to these questions. Throughout all chapters, you may want to remember that the axiom "survival of the fittest" has strong roots in the "world of organizations."

OBJECTIVES

1. To introduce organizations as social structures while discussing their role in coordinating group efforts.

2. To point out the value of viewing organizations as open systems of interrelated components.

3. To discuss the nature of objectives and their influence on organizational behavior.

4. To show how the multiple objectives of organizations exist in a means-end relationship.

5. To examine problems that can arise when setting or implementing objectives.

The organizing function is concerned with combining people, work to be done, and physical resources into a meaningful relationship to achieve organizational goals. Its purpose is to bring order out of chaos when people work together, and regardless of the number of people involved, organizing is required. In this context, organizations may be viewed from the standpoint of (1) who benefits from them, (2) their external and internal environments, (3) organizational members, (4) goals and objectives, and (5) formal and informal authority relationships.

Although an entire book can be devoted to organizing, we limit our discussion of the function to four chapters. In this chapter, emphasis is placed on the role and importance of organizations, the systems approach in viewing organizations, and an analysis of the nature and importance of organizational objectives. The following chapters look more specifically at the organizing function, focusing on the formal dimensions of an organization, the role and scope of authority and responsibility, identifying and grouping jobs to produce a team effort, and the delegation of authority to coordinate relationships among individuals and groups.

MANAGEMENT AND THE ORGANIZATION

Without question, our daily lives are influenced by many business, social, educational, religious, and political organizations. In today's society, most work is accomplished through organizations, rather than being achieved by individuals working separately. Thus, an organization is formed when some endeavor, because of its magnitude or complexity, requires the efforts of two or more people for its accomplishment.

An organization is defined as a social structure designed to coordinate the activities of two or more people through a division of labor and hierarchy of authority for the achievement of a common purpose or goal. This definition emphasizes two important considerations. The first is a group of people working together in a coordinated manner to achieve objectives. The intent in combining forces is to accomplish goals that could not be achieved by individuals working separately. Without goals, there would be no reason for an organization to exist. See Figure 8–1 for a listing of selected organizations whose goals have attracted the memberships indicated.

The second aspect of an organization refers to its framework or structure. An important element of the structure is a division of labor— that is, a specialization of work in which similar activities are generally grouped into various functional or activity units. Each of these units is then assigned to a manager or supervisor who establishes communication flows within and between units. As additional management activities arise, the delegation of authority becomes essential, and a formal hierarchy of authority with communication channels results. All of these management actions are designed to make the organization work

FIGURE 8–1
Selected organizations and memberships

Organization	Membership
Frisbee Association	110,000
Overeaters Anonymous	80,000
Friends of Animals	60,000
American Sunbathing Association	25,000
Muzzle Loading Rifle Association	23,819
Tattoo Club of America	10,000
American Dairy Goat Association	8,500
U.S. Hang Gliding Association	8,000
Zero Population Growth	8,000
Clowns of America	5,200
Amateur Chamber Music Players	5,000
International Lefthanders	5,000
Procrastinators' Club of America	3,500
Electric Railroaders Association	2,100
Citizens for Clean Air	2,000
International Wizard of Oz Club	1,752
National Ding-A-Ling Club	1,600
League for Industrial Democracy	1,500
National Button Society	1,470
American Alpine Club	1,450
Retreads of World War I and II	1,400
American Battleship Association	1,200
American Badminton Association	1,200
American Cemetery Association	1,100
International Jugglers Association	1,000
Goose Island Bird & Girl Watching Society	906
U.S. Monopoly Association	625
American Aging Association	500
International Log Rolling Association	500
Count Dracula Society	500
Desert Protective Council	450
American Feline Society	450
Blizzard Club, January 12, 1888	87

Source: *The World Almanac and Book of Facts, 1980 edition* (New York: Newspaper Enterprise Association, 1980), pp. 336–49. Copyright © Newspaper Enterprise Association, 1970, New York, NY 10166. Used with permission.

smoothly. (Elaboration of these topics and others associated with the organizing function are presented in later chapters.)

In the past, organizations were viewed as stable systems of individuals working together to achieve common goals. They were treated as self-contained entities without regard to the possible impact of outside forces. By assuming relatively stable relationships, organizations were seen as lending predictability to human behavior. As a result, many organization theorists looked into organizations for factors explaining human behavior as they sought to develop organizing design principles.

Today, we realize that to understand organizational behavior, both a search within and a look outside an organization's environment are essential. Research cannot stop at an organization's boundaries.

Because of changes in people, the environments in which organizations operate, objectives to be achieved, and tasks to be performed, organizational structures are becoming increasingly complex and diverse. No longer does an organization, regardless of its purpose, remain stable and unmodified for any extended period of time. Organizational members, however, are more aware of what is stable about an organization than what is changing. Consequently, they often underestimate the rate of change in an organization.

From a managerial perspective, change sometimes causes organizational disorder, friction, and ineffectiveness. In preventing or overcoming these problems, managers must consider change from an analytical and systematic approach.

Organization viewed as a system

Possibly one of the best ways to understand the nature and operation of an organization is to view it from a systems orientation. Although the systems concept (theory) is not new, its applicability to the development of a systematic, theoretical framework for organizations is relatively recent. In just two decades, however, some scholars have come to consider the systems approach as the single most influential concept of contemporary organization theory.[1]

A system has been defined in various ways; and, in many instances, the definitions are not much more than mental exercises in memorization. Yet, by visualizing the human body or an automobile as a complete system with various subsystems, one begins to recognize that a system is a collection of interrelated parts. For an organization, it is a unit of interrelated components, the balance and coordination of which are keys to maximizing performance and optimizing efficiency as a whole. These components may be an identifiable grouping of people, mechanical parts, procedures, and/or resources. Specifically, *a system can be defined as a unit of functionally interrelated components designed to achieve a predetermined objective.*[2]

All parts of a system (in terms of fulfilling their functions) are important, and one part should never become so overemphasized that it works to the detriment of the total system. Maximum efficiency of a particular organizational unit is not as important as achieving optimum efficiency for the entire organization. For example, we have all seen the person who allows the digestive system to overwork to the ill effects of the whole body, or the athlete who becomes a highly coordi-

---

[1] See Seymour Tilles, "The Manager's Job: A Systems Approach," *Harvard Business Review,* January–February 1963, pp. 74–81; and E. M. Rogers and R. A. Rogers, *Communication in Organizations* (New York: Free Press, 1977), pp. 48–76.

[2] See Norman Gaither, *Production and Operation Management* (Hinsdale, Ill.: Dryden Press, 1980), p. 24.

nated system of muscles but fails to train the mental subsystem to be creative and analytical. Thus, the systems-oriented manager is interested in the whole organization and its optimum achievement of total goals.

Characteristics of system design

Based on the preceding discussion, several characteristics can be observed in the design of a system. These include:

1. The need to have meaningful overall objectives.
2. Specialized operating and managerial decisional units (subsystems) must be interrelated in the achievement of objectives. Each subsystem has certain goals that are interdependent in achieving the system's overall objectives. These units may be represented by the physical flow patterns of materials, personnel, money, machines, and communications. Communication, in particular, is an essential element of any system since it links together the interdependent subsystems.
3. A series of *(a)* inputs, *(b)* processes whereby value is added to inputs, and *(c)* outputs are necessary.
4. A set of external environmental relationships exist such as customers, general public, government, labor, suppliers, and stockholders.
5. The system itself is a subsystem since it is a part of an even larger system. For example, the management decision-making system is a subsystem of the larger organizational system. Also, a city's governmental system is a subsystem of the county, which is a subsystem of the state government, which is part of the national political system.
6. Evaluation and control are necessary. Since actual performance of the system may not meet objectives, corrective action may be required.

As indicated by these characteristics, also noted in Figure 8–2, systems contain many variables. Some are not completely understood, and others are subject to influences that cannot be predicted. In any event, the complexity of relationships between management and its environment; the multiplicity of organizational goals; and the interrelationships among groups, individuals, and technology require that organizations be viewed as a total unit—an open system.

Organization—an open system

An organization is best referred to as an open system since it is subject to outside forces of the environment. In definitional terms, *an open system exchanges information with its environment, while a closed system is isolated completely from it.* Rarely is an organization a closed system. Most organizations as we know them are interacting with their environments in the form of exchanging information, drawing upon resources, and providing goods and services. Thus, we can assume that business and social organizations are open systems. If flow

192

FIGURE 8–2
Characteristics of system design

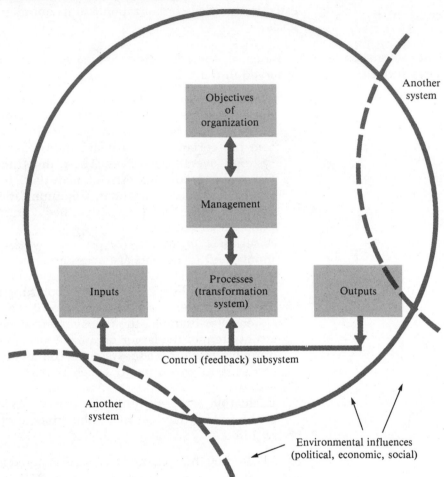

patterns do not exist between these organizations and their environments, they will rapidly decay and soon cease to exist. The phenomena of decay and death of a closed organizational system is referred to as entropy.

An interesting aspect of viewing the organization as an open system is the fast-changing environment in which we live. The statement by Peter Drucker that "organization structures are becoming increasingly short lived and unstable" is quite meaningful when organizations are viewed from an open system approach.[3] Drucker indicates that the

---

[3] Peter F. Drucker, "New Templets for Today's Organizations," *Harvard Business Review*, January–February 1974. Copyright © 1973 by The President and Fellows of Harvard College; all rights reserved.

"classical" organizations of the 1920s and 1930s, such as AT&T, General Motors, duPont, and Sears Roebuck, stood for decades requiring only minor changes in structure and components. In our fast-paced and uncertain world today, however, a major reorganization by these and other companies is no sooner completed than the need for reorganization again becomes apparent. Political and governmental organizations are good examples of groups that are continuously subject to reorganization, almost on a yearly basis.

The key point to recognize is that there are no precise answers or models (textbook examples) that can be applied to all organizations at all times. Each organization is different, each having its own unique and appropriate organizational design. Consequently, developing an organization structure requires systematic analysis in terms of organizational needs, strategy, the work to be done, and a consideration of people within the organization. To determine the one best organizational design and structure for all organizations is impossible and impractical. Thus, designing the organization is more a series of risk-taking decisions than a search for the "one best way." That which works well for others can be used as a guide, but what is done in one particular situation should always be contingent upon circumstances surrounding that situation. By utilizing the open system approach, a framework is provided for studying and analyzing organizational structure and design within a given environmental setting.

Environmental influences

Managers cannot predict the exact influence of most environmental factors even though they act as constraints on all organizations. As an example, a personnel manager may find that a desire to change the length of vacation periods depends on effective collective bargaining with the union.

In most successful organizations, therefore, managers often develop means such as persuasion, lobbying, cooperation, participation, and intercession of higher authority to modify the impact of certain environmental influences.

By utilizing the systems framework, attention is given to forces in the external environment that have an impact on decisions. When these forces and their impact can be identified more clearly, decisions can be made that are more meaningful in terms of employee satisfaction and increased productivity.

Framework of the business organization

The diagram presented in Figure 8–3 provides a framework of the business organization as a system and shows interrelationships among various subsystems. The subsystems of marketing, production, and finance are shown to be interrelated since each contributes to the achievement of an organization's objectives. Outputs of these various subsystems become meaningful only when they contribute to the attainment of overall goals.

FIGURE 8–3
Business organization as a system with interrelated subsystems*

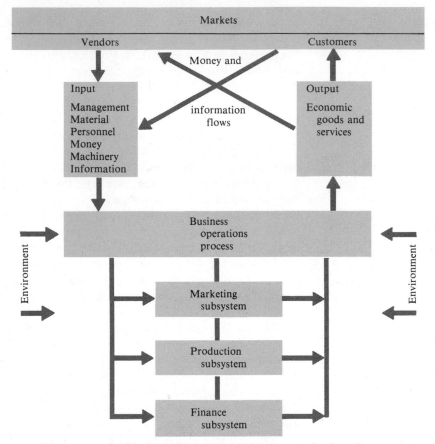

* Figure is applicable to many organizations: prisons, schools, military services, hospitals, and churches.

NATURE AND IMPORTANCE OF OBJECTIVES

The starting point of any organization is the development of objectives by managerial leaders. As a focal point, objectives note the direction the organization is taking, thereby guiding future actions through strategies, policies, programs, and resource allocations. In this section, we will look at objectives as operational guidelines that influence organization behavior.

Since *objectives* provide direction to individual efforts, they *may be defined as the targets people seek to achieve over various time periods.* Viewed in this manner, an essential task of management is the formulation, clarification, and communication of objectives.

Purpose and objectives

Although the words *purpose* and *objective* are generally used interchangeably, a differentiation of the terms is often attempted. When doing so, purpose is defined as the overall reason for an organization's existence. As an illustration, IBM has a stated purpose of solving the various informational problems of its customers. The purpose at du Pont is to be a high-technology company manufacturing and marketing predominately chemicals. Thus, purpose reflects the basic character and direction of organizations. Objectives, on the other hand, are considered to be more specific and direct effort toward the attainment of an organization's purpose.

Within an organizational setting, deciding whether a statement should be regarded as a purpose or as an objective is sometimes difficult. It is hard to know precisely where objectives begin and purposes end. Similar to purposes, a particular objective may also be quite general and its time span could range from the immediate to the long run. Because of these difficulties, we will use the terms purpose and objectives interchangeably.

Objectives and goals

Two additional words that are generally used interchangeably are *objectives* and *goals*. Some managers, however, tend to view objectives as timeless, something to be worked toward in the future.[4] In addition, they feel objectives should be broad and general in setting forth desired future conditions. Goals, on the other hand, are viewed as more specific, being expressed in absolute terms that can be attained in a specified time period. To some degree, the difficulties expressed in making a clear separation between purpose and objectives are the same ones restricting the distinction between objectives and goals. Thus, rather than deciding when to use objective or goal, we will use them interchangeably. Both will pertain to a wide or narrow part of the organization and may be either long range or short range in nature.

Hierarchy of objectives or means-end analysis

The objectives of any organization exist in a hierarchy according to their relative importance. The hierarchy begins with broad overall objectives and concludes with those that are more specific for each element of the organization. Objectives are arrayed in this manner so that each subobjective contributes to the achievement of its immediately higher objective. The result is a hierarchy that reflects a deductive reasoning approach and a structure that may be referred to as a means-end type of analysis. Through means-end analysis, subordinated objectives provide the means for achieving higher-order goals. As a result, each objective in the hierarchy becomes a subobjective that must be accomplished as a means for accomplishing some broader objective.

A means-end chain can be seen in Figure 8–4 that depicts the hierarchy of objectives for the Kane Novelty Company. In this example, top executives establish the main objectives of manufacturing and sell-

---

[4] Peter Lorance and Richard F. Vancil, *Strategic Planning Systems* (Englewood Cliffs, N.J.: Prentice-Hall, 1977), p. 5.

FIGURE 8–4
Means-end chain of objectives, Kane Novelty Company

1. Major objective:	Manufacture and sell novelty chess sets			
2. Means for achieving major objectives become departmental subgoals	**Sales department:** Sell 50,000 chess sets to gross at least $200,000 profit		**Production department:** Produce 50,000 chess sets by October 31 at a variable cost of not more than $1.25 per unit	
3. Means for achieving subgoals become unit sub-subgoals	Direct mail order sales: Priced at $5.99 each	Sales to jobbers: Priced at $2.75 each	Purchasing: Obtain prices, compare bids, place order for raw materials	Product planning and control: Schedule runs for greatest productivity of labor and equipment
4. Means for achieving sub-subgoals are individual objectives	Individual employees' objectives			

ing novelty chess boards. Objectives for the marketing and production managers then become those which provide the means for producing and selling chess boards. This type of analysis continues until the objectives of each person in the organization are set forth in meaningful terms that can be quantitatively measured.

It is important to reiterate that means-end analysis starts with overall objectives and depends on good communications and coordination if it is to operate effectively in a large organization. Unless coordination and central planning are implemented, goal setting at one organizational level may definitely detract from goals at other levels. It is also possible for managers to have goals that are at cross-purposes with overall organizational goals. These actions may not be intentional, but people make decisions differently because (1) they do not perceive overall objectives in the same way, (2) creative powers vary among those involved in the goal-setting process, and (3) each manager has a different frame of reference. Also, some managers show greater allegiance to departmental subgoals than to overall organizational objectives.

In spite of certain limitations, means-end analysis has been very useful to managers. The following are some advantages:

Emphasis is placed on the idea of having goals clearly stated and unified in purpose.

FIGURE 8–5
Organizational participants and their inducements

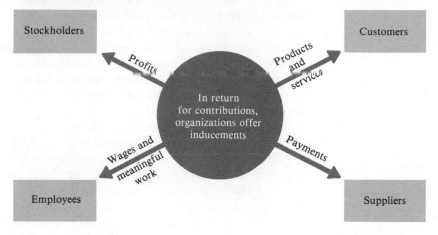

Complex objectives can be viewed as meaningful steps that must be taken to accomplish overall goals.

A proper perspective can be developed throughout the organization as concerns activities that must be completed to achieve goals.

By viewing objectives in a hierarchical relationship, weak links in the chain can often be spotted in sufficient time to reduce losses.

Multiple objectives

The literature is quite complete in showing that organizations have several major objectives. This is especially evident in businesses that have goals of survival, growth, profits, market share, social responsibility, productivity, financial stability, quality of work life, and research and development. New goals that have emerged during the 1980s include resource conservation, multinational expansion, and consolidation of activities as opposed to diversification. Although there is no standard number of objectives that an organization should have, either too few or too many may create difficulties.[5] For example, too few objectives may neglect critical areas, while too many may result in confusion and inconsistency of effort.

The interface of goals with organizational participants is shown in Figure 8–5. Profits are noted as an inducement for stockholders to contribute to an organization, while wages represent the inducement for employees. Suppliers require payment for resources provided, and customers exchange money for products and services. In total, then, organizational goals must be accomplished in such a way that the results

[5] See Y. K. Shetty, "New Look at Corporate Goals," *California Management Review,* Winter 1979, p. 74; and John Child, "What Determines Organizational Performance? The Universals vs. the It-All-Depends," *Organizational Dynamics,* Summer 1974, pp. 10–11.

contribute to the personal objectives of all organizational participants. Likewise, an attainment of participants' goals contributes to the ultimate survival and growth of an organization.

The multiple goal concept is not new to management. The Full Employment Act of 1946, civil rights legislation in the 1960s, and safety and pollution control laws in the 1970s have all caused many managers to develop additional goals within various organizations. Top executives of General Motors Corporation and Republic Steel Corporation, for example, find themselves not only involved with problems of profits but also faced with questions concerning race relations, government regulations, employment levels, inflation, housing, education, medical care, and ecology. Such issues are related to the concept of social responsibility and have brought about an increase in the range of organizational goals to be achieved.

When considering the major objectives of an organization, it is impossible to identify one objective that covers all possible relationships and needs. Organizational problems and relationships cover a multitude of variables and cannot possibly be explained by a single objective. As a result, the recognition of multiple objectives is practical and an analytical necessity.

Setting priorities and balancing objectives

Changing environments coupled with changing internal conditions require the establishment of priorities among objectives. For example, the objective of survival may be of primary importance during periods of adverse economic conditions but may have a lower priority in periods of prosperity. Also, changes in consumer demand, the state of technology, political factors, and societal desires can influence the importance of given objectives. During the last half of the 1970s, the drug and pharmaceutical industry had higher-than-average profits and was accused of profiteering from human misery. In response, many companies in the industry restructured their priorities by emphasizing research and development, product quality, and social responsiveness, rather than profits and growth.

Establishing priorities among objectives can be viewed as a problem of balance. This is illustrated in the work of various state employment services that have the objective of equal opportunity in job placement for older workers, youth, women, the handicapped, and minorities. These objectives are partially competitive. In the spring of each year, emphasis on the placement of youth is highlighted since high school and college students are seeking summer employment. At a later period, the emphasis changes so that there is a balance among the employment objectives affecting each of the other groups.

While objectives are diverse, they must fit within the environmental constraints established by society and not be at cross-purposes with one another. If all goals are not integrated, they can be detrimental to the survival of an organization through the misdirection of managerial effort. Thus, the job of balancing objectives becomes one of the essential activities of top management.

In discussing the balancing of business objectives, a long-standing question concerns the role of profit: Is profit not the major goal of every business from which all other goals are derived? Before formulating your opinion or answer, several views should be discussed. Let us first consider the idea that profit has no meaning until a desirable service is provided.

Service as the first objective of business   There is significant support for the opinion that no business can operate as a going concern unless it considers customer service as its primary objective. Peter Drucker states:

> There is only one valid definition of business purpose: to create a customer. . . . What the business thinks it produces is not of first importance—especially not to the future of the business and to its success. What the customer thinks he is buying, what he considers "value" is decisive—it determines what a business is, what it produces, and whether it will prosper.[6]

In this sense, profitability is viewed as a measure of how well a business achieves its objectives of supplying goods and services to customers. Of course, inherent in the purpose of "creating a customer" is the idea that profit seeking is also an incentive for investing money, time, and effort. However, if all other factors are removed from consideration, the profit motive simply does not explain why entrepreneurs go into business.

Some of our great industrial leaders, such as James F. Lincoln of Lincoln Electric Company, the world's major producer of arc welders, and Henry Ford, followed the consumer service concept. They felt their companies should identify major objectives in the areas of providing jobs and manufacturing better goods for more people at lower prices. In 1919, Henry Ford's objective was to produce an automobile at a price that all wage earners could afford. He viewed profits not as the pure and unadulterated goal of business but as a means by which industry could serve society by providing employment and a satisfaction of consumer needs. James F. Lincoln developed one of the most successful group incentive plans in the United States. The results included higher incomes for employees as well as higher levels of productivity for the company and lower consumer prices on many products.

Profit as the first objective   The flip side of the above view is that profit is the foundation on which other goals are built. If a product is important to customers, profit is essential in manufacturing and offer-

---

[6] Peter Drucker, *The Practice of Management* (New York: Harper & Row, 1954), p. 37.

ing the product on a continuous basis. As a single unitary goal, profit must be maintained as the compensation for the acceptance of business risks and the performance of economic services. Profit can either be reinvested or used as an incentive to attract outside funds for the replacement of used inputs. Without profit, an organization will not survive to fulfill other organizational goals. Thus, profit is essential for the continuity of an organization, even though it does not necessarily assure survival if satisfying customer demand efficiently is excluded from managerial consideration.

Without question, the primary importance of profit can be seen in financially troubled companies. Generally, the first action taken by management in these companies is that of cutting costs to improve profit. In an attempt to create new jobs, acquire new facilities, and develop new products or services, profit certainly becomes the foundation on which survival is dependent.

Profit and the systems approach   Viewed from a systems approach, the profit objective alone may be too general to show the numerous interrelationships among the various parts and complex activities of an organization. Producing desirable goods and services in an organization requires all activities and decisions to be carefully coordinated and interrelated. Yet, equating all efforts to profit is hazardous in evaluating any business.

More than likely, stating overall objectives in terms of profit often disregards the need for interrelating all other goals and plans. For this reason, profit generally provides a poor conceptual framework for bringing together various activities of an entire business organization.

Profit and service: An overview   Serving customers and making a profit are essential in every business. Otherwise, an organization will not continue to exist. Profit, however, does not imply that managers are fixated on earning the maximum profit from all operations. The long-run survival and growth of a company cannot be jeopardized for short-run profits, nor for the maximization of any other objective without the proper regard for total organizational goals.

Kenneth Mason, president of Quaker Oats, feels that the assets of any private economic entity must produce a satisfactory profit because without it the organization would close down.[7] On the other hand, he suggests that making a profit is no more the purpose of a corporation than getting enough to eat is the purpose of life. Hopefully, purpose is something broader and more challenging than eating or making a profit.

In summary, the comments of Professor Herbert Simon are quite appropriate:

---

[7] F. D. Sturdivant, *Business and Society: A Managerial Approach* (Homewood, Ill.: Richard D. Irwin, 1981), pp. 5–6. © 1981 by Richard D. Irwin, Inc.

It has been fashionable in the literature of business administration to debate whether the purpose of a business organization is service or profit. There really is no problem to debate about. Certain individuals, primarily the customers, contribute to the organization because of the service it provides; others, the entrepreneurs, because of the profit they may derive. When the system of organization behavior is examined, it is found that both service and profit areas influence decisions.[8]

Classification of objectives

To facilitate the study of objectives, classification schemes have been developed for use in analyzing organizational activities. Although there is no standard or accepted classification of objectives, such schemes help managers recognize areas in which objectives must be set for organizational growth, survival, profits, and so forth. Three classification schemes are presented for consideration.[9]

Long-run/short-run objectives A dominant classification system is based on time periods where objectives are referred to as either long-run or short-run goals. *Long-run objectives* include those that cover periods of time longer than one year. *Short-run objectives* are those covering 12 months or less, even though their actual accomplishment may require more than one year.[10] Through time, environmental pressures can sometimes change viable long-range objectives into poor ones. Therefore, they must be based on the best possible forecasts of the future and should not commit an organization to irrevocable positions. Likewise, short-run objectives must be sufficiently flexible to allow eventualities to be handled in the long run. In addition, short-run objectives should never be maximized to the extent that they destroy the flexibility required in achieving long-range goals.

Objectives of performance and results For the survival and prosperity of an organization, Peter Drucker suggests that objectives must be established in eight key areas.[11] As set forth in terms of performance and results, these objectives are as follows:

Market standing	Physical resources
Innovation	Productivity
Human organization	Social responsibility
Financial resources	Profit responsibility

While there is no intent to suggest a hierarchy of importance among these eight areas, certain objectives will be more important than others depending on the given conditions, strategies, and risks facing an orga-

---

[8] Herbert A. Simon, *Administrative Behavior* (New York: Free Press 1957), pp. 112–13. Copyright © 1945, 1947, 1957, 1976 by Herbert A. Simon. Used with permission.

[9] For another scheme, see C. Perro, *Organizational Analysis: A Sociological View* (Belmont, Calif.: Wadsworth Publishing, 1970).

[10] George A. Steiner, "Comprehensive Managerial Planning," in *The Management Process* ed. Stephen J. Carroll et al. (New York: Macmillan, 1977), pp. 126–27.

[11] Peter F. Drucker, *Management: Tasks, Responsibilities, Practices* (New York: Harper & Row, 1974), pp. 100–101.

nization during a particular period of time. However, some attention must be given to the objectives in each area if managers are to plan activities, organize events, and evaluate performance to improve future results.

Primary, collateral, and secondary service objectives Professor Ralph C. Davis has presented a classification scheme for objectives based on those values that relate to the necessities of an organization.[12] They are given below in order of importance:

Primary service objectives These objectives refer to the economic value (utility) that an organization must provide to its customers. As such, primary service objectives refer not only to desired products but also to providing products in the right quantities, at the right price, and when and where they are needed. Since these objectives involve all individuals and groups to some extent, they must be subdivided into organizational and operational objectives. Organizational service objectives relate to the values that must be contributed by groups in an organization to its customers over a period of time. Operational objectives refer to the specific goals of all nonmanagerial employees. The cumulative total realized from accomplishing objectives in each area represents the degree to which primary service objectives are accomplished.

Collateral service objectives The values that an organization is expected to provide for the groups that are a part of it are considered collateral in nature. For instance, collateral social objectives might relate to the general public or to some segment of the government, while collateral personal objectives would consider employees, stockholders, suppliers, and financial institutions. In this sense, Professor Davis considers profit as collateral to primary service objectives.

Secondary service objectives These are objectives that must be met if an organization is to accomplish primary and collateral objectives efficiently. An example includes the objectives of service departments in such areas as maintenance, personnel, or research and development.

Difficulties in classifying objectives

Any attempt to set forth a system for classifying the objectives of an organization is plagued with difficulties. For example, it is doubtful that managers within any organization can identify all of the objectives that they are seeking to achieve. Many executives are hard pressed to come up with a written statement of the overall objectives of their organizations, not to mention the difficulties in identifying a complete means-end chain for the entire organization. Thus, while a classification of goals sounds good in theory, things do not fit together that beautifully in practice. There are many decisions and activities in an organization that cannot be analyzed in terms of a patternized classification scheme.

---

[12] Ralph C. Davis, *The Fundamentals of Top Management* (New York: Harper and Row Publishers, 1951), pp. 97–116. Copyright 1951 by Harper & Row, Publishers, Inc.

Consequently, such schemes do not always reflect certain organizational phenomena in an appropriate manner.

Another difficulty with classification schemes is that objectives are not mutually independent. In other words, objectives are interrelated and it is difficult to segment them into clearly defined categories. Furthermore, even similar organizations usually have different objectives, which, in turn, restrict the use of a universal classification scheme. In summary, then, there are certain difficulties in utilizing a classification scheme to analyze and evaluate objectives. One should recognize, however, that such schemes can provide an analytical framework that is useful in examining those areas where objectives have to be established for continued organizational survival and growth.

Practical problems dealing with objectives

All organizations experience problems in developing, balancing, and implementing objectives. In many instances, there are no set answers to these problems. Yet, all individuals within organizations, whether managerial or nonmanagerial, may be faced with some of the following problems:

1. Inconsistencies between stated organizational objectives and actual practice In most organizations, a major reason for this problem arises from stated objectives that are neither clear nor communicated correctly. As a result, misunderstanding and distortion occur at lower levels of authority. When overall goals are vague, managers often make decisions that are entirely inconsistent with the original intent of stated objectives. On the other hand, goals should not be so detailed that they stifle initiative and creativity. Preventing inconsistencies between stated objectives and actual practice requires a clear understanding of what is to be achieved and how operating results are to be measured. In particular, goals should be understood by those who are to develop the means to achieve them.

2. Responsibility for achieving two or more objectives that appear inconsistent This situation presents a balancing problem that is often frustrating for managers. As an illustration, consider the manager of the camera shop in a department store who is not to let a customer wait more than three minutes before being served. The manager also has a goal requiring selling expenses to be less than 8.5 percent of sales. Both goals are clearly understood, but they may be in conflict. Faster customer service may require more sales personnel with an increase in selling expenses. To overcome the problem, objectives should be designed so they are mutually supporting and interrelated to the greatest possible extent. All goals and subgoals must be linked together to achieve the dominant objective effectively. If top executives do not indicate a proper balance among goals, managers are forced to do so.

3. Personal survival may be substituted for goals of efficiency Errors and faulty judgment at top-management levels generally have serious consequences for the total organization. Consequently, these managers are vulnerable to firing when decisions are wrong. Possibly this is why a cloak of conservative decision making is often associated with certain top-management personnel. In any event, the objective of personal survival is sometimes dominant. When this is the case, creativity, inventiveness, efficiency, and imagination are relegated to secondary positions in achieving organizational goals.

4. Unrealistically seeking maximum attainment of goals It is extremely difficult for most managers to determine whether an objective has been maximized. To maximize revenues, for example, a manager would have to make each decision in a perfectly rational manner. This, in turn, would require perfect knowledge about markets, technology, and the total organizational environment. Thus, rather than attempting to maximize results that cannot be accurately measured, managers normally seek levels of achievement consistent with available resources and other organizational constraints. This is not to imply that goals should be set so low that they restrict motivation and inspiration. On the other hand, goals that are unrealistically high do not inspire action nor motivation to achieve.

5. The optimization (best possible achievement) of one objective resulting in a lesser degree of achievement (suboptimization) of other objectives Consider the manager who desires satisfied employees, high productivity, high profits, and a personal workweek of 30 hours. In attaining high productivity and profits, employees may become dissatisfied due to overtime. At the same time, the manager may have to work many more than 30 hours per week. Consequently, an optimization of the productivity and profit objectives can result in a suboptimization of the other goals.

Suboptimization may also result when there is conflict among the goals of organizational subunits. For example, the finance department may be working to restrict capital expenditures for the current budgeted period, while the engineering department has a goal of installing a new production process. Thus, a conflict occurs and proposed solutions may not favor either department.

One way to overcome the problem of suboptimization is to build consistency and flexibility into goals. The further plans extend into the future, the less sure one can be of their outcome. Goals covering long periods of time, therefore, should include a great deal of flexibility. One way to gain such flexibility is to have various contingency actions available for consideration. In this way, responses to change can be more rapid than when managers are fixated on a single course of action.

6. Difficulty of measuring the achievement of some objectives Broad, general objectives present managers with the problem of performance measurement. For example, being a good citizen in the industrial community is an admirable corporate objective, but how do executives measure the degree to which it is achieved? Likewise, to state that the objective is to make a profit is, in reality, meaningless. In contrast, some objectives have built-in measurements such as revenue dollars, products sold, or the tons of iron ore mined in a given period. For example, it is more meaningful to say that the company's objective is to make $1 million in profit within five years. In any event, meaningful objectives must be capable of measurement (preferably in numerical form).

7. Inducements (rewards) to achieve objectives are not related clearly to contributions Workers join an organization for financial, psychological, and social inducements in turn for providing certain contributions to overall goals. Since some tasks are highly specialized in large, complex organizations, individual contributions are not always clearly related to the achievement of organizational goals. Consequently, participants do not see nor are they able to identify how their inducements (money, status, recognition, and social belonging) match their contributions to overall goals. As a result, these workers exhibit little dedication or loyalty to the organization until they feel a part of what is happening and view their activities as meaningful. Thus, it becomes the manager's job to help participants relate their contributions to overall goals and show how desired performance can result in the fulfillment of basic human needs.

SUMMARY

Continued increases in any nation's standard of living now require unprecedented cooperation of effort. Individuals have gone beyond their ability to develop socially and economically without joining together in various organizations. Both nationally and internationally, people need to pool their resources and exchange their output with other organizations if economic and social growth are to continue.

An organization is the vehicle by which disorganized resources of time, energy, people, finances, and materials can be brought together harmoniously to achieve common goals. These organizational units may be hospitals, businesses, governments, churches, or colleges. Regardless of their nature, the increasing complexity and size of organizations require management to be better prepared in achieving a coordination of activities and in harmonizing individual efforts toward common objectives.

Viewing organizations from a systems approach, we find that management is continuously involved with integrating an organization with its environment. Managers must also internally synchronize and balance actions of various organizational subunits (departments). One important aspect of this synchronization is coordinating the efforts of employees who have their own individual values and goals. In general, the systems approach provides managers with a way of looking at an entire organization by putting emphasis on the objectives and interrelationships among units.

For organizational purposes, it is useful to think of objectives as the results people desire to achieve within a specified time period. Objectives result from the planning process and must take changing environmental and internal factors into consideration. The reasons for carefully formulating objectives are that they serve as the directional targets around which activities are coordinated and as the basis for evaluating the effectiveness of employee performance.

No single objective is sufficient for describing the goals of all members who participate in an organization. By having multiple goals, however, conflict among interdependent units can lead to suboptimization.

Within an organization, the process of assigning a portion of the major goals to a particular unit and then subdividing the assignment among small units and finally to individuals creates a hierarchy of objectives. This array of subgoals may be thought of in terms of a means-end relationship. In this way, the goals of each subunit contribute to the goals of the larger unit with which it is associated. Conflicts among goals within the organizational hierarchy can also result in suboptimization.

The question of profit as a goal is not completely settled. We concluded, however, that it is one of the many goals of a business organization and cannot be considered out of context with the service that a company provides.

Due to the changing nature of the environment, managers must be aware of the need to change priorities among goals as well as the need to formulate them on a systematic schedule. Problems associated with organizational objectives include ambiguity, a lack of communication, misunderstanding, and an improper integration or balance among goals. Furthermore, problems often arise because some goals do not lend themselves to measurement. The more concrete and specific goals can be, the more likely they are to be directive, serving as targets around which all people can integrate job accomplishment.

KEY TERMS

Hierarchy of objectives: An array of objectives where the achievement of each subobjective contributes to the achievement of an immediately higher and more comprehensive objective.

Multiple objectives: The concept that organizations have many objectives and that no one objective is of overriding importance at all times.

Objectives: The targets people seek to achieve over various periods of time, thereby providing direction to current effort and future actions.

Open system: An entity, such as an organization that interacts with its environment in the form of exchanging information, drawing upon resources, and providing goods and services.

Organization: A collection of people in pursuit of a common purpose characterized by a division of labor and a hierarchy of authority.

Suboptimization of objectives: Some lesser degree of achievement of a set of objectives resulting from an attempt to attain the best possible achievement of related objectives.

System: A coordinated collection of interrelated parts designed for the purpose of achieving a specific objective(s).

Systems theory: An analytical approach used in understanding an organization's behavior by considering its goals, basic elements of input-process-output, relationship to the larger environment in which it must adapt, and control procedures.

QUESTIONS

1. What is the meaning of an organization?
2. Why is management necessary within an organization?
3. How would you define a system?
4. Note the characteristics of a system.
5. Why is it essential to consider an organization as an open system?
6. What is the relationship between planning and objectives?
7. Discuss the concept of means-end analysis.
8. What is the meaning of multiple objectives?
9. In determining a priority among objectives, is the most important objective service or profit?
10. What value do schemes for classifying objectives have in management?
11. List the practical managerial problems in dealing with objectives.

PROBLEMS

1. Groups are assemblages of individuals who have a relationship to one another, placing them into common classifications of a crowd or a social party. These types of groups are short-lived, have an undefined structure, and have little or no managerial coordination of responsibilities. Based on this information is it adequate to believe that groups and organizations are synonymous terms? Discuss.

2. During the scientific management era, the investigative process by managers was to break a phenomenon down into its parts and then attempt to understand each part. This approach is commonly referred to as "atomistic" research. Systems theory, however, is holistic in nature, assuming the complex interactions among the parts. Thus, systems have to be studied and understood as total units. Based on the above comments, indicate the approach that best fits each of the following statements:

a. The whole is more than the sum of its parts.
b. The whole is the sum of its parts.

3. A few years ago, "hula hoops" were a highly demanded novelty product. Some producers, however, found themselves without a market since this type of product had a short life span.

From the standpoint of the organization's environment (consumer behavioral patterns) and appropriate reaction by the organization, discuss why being highly efficient (being productive) is insufficient to ensure a company's long-run survival.

4. Objectives have been developed by three different middle-level managers of a wholesale company. The objectives are:

"Our company seeks to make a good profit."

"Our objective is to make $5 million profit in the next five years."

"Our objective is to achieve a growth rate in earnings sufficient to be in the top 25 percent of all companies in the industry."

Which objective is *(a)* the least concrete and specific, *(b)* the most measureable, and *(c)* the least timeless in providing a continuous challenge for managers?

5. A relatively new Philadelphia-based optical company with several stores called For Eyes has gained a reputation for selling single-vision glasses for $29 complete. ("Complete" includes choice of top-quality frames and lenses—photochromatic, plastic, or tinted.) One of the owners, David Goldberg, says that the company's philosophy is that "money is not the only thing" and that the secret of success is "we just don't make a lot of money."

State what you feel are the objectives of the company? With profits having such a low profile, do you feel the company has much of a chance for long-run survival?

6. Frederick W. Taylor in his *Scientific Management,* states that it is self-evident that maximum prosperity for the employer and the employee should be two leading objectives of management. What management concept does Taylor have reference to and can Taylor's position be applicable to business enterprises today?

7. John Purdine is president of Purdine Brick and Steel Company. Recently, he spoke to the Business Club members at a local junior college where he commented that he was in business to maximize profits. Furthermore, he stated, "I will never make a decision to do anything that will not produce a maximum profit." Discuss.

8. When Logan T. Johnson took over the reins of Armco Steel Corporation, he initiated two major actions:

a. Reorganized the sales territories of some units and closed one major plant while consolidating others.
b. Ordered major changes in things from the company's trademark to the decor of the reception room.

In another situation, Karl Benetsen took the following action as president of Champion Papers:

a. Trimmed spending to improve profits.
b. Eliminated company planes and Cadillacs.
c. Cut employment by 1,800.

If one argues that a company's objectives are to serve the interests of customers by providing sound products at reasonable prices, how would you explain the actions of Johnson and Benetsen? Shouldn't they have thought first of how to serve customers better while maintaining current employment levels and payrolls?

9. In his book, *An Inquiry into the Nature and Causes of the Wealth of Nations*, the famous economist, Adam Smith, states that "consumption is the sole purpose of all production, and the interest of the producer ought to be attended to, only so far as it may be necessary for promoting that of the consumer." Smith's comments were published in 1776. What relevance do they have in our modern industrial society?

10. A hospital may be referred to as a health restoration system. What are some subsystems that are integral parts of the hospital? Describe a situation in which the hospital is viewed as a subsystem of an even larger system.

SUGGESTED READINGS

Albanese, R. *Managing: Toward Accountability for Performance*. Rev. ed. Homewood, Ill.: Richard D. Irwin, 1978, Chap. 2.

Bowers, D. *Systems of Organization*. Ann Arbor: University of Michigan Press, 1976.

Edmonds, C. P., III, and J. H. Hand. "What Are Real Long-Run Objectives of Business?" *Business Horizons*, December 1976, pp. 77.

Latham, G. P., and J. J. Baldes. "The 'Practical Significance' of Locke's Theory of Goal Setting," in *The Applied Psychology of Work Behavior: A Book of Readings*, edited by D. W. Organ. Plano, Tex.: Business Publications, 1978, pp. 285–90.

Mintzberg, H. *The Structuring of Organizations: A Synthesis of Research*. Englewood Cliffs, N.J.: Prentice-Hall, 1979.

Raia, A. P. *Managing by Objectives*. Glenview, Ill.: Scott, Foresman, 1974.

Rousseau, D. M. "Assessment of Technology in Organizations: Closed versus Open Systems Approaches." *The Academy of Management Review*, October 1979, pp. 531–42.

Schoderbek, C. G.; P. P. Schoderbek; and A. G. Kefalas. *Management Systems: Conceptual Considerations*. Plano, Tex.: Business Publications, 1980.

Sherwin, D. S. "Management by Objectives." *Harvard Business Review*, May–June 1976, pp. 149–60.

Terborg, J. R. "The Motivational Components of Goal Setting." *Journal of Applied Psychology*, October 1976, pp. 613–21.

Tolchinsky, P. D., and D. C. King. "Do Goals Mediate the Effects of Incentives on Performance." *The Academy of Management Review*, July 1980, pp. 455–67.

Viola, R. H. *Organizations in a Changing Society: Administration and Human Values*. Philadelphia: W. B. Saunders, 1977.

9

THE FORMAL
ORGANIZATION

PURPOSE

Although advice from a feng-shui expert may not be considered an essential part of a formal organization in the United States, it is almost mandatory in Hong Kong. Feng-shui is a centuries-old, complicated belief in the selection of grave and building sites according to how they face the wind (feng) and water (shui) to harness good spirits. Many Western business firms operating in the British colony often seek secretly and sheepishly (some openly) advice from feng-shui experts in tackling professional and even personal problems. Consider Chase Asia Ltd. (Chase Manhattan's merchant banking arm) that was having a run of bad luck. The bank had lost some major banking deals, and a senior executive had died in an airplane crash. Since the bank building was not consecrated, the feng-shui expert found two trouble spots—one in the office of the executive director and another in the office of a department manager. In the director's office, daily fresh red flowers are necessary on the desk to chase away devils. In the other office, goldfish are required. Although the fish keep dying, they are supposed to in order to keep the devils busy.

While the director now feels the extreme success of the company is highly coincidental to the feng-shui expert's advice, the practice of keeping fresh flowers and live fish in the offices is maintained. Even Dow Chemical used an expert to choose the day for the opening of a new plant. On that day, the dignitaries were all soaked from a downpour. The rain signified that "the money can't wait to pour down on the firm." Would you believe that the venture has been successful beyond the company's expectations? Regardless of our feelings about such advice, structuring and designing the formal organization in Hong Kong depends upon a feng-shui expert, possibly more so than an organizational consultant.

This chapter does not rely on the advice of feng-shui experts but seeks to develop an understanding of organizing, the rise of complex organizational structures, the meaning of bureaucracy, and the roles of authority and responsibility within formal organizational structures.

OBJECTIVES

1. To discuss formal organizations as planned patterns of authority relationships.

2. To identify the contributions of classical management theorists to organizational design and maintenance.

3. To develop an understanding of organizations as bureaucracies.

4. To examine the nature of authority within organizations.

5. To distinguish between authority and responsibility in the modern organization.

Studying the formal organization structure deserves our personal attention since most of us are already members of various organized groups and, if not now, will in the future be involved in some phase of managing them. The term *formal organization* is used here in the sense that the patterns of work and personal relationships are deliberately set up and officially recognized. Through this process (organizing), managers seek to define the work of different people and to attain a degree of order and coordination in the achievement of goals. At the same time, individuals are better able to communicate and work efficiently since they know where they fit within the organization, to whom they are responsible, and what jobs they must perform. To this extent, organizing produces a synergistic effect—that is, a structure that coordinates independent variables so as to produce an effect greater than the sum of the individual parts.

THE ORGANIZING WORK OF MANAGERS

Although organizing is but one of the functions in the management process, it is important in determining how problems will be prevented or solved in order to reduce the inevitable conflicts that arise when people work together in pursuit of goals. Also, since managers organize all types of enterprises and institutions, their responsibility is to design organizational settings that are conducive to the satisfaction of individual needs and the realization of managerial goals.

In order to understand better how the organizing process results in different organizational designs, we will first examine the foundational framework presented by the classical theorists Henri Fayol and F. W. Taylor. Each of these management practitioners set forth basic guidelines for the design and maintenance of large-scale organizations. At the same time, both realized that structure is only a starting point for the effective and efficient accomplishment of organizational goals.

Henri Fayol identified 16 principles inherent in the organizing function. Assisting in the identification, dividing, and grouping of work, these principles are:[1]

1. Judiciously prepare and execute the operating plan.
2. Organize the human and material facts so that they are consistent with objectives, resources, and requirements of the concern.
3. Establish a single, competent, energetic, guiding authority (formal management structure).
4. Coordinate all activities and efforts.
5. Formulate clear, distinct, and precise decisions.
6. Arrange for efficient selection so that each department is headed by a competent, energetic manager and employees are placed where they can render the greatest service.

---

[1] Henri Fayol, *General and Industrial Management* (London: Sir Isaac Pitman and Sons, 1949), pp. 53–54.

7. Define duties.
8. Encourage initiative and responsibility.
9. Have fair and suitable rewards for services rendered.
10. Make use of sanctions against faults and errors.
11. Maintain discipline.
12. Ensure that individual interests are consistent with general interests of the organization.
13. Recognize the unity of command.
14. Promote both material and human coordination.
15. Institute and effect controls.
16. Avoid regulations, red tape, and paper work.

F. W. Taylor considered the art of management as the molding of relationships between managers and workers.[2] As to the test of a good manager, he mentioned that success depends on the degree to which the satisfaction of both employer and employees is achieved. Furthermore, Taylor implied that satisfaction depends on an organizational structure having a division of work based upon functional specialization, capable employees hired for specific positions, and effective coordination of all functions. In this way, organizing becomes a means for achieving greater efficiency by reducing costs. Yet, Taylor was aware of the difficulty in getting managers to recognize and implement something so intangible as the organizing process. To overcome this problem, he identified the following principles of scientific management for managers:[3]

1. Each element of work is to be analyzed scientifically instead of using a rule of thumb approach.
2. Workers should be scientifically selected, trained, and developed for positions for which they are best suited, rather than letting them select their own work and utilize their own methods in performing jobs.
3. Cooperation should be encouraged between managers who plan the work and those who perform the work to ensure that all activities are carried out in accordance with developed scientific principles.
4. Responsibility of the work must be shared and assumed appropriately between those who plan the work and those who perform it.

Fayol's 16 principles on organizing are quite similar to the aforementioned principles of scientific management set forth by Taylor. Their

---

[2] Frederick W. Taylor, "Shop Management," in *Scientific Management* (New York: Harper & Row, 1947), p. 21. Copyright 1947 by Harper & Row, Publishers, Inc.

[3] Frederick W. Taylor, "The Principles of Scientific Management," in *Scientific Management* (New York: Harper & Row, 1947), pp. 36–37. Copyright 1947 by Harper & Row, Publishers, Inc.

ideas indicate the need to arrange material resources, processes, and people into a structural hierarchy that is more or less permanent. This structure, in turn, provides a starting point for accomplishing organizational objectives.

Both Fayol and Taylor established a foundation for organizing that is still appropriate. While their approach is fairly mechanistic, it remains useful in studying organizations and their operations. Thus, contemporary thought on organizational design does not disregard the work of these two men, but instead, builds on their concepts with findings from the behavioral sciences (psychology, sociology, social psychology, and anthropology). As a result, the following steps are included in most current discussions of the organizing process:

1. *Know the objectives for which one is organizing.* Objectives indicate the type of work to be accomplished, activities to be performed, and the level of technology required.
2. *Divide the work into various activities* to obtain the advantages of specialization of labor. Jobs, however, should provide meaningful work and integrate the responsibility and control aspects of the job. Formalization of jobs should not be so rigid that job flexibility and adaptability are restricted.
3. *Combine the activities into logical units or departments* based upon the technology and tasks to be performed. Membership of units may represent task force arrangements that shift as needs and problems change. The combining arrangement must be consistent with employee needs, personalities, abilities, and interests.
4. *Determine who is to perform the activities* based upon the qualifications and capabilities of the personnel.
5. *Provide an appropriate work place and proper facilities* with which to do the work.
6. *Delegate adequate authority and clarify responsibilities* of each person so that relationships among personnel are understood by all. Communication networks should be used to emphasize consultative relationships rather than overemphasizing command.

These steps indicate the importance of understanding various technical and behavioral factors before deciding how an organization should be designed. More specifically, consideration must be given to the technical makeup of jobs, how managers and subordinates are to perform them, and the need to cope with changing environments. However, putting the right people in the right places to carry out assignments often seems to be an impossible task. After all, what a person seeks from the job may not be consistent with what the job has to offer. Yet, regardless of this difficulty, organizing is necessary if people and jobs are to be combined into a meaningful totality.

FROM SIMPLE TO COMPLEX ORGANIZATIONS

An organizational structure is not determined solely by the number of employees; however, there is a direct relationship. For example, the formal organization portrayed in Figure 9–1 shows four people *(A, B, C, D)*. These individuals are linked together horizontally and are responsible to a group leader and manager. The manager, in turn, coordinates and directs the work of these individuals toward the achievement of organizational goals.

As the organization requires more material and human resources, it may expand on a horizontal basis. If the organization, for example, is a manufacturing concern, new employees are generally made responsible for increased work loads in the areas of production and marketing. In a small owner-manager manufacturing company, the production function often represents the most logical area for expansion. Such expansion continues as long as the manager is able to perform all of the management tasks required in coordinating the work of more subordinates.

In all organizations a point in growth is reached where the manager will have to delegate management authority to one or more subordinates, as shown in Figure 9–2. When this occurs a vertical hierarchy of authority is created. Since coordination now becomes more specialized, we find the emergence of a more complex organization.

The vertical expansion of an organization continues as long as the work load keeps increasing and the complexity of activities expands. There is, however, a limit to the number of organizational levels that are feasible for efficient communication, coordination, and an integration of efforts. Consequently, the organization may return to a horizontal expansion with the creation of various staff specialists, such as an office manager, personnel manager, production planner, and controller.

If the number of employees continues to increase, additional managerial roles are created, both horizontally and vertically, to provide coordination between groups of workers and managers. The larger and more sophisticated the management hierarchy, the more complex

FIGURE 9–1
Simple organization structure

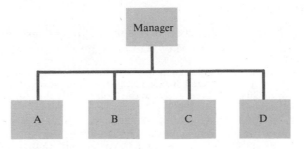

FIGURE 9–2
Complex organization reflecting two levels of management

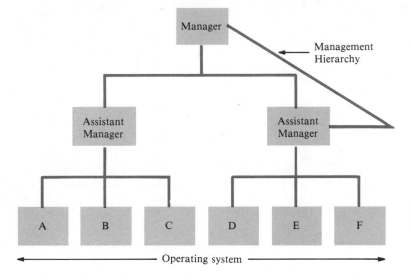

the organization becomes. To overcome any dysfunctional consequences associated with complexity, organizational structures must be evaluated continually in light of changing jobs, environmental influences, and authority relationships. In this sense, management must seek to maintain a structure within which people work because they want to, not because they feel they must.

THE FORMAL ORGANIZATION

The formal organization is basically a goal-oriented entity that exists to accommodate the efforts of individuals and groups. Being formal, it prescribes authority relationships among jobs, outlines the chain of command, and specifies policies and procedures in coordinating activities. In addition, the design of a formal structure is based on the assumption that rationality will lead to an efficient accomplishment of organizational goals. This rationality is considered to be so clearly identifiable that it can be depicted in an organization chart, such as the one noted in Figure 9–3.[4]

Max Weber and bureaucracy

Much of the classical theory of formal organizations can be found in the writings of Max Weber, who lived from 1864 to 1920.[5] Weber

---

[4] A practical modification to the chart is to assign quantitative values to each unit that are then reflected in proportionate sized boxes. See Ronald Fraser, "Q-Charts: How to Give New Perspective to the Organizational Perspective," *Management Review,* December 1979, pp. 28ff.

[5] See *The Theory of Social and Economic Organization,* trans. A. R. Henderson and Tolcott Parsons (London: William Hodge, 1947); and *From Max Weber: Essays in Sociology,* ed. and trans. H. H. Gerth and C. Wright Mills. Copyright 1946, by Oxford University Press, Inc. Renewed 1973 by Dr. Hans H. Gerth.

FIGURE 9–3
Organization chart for an electrical company

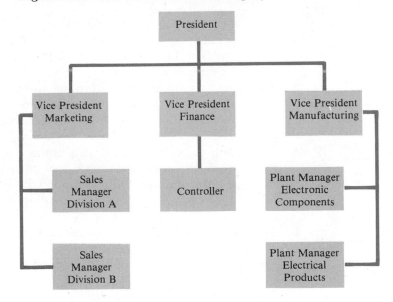

was a German sociologist who presented the first comprehensive theory of bureaucratic organizations. Actually, Weber used the term bureaucracy, rather than organization, with the intent of denoting the ideal arrangement for a formalized structure. In his view, the more formal an organization could become in terms of specifying job assignments, points of coordination, controlling techniques, and plans, the more efficient the organization would be in achieving its goals. Thus, he saw the design and structure of an organization as all important in accomplishing managerial tasks. The ideal bureaucratic structure formulated by Weber, however, did not imply the most desirable arrangement for all organizations. Instead, his intent was to develop a pure, theoretical model that could be utilized as organizations grew larger.

Before examining Weber's formal organization design, some comments about the word bureaucracy should be noted. The term bureaucracy generally has a bad connotation since it is often used when referring to administrative red tape and inefficiency. This is unfortunate, as the bureaucratic structure (the formal organization) is a highly efficient structure in many organizations. In fact, most organizations have some aspects of bureaucracy, although no organization is completely bureaucratic. Certain operational areas within any organization are more bureaucratic than others; and as conditions change, the degree of bureaucracy varies. Consequently, one should not think of an organization as being either bureaucratic or nonbureaucratic. Instead, most organizations should be viewed as falling at various points on a continuum between these two extremes.

Weber noted six characteristics of the large organization with permanent, fixed authority:

1. Specific activities and duties (division of labor) are specified along with the means to achieve them. The extent of authority is delimited by rules and regulations, and each office has a clearly defined sphere of responsibility.
2. A chain of command (hierarchy of authority) exists to promote informational and decisional flows within the organization in the fulfillment of duties. Each lower office is subject to the authority of a higher one.
3. Ownership of private wealth of the manager should be separate from that of the organization. (Today this point has been emphasized in governmental organizations where the official is not to have any vested interest in firms dealing with the governmental unit.)
4. Management is distinct from other types of activities, and managerial training and skills are essential for success. Managers should be selected for their qualifications, knowledge, and technical competence.
5. Management is a full-time activity of those responsible for achieving goals. Promotion of those in office should be based on seniority, achievement, or both—not whim and favoritism.
6. Managers follow specific rules that are applied uniformly and unemotionally in order to regulate each case fairly.

Weber felt that a bureaucratic structure with these characteristics would be technically superior to any other design; and by using them as guides, the advantages of functional specialization would permit complex tasks to be coordinated more simply. Also, with duties and procedures defined, personnel decisions could be based on job-related qualifications, rather than on friendships and personal loyalties. If an employee left an organization, the vacant job would not have to be analyzed. Instead, the manager would merely employ and train another person to fit the standardized position. To this extent, strict rules, disciplinary measures, and controls would outline expected behavior by specifying how various jobs would be performed.[6]

The role of people in the bureaucracy

A criticism often directed to Weber's bureaucratic organization is that it operates according to specific plans without much regard for people. Most of us are familiar with the statement: "Returned goods cannot be accepted without a sales receipt." Specific directives of this type minimize the personal discretion and decision-making authority that can be exercised by an employee. In these instances, a person's

---

[6] See H. H. Gerth and C. W. Mills, eds. and trans. *From Max Weber: Essays in Sociology* (New York: Oxford University Press, 1946), p. 298.

performance level is based on how well specific rules are followed, not on the development of analytical problem-solving skills.

Weber saw rational thought and logic as the building blocks of the formal organization. By requiring people to perform their jobs rationally and exactly as specified, the organization would be structured to eliminate unpredictable, emotional, and irrational behavior. Bureaucracy, therefore, would encourage more impersonal decision making at lower management levels. Weber did not consider such dehumanization a weak point. Rather, he considered it an attribute since employees would have to be objective and rational if goals were to be achieved effectively. Possibly in Weber's day he was correct; however, in dealing with the complexities and multiple competing demands of today's organizations, decision making cannot be totally rational. Without pretense, then, the organization's structure is quite unlikely to be the master tool that can singularly achieve organizational effectiveness.[7] Managers must recognize, therefore, that organizations adapt very slowly and are not highly rational. In this sense, it is not the structure that changes to meet dynamic forces, but the capabilities of people to respond flexibly and rapidly to an unstable business environment. Because of the human element, even Weber did not feel his ideal organization was completely desirable since, as Bendix states, "it could truncate the soul of mankind."[8]

It is also evident that Weber's bureaucratic model did not recognize the more nebulous informal organization as it exists within the formal structure. For example, personal relationships, activities, functions, and other areas not specified and prescribed by formal authority were not considered. In reality, the informal organization exists, even though it is not designated within the formal hierarchy. Informal organizations develop because the formal structure is not perceived as capable nor willing to satisfy completely the needs of individuals and groups who work within the formal structure. (See Chapter 12 for further discussion of the informal organization.)

A final point referred to by Weber is that the bureaucratic organization has a certain degree of permanency built within it. As evident today, this type of social structure exhibits both a high degree of permanence and resistance to change. These characteristics stem from the fact that the formal organization includes not only people who often resist change but also a complex system of fixed policies, procedures, programs, and decision-making systems. Contemporary research has indicated that when organizational emphasis is based strictly on control and stability, flexibility is reduced and organizational behavior is not conducive to innovative thinking and planning. A summary comparison

---

[7] R. H. Waterman, Jr., T. J. Peters, and J. R. Phillips, "Structure is not Organization," *Business Horizons,* June 1980, pp. 14–26.

[8] Reinhard Bendix, *Max Weber: An Intellectual Portrait* (Garden City, N.J.: Doubleday, 1960), pp. 455–56.

FIGURE 9–4
Bureaucratic versus nonbureaucratic characteristics

Bureaucratic	Nonbureaucratic
1. Extensive division of work	1. Less job specialization
2. Hierarchy of authority	2. Greater extent of personal interaction
3. Specified managerial plans to govern functions	3. Employees participate in determining best way to perform functions
4. Impersonal behavior	4. High degree of interpersonal relationships
5. Personnel selected on their qualifications	5. Personnel selected on preference of manager
6. Knowledge of specific job requirements	6. Knowledge of job no more than understanding objectives

of bureaucratic and nonbureaucratic characteristics is shown in Figure 9–4.

In summary, Weber felt that the bureaucratic mechanism was the best structure to help an organization survive. Theoretically, the formal organization with its myriad of trained management specialists would satisfy the needs of goal selection, coordination, and the maintenance of required individual and group behavior. With these problems solved, managers could then focus their talents on any unusual problems with maximum efficiency and speed. In spite of these purported benefits, bureaucracy is not without its limitations. As noted above and discussed more fully in later chapters, a complete reliance on bureaucracy can result in disorder, inefficiency, personal conflict, and job monotony.

BASIC ORGANIZING CONCEPTS

To further an understanding of the formal organization and some of its challenges, certain classical concepts need to be recognized at this point—authority, responsibility, specialization of labor, departmentation, unity of command, and span of control. Together these concepts are essential building blocks of the formal organization and serve to prevent or overcome various organizational problems.

Authority and responsibility are necessary in determining the intended relationships between the vertical and horizontal dimensions of an organization's structure. The *vertical dimension* reflects the ranking of jobs in terms of their scope of authority, which is referred to as the chain of command or the hierarchy of authority. The hierarchy specifies the lines of formal authority, responsibility, communication, and decision making that exist within the organization. On the other hand, the *horizontal dimension* of an organization relates to the specific duties or activities that are found at each level of authority.

The *specialization of labor* relates to determining a division of work (labor) between each job. After all required duties are designated, *departmentation* takes place to determine how various jobs should be grouped together. Thus, a specialization of labor and subsequent departmentation will ultimately affect the functional relationships between all positions and individuals within the structure.

Unity of command addresses the problem of overlapping authority exercised by individual managers. Thus, if a subordinate receives orders in the same area from two superiors, authority and discipline are more likely to break down. A related concept that considers the number of subordinates who should report to a given manager is referred to as the *span of control.*

The remaining sections of this chapter will focus on authority and responsibility. Each of the other concepts will be discussed in the following two chapters.

THE NATURE OF AUTHORITY

Authority is one of the most fundamental, yet misunderstood, concepts of modern management theory. In spite of misunderstandings, however, people can only work together effectively when their efforts are coordinated and interrelated through authority. In this sense, authority is the cornerstone that gives legitimacy to the performance of all organizational activities. Furthermore, no organization can be directed toward an achievement of objectives without a clear definition of authority relationships.

Within a managerial context, authority is defined as (1) *the right to direct others* (emphasizing the superior-subordinate relationship) and (2) *the permission to act* (relating to permission to perform specific duties). Note that this definition emphasizes the idea that authority must include two elements—people and duties (specific areas of involvement).

Some management theorists suggest that authority should be viewed as separate and distinct from duties. This argument states that various duties must first be assigned to employees. Then, authority is delegated for the accomplishment of those duties. By including permission to perform specified duties as a part of our definition of authority, we are not limited to this kind of logic. In fact, from a practical point of view, it is impossible to assign a job without delegating the authoritative right to perform specific duties associated with it. For example, a salesperson would not be assigned to call on customers, take orders, or commit the company to a delivery date unless there was a simultaneous delegation of authority to carry out such activities. Thus, a meaningful definition of authority must include mention of tasks to be performed as well as any specific right to direct others.

Authority is the cohesive element of an organization that promotes coordination of group behavior. Clearly, voluntary cooperation among people is not sufficient by itself. The necessity of authority is seen in situations of conflict, such as a disagreement over the acquisition of new equipment. In this instance, someone in a higher position of authority is often required to settle the disagreement by either moderating a solution or resolving the situation with a managerial directive.

In recent years, it appears that a negative bias has been developing against the exercise of authority, Yet, this does not deny the necessity and importance of authority. The survival of any organization is based on the ability to maintain an authority structure. Consequently, a breakdown of authority will, in most cases, result in a breakdown of the organization itself. When this happens a new organization may form, although it, too, must be based on an established authority structure. Most of us can recall examples of the overthrow of governments in various countries where the new governing body often developed a more rigid structure of authority than that which had existed before. Furthermore, this authority is supported by a formalized, legal system as well as by the informal social norms of various groups within the society.

Sources of authority

Discussions concerning the source(s) of authority are influenced by various theories. Three such theories are suggested here. The more traditional of these is referred to as the formal theory of authority, while the acceptance and situational theories are of more recent origin.[9]

Formal theory   The formal theory views authority as flowing downward through an organization. In a manufacturing corporation, a supervisor receives authority from the plant manager who, in turn, has been delegated authority from the chief executive officer and/or president. The chief executive officer is granted authority by the board of directors who obtains its authority through *the right to hold and manage private property.* Under this theory, the delegation of authority downward must be consistent with the attitudes and value systems of society.

From a historical viewpoint, the right of private property is based on the divine right of kings concept where the master-servant relationship was rigidly followed. Today we realize the right of private property is no longer an absolute right but is bestowed on the owners of property by society and is modified as society demands. If society demands that owners not discriminate as to customers and employees, then these organizational practices must be modified to fit the desires of society. The other alternative is for owners to divest themselves of their property if they do not agree with the modifications desired by society.

Acceptance theory   The acceptance theory of authority was developed by Chester I. Barnard who was an executive in the telephone

---

[9] For an additional discussion of the relationships among various theories of authority, see David D. VanFleet, "The Need Hierarchy and Theories of Authority," *Human Relations,* 1973, pp. 567–80.

industry. Barnard felt that the formal theory of authority was not entirely consistent with what he saw in industry. Thus, he advocated the belief that the acceptance of an order by subordinates represents the true source of authority. According to Barnard, four requirements must be met before a message will be accepted as authoritative:[10]

It must be understood by the recipient.

It must be consistent with the purpose of the organization.

It must be compatible with the personal interests of the recipient.

It must be within the mental and physical abilities of the recipient to comply.

Various scholars suggest that the acceptance theory of authority is misleading. Krupp, for instance, points out that authority based solely on acceptance and consent can cause managers to manipulate conditions and premises so that such acceptance is forthcoming.[11] In other words, attempts can be made to change the value system of the recipient or inculcation can be undertaken to condition the recipient to accept an order. Thus, in a circumscribed manner, we are back to the formal theory where the establishment of rules and regulations (conditions and premises) is a right of the owners of property.

From a practical viewpoint, the formal and acceptance theories are interrelated and both are essential to an understanding of authority. Neither one stands by itself as a complete explanation of the source of authority. By stating the definition of authority as *the permission to act,* the formal theory contributes to our understanding; and, when viewed as *the right to direct others,* the acceptance theory adds another important dimension to the total concept of authority.

Situational theory   This theory of authority was suggested by Mary Parker Follett, a most interesting contributor to management thought. As a social worker and philosopher, she set forth various management principles that relate to organizational behavior while contributing to a better understanding of the source of authority.[12] Follett viewed authority as being offensive to individuals, creating a false unity, and encouraging conflict. Consequently, she felt that authority could not be vested in a superior since this would only result in a position of dominance and power, thereby reducing coordination and a unification of effort. In this context, Follett stated that one person "should not give orders to another person, but both should agree to take their

---

[10] Chester I. Barnard, *The Functions of the Executive* (Cambridge, Mass.: Harvard University Press, 1938), p. 163. See also Herbert A. Simon, *Administrative Behavior,* 2d ed. (New York: Macmillan, 1958), pp. 11, 125–34.

[11] Sherman Krupp, *Pattern in Organization Analysis: A Critical Examination* (New York: Holt, Rinehart, & Winston, 1961), pp. 101–5.

[12] See Mary Parker Follett, *Dynamic Administration,* ed. Henry Metcalf and Lyndall Urwick (New York: Harper & Row, 1942), which is a presentation of a series of her papers.

orders from the situation."[13] This, then, is referred to as *the law of the situation* where the ultimate source of authority rests with the will and consent of all people in an organization.

Additionally, Follett may have been one of our first systems analysts since she was very interested in studying the interrelationships between individual parts and the total organization. For example, she felt that unity is accomplished through integration, including the activities of communication, coordination, and a synthesis of goals, values, and behaviors found in the subparts of an organization. Here Follett used the term *integration* to imply an approach to problem solving where all parties would benefit equally. None would win and none would have to sacrifice or lose, as in situations of dominance or compromise.

Even though Mary Parker Follett felt that personal authority creates an imbalance because one person has dominance and power over others, we should not think of the authority hierarchy as being synonymous with power. In fact, from a managerial viewpoint, it is probably more meaningful to view authority as a coordinating and integrating flow process within an organization, rather than the ability of one person to influence others.[14]

Compliance with authority

An understanding of the source and nature of authority does not explain why people comply with orders or directives. In seeking the reasons for compliance, the phenomenon of power, however, becomes apparent. In this sense, power implies that one individual has the ability to influence the behavior of others. In the following discussion of the reasons for compliance, consideration is given to those elements associated with power, rather than suggesting only the power phenomenon of one person over another.

Sanctions This category refers to the ability of an individual to reward or withhold rewards. Positive reinforcements (rewards) emphasize a satisfaction of individual goals through contributions to organizational objectives. In this respect, rewards offered by an organization must be consistent with employee needs if people are to comply with organizational expectations. Negative connotations of sanctions imply the use of punishment. Punishment may be effective in the short run, but it produces negative results when used on a continuing basis. Lower levels of performance and antagonism toward the organization (a lack of compliance) are especially noticeable if negative rewards are used continuously.

Personal characteristics Personal characteristics, such as knowledge, skills, roles, status, and various environmental aspects, are very

---

[13] Ibid., p. 58.

[14] A review of the literature will show there is not complete agreement on this point. Herbert A. Simon, for example, defines authority as "the power to make decisions which guide the actions of another."

important in gaining compliance. When subordinates have confidence and trust in their superior, they are more likely to comply with authority. Max Weber implied that managers with this kind of power would be technically competent, exercising influence on the basis of knowledge and ability. Personal characteristics, however, do not represent an absolute element. If a particular area of knowledge is no longer important due to technological changes or political events, the degree of influence will be lessened as well as the willingness of subordinates to comply. In such cases, either a new manager will be selected or the original manager will have to develop those new abilities which are viewed as important by subordinates.

Heritage   Many factors cause us to obey those in positions of authority. There are many instances where people are taught by the family unit or other institutions to obey those who have legitimate (socially acceptable) authority. Parents teach their children to comply with orders from police officers, teachers, and employers. Of course, a manager cannot assume that all individuals accept these tenets. Regardless, heritage will always be influential in shaping superior-subordinate relationships.

Group pressure   Peer groups can influence their members to comply with managerial authority if directives are consistent with group norms and standards. Likewise, when group standards are not congruent with organizational goals, peer pressure will have little influence on the goal-seeking behavior of employees.

Persuasion and propaganda   Through a constant repetition of orders coupled with reasons for their necessity, some followers will eventually comply with the directives of a superior. Persuasion is one method for propagating authority and gaining acceptance of that authority by others. Of course, the art of persuasion is a study area in itself and one can see many examples, ranging from campaigning politicians to Fifth Avenue advertising.

In actuality, compliance is based on all of the elements noted above with the importance of each depending on the factors of a given situation. In combination, these factors affect the organization's structure, the style of leadership, the nature of commands, and the objectives and policies that, in turn, influence the structural attributes and established authority relationships within an organization.

RESPONSIBILITY

Any discussion of authority also raises questions concerning the meaning of responsibility. From a managerial viewpoint, responsibility has two interpretations: (1) an obligation and (2) adherence to a moral code.

Obligation

Responsibility can be defined as an obligation to carry out assigned duties within the limits of delegated authority. In this sense, responsi-

FIGURE 9–5
Authority and responsibility

Authority (from and to)	*Responsibility (to and for)*
1. Right to direct (people)	1. Personal commitment of subordinate to superior
2. Permission to act (duties)	2. Shared obligation for carrying out authority in achieving organizational goals

bility becomes a personal commitment on the part of the subordinate to a superior, and it is created when a subordinate accepts the authority to perform specified duties.

Responsibility, however, should be viewed in a broader context than just the personal commitment of an individual. As overall organizational goals are divided into subgoals, they become the responsibility of each individual in the hierarchical structure. Consequently, each unit and position within the hierarchy shares to some extent in the overall accomplishment of objectives. The point is that employees not only have personal commitments (obligations) to carry out their specific duties, but also share an obligation to achieve overall organizational objectives. A professor, for example, is responsible for a specific teaching assignment and also shares with the president, vice presidents, deans, department heads, and other faculty members a responsibility for the achievement of overall university goals. A review of the meanings attached to authority and responsibility are shown in Figure 9–5.

Based on this discussion, authority and responsibility would seem to be commensurate since an obligation is created simultaneously with the acceptance of the delegated authority.[15] Many contemporary situations in management reflect a disparity between delegated authority and responsibility, however. One interesting disparity may be seen in executive techniques used to discharge managers. By delegating authority to do a job that is impossible to achieve, the superior sets up an almost sure-fire way to induce the subordinate to resign. Of course, the opposite approach can also be effective in firing. Here, the manager is assigned to a position that is meaningless; thus, there is authority to do something, but virtually no responsibilities are associated with the position. Most individuals in these situations soon realize that they are being forced out of the organization.

Another example of a disparity between authority and responsibility may be found in organizational environments that have participatory or "bargaining" units. Here, responsibility may purposefully exceed

---

[15] Viewed in a different way, if authority is less than the scope of responsibility, then responsibility will shrink until it is within the limits of authority. In the long run, one cannot be accountable for more than the limits of authority.

authority. In other situations, a manager may be responsible for keeping production on schedule but does not have the authority to prevent a strike nor to direct that raw materials be delivered by a certain date. Reversing the order, situations can also be observed where authority appears to exceed responsibility.

Major disparities between authority and responsibility do not last long since vacuums cannot exist in an organization for any lengthy period of time. If responsibility or authority is not being fully accepted by a particular person, someone else within the organization will step in to assume it. As Barnard has noted, authority is often missing even though managers are held responsible; but the good, promising executive knows how to get results without possessing formal authority.

Barnard also indicated that the best managers are those who are not content with delegated authority and assigned responsibilities and, therefore, continually seek to add to them. Perhaps this attitude is exemplified by Lee A. Iacocca, past president of Ford Motor Company. Iacocca's drive to accept additional authority and responsibility is reflected in the story of how, in his early years with Ford, he recorded on a copy of the corporate organization chart the positions to which he aspired and the dates by which he expected to have advanced to these positions. He set the target of being a vice president by the age of 35, a deadline he missed by only two days. After being exposed to a wide range of responsibilities by Robert McNamara, a former president of Ford, Iacocca was promoted to head the Ford division. In this position he obtained the necessary base from which he could continue his advancement to the top. In the classic sense, Iacocca is not considered an empire builder, but an ambitious individual accepting the challenge of increased authority and responsibility.

Role of moral codes

Chester I. Barnard regarded *responsibility* as the control of one's conduct through adherence to a personal moral code.[16] In this sense, *morals* are referred to as the values and beliefs learned and accepted by an individual. What is important, according to Barnard, is not the specific standards that are used to establish individual morals, but that people act in accordance with their moral codes.

Organizations have both formal and informal codes of moral conduct. In Barnard's terms, individuals who conform to these codes are responsible. The problem most managers face is that of having too many codes to follow as they fulfill various roles. The family unit, the church, business firms, and various social organizations each have codes to direct the behavior of their members. Of course, conflicts do occur among various sets of moral codes, as suggested in the introductory page of Chapter 3 where we discussed the upheaval at Bendix involving

---

[16] Chester I. Barnard, *The Functions of the Executive* (Cambridge, Mass.: Harvard University Press, 1938), pp. 258–84.

William Agee and Mary Cunningham. An ability to reconcile and balance such conflicts is truly one mark of a good manager.

SUMMARY

Organizing is one of the basic functions of management. It deals with establishing a formal structure to coordinate the human and material resources necessary to accomplish desired objectives. One way of viewing the organizing process is to recognize the development that takes place when an organization moves from a simple to a complex entity. As the organization grows, it expands vertically to form a managerial hierarchy that specifies lines of authority and responsibility. In this way, the formal structure provides (1) a clear definition of objectives to be achieved, (2) a framework for coordinating the efforts of organizational members, (3) a definition of intended relationships among the positions in the organization, and (4) a distribution of authority and responsibility.[17]

The formal organization can also be studied from the viewpoint of a bureaucracy. All complex organizations, whether public or private, reveal bureaucratic characteristics. Max Weber considered the bureaucratic model as technically superior over any other organizational design because he felt that his proposed bureaucratic arrangement would enhance communication, coordination, unity of direction, effectiveness, and efficiency.

In order for the formal organization to function properly, authority and responsibility must be defined for all organizational members. Authority implies (1) the right to direct others (emphasizing the superior-subordinate relationship) and (2) the permission to act by performing specified duties. Responsibility is an obligation to accomplish assigned duties. Theoretically, authority and responsibility should be commensurate; however, this is not always the case and many deviations are seen in all types of organizations.

KEY TERMS

Authority: A necessary element for effectiveness that indicates the right to command in the relationships among people and permission to perform specific activities in an organization.

Bureaucracy: A formal organizational design that is characterized as maximizing the stability and predictability of actions.

Formal organization: The officially designated organization structure reflecting the managerial hierarchy, planned interpersonal relationships, and established communication channels.

Organizing process: The steps taken in designing an organizational

---

[17] The delegation of authority and responsibility as a sharing process is discussed in Chapter 11.

structure that combine human and material resources so that an organization can achieve its goals effectively and efficiently.

Responsibility: A personal relationship between positions within an organization and the commitment of the positions' occupants to achieve goals.

Scientific management: A body of literature developed between 1890–1930, noting principles and ideas on improving relationships between workers and managers in order to increase productivity.

QUESTIONS

1. Why is organizing a necessary management function? What is involved in the organizing process?
2. Describe the sequence of events that takes place as an organization grows from a simple to a complex entity. How do the two organizational forms differ?
3. Cite the characteristics of the formal organization.
4. Is there a major distinction between bureaucracy and the formal organization?
5. What are the six characteristics of a bureaucracy noted by Max Weber? How did Weber view human relations within the formal structure?
6. Make a list of advantages that can be derived from the formal organization. Do you perceive any disadvantages or limitations?
7. What is the meaning of authority? Why is it an essential element in any organization?
8. What are three sources of authority? Discuss each.
9. Is compliance to authority based completely on power? Why?
10. Define the two implications of obligation.
11. What is meant by the delegation of authority?
12. Can both authority and responsibility be delegated?

PROBLEMS

1. The bureaucratic structure is often criticized on the grounds that it considers only management wishes and needs and disregards the welfare of other employees. Consider the situation at the U.S. Government Printing Office when it was swamped with complaints from citizens who ordered publications that never arrived. Managers discovered that some employees were simply throwing orders away, rather than filling them. The evidence was there—in the trash cans. The question was, which employees were responsible?

By preparing stacks of secretly marked orders for designated employees, order blanks ending up in the trash can could be traced to particular employees. When certain employees were found to be guilty of such practices, they were suspended or fired.

Exercising their rights as federal employees, the employees appealed their dismissals. There were two days of hearings at the GPO that sustained the firings. Appeals to the Civil Service Commission's field office in Washington were made, where the firings were also upheld. About a year had passed by this time. Appeals began again. This time the commission's Appeals Review Board was petitioned. The employees contended in effect that the evidence against them was only circumstantial since nobody testified that they actually saw them throwing away the orders. This time the employees won. The board ordered that they be reinstated in their old jobs and that they be reimbursed for 18 months of back pay.

Federal agency executives say it has become more and more difficult to fire a federal employee for anything but the most flagrant and outrageous behavior. In a recent 12-month period for which figures are available, the federal government fired exactly 226 employees for inefficiency. It has 2.8 million workers. Federal managers say they are hobbled not only by basic civil service bureaucratic processes that are complex and time consuming but also by union grievance procedures and by new antidiscrimination enforcement regulations that give employees a choice of several different ways to appeal the same action.

Based on the above story, *(a)* Does bureaucracy have any benefits for employees? *(b)* Do you feel civil service employees in the federal government would be willing to opt for fewer, less complex procedures, regulations, and bureaucratic red tape in handling grievance procedures? *(c)* Are there any disadvantages in having such a bureaucratic structure to handle grievances?

2. In the Potemkin mutiny of 1905, Russian sailors refused to eat borsch prepared from meat that they considered maggoty. When the ringleaders of the protest were brought forward before a firing squad, one of them called out to the men in the squad not to shoot their own comrades. The firing squad did not fire, and it was not long before the mutineers had taken over the Potemkin.

Did the ringleader of these men have any authority over the firing squad? If not, why did the squad comply? Can authority be supported indefinitely by this type of compliance?

3. The concept of superior authority states that an order cannot be denied once it is given. Calvin Coolidge was not an advocate of this belief. For example, a young member of Congress was telling President Collidge of the difficulties he had been having with the chairman of a congressional committee. The problem had reached a point where the congressman was told to go to hell by the chairman. At the end of their discussion, Collidge told the young congressman that, after all, he really didn't have to.

Discuss the limitations and merits in the superior authority concept.

4. According to Max Weber, authority is accepted on the following bases:

a. It is traditional. People accept authority because it is a way of life.
b. It is rational and legal. The best qualified person fills the position.
c. Charisma is present. The person has a unique or magnetic personality that attracts followers.

Using this classification scheme, how would you classify the authority of (1) the Queen of England, (2) the president of the United States, and (3) Don Landry, coach of the Dallas Cowboys?

5. The following statement from their chief was received by vision testers and photographers in the Driver's License Bureau of a State Revenue Department:

> We have come to the end of our patience with the sloppy and irresponsible work you have been doing. Some of you don't seem to care what you do as long as the paychecks keep coming. All we hear are complaints to the Director of Revenue. Each time I hear a complaint because a person has not received a driver's license he or she made application for months ago, some one of you is to blame. From now on, there is going to be a monetary charge to each employee for recording mistakes.
>
> If you value your job and are interested in keeping it, things had better improve. Those with continued mistakes must be terminated.

Some of the repeated mistakes referred to in the statement concerned snapshots that did not show the applicant's face, exposed film with no pictures, skipped vision tests, no signatures, and inaccurate numbering. The vision testers and photographers are located in the Revenue Department's main office, its 10 branch offices, and over 140 fee offices around the state.

a. What is the chief's source of authority?
b. On what basis is compliance being requested?
c. Is there a better way to gain compliance with the request for reduced errors?

6. During the Crimean War, the English Light Brigade made its famous charge that had a tragic ending. Tennyson recorded:

> Theirs not to reason why,
> Theirs but to do and die.
> Into the valley of death
> Rode the six hundred.

Considering Barnard's four requirements for accepting an order, how would you interpret this reaction to an order that was suicidal?

7. While serving as president of the United States, Harry Truman was quoted as saying, "The buck stops here!" In terms of responsibility and accountability, what do you think he meant?

SUGGESTED READINGS

Aldrich, H., and D. Herker. "Boundary Spanning Roles and Organization Structure." *The Academy of Management Review*, April 1977, pp. 217–30.

"Bureaucracy in the Eighties." *The Journal of Applied Behavioral Science*, July–August–September 1980, pp. 263–447.

Dalton, D. R.; W. D. Tudor; M. J. Spendolini; G. J. Fielding; and L. W. Porter. "Organization Structure and Performance: A Critical Review." *The Academy of Management Review*, January 1980, pp. 49–64.

Duncan, W. J. *Organizational Behavior*. Boston: Houghton Mifflin, 1978, pp. 263–85.

Hern, W. M.; J. R. Gold; and A. Oakes. "Administrative Incongruence and Authority Conflict in Four Abortion Clinics." *Human Organization,* Winter 1977, pp. 376–83.

Jaques, E. *A General Theory of Bureaucracy.* New York: Halsted Press, 1976.

Katz, D., and R. L. Kahn. *The Social Psychology of Organizations.* New York: John Wiley & Sons, 1966.

Kassem, M. S. "Tolstoy on Organization." *Business Horizons,* April 1977, pp. 9–15.

"The Lordstown Auto Workers." In *Life in Organizations,* edited by R. M. Kanter and B. A. Stein. New York: Basic Books, 1979.

Main, J. "How to Battle Your Own Bureaucracy." *Fortune,* June 29, 1981, pp. 54–58.

Miewald, R. D. "The Greatly Exaggerated Death of Bureaucracy." *California Management Review,* 1970, pp. 65–69.

Milgram, S. *Obedience to Authority.* London: Tavistock Publications, 1974.

Perrow, C. "The Short and Glorious History of Organizational Theory." *Organizational Dynamics,* Summer 1973, pp. 2–14.

Tannenbaum, A. S.; B. Kavcic; M. Rosner; M. Vianello; and G. Weiser. *Hierarchy in Organizations.* San Francisco: Jossey-Bass, 1974.

Urwick, L. F. "That Word Organization." *Academy of Management Review,* January 1976, pp. 89–91.

10

THE DESIGN OF ORGANIZATIONS

PURPOSE

If General Motors were a country, it would rank 20th in national wealth. In 1979, it had revenues of more than $66 billion and some 732,000 employees in 35 foreign countries and the United States. Although the world's number one auto maker's organizational structure and power are awesome, consider Exxon Corporation, now the largest industrial company in the nation. Operating in nearly 100 countries, Exxon has a tremendous impact on the world's energy business. Due to its size, the corporation's chairman and chief executive officer, Clifton G. Garvin, Jr., would clearly have an impossible job keeping up with operations if Exxon's organization were so designed that he had to make all major decisions. Such pressures are eased for Garvin by a highly decentralized authority structure and collective leadership. For example, an eight-member management committee headquartered at Exxon's office in Rockefeller Center provides top-management leadership for the worldwide empire composed of 13 affiliated companies. Regional managers take care of the daily operations, while the CEO and other top officials set corporate objectives, focus on strategic planning, and monitor company expenditures and revenues.

By looking briefly at GM and Exxon, we can see that designing the organization (organizing the company) is an essential function if goals are to be achieved effectively. Even for small organizations, staying on top of a multitude of issues requires an appropriately designed organization. The structure of the organization, in conjunction with the delegation of authority and assistance in decision making, allows managers to track key events, jobs, and performance goals properly. In this chapter, we are primarily concerned with elements involved in identifying and grouping work. Throughout, it will also be clear that organizational design is not a mechanistic, model-building technique that ignores the human element.

OBJECTIVES

1. To point out the role of the design phase of the organizing function.

2. To emphasize the importance of identifying and grouping work in the design of formal organizations.

3. To provide an understanding of situational analysis as related to organizational design.

4. To examine the division of labor and guides to departmentation within organizations.

5. To discuss certain elementary concepts, such as the scalar principle, unity of command, and span of management.

The top administrator of a major department within the federal government stated that organizations in themselves are fine, but when people are put into them, the result is mass confusion. Of course, all organizations include people, but the statement does suggest the importance of constantly reviewing and modifying organizational designs to produce a greater coordination of effort. No organization is flawless, particularly within a dynamic environment where conditions change so rapidly that there is no one best way to design all organizations. In fact, attempts to define the ideal structure are viewed as neither attainable nor desirable, although organizational efforts must be brought together if objectives are to be achieved. How this is accomplished depends on organizational design.

Organizations that are capable of adapting to changes in their environments must be flexible in rearranging their basic parts. This process includes innovative organizational design that depends on (1) identifying, dividing, and grouping tasks; (2) arranging material and human resources into a meaningful structure; and (3) defining responsibilities and delegating authority to coordinate relationships between individuals and groups.

DIVISION OF LABOR   In designing the organization, managers make decisions concerning the division of labor. This concept refers to analyzing work to be accomplished so that it can be divided into separate units or job assignments. More specifically, a division of labor implies making small, simple jobs out of larger, more complex jobs.

The division of labor within an organization is necessary for two reasons. First, the complexity of even small organizations is so great that work must be accomplished by more than one person. In addition, as an organization grows, additional employees are required to complete the various operational and managerial tasks that are identified through the division of labor.

The second reason for a division of duties is to take advantage of increased productivity resulting from a specialization of labor. The classical economist, Adam Smith, was one of the first persons to describe this concept. To illustrate it, consider the objective of making birdhouses. The work of cutting out the pieces, assembling them, and then painting the birdhouses could all be done by one person. However, with specialization of labor, jobs are divided into specific tasks, and the value of the increased output of birdhouses is greater than would be true if one person had to perform all of the tasks (see Figure 10–1). Specialization of labor results in increased productivity due to the following reasons:

1. The ability to become highly skilled at performing a small number of activities. The shorter the work cycle, the larger will be the number of cycles completed, and the greater the opportunity for the worker to learn the activities thoroughly and skillfully.

FIGURE 10–1
Division of labor and production output

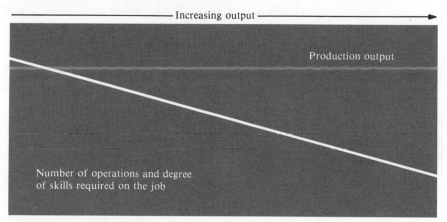

As production output increases, the number of operations and the degree of skills required on the job decrease.

2. The opportunity of many specialized employees to work on different phases of a product or service at the same time so as to reduce the total time required in adding value to the work. Since many specialists are working on the job, the product or service is likely to have greater uniformity and the intricacy of the product may be reduced.

3. The reduction in costs of using mechanical and highly technical equipment that can be used repetitiously for precisely defined functions. When a task requires only a few operations, the work cycle can be repeated many times. Also, the repetitive use of equipment that requires minimal retooling time makes an operation more profitable.

Another dimension of the division of labor includes a specialization of management tasks—that is, a division of the management functions so that a manager can specialize in one or two areas, such as planning and/or controlling. This idea is discussed in the following chapter where line and staff authority relationships are examined.

Division of labor and reduced productivity

With more detailed specialization of each task, costs can increase to the point where they outweigh the additional gains in productivity. This can be seen in a highly specialized manufacturing operation where a bottleneck in one department can result in increased labor and material costs in another. For example, a breakdown on one part of an assembly line may result in the whole line being shut down, while labor costs continue even though no products are being produced. Other economic limitations stem from labor-management contracts that identify specific jobs duties and jurisdictional boundaries that have been agreed on in collective bargaining sessions.

Since each new job must relate to the total objectives of an organization, management's task of integrating and coordinating the various parts becomes increasingly complex and expensive as additional positions are added. Coordination becomes especially critical when increases in specialization cause employees to lose sight of overall organizational objectives. Also, employees may tend to optimize individual goals to the detriment of total organizational goals. In summary, then, a high degree of specialization creates a greater need for coordination and is ultimately limited by reduced productivity.

Physiological and psychological limitations

The responsibilities and interpersonal relationships associated with some jobs may be such that individuals derive a great deal of personal satisfaction from work. Where this occurs, the jobs may be viewed as providing challenge, advancement, increased responsibility, security, a chance to acquire new knowledge and skills, added control over the work environment, or many other attributes. In these instances, *role congruency* exists since the jobs are in line with employee expectations. Unfortunately, many jobs are not of this type, especially if the degree of specialization results in a highly narrow or limited job scope. In other words, if the number of task operations performed on a job are constantly reduced, the point is reached where work for some individuals becomes boring and monotonous.

One of the most critical attacks on the specialization of labor is included in the work of Chris Argyris.[1] After identifying the job rewards needed by the mature and healthy personality, Argyris compares them to the assumptions underlying a high degree of work specialization. He states that the specialization of labor prevents individuals from utilizing their full potential since it permits an expression of only a few limited abilities that do not provide the challenge desired by the healthy personality. In addition, the few skills that do remain in a job are poor substitutes for that which is really desired from work. Mature adults, therefore, are forced to behave in an immature manner and are rewarded for relatively shallow contributions. Consequently, Argyris feels that jobs based on a high degree of specialization cannot be motivational.

The studies of Walker and Guest also describe the interface between the division of labor and various physiological and psychological considerations of humans.[2] This research, conducted in an automobile assembly plant, shows that a high degree of specialization can reach a point where inefficiency occurs in terms of lower product quality and employee disinterest. The research also reveals that various jobs in the plant provided little of what employees sought from their work. As

---

[1] Chris Argyris, *Personality and Organization* (New York: Harper & Row, 1957), pp. 54–75.

[2] Charles R. Walker and Robert H. Guest, *The Man on the Assembly Line* (Cambridge, Mass.: Harvard University Press, 1952); or *Harvard Business Review*, May–June 1952, pp. 71–83.

a result, employee dissatisfaction prevailed, along with a widespread sense of failure and frustration.

To cope with dissatisfaction, failure, and frustration, employees modify their behavior in various ways. Absenteeism, tardiness, work slow-downs, destructive acts, drugs, and alcoholism are examples of outward manifestations of attempts to cope with low morale and frustration. In preventing or overcoming these undesirable behavior patterns, attention should be given to redesigning the organization and reconsidering the degree of specialization. Managers should work to integrate the formal organization with the mature attributes and motivational needs of all employees. In this regard, monotony can be reduced by increasing the content of a job by using management techniques such as (1) job rotation, (2) job enrichment, and (3) employee participation. Since each of these techniques is discussed in Chapter 14, it will suffice at this point to recognize that behavioral responses to job content are directly related to organizational design. Consequently, various physiological and psychological variables must be considered in deciding on the degree to which a specialization of labor is implemented in any organization.

GUIDES TO DEPARTMENTATION

Work that is divided must ultimately be brought back together or grouped in some manner in order to obtain a better coordination of effort. Managers can do a more effective job of coordinating when the activities for which they are responsible are grouped together in some logical form. *The process of grouping or combining jobs is referred to as departmentation.* In general, the forms of departmentation can be classified into six categories: business functions, work processes, geographic area, product or service, customer, and project team.[3]

Departmentation by business functions

Within any business organization the production, marketing, and finance functions must be performed. Production takes place in order to supply appropriate goods and/or services. Marketing is essential in getting all products to the right place, at the right time, and at the right price. Obtaining and maintaining the funds necessary for adequate operations necessitates the finance function. All of these business functions are required whether one refers to a department store, a railroad, a bank, or a public utility, even though the degree of emphasis placed on the functions varies among industries. Similarly, production, marketing, and finance are required in the operation of all other organizations. While not always viewed in the same context, churches, hospitals, and even the American Heart Association must perform these business functions to reach their goals.

---

[3] The material in this chapter shows that no one form of departmentation is best in all situations.

FIGURE 10–2
Departmentation by functions

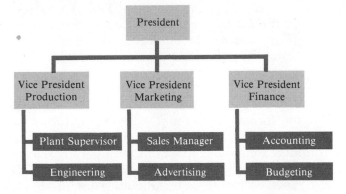

Departmentation by business functions is illustrated in Figure 10–2 where activities are grouped on the basis of the functions performed by each unit. One important reason for grouping activities on this basis is that managers can do a better job of reaching their goals when the activities for which they are responsible are similar in nature. In addition, technical and specialized information can be communicated and utilized more effectively when all business-related activities are grouped together. Major disadvantages, however, can result when departments become so specialized that they are interested in optimizing their own objectives to the virtual exclusion of total organizational goals.[4] Communication problems may develop among departments and the coordination of effort may suffer. Thus, when departmentalizing by functions, policies and procedures are essential in formalizing and standardizing the work of people in similar functional areas.

Beyond production, marketing, and finance, other functional areas may be added by an organization depending on the industry or specific institutional needs. For example, firms in the space and technical industries find that engineering is essential to their success and should, therefore, be given status as a separate department. Similarly, these and other organizations may require large research and development departments. With continued organizational growth, new functional departments may emerge in any organization as managers become unable to handle all of the management responsibilities associated with their positions.

Departmentation by process

Closely associated with grouping by function is departmentation by process lines. This approach views the way work is performed or the processes that must be undertaken to achieve a specific goal. At most state employment offices, for example, job applicants must first

---

[4] This phenomenon is commonly referred to as suboptimization or sectionalism.

FIGURE 10–3
Departmentation by process

see a receptionist who determines the placement interviewers with whom they should talk. By using separate groupings of receptionists, interviewers, and other technical functions in the office, we have departmentation by process, such as that noted in Figure 10–3.

In a manufacturing operation, work may be performed by cutting, shaping, welding, grinding, painting, and assembling. Under departmentation by process, all operations related to each of these processes would be grouped into separate departments. The advantages flowing from such departmentation would include a greater specialization of effort and a more rapid communication of technical information. Coordination, however, can be impaired if employees become so specialized that they lose sight of overall company goals, making it more difficult for them to work together as a team. Another apparent disadvantage of process departmentation comes from the restricted flexibility of employees possessing only limited specialized skills. Even though the degree of specialization may be extremely high, the training period for learning new jobs may be brief, thereby offsetting a portion of this disadvantage.

Departmentation by geographic area

The grouping of jobs according to geographic location emphasizes the areas being served by an organization. The interest of management in geographic departmentation focuses on the location of customers, materials, resources, or suppliers, rather than on the processes or business functions that must be performed. Organizations with branch facilities located away from a headquarters' office find that departmentation by geographic area is extremely useful. For example, most national retail merchandising companies, like A & P, Montgomery Ward, and J.C. Penney Company, divide their operations geographically by both districts and regions. In fact, some of these companies find local groupings feasible when there is a large number of service outlets located in a specific area. (Figure 10–4 illustrates geographic departmentation.)

A major advantage of geographic departmentation stems from the

FIGURE 10–4
Departmentation by geographic area

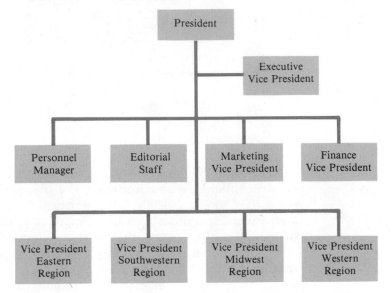

fact that work in a particular area can be conducted by a person whose activities are devoted only to that area. In addition, specific local and regional factors can be considered fully in the decision-making process. These advantages can be outweighed when geographic departmentation is so extensive that there is a costly duplication of facilities and personnel within the various regions.

Departmentation by product and/ or service

As shown in Figure 10–5, departmentation of this type is generally used in large, diversified organizations where emphasis is placed on special groups of products or services. General Motors, duPont, and Westinghouse are illustrative of firms using product line departmentation. Such departmentation is also common in hospitals, department stores, banks, and utilities. For example, a city utility may group activi-

FIGURE 10–5
Departmentation by product

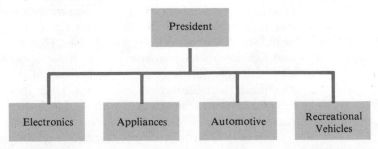

ties around water, gas, electrical, and public transportation facilities. Based on the services offered, departmental groupings for a city chamber of commerce could include economic development, community betterment, public affairs, and membership.

Product departments are generally independent of one another and are responsible for their own sales and production activities. As in other types of departmentation, finance is usually controlled in a centralized manner. Profitability in all departments is the direct responsibility of the respective managers. Since these managers have authority over production and marketing, they can coordinate and affect those activities influencing profits. Yet, the autonomy of these managers is not as great as one might think since complex departmental interrelations may still exist. This is especially true when (1) similar raw materials are used in manufacturing various products, (2) legal questions are similar or identical for each product, (3) contract negotiations are with the same union, (4) engineering designs and production standards are essentially the same for each product, and (5) advertising approaches are similar for all customers. When one or more of the above conditions exist, it is likely that a staff unit will be formed that can perform the particular function for all product managers.

Product and service departmentation has the advantage of providing a coordination of activities as product or service lines expand. In addition, personnel with certain specialized skills can identify with a particular unit. Similar to geographic departmentation, the costs of duplicating activities and personnel for several products or services can ultimately exceed the benefits of this approach.

Departmentation by customer

Organizations that can make a clear distinction among types of consumers may decide to departmentalize by customer. Airlines, for example, have two sales departments—one deals with passenger services and the other serves air freight and cargo customers. As noted in Figure 10–6, the sales manager of a book publishing company may organize activities around customer groups, such as colleges, secondary schools,

FIGURE 10–6
Departmentation by customer

and private commercial schools. In manufacturing and merchandising companies, it is common to find wholesale departments for industrial users and retail departments to service the general public.

A major advantage of this form of departmentation is that a particular customer group is not forgotten nor overlooked. In fact, customer groupings are assured continuous recognition and service. Disadvantages of customer groupings are similar to those of product departmentation—that is, various products or services may not be demanded by customers at certain times of the year, resulting in underutilization of resources. Thus, both seasonal and cyclical variations in customer demand are important variables to consider in determining whether activities should be grouped according to types of customers.

Departmentation by matrix organization design

In some organizations, environmental variables are conducive to departmentation by matrix design. A project or product team may be set up to conduct a personnel study of a particular geographic region, submit a report on a new approach to providing health care services, build a spaceship to explore our solar system, or design and produce a new piece of industrial machinery. In any case, project goals set the stage for what has to be done. The project manager then analyzes the activities that must be performed to achieve established goals and selects personnel in functional areas to fill needed positions. Since personnel who are assigned to each project or product are also members of a functional department, dual authority relationships exist because team members report to two managers. A dual authority relationship of this type can be seen in the matrix structure for Westinghouse's international operation where a factory manager in Brazil reports to the "business unit" (geographic) manager in that country as well as to a stateside "business unit" (product-line) manager.[5]

After formation, the project members work together as a unit, contributing not only to individually assigned tasks but also to all phases of the project. When it is completed, personnel may return to their original departments; or if a new project is under way, they may be assigned to work on it. The advantages of this approach can be seen in the greater ability to respond quickly to rapid changes and in the challenge of new project assignments. Through such arrangements, individuals work toward the achievement of a total goal, rather than the accomplishment of some specialized task. The result is a net contribution to overall productivity and employee satisfaction. For either projects or products, the nature of the matrix design depends on the environment with which it must cope.[6]

---

[5] See Hugh C. Menzies, "Westinghouse Takes Aim at the World," *Fortune,* January 14, 1980, pp. 48–53.

[6] See Norman H. Wright, Jr., "Matrix Management—Fortifying the Organization Structure," *Management World,* May 1980, pp. 24–26.

**GROUPING OF
DEPARTMENTS**

Once the activities essential to an achievement of organizational goals have been assigned to departments, there is still the question of arranging departmental units in order to establish proper relationships among them. This grouping of departments should be done according to an arrangement that will contribute most to the accomplishment of total organizational objectives. The major variables influencing the grouping of departments include (1) the amount of coordination needed, (2) the extent of departmental control required, (3) the need to promote maximum geographic authority, (4) the need to obtain maximum product and/or customer satisfaction, and (5) the perceived impact of the design on employees of the organization.

Two general approaches are available for arranging departmental groupings. One is referred to as parallel departmentation; the other is the balance approach that involves a mixing of forms of departmentation within the organization.

**Parallel
departmentation**

By following parallel departmentation in a single plant, each product department could have its own sales, manufacturing, and purchasing functions. For an organization having multiple plants or stores, a parallel design would reflect identical departmental arrangements in each, as illustrated in Figure 10–7.

**FIGURE 10–7
Parallel departmentation**

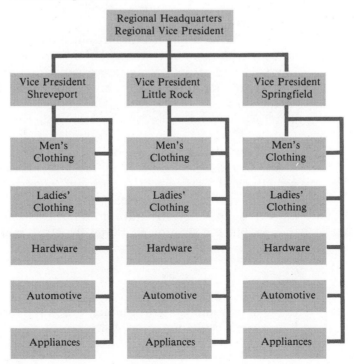

A major advantage of parallel departmentation is found in the control area. Since each department, store, or plant is arranged on an identical basis, its performance can be easily compared to other units. Thus, to a certain degree, the total organization is standardized, and a manager can move easily from one unit to another since there is uniformity among operations and position assignments. For the same reason, communications and the transfer of personnel are more easily coordinated.

The major disadvantages of a parallel arrangement stem from the costs of providing duplicate services in various locations and the loss of flexibility in adjusting to local situations. The criteria of being flexible, adaptive, and creative represent good guides to follow in determining how far one should carry the idea of parallelism. Managers must weigh the benefits of parallel departmentation against the costs of some inflexibility. However, people, tasks, technology, and resources should never be subordinated to a structural design. Change is inevitable, and the successful organization must be capable of perceiving and adapting to change by using resources wisely.

The balance approach

The balance approach takes its name from the concept of balancing different forms of departmentation to arrive at the most effective combination. In actual practice, the design of many organizations reflects such a combination of departmental forms. The organization structure of IBM, shown in Figure 10–8, illustrates managing by product line and geographic area.

Utilizing this approach requires managers to balance the advantages and disadvantages of each form of departmentation in arriving at the most efficient structural design. Again, an overriding guide to follow in determining the proper balance is to consider the net contribution to total organizational goals. The designed structure must promote an effective coordination of activities while contributing to the satisfaction of individual, group, and organizational objectives.

Without question, the growth of any organization is limited by the abilities of its managers. However, organizational coordination and growth can be enhanced by a proper balance between activities and departmental groupings. Along this line, Peter F. Drucker states that a good organization structure does not by itself produce good performance, but a poor organizational structure makes good performance impossible, no matter how good the individual managers may be.[7]

THE SCALAR CONCEPT

As noted in Chapter 9, Max Weber considered the chain of command to be an extremely important element of the formal organization. This hierarchical structure of authority is referred to as the scalar concept. As a chain of direct superior-subordinate relationships throughout the

---

[7] Peter F. Drucker, *Managing for Results* (New York: Harper & Row, 1964), p. 216.

FIGURE 10–8
Organization structure of IBM: Departmentation by product line and geographic area

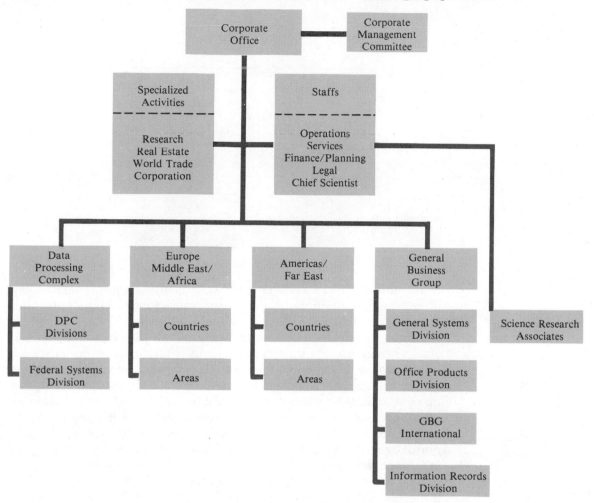

entire organization, the *scalar concept is a series of steps that establish a clear line of authority from the top of an organization to the bottom.* This is illustrated in Figure 10–9 where the graduated steps also reflect that overall responsibilities are held by top managers, but shared with all members within the scalar chain.

Adherence to the chain of command is sometimes not practical. Referring to Figure 10–9, the need to speed up communications may result in person E not going up the chain but going directly across to O.[8] A continued violation of the scalar relationship, however, may

---

[8] Henri Fayol, *General and Industrial Management* (London: Sir Isaac Pitman and Sons, 1949), p. 35. In Coubrough's 1930 translation of Fayol's original French, he used the word *bridge* rather than *gangplank*.

FIGURE 10–9
Scalar concept

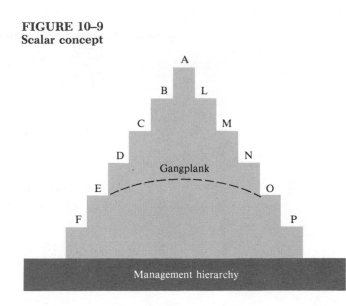

result ultimately in a breakdown in coordination, a misunderstanding of managerial positions, and general inefficiency. Thus, guidelines should be established if gangplanks are frequent.

Another example of bypassing individuals in the chain of command occurs when A picks up the phone and communicates directly with F, rather than going down the chain of command and informing each of the managers in the A–F hierarchy. Such actions certainly speed up communication but can lead to problems if F feels that the arrangement is reciprocal and contacts A directly without following the chain of command. As a general guide, all organizational members should normally follow prescribed communication channels; however, good judgment should be exercised when time is of the essence. Bypassing certain managers in the chain of command may be necessary in some instances, but these managers should still be kept informed through follow-up communications that are initiated as soon as possible.

UNITY OF COMMAND

The concept of *unity of command states that for any specific action or activity a subordinate should receive orders from only one superior.* The purpose, of course, is to prevent conflicts and confusion from arising when a subordinate receives directions in the same area from two or more superiors. In this sense, unity of command seeks to maintain clear authority relationships between superiors and subordinates.

Without question, the unity of command concept has a long history. In the Bible we are told that a person cannot serve two masters. Throughout more recent history, we have observed various problems and conflicts that have resulted from violations of this concept. Interestingly enough, however, there are situations where unity of command is violated without apparent detriment to the organization. For example, General Electric has three individuals who perform the responsibilities of the president's position. In other organizations there are similar cases of multiple direction in various managerial positions. In the project team or matrix organization discussed earlier, individuals working on the project have two "bosses"— a functional department head and a project head. Other violations seem to occur when employees receive directions from their immediate supervisor, the doctor in the infirmary, the production scheduler, the quality control director, the purchasing agent, the personnel manager, or other individuals outside of the normal chain of command.

F. W. Taylor developed a management model—functional foremanship—that is perceived by many to violate the unity of command. Yet, the model is very descriptive of the management levels within most business organizations. As noted in Figure 10–10, Taylor proposed that eight specialists assume the responsibilities of a supervisor. Each

FIGURE 10–10
Taylor's functional foremanship

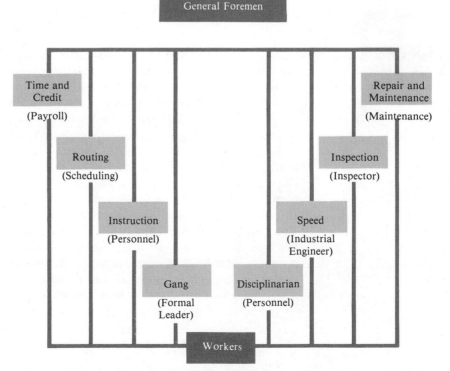

Source: Data for diagram from Frederick W. Taylor, "Shop Management," in *Scientific Management* (New York: Harper & Row, 1947), p. 21.

would have individual authority and would issue orders to workers on matters related to their respective functional specialties. Similar to this arrangement, Taylor also recommended that upper-level line managers have staff personnel to provide assistance in specialized areas of operation.

In reality the employees of most organizations receive directives from many people. This does not imply, however, that the unity of command concept is meaningless in a contemporary organization. In fact, it remains as a viable and useful concept if its meaning is interpreted properly. Note that the unity of command concept does not indicate that subordinates receive orders from only one superior for all actions, but only for any one action. Receiving orders from many individuals is not necessarily a violation of unity of command unless such directives fall within the same area of activity. If one person tells a secretary to use a particular machine while another directs the person to use a different one, then we have conflict and a breakdown of coordination. On the other hand, an employee might be directed to use a certain machining technique by a supervisor, told how many units to produce by someone in production control, and instructed to stop a malfunctioning machine by a maintenance supervisor. In this case, unity of command is not necessarily being violated since each directive is related to a different functional specialty.

SPAN OF MANAGEMENT

Authority, responsibility, the scalar concept, and unity of command have equal impacts on the span of management. *The span of management refers to the number of subordinates reporting to one superior.*[9] The precise number of people involved in the span depends on the superior's level of authority, the type of work being done, the degree of coordination required, and the capabilities of subordinates.

In 1933, A. V. Graicunas, a management consultant, developed a mathematical formula for arriving at the number of possible relationships between subordinates and a given superior.[10] He found that the combination of interactions increases in a geometric progression as the number of subordinates increases in an arithmetical progression. Thus, as shown in Figure 10–11, a manager with two subordinates has two direct relationships, two cross-relationships, and two group contacts for a total of six possible relationships.

Lyndall Urwick, a leader of the British school of scientific management, summarized the work of Graicunas into a so-called *Principle of the Span of Management.* As applied to business, Urwick felt that

[9] The span of management is also referred to as the span of supervision, span of authority, and span of control.

[10] See: A. V. Graicunas, "Relationships in Organization," in *Papers on the Science of Administration,* ed. Luther Gulick and Lyndall Urwick. (New York: Columbia University, 1947), pp. 181–87.

FIGURE 10–11
Possible relationships between a manager and two subordinates

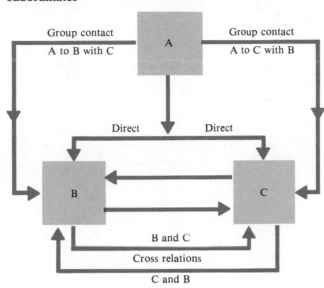

no manager can supervise directly the work of more than five or six subordinates whose work interlocks. By using the word interlocking, Urwick qualified his principle to suggest that the span of management may be larger when there are limited cross-relationships among subordinates whose work does not require frequent interaction. Today, few management scholars attempt to place strict limitations on the span of management. Instead, by following the contingency approach, emphasis is placed on identifying the factors and circumstances that influence the number of subordinates who can be supervised effectively by a given superior.[11] Since conditions vary among organizations, it is natural that wide spans of control are advantageous in some cases while narrow spans are more appropriate in others.

Effects of changes on the span of management

The increased growth and complexity of organizations has resulted in greater organizational problems for top-level managers. The scope of these problems continues to influence the number of subordinates who can be effectively supervised and the number of authority levels in the organizational hierarchy. For example, assume that an organization has 24 nonmanagerial employees and five managers, as noted in Figure 10–12(A). If the span of management is reduced from six to four, the chief executive must be willing to either supervise six manag-

[11] R. D. Dewar and D. P. Simet, "A Level Specific Prediction of Spans of Control Examining the Effects of Size, Technology, and Specialization," *Academy of Management Journal*, March 1981, pp. 5–24.

FIGURE 10–12
Effect upon organization structure when the span of supervision changes

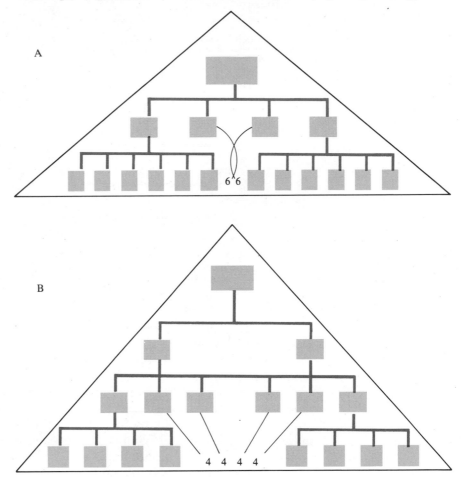

ers or create an additional level of authority, as shown in Figure 10–12(B). The B illustration shows a narrower span of management resulting in a taller structure with more levels of authority and a larger number of managers. Similarly, there is an expansion in the number of organizational offices through which communications must flow.

Some final comments on the span of management

As noted earlier, many management scholars believe that the concept of a theoretically limited span of management is not a meaningful management guide that can be followed effectively in organizing. Some criticisms of the concept are given below:

The number of possible relationships between superiors and subordinates is only theoretical, and the number of direct group relationships may be relatively smaller, particularly at lower levels of management.

Various research studies indicate that some organizations may increase spans of management and experience increased productivity, while others may limit spans and obtain similar results.

By reducing spans of management, the number of managerial levels within an organization may be increased. This may lead to less effective communication and coordination.

Wide spans of management often force supervisors to delegate more authority to their subordinates since they do not have time to get involved in the work of subordinates.

From these criticisms, it is evident that the span of management should not be a controlling factor in organizational design. As a managerial attitude or philosophy, any consideration of spans requires a recognition of those factors that affect performance. These include the capabilities of subordinates, their interactions and interrelationships, the amount of coordinative effort displayed by employees, and the environment within which decision making takes place. Because of these factors, the span of management is not an end in itself but a guide for managers who must consider the impact of spans on human and organizational needs.

ORGANIZATIONAL DESIGN AND BOUNDARY-SPANNING ROLES

As already noted, several variables must be considered in designing the structure of an organization. While all of these variables are influenced by environmental changes, organizational structures are characterized by a certain degree of inertia. Of course, new departments may be created, others rearranged, or horizontal and vertical authority dimensions altered; but, in general, the structure remains relatively stable. Possibly this overall stability is due to the desire of organizational members to maintain consistency. If so, it reflects people's need for stability, as well as a unifying value system. Realistically, however, stability cannot be an overriding factor in times of rapid change. Organizations must develop capabilities for rapid and flexible responses if they are to survive. Such responses to change are required in order to obtain necessary inputs and to market desired outputs. At the same time, survival depends on effectively monitoring information about the environment and transferring technology and innovation across boundaries.

Linkage points between the environment and the organization are referred to as boundary-spanning roles.[12] These roles are often filled

---

[12] See R. Leifer and A. Delberg, "Organizational/Environmental Interchange: A Model of Boundary Spanning Activity," *The Academy of Management Review,* March 1978, p. 138; and Michael L. Tushman and Thomas J. Scanlan, "Boundary Spanning Individuals: Their Role in Information Transfer and Their Antecedents," *Academy of Management Journal,* June 1981, pp. 289–305.

by marketing and sales personnel, purchasing agents, personnel recruiters, advertising and public relations workers, negotiators and bargaining agents, and others whose activities place them at the organization's boundaries to effect transactions with the environment. Clearly, the roles of these people vary, but they are quite different from the roles of people operating primarily within the organization.

Boundary-spanning positions have three distinct and important characteristics.[13] First, occupants of these positions may be more distant—psychologically and physically—from other members within the organization. Second, they represent the organization to its external environment in gathering and processing information. And third, occupants in boundary-spanning roles are their organization's agents of influence over the external environment—other business firms, governments, public and civic organizations, and other social units. Since information from external sources comes to the organization through these specialized boundary-spanning roles, organizations are able to respond more rapidly to environmental changes.

SUMMARY

The division of labor and the grouping of work represent two steps in the dynamic process of designing an organization. Without question, a division of labor can contribute to increased productivity. If carried too far, however, various economic, physiological, and psychological constraints associated with specialization can result in decreased productivity.

Once work has been divided, it must be grouped into appropriate units in order to provide coordination among the resulting activities. This process, referred to as departmentation, requires imagination, creativity, and a sense of purpose among managers. Some of the most common forms of departmentation are by business function, process, geographic area, product, customer, and matrix structure.

Once activities have been grouped, it is still necessary to establish an organizational arrangement of departmental units. Two approaches that may be used are parallel departmentation and the balance approach. Regardless of the approach, the final combination of departments must (1) promote coordination among the interconnected units and (2) assist in the fulfillment of individual and group needs.

The scalar chain, unity of command, and span of management are other important concepts to consider in the design of organizations. However, they do not represent principles in the sense that specific results can be predicted with assurance. Instead, these concepts help managers understand the various elements that must be considered

---

[13] See J. Stacy Adams, "The Structure and Dynamics of Behavior in Organizational Boundary Roles," in *Handbook of Industrial and Organizational Psychology,* ed. Marvin D. Dunnette (Chicago: Rand McNally, 1976), pp. 1175–99.

in designing an organization. Thus, the concepts become means, rather than ends, to be used in designing a structure that will contribute to an achievement of organizational goals. Furthermore, managers must continually develop boundary-spanning roles in order to gain the flexibility needed to adjust and respond to dynamic social, economic, technological, and political changes.

KEY TERMS

Boundary-spanning roles: The linkage points between an organization and its environment that monitor required information in developing rapid and flexible organizational responses.

Business functions: The essential activities of production, marketing, and finance that must be performed in all organizations to achieve goals.

Departmentation: The grouping of work or job assignments so that better coordination of effort can be achieved.

Division of labor: In order to gain greater productivity, work is divided into small, separate, and specialized units.

Functional foremanship: A model developed by F. W. Taylor in which eight specialists would have the authority to issue orders to workers on matters relating to their respective functional specialties.

Guides for departmentation: The bases for departmentation that include function, process, geographic area, product, customer, and matrix organization.

Matrix organization design: An organizational design that integrates various organizational types of departmentation such that an additional structure of authority is superimposed on all or a portion of the organization chart.

Parallel departmentation: A method to arrange departmental groups so that in each plant, store, or other unit identical departmental arrangements exist.

Scalar concept: An established clear line of authority from the top of an organization to the bottom.

Span of management: An organizational design concept referring to the number of subordinates reporting to one superior.

Unity of command: Orders to a subordinate should be received from only one superior for any specific action or activity.

QUESTIONS

1. Is the division of labor regarded as an important element in the design of organizations? Why?
2. Explain how a division of labor is related to increased productivity.

3. Can labor become so specialized that productivity decreases? If so, what factors help bring about this situation?

4. How do employees attempt to cope with dissatisfaction on their jobs? What are some management approaches that can be implemented to overcome these behavioral actions?

5. Once a division of work has taken place, why is the grouping process required?

6. What are the different forms of departmentation?

7. Compare and contrast departmentation by function and by product.

8. How does parallel departmentation differ from the balance approach?

9. What criteria can a manager use in deciding how to group departments in order to achieve a proper relationship among them?

10. What is the current meaning and value of the scalar concept?

11. Is it essential to follow the scalar concept without exception? Discuss.

12. Discuss the meaning of unity of command.

13. "The more uniform and routine the work activity and the lower the organizational level, the greater the span of management can be." Do you agree with this statement? What does it tell you about the span of management?

PROBLEMS

1. The Earth-O Equipment Company sells earthmoving equipment, such as bulldozers, draglines, and tractor-type loaders, through 10 branch offices located in two geographic regions. At present, the regional managers are required to visit the branches fairly often in order to handle problems dealing with sales and service. The president is considering a reorganization that would place all 10 branches in one region. Two specialists would then be added with one responsible for sales and the other dealing with service.

a. Is a division of labor an issue in this problem?
b. What are the apparent advantages associated with the proposed change?
c. Are there any possible disadvantages of the president's plan? Discuss.

2. Philco-Ford Corporation was once organized into four divisions—international, appliances, consumer electronics, and sales distribution. In the fall of 1968, Philco's president, Robert E. Hunter, reorganized the divisions so that the appliances and consumer electronics divisions were completely responsible for the design, engineering, manufacturing, and marketing of their own products.

a. Draw an organization chart of Philco-Ford before and after the change.
b. What forms of departmentation existed after the change?
c. Was parallel departmentation utilized in the new organization structure?

3. Referring to Figure 10–8, the interrelationship between managing by product line and geographic area for IBM could be shown as follows:

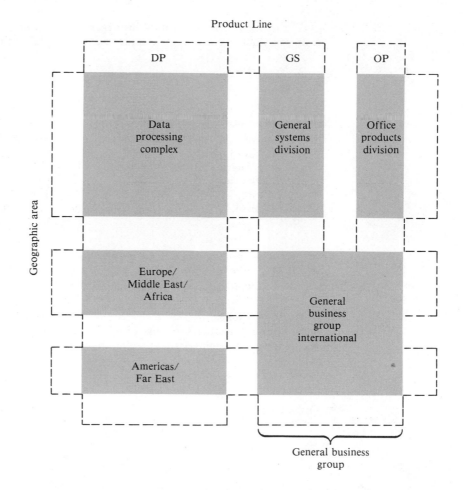

a. Do you feel the above chart is more meaningful than Figure 10–8 in noting the operational aspects of the balance approach?

b. How would this chart be useful to managers?

4. Trimfit Company is a large manufacturing company producing slacks and a variety of other fashion-wear items for women and men. At present, the organization has over 3,000 employees. As the organization has grown in size, the number of people required to support the activities of the business has also increased. During the past year, the president decided that the purely functional organization was becoming unwieldy and felt that some other organizational structure was needed in order to measure profit performance more accurately.

Currently, there are five major product lines in the company. Functional activities include sales, design, manufacturing, and quality control. Legal counsel, financial services, and employee relations are centralized at the top-management level.

With this information, draw an organization chart to reflect suggestions that you would give to the president for reorganizing the Trimfit Company.

5. Typical ratios of subordinates to superiors in various functional areas include the following:

Function	Range of ratio
Marketing and research	8:1 to 10:1
Purchasing, finance, employee relations, and engineering	10:1 to 12:1
Manufacturing	15:1 to 20:1
Quality control	12:1 to 14:1

a. What generalizations can be made about these ratios?
b. If you were designing the organizational structure of a new company, do you feel that you would be justified in following ratios of this type?

6. Loray Stokes, president of Quik-Print Photofinishing Company, made sweeping organizational changes in flattening the management structure of the company by eliminating the multilayered structure noted in Figure A and replacing it with the arrangement shown in Figure B. In the reorganization process, some senior management people were retired while others were

Organization chart of Quik-Print Photofinishing Company

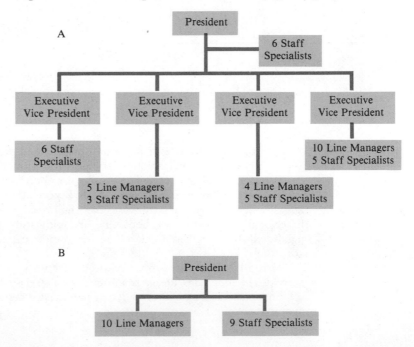

placed in different jobs. Several managerial positions were also eliminated. As a result, salaried employment was cut by 20 percent and administrative overhead dropped by $5 million in one year.

Stokes believes that the reduced number of authority levels will improve the reaction time of employees within the organization while increasing their individual responsibilities. The president also feels that the "flat" structure is more consistent with the idea that most staff and management jobs are peripheral to the main purpose of the company and are only justified when they help employees produce and sell more products.

a. How can a person distinguish between the "flat" and "tall" organizational structures?
b. What do you think Stokes means by the statement that staff and management jobs are peripheral to the main purpose of the company?
c. Do you feel that the flat structure is workable with any type of leadership style?

7. The formula to determine the number of possible interrelationships associated with any given span of management is given below:

$$C = n\left(\frac{2^n}{2} + n - 1\right)$$

where C is the total number of possible interrelationships and n is the number of subordinates reporting to one superior.

a. As the number of subordinates increases from 1 to 3, what is the increase in possible interrelationships?
b. Do you think that all of them have the same intensity of involvement?
c. What impact does your answer have on Urwick's principle of the span of management?

8.

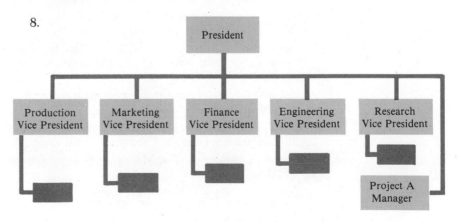

a. Using the organization chart above, show how the matrix-type organization would look if project A manager had to draw upon personnel in production, marketing, finance, engineering, and research.

260

b. Describe the new arrangement in terms of authority relationships, communication, and the value placed on cooperation within the organization.

SUGGESTED READINGS

Boileau, O. C. "Program Management in the Space Age." *Management Accounting,* May 1977, pp. 13–16.

Cascino, A. E. "How One Company 'Adapted' Matrix Management in a Crisis." *Management Review,* November 1979, pp. 57–61.

Davis, L. E. "Individuals and the Organization." *California Management Review,* Spring 1980, pp. 57–61.

Etzioni, A. *A Comparative Analysis of Complex Organizations.* New York: Free Press, 1961.

Galbraith, J. *Designing Complex Organizations.* Reading, Mass.: Addison-Wesley Publishing, 1973.

Gyllenhammar, P. G. "How Volvo Adapts Work to People." *Harvard Business Review,* July–August 1977, pp. 102–13.

Hellriegel, D., and J. W. Slocum, Jr. "Organizational Design: A Contingency Approach." *Business Horizons,* April 1973, pp. 59–68.

Ivancevich, J. M., and J. H. Donnelly, Jr. "Relation of Organizational Structure to Job Satisfaction, Anxiety-Stress, and Performance." *Administrative Science Quarterly,* June 1975, pp. 272–80.

Jelinek, M. "Technology, Organizations, and Contingency." *The Academy of Management Review,* January 1977, pp. 17–26.

Knight, K. "Matrix Organization: A Review." *Journal of Management Studies,* May 1976, pp. 111–115.

Kolodny, H. F. "Evolution to Matrix Organization." *Academy of Management Review,* October 1979, pp. 543–53.

————. "Matrix Organization Designs and New Product Success." *Research Management,* September 1980, pp. 29–33.

Mandt, E. "Managing the Knowledge Worker of the Future." *Personnel Journal,* March 1978, pp. 138ff.

Mashburn, J. I., and B. C. Vaught. "Two Heads Are Better than One: The Case for Dual Leadership." *Management Review,* December 1980, pp. 53–56.

McCaskey, M. B. "An Introduction to Organization Design." *California Management Review,* Winter 1974, pp. 13–20.

Ouchi, W. G., and J. B. Dowling. "Defining the Span of Control." *Administrative Science Quarterly,* September 1974, pp. 357–65.

Urwick, Lyndall F. "The Manager's Span of Control." *Harvard Business Review,* May–June 1956, pp. 39–47.

Von der Embse, T. J., and W. H. Toliver. "Contingency Organization Design: What It Is and How It Works." *Research Management,* September 1979, pp. 31–36.

Walker, A. H., and J. W. Lorsch. "Organization Choice: Product vs. Function." *Harvard Business Review,* November–December 1968, pp. 129–38.

Wolff, M. "Managers at Work—The Day (and Woe) of Matrix." *Research Management,* March 1980, pp. 10–12.

11

AUTHORITY
RELATIONSHIPS

PURPOSE

Aristotle urged all of us to "know thyself." This truth is particularly important to managers in evaluating their ability to delegate authority to subordinates. Consider the performance appraisal and evaluation report on the operations vice president of a large department store based in Los Angeles. As the report noted, this manager had difficulty delegating authority to subordinates and took an active role in defining goals and specifying how they were to be achieved. The report also suggested that by having subordinates clear the slightest deviation from standard operating procedures, creativity was stifled and personal growth inhibited.

After being confronted with the appraisal results, the executive declared, "One of my greatest strengths as a leader is my ability to delegate." Even after several examples were provided showing how subordinates' activities were being overstructured, the executive was never able to admit that the delegation of authority was being restrained.

Possibly some professional counseling would have helped this executive, but the company did not see the alternative as a realistic approach. Instead, the manager was demoted to a position that involved limited decision making and little need for the delegation of authority. Contrasted with this example, we now turn to an examination of how authority relationships can strengthen coordination within an organization.

OBJECTIVES

1. To provide an understanding of the common authority relationships that exist in most organizations.

2. To discuss the delegation of authority within organizations.

3. To develop an understanding of line, staff, and functional authority relationships.

4. To examine the centralization and decentralization of management decision making.

5. To present factors to consider before moving toward decentralization.

Organizing a missile system closely parallels that of designing an organization. The system must first be divided into manageable tasks or subsystems, such as guidance, propulsion, structure, and control. Each subsystem is then designed according to input-output requirements, environmental constraints, and required interfaces with other subsystems. The ultimate purpose of these steps is to assure proper performance of the missile system when all components are assembled.

Likewise, organizations must be designed so that objectives will be met in the most economical and timely manner. As discussed previously, establishing the organization depends on (1) dividing the system into manageable tasks, (2) grouping the tasks based on input-output requirements and environmental constraints, and (3) establishing an interface among units by delineating authority relationships within the management hierarchy. The third element is the subject of this chapter.

DELEGATING AUTHORITY FOR OPERATING AND MANAGEMENT TASKS

As an organization grows and becomes larger, the number of management levels increases. This vertical expansion requires that the proper scope and type of authority rest with those who are responsible for carrying out assigned tasks. Achieving this mission depends upon the "delegation of authority."

In a managerial context, *delegation is defined as a sharing process where a superior entrusts certain authority to others.*[1] Authority can be delegated for the performance of specific operating tasks, as well as for the discharge of management responsibilities. The need for delegation is easily seen in organizations that are growing in terms of operations and employment levels. In such growth situations, managerial jobs become more demanding, with a smaller proportion of time going to the solution of an ever-increasing number of problems. Through delegation, however, the manager can spend less time on specific routine activities and place greater emphasis on nonprogrammable managerial decisions that have to be made for successful operation of the organization. In turn, the authority delegated to new employees grants them permission to perform assigned duties. Consistent with the delegation of some aspects of the management functions, managers will have even more time to concentrate on pressing management problems. These points are summarized in Figure 11–1.

We should also note that the delegation of authority does not in any way relieve managers of their original responsibilities since each manager still retains ultimate responsibility for all work delegated to others. Similarly, delegation does not reduce the manager's overall authority since delegated authority may be withdrawn at any time. Withdrawal of this type does not generally happen, as the original

---

[1] Some management writers use *granting* and *conferring* rather than *sharing*. However, sharing seems more indicative of a two-way process.

FIGURE 11–1
Delegation provides more time for managing

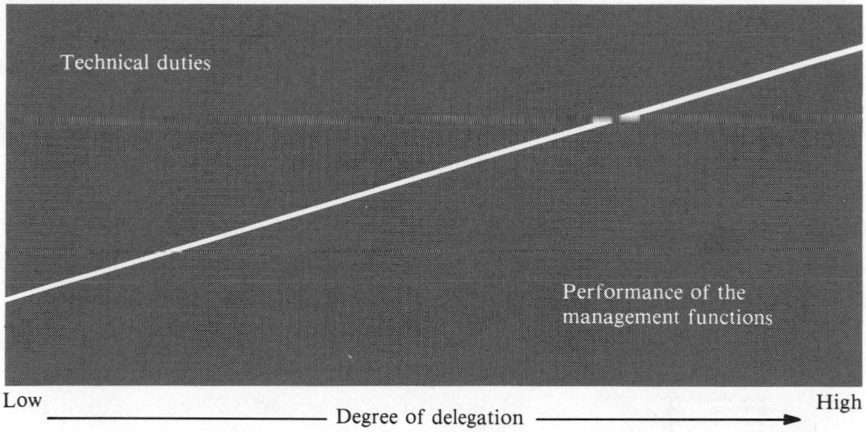

intent of delegation is to share assignments with others so that work can be accomplished more efficiently.

Delegation is a planned activity and cannot be left to chance. It must be undertaken rationally; however, entrusting part of the operational and/or managerial work to others is not without its problems. Two major barriers seem to hamper the delegation process.

Barriers to delegation

The first major barrier to delegation is the unwillingness of superiors to delegate because of a fear that subordinates will not do a job satisfactorily. This lack of confidence may be related to the manager's own inability to encourage cooperation among subordinates or an absence of controls to warn managers about impending difficulties. Some managers have the attitude that delegation diminishes managerial authority, thus failing to realize the obligation of developing subordinates for future managerial positions. On the other hand, some executives may actually think they are delegating authority, while in reality they are overstructuring and constraining the activities of those reporting to them.[2] Whatever the cause of unwillingness, subordinates do not have the autonomy and freedom to make decisions in the absence of delegation.

The second major barrier to delegation is the unwillingness of subordinates to accept delegation. Of course some people do not wish to have greater authority, but in many situations unwillingness is based on past experiences that condition subordinates to feel they have no role in the decision-making process. In these instances, management is at fault for not getting subordinates involved. In addition, subordi-

---

[2] Robert N. McMurray, "What to do about Executives Who Can't Delegate and Won't Decide," *Nation's Business*, May, 1980, pp. 70–73.

nates may also experience the fear of being criticized if a mistake is made, a very distinct possibility in every superior/subordinate relationship.

Managers should also recognize that subordinates' unwillingness to accept delegation may hinge on a lack of information or resources to utilize authority properly. Likewise, inadequate incentives (financial as well as nonfinancial) may cause subordinates to reject additional responsibilities.

Overcoming barriers to delegation

While barriers to delegation result from both managers and subordinates, they are not insurmountable. The following guidelines can assist in preventing or overcoming such barriers:

1. Realize that subordinates have much to contribute to decision making in their areas of specialization.
2. Learn to plan ahead so that delegation can take place before, rather than after, the fact.
3. Build confidence in employees through training, recognition, counseling, and a willingness to delegate more than insignificant decisions.
4. Be willing to take a chance on subordinates and force subordinates to make decisions while giving them help when needed.
5. Do not be overly critical when subordinates make mistakes.
6. Develop control systems that will point out impending problems and let subordinates know what is to be done and the results that are expected.
7. Do not continuously delegate and then withdraw authority since subordinates may become confused and hesitant to exercise initiative.
8. Supply subordinates with adequate resources to fulfill their responsibilities.
9. Provide adequate incentives so that employees are willing to accept increased delegation.
10. Develop an organization structure that provides for personal growth and challenge, thereby helping subordinates become more self-reliant.

Implied in the above is the point that the success of delegation depends on managers who decide the extent to which authority will be delegated. Unfortunately, some managers are unable to delegate because of the popular stereotype that they are supposed to be strong, decisive, and self-confident. When such a psychological problem exists, these managers are likely to be either demoted or terminated.

Authority delegated to fulfill management responsibilities can be viewed from the standpoint of line, staff, and functional relationships. Some management scholars feel that such distinctions are not useful since authority relationships have become very blurred in complex organizations.[3] However, we take the position that the complexities of modern organizations require an even greater recognition and understanding of all facets of authority relationships.

LINE AUTHORITY

Any structure of superior-subordinate relationships represents a gradation of authority from the top to the bottom of an organization. Stated another way, this line of authority represents a chain of command among individuals within the formal organization structure. Thus, line authority derives its meaning from the direct and continuing relationships between superiors and subordinates. Based on this relationship, line managers are viewed as having relatively complete authority to direct their immediate subordinates.

An additional meaning sometimes attached to line authority refers to those activities within an organization that are directly related to an achievement of primary objectives. In this sense, managers who are directly involved in accomplishing primary organizational objectives are said to possess line authority. If, for example, an organization's major objectives are to produce and sell certain goods, then the areas of production, marketing, and finance would be line functions since they are basic to an accomplishment of primary objectives. If separated from these basic functions, activities of inspection, personnel, and purchasing would be viewed as having indirect involvement in achieving primary objectives and would be classified as staff functions. Unfortunately, much confusion arises from this approach due to the extreme difficulty in identifying the activities that make the most direct contribution to an achievement of major organizational objectives. Clearly, the overall relationship between line and staff is situational or contingent in nature; but, if the design of the organization indicates a meaningful distinction between line and staff and it is useful to the company to make such a distinction, it should be made.[4]

STAFF AUTHORITY

In its purest form, staff authority represents an advisory relationship among individuals and carries no command prerogatives. Authority of this type provides only the right to advise or assist other individuals in the performance of their duties. Staff personnel bring specialized knowledge and expertise to an organization. Acting in an advisory capacity, they assist other managers in discharging their responsibilities. In fact, most large-scale organizations are supported by staff personnel since managers cannot possess all of the abilities and knowledge required in the performance of their duties. The partial organization

---

[3] G. G. Fisch, "Line-Staff Is Obsolete," *Harvard Business Review,* September–October 1961, pp. 67–79.

[4] Vivian Nossiter, "A New Approach Toward Resolving the Line and Staff Dilemma," *The Academy of Management Review,* January 1979, pp. 103–6.

chart of a small manufacturing company pictured in Figure 11–2 serves to show certain prescribed line and staff authority relationships.

Scope of staff authority

The scope of staff authority possessed by various individuals is dependent on an organization's objectives and functions. Consequently, there are several possible types of staff arrangements. The following arrangements are generally found in actual practice: specialized staff, service departments, and general staff.

Specialized staff   When a manager has neither the knowledge nor the technical ability to handle a specific problem, expert assistance may be provided by a specialized staff member. Examples of such specialized staff services include the following:

Legal counsel	Forecasting and planning
Quality control	Contract negotiations
Public relations	Internal control
Personnel	Organizational planning
Industrial relations	Accounting

In a pure line-staff relationship, line managers may either accept or reject the advice offered by specialized staff members. However,

FIGURE 11–2
The line-staff relationship

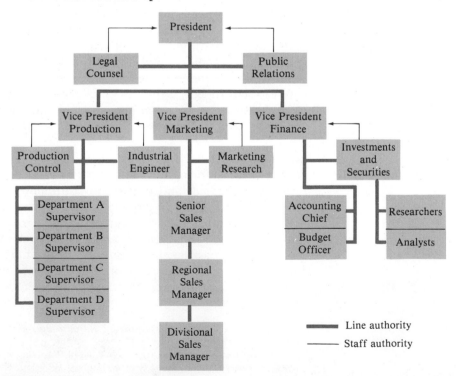

staff personnel are of the opinion that they are hired for their expert knowledge and often feel that line managers should be obligated to accept their advice. As we will see later, such feelings sometimes reach the point where they result in conflicts between staff personnel and line managers. In other situations, the role of staff personnel is strengthened by requiring concurring approval from them before a decision can be made. Familiar examples of such approval are seen in decisions dealing with legal matters or quality inspections of raw materials and finished goods.

Service departments The concept of specialized staff can be expanded to include specialized service departments. A difference occurs, however, since these departments are not always strictly advisory. In some cases their services may be mandatory, such as those provided by a purchasing department. In another example, the manager of a maintenance department may be asked for advice about an addition to physical facilities or the purchase of new plant equipment. This individual may also have the authority to require production (line) managers to follow specific steps in maintaining their equipment. A personnel department could be advisory in nature if its authority was limited only to assisting other managers in the recruitment and training of employees. But it could also possess mandatory authority if made responsible for establishing and implementing an affirmative action program to be followed in the hiring and promotion of employees. Several typical service departments are noted below, although we should recognize that they can be classified as either staff groups or service departments depending on the scope of their authority:

Research and development	Food service
Industrial relations	Legal counsel
Customer service	Transportation
Personnel	Accounting
Public relations	Advertising
Maintenance	Market research
Purchasing	Budgetary control
Engineering	

General staff A common reference to general staff is the traditional military classifications of G–1 (personnel), G–2 (military intelligence), G–3 (operations), and G–4 (training and supply). Each major command officer has these four general staff positions to provide assistance in the planning function. In addition, the general staff concept is also widely used in the federal government and in large-scale industrial organizations. For example, major administrative officials in the federal government often have a general staff composed of (1) budget and fiscal officers, (2) personnel officers, and (3) administrative assistants or planning officers.

At General Motors, the general staff includes (1) an operations staff,

(2) a financial staff, and (3) a legal staff. The operations staff is divided into marketing, engineering, personnel, manufacturing, public relations, styling, research, motor holdings, and patents. All general staff personnel advise top corporate officals and the executive vice presidents. By having a centralized general staff, executives in the Chevrolet Motor Division, for instance, do not make major policy decisions in manufacturing or finance unless they consult with members of the general staff. Thus, the general staff cooperates with the operating divisions to see that a coordination of effort is achieved.

In smaller organizations, a general staff grouping may not be economically feasible. However, a corollary to the general staff is found in the use of a staff assistant, often referred to as an *assistant-to* or *administrative assistant*. The title of administrative assistant is used in governmental organizations while the assistant-to position is more common in business firms. In any event, staff assistants should not be confused with assistant managers. An assistant manager possesses line authority and normally stands between the manager and a group of immediate subordinates. Staff assistants usually provide only advice and assistance for the manager to whom they are assigned. This distinction is illustrated in Figure 11–3.

FIGURE 11–3
Distinction between staff assistants and line assistants

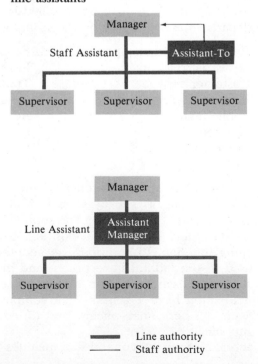

────── Line authority
────── Staff authority

Some of the major responsibilities of staff assistants include investigation, report writing, and the development of recommendations concerning various problems such as excessive labor turnover, a breakdown in communications, or unexplained budget variances. Thus, staff assistants must be able to communicate well, both orally and in writing, as they interrelate with personnel throughout an entire organization. Through such contacts, staff positions of this type provide individuals with frequent opportunities to view a wide variety of organizational processes and managerial practices.

Using staff authority wisely

The use of staff personnel must be justified economically. This requires top management to balance the costs of staff positions against the anticipated benefits from their use. In this calculation, costs must include not only salaries but also other qualitative considerations. Some additional cost considerations include (1) any possible increases in the complexity of the organization; (2) potential status problems between line and staff personnel, since people must be seen doing measurable work contributing to profits if recognition is to be received; (3) "power plays" that can develop if staff personnel try to usurp the authority of other managers; (4) the creation of additional communication links in the organization; and (5) the dangers of stagnation associated with staff personnel who become "yes men."[5]

In general, the benefits of staff authority depend on the interrelationships among various managers. To ensure a greater probability of success, managers should do the following:

Carefully select staff members for their technical competence and ability to work with others, while explicitly stating their authority relationships to other organizational members.

Encourage line managers (who may have more decision-making authority, but less communicative skill) to understand the importance and purpose of staff members.

Assure staff members of their relative importance in the strategic timing of long-run courses of action.

Provide staff personnel with the information they will need to perform their jobs.

See that authority and responsibility of staff managers are commensurate with the tasks to be done.

Consult with staff specialists in areas where their expertise is relevant before making decisions.

Encourage staff personnel to recognize that their ideas can be implemented by making recommendations to managers and by trying

---

[5] For additional discussion of factors, see E. H. Potter, III, and F. E. Fiedler, "The Utilization of Staff Member Intelligence and Experience under High and Low Stress," *Academy of Management Journal*, June 1981, pp. 361–76.

to secure voluntary acceptance of suggestions. These two actions are better than attempting to command or use the power that might flow from staff association with other managers.

FUNCTIONAL AUTHORITY

Functional authority exists when managers have the right to issue orders in a specific area of activity to others who are outside their normal scope of authority. Instead of making recommendations to their superiors or to some other person, managers with functional authority can direct the efforts of others over whom they have no continuing line authority. The effect is the same as if a directive had come down through the normal chain of command. The exercise of such authority, however, should be limited in two ways. First, it should be restricted to the performance of carefully defined duties; and second, it should be granted for a specified period of time.

The term *functional authority* was first considered in Taylor's functional foremanship.[6] Although somewhat different in form from that noted by Taylor, functional authority still exists to a large degree in most organizations. Its use is particularly essential and necessary when technical competence is required and consistency of decisions is essential in several operating departments. However, it cannot be extended to the point where the effectiveness of line authority is destroyed. This is particularly true if it undermines the authority of line supervisors and results in conflicting orders. An example of the creation of functional authority will help clarify its importance in the operation of a business.

Consider the situation of E. J. Moak, who has converted his small dairy plant into a country meat market. He slaughters cattle and hogs and sells fresh meat through a retail market. At various points in the growth of his business, Moak found himself unable to perform some of the management functions. Thus, he hired an accountant to help develop various control techniques and brought in consultants to assist in analyzing alternative equipment choices for a plant expansion. A lawyer was hired to provide advice in preparing contractual arrangements between the business and its customers. Each of these positions represents the use of staff authority by outside professionals.

With the enactment of laws affecting meat packaging firms, Moak is now faced with a need to add two certified meat inspectors. Even though these inspectors are granted staff authority, they also possess functional authority, as shown in Figure 11–4. In fact, they can only be effective when they have functional authority to make decisions about accepting or rejecting carcasses, cleanliness of the plant, and how meats may be displayed and sold over the counter. With functional

---

[6] Frederick W. Taylor, "Shop Management," in *Scientific Management* (New York: Harper & Row 1947), pp. 92–109.

FIGURE 11–4
Line, staff, and functional authority: Moak's Meat Market

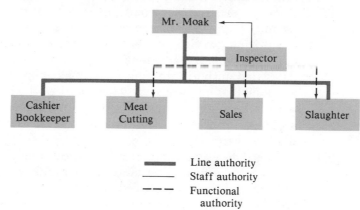

authority, the inspectors need not seek the advice of the owner before making decisions concerning sanitation and quality in meat processing. Their authority is even binding on the owner; and, thereby, they exert direct influence over the entire organization. In situations of this type, functional authority can bring order and efficiency to an organization, but the greater complexity of authority relationships remains as a potential source of future problems.

Summarizing, functional authority is a reality in both large and small companies, but its use can be justified only when its benefits outweigh its potential dangers. The benefits can be easily seen in the need for greater consistency, technical competence, and formal approval of authority that is generally accepted most of the time by others. Dangers to be balanced against the benefits include increased complexity of decision making, empire building, and possible violations of unity of command. In spite of these dangers, the role of functional authority may become even more firmly established, particularly as organizations develop task forces or project teams (a matrix organization) that cut across departmental lines. In such cases, members of the team normally possess functional authority to direct others but are limited to their individual areas of specialization in exercising such authority.

CENTRALIZATION AND DECENTRALIZATION OF AUTHORITY

The degree to which managerial authority is delegated determines the extent of centralization or decentralization within an organization. Centralization implies a minimal delegation of authority, while decentralization refers to the release of greater scopes of authority. In a decentralized organization, managers delegate decision-making authority to lower-level managers. In a highly centralized structure, top management retains a majority of such authority. Within any one organization, however, some activities may remain centralized while others are decentralized.

To emphasize these points, let us look at the K mart discount chain again. A highly centralized set of corporate policies dealing with product pricing, service, and procurement decisions for individual stores are set by top management. Each store manager, however, has been delegated authority to make decisions about the selection of specific products that best suit a particular market, the hiring of sales personnel, work schedules, and many in-store operational policies. The result is a combination of both centralization and decentralization within the K mart chain.

The difference between centralization and decentralization of authority can be further visualized by considering a continuum, as shown in Figure 11–5. Complete centralization is at one end of the continuum, and full decentralization is at the other. Generally, most organizations fall some place between the two extremes since none can be either completely centralized nor totally decentralized. Obviously, an organization cannot be completely centralized because all authority would be retained in the office of the chief executive. A complete decentralization is also untenable since all authority would be pushed downward to the lowest organizational level. In practice, then, an infinite number of variations in degrees of delegation exist.

The degree of decentralization implemented in a given organization reflects a series of circumstances or factors unique to each organization. Size, existing equipment, competence of individuals to whom authority is delegated, the ability to obtain adequate and reliable information in decision making, and the potential impact of decisions in terms of competitive strategy are important factors in determining the degree to which decentralization is practiced. From a contingency viewpoint, each organization must decide on how much delegation best fits its specific situation.

It is generally agreed that a decentralization of authority develops initiative, promotes flexibility in maximizing individual and group decision-making contributions, increases independence of thought, and develops future managers by allowing subordinates to learn management skills. Believing in these benefits, A. W. Clausen, the former chief execu-

FIGURE 11–5
Centralization-decentralization continuum

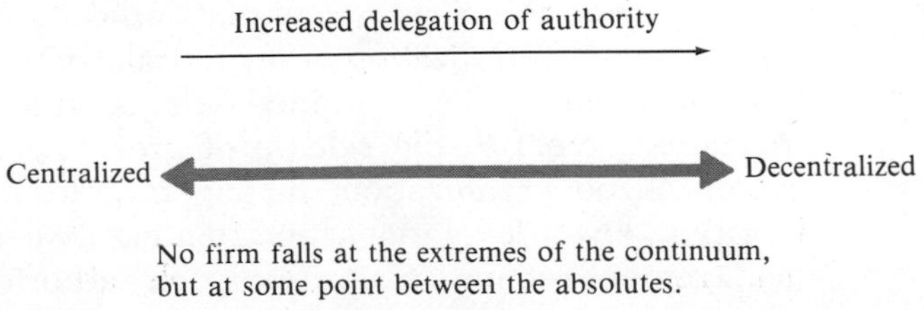

Increased delegation of authority

Centralized ←——————————→ Decentralized

No firm falls at the extremes of the continuum,
but at some point between the absolutes.

FIGURE 11–6
**Is the organization centralized or
decentralized?**

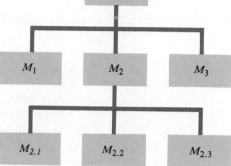

tive officer of BankAmerica Corporation, undertook a decentralization
program to shift responsibility as far down the executive ladder as
practical. In Clausen's view, his job was to help other managers make
the right decisions rather than to reserve them for himself.

One way of determining the degree of decentralization practiced
in an organization is to identify the extent to which subordinates must
refer matters to their superior for a decision. Consider an organization
where the scope of authority in various management positions permits
little more than performing routine functions. These might include
the duties of scheduling production runs, assigning company cars to
employees, and approving departmental expenditures of not more than
$25. All of these activities indicate that higher-level managers are regi-
menting work via organizational objectives, policies, and standard operating procedures. In this organization, the degree of delegation is
relatively insignificant and we can conclude that authority is more
centralized than decentralized.

Interestingly, an organization chart does not clearly indicate
whether authority is centralized or decentralized. By looking at Figure
11–6, there is no way to determine the degree of centralization or
decentralization that exists. It can only be done by reviewing job descriptions and identifying through direct observation the scope of decision-making authority in each position. Still, an organization chart can
help in determining the extent to which decentralization might be
implemented. For instance, grouping activities that relate to types
of customers served, kinds of products sold, or to the territories covered
usually encourages greater decentralization than departmentation by
function where the need for overall coordination is much greater.
By knowing the type of departmentation, managers have a better idea
of possible limits on decentralization. From this discussion, we can
conclude that centralization and decentralization:

Exist in varying degrees within organizations.

May vary within and among specific organizational units.

Will vary as managerial capacities and environmental conditions change.

Examples of centralization-decentralization

A noteworthy example of centralization-decentralization is found in General Motors Corporation (GM). Being the largest auto maker in the world, good organization is essential in the coordination and control of GM's employees, numbering approximately 750,000. Much of GM's success through the years must be credited to the organizational genius of Alfred P. Sloan, Jr., who was president of the company from 1923 to 1937. Under Sloan's leadership, GM sought to realize the benefits of centralized policy determination with decentralized decision making at the divisional levels.

The overall organizational structure of GM is shown in Figure 11–7. Again, we cannot determine the degree of decentralization in GM

FIGURE 11–7
Partial organizational structure of General Motors

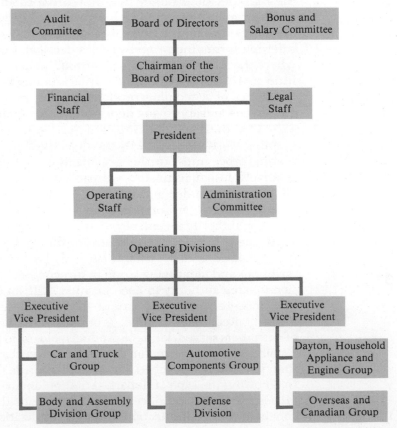

by simply viewing the organization chart, but we can see that the major operating divisions are divided on a product basis. This form of departmentalization allows for a substantially greater degree of decentralization than would be true if functional departmentation existed at the divisional level.

Thomas A. Murphy, the past chairman of the board of GM, managed the system not simply from the standpoint of decentralization but also in terms of coordinated control. In this regard, coordinated control means the integration of operating units through centralized policies. Major policy and strategy considerations, such as union negotiations, dealer relations, antipollution, and safety issues, are coordinated at the top-management level. Through this approach, work can be shifted from one division to another, assignments changed, and even divisions restructured by the central staff. Yet, day-to-day operations remain on a decentralized basis by division.

The General Electric Company (GE) illustrates a decentralized operation. Within GE emphasis is placed on the development of profit centers. These centers are manageable divisions of the company that are responsible for earning a satisfactory return on investment. Managers of these profit centers are given wide latitude in making operating decisions since they are responsible for the profit of their respective divisions. Through decentralization it is felt that better corporate planning, increased flexibility, faster decisions, effective leadership, and a more competitive market position will be attained. GE executives, however, still rely on several thousand centralized staff members for assistance in promoting profit center effectiveness. Emphasizing a decentralized arrangement, GE reflects a unique combination of centralized policy making with decentralized profit centers.

The Philco-Ford Corporation provides another example but with a more centralized structure. When Robert E. Hunter became president of Philco-Ford he reorganized the corporation, following the belief that more companies had been hurt than helped through a decentralization of authority. His approach to a centralized reorganization included the following:

1. Centralizing all of the consumer product divisions into one profit center. One vice president was placed in charge of all sales and marketing, and another became responsible for all engineering, manufacturing, and distribution.

2. Making the engineering department responsible for all product development and design within the organization. The feeling here was that an engineering group developing communication satellites should also be able to develop better consumer products.

3. Coordinating physical distribution by making the production control staff responsible for a component from the time it arrived at a plant until the finished product was billed to a dealer.

Based on the above examples, we can see that centralization and decentralization are not absolutes—that is, neither is an end in itself. Instead, when judiciously mixed within the organization, both centralization and decentralization represent important means to assist in the accomplishment of objectives.

Contingency considerations in centralization-decentralization

We have identified the advantages of both centralized and decentralized organizations. To realize any of these advantages, however, one must consider the causal factors influencing the degree of centralization or decentralization that is practical for a given organization.[7] The situational variables that determine where in the management hierarchy decisions will be made are discussed below:

1. As noted earlier, organizations marketing diverse product lines in several different locations may find decentralization to be more efficient than centralization. Likewise, if customer or territorial departmentation is utilized, a centralized coordination of policies may not be as essential as when departmentation is based on the business functions.

2. The ability of managers to collect data, analyze alternatives, and make decisions suggests the extent to which decentralization can be implemented. Some complex decisions may require centralization while others, such as when to replace the coffee urn in the employee's lounge of a hospital, could be easily delegated.

3. The necessity for flexibility and speed in decision making due to frequent changes in competition, technology, and consumer demand may indicate that decentralization would be advantageous.

4. For organizations that require managerial creativity and initiative in the attainment of profit, decentralization is often appropriate. In this situation, supervisors must be willing to accept some mistakes, particularly if subordinates are to improve their skills and confidence while demonstrating initiative in decision making.

5. Information that passes through many offices and communication centers is subjected to distortion. This need to improve communication may suggest a move toward greater decentralization.

6. If the cost of a poor decision is less than the cost of referring the matter upward for a decision, an increased delegation of authority may be appropriate.

7. When numerous interrelationships among operational subsystems exist, an organization tends to require more centralization. Here, a coordination of effort is achieved through centralized policy making and budgetary controls. Even as decentralization becomes more feasible, appropriate feedback and evaluation procedures are still essential at the top-management level.

---

[7] Based on a contingency approach, decentralization is treated as a dependent, rather than an independent, variable in structuring an organization. See D. C. Murphy, "Decentralization: The Effects of Complexity," *The Southern Journal of Business*, November 1972, pp. 79–86.

In conjunction with the above, we have found that when a relatively large number of subordinates report to a manager, the amount of direct supervision that they receive decreases and the scope of their decision-making authority increases. Furthermore, research studies have shown that morale and productivity are low when managers and workers are subjected to close supervision and rigid controls. With increased autonomy, people are more prone to accept responsibility, use independent judgment, and initiate action. For these reasons, it is possible to hypothesize that increased productivity results from a decentralization of authority because (1) the scope and/or depth of jobs is increased, (2) people are required to accept greater responsibility, (3) decision-making skills are enhanced through practice and the freedom to learn from mistakes, and (4) organizations can respond more quickly to the needs of employees and customers. In spite of these potential benefits, organizations have been slow in moving toward a decentralization of authority. Perhaps this is wise, because decentralization does not solve the structural problems of organizations nor assure top management that subordinate managers are properly trained to perform the management functions. If the organizing function is not done well by top-level executives, changing the scope of delegation will not improve anything.

Finally, as we have defined it, decentralization has reference to only the delegation of authority. This definition is not meant to include situations where an organization has several plants or offices located throughout the country, nor does it include profit centers per se that are established within an organization. In the first situation, we are referring to a geographic decentralization of plants or offices. The second merely refers to organizing around profit centers. Neither is necessarily accompanied by a decentralization of authority.

Impact of environment and computer technology on centralization

Today, large-scale organizations are faced with numerous pressures from a variety of sources. The issues surrounding pollution, safety and health, price inflation, and affirmative action have produced many new problems for most organizations. Centralization of authority has recently become an important consideration as organizations seek ways of adapting to change and solving these problems in a coordinated manner. Automotive companies have standardized certain parts and instituted more coordination of design to meet federal safety and antipollution requirements. As a result, various managers in these companies have experienced some reduction in their authority.

Advances in computerization have made possible more refined management information systems that also permit a greater centralization of many decisions at top-management levels. With these advances in computer technology, the need for certain middle-management positions may be reduced in some organizations. At present, the scheduling of output in oil refineries, the design of textile patterns, and the development of engineering specifications for special-purpose products is often done by computers with a resultant elimination of many staff planners. Similarly, many lower-level line managers are finding that computers are handling many of their programmable-type decisions. While these changes are dramatic, the cumulative impact of computerization will not be known for quite some time. During the interim, it is apparent that a centralization of authority will continue to receive renewed interest in the design of management hierarchies.

SUMMARY

Authority is delegated for the performance of specific operating tasks, as well as the discharge of management responsibilities. In this context, the performance of all organizational activities depends on the delegation of authority from superiors to subordinates. The degree of delegation depends on the abilities of each superior, the perceived capabilities of subordinates, the nature of the work to be completed, and other relevant organizational constraints.

The authority vested in any position can be line, staff, functional, or a combination of these types. Whether considered individually or in combination, they refer to authority relationships among individuals in an organization. Line authority relates to the direct and continuing right of a manager to direct subordinates toward the accomplishment of specified objectives. Staff refers to the authority of one individual to advise or assist another. A pure staff relationship carries none of the prerogatives associated with line authority. (Within a staff department, however, line authority may exist.) Functional authority is best characterized as modified line authority in that it involves a right to direct others, although this right is limited to carefully defined areas and is normally granted for a specific period of time.

There are several possible styles of staff arrangements with specialized staff groups, service departments, and general staff arrangements being the most common. In smaller organizations where staff groupings in departmental units are not feasible, staff assistants may be used. Of course, the use of all staff personnel should be justified economically by balancing the costs of such individuals against the benefits anticipated from their use.

Decentralization of authority refers to the scope of authority delegated downward in an organization. In the early part of this century, authority was highly centralized at the executive levels of most organizations. Following World War II, there was a move toward more decentralization of authority to accommodate the rapid growth of organizations and managerial shortages that prevailed at that time. More recently, computerization and the development of more sophisticated management information systems have permitted a return to more highly centralized forms of organizations.

There are many purported advantages of both centralization and decentralization of authority. However, certain actions must be taken before seeking the benefits of either. First, individual differences must be considered—an increased scope of authority is not sought by all people. Second, an assessment of the total organizational environment must be conducted to isolate constraints that would hamper an implementation of either increased centralization or decentralization. Finally, the management philosophy exhibited by top executives must be considered. In short, much time, thought, and effort must precede any decision to move in the direction of either increasing or decreasing the decisional authority delegated to subordinate managers. Only in this way can the resulting decision be expected to meet the unique problems of given organizational environments.

KEY TERMS

Assistant-to: A staff assistant who generally provides advice and assistance for the manager to whom he/she is assigned.

Decentralization: The delegation of managerial decision-making authority to the lowest managerial levels possible.

Delegation: The management practice of entrusting the performance of specific operating tasks and/or managerial functions to subordinates, thereby creating a shared authority relationship.

Functional authority: In either line or staff positions, managers are delegated the right to issue orders in a specific area of activity to others who are outside of their normal scope of authority.

Line authority: The direct and continuing authority relationship between superiors and subordinates within the formal organization.

Service department: Normally a department in an advisory capacity to other organizational units, but the department's advice may be mandatory if its knowledge and expertise are vital to the successful achievement of organizational goals.

Staff authority: The right of individuals who have specialized knowledge and expertise to assist others in the performance of their duties.

QUESTIONS

1. What is the meaning of delegation and what relationship does it have to authority?
2. List the barriers to delegation that can arise in any organization.
3. Define the meaning of line authority.
4. What is the meaning of staff authority? Why does it exist?
5. "All staff authority originates from line authority." Discuss.
6. Briefly outline the problems that can exist among individuals in line and staff positions.

7. What are three types of staff arrangements? How do they differ from each other?

8. Distinguish between the positions of "assistant to" and "assistant manager."

9. What major factors should managers consider in deciding on the desirability of using staff authority?

10. Define functional authority. Is its use restricted to any particular type or size of organization?

11. Distinguish between centralization and decentralization of authority. Why can neither exist in pure form?

12. Does an organization chart indicate whether authority is centralized or decentralized? What factors should a person consider when attempting to determine the degree of decentralization in an organization?

13. What are the advantages of centralization of authority? Decentralization?

14. List the variables that are important in determining the extent to which a decentralization of authority would occur.

15. What changes are now taking place that may cause organizations to move toward a greater centralization of authority?

PROBLEMS

1. Multinational companies located in the United States find that one of the difficulties in using foreign national managers is their unwillingness to delegate decisional authority.

a. Why do you think foreign managers are this way, particularly in developing countries?

b. How might these obstacles be overcome?

2. A salesperson in the record and tape department of a retail store is responsible for submitting daily cost reports on departmental activities. However, these reports do not go to the department head but are submitted to the cost accountant who establishes the regulations and procedures for filling them out. Recently a problem arose about the reporting of these data, and the cost accountant went directly to the salesperson, thus bypassing the department head in the process.

a. Who is the salesperson's immediate superior?

b. What authority relationships are involved in this situation?

c. Is bypassing the salesperson's superior a sound management practice?

d. How might potential conflicts of this type be avoided?

3. Consider the following illustrations:

a. A recent study of Harvard graduates found that many MBAs could not easily classify their jobs as definitely line or staff.

b. In a matrix organization, a line manager may work in a staff capacity on a project.

c. Studies conducted in specific organizations show that managers do not always agree as to the number of line and/or staff personnel in their company, although each feels confident of the meaning and interpretation of line and staff.

These three illustrations can be expanded in number, suggesting the blurred distinctions between line and staff. Is the implication that the concept of line/staff is not useful in the modern-day organization? Or, can the gap between theory and application be overcome by being more sensitive to the organizational situation, recognizing that differences in design may call for different ways of viewing and designing line-staff relationships?

4. Indicate the appropriate type of staff arrangement for each situation:

Situations	Types of arrangement		
	Specialized staff	Service dept.	General staff
a. Due to new EPA interpretations of regulations, the company has hired an additional public relations person to deal with air quality standards.			
b. Several positions have been developed to advise top corporate officials in a large organization.			
c. The inventory control department provides advice on EOQ and ordering dates. At the same time, specific procedures designated by the manager must be followed in reporting usage and receipt of materials.			
d. An administrative assistant to the dean of the college was appointed.			

5. Consider yourself as an eager and ambitious individual serving as an assistant to the president of a small business organization. You have been assigned to work on a variety of projects ranging from helping develop the annual budget and major policy statements to entertaining plant visitors, including relatives of the president. Recognizing your eagerness to do a good job while obtaining as much managerial training as possible, what organizational problems could arise from your enthusiasm and initiative?

6. Gold Oil Corporation is divided into four regional companies, each with its own president, and a fifth company, also headed by a president that operates on a worldwide basis. Authority relationships are guided by a corporate concept referred to as "The Executive." The implication here is that top officers acting individually within each regional company are given the authority to make final decisions on major corporate matters. In other words, they have broad authority that is not restricted to decisions within particular company areas.

Recently, a top executive of the company stated that an extreme decentralization of authority can destroy the essential character and meaning of a corporation. Delegation, the executive said, can be carried to the point where top management is nothing more than a holding company.

Comment on this statement and decide if it is consistent with corporate practices.

7. A concept that Honeywell Information Systems practices is called mission concept. Through this concept, various specialists, no matter where they are located, are given a worldwide mission to plan, design, develop, manufacture, and market computer systems. Thus, the company can capitalize on existing expertise, whether it is in Italy or Arizona. For example, a French specialist based at Honeywell-Bull's small computer plant in Paris may show up in Chicago to help correct a problem involving the small computer. Similarly, executives based in Phoenix have worldwide responsibilities for Honeywell's Series 6000.

The mission concept is also applied to Honeywell's management information systems. Here, an operating committee composed of the executive vice president of information systems and the manager of the French, Italian, British, and North American divisional operations participate in making all major decisions.

a. Would you classify Honeywell as being more centralized than decentralized? Substantiate your answer.
b. Is functional authority utilized in Honeywell?

8. In preparing a memorandum for the board of directors, Jack Star, assistant to the president, included the following statement:

> Companies with a high volume of unit sales tend to be more centralized than those with a lower volume of unit sales. In addition, companies with a larger number of operating employees tend to be more decentralized than those with fewer operating employees.

One of the company's operational line managers disagrees with Star's assertions and has presented a report to the president quoting empirical research to indicate that neither sales nor the number of operating employees is significantly related to a decentralization of authority.

a. Which major assertion do you think is correct?
b. Assume that this company has (1) standardized employee relationships through strong unionization and established personnel policies, (2) high task standardization, and (3) plant operations substantially below capacity. Would these elements cause you to change your answer?
c. If the president and the board were making a decision to move toward greater decentralization, what potential conflict could arise between line and staff positions.

9. The "Federal Principle" has its origin in *The Federalist*, written by Alexander Hamilton, and in Hamilton's letters dealing with the "Insufficiency of the Present Confederation" and the "Necessity of an Energetic Government." The essential issue was that the 13 colonies were too small and weak to provide a strong government for each one.

    a. Could Hamilton's argument be applied to the decentralization of a company like General Motors into 13 separate operating units?

    b. What factors should be considered in a decision of this type?

10. A rule of thumb states that every effort should be made to decentralize unless the purely economic costs of operating a centralized organization are at least 25 percent less than those of operating a decentralized organization.

    Discuss the meaning of this rule and the problems involved in applying it.

11. As business increased in size and output immediately after World War II, there was a large movement toward decentralization. The results were disastrous for many companies. Since then, studies have shown that the two most common causes of failure of decentralization are (1) the lack of written and clearly understood objectives and policies and (2) the diminution of a pool of managerial talent.

    a. Why do you think these two factors are so important to successful decentralization?

    b. What other variables should be considered?

SUGGESTED READINGS

Atherton, R. M. "Centralization Works Best When Managers' Jobs Are Improved." *Human Resource Management,* Summer 1977, pp. 17–20.

Burack, E. H. "Supervisory Authority and Delegation." In *Supervisory Management: Tools and Techniques,* edited by M. G. Newport. St. Paul: West Publishing Company, 1976, 113–36.

Burns, T. S. "Line and Staff at ITT." In *Management: Concepts and Controversies,* edited by J. A. Litterer. Santa Barbara, Calif.: John Wiley & Sons, 1978, pp. 162–70.

Cooper, C. L. "Humanizing the Work Place in Europe: An Overview of Six Countries." *Personnel Journal,* June 1980, pp. 488–91.

Davis, S. M., and P. R. Lawrence. "Problems of Matrix Organizations." *Harvard Business Review,* May–June 1978, pp. 131–42.

Dodson, D. C., V. R. Ewing, and O. R. Crocker. "The Changing Role of the Administrative Assistant." *Applied Business and Administrative Quarterly,* Spring 1981, pp. 2–7.

Drucker, P. F. *An Introductory View of Management.* New York: Harper & Row, 1977, chap. 36.

Hayes, R. H., and R. W. Schmenner. "How Should You Organize Manufacturing?" *Harvard Business Review,* January–February 1978, pp. 105–18.

Hill, R. "The Relaxed Management Style of a High Technology Company." *International Management,* March 1978, pp. 12–15.

"ITT's New Chief Executive Gets Down to Work." *International Management,* January 1978, pp. 18–23.

Powell, G., and B. Z. Posner. "Resistance to Change Reconsidered: Implications for Managers." *Human Resource Management,* Spring 1978, pp. 29–34.

Scott, W. G. "Organization Theory: A Reassessment." *Academy of Management Journal*, 1974, pp. 242–54.

Starkweather, D. B. "The Rationale for Decentralization in Large Hospitals." In *Readings in Organizations: Behavior, Structure, Processes*, edited by J. L. Gibson, J. M. Ivancevich, and J. H. Donnelly, Jr. Plano, Tex.: Business Publication, 1976, pp. 262–78.

Weick, K. E. "Amendments to Organizational Theorizing." *Academy of Management Journal*, September 1976, pp. 487–502.

"What It's Like to Run Biggest U.S. Companies." *U.S. News and World Report*, October 27, 1980, pp. 83–86.

Super Food Corporation

From the 1940s to the mid-1960s, Super Food Corporation (SFC)—a leader in packaged convenience foods—had a thriving business. After the 1960s, however, competition grew tougher and sales for SFC dropped off in several markets. In order to strengthen sales, new business acquisitions were undertaken but with little success.

The new president of SFC who came on board in 1980 diagnosed the problem as a structural one. The company's products were seen as competing with each other rather than augmenting one another in the consumer's diet. Consequently, the company's marketing, technological, and management efforts were not being coordinated effectively.

ORGANIZATIONAL DESIGN (1980)

Products were divided along divisional lines, based on brands or brand names. For example, since SFC's powdered breakfast drink, powdered soft drink, and frozen orange juice had different brand names, they were marketed by different divisions. In order not to miss opportunities for new products and to analyze products in the context of the total consumer market, cross-divisional task forces were utilized. Although there was some discussion that the organization restricted managers in dealing with the interaction of the company's brands, a sweeping reorganization was thought to be too disruptive to existing communication and authority relationships.

A VISIT TO UNITED COFFEE COMPANY

On a business trip to New Orleans, the president was invited to tour the United Coffee Corporation. The company had a variety of brands and blends—regular, decaffeinated, ground, instant, and flavored. Their grouping was not based on technology nor distribution modes, but by their natural interrelationship on the consumer's menu. The total organization was designed or structured around strategic business units.

PROPOSED REORGANIZATION FOR SFC

Being impressed with the organizational design of United Coffee, and recognizing that competitors marketed their established and new products on the basis of the market as a total arena, the president proposed the formation of three new divisions. These divisions would bring together some of the existing brands that were complementary in nature. The various brands would be treated as strategic business units (SBU) with a manager being responsible for the performance and competitive standing of each unit, the identification and exploitation of opportunities, and contribution to corporate profits. The SBU managers would also develop and execute long-term strategies and plans with the approval of divisional vice presidents.

The three new divisions would be the food products division (emphasizing main meals and desserts), the beverage and breakfast division, and the pet foods division. Each division was to be given its own research capability geared to supporting existing businesses and developing line extensions and new products. One sales force would be used for the beverages and breakfast and the pet foods divisions and one for the food products division.

ENVIRONMENTAL CONCERNS

With the proposed new organization, SFC intends to double its efforts in new product development and increase investment in research and development. The company sees the expanded awareness of nutrition as creating more opportunities for new products. Other concerns for future product development involve weight control and the relationship of meat products to health. Also, the president thinks that there is an expanding need for convenience foods since there are more households where husbands and wives both work.

MANAGEMENT PHILOSOPHY

SFC operates on the philosophy that a good and innovative marketing program must be based on a product that has a reason to exist. In this sense, the product must have some superiority or quality that commends it to the consumer.

In analyzing any new problem, several questions are asked at SFC: What is the product like, how is it different, and will it stand up to the competition? Thus, most general business propositions are analyzed from a marketing standpoint. Additional questions are then asked: What are the margins? and What are the capital requirements?

Questions

1. Is the argument of avoiding a disruption of existing lines of communication and authority sufficient to discourage a substantial reorganization when the record shows that the current structure is simply not functional?
2. Assess the idea of organizing around basic menu segments.
3. Are you in agreement with the president that a reorganization is needed and that the new approach deserves consideration by the board of directors?

4. Is the proposed reorganizational structure functional in dealing with environmental concerns and consistent with SFC's management philosophy?

The Hanging-On Syndrome

The Waterfront Barge Line was founded by Adam J. Rivers in 1937 and has now grown to one of the largest lines in the United States. It also operates a large fleet of high-speed commercial, oceangoing container ships. The firm is very profitable, financially sound, and one of the most competitive organizations in a fast-growing industry.

At the age of 72, the genial but iron-willed Rivers decided to step down from the presidency of the company. He then spent over a year trying to decide who should succeed him as president. His major criterion in selecting a successor was to find someone who would run the organization just as he had always done it. Thus, with a smooth transition in presidents, the company would experience few noticeable changes in either operations or policies.

Rivers finally chose William E. Ahab, manager of Waterfront's ship division, to succeed him. After Ahab became president, he managed the company his own way, but the changes he implemented often piqued the board of directors. The board was dominated by individuals who had been selected by Rivers, and they continued to maintain close contact with him.

Last year, revenues totaled $151 million with profits of $14.4 million for a new high. Yet, the board complained that Ahab was not generating sufficient sales and that the future profit picture of the company looked bleak. During the past three months, there have been frequent arguments over (1) a new organizational arrangement that Ahab feels will clarify employee relationships, (2) a revised retirement policy for all employees, (3) a new management compensation plan, and (4) a program of executive appraisal and development. Consequently, Ahab feels that Rivers' influence will prevent him from getting his own programs and plans off the ground.

Throughout the total organization, morale has been poor and a high turnover of middle managers has continued since Ahab became president. One of the division managers stated that "The company has a good reservoir of number two executives. However, no potential executives are available since the best management talent has constantly been driven off through the years."

Ahab's management philosophy is built on the idea that the chief executive should not fight fires and meddle in the everyday operations of other executives. Instead, the job of the president should focus on policy decisions, long-range planning and strategy, and on the development of key management personnel.

Unfortunately, the conflict between Ahab and the board of directors has become so unreasonable that Ahab now feels his only alternative is to resign as the company's president. He wants to make a final decision before the board of directors meets again in two weeks.

Questions

1. Do you feel that Ahab has proven to be an effective president?
2. Does the conflict between Ahab and the board of directors stem from *(a)* the criterion on which Ahab was selected, *(b)* Ahab himself, or *(c)* Rivers?
3. What short-range actions seem to be required? What long-term actions?
4. What will have to change before real progress can be made in either the short or long run?

Zappa Grain and Seed Company

Zappa Grain and Seed Company is a well-established seed packaging and sales company. Company sales and revenue transactions in 1981 were well over $25 million. The firm is headed by Walter Zappa who founded the company 19 years ago. He is assisted by the plant superintendent and six departmental supervisors. The organization chart of the management hierarchy is shown in Exhibit 1.

Fescues, bluegrass, and ryegrass are some of the types of seeds handled by the Zappa plant. Although grains are purchased and sold, the majority of business is in seeds. Shipments of seeds are made throughout the continental United States and to several Latin Ameri-

EXHIBIT 1
Organization chart for Zappa Grain and Seed Company

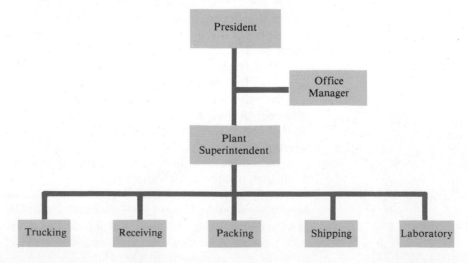

can countries. Zappa's largest customers are seed houses and operators of large-sized farms. Some customers pick up the seeds themselves; however, the company has three large trucks for regional delivery and a rail spur for long-distance shipping. Latin American orders are shipped by ocean vessels.

Seeds are purchased from large mill houses in the United States and processed at the Zappa plant. Upon receipt of seeds, samples are taken and tested by the company in cooperation with requirements of the United States Department of Agriculture. After verification of purity and germination, the seeds are packaged in 50 and 100-pound bags.

The packing department has the largest number of workers. Under the supervision of Bob Ewell, 34 employees in the department work without representation from a union. Because of the hard manual labor involved and the low pay, the turnover of packers is high. Generally, packers remain with the company less than one year. In a recent attempt to find out why there is such a high labor turnover in the department, Mr. Zappa was told by employees who were called into his office for an interview that they had nothing to look forward to in coming to work. Several indicated they stayed on the job only because they probably could not find work elsewhere. Four packers noted that people do not like to be treated as though they cannot think for themselves and make appropriate decisions concerning their work. In summarizing the packer's comments, Mr. Zappa noted to himself that employees do not remain loyal to an organization that treats them as something less than human.

Two months after the interview session, Gene Whittier complained that another man had been hired for a position for which he felt he was qualified. The following conversation occurred:

Whittier: Mr. Ewell, I have been a packer here for six months, and I thought that I would be promoted to shipping clerk as soon as there was an opening. Yesterday, a person was hired for that job without having first served as a packer.

Ewell: Well, Whittier, who told you that you would be promoted?

Whittier: Mr. Zappa did about two months ago when I talked to him about why people are so prone to leave the packing department. He said that I was a good worker and would be the next packer promoted.

Ewell: You go back to work for now, and I will go talk to the plant superintendent. I will talk with you later.

After Ewell had explained the above conversation to the plant superintendent, he was told, "I really don't care what you do about this, it is your problem. Zappa never said anything to me about promoting Whittier. Why don't you go tell Zappa about it; he is the one who sets policies around here." Ewell's conversation with the superintendent ended at this point. Furthermore, Ewell did not talk with Zappa nor did he discuss the situation with Whittier. In one instance, Whittier mentioned the promotion to Ewell, but he was cut off when Ewell said he was going for a cup of coffee.

Three weeks after the above discussions occurred, another opening existed in the shipping department. The following day Ewell informed Whittier that if he was interested in the position he would get it. Overjoyed with the good news, Whittier told the other packers about his promotion and said that he would miss working with them. Another packer, however, who had been employed by the company for a little over a year complained to the plant superintendent that he should be transferred before Whittier since he had seniority. The plant superintendent then called Ewell to his office and informed him that transfers within the plant had always been based on who had been with the company the longest. Ewell did not say anything and returned to the packing department. The following conversation then occurred:

Ewell: The plant super just told me that the one who has been with the company the longest will get the promotion.

Whittier: But you told me yesterday that the opening in the shipping department was mine if I was interested. You know how much I want that job. I have done a good job as a packer, and I feel that I can do a good job in shipping.

Ewell: I am sorry, but you know the policy we follow if there is a transfer from one department to another.

Whittier: I am not talking about a transfer, but a promotion. What kind of runaround am I getting?

Ewell: Look here, Whittier, you don't seem to be very happy with your job. Why don't you just collect your paycheck and go home?

Questions

1. Why did Mr. Zappa tell Whittier that he would receive the next promotion but not inform the plant superintendent?

2. Is there any inconsistency within policy statements?

3. Is Whittier being unreasonable in his demands? What should he do now?

4. List the problems that you feel are causing the present difficulty, and indicate some alternative solutions to prevent similar incidents in the future.

PART
FOUR

ACTUALIZING
ORGANIZATIONAL
COMPONENTS

12

THE INFORMAL ORGANIZATION

PURPOSE

In small organizations, the right hand always seems to know what the left is doing. Employees interact frequently, lines of communication are shorter, and a common sense of purpose seems to exist. As an organization grows, however, people are added to fill jobs that are more specialized; staff departments develop to provide advice and assistance to other units of the organization; communication is slower and less accurate; and employees begin to feel they are little more than a payroll number in the computer. To deal with such changes, employees often seek security and a satisfaction of other needs through the formation of informal groups. These groups function outside of the departments, units, and formal authority relationships of an organization and are called the informal organization.

The purpose of this chapter is to provide an understanding of the informal organization and to show how informal relationships influence attitudes and behavior in an organization. Throughout the chapter we will emphasize that informal groups are an important part of organizational life. By influencing individual actions and roles, they can contribute to, or detract from, the success of the formal organization.

OBJECTIVES

1. To create an awareness of the social relationships within an organization that are not prescribed by the formal structure.

2. To develop an appreciation of informal organizations and their impact upon the behavior of organizational members.

3. To discuss the purposes of informal organizations.

4. To examine the stages of development and characteristics of informal groups.

5. To analyze the emergence of leaders within informal organizations.

The following conversation took place among three workers in the cafeteria of the Econo-Pak Candy Company:

Monty: Right now I'm turning out about 3,500 units a day, and some of my friends are kicking. They want me to come down to about 2,600, but I don't see why I should. If I did, I'd be producing only 100 over standard and my boss would get on me.

Bruce: You fast people really bug me. I think it's foolish to work so fast. It won't do you any good, and it will probably do the rest of us a lot of harm.

Brenda: How do you figure that?

Bruce: Well, if each of us start turning out 3,500 units a day, that's a total of 10,500 units. Then the boss might lay one of us off since three can do the work that four are now doing at 2,600 units apiece.

Monty: I see what you mean and it makes sense. Our department is now receiving fewer orders, too. If the boss sees that three people can do the work of four, some of us are going to be laid off. Then, when things pick up, they will still expect us to keep doing the same amount of work.

Brenda: And you know what that means! The next step will be to raise the standard on us so we won't have a chance to make more money.

Bruce: Now you see why we have to stick together as a group if we are going to get along. We have to know what to expect from each other. That's the only way we can protect ourselves!

Discussions like this point out some of the daily interpersonal relationships among people working together in an organization. These kinds of social relationships are expressed through the informal organization and reflect attitudes and behavior that may not agree with expectations of the formal organization.

FORMAL ORGANIZATIONS IN THE REAL WORLD

As noted in previous chapters, a task of all managers is to define the formal roles of their subordinates. These roles and their planned relationships to one another make up the formal organization structure that provides guidelines for cooperative behavior. Ideally, behavior of this type would result from the following:

A proper assignment of duties and decision-making authority.

An accurate description and defined role for each job.

Clear lines of authority and responsibility among all management positions.

Guidelines for coordinating the functions of planning, organizing, actuating, and controlling.

A clear and uninterrupted two-way flow of communication.

Clearly stated objectives, policies, procedures, and methods to guide all employees.

Unfortunately, as we know from the real world, there are few, if any, organizations that enjoy total cooperation from all employees. Even with the finest organizational design, goal achievement is never assured. Various reasons show why the perfect formal organization does not exist. One concerns the problems associated with defining specific job duties. Jobs change through time, but job descriptions are not always updated often enough to reflect all important changes. Employees are then caught in the middle. They may find that there are different and conflicting views of what they should be doing. Stated another way, employees carry out one role while management expects another. The results often include employee frustration, job dissatisfaction, and low levels of performance.

A second reason for something less than the perfect formal organization stems from the many informal groups that are found in most work situations. When the activities of such groups are in line with those of the formal organization, we say that their roles are *congruent*. In such situations, members of informal groups are not at odds with other managers or employees. However, when the role of an informal group is in conflict with that of the formal organization, relationships between the two are often strained. Here, it soon becomes apparent that behavior is being influenced more by informal group pressure than by the authority structure, goals, or policies of the formal organization. The result is one of *role incongruency*.

NATURE OF THE INFORMAL ORGANIZATION

In management literature, the term *informal organization is normally used to describe groups that fall outside of the planned organizational structure.* As mentioned earlier, this refers to the many "people arrangements" that do not appear on an organization chart. Consider, for example, employees who become informal leaders because of their job skills, as opposed to a formal delegation of authority. Even though they do not have a title like supervisor or manager, other employees may seek them out for advice on job problems. The advice received may be good, or it may lead to job performance that differs from that expected by management. In either case, the informal leader is influencing the performance of the formal organization.

It is almost impossible to show on paper the exact structure of informal organizations because of the numerous reasons that lead to their formation and continuity. However, informal organizations can be studied by looking at their purposes, social interests and geographic locations of their members, and other related factors. Through such study, we see that informal organizations actually become rather formalized through time. They have their own goals and leaders. An authority structure and communication channels come into being, and group norms are used to guide the behavior of individual members. Each of these characteristics will be examined in later sections of this chapter. Before going on, however, we need to look at two major points that must be considered when working with informal organizations: (1) they have purposes and (2) they must be recognized by managers.

Purposes of informal organizations

Informal relationships are meaningful in satisfying both individual and group needs. Social gatherings, like the lunch-hour bridge group, or the water cooler/coffee lounge gang, all have their purposes. Among other things, group interaction provides a reduction of boredom and tension, a sense of belongingness (companionship), recognition, status, and a communication link. To satisfy these needs, role prescriptions and group norms are developed to control and regulate the behavior of members. Thus, informal organizations are active in fostering group values while satisfying various social and psychological needs of the people involved. In order to be most effective in these areas, informal organizations tend to stay small. As a result, large formal organizations will usually include many small informal groups at both the managerial and nonmanagerial levels.

Managerial recognition of the informal organization

Within any formal organization, informal groups will arise and they cannot be abolished. People bring an organization to life, and their efforts to develop and maintain personal relationships eventually override any formal structure. Barnard aptly describes how the informal organization affects and is partly expressed through the formal organization:

> They are interdependent aspects of the same phenomena—a society is structured by formal organizations; formal organizations are vitalized and conditioned by informal organizations . . . there cannot be one without the other.[1]

As permanent elements of any organization, informal groups are potential aids to assist in achieving organizational objectives. In fact, there is no reason to believe that informal and formal organizations must be at odds with one another. If there is proper cooperation between the two, an alignment of objectives can exist. Informal groups can help make an enterprise work more effectively since formally structured duties cannot cover every conceivable problem that might arise. Of course, such cooperation depends on managerial attitudes that neither deny nor reject the natural existence of the informal organization.

Managers can do several things to understand the informal organization better. They can listen to members of the informal organization, observe group behavior, seek to understand why certain behavior occurs, and identify informal leaders. In dealing with the informal group,

---

[1] Chester I. Barnard, *The Functions of the Executive* (Cambridge, Mass.: Harvard University Press, 1938), p. 114.

managers can gain support if they are willing to work through informal leaders and keep group members informed of management's position. Particularly important is asking for advice from the group and promoting participation in decisions directly affecting the informal organization. In addition, all efforts should be integrated so that formal and informal roles are congruent in the achievement of goals.

Linking the formal and informal organizations

Efforts to involve informal organizations in reinforcing formally prescribed behavior are quite diverse. One interesting example concerns the recreation program (Texins Association) sponsored by Texas Instruments. The program offers job-oriented involvement in various sports and self-improvement programs. While backed by the company, the program is largely financed and completely managed by the employees themselves. Employees choose and organize their own sports and self-improvement activity clubs. The company provides a large modern gymnasium, but there is no direction from top management concerning the program's operation. At present, about 44 different activity clubs are coordinated by the Texins Association. Even though the Texins Association is not shown on the company's organization chart, it is becoming more closely linked to the formal organization.

Many other companies in the United States currently provide extracurricular activities for their employees. These activities foster increased interaction among employees and can lead to a closer identification with the formal organization. They are insufficient by themselves, however. Many of today's employees are better educated than ever before. They seek new challenges and ways to become actively involved in the affairs of their organizations. Opportunities for such involvement must go beyond recreational programs and other extracurricular activities. Job enrichment, management by objectives, or other participative management techniques must also be available. Otherwise, efforts to link the informal and formal organizations together will be viewed as manipulative in an attempt to keep employees happy without really involving them in meaningful ways.

THE HAWTHORNE STUDIES

The Hawthorne Studies were the first systematic investigations into altering social (informal) relationships in the work place. Conducted by Elton Mayo and his colleagues from Harvard University, the studies ran from 1924 to 1932 at the Hawthorne plant of the Western Electric Company in Chicago.[2] The most significant results produced by the

---

[2] The data reported are found in F. J. Roethlisberger and W. J. Dickson, *Management and the Worker* (Cambridge, Mass.: Harvard University Press, 1938). Reading only a part of this book often results in less than a full understanding of the entire work, while a reading of the entire volume is a formidable task. An excellent summary of the entire book is presented in Henry A. Landsberger, *Hawthorne Revisited* (Ithaca: Cornell University, New York State School of Industrial and Labor Relations, 1968), chap. 2.

studies are: (1) workers organize into informal social groups when the work arrangement allows them to do so and (2) factors outside of the job can affect worker behavior more than the job itself.

The earliest experiments were undertaken to examine the question: "What is the relationship between working conditions (illumination, temperature, humidity, etc.) and the incidence of fatigue and monotony?" Based on this question, the first experiment sought to test the effects of illumination on the output of workers.

Effects of illumination on worker output

The illumination experiments failed to find data to support what had been expected; namely, a direct relationship between illumination and productivity. Instead, as illumination was increased in three different departments, productivity increased erratically in two of them. In the third, the increase varied without direct relation to the amount of illumination. To determine if the results were due to the type of work in the different departments, a second study was undertaken. It involved putting two groups of workers from the same department in two different buildings. The results showed that output increased in the experimental group as illumination was increased. Within the control group, production also increased almost identically, although illumination was held constant.

A third study was made to determine whether these findings resulted from a combination of natural and artificial light. The results showed that output in both groups continued to increase—even when lighting in the experimental room was reduced to the point of insufficient illumination for employees to see their work. The general conclusion indicated that changes in productivity were not due to illumination. In fact, other uncontrolled variables had apparently influenced output. This conclusion resulted in a new experiment referred to as the Relay Assembly Test Room.

Relay Assembly Test Room experiment

In order to gain greater control over the variables, six women were separated from a larger group assembling small relays (a single and highly repetitive task). Accurate records were kept in order to measure output as the variables were changed. For example, rest pauses and hot lunches were scheduled, then taken away. The length of the workday and the workweek were varied. Even after continuous changes in the variables, the general trend of the women's output was upward.

Through this experiment, researchers found that they were dealing with a team of women (a work group) that had experienced improved human relations. This was seen by the fact that the women had their own leader, group spirit, and social relationships. Particularly interesting were comments by the women that freedom from supervision was an important factor affecting their attitudes toward work. Cohesiveness of the group was also observed as the women helped one another in their work.

The general conclusion reached by the researchers was that neither improved working conditions nor monotony of work were significantly correlated to changes in output. At this point in the Hawthorne Studies, both researchers and managers realized that productivity was not related to a single factor but was a function of many variables.

Interviewing program

Although top management felt that supervision in the Relay Assembly Test Room was especially good, employees were not happy with their supervisors. The interviewing program involving over 21,000 employees sought to find out more about the relationships between employees and their supervisors. Using a new technique called *nondirectional interviewing*, employees were allowed to talk freely to gain information concerning supervision, working conditions, and jobs. Even though no changes were made in the physical environment, it was evident that the interviews provided psychological satisfaction, as evidenced in the improved attitudes of employees. It was concluded that status, informal leaders, and group pressures affect attitudes toward management, working conditions, and job requirements.

The Bank Wiring Observation Room experiment

This experiment was undertaken in order to learn more about how informal groups influence workers and how group norms and controls are established. Involving 14 workers operating under experimental conditions, information was gathered in two ways: (1) an observer stationed in the room with the workers and (2) interview sessions conducted outside the room.

Observation of informal organization The observer noticed certain uniform behavior patterns that deviated from those specified by the formal organization. As an example, the elaborate wage incentive plan established to increase productivity was invalidated when the workers established their own standards to control production levels.

Two interesting reasons were noted for the development of production norms by the group. The first was a belief that greater output would imply that fewer workers were needed to do the required work, resulting in some workers being laid off. Here, group norms were perceived as a way to increase job security. A second reason for the development of group norms stemmed from a belief that increased output could cause management to set higher piece-rate standards. Therefore, more work would be expected for the same pay.

Development of cliques Within the group two distinct interpersonal patterns (cliques) appeared among the workers as they played games, talked, and gambled. Membership in either clique was determined by (1) not being a rate buster (turning out too much work), (2) not being a chiseler (turning out too little work), (3) not being a squealer (informing on a co-worker), and (4) not acting officially (acting bossy or like a management type). Basically, these four agreements were norms within each clique and served to guide member behavior.

As shown in Figure 12–1, clique A included four wirers, a solderer, and one inspector. W_2's membership in clique A was not clear, since the person participated in games with the clique but was not considered a bona fide member in other respects. Clique B consisted of one solderer and either three or four wirers depending on the group's activities. For example, W_6 was a member of clique B in terms of horsing around but was outside the clique in other ways. Finally, workers I_3, W_5, and S_2 were considered isolates since they did not belong to either of the cliques.

The primary motive in the development of the cliques was to resist changes introduced by management. With additional research, it was found that plant managers were actually not concerned about how workers would react to changes or perceived threats. Since consideration was not given to the behavioral consequences of timing and methods for introducing organizational changes in the plant, cliques were important to the workers for security purposes.

Contemporary implications of the Hawthorne Studies

The Hawthorne Studies have shown that increases in production can result from greater work satisfaction and are not necessarily related to physical considerations. The studies also indicate that employee attitudes toward their jobs and supervisors are important in improving production levels. Similarly, the nondirective interviewing program suggests that people feel better when they are given a chance to discuss a problem, even when the trouble is not corrected. Findings of the Bank Wiring Observation Room experiment give us a much better idea about how the informal organization influences employee behavior and production standards.

In total, these findings indicate that modern business organizations should be viewed as both economic and social institutions. From a social standpoint, informal groups permit individuals to increase their control over the work situation while reducing their dependence on the formal organization. Such groups can also increase the cohesiveness

FIGURE 12–1
Informal organizational arrangements of the Bank Wiring Observation Room

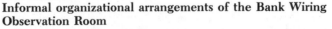
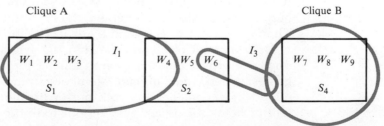

Source: Adapted with permission from F. J. Roethlisberger and William J. Dickson, *Management and the Worker* (Cambridge, Mass.: Harvard University Press, 1938), p. 518.

of employees by limiting competition among them that could work against the goals of the entire group. With this knowledge, managers can develop a better understanding of informal social relationships among people at work. In turn, possible employee reactions to changes in working conditions, wages, job requirements, or hours of work can be predicted with more accuracy.

Criticisms of the Hawthorne Studies

In spite of their impact on management thought, the Hawthorne Studies have been subjected to various criticisms.[3] Some of these include:

1. Favorable, but only temporary results occurred because the experiments gave special attention to workers. The biasing of results by the observers' personal involvement in an experiment is referred to as the *Hawthorne effect.*
2. The method of research and the small sample upon which major conclusions were reached were not statistically appropriate. Much of the research employed relatively unsophisticated design concepts and focused on only small portions of organizational life.
3. The premises on which the research was conducted were unrealistic. For example, one assumption was that organizational members exist in such a condition of *anomie* (a state of confused individuals in a disorganized society) that they revert to the group for solidarity.

Although these and other criticisms are valid, the Hawthorne Studies contributed greatly to the development of management thought at a time when serious research in the area was still in its infancy. One result was the "human relations movement" that stimulated further research on behavior in organizations. Such research continues today and is increasingly important to managers in all organizations.

GROUP STRUCTURE

While much of the information in this section holds true for formal relationships, it is presented as a framework for understanding informal organizations. T. N. Whitehead has made three astute observations within this framework:

1. The informal group is usually not oriented toward the formal manager but toward some informal leader within the group.
2. Managers of formal organizations have sentiments and attitudes that reflect radically different experiences than the members of nonmanagerial informal groups.

---

[3] For a discussion of different criticisms of the Hawthorne Studies, see Landsberger, *Hawthorne Revisited,* pp. 48–79. See also Alex Carey, "The Hawthorne Studies: A Radical Criticism," *American Sociological Review,* vol. 32, 1967, pp. 403–16; and J. M. Shepard, "On Alex Carey's Radical Criticism of the Hawthorne Studies," *Academy of Management Journal,* vol. 14, 1971, pp. 23–32.

3. A group acceptance of change is related more to the group leader, loyalty to the leader, and group sentiments than to a thorough understanding of factors associated with the change itself.[4]

To understand these points more fully, groups, group norms and rules, group cohesiveness, group status, and group leadership will be examined in the remaining parts of this section.

Groups defined

Since reference in this chapter is to human groups, we can state that *a group is composed of two or more people interacting with one another and having common identifying characteristics.* Our particular interest is with work groups that support and influence the behavior of their members within a formal organization setting.

The individual and the group

A primary motive for people interacting with one another is to verify personal beliefs and attitudes. In this sense, it is reasonable to assume that individuals will choose to associate with those who are most likely to be in agreement with them. Thus, group interaction permits us to determine whether or not a given group is in agreement with our perceptions and beliefs. Under these circumstances, a person will remain in a group only when a need for dependence outweighs the negative value of group criticisms.

In order to achieve a favorable self-concept, members must engage in activities that group members evaluate favorably. An early study of the restaurant industry pointed out that persons who cannot identify with the common interests of any work group will find themselves isolated and may eventually leave to seek employment elsewhere.[5]

At this point, we see groups providing their members with social support and a feeling of personal worth. They provide social satisfaction through status, recognition, and a chance to relate to others. Since productivity and employee satisfaction can be influenced by these things, they are as important as an organization's formal reward system. Again, this points out that work can be more rewarding to many employees when informal groups are properly integrated with the formal organization structure.

Characteristics of groups

Various scholars of group behavior emphasize the importance of interactions among members. Factors associated with effective interaction can be characterized as follows:

1. *Predictable interaction* To be effective, individuals must be able to predict how group members will react in various situations. All individuals must know how the group expects them to react. Therefore,

---

[4] T. N. Whitehead, "The Inevitability of the Informal Organization and Its Possible Value," in *Readings in Management,* ed. Ernest Dale (New York: McGraw-Hill, 1970), p. 213.

[5] William F. Whyte, *Human Relations in the Restaurant Industry* (New York: McGraw-Hill, 1948).

each member must have some reasonable idea of what other members are going to do and how their individual efforts fit into total goal achievement.

2. *Group goals or purposes*   The behavior of any group is purposeful and rational even though it may not be viewed that way by outsiders. Consider the Bank Wiring Observation Room experiment of the Hawthorne Studies where employee behavior may have seemed irrational to management since the entire group was holding down production levels. Such behavior, however, was directed toward retaining jobs during a period of time when workers were being laid off due to poor economic conditions.[6] This, then, was a common group goal.

3. *Group norms*   In spite of an apparent informality among members, group effectiveness depends on behavior that is predictable. Consequently, norms or standards ultimately develop and are used as a basis for guiding and evaluating the behavior of members.

4. *Group roles*   Although not specified by the formal organization, a hierarchy of authority develops within informal groups. Two apparent roles arise; namely, that of the informal leader and that of the followers.

5. *Group cohesiveness and attractiveness*   Members of a group are bound together by some common purpose. An increased identification with the purpose makes the group more attractive to current and potential members. As a result, group members become more closely bound together (cohesive).

Multiple group interaction

Group interaction does not imply that a person belongs to only one group. In fact, multiple group memberships are quite common and employees may belong to groups that cut across various organizational lines. Even here, however, the work group is usually the major one for each employee within an organization. Aside from intraorganizational groups, workers may also be members of social groups including fraternal orders, clubs, educational associations, and religious organizations.

Since a group includes two or more people seeking a satisfaction of common needs, the behavior of all members must be in line with group goals. To ensure coordinated action, therefore, informal organizations ultimately develop a set of norms to guide the behavior of their members. Consequently, employees who are members of multiple informal groups are influenced by the norms of each.

Group norms and rules

Group norms and rules represent the standards of behavior expected of informal group members. They specify behavior that is allowed, or not permitted, within the group. As such, they can result in behavior

---

[6] Roethlisberger and Dickson, *Management,* p. 531, note that the restriction in output in the Bank Wiring Observation Room experiment may have been related to the depression of the 1930s. But, it was pointed out that restrictions in output occurred in good times as well as bad.

that either contributes to, or detracts from, goal achievement of the formal organization. While norms are neither formally agreed upon nor written down, group members can usually state them orally.

There is also a major difference between norms and roles in terms of group activities. Norms usually apply to all group members without exception. Roles, however, are more individualistic and refer to the behavior expected of persons holding given positions within the group.

Reasons for group norms By specifying the behavior of members, norms promote group stability and cohesiveness. The resulting solidarity helps groups survive. Consider a period of economic recession where employee layoffs are common. In a situation of this type, there is a natural drive to keep one's job. Without norms to control individual behavior, conflicts could develop among employees as some try to outdo others in order to keep their jobs as long as possible. With norms, groups faced with conditions of this type have a better chance of providing security for all members.

Finally, it should be noted that norms serve to perpetuate behavior that has been acceptable to group members over some period of time. When confronted with a situation not covered by past experience, however, the group must develop new norms. Sometimes this is done solely by trial and error. For example, a group of employees wanted to start playing poker during their lunch period. There was no written company rule against gambling, so the group started playing a few hands of poker after lunch each day. When no one stopped them, the employees assumed that gambling on their own time was acceptable. Playing poker during the lunch hour then became an accepted norm within the group.

Enforcing group norms Various pressures are used to enforce group norms, and they vary from open actions to more subtle methods. Milder forms of open action include arguing, antagonizing, criticizing, kidding, cursing, and spreading rumors. Or the silent treatment may be a way of pressuring group members into conforming. Damage to personal possessions such as lunch boxes, clothing in lockers, or automobiles is also used to get messages across to group members who are not following accepted norms. In extreme cases, group pressure can become so strong that employees are forced to resign, or pressure is brought on management to have certain workers fired.

The Hawthorne Studies provide other examples of group enforcement of norms. Name calling was utilized by some employees in the plant. "Rate Buster," "Slave," and "Speed King" were popular names for employees who worked too fast. Minor physical pressure called "binging" (a hard blow on the muscle of the upper arm) was also used in bringing members into line with group standards. Even today, it is not uncommon for fast workers in production plants to slow down toward the end of the day so that they do not violate group norms. In these instances, we see group norms having a greater influence on production levels than the desire of individuals to maximize their income.

Rewards for conforming   Rewards given to members who conform to group norms also take many forms. Some take the form of greater popularity, group acceptance, or status. Generally, new members of a group seek rewards of this type. Members with longer tenure and more status within a group find it easier to resist pressures calling for compliance and can often exert enough influence to change certain norms. However, these members will lose status if they continually fight or disregard group norms. In fact, some norms are so important to a group that even the most influential members are not permitted to violate them.

Finally, it is necessary to consider the "righteousness" of norms when looking at the reward systems of informal groups. Some norms produce behavior that is good for all group members. Others may guide persons toward undesirable ends. At the same time, norms may require too much conformity and lead to autocratic leadership within the group. When this happens, norms often become ends in themselves, rather than the means for satisfying those goals that attracted members to a group in the first place.

Group cohesiveness

The concept of cohesiveness can best be understood by viewing it as the "glue" that holds group members together. This glue includes the number and strength of common attitudes among group members, as reflected in their unity of purpose. Viewed in this manner, increased cohesiveness causes individual members to assume more responsibility for achieving group goals.

Conditions leading to cohesive groups   James Webb, past administrator of NASA, has stated that the process of management in large-scale organizations becomes that of fusing a large number of forces at many levels into a cohesive unit. From a managerial perspective, the question is, "What generates cohesiveness within a group?" One condition contributing to cohesiveness is a homogeneity of interests or other factors that are important to group members. In a university setting, for example, a homogeneity of degrees held by faculty members in a management department might assist in the development of cohesive bonds among departmental members.

Cohesiveness also increases when the achievement of group goals leads to the fulfillment of individual goals; and, many times, fulfillment of personal goals is directly related to the interdependencies among members of a group. For instance, the team concept in management requires a high degree of cohesiveness since the success of any one person usually depends on the success of the entire group. The U.S. space program illustrates a situation of this type, and the result is a network of cohesive groups with a high degree of productivity. Other conditions determining cohesiveness include the ability of group members to communicate with one another and the size of the group (the larger the group the more impersonal it becomes).

Cohesiveness, social support, and productivity Two important benefits are associated with group cohesiveness. First, members of highly cohesive groups tend to provide social support for one another. Through this support an element of security is also provided to group members. A second important benefit of cohesiveness relates to higher productivity levels in the achievement of group goals.[7] As concerns this benefit, increased productivity is sometimes attributed to a greater degree of personal satisfaction among members of highly cohesive groups.

To understand the possible relationship between group cohesiveness and productivity, it is also important to look at how and by whom productivity is being measured. If group members are attracted to one another for the purpose of socializing, extra long coffee breaks and other social activities might be viewed as highly productive from the group's point of view. As seen by management, however, the same individuals might be regarded as lazy and inefficient.

Where group goals are more closely aligned with those of management, productivity will be perceived in a somewhat similar manner by both managers and group members. This is illustrated in Figure 12–2. To expand further, assume that a group has goals of being punctual and of not missing work except for sickness. If the group is highly cohesive, members will strive harder to reach these goals; and since managers look favorably on such behavioral patterns, they are also more likely to view group productivity as being high.

A final illustration of the relationship between cohesiveness and productivity can be found in the novel, *Bridge over the River Kwai.*[8] In this book, British prisoners of war held by the Japanese developed into a cohesive group. The objective of the Japanese was to have the prisoners build a railway bridge across the Kwai River for the movement of troops and supplies. To the prisoners, however, the bridge symbolized a chance to utilize their skills and abilities while keeping themselves together as a unit. In spite of great odds, the group's cohesiveness resulted in a highly productive work force of prisoners that completed the bridge within a specified time limit. Thus, the ultimate objective for both the prisoners and the Japanese was that of completing the bridge; however, the bridge symbolized the fulfillment of different needs for each group.

[7] See Joseph A. Litterer, *The Analysis of Organizations* (New York: John Wiley & Sons, 1973), pp. 212–18 for research studies relating to cohesiveness and productivity. Not all studies suggest that there is a direct relationship between the two variables; however, many studies indicate that there is some relationship. See Stanley E. Seashore, *Group Cohesiveness in the Industrial Work Group* (Ann Arbor: University of Michigan, Institute for Social Research, 1954), pp. 63–80.

[8] Pierre Boulle, *The Bridge over the River Kwai* (New York: Vanguard Press, 1954).

FIGURE 12–2
Management's perception of group productivity depends on the similarity between management and group goals

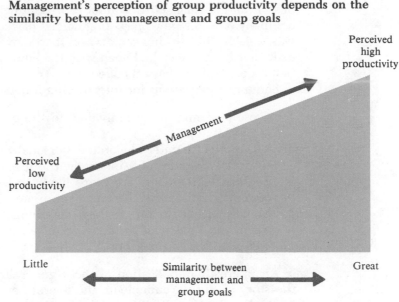

The relationships in this figure are based on the assumption that group goals are being effectively achieved.

Status of group members

The status hierarchy among members of a group refers to the ranking of each member relative to all others. It is an important characteristic of group behavior that is necessary for achieving group stability and an efficient accomplishment of goals. The status afforded to given individuals is based on the value attached to their contributions in achieving group goals. Thus, higher status is usually enjoyed by those who conform most closely to group norms. Other important factors used to establish an informal status structure include occupational groupings, the specific job of an individual, seniority on the job, skill in performing a job, and wages received. Of course, the importance attached to any of these factors will usually vary among groups according to their value structures.

Status symbols

To assist individuals in determining where they rank among group members, status symbols are extremely important. In order for them to be meaningful, however, they must be visible, rational, recognizable, and acceptable to a majority of the members. For informal work groups, status symbols can include dress, type of work, equipment and tools used, secretarial help, location of work place or office, seniority, accuracy in performing work, and title.

Many examples of status symbols are also apparent in the formal organization. Office size, the type of desk, pictures, leather desk chair, carpeting, and drapes are just a few of the status symbols used by some organizations. In one company, a coffee pot on an executive's desk is an informal status symbol representing long service with the company. When a new marketing official placed one on her desk, she was quickly told by her supervisor to remove it. It seems another executive in the office had been with the company seven years before being permitted to have a coffee pot.

Some generalizations for interpreting a person's status include:

1. Close proximity of an individual to the group leader is a symbol of high status.
2. The more elaborately decorated, personalized, and leisure oriented the office facilities of a manager, the greater the status position.
3. High-status members are more likely to be in the direct line of communication from the top of an organization.
4. Members tend to direct their communications to higher-status members, or at least to members of equal rank, to further their own standing in the group.[9]

An interesting application of these generalizations can be seen in the story of Rufus Youngblood, the Secret Service agent, who threw his body over Vice President Johnson at the time of President John F. Kennedy's assassination. As a White House agent, his status decreased when President Nixon entered office. This was reflected by changes in his status symbols, even though he remained as assistant director of protective forces. His office was moved from the White House to another office across the street. Communications about meetings were not directed to him until they were over. Memos came by his office for signature only after important decisions relating to the issues had been made. In all of these cases, it was evident that the status position of Youngblood was being drastically reduced to fit a new ranking among members of the Nixon administration. Ultimately, the reduction in status reached the point where Youngblood felt compelled to resign from the Secret Service.

Inevitability of status symbols   Generally, the greater the authority and responsibility of group members, the more common it is for them to have recognizable status symbols. If the formal organization does not provide such recognition, informal interactions will create new status symbols to embellish the positions of various group members. Thus, status symbols are an inevitable part of any group structure and they are always present.

At times certain status symbols may be at odds with formal organization policy. Managerial efforts to change these symbols often meet with resistance from the group, and if they are changed, new ones are ultimately created to replace them. Unfortunately, symbols created

---

[9] For additional discussion of group behavior, see Richard M. Steers, *Introduction to Organization Behavior* (Santa Monica, Calif.: Goodyear, 1981).

in this manner may become even more inconsistent with goals of the formal organization. Thus, management should try to recognize and utilize existing status symbols before attempting to change them. The key in this instance is to deal with real problems rather than treating symptoms by trying to change group status symbols.

Status consensus   Group behavior is also influenced by status consensus or agreement on the status positions of group members. Such a consensus among members is extremely important in providing group stability and in determining the level of member satisfaction. Generally, if status consensus is high, the satisfaction associated with group membership will also be high. Similarly, individuals are more likely to retain membership in a group where such conditions prevail. For any group leader, efforts to maintain status consensus represent an important function.

Role of the leader in small groups

Leadership in an informal group is based on a self-motivated process where certain members compete for the role. Thus, individual prominence is an important variable influencing the ultimate choice of a leader. Obtaining prominence depends upon behavior patterns reflecting aggressiveness, good verbal communication, confidence, and a desire for recognition. In the final analysis, positive group sociability and an ability to accomplish group goals are probably the most important variables in selecting informal group leaders.

Since leadership depends upon needs of the moment, an appropriate leader in one situation may not necessarily be qualified to lead in another situation. There are many group settings requiring different leadership roles. For example, the union representative who must deal with management plays a leadership role quite different from the informal group leader who provides technical assistance and advice. Other leadership roles include the social mediators who can moderate opposing views and bring the group back together, the sergeant-at-arms type who persuades members to conform to group norms, and the crisis leaders who can reason under pressure and provide leadership in situations of emergency or threat. From this we see that groups have many leadership roles. Although one group member might fulfill all of them, several members will probably lead the group at various times.

The selection of informal group leaders provides an excellent opportunity to see the acceptance theory of authority in operation. This theory states that authority depends largely on the willingness of group members to accept and follow another member as their leader. To be accepted, the goals of a potential leader must agree with those of the group. Beyond this, persons chosen as informal leaders must be perceived as having the knowledge and skill to assist the group in accomplishing common goals. While these are demanding requirements, there are also rewards. Like all leaders, those in informal groups can satisfy certain personal needs while contributing to the success of the total group.

FRAMEWORK FOR DEVELOPING NEW GROUP THEORIES

In the last 20 years, increased efforts in several areas have added to our present knowledge about groups. *Group dynamics* is one of these areas. Following the early leadership of Kurt Lewin, further research has assisted us in understanding why groups develop, how they are formed, how they affect the behavior of their own members and other groups, and how to improve their effectiveness. Unfortunately, a complete discussion of Lewin's findings would go beyond the purpose of this section. In general, however, he concluded that democratic groups that stress the participation of members are more effective in achieving their goals.

Additional knowledge about informal group processes is very important since such groups provide a source of satisfaction to employees that the formal organization may not offer. As discussed earlier, security and support, reduction of boredom, lessening of tensions, and opportunities for self-expression can be provided by informal groups. Also, more knowledge about group behavior allows managers to be more effective as they work to achieve formal organizational goals. However, the advancement of knowledge concerning groups requires the development of a general theoretical framework that is both practical and workable. Without such a framework, it becomes very difficult either to understand or to predict behavioral patterns within groups.

A CONCEPTUAL SCHEME FOR DESCRIBING GROUP BEHAVIOR

George C. Homans, a small group theorist, has set forth a systematic framework for analyzing small groups.[10] The model he proposes is basically a general description of human behavior in the smallest of groups—those which he considers to be the most familiar and basic of social units. Through the model, Homans points out three elements common to all small groups:

1. *Activity*—what members of a group do.
2. *Interaction*—relations between and among group members.
3. *Sentiments*—the physical and mental feelings that a group member has in relation to group activities.

Relationships among these elements can be seen in a situation where the actions of some group members go against group norms (sentiments). One result is increased activity, as the group tries to bring the behavior of deviating members back in line with group sentiments.

To understand the interrelatedness of activities, interactions, and sentiments, it is also necessary to note the distinction drawn by Homans

---

[10] George Homans, *The Human Group* (New York: Harcourt, Brace, Jovanovich, 1950), chap. 2. For another model of group behavior, see Linda N. Jewell and H. Joseph Reitz, *Group Effectiveness in Organizations* (Glenview, Ill.: Scott, Foresman, 1981).

FIGURE 12–3
Homans' model: a way of viewing small groups

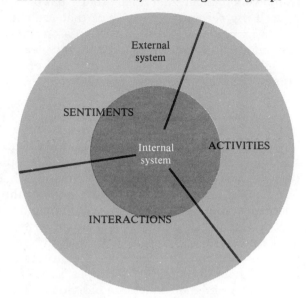

External system—Required behavior in terms of job specifications, work methods, prescribed layouts, and selection of personnel.

Internal system—Emergent behavior that results from friendships and cliques, socialization, and helping one another with work, etc.

Activities—The things people do, the acts they perform.

Interactions—The effect one person has on another when two people come together. Interaction is differentiated in three ways: duration, frequency, and direction.

Sentiments—The internal states of a person's emotions or feelings, beliefs, objectives, frames of reference, and needs.

Source: Data for diagram from George C. Homans, *The Human Group*, Harcourt Brace Jovanovich, Inc., New York, 1950, p. 82. By permission of the publisher.

between external and internal systems. The external system includes contact points between the group and outside influences—managers, governmental regulations, consumer demand, technology, and so forth. In short, the external system is a constraint on group behavior. The internal system is concerned with the sentiments of group members toward one another. Thus, within the internal system, we refer to emergent behavior in contrast to the required behavior outlined by the external system. Figure 12–3 shows these distinctions and interrelationships.

The Homans' model not only provides managers with a general framework for analyzing small groups, but possibly larger organizations as well. By recognizing variables that are common in small groups, it is easier to identify more possible reasons for behavior in both formal and informal organizations. At the very least, such a systematic approach can replace some of the trial and error involved in managing human behavior in organizations.

IMPACT OF BEHAVIORAL THEORY ON ORGANIZING

Earlier chapters on organizing discussed the classical organizational models of Max Weber, Frederick W. Taylor, and Henri Fayol. While these models have contributed to the development of management thought, they are now viewed by many as being too simplistic for our complex society. In this regard, none of the classical models give adequate attention to the realities of human behavior in organizations.

Since the works of early management writers first appeared, behavioral research has grown in both quantity and quality. Much of this research continues to emphasize the importance of understanding human behavior in organizations. Rules, procedures, and policies do not stand alone, and the behavior of individuals is not necessarily irrational when it does not conform to such organizational guidelines. Personal values, perceptions, and needs must also be considered.

With more knowledge of behavior in organizations, most managers now realize that there is no "one best way" to organize human and material resources. As we will see in the chapter on motivation, organizational effectiveness can be improved by modifying the formal organization to recognize employee needs for independence, achievement, recognition, and self-esteem. Likewise, the chapter on leadership points out the influence of managerial attitudes, perceptions, and assumptions on organizational structures.

If organizations are to cope with problems and challenges of the future, they must be behaviorally oriented. The classical view of organizations as rational economic entities will not suffice. Organizations will need to adapt to a host of changing situational variables. A recognition of these variables and an understanding of their impact on organizational design is another example of a contingency approach to management.

SUMMARY

The initial thrust behind research into human behavior in organizations was provided by the Hawthorne Studies. These studies were somewhat crude by today's standards but they pointed out that various social factors are important in understanding individual and group behavior in the work place. Since the Hawthorne Studies, improved sociological and psychological research techniques have produced new findings to expand our knowledge of behavior in formal and informal organizations.

There is always a reason for the development of informal organizations. A major reason is based on the belief that such groups can satisfy certain employee needs better than the formal organization. As long as this belief persists, informal groups will remain a permanent part of any organization. Consequently, managers must deal with these groups in a positive way since attempts to destroy them will usually fail. A positive approach by management is one that recognizes the goals of informal groups and seeks to understand any underlying problems caused by employee dissatisfaction. Through this approach, managers are also in a better position to see where improvements may be needed in the policies, programs, or practices of the formal organization. The result is one that lets the formal and informal organizations work together, rather than setting them apart as competitors.

KEY TERMS

Cliques: A small exclusive group bound together by the common interests of its members.

Group: Two or more people interacting with one another and having common identifying characteristics.

Group cohesiveness: The unity of members that holds a group together. Common goals, attitudes, and perceptions contribute to this group unity.

Group norms: The standards of behavior expected of group members.

Group status: The social ranking of a group member relative to all others in the group.

Informal organization: Groups or "people arrangements" that function within the formal organization structure but are not a planned part of the structure.

Nondirectional interviewing: Permitting a person to talk freely in an interview situation with only limited guidance or structure provided by the interviewer.

Role congruency: The situation that exists when the activities of individuals or groups are in line with expectations of the formal organization.

Status symbols: Any item or title that is accepted by group members as a sign of social ranking within the group.

QUESTIONS

1. Both formal and informal organizations provide guidelines for the behavior of their members. How do these guidelines differ?
2. Does the informal organization always operate within the structure of a formal organization? Explain.
3. How can managers gain the support of informal organizations? Be specific.
4. What did the Hawthorne Studies contribute to management knowledge about human behavior in organizations?

5. Why do individuals join groups? Is it possible for an individual to survive without joining some group?

6. How do informal groups become more formal with the passage of time?

7. Discuss the importance of group norms. How are norms enforced?

8. Can an informal group be highly cohesive without contributing to the goals of the formal organization? How?

9. "Informal groups exist only because of some failure on the part of the formal organization." Do you agree?

10. How do members of informal groups obtain status within such groups? Can members have a higher status in one group than in another?

11. Do you agree with the statement, "informal groups are inevitable and cannot be abolished." Why or why not?

PROBLEMS

1. One author has stated that much of the work in an organization actually takes place in the blank spaces between the boxes shown on the organization chart.

a. Draw a simple organization chart.
b. By referring to your chart, discuss why this statement is true or false.

2. Various research studies point out the importance of understanding informal group structures and processes. In a study of military personnel, for example, it was found that men who trained together under the same group of officers were more effective in battle than those who had not remained together throughout their training. Also, it was concluded that fewer psychiatric cases developed among men who were members of close-knit groups.

a. Can you draw any generalizations about group cohesiveness from studies such as these?

b. What implications do these findings have for managers in other organizations?

3. Based on interviews with group members, the following norms were identified in two informal work groups within the same organization:

First group: *a.* "No person will work so hard that other members will appear to be dragging their feet."

    b. "The company is rich enough that the few items in inventory that 'walk off' will never be missed."

Second group: *a.* "Equipment should always be covered and desks cleared before leaving for the day."

    b. "Personal appearance and quality of work should never be so unacceptable that management would have reason to transfer or dismiss a group member."

In terms of importance to group members, are these norms similar? Would management have the same opinion of both groups after a review of their norms?

4. A recent survey conducted by Opinion Research Corporation shows that middle managers are being forced to become passive mediators in their specialty fields. They pass problems upward in their organizations, wait for responses, and then pass decisions down through layers of subordinates. Although they may be well aware of the problems around them, they lack the autonomy and authority to tackle problems by themselves.

At lower levels of organizations, dramatic changes are also taking place. Robots that can work almost like people are approaching faster than many people realize. Renault, the French automaker, now has a robot with a television camera "eye" that can identify each of 200 parts presented to it at random, then reach out and grasp each part at the proper time for whatever the next operation might be. Other leading contenders for the robot market include Hitachi, Texas Instruments, IBM, and General Motors.

a. Will changes like these have any impact on informal organizations in the future?
b. Is it possible that such changes will actually eliminate informal groups in some organizations?

5. In a study conducted with a group of college students, participants were asked to match the lengths of several lines to a standard line. All of the students, except one, were told to give the wrong answers at various times. The student who had not been told to give the wrong answers went along with the group and gave incorrect answers 32 percent of the time.

a. What can cause persons to agree with other members of a group, even when they know the members are wrong?
b. What can managers learn from experiments of this type?

6. When Royal McBee, a division of Litton Industries, was manufacturing typewriters in Springfield, Missouri, its employees were on a wage incentive system. Yet, it was an unwritten group norm that no one was ever to produce more than 150 percent of standard. As a result, take-home pay was fairly constant.

a. How would you explain this voluntary limitation on wages?
b. What might account for behavior of this type since employees could have made more money by producing more?
c. Under what conditions might employees choose not to abide by a group norm that would limit their income?

7. In a study of two groups of carpenters and bricklayers, each worker was given the chance to rank preferences for three work partners. Work assignments were then made by pairing the workers as nearly as possible according to their preferences. In pairing the groups, 22 workers received their first choice, 28 their second, 16 their third, and 8 nonchosen isolates were paired. The sociometrically selected work groups showed the following results:

a. Labor turnover decreased from 3.11 to 0.27.
b. Labor cost index decreased from 36.66 to 32.22.
c. Material cost index decreased from 33.00 to 31.00.

How could the choice of work partners have influenced productivity in such positive ways?

8. It has been recommended that simulation models be used by managers to determine how employees might react to proposed changes in an organization. Such models could help provide information about changes in (1) authority relationships, (2) communication channels, (3) decision-making systems, and (4) group influence patterns. The benefits would be those of spotting possible trouble areas before introducing changes, while providing training for those managers responsible for implementing the changes.

a. Since human behavior is so unpredictable, is it reasonable to assume that it can be simulated through the use of models?
b. Are there benefits from simulating behavior even though such simulation may be far less than perfect?

9. A Chicago banking consultant has stated that banks need more customers who can maintain $3,000 to $5,000 on deposit at all times if they are to stay profitable. Banks around the country apparently agree since many are now offering incentives to prosperous customers who open new accounts or increase existing deposits.

The North Valley Bank in Redding, California, hosts "Monday Night Football" parties each week. Some 40 doctors, lawyers, and other leading citizens are guests at a local motel for drinks and a buffet meal during the televised football games. Clients of Brookhaven Bank and Trust in Brookhaven, Mississippi, include many well-to-do retired persons. The bank recognizes them each year with birthday cards and organizes various low-cost outings for senior citizens. In Augusta, the Georgia Railroad Bank and Trust welcomes new executives and their families to the city with a box supper of southern fried chicken on moving day.

a. Since many of the customers being courted are quite wealthy, why do they respond favorably to the offers being made by these and other banks?
b. Is there any relationship between this information and the discussion of informal groups presented in this chapter?

SUGGESTED READINGS

Alexander, C. N., Jr. "Status Perception." *American Sociological Review,* 1972, pp. 767–73.

Hamner, W. C., and D. W. Organ. *Organizational Behavior: An Applied Psychological Approach.* Plano, Tex.: Business Publications, 1978, chaps. 13 and 14.

"Hawthorne Revisited: The Legend and the Legacy." *Organizational Dynamics,* Winter 1975, pp. 66–80.

Hockman, J. R. "Group Influence on Individuals." In *Handbook of Industrial and Organizational Psychology,* edited by M. D. Dunnett. Chicago: Rand McNally, 1976.

Homans, G. C. *Social Behavior: Its Elementary Forms.* Belmont, Calif.: Wadsworth, 1971.

Jackson, J. *Norms and Roles Studies in Systematic Social Psychology.* New York: Holt, Rinehart & Winston, 1976.

Jurma, W. E. "Leadership Structuring Style, Task Ambiguity, and Group Member Satisfaction." *Small Group Behavior,* February 1978, pp. 124–34.

Keller, R. T. "Role Conflict and Ambiguity: Correlates with Job Satisfaction and Values." *Personnel Psychology,* Spring 1974, pp. 57–64.

Likert, R., and J. G. Likert. *New Ways of Managing Conflict.* New York: McGraw-Hill, 1976.

Luthans, Fred. *Organizational Behavior.* New York: McGraw-Hill, 1981.

Porter, L. W.; E. E. Lawler; and J. R. Hackman. *Behavior in Organizations.* New York: McGraw-Hill, 1975.

Salancik, G. R., and J. Pfeffer. "Who Gets Power—and How They Hold on to It: A Strategic-Contingency Model of Power." *Organizational Dynamics,* Winter 1977, pp. 2–21.

Schuler, R. S. "Role Perceptions, Satisfaction, and Performance: A Partial Reconciliation." *Journal of Applied Psychology,* December 1975, pp. 683–87.

Steiner, I. D. *Group Process and Productivity.* New York: Academic Press, 1972.

White, H. C., and G. Bassford. "Industrial Effectiveness: Leadership Style and Small Groups." *Industrial Management,* January–February 1978, pp. 5–9.

13

COMMUNICATION
AND
INFORMATION
SYSTEMS

PURPOSE

While serving in the Merchant Marine during World War II, John Diebold was intrigued by the precision of remote-controlled, antiaircraft guns. This interest led to his founding and current chairmanship of the management consulting firm, the Diebold Group, Inc. The business pioneered in the areas of automation, management information systems, and computers while growing to over 600 employees. With offices in the United States, Frankfurt, Paris, Vienna, and London, the Diebold Group has been influential throughout the world in shaping the growth of computers and communication technology in the information processing field. Diebold warns, however, that few corporations will prosper in the next decade without developing an overall strategy for acquiring, utilizing, and managing information. Automation (a word coined by Diebold), computerized data-processing, and communication technology are, as he sees them, the important variables in providing access to information required in managerial decision making.

This chapter recognizes the ever-present importance of communication within organizations. The purposes of communication are discussed along with barriers and guidelines for their prevention. In addition, the role of management information systems is examined, as are the steps included in the design and implementation of such systems.

OBJECTIVES

1. To examine the meaning and importance of communication to management.

2. To discuss communication as the two-way process of transmitting and receiving information.

3. To develop an understanding of the flow of communication within organizations.

4. To identify common barriers to communication.

5. To outline guidelines to follow for increasing communication effectiveness.

For an idea to become a reality, there must be a plan; and once a plan is developed, it must be communicated to others who will be involved in its implementation. Communication is also required if results are to be evaluated in terms of what was sought through a given plan. In this managerial context, *communication* is the means for obtaining, willingly, action from others and is defined as the *process of transmitting and receiving information.* Through the use of symbols, this process provides a way of developing understanding among people through an exchange of facts, opinions, ideas, attitudes, and emotions.

From the standpoint of leadership, communication is essential in motivating individuals and groups to follow certain behavioral patterns. It is required for the effective coordination of group activities and is essential in the performance of all management functions. Thus, the success of any manager is dependent on an ability to communicate effectively with other organizational members.

THE PURPOSES OF COMMUNICATION

Most of our daily activities require communication with others. Within an organization, communication is essential in (1) providing employees with the necessary information to do their jobs and (2) developing attitudes that promote coordination, performance, and job satisfaction.[1] More generally, organizational communication is involved with bringing about desired changes in individual behavior or other matters over which the organization has control.

Communication is also of prime importance in the performance of all management functions. It is impossible to plan, organize, or control without communication since understanding and acceptance of information are essential to each. Likewise, communication lies at the heart of both motivation and leadership—the subjects of the next two chapters.

COMMUNICATION AS A TWO-WAY PROCESS

Like many other management concepts, communication can best be explained by viewing it as a process. In fact, it must be considered as a two-way process if there is to be true communication. We often talk about one-way communication; however, such communication does not exist.[2] By definition, the transmitting and receiving of information must take place between two or more people. Basically, the process requires a sender who transmits a message through a channel to a

---

[1] R. Farace, P. Monge, and H. Russell, *Communicating and Organizing* (Reading, Mass.: Addison-Wesley Publishing, 1977).

[2] See Douglas McGregor, *The Professional Manager* (New York: McGraw-Hill, 1967), p. 153, where mass media advertising is considered to be one-way communication. However, unless individuals respond (buy advertised products or change attitudes), there is little effectiveness in the process.

FIGURE 13–1
The communication process

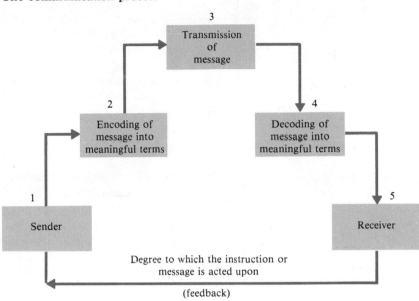

receiver. The receiver, as illustrated in Figure 13–1, then decodes the message and sends back some type of signal or feedback. In this sense, all parties are both senders and receivers in the process. Various channels may be used to transmit messages, and they may pass through several people before reaching intended recipients. But, even in the most sophisticated systems, communication remains a two-way process.

TRANSMITTING AND RECEIVING THE MESSAGE

In communicating, the message must be encoded into meaningful symbols by the sender. This might involve writing, speaking, body language, or a computer program. After a message has been encoded, it is sent through communication channels or paths. These paths are represented by such elements as sound waves, electrical waves, or light waves that can be tuned to the human senses of sight, sound, taste, touch, and smell. The choice of channels to be used is influenced by past experience, prior knowledge, values, perceptions, and the total environment surrounding the sender. The channels selected, however, must be fitted to the receiver in order to provide the greatest accuracy of the message as it is transmitted.

The receipt of a message requires the receiver to decode it into meaningful terms. Of course, decoding may not result in the type of understanding that was originally anticipated, especially if the receiver interprets the meaning of certain symbols differently from the sender. Thus, for a message to be understood, the receiver must interpret words, signs, and gestures in essentially the same manner as intended by the sender.

As a two-way process, the transmission of information alone is not sufficient for communication to occur. The sender must also know whether the message has been received and understood. This knowledge is provided through feedback from receivers. One way of obtaining feedback is to ask them if they understand the message. Other ways of determining the level of understanding among receivers include the observation of facial expressions and an evaluation of the type and number of questions evoked by a message.

ORGANIZATIONAL COMMUNICATION

All social interaction involves communication, and without interaction there would be no organization. The volume of communication in any large organization is almost incomprehensible to perceive. Consider the numerous interactions that take place among a sales manager and 15 salespeople who, in turn, communicate with hundreds of customers. Furthermore, the sales manager may communicate with superiors, government officials, customers, other managers, and stockholders. When such relationships are multiplied by the number of managers in an organization, the volume of communication becomes staggering.

As another example, consider the automobile industry where companies communicate with the general public to (1) identify their particular fuel-efficient automobiles and (2) explain their product superiority, what research is underway, and what remains to be done in the future. The industry also communicates with consumers to provide information on new styles, repair services, warranties, and product standards. Employees need information to do their jobs, and understanding is essential in the development of attitudes conducive to work.

Managers often do a poor job in communicating with their own subordinates. Part of this problem results from a limited awareness of *what* needs to be communicated and *why* a particular message has to be sent. For example, some managers may concentrate on simply blowing off steam, rather than on what truly needs to be communicated. When this occurs, managers may feel better, but there is serious doubt that the communication will be effective. In addition, communication problems tend to arise when managers take employees for granted in terms of their willingness to listen, interest in the message, capacity to comprehend, ability to take action, freedom from distractions, and understanding of the message.

THE FORMAL COMMUNICATION SYSTEM

The formal communication system refers to those channels officially designated by the organization for transmitting information within and outside the system. For quality decision making, coordination, and an effective performance of all management functions, these chan-

FIGURE 13–2
Formal organization showing downward, upward, lateral, and outside communication flows

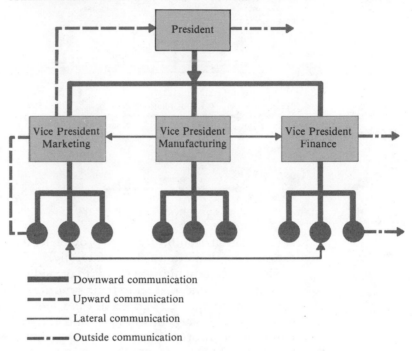

━━━━━ Downward communication

╺╺╺╺╺ Upward communication

───── Lateral communication

━╸━╸━ Outside communication

nels must be open so that information flows freely. This is analogous to the central nervous system in the human body. When the system becomes clogged or out of adjustment, the coordination of activities breaks down, decisions are illogical, and goals are not achieved effectively.

Directional flow of information

Formal organizations use downward, upward, and lateral communication flows. These are illustrated in the organization chart shown in Figure 13–2. In downward communication, messages normally consist of (1) instructions including policies, procedures, rules, work schedules, and so forth, (2) requests for information, and (3) attempts to provide information that will achieve a group consensus on given matters. Some of the commonly used downward communication channels are group meetings, posters, bulletin boards, employee handbooks, company periodicals, and interoffice communications.[3] Since there is always a chance that information can become distorted or even lost in downward communication, decentralization can be used to reduce the number of authority filters. The flatter organization structure produced by a de-

---

[3] "How to Keep Employees Well Informed," *Personnel Management,* July 1977, pp. 13–15.

FIGURE 13–3
**Different kinds of information reflect
different communication flows**

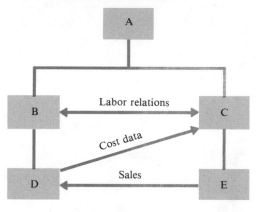

centralization of authority helps provide for a more balanced communication flow—both upward and laterally.[4]

Upward communication serves to provide subordinates with a means for conveying information to their superiors. This communication flow can be encouraged by various devices such as suggestion boxes, group meetings, grievance procedures, and the open-door policy. Unfortunately, in many organizations these approaches are not properly implemented and become quite ineffective.

Lateral communication refers to the flow of information among individuals on the same organizational level and is valuable in coordinating activities within and among various organizational units. A final way of viewing the directional flow of communication is to consider the types of information transmitted. Referring to Figure 13–3, we see that various kinds of information can reflect different communication flows, none of which necessarily follow the exact channels specified by the formal organization (the official chain of command). To expand, consider a vice president of production who needs to know the status of engineering specifications for an experimental engine. A request for such information may not go through each link in the chain of command, but directly to the engineer working on the project. Even though managers in the hierarchy are bypassed, direct contacts of this type are often necessary in order to keep the system from becoming overloaded with unnecessary messages. Such deviations from the chain of command are called cross communication, as illustrated in Figure 13–4. In the figure, Bs communication with F and G would result in wasted time if it were necessary to go through C, D, and E. Although C, D, and E should be informed of the cross-communica-

[4] See K. H. Roberts and C. A. O'Reilly III, "Measuring Organizational Communications," *Journal of Applied Psychology*, June 1974, p. 325.

FIGURE 13–4
Cross communication

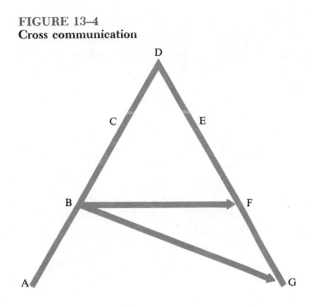

tion, the resultant decrease in the upward-downward movement can actually increase the accuracy of the informational flow.

Channel selection

Selecting a specific communication channel depends on situational analysis. In this process, managers must consider the (1) nature of the communication to be sent; (2) ability of the parties to communicate; (3) type of audience addressed; (4) interrelationships within and among groups; and (5) channel characteristics in terms of selectivity, speed, and acceptability. Upon examination, the inability of some parties to encode and decode messages properly may restrict the use of certain channels. Also, managerial attitudes toward various channels are influential in the selection process and must be recognized. Some managers use only officially designated channels, while others are more inclined to deviate from prescribed patterns. In addition, some channels have intermediaries who create more distortion and confusion than those in other channels.

The degree of cohesiveness among group members also helps determine the selection of channels. If a group is highly interactive, informal channels may be much more desirable than those which are formally prescribed. Similarly, managers who interact well with their subordinates may be more effective with a free flow of communication by avoiding formal channels that sometimes imply a sense of managerial aloofness.

When speed is essential, the manager may reduce the time spent in communicating by selecting channels that provide less feedback. One way of reducing feedback is to hold down the amount of face-to-face communication. To this extent, written messages are sometimes

328

much faster. Also, in ascertaining employee feelings, questionnaires are often used, rather than personal interviews. Remember, though, that the accuracy of the informational flow may be impaired when employees do not have a chance to ask questions that come to mind as they read a message or complete a questionnaire.

Another factor to consider in the selection of a channel is the selectivity associated with certain channels. In this context, *selectivity refers to those who are, or are not, supposed to receive certain types of information.* The routing forms used to send information only to designated organizational members illustrate such selectivity.

The economics of channel selection are also important and the cost of using various communication channels must be compared to the benefits derived from each. In universities, some courses are taught by closed-circuit television or by newspaper when enrollment is high or students are geographically dispersed. Written communication may be used exclusively for still other courses, such as those taken through correspondence. Similarly, business firms that are geographically dispersed may find that travel time and transportation costs prohibit the use of face-to-face communication, causing them to use telephone and written communication channels.

Interpersonal relationships and communication networks

As noted earlier, managers faced with selecting communication channels must have some idea of the network or pattern of relationships that exists among people within given channels. Through such knowledge, managers can better understand the impacts of interpersonal relationships such as:

1. *The higher a manager's rank and status, the greater the volume of communication received from both superiors and subordinates.* Conversely, as the number of interactions increases, the time available for reading, writing, and thinking about each message is greatly reduced.

2. *Lower-ranking managers initiate much of the interaction that takes place within the managerial hierarchy.* Think of a subordinate who completes an assigned task and asks the manager for instructions on what to do next. The superior must then initiate new activities by issuing orders that flow downward through the chain of command.

If approval is required before a specific action can be undertaken, the manager is forced to initiate interaction with higher-level management. Managers generally initiate more activity than nonmanagers. Yet, as participative leadership becomes more popular, nonmanagers may play a greater role in initiating interactions of this type.[5]

3. *The percentage of lateral communication compared to total communication decreases as managers advance in an organization.* This

[5] W. E. Bennis, "Changing Organizations," in *Groups and Organizations: Integrated Readings in the Analysis of Social Behavior,* ed. B. L. Hinton and H. J. Reitz (Belmont, Calif.: Wadsworth Publishing, 1971), pp. 583–90.

FIGURE 13–5
Four basic network patterns of communication

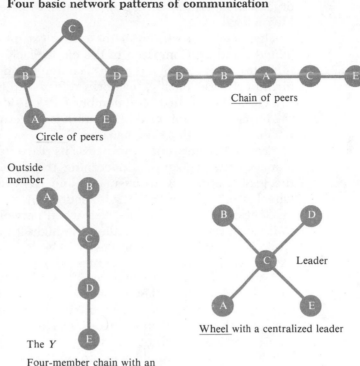

Circle of peers

Chain of peers

Outside
member

The *Y*

Four-member chain with an
outside member who communicates
with only one member in the chain

Leader

Wheel with a centralized leader

statement recognizes that there are fewer peers at the top levels of an organization with whom managers can interact.

4. *An increase in lateral communication can result in greater individual and group status.* Status and influence are often related to the volume of communication received. This relationship is due to the amount of desired, relevant information possessed by an individual or group. Thus, the interactions generated by communication not only influence the effectiveness of the communication itself but also the status of individuals and groups.

Another way to understand the impact of interpersonal relationships on communication is to view the four basic networks illustrated in Figure 13–5.[6] In the *circle* network, communication may be initiated on either side of a given individual. It is representative of lateral communication systems without an apparent leader who communicates with each subordinate; however, subordinates are unable to communi-

[6] Harold J. Leavitt, "Some Effects of Certain Communication Patterns on Group Performance," in *Readings in Social Psychology,* ed. Swanson, Newcomb, and Hartley (New York: Holt, 1952), p. 114. Also see E. M. Rogers and R. A. Agarwala-Rogers, *Communication in Organizations* (New York: The Free Press, 1976), pp. 108–48.

cate with one another. This network is characterized in traditional organization charts where superior-subordinate relationships are rigidly defined.

The *chain* is a version of the circle, except that the links are not joined together. Compared to the circle, each open end of the chain tends to reduce the total volume of communication that can be initiated in the network. Finally, networks referred to as the *Y* are similar to the chain, except that one member falls outside of the chain. Within the formal organization, the *Y* pattern is reflective of the staff specialist who interacts with a line manager.

Each of the network patterns has its place in solving or preventing management problems.[7] Concerning the speed of problem solving, the least number of errors made, and the clarity of directives, the wheel is considered the best selection. In most instances, the least efficient pattern is the circle. Yet, when network members are asked to indicate the pattern providing the highest level of satisfaction, the circle is generally their first choice. The least desirable is the wheel except for the person in the center who is normally quite happy.

When considering creativity and flexibility, new ideas are likely to be accepted more quickly in the circle than in the wheel. The restriction of new ideas in the wheel is often due to the person in the middle who feels that the group is already efficient and that innovations will only introduce complexity into a routine and patternized network.[8]

While the wheel would seem to be the best network in a task-oriented work environment, it is generally considered unsatisfying to its members. Thus, if the primary criterion is satisfactory work relations, a communication network other than the wheel might be a better selection. In any event, the most effective network depends on the situation and whatever network is selected, it will have a direct impact on the performance, attitudes, and roles played by individuals within the organization.

INFORMAL ORGANIZATIONS AND COMMUNICATION

Formal communication systems generally identify those who are to receive certain information, what specifics are to be included, and how information is to be transmitted.[9] Within such well-defined systems, however, the information needs of organizational members are

---

[7] Harold J. Leavitt, "Unhuman Organizations," in *Readings in Managerial Psychology*, ed. H. J. Leavitt and L. Pondy. (Chicago: University of Chicago Press, 1966), pp. 542–56.

[8] Some interesting findings about the decision process in modified forms of the basic networks may be found in M. E. Shaw, G. H. Rothschild, and J. F. Strickland, "Decision Processes in Communication Nets," in *Studies in Organizational Behavior and Management*, ed. P. E. Porter, P. B. Applewhite, and M. J. Misshauk (Scranton, Pa.: International Textbook, 1971), pp. 489–504.

[9] See J. R. Meredith and T. E. Gibbs, "The Systems Interface: Information and Computers," in *The Management of Operations* (New York: John Wiley & Sons, 1980).

FIGURE 13–6
Informal communication system within the formal organization

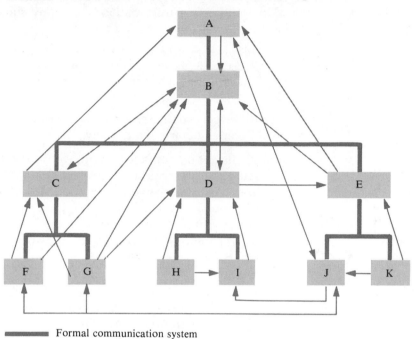

Formal communication system

Informal communication system

not always met. As a result, unofficial communication systems are created around existing social relationships to satisfy requirements for additional information throughout an organization. These systems include informal networks and serve to process nonsystematic group communication.[10] In contrast to the formalized management information system, informal channels often provide a large proportion of the additional information needed by managers to make decisions.

The extent and complexity of informal communication networks are illustrated in Figure 13–6. As noted in the figure, many informal networks can be established. In some cases, a message may be passed to selected individuals and friends (a cluster chain), or a person may communicate with everyone that comes along (the gossip chain). Regardless of the chain selected, an important element of informal communication is referred to as the *grapevine*, a term originating during the Civil War.[11] Although information from the grapevine may not

---

[10] David L. Kurtz and Lawrence A. Klatt, "The Grapevine as a Management Tool," *Akron Business and Economic Review*, Winter 1970.

[11] During the Civil War, telegraph lines were loosely strung from trees and the effect resembled grapevines. As a result, messages were often unclear and distorted. Thus, it became common to attribute rumor to the grapevine.

always be reliable, employees use it to send and receive messages that assist them in coping with an organization's internal environment.

In transmitting information about any subject, the grapevine can be described as follows:

> It moves with impunity across departmental lines and easily bypasses superiors in the chain of command. It flows around water coolers, down hallways, through lunch rooms, and wherever people get together in groups.[12]

With respect to the foregoing description, some basic characteristics of the grapevine are given below:

A significant percentage of employees consider it to be their primary source of information about organizational affairs. Since the grapevine is perceived by employees as a personal type of communication, it frequently has a stronger impact on them than formal channels of communication.

The grapevine is much more flexible than formal channels, and it embellishes information and supplies inferences that are otherwise unavailable.

The grapevine transmits information rapidly. After a "newsy" event occurs in an organization, the grapevine makes information available almost immediately. The speed of transmission appears directly related to each situation and to the perceived importance of the information. Generally, identical information travels more quickly through the grapevine than through formal channels.

Although the grapevine can be accurate in many cases, it is still more likely to produce a low level of understanding among recipients. This is especially true where rumors are concerned. Many times rumors are fragmented with the missing parts being filled in by individuals in the communication channel. The result is a distortion of the original message as it passes from person to person. Since there are no formal authority relationships involved in the grapevine, clearly none of the people participating in the rumor are accountable for its truthfulness. Although most rumors do not start with the intent of being perversive or destructive, they often end up that way.

In the grapevine, information is usually transmitted through oral channels. Written channels may be utilized when word of mouth is not convenient or may be too obvious.

A person in the grapevine who passes on information usually communicates with several individuals, rather than with only one. Of the people receiving a message, however, only a limited number will be involved in passing it on to others.

[12] Keith Davis, "Grapevine Communication among Lower and Middle Managers," *Personnel Journal*. Reprinted with permission of *Personnel Journal*, copyright April 1969.

The grapevine may be a convenient way for managers to pass on information that they may not wish to transmit formally. When the boss looks around the office with a scowl, the word spreads quickly that this is not a day that mistakes will be tolerated. Likewise, the grapevine can be valuable in assessing the reaction of employees to an announcement before it is made through formal channels.

In order to reduce problems associated with the grapevine, managers should first make every attempt to close existing gaps in the formal communication system. When employees have proper information, they feel better informed and more secure about their role in the organization. Also, by eliminating ambiguous formal messages, the incidence of rumors is reduced, thereby preventing distortion in the grapevine.

To summarize, informal communication networks arise when formal channels do not transmit desired information. How and when informal links develop depends on the perception, innovativeness, and motivational needs of organizational members. In any case, managers can neither fully depend on, nor ignore, the impact of informal communication systems. Within any effective communication system, informal networks should be recognized and permitted to operate in harmony with formal channels.

BARRIERS TO COMMUNICATION

As with most management systems, barriers arise in a communication network, and when managers are unaware of such barriers, misunderstandings are more likely to enter the communication process. By recognizing these barriers, managers are in a better position to overcome the dysfunctional consequences of faulty communication.

Frame of reference and semantics

Although communication refers to the transmission and reception of information through the use of symbols, there is no assurance that the symbols used will be interpreted identically. Misunderstanding may occur because some symbols mean different things to different people. Either the sender or the receiver may define a particular word differently due to past experiences, educational background, attitudes, biases, or perceptions. Thus, understanding is not transmitted in symbols but depends upon the receiver. Consider the manager who perceives the coffee break as a fringe benefit that contributes little to the accomplishment of organizational goals. Employees, on the other hand, may see the coffee break as an important aspect of their jobs that satisfies certain physical and social needs. Due to these different frames of reference, the communication required to reach a meeting of the minds on coffee breaks may be doomed at the outset.

Words also have different meanings because some do not have specific references with which receivers can readily relate.[13] Managers are recognizable and can be touched; however, we cannot touch planning, control, or a perfect circle. Consequently, both senders and receivers may arrive at different interpretations of the same word. In addition, certain words have no meaning to some receivers. As an illustration, the term *profit* is meaningless in some primitive cultures.

Distorted messages

When messages become distorted, we cannot expect people to understand them fully. Yet, distortion is common and occurs for a variety of reasons. One of the most common occurrences is due to the number of organizational levels through which many messages must travel. Since different people must encode, transmit, and decode a message, the original meaning can be distorted easily before the message reaches its intended recipient.

Poor listening

Although a large percentage of our time spent in communicating is devoted to listening, many individuals are poor listeners. From the managerial side, leaders must acquire the skills of openness and receptiveness. Some organizations are adopting the concept of having a special officer under the president to hear and to report employee complaints, problems, and concerns.[14] Unfortunately, employees are also poor listeners. One reason for this problem is related to the way many decisions are made. When people are not permitted to participate in making decisions that affect them, their responsiveness to orders is greatly reduced. If orders are unexpected, or perceived as unpleasant, people may actually refuse to listen.

Interdepartmental friction

All organizational units must be tied together through a coordinated network of authority relationships. The extent to which these relationships are integrated often depends on the effectiveness of communication in developing mutual understanding and trust. When friction occurs due to faulty communication, the results are often expressed in terms of dissatisfaction, mistrust, and a lack of cooperation among units. The next step is usually that of avoiding all communication as much as possible—a situation that is unhealthy within any organization.

Technical difficulties

Most communication channels are far from efficient, since various technical disturbances and human errors cause messages to be lost, delayed, or misinterpreted. Such defects are referred to as *entropy*, a term borrowed from thermodynamics that refers to the randomness and chaos existing in a system. One particularly annoying disturbance

---

[13] See S. I. Hayakawa, *Symbol, Status, and Personality* (New York: Harcourt, Brace, Jovanovich, 1963).

[14] "Where Ombudsmen Work Out," *Business Week,* May 3, 1976, pp. 114–16.

is noise that includes anything that distorts or detracts from the message being transmitted. The clatter of a typewriter, a four-party telephone line, music played over an intercom system, or sounds from a drill press are examples of noise that can cause communication problems.

One way of preventing noise and interference is to avoid overloading channels with unnecessary information. Another technique is to have messages repeated, a process known as *redundancy*. Although redundancy takes time, it definitely helps to improve the chances that responses to a given communication will meet expectations.

Communication screens

Communication screens exist in all organizations and often contribute to distorted messages since their purpose is to allow only certain information to flow through a channel. For example, if a manager fears the reaction of subordinates to a particular message, some information will be filtered out in order to reduce challenges to the message. Other examples of screens are found in situations where only limited information is presented about profits, operating performance, or the rationale for specific decisions. Most annual reports filter information communicated to employees, stockholders, and the general public since they tell very little about the internal operations of an organization.

In responding to management, screens are equally useful to employees. One example of screened feedback occurred in a southern paper mill where a management consulting firm was retained to help reduce labor costs. Employees were told by the consultants that personnel in each department would probably be cut by 20 percent. To block efforts by the consultants to determine how valuable each employee was to the organization, many employees concealed their true responsibilities by screening job information that might have threatened their job security.

In upward communication, screening becomes a serious problem when subordinates fail to transmit information that might put them in an unfavorable light with their superiors. This point is emphasized by the old adage that says, "pass up only information that the boss wants to hear so that it may be perceived as positive." By omitting facts that are unfavorable, control information for performance evaluation can be seriously distorted when it reaches the intended receiver.

TOWARD IMPROVED COMMUNICATION

Overcoming, or preventing, communication barriers requires that all organizational members commit themselves to improved communication effectiveness. This commitment must include efforts to improve the understanding of messages transmitted between senders and receivers throughout an organization.

Better encoding and decoding of messages

By following appropriate guidelines for encoding and decoding messages, managers can become more effective in directing the behavior of others. Some of these guidelines include:[15]

The intent of each message must be clearly defined. This means that we determine why the message is being sent, who is to receive it, the exact relationship between the sender and receiver, and when the message should be sent. When these determinations have been made, the sender should have no doubt about either the nature of the message or its purpose.

In order to encode and transmit messages satisfactorily, the sender must determine whether information is to inform, to stimulate thought, or to persuade others. Once this is decided, the sender can then select the appropriate symbols (words, etc.) and the channels to achieve understanding of the message.

The basic message must be appropriately formulated so that receivers are able to respond in the desired manner. Likewise, each message must be tailored to particular receivers and all relevant information provided to help ensure understanding.

For the benefit of both sender and receiver, the verification of communication is also important in reducing errors. This can be achieved by encouraging the sender to read messages before they are transmitted and by asking receivers to repeat them upon receipt. Verification is clearly important in the use of electronic data processing equipment as indicated by verifying machines that check data punched on cards and computer programs that verify the flow and sequencing of input data.

Written communication should be used whenever practical. Policies, procedures, rules, orders, and instructions often have a much better chance of being understood when they are in writing. Beyond this immediate use, written messages also serve as records that can be filed for later reference.

All of these guides emphasize the need for people to be situationally sensitive to one another. Basically, the more sensitive we are to differences in experiences, frames of reference, and behavioral characteristics, the greater the probability that we will be able to prevent barriers and to improve communication effectiveness.

Behavioral considerations

Managers must recognize various behavioral considerations in order to reduce misunderstanding while improving credibility and trust. As much as anything, they should (1) listen with sensitivity, (2) discuss problems with subordinates, and (3) fit messages to the needs of

---

[15] *A Guide to More Effective Communication*, General Electric Company, Engineering Services, 1972.

receivers.[16] These types of communication skills are particularly essential if participative management and organizational development are to become operational realities.

Since value judgments always enter the communication process, barriers can also result when facts are not considered objectively. For example, a manager may generalize that many of the operators in the computer center are loafers. Others may then be tempted to view them in this same light. Unfortunately, such a tendency often remains even after the original assumption is proven false. The net result is that people become what we perceive them to be, regardless of what they are really like.

Because value judgments enter all performance appraisals, managers should not try to persuade subordinates to accept their evaluations as final and binding. This is particularly true when appraisal results are contrary to the opinions held by subordinates. In these cases, managers must not only listen effectively in order to evaluate the personalities of employees—they must also recognize the impact of their words on the feelings of others. What they communicate should be conditioned by what they think receivers will accept. Similarly, all managers should realize that feedback from subordinates is conditioned by their perception of given situational factors.

Developing perception

As emphasized earlier, effective communication requires that managers be sensitive to the feelings of others. Both parties in the communication process must see the position and viewpoints of the other side.[17] To be genuine, sensitivity must be based on an understanding of oneself as well as on the personalities of others within an organization's social system. After all, learning about oneself depends on information received from others, just as obtaining a true perception of others requires that we see them as they see themselves.

To round out this discussion, we can state that perception and sensitivity depend on skillful listening, a recognition of the impact of one's behavior on others, an awareness of how others perceive us, and proper evaluation of what is actually taking place in the total communication process.[18]

MANAGEMENT INFORMATION SYSTEMS

Thus far the general focus of our discussion has been on the transmission, reception, and understanding of information among people. In this section, the discussion is expanded to include a consideration of

[16] See F. J. Roethlisberger, *Man-in-Organization* (Cambridge, Mass.: Belknap Press of Harvard University Press, 1968), p. 174.

[17] For a discussion on how people can acquire and improve their communication skills, see Gary T. Hunt, *Communication Skills in the Organization* (Englewood Cliffs, N.J.: Prentice-Hall, 1980), pp. 303–30.

[18] For a discussion of the varying degrees of information held in common between two people (referred to as the *Johari Window*), see Jay Hall, "Communication Revisited," *California Management Review*, Spring 1973, pp. 56–67.

the systematic relationship between people and machines. As organizations become larger and more complex, communication networks must be modified if they are to provide required information rapidly.[19] Clearly, the communication networks used by managers in a two- or three-person operation are not sufficient when the organization grows to 25 or 30 employees. Without necessary modifications, informational requirements will outgrow the capacity of existing communication channels. Also, organizations facing varying degrees of environmental uncertainty need to adjust their information processing capacity in order to meet successfully changes that are occurring.[20]

Management information systems refer to the people and equipment used in the selection, storing, processing, and retrieving of information required in the management decision-making process.[21] The system connotation implies that these elements are functionally and operationally united to provide a needed flow of information. In a broader sense, the objectives of an information system are to supply decision makers with required information while also providing information to people outside of the organization. To achieve these objectives, an information system must unite all sections of an organization.

Norbert Wiener was one of the first individuals to study organizations, communication systems, and operational controls in a systematic manner. His approach is known as *cybernetics* and purports the central theme that people can control and modify their environment only through an effective information system.[22] Important elements within the total conceptual framework of cybernetics concern the role of messages and subsequent feedback.[23]

The necessity of information in the decision-making process cannot be overemphasized. However, information alone is not sufficient to assure good decisions. Instead, it is important to have complete, accurate, and timely information about internal operations and environmental events. For example, determining the feasibility of producing a new product, or the impact of a 10 percent increase in sales, requires reliable and meaningful information at the time a decision is required.

The management information system in the Chevrolet Division of General Motors further illustrates the importance of timely information. When increasing the production of various Chevrolet models, inadequate information about parts inventories occurred. This caused material shortages on assembly lines, and needed parts had to be flown

[19] Arnold M. Kneitel, "MIS—the Big Bang," *Infosystems*, March 1978, p. 93.

[20] J. Galbraith, *Organizational Design* (Reading, Mass.: Addison-Wesley Publishing, 1977).

[21] See Bonita J. Campbell, *Understanding Information Systems: Foundations for Control* (Cambridge, Mass.: Winthrop Publishing, 1977).

[22] Herbert Wiener, *Cybernetics,* 2d ed. (Cambridge, Mass.: MIT Press, 1961).

[23] For a discussion of feedback in cybernetic systems, see Leroy H. Mantell, "On the Use of Cybernetics in Management," *Management International Review,* 1973, pp. 33–41.

in on chartered aircraft. The subsequent development of an information system that was more timely led to improvements in the recording, storing, and processing of information on material usage. As a result, a lower response time was achieved in (1) placing orders for parts, (2) assigning orders to various assembly plants, and (3) delivering vehicles to customers.

The one area in which management information systems have not been particularly successful is where problems are highly unstructured.[24] In such instances, alternatives and their consequences are neither completely known nor defined quantitatively. A partial explanation of why this happens is that computerized systems are not designed to fully support independent, nonstructured decision-making activities. A total management information system must have access to important outside data, as well as internal organizational information, for effective strategy decisions. Unfortunately, such systems are a long way from being developed.[25]

Beyond design, determining when a management information system becomes ineffective is also important. One method of spotting such deterioration is to be aware of various warning signs, such as complaints that indicate that present informational flows are inadequate. Some of the complaints heard most frequently include the following:

1. "I receive ample information, but it is never relevant to the decisions that I have to make."
2. "In my position, specific facts are needed, but you must be a detective to discover who has them."
3. "Various departments in our organization are performing badly, but someone is doing a beautiful job covering up the true facts by suppressing certain information."
4. "I always receive the necessary information. Unfortunately, it arrives two or three days after I really need it."
5. "We receive information, but there is no indication of where it comes from, who authorizes it, or whether it is even true.

Information overload may also create problems that result in poor decision-making performance.[26] Evidently, there is an optimal amount of information that is useful in decision making—not necessarily suggesting less or more information, but more careful communication of information within the organization.

---

[24] See: V. Neumann and Michael Hodars, "DDS and Strategic Decisions, *California Management Review*, Spring 1980, pp. 77–84.

[25] P. H. Pheney and N. R. Lyons, "MIS Update," *Data Management*, October 1980, pp. 26–32.

[26] Charles A. O'Reilly III, "Individuals and Information Overload in Organizations: Is More Necessarily Better?" *Academy of Management Journal*, December 1980, pp. 684–96.

DEVELOPMENT OF A MANAGEMENT INFORMATION SYSTEM

Management information systems do not just happen—they must be carefully designed, implemented, and monitored. Two basic but essential steps in developing the system are organizing the information and designing the system.

Organizing information

Organized information refers to that which is stored systematically, processed accurately, and retrieved rapidly. In other words, information is not useful until it is put into some logical and meaningful order. In complex systems, the establishment of a rationale for the organization of data is influenced by the availability of certain equipment such as typewriters, filing cabinets, copying machines, word-processing equipment, and high-speed computers.

Designing the system

This step involves the design of a system that is compatible with existing and anticipated needs and resources. By utilizing the system construct of input-process-output, the resultant information system should (1) determine what informational outputs are desired; (2) determine the inputs that are required in providing desired outputs; and (3) establish the system, including capacity, procedures, and routing.

The determination of inventory levels illustrates how the input-process-output construct can be used in designing an information system. As indicated in Figure 13–7, the desired *output* is information that shows the quantity of each item in inventory at the end of a designated period. Next, *inputs* are determined. Here, an inventory subsystem would include inputs on the current level of each item in stock at

FIGURE 13–7
Management information subsystem for determining inventory levels

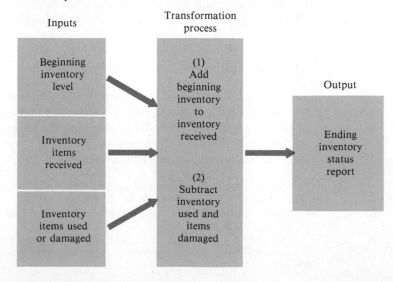

FIGURE 13-8
Integration of information subsystems into a total information system

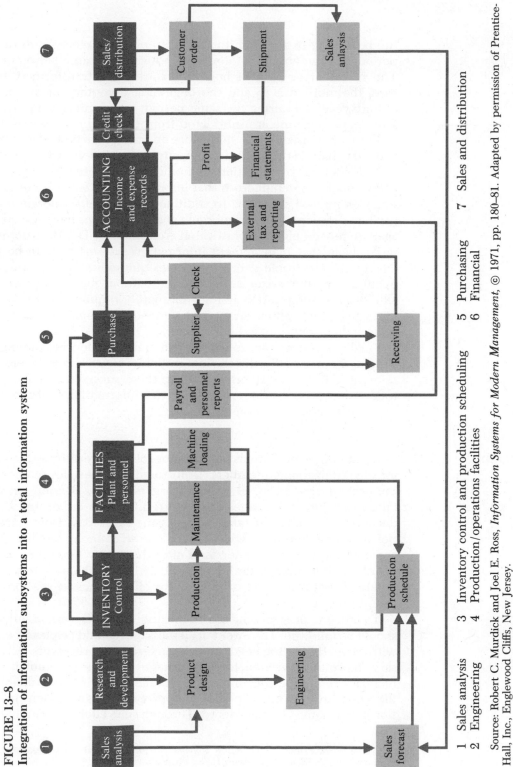

1 Sales analysis   3 Inventory control and production scheduling   5 Purchasing
2 Engineering   4 Production/operations facilities   6 Financial
                                                                        7 Sales and distribution

Source: Robert C. Murdick and Joel E. Ross, *Information Systems for Modern Management*, © 1971, pp. 180–81. Adapted by permission of Prentice-Hall, Inc., Englewood Cliffs, New Jersey.

the beginning of a period, the quantity of items received during the period, and the number of items used during the same period of time. The *process* stage outlines how inputs are to be transformed. In this case, the method is to add the beginning inventory to the number of units received during the same period; then, units used during the same period of time are subtracted from the total.

To make an inventory system more operative, the type of equipment needed to handle the input-process-output components must be considered. For a large organization, equipment is absolutely necessary since transactions are so numerous that information systems cannot depend solely on manual dexterity. In addition, international operations, new product development, and mergers and acquisitions have forced managers to rely on highly sophisticated equipment.[27] This does not necessarily mean that management information systems have to be interfaced with electronic data processing equipment. In fact, there are many information systems that operate without such equipment. Yet, all advanced information systems ultimately require special data manipulations that call for an interface between manual-machine operations and computer-based equipment.

Finally, it is necessary to consider the interrelationships among subsystems. Figure 13–8 notes the integration of an inventory level subsystem with other subsystems. Together, these subsystems make up the total system that provides managers with information that is essential in making effective decisions.

SUMMARY

Communication systems play a major role in determining the behavior of organizational members. Unfortunately, examples of poor communication abound in all types of organizations. Barriers arise and take many forms. Messages are distorted through either encoding or decoding, and filtering takes place as messages pass from person to person with an ultimate reduction in the level of understanding. People are notoriously poor listeners and often hear only what they want to hear. In other cases, interdepartmental friction, channel noise, or semantics lead to barriers that impede the effectiveness of the communication process.

To prevent, or overcome communication barriers, various guidelines should be followed. The intent of all messages should be clearly defined with each fitted to the needs and characteristics of receivers. All necessary information related to the message must be accumulated, and feedback should be encouraged. Simultaneously, timing, available media, costs, and the development of appropriate management information systems must be considered. Through such efforts, communication

---

[27] Thomas R. Prince, *Information Systems for Management Planning and Control* (Homewood, Ill.: Richard D. Irwin, 1975), chap 3.

comes much closer to the ideal of transmitting information that is both understood and accepted by receivers.

KEY TERMS

Communication: The process of transmitting and receiving information through the use of common symbols so that understanding takes place.

Communication screens: A filtration effect that allows only specific information to flow through a channel.

Cross communication: Directional flows of information within the formal organization that do not follow the official chain of command.

Decoding: A mental process that the receiver of a message follows in interpreting the meaning of certain symbols.

Downward communication: The flow of information within an organization structure from people in higher-level positions to those at lower levels.

Encoding: Converting a message or an idea into understandable symbols by the sender.

Information overload: An amount of information greater than that needed by the decision maker that may result in poorer decision-making performance, but possibly a greater sense of job satisfaction.

Lateral communication: The flow of communication among individuals on the same organizational level.

Management information systems: The people and equipment used in the selection, storing, processing, and retrieving of information required in decision making.

Network models: Communication patterns that reflect the designs of a circle, wheel, chain, and Y, all of which are used within the organization with varying degrees of effectiveness.

Perception: Organizing and interpreting various stimuli so that meaning and understanding are given to a person's environment.

Semantic barriers: Due to different past experiences, attitudes, biases, or perceptions, senders and receivers define specific words differently.

Upward communication: The flow of communication that provides subordinates with the means for conveying information to their superiors.

QUESTIONS

1. What is communication? Why is it important in management?
2. Why is communication considered a two-way process? Can it ever be one way?

3. List the steps involved in the communication process.

4. Describe upward, downward, and lateral communication.

5. What factors influence the selection of formal communication channels?

6. Describe the four basic communication networks that can exist among people.

7. Note some of the major characteristics of the grapevine.

8. Discuss major barriers to communication.

9. What three approaches can be used to help improve the effectiveness of communication?

10. Note five communication guidelines that managers can follow in reducing misunderstanding.

11. What is the meaning and importance of a management information system?

12. Describe the steps used in developing a management information system.

13. Note some of the major factors that must be considered in making an information system operative.

PROBLEMS

1. The rather hidden meaning of communication is seen in the fact that one researcher has found over 95 definitions of the concept, some pointing in rather contradictory directions. The term *communication,* however, comes from the Latin word, *commanis,* meaning common. Although we are unable to arrive at a "common" definition of the word, how does the Latin meaning relate to the definition of the term provided in this chapter?

2. What accounts for the communication gap that seems to exist between management groups and labor unions? What can be done to narrow this gap?

3. The *Management Handbook* for Saga Airlines contains a section on improving supervisory communication. The focus of the two-page section is on the importance of downward communication. Basically, the section states that downward communication lets subordinates know what is expected of them, how they are to do their jobs, and how well they are performing. The section also implies that supervisors must encourage subordinates to *(a)* ask questions about instructions or the progress of their work, *(b)* feel that their ideas and comments are respected, and *(c)* think of themselves as part of the overall management team.

(a) Is downward communication the only directional flow emphasized in the handbook?

(b) What guidelines could supervisors follow to develop an atmosphere of free and open communications?

4. Think of the 50 plus American hostages who were held in Iran. Assume that all formal communication channels had been destroyed and communication by word of mouth was prohibited. Would it have been possible for the hostages to communicate with one another under these circumstances? Why or why not?

5. The Federal Paperwork Commission estimated the paperwork cost to private industry in communicating with federal agencies to be approximately $25 to $32 billion per year. The 10,000 largest companies expected to have spent $10 to $12 billion on paperwork and to have filled out more than 10 billion sheets of paper a year. If the cost of collecting data continues to grow at the present rate, it could reach 5 percent of our GNP by the mid- to late-1980s.

(a) The word *data* refers to recorded facts and figures on some activity, while *information* is regarded as the processing of these facts and figures so that they are meaningful to the person using them. Do you feel that the data collected by federal agencies turn into information?

(b) Can the cost of $25 to $32 billion a year ever be justified, particularly since the final consumer may eventually pay for the cost?

6. When people are asked to describe the personal characteristics of an individual by looking at a photograph, their replies vary widely, but predictably, according to whether they are told the picture is of a union leader or a business executive. What accounts for this phenomenon?

7. By using Figure 13–8, develop the informational flow system diagram into a conventional organization chart that shows only the hierarchical lines of authority. Put the two figures side by side and note how they differ from one another. Which chart do you think management would want to develop first?

8. Mr. Phillip Broughton, an official in the U.S. Public Health Service, developed the Systematic Buzz Phrase Projector, as noted below:

Column 1	Column 2	Column 3
0. Integrated	0. Management	0. Options
1. Total	1. Organizational	1. Flexibility
2. Systematized	2. Monitored	2. Capability
3. Parallel	3. Reciprocal	3. Mobility
4. Functional	4. Digital	4. Programming
5. Responsive	5. Logistical	5. Concept
6. Optional	6. Transitional	6. Time-phase
7. Synchronized	7. Incremental	7. Projection
8. Compatible	8. Third-generation	8. Hardware
9. Balanced	9. Policy	9. Contingency

Its use is simple: Think of any three-digit number. Then select the corresponding "buzz phrase" by matching the sequence of each digit to the column number. For instance, number 734 produces the phrase "Synchronized Reciprocal Programming," a phrase that can be dropped into virtually any report with a decisive ring of authority. Of course, no one has the slightest idea about what is being discussed, but no one is about to admit it.

Is Mr. Broughton's scheme a meaningful communication device? Is it applicable in any way toward improving management decision making?

9. The following is an elementary experiment in reading and following directions.

Instructions: Use the accompanying map and follow the instructions given below. Place each X exactly over the intersections of the streets and proceed with each successive instruction by starting from the last X recorded, except in instances where you are instructed otherwise. Number each X as you write it. When you write an X, let it stand. Make no erasures.

A. Place an X at the corner of Jason and 5th streets.
B. Walk two blocks east, three blocks south, two blocks west, one block north and place an X at the corner where you arrive.
C. Walk one block east, three blocks north, one block east and place an X at the corner where you arrive.
D. Walk five blocks south, two blocks west, three blocks north, one block east and place an X at the corner where you arrive.
E. Walk three blocks west, one block south, five blocks east and place an X at the corner where you arrive.
F. Walk one block east, three blocks west, three blocks north and place an X at the corner where you arrive.
G. Place another X as far from the west and south borders of the map as your last X is from the west and north borders of the map.
H. Start north, zig-zag north and east, alternating one block at a time and walking five blocks in all, then place an X at the corner where you arrive.
I. Start at the opposite corner of the block southeast of where you placed the last X, walk two blocks west and place an X at the corner where you arrive.

Map-communication experiment

North

1st Street	2d Street	3d Street	4th Street	5th Street	6th Street	7th Street	8th Street	
				Jason St.				
				Johns St.				
				Jarvis St.				
				James St.				
				Jackson St.				

J. Go three fourths of the way around a square that has the length of two blocks on each side, starting where you placed the last X and ending due south of the starting point. Place an X at the corner where you arrive.

a. Were the instructions clear and simple?
b. Did you end up at 7th and James streets?
c. What communication implications can be derived from the experiment?

10. In a study by the Opinion Research Corporation, it was found that *(a)* over one half of all employee respondents believed that telling the supervisor everything they felt about the company would get them into trouble, *(b)* almost three fourths of all respondents felt that management was not interested in employee problems, and *(c)* supervisors felt they needed more training in communication practices, particularly listening.

What communication barriers do these findings have reference to, and what could be done by management to overcome these barriers?

11. Communicating depends upon a variety of symbols to achieve understanding of information. Some of the most common are speaking, drawing, acting, and writing. Give some examples of how the various symbols could be used in management. Some examples to help start your thinking are population density maps, moving an employee from a private office to an open area, and having to wait 40 minutes to see the boss who is finishing his coffee break.

12. The Flesch system provides an analysis of sentence length, number of affixes, and the number of human interest words used in written sentences. For example, the standard sentence length is 17 words. The "fog index" relates to the number of years of formal education required to read a passage easily and with understanding. Specifically, the index is derived by multiplying 0.04 by the number of three or more syllable words in a 100-word passage. In a similar vein, the average speaking speed is 120 words per minute, and our listening comprehension is about 480 words per minute.

What implications do these facts have for managers in writing employee directives and handbooks or in presenting employee training sessions?

SUGGESTED READINGS

Ackoff, R. L. "Management Misinformation Systems." *Management Science,* December 1967, pp. 147–56.

Athanassiades, J. C. "The Distortion of Upward Communication in Hierarchical Organizations." *Academy of Management Journal,* June 1973, pp. 207–26.

Bass, B. M., and R. Klaus. "Communication Styles, Credibility, and Their Consequences." *The Personnel Administrator,* October 1975, pp. 32–35.

Burck, C. G. "How Frank Considine Runs a Billion-Dollar Small Company." *Fortune,* July 3, 1978, pp. 74–77.

Colbert, B. A. "The Management Information System." *The Price Waterhouse Review,* Spring 1967, pp. 4–14.

Di Gaetani, J. L. "The Business of Listening." *Business Horizons,* October 1980, pp. 40–46.

French, R. L. "Making Decisions Faster with Data Base Management Systems." *Business Horizons,* October 1980, pp. 33–36.

Goldhaber, G. M.; H. S. Dennis, III; G. R. Richetto; and O. A. Wiio. *Information Strategies: New Patterns to Corporate Power.* Englewood Cliffs, N.J.: Prentice-Hall, 1979.

Huebner, A. "The Worldwide Struggle over Information." *Business and Society Review,* Summer 1980, pp. 59–62.

Keen, P. G., and M. S. Scott Morton. *Decision Support Systems: An Organizational Perspective.* Reading, Mass.: Addison-Wesley Publishing, 1978.

Kelly, C. M. "Empathetic Listening." In *Small Group Communication: A Reader,* edited by R. S. Cathcart and L. Samovar. Dubuque, Iowa: Wm. C. Brown, 1974, pp. 340–48.

Kikoski, John F. "Communication: Understanding It, Improving It." *Personnel Journal,* February 1980, pp. 126–31.

Lee, H, C., and J. J. Grix. "Communication: An Alternative to Job Enrichment." *The Personnel Administrator,* October 1975, pp. 20–24.

Mandell, L. "The Management Information System Is Going to Pieces." *California Management Review,* Summer 1975, pp. 50–56.

O'Reilly, C., and L. Pondy. "Organization Communication." In *Organization Behavior,* edited by S. Kerr. Columbus, Ohio: Grid, 1979, pp. 119–50.

Samaras, J. T. "Two-Way Communication Practices for Managers." *Personnel Journal,* August 1980, pp. 645–48.

Welling, P. "Introducing the MISA." *Management Accounting,* February 1977, pp. 31–33.

14

MOTIVATION WITHIN ORGANIZATIONS

PURPOSE

While president of du Pont, Crawford Greenewalt wrote a delightful book entitled *The Uncommon Man*. Over 20 years later, the book's message is as powerful as ever. The thrust of the message is that all organizations, nations, societies, and civilizations will prosper and advance only to the extent that they encourage common people to perform uncommon deeds. To stimulate uncommon efforts, there is a need for adequate incentives combined with maximum personal freedom. Even in 1959, however, Greenewalt saw some financial incentives losing their appeal due to the increased share of monetary rewards being taken by income taxes. At the same time, forces within both the internal and external environments of organizations were restricting the personal freedom of many employees and managers.

Today, the role of financial incentives is still questioned in our society. Those who seek financial rewards are sometimes called money chasers, while those who do not are labeled as lazy. In addition, the leisure ethic is replacing the work ethic for many persons since higher income, social security, and estate taxes penalize those who work harder to earn more money. When combined with a continued loss of personal freedom at work due to a maze of government regulations, growth in the size of organizations, and increased job specialization, the motivational climate of many organizations is quite bad. Consequently, we see fewer uncommon efforts from common people.

This chapter looks at motivation within organizations. The relationship between needs and behavior is discussed, and a general approach to motivation is presented. Specific management approaches to motivation are also included since a knowledge of needs and behavior is of little value unless it can be applied in organizational settings.

OBJECTIVES

1. To outline current management thought on individual behavior and motivation.

2. To discuss the hierarchy of needs concept as one approach to understanding motivation.

3. To present a general approach to the motivation of organizational members.

4. To assist in developing an understanding of participative approaches to motivation.

5. To examine job enlargement, job enrichment, management by objectives, and other participative management techniques.

In addition to being members of various groups that influence behavior within an organization, employees are unique individuals unto themselves. All have needs, experiences, values, and attitudes that cause them to behave differently. Their behavior is sometimes directed toward goals of the formal organization; at other times, it is not.

Current approaches to motivation are based on a greater awareness of behavioral differences than was seen in earlier management philosophies. Job enrichment, management by objectives, and other participative approaches focus on needs for recognition, esteem, accomplishment, and self-actualization. Having received limited attention prior to the last 25 years, some satisfaction of these needs is now considered essential in developing an organizational climate within which employees will be motivated to carry out their prescribed roles.

MANAGEMENT THOUGHT ON INDIVIDUAL BEHAVIOR

Many early management scholars and practitioners felt that people worked only to feed and clothe themselves. Thus, the way to get more work out of employees was either to provide additional money or to threaten to withhold money for poor performance. From the late 1930s through most of the 1950s, this feeling slowly changed to one suggesting that people worked out of loyalty to the organization. Since loyal workers were supposed to be more productive, attempts to increase employee loyalty were numerous. Recreational programs were organized, and annual company picnics were common. Company newspapers and magazines were published in an effort to improve communication with employees, while giving them recognition for their accomplishments. Physical working conditions were given more attention, and fringe benefit packages were expanded. While still found in many organizations, these efforts alone have not increased employee loyalty as originally thought.

Most behavioral theories now suggest that people are purposeful in their behavior. They do not act in a particular way unless there is some reason behind the action. Determining the real reason for a certain action is not easy, however. Casual observations of behavior do not always indicate the true motivation of persons with whom we are dealing. When their behavior is examined in more depth, we often find one or more basic, yet unapparent, reasons for certain actions. This brings us to that portion of current management thought that suggests behavior is directed toward specific goals in response to individual needs.

Need-behavior cycle

The relationship between needs and behavior is shown in Figure 14–1 with the starting point being the recognition of a *need* within an individual. For example, the need for clothing creates a state of tension within an individual that continues until it is satisfied. Of course, clothing is generally required by all individuals, but the need is modi-

FIGURE 14–1
The need-behavior cycle

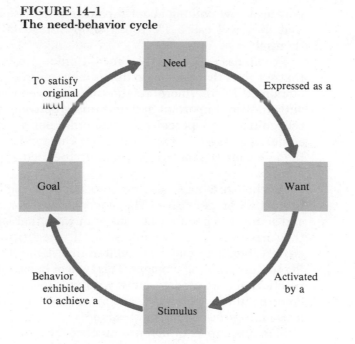

fied by social and economic factors. As a result, it is expressed differently in terms of individual wants. Some people want to dress conservatively, while others desire a different look. A stimulus, such as an advertisement about clothing, activates the motivational drive of the individual. In this example, as well as in others, the strength of the motivational drive depends primarily upon the perceived importance of the need.

The need-behavior cycle is a starting point for understanding behavior. It recognizes that individual behavior is directed toward the satisfaction of needs and serves as a basis for explaining why people react as they do to various motivational forces. At the same time, it assists managers in identifying approaches for directing behavior that will produce the greatest benefits for both the organization and its employees. In this context, managers must understand human needs in order to deal most effectively with all organizational members.

Need satisfaction—a partial explanation

By no means should one consider the need-behavior cycle as a complete explanation of behavior since many different factors are responsible for individual actions. The leadership styles of managers impact on the behavior of subordinates just as working conditions, policies, and authority structures influence employee responses to various situations. Consequently, behavior is directly related to individual perceptions and knowledge of these and other factors.[1] For example, if two

---

[1] See B. S. Georgopoulas, G. H. Mahoney, and N. W. Jones, "A Path-Goal Approach to Productivity," *Journal of Applied Psychology*, 1957, pp. 345–53.

persons know nothing about repairing a television set, we can predict that they will call a TV repair shop instead of trying to fix the set themselves.

Vroom has expanded this line of thinking in his motivational model that suggests that people do things (behave) in expectation of a specific outcome.[2] Furthermore, relationships between first- and second-level outcomes are important in determining behavior. A person may desire recognition and perceive outstanding performance (first-level outcome) as a way to achieve this goal. Outstanding performance would then become the means for attaining the second-level outcome of recognition.

Psychologists have also pointed out that some behavior is simply protective or defensive. This concept was first presented by Freud and states that people will behave in ways that agree with the picture they have of themselves. Because of insecurity, hurt, frustration, or anxiety, behavior may be exhibited that denies that which is threatening to a person's self-concept. This type of behavior is called a defensive reaction and is used to cope with the fear of being overwhelmed. Some common defensive reactions are rationalization, repression, projection, regression, and aggression.[3]

Many examples of defense mechanisms are found both on and off the job. Employees who do not receive desired promotions may react by rationalizing that they really did not want the added responsibilities, or by stating that they were discriminated against. In either case, the employees are attempting to cover up and protect themselves from the reality that they may not be as good as the employees who received promotions. Another example is the person with marital problems who may vent frustrations on other employees or may withdraw from the situation by abandoning the family. Thus, rather than solving problems logically, the person uses other mechanisms in an attempt to defend against a threat that appears to be overwhelming.

Hierarchy of needs   An approach to motivation that explains behavior in terms of individuals seeking satisfaction of a hierarchy of needs has been formulated by Abraham H. Maslow.[4] According to Maslow, humans have definite categories of needs that can be arranged in a natural hierarchy of urgency. The most basic and potent needs are located at the bottom of the hierarchy, and until these needs are satisfied, they are the most important. Beyond these physiological needs, Figure 14–2 shows the

[2] See Victor H. Vroom, *Work and Motivation* (New York: John Wiley & Sons, 1964); and J. C. Hunt and H. W. Hill, "The New Look in Motivational Theory for Organizational Research," *Human Organization*, 1969, pp. 100–109.

[3] For a discussion of defense mechanisms, see Chris Argyris, *Personality and Organization* (New York: Harper & Row, 1957), pp. 36–47.

[4] A. H., Maslow, *Motivation and Personality*, 2d ed. (New York: Harper & Row, 1954).

FIGURE 14–2
Maslow's hierarchy of human needs

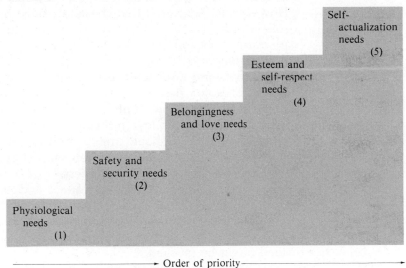

Source: Data and material for diagram based on Hierarchy of Needs in "A Theory of Human Motivation" in *Motivation and Personality,* 2d ed., by Abraham H. Maslow. Copyright © 1970 by Abraham H. Maslow. Adapted by permission of Harper & Row, Publishers, Inc.

safety, belongingness and love, esteem, and self-actualization needs in the order of their priority.

Maslow's general proposition is that all needs do not emerge at the same time. When the physiological needs have been satisfied, an individual may then engage in other forms of behavior to satisfy safety needs at the next level. After the safety needs are fulfilled, the needs of love, esteem, and self-actualization arise. An important point to recognize here is that each level of needs must be dealt with adequately before an individual seeks needs at the next higher level. When relatively satisfied, the dominant needs then submerge and allow the next higher level of needs in the hierarchy to become dominant. In addition, once a need is satisfied, it no longer motivates behavior.

The five basic categories of needs presented by Maslow can now be discussed more fully as follows:

1. *Physiological*—The biological aspects of the human body, such as the need for food, water, protein, oxygen, rest, and sex, make up this group of needs. As to the satisfaction of these needs, Maslow states, "They now exist only in a potential fashion in the sense that they may emerge again to dominate the organism if they are thwarted."[5]

2. *Safety*—The threat of danger, terror, and illness results in a need

_____
[5] Ibid., p. 87.

for a predictable and organized world. Maslow indicates that for the healthy, normal adult in our culture, the safety need is largely satisfied. However, he points out that the safety need is dominant *(a)* in a neurotic, *(b)* for the economically and socially deprived individual, and *(c)* during war and natural catastrophies.

3. *Belongingness and love*—The desire for affectionate relations with others and a recognized place in a group are classified as social needs. Maslow's position is that an inadequate satisfaction of these needs is the most commonly found cause of psychological maladjustment. In this respect, love refers to the desire for affection and acceptance by others. It should not be considered synonymous with sex, even though sexual behavior is determined by both the sex drive and the need for love and belongingness.

4. *Esteem*—People seek self-respect and esteem from others. Esteem can be obtained through competence, independence, status, recognition, and dominance. Gaining status by earning a recognized title, such as president within an organization, is an example of how this need might be satisfied.

Deprivation of the esteem need creates inferiority, helplessness, frustration, and conflict which can lead to discouragement and neurotic tendencies. The person who cannot obtain satisfaction of this higher-level need may become just as ill as one who is deprived of physiological needs. However, the satisfaction of the esteem need can prevent feelings of inferiority and weakness.

5. *Self-actualization*—Self-actualization refers to the need of individuals to become what they are capable of being. If, for example, you feel capable of being the best manager in your organization, you must be given the opportunity and responsibility to manage if you are ever to be self-fulfilled.

In summary, Maslow's theory is not built upon the uniqueness of the needs to which he refers, but upon the idea that these needs are arrayed in a natural hierarchy of urgency. A practical example of the operation of Maslow's model can be seen in the very apparent and continuous switching and changing of careers by many workers.[6] Rising incomes have enabled many people to shoulder the financial burden of training for a new job. Thus, once basic lower-order needs are satisfied, individuals are able to move from jobs that are routine and boring to those that hold more potential for satisfying their higher-order needs.

Evaluation of Maslow's hierarchy

Two major questions can be asked about Maslow's theory: (1) Must a need be completely satisfied before the next level need emerges? (2) Is the hierarchy actually fixed in a rigid order, or are there some exceptions? Let us take a look at these questions to clarify the nature of the hierarchy of needs further.

---

[6] R. E. Hill and E. L. Miller, "Job Change and the Middle Seasons of a Man's Life," *Academy of Management Journal*, March 1981, pp. 114–27.

FIGURE 14–3
Importance of needs relative to a person's degree of satisfaction

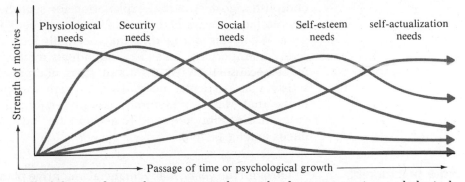

All of the needs are always present, but with advancements in psychological growth, higher needs dominate the hierarchy and the basic ones decline in importance.

Source: David J. Lawless, *Effective Management: Social Psychological Approach.* © 1972, p. 87. Reprinted by permission of Prentice-Hall, Inc., Englewood Cliffs, New Jersey.

Overlapping of needs   Based upon the concept that a single behavior may have a large number of associated needs, a given need does not have to be fully satisfied before a higher-order need becomes urgent or potent. From a practical standpoint, individuals neither choose nor desire a maximum satisfaction of needs. Instead, they are usually content with a satisfactory level of achievement. Maslow emphasizes this point by stating that a normal person's basic needs are partially satisfied, and at the same time, partially unsatisfied. For any particular person, needs are inseparable and interrelated, just as the mind and body are interconnected.

In terms of their potency, one way to express the interrelationships among needs is shown in Figure 14–3. This figure shows various levels of satisfaction for the basic needs as well as the number and relative urgency of needs existing at any one level. As the basic physiological needs are fulfilled, other needs arise and the peak of satisfaction for each previous need must occur before the peak of the next higher order need can be reached.

Rigidity of the hierarchy   If a person has been unable to satisfy two different needs, will fulfillment of the more basic of the two ultimately occur first? While it is possible that this may happen, there is no assurance. Although Maslow specified a universal ordering of needs, he realized that the creative person, for example, may experience the self-actualization need long before the lower-level needs are even partially satisfied. Similarly, other people know what they want and set out to achieve it, regardless of the level of satisfaction among other needs.

No doubt you are aware of people who have been willing to sacrifice self-esteem, love, safety, and physiological fulfillment in order to accomplish a goal. A partial explanation for such behavior is that many people have always had their lower-level needs satisfied to some degree. When this is true, they may normally look at such needs as relatively unimportant. Likewise, individuals might jump a certain need level because their environment does not provide opportunities to satisfy that particular need. Due to such exceptions, some scholars imply that Maslow's hierarchy is an oversimplification; and, in some cases, it is possibly too rigid to account for individual learning experiences among people.[7]

Role of financial incentives

Through the years, many financial incentive plans have been devised by industrial engineers and compensation specialists. To their dismay, many of these plans have not consistently brought forth high levels of productivity.[8] In addition, research studies show that the relationship between wages and increased productivity is extremely indirect and remote.[9] Many managers, however, continue to adhere to the philosophy that the more pay individuals receive the harder they will work.

By looking at Maslow's hierarchy of needs, we also see that monetary rewards alone may not lead to desired behavior. If an employee has enough income to buy adequate food, more money to buy additional food is not necessarily an incentive to work harder. Likewise, money may not be an important motivator beyond the satisfaction of basic physiological needs if it is not a true reflection of job performance. Expectancy theory points this out by suggesting that individuals behave according to perceived relationships among effort, performance, and rewards.[10]

In spite of these comments, there is no evidence that most people have ceased to have a strong desire for the comfort and possessions that money can buy.[11] There are also instances where money is important as a status symbol or a means for achieving recognition. If two workers with the same seniority are doing the same job, but one earns 10 cents more per hour, the lower wage earner can become frustrated and dissatisfied. An increase of 10 cents an hour might be important to this worker since it could lead to more social status while indicating

---

[7] K. H. Roberts, G. A. Walker, and R. E. Miles, "A Factor-Analysis Study of Satisfaction Items Designed to Measure Maslow Need Categories," *Personnel Psychology*, 1971, pp. 205–20.

[8] Edward L. Deci, "Paying People Doesn't Always Work the Way You Expect It To," *Human Resource Management*, Summer 1973, pp. 28–32.

[9] See William Foote Whyte, *Men at Work* (Homewood, Ill.: Richard D. Irwin and Dorsey Press, 1966), pp. 98–99.

[10] C. W. Cook, "Guidelines for Managing Motivation," *Business Horizons*, April 1980, p. 63.

[11] "The Mysteries of Motivation," *Success Unlimited*, October 1980, pp. 36–40.

equity and fairness in the organization's wage and salary structure.[12]

At this point, we can only conclude that the exact role of money as a motivator is uncertain. Just as individuals are different, their responses to financial incentives differ. Money is very important to some persons and less important to others. In all cases, however, it is but one of many factors affecting the motivation of people at work.

HERZBERG'S TWO-FACTOR THEORY

An interesting corollary to Maslow's work is the Two-Factor Theory of Motivation, developed by Frederick Herzberg.[13] His model is based on research conducted among middle managers in engineering and accounting and presents the view that factors in the work environment that provide job satisfaction are not necessarily the same as those that cause dissatisfaction.[14] Characteristics of the work environment that may lead to dissatisfaction are called hygiene factors and include the following:

1. Company personnel policies and management practices under which a job is performed.
2. Technical supervision received on the job.
3. Interpersonal relations with supervisors and peers.
4. Quality of working conditions.
5. Salary received for doing a job.

When these factors are absent in the work situation, Herzberg feels that employee dissatisfaction is likely. However, the presence of hygiene factors does not necessarily motivate employees. Instead, they help prevent dissatisfaction and, in this sense, are similar to preventive practices recognized in medicine.

The job content factors that produce satisfaction are called motivators and include the following:

1. Achievement on a job
2. Recognition for job achievement.
3. Nature of the job and the work itself.
4. Responsibility for job achievement.
5. Advancement and growth in job capability.

---

[12] For further discussion on the relationship between behavior and perceived equity and fairness of payments, see J. S. Adams, "Toward an Understanding of Inequity," *Journal of Abnormal and Social Psychology*, 1963, pp. 422–36; and P. S. Goodman and A. Friedman, "An Examination of Adams' Theory of Inequity," *Administrative Science Quarterly*, 1971, pp. 271–88.

[13] Frederick Herzberg, *Work and the Nature of Man* (Cleveland: World Publishing 1966).

[14] The empirical work may be found in Frederick Herzberg, Bernard Mauser, and Barbara B. Snyderman, *The Motivation to Work* (New York: John Wiley & Sons, 1959). See especially pp. 113–19.

Herzberg states that the absence of these motivational factors in the work situation does not bring about dissatisfaction on the job; but, when present, they relate to a high level of motivation and job satisfaction. As such, motivators relate to the intrinsic factors or actual content of a job, not just to extrinsic factors of the job environment. In this light, motivators are closely linked to the esteem and self-actualization needs expressed by Maslow.

Implications of the Herzberg model

Herzberg's findings indicate that responsibility, work itself, and advancement are the most important job conditions contributing to lasting satisfaction with a job. As indicated above, these factors are not the same ones that make people unhappy on a job. However, as we can see in Figure 14–4, there is an overlap of the motivators and the hygiene factors. Consequently, a few of the factors associated with good feelings about jobs also appeared in descriptions of job conditions that caused dissatisfaction. Herzberg's explanation is that a work or job-oriented factor can result in a dissatisfied feeling if an employee

FIGURE 14–4
Comparison of factors resulting in job dissatisfaction and job satisfaction

Source: Adapted from F. Herzberg et al., *The Motivation to Work* (New York: John Wiley & Sons, 1959). By permission of the publisher.

has too little work to do or has been stereotyped by a superior for only a particular kind of work. Such overlapping among factors, however, has resulted in criticisms of the Herzberg model. Later research also suggests that these factors do not reliably predict whether an employee's feelings are positive or negative about a job.[15]

Criticisms of the Herzberg model

The Herzberg model has been criticized on many counts including methodology and inconsistency with past evidence concerning employee satisfaction and motivation.[16] From a managerial viewpoint, we are interested in knowing whether highly satisfied employees are always the most productive. Herzberg noted in his own research that only 14 out of 27 cases revealed a positive relationship between a good job attitude and productivity.[17] In addition, one of the most complete studies compiling research findings on job satisfaction and job performance indicates that, at best, there is only a small relationship between these two variables.[18]

Even though the relationship between job satisfaction and productivity is not clear, three theoretical positions are possible. The first is that a satisifed worker is likely to be more productive in the long run than one who is dissatisfied. A second position holds that the direct influence of worker satisfaction on performance depends on various situational variables. The third is that a productive worker is more likely to be satisfied as a direct result of the rewards and sense of achievement that accompany good performance.

The first two propositions show only a casual relationship between employee satisfaction and performance. Perhaps this explains why some employees who seem quite satisfied with their jobs are actually poor performers. More important, these propositions point out that job satisfaction is a function of many factors. What may be a motivator for one person may be a hygiene factor for another.[19] In this respect, there is some doubt that the Herzberg model is correct in presenting a fixed preference of motives underlying behavior. The model does, however, offer managers much food for thought concerning their relationships with subordinates. With the model, managers can see that

---

[15] V. M. Bockman, "The Herzberg Controversy," *Personnel Psychology*, 1971, pp. 115–89.

[16] R. J. House and L. A. Wiglor, "Herzberg's Dual-Factor Theory of Job Satisfaction and Motivation: A Review of the Evidence and a Criticism," *Personnel Psychology*, 1967, pp. 369–87. See also J. Scheider and E. A. Locke, "A Critique of Herzberg's Incident Classification System and a Suggested Revision," *Organizational Behavior and Human Performance*, 1971, pp. 441–57.

[17] Frederick Herzberg, *Work and the Nature of Man* (Cleveland: World Publishing, 1966), pp. 92–162.

[18] Victor H. Vroom, *Work and Motivation* (New York: John Wiley & Sons, 1964), pp. 9–18.

[19] M. G. Wolf, "Need Gratification Theory: A Theoretical Reformulation of Job Satisfaction, Dissatisfaction, and Job Motivation," *Journal of Applied Psychology*, vol. 54, 1970, pp. 87–94.

the best way to increase motivation may not include a greater emphasis on wages, fringe benefits, or other personnel practices. A sense of accomplishment and other personal experiences associated with work are also important when one considers the psychological growth of organizational members.

MOTIVATION AND PERSONALITY

Personality affects the way people do their jobs and how they interact with other organizational members. Thus, managers must understand the attitudes, values, and perceptions of people in their organizations since relationships between motivation and personality cannot be considered apart from such factors.

One interrelationship between personality and motivation concerns the way a person selects a particular behavior to satisfy certain needs. While Maslow and Herzberg have categorized needs that motivate individuals, they say very little about how motivation is actually expressed. As touched on earlier, a better way to view expressions of motivation may be through *expectancy* or *instrumentality theory*. According to this theory, external goals act as forces that "pull" people to act in a certain way to satisfy their needs.[20] Behavior, then, is guided by the expectation of achieving results that will satisfy given needs. Accordingly, individuals exhibit that behavior perceived as having the greatest payoff relative to their needs.

Since all people do not perceive things in the same way, we see why their behavior often differs even in similar situations. Perceptions vary, of course, because of people's knowledge, experiences, sensitivities, organizational authority, group memberships, and a host of other factors. To determine the influence of such factors on perception is very difficult, but managers must make the effort. Otherwise they will not understand relationships between motivation and the perceptions of different personality types within their organizations.

A GENERAL APPROACH TO MOTIVATION

Two questions arise when one seeks to strike a balance between some satisfaction of employee needs and an accomplishment of organizational goals:

1. Are employees similar enough that the same incentives can be used for all of them?
2. Do managers have the time to determine the active needs of each subordinate?

To answer the first question, we have already seen that the same incentives will not work equally well for all employees. Just as people

---

[20] L. L. Cummings and Donald P. Schwab, *Performance in Organizations: Determinants and Appraisal* (Glenview, Ill.: Scott, Foresman, 1973); Lyman W. Porter and Edward E. Lawler, III, *Managerial Attitudes and Performance* (Homewood, Ill.: Richard D. Irwin, and Dorsey Press, 1968); and Vroom, *Work and Motivation*.

are different, the strength of given needs varies from person to person. When such differences are compounded by the growing complexity of organizations, it becomes very difficult to generalize about behavioral responses to the same incentives. Understanding subordinates as individuals is, therefore, important to the success of most managers.

The second question points to time constraints faced by managers. It is obviously impossible for managers to spend the time that would be required to know each employee intimately. Common sense also dictates that few people fully understand their own actions, to say nothing about the behavior of others. Yet, since the needs of employees differ, managers must try to deal with them as individuals. A step in this direction can be taken by looking at the impact of various management practices on need satisfaction. Through such efforts, practices that have a positive impact can be supported, while those regarded as negative can be eliminated.

Eliminating unhealthy management practices

Some of the unhealthy management practices that can be eliminated include discrimination, an unwillingness to let employees present their ideas, an inability to change when shown to be wrong, and a lack of management knowledge and skill. Figure 14–5 presents these and other unhealthy management practices while indicating employee needs that tend to go unsatisfied as a result. The listing shown is not

FIGURE 14–5
Management practices that restrict need satisfaction

Management practices	*Individual needs restricted*
Discrimination	Security, self-esteem, belongingness, self-actualization
Inability and/or unwillingness to communicate and personally interrelate with subordinates	Security, belongingness, recognition
Lack of managerial knowledge and skill	Achievement, recognition, self-actualization
Lack of time or ability to understand employees	Physiological, safety, belongingness, esteem, self-actualization
Makes decisions strictly by the book and follows inept policies	Recognition, belongingness, self-actualization
Builds status symbols of power and authority to achieve recognition	Security, recognition, belongingness
Inability to change when shown to be wrong	Security and belongingness
Provides improper working conditions	Physiological and security
Criticizes so that employees lose face and status in the work group	Security, belongingness, and self-esteem

all inclusive, of course, and can be expanded through your own knowledge and experience.

Supporting positive management practices

Some of the general management practices that can be followed to help satisfy the needs of employees are shown in Figure 14–6. An important point to remember about these practices is that the most successful incentives are those which are simple. When employees can directly connect a management practice with the fulfillment of personal goals, motivation becomes mutually effective for them and the organization. Figure 14–6 also shows working conditions and financial incentives as positive management practices; however, if physiological needs are partially satisfied, a further extension of these incentives may not produce the level of motivation desired by management. In the long run, money alone does not usually buy job satisfaction, loyalty, or dedication. Instead, these normally come from feelings of accomplishment and opportunities to satisfy a wide range of other needs on the job.

FIGURE 14–6
Management practices that positively support fulfillment of individual needs

Management practices	Individual needs fulfilled
Promote sense of accomplishment	Esteem and self-actualization
Provide growth potential for employees	
Help employees achieve the best possible way	
Provide feedback on how well subordinates are performing	
Willing to delegate authority and responsibility to others	
Provide legitimate recognition, awards, and status within the company	Esteem, self-actualization, and recognition
Grant employees freedom and creativity	
Develop promotion programs	
Communicate about things that affect employees	Security, belongingness, and esteem
Gain employee trust and respect	
Request employee ideas so as to promote participation and involvement	
Set up equitable pension funds, grievance systems, seniority, and retirement programs	Security
Provide adequate working conditions and monetary rewards for adequate standard of living	Physiological and security

Considering macromotivation

Keith Davis states that there are two types of motivation.[21] *Micromotivation* relates to conditions within a single organization that influence performance on the job. *Macromotivation* considers factors in the social environment outside the organization that may influence job performance. With micromotivation, the focus is on incentive plans, fringe benefits, working conditions, personnel policies, and other programs that management can offer, expand, or eliminate.

Macromotivation looks outside the organization and considers such things as the attitudes of society toward work and leisure; national, state, and local tax structures; economic inflation and recession; and the growing burden of government regulations. Since the impact of these factors on motivation within organizations has grown more negative in recent years, they, too, must be considered in outlining a general approach to motivation.

Where job conditions are poor, motivation will probably be lacking regardless of how supportive an organization's external environment might be. The opposite of this is also true. When factors in the external environment are perceived as being negative, employee motivation will suffer in spite of favorable job conditions within the organization. Therefore, improved performance is a function of both macro- and micromotivation. One without the other is something less than a complete approach to the motivation of employees.

PARTICIPATIVE APPROACHES TO MOTIVATION

Although participative techniques have not replaced autocratic management styles in many organizations, their value in the motivation of employees is more widely recognized than ever before. Through participative methods, employees are given opportunities to be involved in making decisions that affect their job performance. Originally, participative management was based on the idea that people are more likely to support decisions when they have played a part in making them.[22] During the 1960s, this line of thinking was expanded to suggest that joint problem solving also results in better decisions than those made by staff planners. However, it is not yet clear that creativity and the quality of decisions are directly related to participative management.[23]

Realistically, participative approaches have limitations and should not be seen as the answer for all motivational problems. Their application is restricted by the constraints of leadership styles, organizational structures, employee attitudes, working conditions, and other variables.

---

[21] Keith Davis, "Low Productivity? Try Improving the Social Environment," *Business Horizons,* June 1980, pp. 27–29.

[22] Rensis Likert, *New Patterns of Management* (New York: McGraw-Hill, 1961), pp. 9, 20–21.

[23] John B. Miner, *The Management Process: Theory, Research, and Practice* (New York: MacMillan, 1978), pp. 431–33.

In all cases, however, efforts to use participative approaches must be genuine. Token efforts will not work. As Argyris states, "A dilution of the real stuff will taste funny and people may not like it."[24]

Specific participative approaches to motivation include job enlargement, job enrichment, management by objectives, and team management. While different in concept, each of these approaches focuses on (1) developing jobs that give employees opportunities to be more responsible and creative in their work and (2) delegating added decision-making authority to lower organizational levels.

Job enlargement

Job enlargement is an approach to job design that reverses task specialization. Through this approach, job duties are enlarged or combined rather than being divided into smaller tasks. In addition, an element of job enlargement can be provided through job rotation.

An example of combined tasks can be seen at the Indiana Bell Telephone Company where the assembly of telephone books was previously completed in 21 steps, each performed by a different clerk. Now, each clerk is given the responsibility for assembling an entire book. Although the new task assignment may not seem much more meaningful than the old, monotony is relieved. One result has seen employee turnover cut by as much as 50 percent in recent years. General Motors, however, has had less success in enlarging jobs to include additional tasks.[25] Workers often found that they had less rest time and that enlarged jobs were not any more challenging. Although workers were no longer performing only one small part of an operation, they still felt that their jobs were too routine, thereby limiting their control over what was to be done and how it was to be accomplished.

Through job rotation, employees are given training in various operations enabling them to move from one job to another. With proper scheduling, job rotation can be effective in reducing the monotony and boredom found in various operating positions. At managerial levels, job rotation can also be very useful. Radio Corporation of America rotates managers horizontally from one position to another until they have sufficient experience to move upward into a higher position. In this way, individuals do not feel isolated nor locked into a particular position. Job rotation also gives employees an opportunity to broaden their understanding of other parts of the organization so that coordination among all units can be enhanced. As an added incentive, job rotation can serve to restrict empire building within segments of an organization.

Job enrichment

Job enrichment can provide employees with a greater sense of accomplishment, recognition, and involvement in their work. Through

---

[24] Chris Argyris, *Management and Organizational Development: The Path from XA to YB,* p. 145. Copyright © 1971 by McGraw-Hill Book Company. Used with permission of McGraw-Hill Book Company.

[25] "The Spreading Lordstown Syndrome," *Business Week,* March 4, 1972.

this approach, employees are given opportunities to plan, organize, and/or control portions of their jobs. Thus, job enrichment is a vertical approach to job design that has the result of moving tasks and authority downward from one organizational level to another. For example, employees may be permitted to schedule their own operations, reorganize their work places, inspect their own work, or perform other tasks previously carried out by persons at higher levels of authority in the organization.

In practice, elements of job enrichment and job enlargement may be combined to seek benefits of both vertical and horizontal job design. When this is done successfully, the knowledge, ingenuity, creativity, and skills of employees are utilized even more completely.

While various ways to enrich the content of jobs have arisen through the years, most are covered in the following suggestions offered by Herzberg:[26]

1. Remove some controls while retaining employee accountability.
2. Increase individual accountability for work performed.
3. Create a natural unit of work for each employee.
4. Provide greater job freedom by granting additional authority to employees for their duties.
5. Make periodic reports available to employees, rather than to their supervisors.
6. Introduce new and more difficult tasks not previously handled.
7. Allow employees to become experts by assigning specific or specialized tasks to some of them.

While a blanket application of these suggestions in all situations can be questioned, they do provide a starting point for balancing employee needs with organizational goals. By focusing on the nature and value of work, they certainly cause managers to think of employee needs beyond those addressed by wages, working conditions, or personnel policies.

Experiments in job enrichment   McGregor notes three studies of job enrichment, one conducted in British coal mines, another in an Indian textile weaving plant, and a third in a U.S. manufacturing plant.[27] In all of these studies, enriched jobs produced positive results that contributed to the accomplishment of organizational objectives.

Some of the best-known and most successful job enrichment programs are currently found at the Gaines Pet Food plant in Topeka, Kansas; Traveler's Insurance Company in Hartford, Connecticut; and the Motorola Corporation plant in Fort Lauderdale, Florida. One of the most extensive job enrichment projects ever undertaken was at

---

[26] Frederick Herzberg, "One More Time: How Do You Motivate Employees," *Harvard Business Review*, January–February 1968. Copyright © 1967 by the President and Fellows of Harvard College; all rights reserved.

[27] Douglas McGregor, *The Professional Manager* (New York: McGraw-Hill, 1967), pp. 84–90.

American Telephone and Telegraph.[28] Frederick Herzberg worked closely with the company in setting up the project that was under the direction of R. N. Ford, a personnel executive of AT&T. The impetus for the program was provided by a large number of exit interviews where employees had expressed the desire for more responsibility in their jobs.

The first experiment to make "work itself" more important to employees was conducted in the home office treasury department of AT&T where 120 nonmanagerial women were employed. More than 70 percent of these women were college educated, but their work and morale were poor. Herzberg's suggestion was to change the jobs of the women so that they could research, compose, and sign their own letters without having their work checked by a supervisor. In this way, employees were permitted to run their own show. The results were dramatic. Turnover dropped by 27 percent, 24 clerks accomplished the work that had previously required 46, and 8 management and 4 verifier jobs were eliminated. Job satisfaction, measured on a scale of 100, soared from 33 to 90 in 6 months without pay increases. From the cost side of the ledger, calculable savings were estimated at $558,000 over an 18-month period.

Dramatic benefits were also seen in other areas of the AT&T system where job enrichment programs were implemented. Similarly, companies elsewhere in the United States, Japan, and the United Kingdom have reported favorable results from job enrichment. Rather than merely focusing on specific outcomes, however, it is also necessary to look at the length of time through which stated results have been observed.

Increased production, reduced labor turnover, and improved job satisfaction are usually among key results attributed to job enrichment programs. Unfortunately, the time spans during which many of these results have been observed are quite short, ranging from six months to two years. This makes it dangerous to assume that such results will continue over longer periods of time. It is quite possible, for example, that results of job enrichment programs are biased by the personal attention given to employees during their implementation. When these programs are fully operational, employees are left with new duties but gradually receive less personal attention from management. Employee satisfaction, production levels, and other measures may then return to levels comparable to those existing prior to the implementation of job enrichment programs. Therefore, caution must be exercised when looking at the results of short-term job enrichment experiments, or when examining the results of a single isolated experiment.

Additional points on job enrichment   It should be obvious by now

[28] Robert N. Ford, *Motivation* (New York: American Management Association, 1969); and "Job Enrichment Lessons from AT&T," *Harvard Business Review*, January–February 1973, pp. 96–100.

that knowledge concerning job enrichment is far less than perfect. Clearly, the variables affecting work, motivation, and employee satisfaction are not completely understood. Some employees prefer jobs with repetitive tasks and low levels of responsibility. Others do not. Designing jobs to fit human needs while achieving organizational goals is, therefore, quite complex. There are no packaged models that can be applied in all situations. Instead, all job enrichment programs must be developed to fit the characteristics of specific situations.

The complexities of job enrichment are further increased as change affects the expectations, social positions, lifestyles, and education of employees.[29] In large companies, for example, the complexity of many jobs and the differences among employees are so great that 100 percent job enrichment is impractical. Here, granting assembly-line workers the authority to decide production schedules, assembly-line speeds, and observance of holidays could easily result in mass confusion. Consequently, most companies do not apply job enrichment on a company-wide scale, but rather on a localized basis.

It is also important to note that job enrichment programs will not work well where managers do not understand the behavioral considerations of participative approaches to job design. The concept includes far more that simply adding tasks or authority to a job. On one hand, it can help employees satisfy certain needs, while on the other, it can assist organizations in becoming more productive and competitive. In the absence of a supportive environment where everyone understands the total concept, job enrichment will probably become an experimental failure causing more harm than good.

Management by objectives

One participative management technique that has contributed to higher levels of job satisfaction is management by objectives (MBO). While applicable to both managerial and nonmanagerial employees, the technique is used most often with managers. As such, MBO is basically a process by which managers and their subordinates participate jointly in setting goals, activities, and target dates as well as the evaluation of performance as it relates to established objectives.

Peter F. Drucker first publicized the MBO concept as a way to integrate activities and balance organizational objectives. Other management theorists have emphasized its value as a performance appraisal technique where participants are evaluated on the basis of their contribution to overall goals, rather than on such characteristics as personality traits. In any event, the philosophy behind MBO is that organizational effectiveness is influenced by the degree to which individuals are motivated to use their abilities in the achievement of organizational as well as personal goals. Furthermore, fairer and more valu-

---

[29] See Fred Foulkes, *Creating More Meaningful Work* (New York: American Management Assn., 1969).

FIGURE 14–7
The management by objectives process

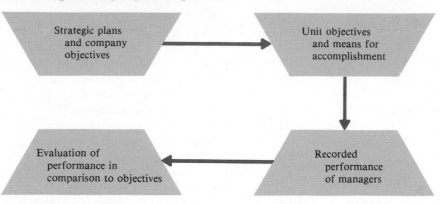

able appraisals of performance are likely to occur. However, research relating MBO programs to productivity is highly limited and without definite conclusions.[30]

Although the purposes of MBO may be varied, the technique can be thought of as a continuous, ongoing process, such as that noted in Figure 14–7. In addition, if the process is to be functional, it should be reflective of the following elements:

1. Superiors and subordinates critically review organizational strategy and then jointly establish *(a)* expected goals and *(b)* job improvement plans for a specified period of time.

2. Established goals must be measurable and realistic while contributing to overall, divisional, and departmental objectives.

3. Management information systems must be designed for maximum flexibility and speed in order to provide the feedback necessary for effective decision making and control.

4. Superiors and their subordinates meet on a systematic basis to evaluate actual achievement in terms of established goals. Such appraisals help subordinates assess past performance in order to outline future courses of action designed to achieve goals more effectively.

5. If performance reviews indicate managerial weaknesses, training plans are developed and put into action to help build strengths while indicating the values of continued self-development.

Instituting an MBO program Starting an MBO program takes time and requires the full support of top-level managers. They must understand the approach and be dedicated to making it work. Since MBO is expensive to implement, costs must be weighed against expected benefits. All persons affected by MBO must be trained in its use, and all levels of authority must be coordinated to implement the process

---

[30] See J. N. Kondrasak, "Studies in MBO Effectiveness," *The Academy of Management Review,* July 1981, pp. 419–30.

effectively. Furthermore, changing social and economic environments require that managers be prepared to review the program on a frequent and regularly scheduled basis.

For illustrative purposes, let us look at the actual institution of an MBO program in a large manufacturing company with processing plants in each of several divisions. Establishing overall corporate objectives was the first step. This was accomplished by division and corporate managers who consolidated and balanced sales and profit goals for the entire organization. Based on these goals, overall divisional objectives were established and communicated to the plants within each division. Plant objectives were then determined, as were the goals of all departments within each plant. Consequently, line managers throughout the organization had a personal role in setting the objectives against which their performance would be measured. Similarly, staff managers at all levels were able to establish goals that reflected those of their respective unit managers.

Figure 14–8 presents specific guidelines that can be used in establishing objectives. Once established, progress toward their achievement can be aided by the following:

1. *Adjusting objectives to time periods.* Objectives usually cover a one-year time period. However, activities already under way when objectives are being established may influence their accomplishment during the year. Therefore, adjustments for programs carried over from preceding time periods must be considered in determining realistic objectives.

2. *Developing ideas to achieve objectives.* Generating new ideas can be facilitated through interviews with managers. Prior to the session,

---

FIGURE 14–8
MBO guidelines to follow in establishing objectives

---

1. Objectives should be established for each level and area of management.
2. All managers should know overall organizational objectives as well as their own.
3. Objectives should act as a stimulus; thus, they should be
    a. Personal ("Tom, your objectives are . . .").
    b. Few in number (two to five).
    c. Reasonable and attainable, but at the same time, requiring some improvement from every person each period.
    d. Weighted, if possible. Of three objectives, for example, two may represent 40 percent each and the third 20 percent of the total job.
    e. Specific in terms of results expected.
4. Superior and subordinate should participate jointly in determining the objectives to be sought. This joins the planning of both and contributes to better coordination and control.
5. Goal accomplishment should be the measure of job performance.

---

each manager is asked to come prepared with ideas that could be helpful in achieving objectives. All suggestions are then evaluated in terms of their feasibility and utility. Those who submitted ideas should then be told about what happened to their suggestions, including reasons for their acceptance.

3. *Coordinating performance.* MBO committees are often formed to monitor results and to recommend adjustments in either performance or objectives. By serving on these committees, managers in one organizational unit are kept informed of the progress of others.

Limitations of MBO programs Like most managerial techniques, MBO has its limitations. In this respect, there are two major difficulties: (1) the problem of one manager attaining goals at the expense of others and (2) the need of obtaining valid measures to determine whether objectives have actually been achieved. An additional limitation is that the technique is not highly applicable to lower-level jobs where tasks are tightly programmed and structured. Furthermore, the approach cannot be viewed independently of other activities but must be thoroughly integrated with other organizational systems if it is to work properly.

Management by group objectives Participative management involves subordinates in the decision-making process. MBO focuses this involvement on a joint establishment of objectives against which the performance of subordinate managers will be measured. In the process, however, MBO can create competition among these managers since the emphasis is on individual performance rather than group accomplishments.

According to Rensis Likert, "groups rather than individuals in isolation, are the key to improving organizational effectiveness and problem solving."[31] Thus, where the proper participative management climate exists, Likert argues that management by group objectives (MBGO) is more effective than MBO. Both approaches use the same information in setting objectives. Through MBGO, however, objectives result from group discussions and reflect a shared interest in seeing the group succeed. Similarly, the evaluation of performance is also a group process. With this emphasis on group participation, MBGO encourages teamwork rather than competition. Organizational, group, and individual goals are, therefore, more closely integrated with significantly better results for all concerned.

Other techniques

Although the participative approaches discussed so far include some of the most important ones, there are other useful and valuable techniques. Among these, employee attitude surveys, suggestion systems, grievance procedures, and committees represent techniques that can also be used to increase organizational effectiveness.

---

[31] "No Manager Is an Island," *International Management,* January 1979, p. 22.

Employee attitude surveys   Attitudes can have a positive or negative influence on employee behavior. With information provided by attitude surveys, managers can better understand employee reactions to decisions, policies, working conditions, salaries, and other factors in the work environment. As a systematic approach to assessing employee feelings, attitude surveys also have the potential to provide management with more valid information on attitudes than is available from other sources.

Several other important behavioral considerations are associated with attitude surveys. They definitely improve upward communication between subordinates and superiors. Information is made available that can assist managers in improving their leadership styles while helping them learn more about the needs of their subordinates. Above all, perhaps, attitude surveys can improve the level of trust and support between superiors and subordinates when their results are used correctly.

Suggestion systems   Employee suggestion systems are part of the formal communication system designed to provide management with new ideas and approaches. Their use gives employees an opportunity to participate in suggesting improvements and solutions to organizational problems. In general, suggestion systems show that management views employees as being capable of making real contributions to the organization. They also reflect a managerial philosophy that under proper conditions, employees are eager to make greater use of their own abilities.

For suggestion systems to operate effectively, recommendations must be evaluated by a standing committee. Adequate rewards should also be given when suggestions are judged to be valuable in improving methods and procedures. Regardless of whether a suggestion is implemented, the final disposition of each should be communicated to the person who submitted it.

Grievance procedures   Another possible way to improve employee satisfaction and performance is to establish a viable grievance procedure. When employees feel that they have a legitimate complaint, machinery should be available to handle the matter fairly and equitably. Although most union contracts provide for a grievance procedure, nonunion organizations also find such a system to be an important participative technique. As such, it promotes confidence and trust in management's desire to examine and to correct employee dissatisfaction.

Effective grievance systems require that management and employees support them fully. Gaining employee support requires management sensitivity to improving personnel practices while abstaining from reprisals. Surely employees would not consider using a grievance procedure if they would be subjected to negative sanctions or management retaliation. Like all other participation techniques, then, suggestion systems must be tailor-made to fit a particular organization; and, if they are to eliminate dissatisfaction and to improve performance, their effectiveness requires hard work by all organizational members.

Committees Although the advantages and disadvantages of committees are discussed in Chapter 19, a few brief comments about their use as a participative technique will be presented here. Basically, committees permit various organizational members to be involved in the decision-making process. While research has indicated that decisions by committees are much more risk oriented and less conservative than those made by only one person, this fact may lead to better decisions. In addition, people are often more motivated to accept and carry out those decisions that they have helped make since such participation provides them with an opportunity to satisfy certain needs.

AN OVERVIEW OF PARTICIPATION

Likert suggests that the most productive and satisfied employees of an organization are those who are managed with a participative approach that he calls System IV.[32] This system, outlined briefly in Figure 14–9, includes a management style that places confidence and trust in subordinates. Workers feel free to discuss their jobs with superiors who, in turn, are able to apply ideas and suggestions offered by subordinates.

Unfortunately, the involvement of employees in planning and controlling their work has not produced guides on how far managers should go in applying participative techniques. All organizations probably have some limited degree of employee participation. However, managers must evaluate their employees carefully before starting extensive programs. In addition, the total organizational environment must be examined before new participative approaches are considered. Physical limits also influence how far managers can go in providing opportunities for more independence in the work environment.

Since the use of participative techniques depends on time constraints, management philosophies, employee attitudes, and a host of other factors, implementation is not easy. At a minimum, it takes patience, support, and a willingness to change. More important, however, there must be a realization that participative approaches do not work equally well with all persons nor in all organizational settings.

SUMMARY

Understanding human behavior is difficult, but a study of motivation theory can help. As discussed, people are motivated because of an internal state created by unsatisfied needs. Since employees work to satisfy certain basic needs, managers must provide incentives that will

---

[32] Rensis Likert, *The Human Organization* (New York: McGraw-Hill, 1967), pp. 4–10.

FIGURE 14–9
Likert's participative management system: System IV

Organizational elements	*Characterized as*
1. Leadership process	1. High task involvement along with a high degree of personal relationships with subordinates.
2. Motivational forces	2. Economic rewards based on a compensation system developed through participation.
3. Communication processes	3. Uninhibited flow of information among all levels—upward, downward, and horizontally.
4. Interaction-influence processes	4. High degree of mutual confidence and trust between superiors and subordinates. As a result, employees are more willing to accept responsibility. The informal organization is accepted as part of the formal organization and recognized as being supportive in achieving organizational goals.
5. Decision making	5. Widely dispersed and well integrated throughout the organization. Employees participate in setting goals, work methods, and decisions relating to their work.
6. Control processes	6. Wide responsibility for review and control at all organizational levels. Responsibility for implementation of the control function is dispersed to all employees throughout the entire organization. Control data, such as productivity, costs, etc., are used for self-guidance and coordinated problem solving, rather than entirely for punitive purposes.

Source: Adapted from Rensis Likert, *The Human Organization*, pp. 4–10. Copyright © 1967 by McGraw-Hill Book Company. Used with permission of McGraw-Hill Book Company.

be perceived as contributing to need satisfaction. Money can sometimes be an important incentive, but its actual importance remains unknown since it can satisfy different needs for different people. Thus, it should be considered in relationship to other incentives, not in isolation.

Both Maslow and Herzberg have shown that satisfied needs are not motivators. The message for managers is that continued efforts to provide lower-level need satisfaction may actually detract from the fulfillment of higher-level needs. Typically, behavior has more than one motivation and there may be multiple paths for achieving the same goal. Managers must, therefore, offer various incentives if they are to motivate individuals effectively. Among these incentives, participative management techniques may be of value. As with other techniques, they are not desired by all persons in all organizations. Accordingly, situational analysis is necessary when considering participative techniques versus other possible approaches for dealing with the motivational problems of a given organization.

KEY TERMS

Defensive reactions: Protective behavior patterns that are followed to cope with situations that threaten a person's self-concept.

Expectancy theory: A theoretical explanation of behavior, suggesting that people behave in expectation of certain outcomes from perceived relationships between performance and rewards.

Job enlargement: A participative approach to job design that reverses task specialization by involving employees in expanding or combining their job duties.

Job enrichment: A participative approach to job design that involves employees in planning, organizing, and/or controlling portions of their job.

Macromotivation: The approach to motivation that considers factors in the social environment *outside* an organization that influence job performance.

Management by group objectives (MBGO): A process that encourages teamwork by emphasizing group participation in setting objectives and evaluating performance.

Management by objectives (MBO): A process by which managers and their subordinates participate jointly in setting objectives and evaluating performance in relationship to them.

Micromotivation: The approach to motivation that focuses on conditions *within* an organization that influence job performance.

Need-behavior cycle: A way of looking at the relationships among needs, wants, stimuli, and goals as a starting point for understanding behavior.

Need-hierarchy: Categories of needs ranked from basic physiological needs through safety, belongingness and love, esteem, and self-actualization.

QUESTIONS

1. What are the steps in the need-behavior cycle? What are the shortcomings of this approach in explaining behavior?

2. What questions can be raised about the hierarchy of needs concept?

3. Since the role of money in motivation theory is not clear, why do financial incentives receive so much attention in most organizations?

4. Distinguish between motivators and hygiene factors in Herzberg's Two-Factor Theory of Motivation.

5. What are the differences between micromotivation and macromotivation?

6. What is the rationale behind participative approaches to motivation?

7. Distinguish between job enlargement and job enrichment.

8. What are the major objectives of MBO? Are there limitations to this participative technique?

9. How does MBGO differ from MBO? Does the difference seem to be a significant one?

10. Why is situational analysis important when considering the implementation of participative approaches to motivation?

PROBLEMS

1. A recent study of 73 women and 50 men who received masters' degrees from the Stanford business school in 1977 and 1978 points out that nightmares, depression, and stress are the price paid by many women who enter the business world. As managers, women graduates are very hard on themselves and feel that they must constantly prove their worth in male-dominated corporate structures.

These women and others face the strain of building a career while managing a family at the same time. They have to worry a lot about what is happening at home while they are at work. At the same time, women in the study tended to earn less and were sometimes given fewer responsibilities than male colleagues with the same training. All of these factors in combination may explain why the study also found that women were four times more likely to seek psychological help than men.

a. When faced with such problems as those found in this study, what can possibly motivate women to enter management positions?

b. How are both micro and macromotivation evident in situations of this type?

2. During the transition from the Carter presidency, former State Department spokesman Hodding Carter III gave some advice on the federal bureaucracy to the incoming Reagan administration. He stated that efforts to trim fat from the bureaucracy would result in an unequal contest with the odds stacked against the newcomers in staggering proportions.

By law, the president can appoint only a few thousand people at all levels. Yet, they must manage a federal bureaucracy that includes hundreds of thousands in Washington alone. The latter persons also know that they will be around from one administration to the next. Consequently, there is little incentive to change, and attempts by the administration to initiate changes can often be delayed for years. Therefore, it seems the power of the bureaucracy has become so great that it is a common danger for both major political parties.

a. Based on this information, can we say that goals of the federal bureaucracy are consistent with those of its employees?

b. From the viewpoint of motivation theory, can anything be done to overcome the resistance to change that exists in situations of this type?

3. A small manufacturing plant in southeast Texas with 150 employees was closed after being purchased by a large conglomerate. Some of the company's employees sought new jobs within the community by checking with friends, employment agencies, and the personnel departments of other companies. Other employees, however, stayed at home for several weeks before making any attempt to find new jobs.

a. Why did some of the employees show more initiative than others in seeking new jobs?
b. If both groups were faced with satisfying their physiological needs, would differences in their behavior have been as noticeable?

4. Texas Instruments, Inc., instituted a job enrichment program in the production-line assembly of radar equipment. In setting up the program, the first step was to brief workers on products produced and their contributions to company profit. Second, employees were asked to help set their own goals and make suggestions as to how production procedures and methods might be improved. The group worked closely with supervisors and engineers to determine which ideas could be implemented. In the third step, workers were assigned jobs that involved both their minds and physical abilities. Success of the program was noted in the reduction of labor turnover and in increased output per work hour.

a. What are some possible reasons for the increased performance?
b. Would the job enrichment program be applicable throughout the entire plant? Explain your answer.

5. Some productivity increases are referred to as *The Hawthorne Effect.* This term refers to situations where increases in output are not maintained over time. It has been stated that the real causes of increased performance in the Hawthorne Studies were *(a)* the novelty of the situation, *(b)* the great interest shown by higher management in the experiments, and *(c)* the status that accompanied the unique treatment of these workers. When these causes were removed, performance reverted back to normal. Could the same charges (The Hawthorne Effect) be directed against job enrichment and other participative approaches to motivation?

6. One of the earliest and best-known company-wide participation programs is the Scanlon Plan. Joseph N. Scanlon developed the plan in 1938 at a small steel company, and it has been directly related to increases in productivity. The plan was originally a management and union agreement to *(a)* increase employee suggestions, *(b)* develop employee and management participation, *(c)* encourage more meaningful communication, *(d)* increase productivity, and *(e)* share in labor-cost savings.

Although Scanlon stressed the importance of financial incentives, success of the plan is generally attributed to the role played by the production committees. Employee participation in these committees is sought to help solve cost, scheduling, waste, and other problems. The committees have the authority to make production decisions appropriate to their level in controlling certain production problems. By having access to staff personnel through committees, resentment to outside control is held down, which is often a major cause in restricting output. In short, Scanlon recognized the need to have consultation and participation in planning and controlling production decisions; and, where the Scanlon plan has been used, the results indicate increased profits, greater employee benefits, and improved worker satisfaction.

a. Would the Scanlon plan be applicable in all organizations?
b. The plan calls for employee bonuses to be calculated each month by comparing the actual ratio of payroll cost to total sales dollars to a predetermined ratio. When the actual ratio is reduced, the savings are shared, with employees receiving 75 percent of them. Without this financial incentive, do you think the plan would be successful?

7. Williams Manufacturing Company makes specialized wooden toys for preschool children. Recently, it abandoned the assembly line in order to allow teams of four to five persons to assemble, inspect, and package toys from start to finish. Teams worked in separate rooms and took charge of organization, production, product quality, product control, and group discipline. When individual members did not measure up to standard, group pressure was used to make them conform. If this did not work, managers were asked by the group to have them dismissed. Workers received a salary that would increase with substantial increases in performance. Most of the workers, who were women, *(a)* developed a high identification with their work groups, *(b)* shared information among themselves and among groups, *(c)* thought in terms of company objectives, and *(d)* introduced new production methods and ideas. The change from the assembly-line production strategy resulted in a 50 percent reduction in hours devoted to assembly, inspection, and packaging of toys.

a. What specific behavioral aspects are apparent in the new assembly process?
b. Characterize the role and duties of management in this situation.
c. How would you account for the increase in productivity?

8. Assume that you have been asked to help set up a Management by Objectives program for your company. The overall corporate objective is to obtain a 25 percent sales profit margin, mathematically expressed as follows:

$$\frac{\text{Net income after taxes}}{\text{Sales}}$$

One way of seeking this objective is for the manufacturing division to reduce manufacturing costs by 4 percent within the year. Briefly explain the steps that will have to be followed in implementing the MBO program.

SUGGESTED READINGS

Albrecht, K. *Successful Management by Objectives.* Englewood Cliffs, N.J.: Prentice-Hall, 1978.

Cook, C. W. "Guidelines for Managing Motivation." *Business Horizons,* April 1980, pp. 61–69.

Gayle, J. B., and F. R. Searle. "Maslow, Motivation, and the Manager." *Management World,* September 1980, pp. 19–25.

Hackman, J. R. "Is Job Enrichment Just a Fad?" *Harvard Business Review,* September–October 1975, pp. 129–38.

Herzberg, F. "Motivation and Innovation: Who Are Workers Serving?" *California Management Review,* Winter 1979, pp. 60–70.

McConkie, M. L. "A Clarification of the Goal-Setting and Appraisal Processes in MBO." *Academy of Management Review,* January 1979, pp. 29–40.

Parke, E. L., and D. Tausky. "The Mythology of Job Enrichment: Self-Actualization Revisited." *Personnel,* September–October 1975, pp. 12–21.

Patten, T. H., Jr. "Job Evaluation and Job Enlargement: A Collision Course?" *Human Resource Management,* Winter 1977, pp. 2–8.

Peterson, R. B. "Swedish Experiments in Job Reform." *Business Horizons,* June 1976, pp. 13–22.

Pinder, C. C. "Concerning the Application of Human Motivation Theories in Organizational Settings." *The Academy of Management Review,* July 1977, pp. 384–94.

Reif, W. E. "Intrinsic versus Extrinsic Rewards: Resolving the Controversy." *Human Resource Management,* Summer 1975, pp. 2–10.

Steers, R. M., and R. T. Mowday. "The Motivational Properties of Tasks." *The Academy of Management Review,* October 1977, pp. 645–57.

Steers, R. M., and L. W. Porter. *Motivation and Work Behavior.* New York: McGraw-Hill, 1975.

Tavernier, G. "France Proclaims the Role of the Manual Worker." *International Management,* December 1977, pp. 26–29.

Turney, J. R. and S. L. Cohen. "Participative Management: What is the Right Level?" *Management Review,* October 1980, pp. 66–69.

West, G. E. "Bureaupathology and the Failure of MBO." *Human Resource Management,* Summer 1977, pp. 33–40.

15

THE DYNAMICS
OF LEADERSHIP

PURPOSE

Extensive discussions about leadership in scouting, extracurricular school progams, and other organizations have resulted in most of us having the attitude that no human practice may be more important than leadership. In fact, we often assume that the effective functioning of *all* social systems is dependent upon capable leaders. This assumption is reflected in our tendency to blame a baseball coach for a losing season or to credit a commander for daring military victories.

Since we attach so much importance to leadership, it would seem valuable to society if we could identify and effectively train future leaders. Possibly psychologists could develop a test to select people for training who possess leadership talents. Unfortunately, what we now know about leadership suggests that the precise identification of potential leaders is not a realistic hope since leadership is not a unidimensional personality trait. To diminish our hopes further, research findings have not demonstrated any consistent, direct correlation between leadership and improved organizational effectiveness. At best, effective leadership may account for only 10 to 15 percent of the variability in organizational performance. In spite of its unknowns, however, leadership is still essential in management and this chapter looks at its complexity. Specifically, we will look at certain value assumptions and normative assertions that are questioned in discussions of leadership as well as various theories that are useful in explaining and predicting leadership roles.

OBJECTIVES

1. To discuss leadership as a process of interpersonal relationships that influences individual and group behavior.

2. To emphasize the need for effective leadership to be responsive to the needs of the organization, its members, and environmental changes.

3. To outline historical approaches to the study of leadership.

4. To examine various contemporary models of leadership.

5. To point out that the most effective leadership style is one that best fits existing situational factors.

Leadership is a universal phenomenon that results in observable behavior wherever people work together to achieve common goals. Even the animal kingdom has its leaders with positions of authority and responsibility. In management, leadership is one of the most dynamic elements in the life of any organization, since it can either motivate followers to high levels of organizational performance or drain strength from an organization and limit its survival. To some extent, then, the effectiveness of an organization depends on the quality of managerial leadership.

As a dynamic force, leadership is contingent upon the needs of organizations and their members. In formal organizations, the leader may be exemplified by the manager, administrator, executive, or supervisor who attempts to influence organizational members to fulfill prescribed roles. In this context, *managerial leadership is defined as a process of interpersonal relationships through which a manager attempts to influence the behavior of other people and, in turn, to direct organizational behavior toward the attainment of predetermined objectives.*

THE NATURE OF LEADERSHIP

Leadership takes place within specific situations and reflects contingency relationships between leaders and followers seeking the achievement of objectives. Through leadership, managers are better prepared to (1) give meaningful direction to the work of others in relation to organizational goals, (2) solve present problems, and (3) interpret external forces in order to plan for the future.

Within particular situations, leaders must also provide the influence that stimulates cooperation among organizational members in achieving objectives. This is true for both formal and informal organizations. Informal leaders are primarily concerned with satisfying the needs of their group members. Beyond attempts to satisfy these same individual needs, management must seek to accomplish objectives of the formal organization as well. Consequently, distinctions between these two types of leaders are not necessarily based on their specific jobs but on the extent of their roles.

In all organizations, successful leadership depends on an ability to apply skills acquired through experience, study, and observation. It cannot be based solely on the strict use of a position's authority, prestige, or power. In fact, the effectiveness of leaders often diminishes in proportion to dependence on the authority of their positions. Demanding obedience, rather than securing cooperation, has produced the saying, "the poor manager drives; the good manager leads." This points out the fact that effective leadership must be based on earned authority.

DYNAMIC LEADERSHIP SKILLS

One approach to studying leadership suggests that the behavior of an effective leader in one situation may not be effective in another.

FIGURE 15–1
Dynamic leadership skills model

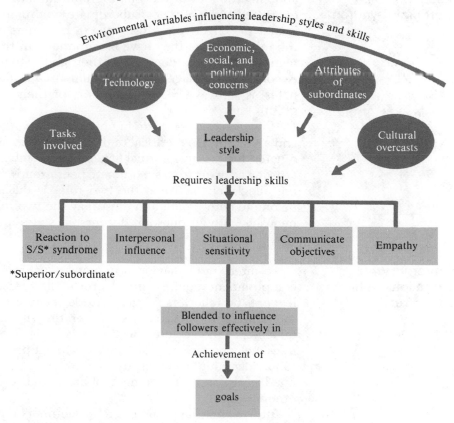

*Superior/subordinate

However, certain leadership skills are essential regardless of the situation if the needs of both the organization and its members are to be met. In this respect, the following skills are important:

Reacting appropriately to the superior/subordinate syndrome.
Providing interpersonal influence.
Having situational sensitivity.
Communicating and facilitating the accomplishment of objectives.
Being empathetic.

Although these five skills are not totally inclusive, it is important to understand their role in the leadership process. This role is shown in Figure 15–1, which presents a model of leadership skills. Being dynamic in nature, the use of these skills will vary among leadership styles and will be influenced by variables within an organization's internal and external environments. The following sections consider these skills individually and their interfaces with environmental variables.

Reacting to the superior/subordinate syndrome

Managers in the chain of command must be loyal to both superiors and subordinates in the hierarchy of authority. This concept is best expressed as the superior/subordinate syndrome. The implication here is that the effective performance of managers as leaders depends on the influence that they have on superiors. In turn, acceptance within management ranks depends on their ability to influence subordinates. Accordingly, managers must be influential leaders over their subordinates as well as effective members of their own peer (managerial) groups.[1]

How managers perform in positions where they are both a superior and a subordinate is critical to their leadership effectiveness. To subordinates, for example, formal leaders are members of management and are viewed apart from subordinate peer groups. For this reason, balancing allegiances between the two roles is difficult; yet, most leaders belong to both groups and must play the two roles somewhat simultaneously. Without question, leadership styles are affected in the process.[2]

Interpersonal relations with followers

To direct the behavior of organizational members toward goal accomplishment requires some degree of interpersonal relations between leaders and followers. Through these relationships, managers become more aware of employee needs, operating situations, and environmental factors. Open communication is essential in this regard. Other avenues include searching for new ways to get people involved, providing sound planning, avoiding dysfunctional controls, specifying well-defined goals, and developing cooperative attitudes about oneself and others.

Interrelationships among group members result naturally in an expression of attitudes toward the leader. When these attitudes are negative, leaders soon lose their power to influence. Managers, therefore, need an accurate reading of group attitudes toward them if they are to be effective. In this sense, different leadership styles reflect varying degrees of power to influence group members.

Situational sensitivity

Situations in which leaders function are affected by changing environmental factors (stimuli). Organizational structure, technology, job design, cultural characteristics, economic-political forces, and individual needs represent realistic variables that can cause situations to change. The arrangement of these variables and their relationships to one another are so diverse that no two situations are ever identical.

---

[1] On the assembly line the supervisor often battles with the union, keeps pressure on workers to achieve maximum production, and maintains quality while being considered supportive, reasonable, and fair by subordinates.

[2] Aaron Lowin and James R. Craig. "The Influence of Performance on Managerial Style: An Experimental Object-Lesson in the Ambiguity of Correlation Data," *Organizational Behavior and Human Performance*, 1968, pp. 440–58.

Situations are unique unto themselves; therefore, they must be considered individually in light of the particular variables affecting them. When leaders are situationally sensitive, they are better prepared to perceive changing environmental forces in time to modify behavior accordingly. This type of sensitivity permits managers to be more realistic in fitting their leadership styles to given situations.

Leaders must also be sensitive to other differences found in organizational settings. In the military, for example, organizational philosophies are normally different from those found in educational institutions. Even among similar types of organizations, various philosophical and managerial differences can be found. Although leaders must be able to perceive and to adapt to these organizational differences if they are to be effective, most find the task to be difficult. For this reason, previously proven successful leaders may fail when placed in situations that impose demands inconsistent with their personalities or past patterns of interaction and performance.

Communicating objectives

In any organizational situation, at least three groups of objectives must be considered. These include objectives of the organization, the leader, and the followers.[3] The coexistence of such objectives and their satisfactory accomplishment will result in some group members being satisfied with the leader. On the other hand, some will be dissatisfied since all goals cannot be met at the same time. To be effective in accomplishing these various goals, the leader must clearly define and communicate them and think in terms of composite objectives that may not be those of any one group. This is the type of thinking found in team effort where functional groups, project teams, and professional specialists work together in a unified manner.

Empathy

Although closely related to situational sensitivity, *empathy* is considered as a separate leadership skill and is equally important in achieving individual and group objectives.[4] It is defined as *the ability to sense and understand the needs, wants, and feelings of others.* Empathy goes beyond sympathy since it implies a mutual understanding of the needs and feelings of other people, rather than just an expression of compassion.

By understanding the reactions of others to various situational factors, managers are in a better position to exhibit leadership behavior

---

[3] Robert Tannenbaum and Fred Massarik, "Leadership: A Frame of Reference," *Organizational Behavior and Management,* ed. D. E. Porter and P. B. Applewhite (Scranton, Pa.: International Textbook, 1968), p. 413.

[4] The concept of empathy was introduced in psychology by Lipps in Germany about the turn of the century. However, it was not until the late 1940s that empirical research was undertaken to determine its importance in leadership. Research has not definitely proven that empathy (the degree of insight into the feelings and motivation of followers) is important in predicting leadership effectiveness; however, this may be more a problem of measuring empathetic ability than the validity of the concept.

FIGURE 15–2
Some of the traits of leadership considered by advocates of the great man theory

Physical traits	*Social traits*
Height	Empathy
Weight	Tact
Physical attractiveness	Patience
Vitality	Trust
Physical endurance	Status
	Participativeness
Personality traits	*Personal traits*
Ambition	Verbal skills
Confidence	Wisdom
Integrity	Judgment
Initiative	Intellectual ability
Persistence	Capacity for work
Imagination	Achievement
	Responsibility

that will secure the cooperation and support of followers. As such, empathy assists managers in determining the appropriate stimuli to influence individual and group performance effectively within organizations.

HISTORICAL APPROACHES TO STUDYING LEADERSHIP

In the preface of *The Human Side of Enterprise,* Douglas McGregor notes a series of questions once asked by Alfred P. Sloan.[5] These questions relate to the age-old problem of determining whether or not managerial leadership is a property of the individual, or a term describing relationships among members of a group. To appreciate the depth and complexity of this problem, let us briefly trace several approaches to studying leadership.

Traitist theory

In 1910, Thomas Carlyle postulated the "great man theory" of leadership that stated that world progress is a product of the individual achievements of great persons.[6] Advocates of this theory feel that certain individuals possess a combination of traits that can be determined and used in identifying potential leaders and leadership effectiveness. As shown in Figure 15–2, the theoretical basis for this approach is that certain physical, social, personality, and personal traits are considered to be inherent within some individuals and can, therefore, be used in distinguishing leaders from nonleaders.

Innumerable studies have been undertaken to determine the relia-

---

[5] Douglas McGregor, *The Human Side of Enterprise* (New York: McGraw-Hill, 1960), p. v.

[6] Thomas Carlyle, *Lectures on Heroes, Hero-Worship, and the Heroic in History,* ed. P. C. Parr (Oxford: Clarendon Press, 1910).

bility of the traitist approach.[7] Although some research studies suggest the relative importance of traits, others have failed to identify leadership traits that can consistently be used as standards for designating individuals as either leaders or nonleaders.[8] In a survey of 124 leadership studies based on the traitist approach, another researcher concluded that there were few similarities among the traits noted in the various studies.[9]

A major criticism of the traitist approach focuses on determining the relative importance of physical and personality characteristics. For example, vitality, height, and physical endurance factors have not shown a consistent correlation with managerial effectiveness.[10] On the other hand, certain personality and personal traits, such as a capacity for work, achievement, self-confidence, enthusiasm, and inspiration are seen by some writers to be associated with leadership effectiveness.[11]

Psychological studies of various leaders show, however, that no two are exactly alike. The temperaments and personal characteristics of military leaders, for example, are as different as their names. Likewise, the things leaders do to influence others vary from person to person and from one situation to another. Consequently, generalizations about traits are difficult to substantiate.

Including the situation

After the 1930s, theorists began suggesting that leadership effectiveness is more complicated than just a set of qualities possessed by an individual. They postulated that specific leadership traits are related to a given situation and should be viewed as outputs, rather than inputs. The rationale here is that the nature of any situation will determine which traits are necessary for success, and the person within a group who possesses these traits will be chosen as the leader. By letting the situation act as a theoretical base to show which traits are important, the idea of considering them in the selection of leaders becomes more palatable.

Additional factors of leadership

Contemporary theorists suggest that the leadership context must be broader than just the leader and the situation if realistic theories

---

[7] See Edwin E. Ghiselli, *Exploration in Management Talent* (Pacific Palisades, Calif.: Goodyear, 1971); and H. L. Smith and L. M. Krueger, "A Brief Summary of Literature on Leadership," *Bulletin of the School of Education*, Bloomington: Indiana University, 1933, pp. 3–80.

[8] Eugene E. Jennings, "The Anatomy of Leadership," *Management: A Book of Readings*, ed. Harold Koontz and C. O'Donnell (New York: McGraw-Hill, Co., 1968), p. 454.

[9] R. M. Stogdill, "Personal Factors Associated with Leadership: A Summary of the Literature," *Journal of Psychology*, 1948, pp. 35–72.

[10] James A. Mahoney, *Building the Executive Team* (Englewood Cliffs, N.J.: Prentice-Hall, 1961), pp. 190–97.

[11] Harold Koontz, Cyril O'Donnell, and Heinz Weihrich, *Management* (New York: McGraw-Hill, 1980), pp. 664–65.

FIGURE 15–3
The leadership process

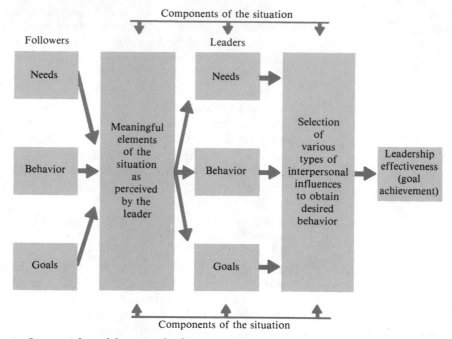

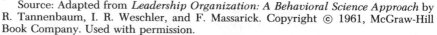

Source: Adapted from *Leadership Organization: A Behavioral Science Approach* by R. Tannenbaum, I. R. Weschler, and F. Massarick. Copyright © 1961, McGraw-Hill Book Company. Used with permission.

of leadership are to be developed. The expectations of *followers* and their subsequent motivation to work are additional variables in this regard. Thus, effective leader behavior is viewed as a function of many factors that interact to make up the leadership process.[12] The interrelationships among these factors are noted in Figure 15–3. As indicated, the needs, behavior patterns, and goals of followers must be combined with characteristics of the situation to provide a framework of variables within which the leader must operate. In addition, leaders' perceptions of these elements and of their own needs, behavior, and goals determine the style (influences) used to affect behavior.

In summary, the study of leadership cannot ignore leader/group interaction. Since 1950, research has moved from trying to identify differentiating leader traits to the study of leader behavior. This shift occurred because there had been little success in selecting leaders in terms of traits. Furthermore, researchers found that personality traits varied from one situation to another. Thus, a more realistic approach views leadership in terms of the relationships that exist among people

---

[12] Tim R. V. Davis and Fred Luthans, "Leadership Reexamined: A Behavioral Approach," *The Academy of Management Review*, April 1979, pp. 237–48.

in a given social structure, rather than by examining a series of isolated individual traits.

In the following sections, our concern is with broad models of leadership that can be utilized to influence human behavior. These models are important because they provide descriptions of leadership and explanations of why certain behavior can be either effective or ineffective.

MODELS OF LEADER BEHAVIOR

Before examining various models of leadership, we should realize that an individual rarely fits perfectly into any one specified behavior pattern. Also, no one model is adequate in totally explaining leadership effectiveness, although each offers some insights. In this sense, models can be used to describe certain types of leader behavior. Realistically, however, leadership styles cannot be categorized as good or bad without reference to a particular situation.

Two leadership roles in the group—Bales

Group arrangements in which more than one leader is involved are quite common in organizations. Informal leaders may arise at different times, or the group may select two or more leaders to serve simultaneously. However, the roles these leaders fulfill do not necessarily overlap. For example, routine work might be handled by the leader with personal characteristics of charisma, sound judgment, and valued experience. Yet, when there is a need for creativity and innovation within the group, the more imaginative, decisive, and self-assured leader might come forward to fill that role.

One of the most interesting research studies dealing with dual informal leadership roles was conducted by Professor R. F. Bales with a group of students.[13] He found that two leaders tended to emerge within the study groups. The behavior of one leader was related to the task to be achieved, while the other leader was human relations oriented. Bales further indicated that groups function more effectively if these two roles are filled by two distinct leaders, rather than by the same person. Even though the two behaviors are actually quite different, both are essential for building group solidarity. In addition, Bales's study indicates that these two distinct dimensions of leadership remain whether filled by one or more leaders. Consequently, the number of leaders to emerge in a situation depends on the degree of differentiation between task and member satisfaction.

Employee-centered versus job-centered supervison—Likert

After extensive research of leaders in various fields, Rensis Likert feels that each leader should view the organization as supportive in building and maintaining employee feelings of personal worth and

---

[13] Robert F. Bales, "Task Roles and Social Roles in Problem-Solving Groups," *Readings in Social Psychology*, eds. E. E. Maccoby, T. M. Newcomb, and E. L. Hartley (New York: Henry Holt, 1958), pp. 437–47.

FIGURE 15–4
Production related to different leadership styles

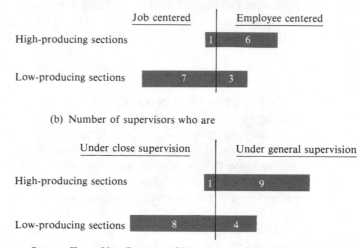

(a) Number of supervisors who are

Job centered | Employee centered

High-producing sections   1   6

Low-producing sections   7   3

(b) Number of supervisors who are

Under close supervision | Under general supervision

High-producing sections   1   9

Low-producing sections   8   4

Source: From *New Patterns of Management* by Rensis Likert. Copyright © 1961, McGraw-Hill Book Company. Used with permission.

importance. In this sense, building a supportive structure requires (1) group-oriented leaders, (2) trust and loyalty between managers and subordinates, and (3) a sharing of information up and down the organizational hierarchy.

Likert's research shows that supervisors with the best performance scores focus their attention primarily on human aspects of subordinates' problems and on building effective work groups.[14] He classifies these leaders as *employee centered.* See Figure 15–4(a) where this behavior is compared to the *job-centered* leader who emphasizes a high division of labor, close job supervision in controlling tasks, and the use of incentive systems.

The relationship among leaders who are under close supervision and general supervision is noted in Figure 15–4(b). The general implication in this comparison is that leaders in charge of low-producing units tend to issue orders to subordinates while giving them very little freedom to do their jobs. To improve organizational effectiveness, Likert believes that managers should develop an employee-centered leadership style. Thus, job-centered leaders may be more influential in bringing about effective goal achievement if they can develop employee-centered behavior.

---

[14] Rensis Likert, *New Patterns of Management* (New York: McGraw-Hill, 1961), pp. 113–14.

Continuum of leadership behavior—Tannenbaum and Schmidt

One of the first attempt to differentiate among leadership styles was through the leadership behavior continuum developed by Tannenbaum and Schmidt.[15] As shown in Figure 15–5(a), the left end of the continuum depicts the authoritarian, boss-centered manager; the other end is the democratic, subordinate-centered manager. Various possible combinations of leadership styles exist between these two extremes. A particular pattern of leadership behavior is related to the degree of authority exercised by the leader coupled with the amount of authority granted to subordinates. Behavior at the extreme left of the continuum characterizes the leader who exercises a high degree of authority and control. Conversely, the "democratic" leader on the extreme right exhibits a behavior pattern that grants subordinates freedom to participate in the decision-making process. Regardless of the leadership style selected, the manager should be sufficiently flexible to adapt to different situations.

As shown in Figure 15–5(b), the original continuum model was modi-

FIGURE 15–5
(a) Continuum of leadership behavior

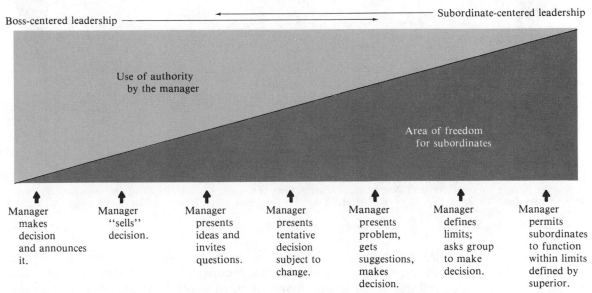

Source: Robert Tannenbaum and Warren H. Schmidt, "How to Choose a Leadership Pattern," *Harvard Business Review,* March–April 1958, p. 96. Copyright © 1958 by the President and Fellows of Harvard College; all rights reserved.

[15] Robert Tannenbaum, and Warren H. Schmidt, "How to Choose a Leadership Pattern," *Harvard Business Review,* March–April 1958. Copyright © 1958 by the President and Fellows of Harvard College; all rights reserved. A retrospective commentary on this article can be found in Robert Tannenbaum and Warren H. Schmidt, "How to Choose a Leadership Pattern," *Harvard Business Review,* May–June 1973. Copyright © 1973 by the President and Fellows of Harvard College; all rights reserved.

394

FIGURE 15–5 *(continued)*
(b) Continuum of manager-nonmanager behavior

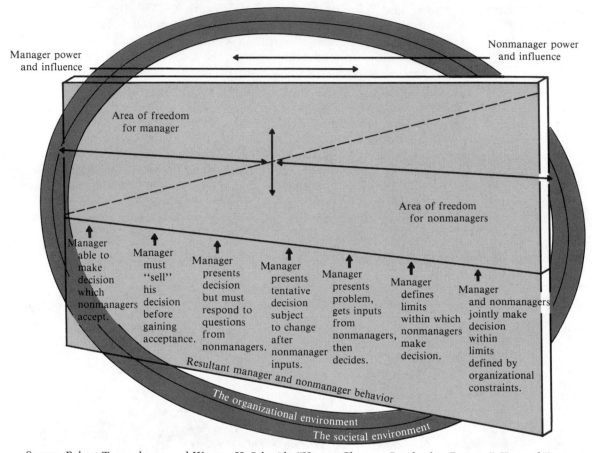

Manager power
and influence

Nonmanager power
and influence

Area of freedom
for manager

Area of freedom
for nonmanagers

Manager able to make decision which nonmanagers accept.

Manager must "sell" his decision before gaining acceptance.

Manager presents decision but must respond to questions from nonmanagers.

Manager presents tentative decision subject to change after nonmanager inputs.

Manager presents problem, gets inputs from nonmanagers, then decides.

Manager defines limits within which nonmanagers make decision.

Manager and nonmanagers jointly make decision within limits defined by organizational constraints.

Resultant manager and nonmanager behavior

The organizational environment

The societal environment

fied to emphasize the need for managers to understand themselves, the capabilities of subordinates, groups, the organization and its goals, and the broad social environment in which management operates. A knowledge and understanding of these elements helps the leader choose a style that is most appropriate and effective in achieving goals. Thus, the insightful and adaptive manager can properly assess the forces that determine what the most appropriate leader behavior should be at any given time.

In summary, the Tannenbaum and Schmidt continuum emphasizes a flexible leadership style and the importance of assessing the relevant forces affecting a particular style. Some of these forces are (1) personality variables of subordinates, (2) expected leader behavior in terms

FIGURE 15–6
Ohio State behavior factor leadership quadrants

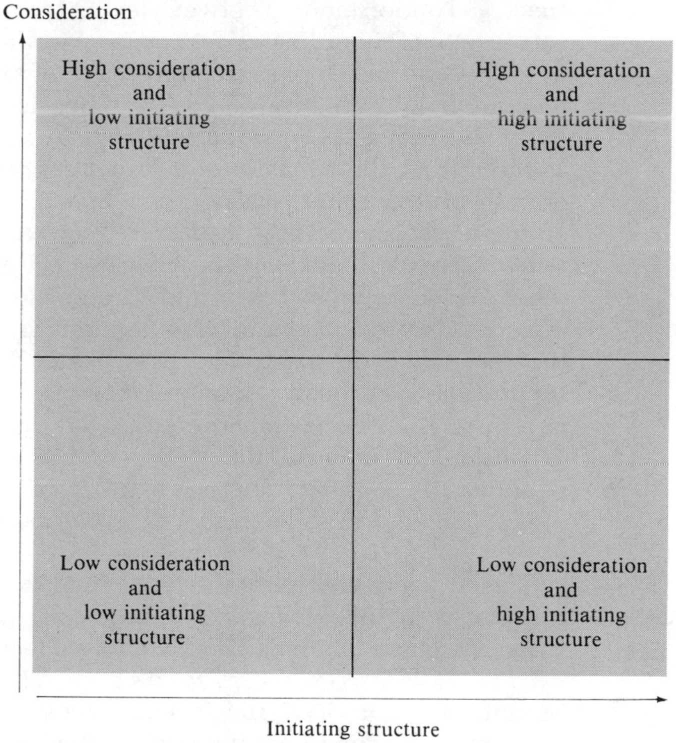

Consideration

High consideration and low initiating structure	High consideration and high initiating structure
Low consideration and low initiating structure	Low consideration and high initiating structure

Initiating structure

Source: Ralph M. Stogdill and Alvin E. Coons, eds., *Leader Behavior, Its Description and Measurement*, No. 88, Bureau of Business Research, The Ohio State University, Columbus, Ohio, 1957. By permission of the publisher.

of how subordinates think the leader should act, (3) ability of the work group to solve problems, and (4) willingness of subordinates to accept responsibility.

Ohio State leadership studies

Limitations of the Tannenbaum and Schmidt continuum model can be seen in studies conducted at The Ohio State University.[16] The central findings of these studies reveal that the major attributes of leadership can be depicted in two dimensions. These are *initiating structure* and *consideration*. Initiating structure, as represented in Figure 15–6, refers to letting followers know what to expect. A high emphasis on this dimension characterizes the manager who establishes and demands rigid adherence to channels of communication, patterns of organiza-

---

[16] Ralph M. Stogdill and Alvin E. Coons, eds., *Leader Behavior, Its Description and Measurement*, no. 88 (Columbus: The Ohio State University, Bureau of Business Research, 1957).

tion, control systems, and organizational policies. Contrasted to this dimension, consideration refers to the degree of friendship, trust, respect, and understanding between leaders and their followers. By being considerate of subordinates' feelings and welfare, having personal trust in others, and developing an atmosphere of respect, a manager would measure high on the consideration dimension.

By examining the quadrants shown in Figure 15–6, it should be apparent that the behavior of a leader represents some combination of both structure and consideration. Specific behavior can be plotted at any place between the two axes. Viewed in this manner, a major difference exists between The Ohio State University studies and the other models noted by Likert and Tannenbaum/Schmidt; namely, that a leader may exhibit both consideration and initiating structure at the same time. In short, The Ohio State University studies do not support the idea that a person exhibits only one leadership dimension at a time (an either/or situation). Instead, research stimulated by the original studies indicates that leaders with high scores in both initiating structure and consideration tend to promote higher degrees of follower satisfaction, and in some instances, group performance.[17]

**Managerial Grid®–
Blake and Mouton**

The interactive effect of the leader and the organization is logically considered in the *Managerial Grid*® concept developed by Robert Blake and Jane Mouton.[18] Their analysis of leadership styles recognizes two major factors: (1) *concern for people* and (2) *concern for production*. As noted in Figure 15–7, the grid includes two nine-point scales reflecting degrees of concern for these two factors. Thus, there are 81 possible relationships between the concerns for production and people. Five of the major styles of leadership resulting from these combinations are characterized as follows:

9,1   *High concern (9) for production, low concern (1) for people*— Manager concentrates on maximum production in accomplishment of objectives but overlooks the satisfaction of human needs. The result can be an ultimate deterioration of morale and productivity.

1,9   *Low concern (1) for production, high concern (9) for people*— Maximum concern for people leads to satisfying relationships by promoting good feelings among members of the group. Little emphasis is placed on the production goals of the organization.

1,1   *Low concern (1) for production, low concern (1) for people*— These leaders go through the motions of leadership, but they

---

[17] See Ralph M. Stogdill, *Handbook of Leadership, A Survey of Theory and Research* (New York: Free Press, 1974), pp. 128–41; and "The Ralph M. Stogdill Memorial Symposium: Reflection on the Origins of Leadership Models, Concepts, and Approaches." *Journal of Management*, Fall 1979, pp. 125–65.

[18] R. R. Blake and J. S. Mouton, *The New Managerial Grid* (Houston: Gulf Publishing Co., 1978).

FIGURE 15–7
The Managerial Grid®

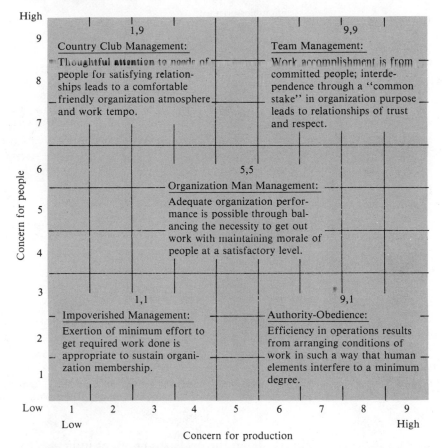

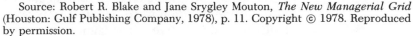

Source: Robert R. Blake and Jane Srygley Mouton, *The New Managerial Grid* (Houston: Gulf Publishing Company, 1978), p. 11. Copyright © 1978. Reproduced by permission.

do not contribute to the achievement of the goals of the organization or the group. The manager does only the minimum required to remain in the organization.

5,5 *Middle of the road*—The leader follows a theory that adequate performance can be achieved by balancing the necessity to get the work out and maintaining satisfactory employee relations. The leader follows the philosophy of conforming to the status quo.

9,9 *High concern (9) for production, high concern (9) for people*— The leader stresses the team approach to problem solving. The style is goal oriented and seeks to gain high quantity and quality through participation, commitment, and conflict resolution.

FIGURE 15–8
Reddin's four basic styles of leadership

Relationships-oriented

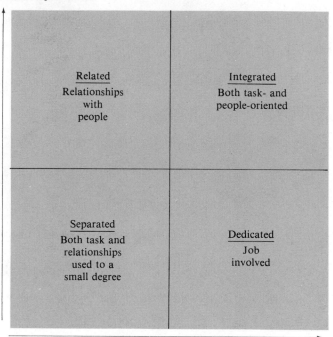

Task-oriented

Source: From *Managerial Effectiveness* by W. J. Reddin. Copyright © 1970 McGraw-Hill Book Company. Used with permission.

Although the grid arrangement indicates that leadership styles vary in their orientation toward people and production, Blake and Mouton feel that the 9,9 style is the soundest way to achieve organizational excellence.

The 3-D theory— Reddin

Reddin's three-dimensional theory of leadership is also built around (1) the tasks to be accomplished and (2) relationships with other people.[19] The task-oriented approach refers to leaders who structure work relationships, while the relationship-oriented leader characterizes those who are interested in building and maintaining interpersonal relations among people. These two elements result in four basic styles of leadership (see Figure 15–8):

Separated leader—These leaders combine low task and low relation-

[19] W. J. Reddin, *Managerial Effectiveness* (New York: McGraw-Hill, 1970).

ship orientations while identifying with the organization as a whole, rather than with individual members. They do things by the book, adhering to policies and rules without developing interpersonal relations.

Related leader—These leaders exhibit a high relationship orientation with a low task orientation. They accept others willingly and are not too concerned with time. Harmonizing differences, working with people, and being dependent on others are characteristics of the related leader.

Dedicated leader—Task accomplishment, rather than satisfying the needs of subordinates, is characteristic of the dedicated leader. The management functions of planning, organizing, and controlling are readily observed in the dedicated leader's behavior. Authority of the position is used to tell people what to do, and the motivational approach is basically built around the power to reward and punish. In addition, these leaders are often argumentative since they deal with stressful situations by dominating others.

Integrated leader—Demonstrating more than average task and relationship orientations characterize integrated leaders. They become deeply involved with, and dependent on, teamwork to satisfy organizational and subordinate needs. However, their close identification with others does not cause them to lose sight of the need to establish group performance standards. This style of leadership is not suited for routine, detail work, nor for stressful situations where participation might tend to restrict the decision-making process.

Reddin notes that none of these individual styles is the most effective in all situations. One style may be very effective in a given situation, but ineffective in another. However, when a particular style is used inappropriately, the result is ineffective leadership. The names given to the various styles when used appropriately and inappropriately are noted in Figure 15–9. By using Reddin's 3-D approach, the four basic styles are located in the center of the figure; the four less effective equivalent styles are located left of center; and the more effective equivalent styles at the right of center in the figure. For example, when the high task orientation is used appropriately, the style is that of the benevolent autocrat; when it is used inappropriately, the style is autocratic.

The three-dimensional theory of Reddin is a useful model since it identifies some of the variables that are important in leadership effectiveness. In a capsule form, the theory emphasizes the importance of (1) being aware of situational problems, (2) determining the style of leadership that will be most effective in solving those problems, and (3) being sufficiently flexible to change leadership styles in order to achieve higher output for the organization and greater rewards for subordinates.

FIGURE 15–9
Names of the basic styles of leadership when used appropriately and inappropriately as measured by leadership effectiveness

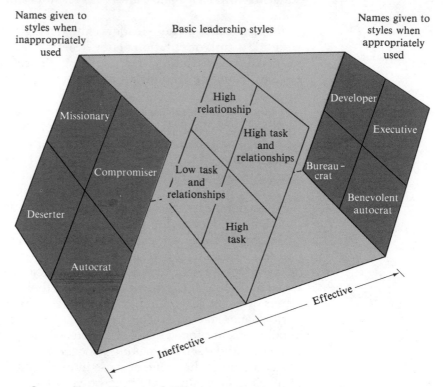

Source: From *Managerial Effectiveness* by W. J. Reddin. Copyright © 1970 McGraw-Hill Book Company. Used with permission.

COMPARISON OF THE VARIOUS LEADER BEHAVIOR MODELS

The commonality of the various models discussed above is presented in Figure 15–10. All of the models emphasize two major leadership dimensions—job and human considerations. Although Likert labels the dimensions differently, he claims that the most successful leader in all situations is one who is employee centered. Similarly, the Managerial Grid® purports that the most effective style is a 9,9. Other than claims for the one best leadership style, the major difference among the models is that of a continuum versus a multidimensional approach. Tannenbaum and Schmidt's continuum model is fairly restrictive in the sense that only one leadership dimension is expressed at a time, while a combination of human and technical skills can be presented through a multidimensional approach. This latter approach is particularly useful since it shows leadership positions of a high or low task orientation combined with either a high or low concern for people. In utilizing multidimensional models, we note that (1) an appropriate relationship must be developed between job and human dimensions and (2) the

FIGURE 15-10
Commonality of the various leadership models

Theorists	Leadership dimensions	
	Job or technical	Human
R. F. Bales	Work oriented	Human relations oriented
Rensis Likert	Job centered	Employee centered
Tannenbaum and Schmidt	Authoritarian	Democratic
Ohio State Studies	Initiating structure	Consideration
Blake and Mouton	Production concern	People concern
W. J. Reddin 3-Dimension	Task	Relationships

models of leadership vary as to what is considered to be the "ideal" style.[20]

SITUATIONAL MODELS IN PREDICTING LEADERSHIP EFFECTIVENESS

Each leader must ask whether social and psychological needs exhibited by employees can be satisfied through greater job responsibility, freedom, and/or participation in the organization's decision-making process. In some instances the answer may be yes, especially if jobs can be redesigned to assist in fulfilling such needs. Caution is necessary since some employees do not desire a greater degree of responsibility nor a more important role in the decision-making process.[21] They may prefer to do their jobs by following detailed orders and directions from supervisors. This indicates that some followers actually prefer an authoritarian leader because they feel more secure or lack the motivation to influence the variables affecting their environment. For these employees, a highly participative leadership style may actually produce apathy, tension, and frustration since followers are asked to fill roles in which they are uncomfortable.

This discussion suggests that leadership effectiveness is not based on stereotyped or unchanging leadership styles. Instead, it depends on matching the appropriate style to a specific situation, and leaders must be sensitive to the environments in which they function in order to determine which style will be most effective. To date, three situational models of leadership have proven to be fairly successful in pre-

---

[20] For a further discussion of the research in this area, see Paul Hersey and K. H. Blanchard, *Management of Organizational Behavior: Utilizing Human Resources* (Englewood Cliffs, N.J.: Prentice-Hall, 1977), pp. 107–8.

[21] See Abraham H. Maslow, *Eupsychian Management* (Homewood, Ill.: Richard D. Irwin, 1965), pp. 54–56.

dicting leadership effectiveness—the Path-Goal Theory, the Fiedler Contingency Model, and the Vroom-Yetton Decision Model. The Fiedler and Vroom Yetton models are somewhat similar in their approach and will be contrasted to the Path-Goal Theory.

Path-Goal Theory of leadership

According to this theory, leaders are effective because of an ability to enhance their subordinates' motivation to perform, job satisfaction, and acceptance of the leader.[22] By following various leadership styles, the leader exhibits (1) "consideration" that determines the perception of the abundance of available rewards and (2) "task orientation" that determines followers' perception of the paths (behaviors) through which rewards may be attained. Thus, performance depends on how well the leader clarifies the path to desired rewards while making such rewards contingent on effective performance. This kind of leadership behavior suggests the importance of recognizing potent needs coupled with an ability to assist in satisfying them. To develop realistic paths, rewards must be related to work and personal goals; subordinates must be helped in identifying paths to these goals; leaders need to support subordinates' efforts; and barriers to goal achievement must be reduced.

Basically, then, the Path-Goal Theory is built on the relationship among various leadership styles, characteristics of subordinates, and other situational factors. In turn, all of these combine to influence the attitudes and behavior of subordinates. For example, the theory suggests that effective leadership varies with different task situations (ambiguous-nonroutine versus unambiguous-routine) and personal characteristics of subordinates in relationship to particular styles of leadership. Although the Path-Goal Theory is relatively new, and additional testing is necessary, it is a potentially valuable approach for determining the most effective leadership style for a specific situation.[23]

Changing leadership styles The Path-Goal Theory suggests that the same leader can exhibit different leadership styles in various situations. However, if psychologists are correct that individual personalities are structurally formed by the time a person is eight years old, changing leader behavior may be as difficult as suddenly trying to become Superman. Learned habits or actions are based on a complex history of past experiences, and any new information is profoundly influenced by that history. Furthermore, psychologists have found that two or

---

[22] Robert J. House and Terrence Mitchell, "Path-Goal Theory of Leadership," *Journal of Contemporary Business*, Autumn 1974, pp. 81–97. The theory was proposed by Martin G. Evans. See "The Effects of Supervisory Behavior on the Path-Goal Relationship," *Organizational Behavior and Human Performance*, May 1970, pp. 277–98; and "Leadership and Motivation: A Case Concept," *Academy of Management Journal*, 1970, pp. 91–102.

[23] Chester Schriesheim and Mary Ann VonGlinow, "The Path-Goal Theory of Leadership: A Theoretical and Empirical Analysis," *Academy of Management Journal*, September 1977, pp. 398–405.

three years of intensive psychotherapy may be necessary to bring about a lasting change in personality patterns.

In addition to personality, leader behavior is also influenced by important and pressing needs that require fulfillment. The actions selected to satisfy these needs are based on experiences and behavior patterns that have been successful in the past. Thus, leaders may rationalize that a style that has worked in the past will continue to work in the future. Unfortunately, rationalization of this type makes behavior difficult to change since leaders normally receive little feedback in specific situations as to why followers do not behave as expected. As a result, they begin to blame their subordinates, rather than taking an inward look at themselves.

Another reason for a lack of motivation to change leadership styles stems from the patterns set by top management. Managers who are chosen to advance in an organization often exhibit behavior patterns closely related to those of top executives. In looking for potential leaders, top executives are often attracted to those subordinates who more nearly portray the same leadership style as themselves. An interesting story to illustrate this point is told by the training director of a large corporation who had set up several leadership programs for young managers. After two years, the training director began asking why some divisions were sending the same managers. One vice president stated that by sending the same managers, those needed to get the work out in the division could be kept on the job. In this case, it is evident that the vice president saw no need to have managers change their leadership styles since they were already fulfilling the roles expected of them.

Even though changes in leadership style may be difficult to achieve, training can be useful in bringing about some improvements in leader effectiveness. For example, leadership training can emphasize the techniques to deal with people problems, as well as to introduce changes in leader behavior. The key here is to inform managers about the variables that influence leadership, how such variables affect goal perception, and the importance of clarifying paths to goal attainment.

Leadership training Leadership training represents a large percentage of the management development activities conducted in organizations today. The content of such training is generally directed toward (1) increasing technical knowledge within specific functional areas; (2) learning new managerial techniques for performing the management functions; and (3) improving personal relationships with others through better communication, increased participation, and a more comprehensive understanding of motivation.

Several training methods are available for achieving these results. The lecture and lecture-discussion methods are quite common. With motivated participants, the lecture method can be effective. Other training methods include experiential training sessions, on-the-job training, coaching, and counseling. The conference method also provides a viable technique when it is organized around permissive and leaderless sessions.

Determining which training method to utilize depends on the participants, learning objectives, time, money, and other situational factors. For some people, leadership growth occurs without formal training. In other cases, little improvement is noticed in spite of expensive and sophisticated programs. Regardless of the method used, however, a key element in any training program is the motivation of participants. Many times top-level managers become so enthusiastic about leadership training that they feel it is something for all individuals in positions of leadership. But, unless participants are sufficiently motivated, even the more exacting approaches may be of little value in learning.

Sensitivity training   Sensitivity, or T-group (training group), sessions are built around intimate personal interaction and open communication among participants in small groups.[24] The groups are composed of 10 to 15 participants who meet for several successive daily sessions. The objectives of T-groups are to assist participants in understanding (1) themselves, (2) the impact of their behavior on others, (3) the feelings and needs of others, (4) group processes, and (5) organizational complexities and the dynamics of change.

In seeking these objectives, sensitivity groups are organized around a self-help concept. To learn more about oneself and to overcome emotional problems with others, each person in the group depends on comments from people in the session. Participation by all members is especially important, and all members are asked to be open and frank. Unstructured meetings without an agenda are utilized so that the group may explore various avenues in a nonthreatening atmosphere. However, the lack of structure can become exceedingly frustrating to those who like to follow a definite agenda.

In the absence of any prearranged schedule, sensitivity groups usually establish their own ground rules concerning feedback that is allowed, such as telling individual participants how their behavior is viewed by other members of the group. By understanding how others view their behavior, individuals learn about themselves, a first step toward understanding other people. Through such feedback, change becomes an experience where old values are questioned and new values, feelings, and desires are developed and reinforced.[25]

Evidence is quite meager as concerns the real effectiveness of sensi-

---

[24] For a complete discussion of this method, see E. H. Schein and W. G. Bennis, *Personal and Organizational Change through Group Methods: The Laboratory Approach* (New York: John Wiley & Sons, 1966); and L. P. Bradford, Jr., R. Gibb, and K. D. Benne, *T-Group Theory and Laboratory Method* (New York: John Wiley & Sons, 1964).

[25] Irving Borwick, "Team Improvement Laboratory," *Personnel Journal*, January 1969, pp. 18–244; and Schein and Bennis, *Laboratory Approach*.

tivity programs, particularly when participants return to their jobs.[26] One problem is that of measuring leadership effectiveness. The ideal measure is to determine whether those who have completed such training are more effective in achieving group goals than those who have not participated. Unfortunately, this type of measure is practically impossible because the variables influencing leader effectiveness are never identical in any two situations. Another problem in determining the effectiveness of sensitivity programs is that the organizational environment to which people return remains the same. Thus, what has been learned cannot be truly put into practice. Since the organizational environment is likely to be much more authoritarian and less supportive than the sensitivity sessions, managers may experience frustration and anxiety. Consequently, they may become less effective leaders than before training took place. These and other problems have been significant enough to cause many companies to discontinue sensitivity training.

Fiedler Contingency Model of leadership

An alternative to improving leadership effectiveness through training is that of fitting the leader's style to the situation, rather than attempting to change the style itself. In this respect, widespread recognition has been given to two situational or contingency models—the Fiedler Contingency Model and the Vroom-Yetton Model. Both models suggest that a number of styles may be effective depending upon elements of the situation.

Based upon his research, Fiedler holds that the effectiveness of a group depends on the personality of the leader and the degree to which the situation gives the leader power, control over sanctions, and influence over the task structure.[27] As concerns the leader's personality, Fiedler describes various types of individuals ranging from those who are relationship motivated to those who are task motivated. Relationship-motivated leaders are fairly open, permissive, and approachable, while task-motivated leaders are more oriented toward control and task accomplishment.

Through laboratory and field tests, Fiedler and Chemers have found that leadership styles are revealed in the way people feel toward their least preferred co-worker (LPC rating).[28] The rating is computed by evaluating 18 attributes of the co-worker, such as pleasantness and sincerity, on a scale of 1 to 8. A score of 64 or above is considered to be high, and consequently, people are regarded as relationship ori-

---

[26] P. B. Smith, "Controlled Studies of the Outcome of Sensitivity Training," *Psychological Bulletin,* July 1975, pp. 597–622.

[27] See Fred E. Fiedler, *A Theory of Leadership Effectiveness* (New York: McGraw-Hill, 1967), pp. 247–60; and F. E. Fiedler and M. M. Chemers, *Leadership and Effective Management* (Glenview, Ill.: Scott, Foresman, 1974).

[28] Fred E. Fiedler and Martin M. Chemers, with Linda Mahar, *Improving Leadership Effectiveness: A Leader Match Concept* (New York: John Wiley & Sons, 1976).

ented. When LPC scores are high, individuals are better able to differentiate between their negative reactions to people who are least preferred co-workers and their appreciation of them as individuals.

In contrast, low LPC persons—scoring under 57—generally are more concerned with their tasks than the quality of their interpersonal relations. Both types of leaders, however, are effective in situations that match their style, but neither are outstanding in all situations. For example, low LPC leaders tend to perform best in a predictable environment where the task is highly structured and decisions are viewed as leading to intended outcomes. High LPC persons do well in situation that require flexibility and creativity as well as diplomacy and tact in dealing with co-workers. If the leader is in a situation that is incompatible with the recognized style, it is preferable to modify the task or change the relationship with co-workers.

An important aspect of the Contingency Model concerns the degree of favorableness that a situation provides for the leader. The degree to which a situation is favorable can be assessed by examining the following:

1. *Leader-member relation*—the degree to which a group is willing to accept the leader.
2. *Task structure*—the degree to which tasks are defined and structured.
3. *Position power*—formal authority as distinct from personal power of the leader.

The most favorable situation is one where the leader is accepted, the task is structured, and the leader has high position power to control sanctions. In a highly favorable situation, the task-motivated leader would generally perform best. Such behavior will also be best when leader-member relations are poor, the task unstructured, and the leader's position power is weak (an unfavorable situation). On the other hand, relationship-motivated leaders tend to perform best in situations where they have moderate situational favorableness in terms of power, control, and influence.

A description of the Contingency Model is shown in Figure 15–11. The situational favorableness dimension is indicated on the horizontal axis, and the vertical axis shows group or organizational performance. The solid line on the graph is the performance curve of relationship-motivated leaders under various situational conditions, while the broken line represents the performance of task-motivated leaders. The model clearly suggests that leaders avoid situations in which they will not be effective and seek out those situations where they can be successful. Since leadership styles are not polarized as bad or good, a leader may perform well in one situation but be ineffective in another.

Under this theory, a leadership style is made more effective by altering various situational factors, such as subordinate relations, the routini-

FIGURE 15–11
The performance of relationship and task-motivated leaders in different situational-favorableness conditions

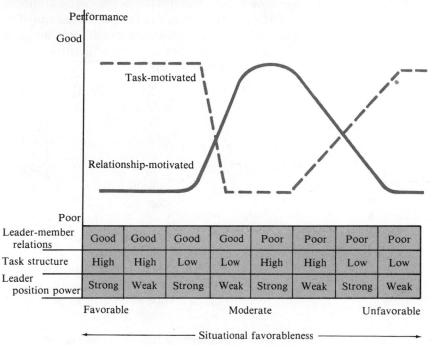

Leader-member relations	Good	Good	Good	Good	Poor	Poor	Poor	Poor
Task structure	High	High	Low	Low	High	High	Low	Low
Leader position power	Strong	Weak	Strong	Weak	Strong	Weak	Strong	Weak

Source: Adapted from Fred E. Fiedler, "The Contingency Model—New Directions for Leadership Utilization," *Journal of Contemporary Business,* Autumn 1974, p. 71. Reprinted with permission of the *Journal of Contemporary Business.* Copyright 1974.

zation of tasks, and the power to reward and punish. Fiedler believes that this approach is much better than having people go through leadership training intended to change personality/leadership.

The process of changing a situation to suit the leadership style is called organizational engineering.[29] Each organization has its own technology, competition, and personality that reflect patterns of behavior based on established policies, procedures, methods, and control systems. Changes in these areas, by necessity, take time. Likewise, institutionalized images and values that are held by organizational members cannot be easily modified. In particular, large organizations are more difficult to change, or at least require more time to change, than smaller ones. For these reasons, changing the situational dimensions of a leader's relations, task structure, and position power may be more theoretical than practical. In addition, organizational engineering may be utopian at this time because we have not yet validated those situational dimensions that have the greatest impact on leadership performance.

[29] Fred E. Fiedler, "Engineer the Job to Fit the Manager," *Harvard Business Review,* September–October 1965, pp. 115–22.

The Vroom-Yetton Decision Model

The Vroom-Yetton Model is relatively new.[30] It attempts to determine the degree to which the leader should share decision-making power with subordinates. Thus, leadership styles are defined in terms of the degree subordinates participate in decision making. Basically, the model develops an approach for matching a manager's leadership behavior to the demands of the situation. The following five styles are identified.[31]

Autocrative I(AI)	Leader makes the decision using information available at the time.
Autocrative II(AII)	Leader obtains necessary information from subordinates and then decides. Subordinates are not involved in developing or evaluating alternatives.
Consultive I(CI)	Leader shares relevant problem with subordinates individually, obtains suggestions, and then makes decision.
Consultive II(CII)	Leader shares problem with subordinates as a group, collectively obtaining ideas and suggestions, and then makes the decision.
Group II(GII)	Leader shares problems with group in generating and evaluating alternatives in an attempt to reach agreement on a solution. Leader accepts and implements solution that has support of the entire group.

Determining which style to follow depends upon answers to seven situational questions that relate to the problem itself and subordinates. The first three questions shown in Figure 15–12 are intended to protect the quality of the decision, and the final four are designed to restrict styles that would unduly jeopardize subordinate acceptance. One version of the model is expressed in the form of a decision tree (Figure 15–12). To use it for a particular decision-making situation, the leader starts at the left-hand side and works to the right to each successive box asking the question related to the letter above the box. When a terminal node is reached, the first number encountered represents the problem type. The other symbols following the colon designate the feasible leadership styles (noted earlier) that may be followed. For example, AI is prescribed for problem types 1, 4, and 5.

The Vroom-Yetton Model is an exciting new addition to the leadership field. Although the model has not been tested completely, it attempts to identify leadership styles that a manager should use to deal effectively with problems encountered on the job.[32] By following the analytical approach outlined in the model, managers have an opportu-

---

[30] Victor H. Vroom and Philip W. Yetton, *Leadership and Decision Making* (Pittsburg: University of Pittsburg Press, 1973).

[31] Since Group I is a special case, it is excluded in this discussion.

[32] R. H. George Field, "A Critique of the Vroom-Yetton Contingency Model of Leadership Behavior," *The Academy of Management Review*, April 1979, pp. 249–57.

FIGURE 15–12
Vroom-Yetton Decision Model

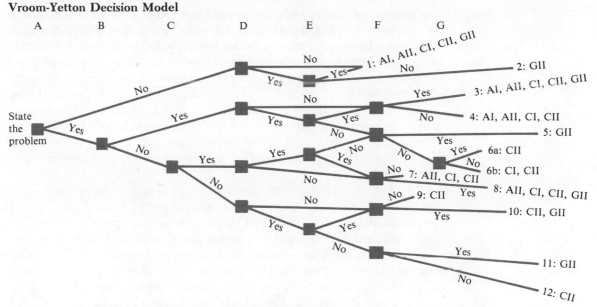

A. Does the problem possess a quality requirement?
B. Do I have sufficient information to make a high-quality decision?
C. Is the problem structured?
D. Is acceptance of the decision by subordinates important for effective implementation?
E. If I were to make the decision by myself, am I reasonably certain that it would be accepted by my subordinates?
F. Do subordinates share the organizational goals to be attained in solving this problem?
G. Is Conflict among subordinates likely in preferred solutions?

Source: Victor H. Vroom, "Can Leaders Learn to Lead?" *Organizational Dynamics,* Winter 1976, p. 19. © 1976 by AMACOM, a division of American Management Association; all rights reserved. Used with permission.

nity to select a style that should result in decisions that are more rational and effective.[33]

SUMMARY

Three major points about the dynamics of leadership are identified in this chapter. First, leadership is a process that is necessary in any undertaking where two or more people seek to accomplish a common goal. Leadership effectiveness, however, is only one component of managerial effectiveness. In this respect, leadership is built on a mutually dependent relationship. Subordinates depend on the leader, and leadership success depends on the performance of subordinates. It becomes

---

[33] Arthur G. Jago and Victor H. Vroom, "An Evaluation of Two Alternatives to the Vroom/Yetton Normative Model," *Academy of Management Journal,* June 1980, pp. 347–55.

obvious, therefore, that effective managers require a combination of leadership, technical, and managerial knowledge. Certainly, all managers perform many activities that are not regarded as leadership acts; but, when leadership must be exercised, a manager's success depends on a combination of the leadership skills discussed in this chapter.

Second, there are no physical characteristics or personality traits that are universally evident in all leadership situations. A specific leader emerges because there is a blending of the attributes of the leader, the elements of the situation, and the characteristics of the followers. For this reason, managers must develop good diagnostic skills if they are to adapt their leadership styles to fit situational requirements realistically.

Our last point deals with the ability of managers to influence the behavior of others. In most instances, changes in wage rates are not left to the discretion of individual managers, nor are promotions, working conditions, job technology, pension plans, or a host of other changes. Thus, leaders must be creative, innovative, and venturesome in influencing behavior in the desired direction; and, they can improve their effectiveness in these areas by understanding themselves, subordinates, and the specific situations in which they must function.

KEY TERMS

Consideration: Leadership acts showing concerns for people (employee-centered behavior).

Contingency Model of Leadership: Assuming that a person generally follows a particular leadership style, then that style must be matched to the situation that gives the leader power, control over sanctions, and influence over the task structure.

Dynamic leadership skills: The five essential leadership skills of reacting to the superior/subordinate syndrome, interpersonal influence, situational sensitivity, communication, and empathy.

Empathy: The ability to sense and understand the needs, wants, and feelings of others.

Initiating structure: Leadership acts relating to job-centered behavior emphasizing production.

Leadership: The process of interpersonal relationships through which a person attempts to influence the behavior of others and, in turn, to direct organizational behavior toward the attainment of predetermined objectives.

Managerial Grid®: A representation of leadership styles on two nine-point scales reflecting degrees of concern for people and concern for production.

Path-Goal Theory: A situational model of leadership suggesting that the same leader can follow different styles in various situations by exhibiting consideration and task orientation.

Situational approach to leadership: Leaders must understand their own behavior, the behavior of their subordinates, and the organizational situation in selecting the particular leadership style they should follow.

Trait Theory: An attempt to specify the physical, personality, social, and personal traits that are associated with leadership success.

QUESTIONS

1. Define leadership. What are the important elements of your definition?
2. Are all managers also leaders? Why or why not?
3. Discuss the five important skills in the dynamic leadership skills model presented in this chapter.
4. What is the traitist approach to studying leadership?
5. What are the two leadership roles presented by Bales?
6. Which leadership type is recommended by Rensis Likert? Why?
7. Discuss the continuum models developed by Tannenbaum and Schmidt.
8. How do the leadership quadrants shown in the The Ohio State University studies differ from the continuum model?
9. Which one of the 81 possible leadership behaviors does Blake and Mouton consider to be the most successful?
10. How does the Reddin 3-D theory differ from the Managerial Grid®?
11. Compare and contrast the Path-Goal Theory, Fiedler's Contingency Model, and the Vroom-Yetton Decision Model in terms of:

    a. Contingency (situational) approach.
    b. Leadership training as an important model element.
    c. Utilization of organizational engineering.

12. What are some of the barriers that must be overcome in changing a leader's style?
13. What is the value of sensitivity training in developing leadership qualities? Are there possible limitations?
14. Discuss the advantages and disadvantages of changing situations to fit leadership styles.

PROBLEMS

1. U.S. military leaders display a wide range of personal characteristics. Their moral habits are quite different; also their degrees of modesty. Some are more robust than others. For example, General Ira C. Eaker, a soft-spoken, sober man in military battle, is quite a contrast to General Curtis E. LeMay whose nicknames include "Ole Iron Pants," and "The Man the Russians Fear the Most."

a. What generalizations about leadership do such individual differences suggest?

b. How do the factors of interpersonal relations, situational sensitivity, and communicating objectives fit with your answer to *(a)?*

2. Do you feel that personal traits such as intelligence, individuality, initiative, and emotional maturity affect leadership effectiveness? Is it the presence of such traits, or the way in which they are used, that influences effectiveness?

3. Winston Churchill noted the obligation of leadership when he stated: "The Nation will find it hard to look up to leaders who keep their ears to the ground." Why is it impractical to discuss in isolation the leadership elements of the leader, the situation, and the followers?

4. Assume the following situations:

A. Good leader-follower relationships.
   High task structure (routine work).
   Strong authority position power of leader to withhold rewards and punishments.
B. Moderate to good leader-follower relationship.
   Low task structure (unstructured work).
   Weak authority position power of leader to withhold rewards and punishments.
C. Poor leader-follower relationship.
   High task structure.
   Low authority position power of leader to withhold rewards and punishments.

a. In which of these situations would the task-oriented leader be most effective?
b. In which of these situations would the relationship-oriented leader be most effective?

5. The laissez-faire leadership style is often discussed. This behavior pattern allows individuals to do their own thing without guidance from policies, procedures, and rules. Everyone in the group is completely free. Would you say that there is leadership in this type of situation?

6. Before he was promoted to a supervisory position, Jed Williams had always thought that he would approach supervision as an employee-centered leader. Three months after Jed was named supervisor of the shipping and receiving dock, he found that his subordinates were confused and frustrated. In addition, productivity within the department was falling and the actions of his group reflected negative, rather than positive, feelings about the work.

In explaining the performance of his department to the plant superintendent, Jed stated that he knew his managerial style was not causing the problem since he was following the principles of employee-centered leadership.

a. Could Jed be mistaken about the cause of the problem in his work unit?
b. If he is mistaken, could Jed be basing his leadership style on false assumptions? Why?
c. Where might Jed be placed on the Managerial Grid®?

7. "Managers should change the shape of the hole rather than try to change the shape of the peg." From the standpoint of leadership theory, what are some of the implications of this statement?

8. Spence and Helmeich of the University of Texas have conducted studies on masculinity and femininity. Viewed as acquired characteristics of behavior, they feel that masculinity and femininity are parallel characteristics of personality rather than opposite ends of a single continuum. They have shown that androgynous people (those who score high on both masculine and feminine dimensions) have generally been high achievers and accomplishment oriented.

Is this type of evidence—assuming that task behavior is essentially masculine and relationship behavior is essentially feminine—more consistent with the Blake and Mouton Model or the Path-Goal Theory?

9. A group of graduate students in psychology at the University of Utah studied the lives of famous historical and contemporary figures in order to calculate their possible LPC scores. Although long-distance psychoanalysis is difficult, the speculation of how LPC scores may have affected their careers is interesting. How would you rate (either as high or low) the LPCs of the following leaders: Mao Tse-tung, Napoleon, Lyndon Johnson, Richard Nixon, and Jimmy Carter?

In making your decisions, consider these aspects:

Low LPC—Single-minded in obtaining objectives or historical mission.
   Task oriented.
   Retreats from others.
   Becomes irritable and tense under pressure.

High LPC—Good personal relations.
   Wins admiration of followers.
   Open communications and innovative.
   Compassion and requires personal support.

10. Assume that the president of the United States encounters a situation that does not match the leader's particular style and the organizational setting cannot be reengineered. What are some ways to compensate for the unmatched leadership style with the particular situation?

11. Indicate your agreement or disagreement with the following statements.

a. Leadership comes with the position.
b. Leadership should be exercised exclusively by persons in titled positions.
c. No one can perform a leadership act unless it is expressly permitted by higher authority.
d. Leadership must be democratic.
e. Leadership is the process by which a member helps a group meet its goals.

12.
Leader A's	*Leader B's*
attitudinal values	*attitudinal values*
Disregards individual employee differences.	Recognizes individual differences and needs.
Authority and power in gaining compliance is important.	Downplays authority in relations with others.
Uses commands in communication.	Empathetic in dealing with individuals.
Intolerant of human errors.	Understanding of risks in delegating authority.
Unwilling to accept employee limitations and defects.	Recognizes human limitations and assists others in overcoming them.
Unwilling to delegate because of chance of errors.	Communicates in a realistic and human manner.

Of the two leaders, which one would have the better outlook essential to establishing productive interpersonal relations with followers? Which leader is likely to be the most effective in terms of performance? Based on your previous answer, is there anything to be said for the other attitudinal set?

SUGGESTED READINGS

Barrow, J. C. "The Variables of Leadership: A Review and Conceptual Framework." *The Academy of Management Review*, April 1977, pp. 231–51.

Bass, B. M. *Stogdill's Handbook of Leadership: A Survey of Theory and Research*. New York: The Free Press, 1981.

Blake, R. R., and J. S. Mouton. "Toward Resolution of the Situationalism vs. 'One Best Style' . . . Controversy in Leadership Theory, Research, and Practice." Austin, Tex.: Scientific Methods, Inc., 1981.

Burke, W. W. "Leadership: Is There One Best Approach?" *Management Review*, November 1980, pp. 54–56.

Ford, J. D. "Departmental Context and Formal Structure as Constraints on Leader Behavior." *Academy of Management Journal*, June 1981, pp. 274–88.

Green, S. G.; D. M. Nebeker; and M. A. Boni. "Personality and Situational Effects on Leader Behavior." *Academy of Management Journal*, June 1976, pp. 184–94.

Hill, W. "Leadership Style: Rigid or Flexible?" *Organizational Behavior and Human Performance*, 1973, pp. 35–47.

Hollander, E. P. *Leadership Dynamics: A Practical Guide to Effective Relationships*. New York: Free Press/Macmillan, 1978.

Jago, A., and V. H. Vroom. "Hierarchical Level and Leadership Style." *Organizational Behavior and Human Performance*, February 1977, pp. 121–45.

Manz, C. C., and H. P. Sims, Jr. "Self-Management as a Substitute for Leadership: A Social Learning Theory Perspective." *The Academy of Management Review*, July 1980, pp. 361–67.

Mitchell, T. R.; J. R. Larson, Jr.; and S. G. Green. "Leadership Behavior, Situational Moderators, and Group Performance: An Attributional Analysis." *Organizational Behavior and Human Performance,* April 1977, pp. 254–68.

Ouchi, W. *Theory Z: How American Business Can Meet the Japanese Challenge.* Reading, Mass.: Addison-Wesley, 1981.

Schneier, C. E. "The Contingency Model of Leadership: An Extension to Emergent Leadership and Leader's Sex." *Organizational Behavior and Human Performance,* April 1978, pp. 220–39.

Schriesheim, C. A.; J. M. Tolliver; and O. C. Behlins. "Leadership Theory: Some Implications for Managers." *MSU Business Topics,* Summer 1978, pp. 34–40.

Smith, P. B. "The T-Group Trainer—Group Facilitator or Prisoner of Circumstance?" *The Journal of Applied Behavioral Science,* January–February–March 1980, pp. 63–77.

Vroom, V. H. and A. G. Jago. "On the Validity of the Vroom/Yetton Model." *Journal of Applied Psychology,* 1978, pp. 151–62.

The Sure Way

Ten years ago, Ms. Lea Long and her husband were in their late 40s. They did not have children, and both were unemployed due to the closing of the town's major employer, a shoe factory. During this period, the Longs were invited to attend a meeting that they were told dealt with a new investment opportunity that would provide them financial security, a tax shelter, and extremely high profits. At the meeting, the speaker described a pyramid distribution plan whereby distributors make money two ways: (1) commissions based on their own sales volume and (2) commissions earned on the sales of distributors they sponsor. People who signed up as distributors were encouraged to recruit other distributors so that they could become their wholesale suppliers. No restrictions as to territories were involved, nor were there any franchise fees or capital requirements, other than what the person purchased.

The director of the meeting told the Longs that there were no failures in the business—only quitters—and that the opportunity to earn bonus checks of $50,000 to $100,000 a year was common. Although participants were encouraged to develop their businesses at their own pace, it was noted that success depended on the time invested, the effectiveness of their independent organization, and the development of permanent clientele. The Longs accepted the challenge presented to them and have been distributors of SWAY products since that time.

SWAY Corporation

Based in Chicago, Illinois, the SWAY Corporation is a direct sales company that sells its own home care products, ranging from detergents to jewelry. Basically, the company's public image is of a business specializing in high-quality household cleaning products that are developed through extensive research. Each product has a 100 percent guarantee associated with it.

Since the 1955 inception of SWAY in the garages of its founders, the corporation has had a phenomenal growth rate. Gross sales by years are as follows:

Year	Sales volume (in $millions)
1966	$ 20
1970	100
1976	275
1981	850

SWAY distribution

The success of the SWAY distribution system is in providing top-quality, easily sold products that maintain a demand for repeat sales. Typically, a SWAY distributor is a man and wife team who work together. In recent years, however, single persons have comprised about 25 percent of all new distributors. Generally, $60 to $80 is required to go into business, depending on the quantity of products originally ordered. SWAY claims more than 300,000 distributors worldwide.

Each distributor is not only encouraged to sell directly to customers, but more important, to become a wholesale supplier by recruiting others to be distributors. Basically, sponsoring more people means making more money. For example, when three distributors sell $8,400 worth of products for three consecutive months, their sponsor becomes a "Direct Distributor" who receives a 3 percent commission on this sales volume. Six distributors at that level for six months makes the sponsor a "Super Distributor," who is entitled to an even higher percentage of each distributor's sales volume. The system progresses to different levels, each earning the distributor gold pins encrusted with gems. Higher levels mean more expensive pins, more money for the sponsoring distributor, and more rewards from the company.

Ms. Long's success

Since the death of her husband, Lea Long has taken full responsibility for the business and has reached the notable position of a "Super Distributor." Over the years, she has been directly or indirectly responsible for putting hundreds of SWAY distributors into business.

Recently, Ms. Long was invited to attend a meeting at SWAY's headquarters in Chicago. Held on a weekly basis, meetings of this nature are intended to be motivational, as well as inspirational, for distributors. Although Ms. Long had attended two such meetings in the past, she continued to be impressed with the lavish auditorium, decorated with flags from all over the world and furnished with the latest audio-visual equipment. Prior to entering the auditorium, the group she was with was cheered by corporate employees as they passed by the company's opulent office complex and research center.

At the meeting the president of SWAY exhorted the distributors to "keep signing new distributors." Furthermore, the president said:

> If you are not feeding people into the system, you are going to find yourself with about one half of the business you think you have. Remem-

ber, there is nothing that will do more for your attitude than signing up a new person.

During the meetings, many ovations were given for corporate managers who addressed the cheering, whistling crowd. As viewed by Ms. Long, SWAY's success lies in (1) keeping people highly motivated and (2) inspiring distributors by showing them bonus checks that have been processed and slide shows about the SWAY story. Although corporate officials praised product quality, they generally pitched "the system" as hard or harder than products. As an example, one official stated that "Super Distributors" are provided a one-week, all-expense-paid vacation trip to Palm Springs. When the "Double Super" level is reached, the corporate jet is sent to the distributor's home town so the distributor may be flown to Chicago for a day of honor. Later on, a paid tour to Hawaii is provided. As is true with many distributors, Ms. Long is looking forward to the day when the corporate jet will land in her town and take her to Chicago.

Questions

1. Do you think selling SWAY products on a door-to-door basis would be a challenging and satisfying job?
2. What type of techniques might be used to encourage people to become distributors?
3. What motivational incentives do you feel encouraged the Longs to become SWAY distributors?
4. Many SWAY distributors never make it to the top in terms of receiving large bonus checks. What, then, causes people to be so enthusiastic about SWAY and to exhibit such high degrees of motivation?
5. Given the dynamics of the marketplace, should SWAY's top-level managers feel complacent about the company's performance and successful distribution system? What types of macromotivational issues should be considered that may have an impact on the company's future success?

Velda University

The women faculty members at Velda University have taken the position that the administration is chauvinistic in its relationships with female employees. Discrimination charges concerning pay levels, working conditions, fringe benefits, teaching loads, promotions, tenure, and hiring practices have been discussed with the State Association of Educators. Even though some of the charges are considered to be unfounded, there is good reason to believe that the president of Velda University discriminates against women employees. At a reception for new faculty members, the president was heard to say that he was trying to hire a woman faculty member for less money than a male, due to a tight budget. He also stated that she should be willing to accept the lower sum, particularly since she is married and can afford to work for less money.

Dr. Claudine Smith, an assistant professor of management, has been studying salary schedules within the School of Business Administration for the past five years. She has not been able to obtain all of the desired data but has found a significant number of cases where women with higher degrees and more teaching experience received substantially less pay than their male counterparts.

At a recent meeting of faculty women, Dr. Smith presented a paper showing that women accounted for only one fifth of the nation's 533,000 faculty members. Additional data quoted in her report are presented in the following table:

Percentage of academic women and men holding ranks of instructor and full professor

	Lowest rank instructor (percentage)	Highest rank full professor (percentage)
Women	35	9
Men	16	25

As support for her position, a recent research report states that 63 percent of faculty women were paid less than $20,000 a year, while only 28 percent of faculty men earned less than that amount. In some respects, academic women have actually lost ground, concludes another report, while stating that within the past five years men have replaced women as presidents of the prestigious Sarah Lawrence, Bryn Mawr, and Vassar colleges.

One of the present university policies that Dr. Smith considers discriminatory is the antinepotism policy. The policy states that if a female faculty member marries a male faculty member within the university system she must resign her position, or if she wishes to continue to teach she must work at lower pay with no regular academic rank. As such, the policy results in the university obtaining equally qualified female faculty members at a lower salary than that paid to the regular full-time faculty.

In a conversation with Dr. Smith, Dr. Max Fedium, president of Velda University, stated that her statistical comparisons are not necessarily an indication of male chauvinistic discrimination as she had claimed. In addition, he indicated that his reluctance to hire female faculty members is based on the belief that young women usually quit to marry and raise families. "For a woman who wants to teach, a husband or child can be a liability, particularly if the woman is a department's only specialist and must leave for a year," he stated.

"Furthermore," he said, "women aren't really able to earn a scholarly reputation. Family responsibilities, you know, make it hard for them to keep up to date in their field and to turn out as much research as men do."

Dr. Smith retorted: "This may be true in some cases, but it is hardly a meaningful generalization. The small number of women in many academic areas stems directly from biases in hiring and promoting women. The hiring practice at Velda is so discriminating that the application form may as well be stamped *male only.*"

Dr. Fedium then stated, "Dr. Smith, your problem is that you hold no loyalty to this fine institution that is paying you a salary that you could not earn elsewhere. Besides, we tried to hire a woman faculty member for this past fall semester, but she wanted us to hire her husband, too. Now what were we going to do with him?"

Referring to the nepotism policy that prevents both husband and wife from working as full-time faculty members in the same institution. Dr. Smith said, "This nepotism policy is unbearable as a discriminating device against women. When an academic woman marries an academic man, her career becomes that of the sacrificial cow. How can this be fair to any of the single female professors, as well as to those who are teaching here and happen to be married to men on the university faculty? It is the woman who loses her rank, respect, dignity, and career."

"You know full well, Dr. Smith," Dr. Fedium retorted, "that this rule is designed to prevent problems such as one spouse having to pass judgment on another, and it does not discriminate on the basis of sex."

Dr. Smith then replied that nepotism rules, such as the one at Velda University, had been revised at some of the major universities and that it was time for a change at Velda. She then informed the president that unless a change was made by the end of the semester, a discrimination complaint would be filed.

As a closing remark, she reminded him of how $6 million in federal research funds were withheld from a sister university until it came up with an acceptable plan to end sex discrimination. At that point, she slammed the president's office door and was met in the hall by Dr. Fred Jacon who said, "Sweetheart, how did things work out?" As the door slammed, Dr. Fedium said to himself, "That woman wouldn't dare do that to this university!"

Questions

1. What are some of the reasons behind the behavior exhibited by Dr. Smith and Dr. Fedium?
2. What changes could be implemented to improve conditions at Velda University?
3. What is President Fedium's responsibility in this situation? What should he do at this point?

4. What is Dr. Smith's responsibility in this situation? What do you think she will do now?

Leadership Training at SRW, Inc.

Twelve executives from 10 major industrial companies agreed to meet at a rather remote lake resort for two weeks to participate in a T-group session sponsored by an East Coast management consulting firm. One of the participants was James A. Parker, a vice president from SRW, Inc. All of the executives were informed that T-group members are normally given a minimum of direction so that they can clarify their personal values, specify group norms, and note sanctions on their own behavior. Thus, the objective of the T-group is to help individuals lower their defense mechanisms, thereby beginning to learn more about themselves and others through feedback from the group.

None of the participants were very clear about what to expect as they met in a large assembly room on Monday at 9:00 A.M. At 9:50 A.M., a man entered the room and stated that he was the director of the session but that he did not plan to be the leader of the group. He stated that the organization of the group was up to the participants and that the training to be accomplished would result from the group's efforts. The director further noted that he would periodically enter into the discussion to encourage feedback on (1) the effectiveness of the group and (2) the reaction of participants to one another. At 10:10 A.M., he walked to the back of the room and sat down. He said nothing until 11:00 A.M. when he told the group to break for the morning.

A portion of the discussion that occurred among the T-group participants between 10:10 A.M. and 11:00 A.M. follows:

A: What are we supposed to do?

B: I don't know, but my brother who teaches at Cornell told me to expect something like this.

C: I think the whole thing is ridiculous since I have a helluva lot of work to do at the office that I will have to make up.

D: For myself, I have the time off and I am going to make the most of it. What about you? I think your name is "J," isn't it?

J: Well, I don't know; I assume there is a point to all of this, but I would like to have the director's job. He doesn't do anything but make a lot of dough out of this deal. It scares me to think about the amount of graft that goes on in industry today.

D: That may be so, but I think that this is a legitimate operation and have you thought about the graft that goes on daily in your own organization? Have you ever padded your expense account?

J: Hell, no! Besides, what business is it of yours if I do?

D: I guess it's none of my business. I was just making a general statement. Some of my subordinates do say that I am too nosy about their personal lives.

A: Intrusiveness is not a bad trait if one knows how to use it at the appropriate time.

As the days went by, the group discussed various issues and the participants became very frank with one another. By the end of the first week, the director had noticed some change in three of the participants.

Upon returning to his office at SRW, Inc., Parker submitted a written report to the corporate president about his T-group experience. His recommendation was that SRW should not move in the direction of T-group sessions for its leadership training. Instead, he concluded that the company should continue to use, as it had in the past, the task or work-oriented programs where the emphasis is on solving company problems.

Based on the Parker Report, the president of SRW established a development program for a group of employees working on a governmental satellite project. The president said in the ground rules that no form of sensitivity training was to be used and that there would be no probing into the personal feelings and behavior of the team members. All discussions were to be job oriented with the basic objective of reducing the project time for the satellite program by one month while reducing its cost by $250,000.

Jake Atson was chosen to conduct the sessions. Most of the employees in the group characterized Jake as being extremely aggressive. He was considered to be very knowledgeable but was known to verbally attack project employees who made suggestions or remarks with which he did not agree. Two of the 10 people in the group expressed the opinion that they were "really scared of Jake."

For the first two days of the session, discussions were based on problems dealing with the company's suppliers and its customer, the U.S. government. Parker visited the sessions periodically during the first two days. At the end of the second day, he reported to the president that in his opinion things were not progressing rapidly enough for a five-day session. He stated that if Jake didn't "get them knuckled down," the entire program would be another week behind schedule.

Questions

1. What type of personal experience do you feel Parker had at the T-group session?
2. Do you believe that the satellite group will develop the degree of efficiency desired by the president?
3. Characterize the leadership styles of Parker and Jake Atson.

The Springdale Medical Association

The Springdale Medical Association is a regional medical organization whose membership is made up of medical doctors, therapists, technicians, nurses, and administrators of nursing homes and hospitals. Meetings are generally held monthly. The major objective of the association is to investigate, analyze, and implement new approaches for improving the delivery of medical care in rural areas.

Monthly programs feature speakers from the state medical school and the various national medical associations. At least four times a year workshops and seminars are set up to highlight innovative approaches that are being used in rural health care programs.

The central theme of the July meeting was a discussion about the change in the system of accounting for the organization. The Springdale Medical Association is a nonprofit corporation and has accumulated over $100,000 in assets during the last several years. The Internal Revenue Service has granted the association an exemption from paying taxes. However, it is also requiring the organization to keep a more meaningful and accurate set of records. In order to make a step in this direction, the association is changing from a cash accounting to an accrual accounting system. This change will precipitate a reorganization of the management structure. Specifically, the office of the treasurer is to reflect greater responsibility to the membership. As proposed, all accounting records will be handled by a designated public accounting firm, and the treasurer will submit all bills to the accountant for vertification before they are paid. To provide for further control, all revenue receipts will be documented and submitted to the accountant along with a copy of the bank deposit slip.

In the proposal being submitted to the membership for vote, both the signatures of the president and the treasurer will be required on all checks written by the treasurer. Prior to the July meeting, a certified public accountant (CPA), Ms. Binderdown, was asked by the president to present the treasurer's report that incorporated the proposed new accounting system.

The charge of discrepancy

The meeting began with a sense of joviality. Then the president asked for the treasurer's report and immediately recognized Ms. Binderdown who gave a complete accounting of income, expenses, and budget variances. After the report was presented, the president asked for any discussion or corrections that should be noted. Mr. Lightfoot, who is the present treasurer, asked to be recognized. He stated that during the past afternoon he had added up the expenses that totaled $3,100, rather than the $2,100 as noted in the Binderdown report. Presently, the accounts are kept by Mr. Lightfoot's bookkeeper who is also the bookkeeper for the Midville Nursing Home of which Mr.

Lightfoot is administrator. Ms. Binderdown retorted that she is a CPA and that her analysis reflected accurately the accounts as reported.

One of the members in the audience commented that the difference in totals might be due to the fact that the bookkeeping system had been changed recently from a cash system to an accrual system. Thus, accounts payable that would not be paid until the next period would be charged as current rather than past expenditures. Mr. Lightfoot, then commented that he had taken recognition of this fact and that he still totaled expenses of $3,100 for the month. He stated, "There is a serious discrepancy in the CPA report, and I am highly concerned about the misrepresentation of the association's reported financial position." Ms. Binderdown, who was a guest at the meeting, became quite irritated at this point, commenting that she personally guaranteed to the members that the books were correct, balanced, and without error. "There has never been one instance in 15 years of professional accounting work in which there has been a question regarding the accuracy of my skills and knowledge," she said. Ms. Binderdown further noted that she did not have the association's books with her and could not explain the difference at this time between her report and the figures noted by Mr. Lightfoot. She assured the members, however, that the books accurately reflected the true financial position of the association.

The vote

Later during the meeting, the membership was asked to vote officially for a reorganization of officers in the form of a revision to the bylaws. As proposed by the board of directors, the following management structure was moved for adoption: board of directors, president, president elect, treasurer, secretary, membership director, and audit committee chairperson. The motion was seconded and before too much discussion occurred, Mr. Lightfoot called for the "question." The question received a majority of affirmative votes that allowed for the vote on the motion.

The vote on the motion was taken by secret ballot; and after an extended period of time during which the ballots were counted, the president came back into the room and announced that the motion had won by two votes—61 to 59 votes. At this moment, Mr. Lightfoot and one of the directors who was the immediate past president stood up and submitted their resignations from the association's board of directors. They implied that their actions were a result of the outcome of the election. They then immediately walked out of the meeting. For a few seconds the air was heavy, and anxiety existed among all those present. The president then stated that he would not accept the resignations of the members until they had given more thought to the matter. Following these remarks, the meeting was adjourned without the customary motion for adjournment.

Questions

1. What management concepts could have been employed to make the meeting more effective?
2. How would you rate the leadership skills of the president of the association?
3. What do you believe are the reasons for the conditions existing at the present time within the association?
4. Are there any long term actions that could be taken to prevent similar problems from occurring in the future?

PART FIVE

CONTROLLING PERFORMANCE FOR BETTER RESULTS

16

THE NATURE
OF CONTROL

PURPOSE

Robert Owen, a Scottish textile manufacturer, knew the importance of determining whether actual performance conformed to plans (the control process). He devised a system that enabled all workers to see how well they were doing at their jobs. The method was simple, but it worked so well that thousands of persons visited his company in New Lanark, near Glasgow, each year to see it operate.

Over all job stations hung a wooden block with each of the four sides painted a different color. If a worker's performance was excellent, the white side was turned outward for all to see. A different color was shown for "good," another for "indifferent" work, and a fourth for "bad." Not only could the factory manager see at a glance how the work force was doing, but each worker had the satisfaction of receiving recognition by having excellent work labeled as such. Each worker could also inspect the books in which job performance was recorded; if there was a feeling that the rating was unjustified, an appeal could be made. In addition, wage rates in the Owen plant were relatively high when compared to others in the area.

Contrasted with today's control techniques, those used by Owen may seem rather old-fashioned. Yet, in the early 1800s, control problems associated with the Industrial Revolution caused Owens techniques to gain widespread attention. More important, Owen's early contributions point out that the need for control in organizations is not unique to the 1980s.

In this chapter, we discuss the controlling function and its role in the management process. Later chapters examine specific control techniques along with guidelines for developing and implementing effective control systems.

OBJECTIVES

1. To discuss the importance of control in the accomplishment of objectives.

2. To identify steps in the control cycle while showing the relationship between control and all other management functions.

3. To examine the nature of precontrols, concurrent controls, and postcontrols.

4. To analyze the steps in the control process.

5. To relate cost considerations to the control process.

Henri Fayol noted that control involves "whether everything occurs in conformity with the plan adopted, the instructions issued, and the principles established."[1] Stated another way, the goal of managerial control is to have organizational members do the right things, at the right times, with the right resources. By necessity, then, managers must not only *correct* errors in performance but must also work to *prevent* them from happening if this goal is to be met.

AN OVERVIEW OF CONTROL

When discussing *management control,* one must be careful not to confuse the meaning of the term with others, such as *power, coercion, authority,* and *influence.* These words have meanings that are too narrow to describe clearly the nature and meaning of control as a management function. For example, behavioral scientists sometimes use the word *control* when referring to a process through which a person or group affects the behavior of another person, group, or organization.[2] While this meaning is implied to some extent in a managerial definition of control, it is not complete enough to describe control as a management function.

For our purposes, *the control process includes all activities that try to match performance with established objectives.* Due to such breadth, the nature of control must be described by looking at the steps involved in controlling organizational resources. Although a more complete discussion will be presented later, the most important steps of the control process are shown in Figure 16–1. To highlight these steps, consider the evaluation of sales performance. When quotas are assigned to salespersons, they are usually expected to meet them within a certain period of time. Actual sales are recorded through this period and are compared to assigned quotas. Three possible conditions may result from such comparisons:

If actual performance is on target, action can be continued without change.

Action can be continued with only minor changes if actual performance does not differ greatly from standards and if causes for the difference can be found rapidly.

Action must be halted if actual performance is not within acceptable limits, and causes cannot be identified quickly. (If this condition occurs, the sales manager has a new problem and the decision-making process must be repeated.)

Regardless of who is performing the control function at a given point in time, there are no differences in the steps of the process.

[1] Henri Fayol, *General and Industrial Management* (London: Sir Isaac Pitman and Sons, 1949), p. 107.

[2] Arnold S. Tannenbaum, *Control in Organizations* (New York: McGraw-Hill, 1968), pp. 4–6.

FIGURE 16–1
The decision making—control cycle

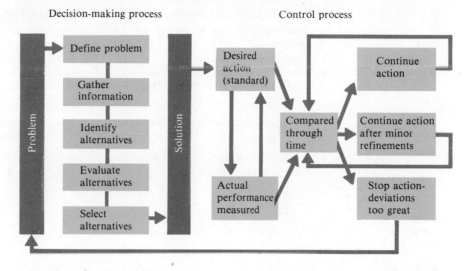

To correct undesirable performance shown in monthly progress and budget reports, middle managers must follow the same steps as individuals on an assembly line who may correct their actions immediately in order to meet quality standards. Also, the degree to which the control process is automated has no bearing on these steps. The thermostat in the cooling system of an automobile, the guidance system of a spaceship, and the physiological control of body temperature depend on the same basic steps, even though their mechanisms may differ.

It should also be noted that control is interrelated with all other management functions. Controlling performance implies that planning has taken place since the process begins with an established plan or standard. Likewise, the development of control systems depends on organizational design and related behavioral considerations. In this sense, control is but one part of the total management process, and effective control systems are always dependent on the successful performance of all of the other management functions.

THE NEED FOR CONTROL

A major purpose of managerial control is to ensure that programs are carried out in such a way that objectives will be met successfully. But why is control needed if activities were carefully planned in the first place? An interesting answer to consider is found in "Murphy's Law," which states that one can be almost certain that events will not go according to plan. This law implies that environmental factors often seem to conspire to produce problems that will prevent performance from meeting established standards. Since managers can never be sure that standards will be met as planned, the safe thing to do is to check and to evaluate performance on a continuous basis in order to guard against undesirable surprises.

Not only are control systems needed in all organizations but they must also cover all major activities related to an organization's inputs, processes, and outputs. In more specific terms, control is needed to achieve the following:

Standardize performance to increase efficiency.

Safeguard organizational assets from theft, waste, and misuse.

Standardize quality to meet engineering and customer specifications.

Set limits through job descriptions and auditing systems within which delegated authority can be exercised.

Measure the job performance of all organizational members.

Determine the effectiveness of top-management plans and programs.

THE SCOPE OF CONTROL

The scope of all control systems is determined, in large part, by the dominant personal philosophies of managers who design, implement, and review them. At the same time, these philosophies are modified by environmental factors, such as legislation, social values, consumer interests, and competitive practices that also influence the scope of control within an organization. In response to public concern after the Watergate scandal, for example, the U.S. Congress approved expanded control systems designed to prevent graft in political campaigns.

In most business firms, production, purchasing, sales, personnel, research, transportation, and capital funds represent some of the most important areas requiring control. By themselves, however, these areas are not directly controllable. Instead, basic elements within each area are controlled—that is, quality, quantity, time, and costs. Production and marketing goals, for example, can be stated in terms of *quality* standards (meeting various classifications of grade and size), *quantitative* budgets (producing and selling a stated number of units), *time* standards (determining when various operations should be started and completed), and *cost* standards (staying within established cost boundaries). It is important to note that these standards must be measurable. If appropriate measurement is not possible, taking corrective action is difficult and the control process becomes ineffective.

Beyond this discussion, the full scope of the control process can be shown even more completely by dividing it into three separate time phases—precontrol, concurrent, and postcontrol.

Precontrols

When controlling takes place prior to the performance of specific duties or activities, it is called *precontrol*. William Miller, while president of Textron, Inc., best expressed precontrols by stating that good control means that surprise losses of $25 million do not show up some Monday morning. Obviously, the intent here is to prevent or to limit undesirable actions before they occur. As an example, a PERT network can be used by marketing managers to keep advertising programs from being started until new products are actually available and salespeople have the necessary product information, suggested prices, and lists of potential customers. Similarly, policies, procedures, budgets, and time schedules can be very useful to managers in preventing deviations from predetermined standards.

Airlines and road construction companies seek to avoid breakdowns and to prevent accidents through regularly scheduled maintenance programs. In these and many other organizational situations, managers simply cannot wait until things are out of control before taking corrective action. Therefore, preventive controls are used to reduce the occurrence of deviations through good system design.[3]

Concurrent controls

Concurrent controls monitor activities or projects while they are being carried out; thus, the control cycle is much more apparent with these types of controls. Results are measured and compared against standards. When necessary, corrective action is then taken. Employee performance and automatic equipment operations are examples of activities that are usually monitored through concurrent controls.

By checking employee performance, managers determine whether subordinates are accomplishing objectives as planned. At American Airlines, for example, senior vice presidents are evaluated every three months on how well they have achieved 10 priority goals established earlier in the year.[4] If undesirable results are seen, corrective action in the form of guidance and suggestions is taken by the president to bring performance back in line with standards.

In some organizational settings, subordinates have the authority and responsibility to take corrective action on their own. Operating a machine or piloting an airplane often requires such adjustments in performance or speed. Many salespeople also apply their own concurrent controls regarding hours worked and customers contacted. With reference to equipment, thermostats and other automatic devices can make self-adjustments to keep performance within prescribed limits.

As with precontrols, managers using concurrent controls do not have to wait until the end of a designated time period before corrective action can be taken. Correcting deviations as they occur, however, requires meaningful standards and rapid feedback systems that keep

---

[3] R. R. Meredith and T. E. Gibbs, *The Management of Operations* (New York: John Wiley & Sons, 1980), pp. 507–8.

[4] "Competition, Streamlined Management Marks Style of American Airlines Chairman," *The AMBA Executive*, April–May 1978, p. 11.

managers informed on performance. For this reason, instantaneous feedback is essential in many concurrent control systems.

Postcontrols

If evaluation and corrective action take place only after the activity is completed, the time relationship is one of *postcontrol*. Generally, this is the least desirable type of control since performance has already been completed and corrective action cannot improve past results. As expressed through financial statements and other types of reports, controlling after the fact does permit managers to look at undesirable results and make adjustments for future operations.

In most organizations, postcontrols do not exist by themselves. Instead, we usually find them in some combination with precontrols and concurrent controls. Students, for example, apply precontrols when they develop good study habits. Concurrent controls are applied by having early testing programs that indicate acceptable progress. The final grade acquired at the end of the course reflects postcontrols. Likewise, the combination of time-related controls can be seen in a hospital, particularly for surgery patients in the preoperative, operative, and postoperative phases.

STEPS AND PROBLEMS IN THE CONTROL PROCESS

The control process does not operate as smoothly as the logic of the steps might tend to indicate. Major problems often arise, with some being greater than others. Thus, managers are constantly involved in overcoming barriers to effective control in order to maintain the smooth operation of the total process. The following sections present a discussion of the steps in the control process and identify some of the problems associated with each.

Standards as the basis for control

The standards used in controlling can be quality standards, budgets, quotas, objectives, or other desired results that are to some degree measurable. To be most effective, the standards used must also be realistic and acceptable to the people whose performance is evaluated.

Past results or industrial averages are often used as the standards for a particular operation. Such norms may or may not be realistic. For example, monthly overtime pay in the accounting department of a large midwestern railroad had traditionally been no larger than 1 percent of the monthly payroll. This situation changed when records showed that overtime compensation for the current month stood at 8 percent of the payroll. The deviation, however, was not critical because the payroll officer observed that business had been much heavier that month than in the past with freight revenues increasing over 12 percent. As discovered by this railroad, historical standards should not be used as the only basis for evaluating current performance. For most organizations, the search for meaningful standards is extremely important and must consider past, present, and future conditions.

Measuring actual performance

Possibly one of the most difficult steps in the control process is that of measuring performance. A part of the measurement problem lies in the fact that each unit within an organization may use different measures in evaluating performance. This causes the measurement process to range from simple observations by an inspector or supervisor to rather complex reporting systems, such as the one required by the top management of International Telephone and Telegraph. At ITT, monthly progress reports submitted by subsidiaries of the company may total 50 pages or more. President Reagan, on the other hand, prefers that staff members include no more than one or two pages of information in their progress reports. Regardless of the system, however, certain basic conditions are necessary for effective measurement. These include a determination of (1) the specific characteristics to be measured, (2) the accuracy of measurement, and (3) who will use the measurements.[5]

One way to understand the difficulties involved in measuring performance is to consider statements made by students that grades are really not a true measure of what is actually learned in a course. Exams and other measuring devices used in college courses are criticized by many students—and rightly so in some instances. Likewise, factory workers and hospital personnel feel that their productivity is much greater than can be measured by a mere count of items produced or patients served.

In many instances, an exact measurement of the productivity of certain professional and technical personnel is not possible. In this regard, appraising the teaching abilities of college professors is no easy task. Performance is often measured primarily in terms of the number of articles published in refereed journals, papers presented at professional meetings, or books and monographs written during a given time period. This is not to say that there is anything wrong with this approach; but in colleges, as well as in other organizations, measurement often emphasizes those aspects of performance that can be easily quantified.

Management personnel in businesses are generally evaluated against such standards as the level of profits, costs, units produced, or divisional sales. These standards, of course, relate to only portions of the total objectives of an organization and are of a short-term nature. But again, note that they are performance areas that can be easily quantified. Where managerial responsibilities require extensive creativity and conceptual planning, the measurement process becomes more difficult. Furthermore, organizational activities that are intangible, such as public relations, social responsiveness, management development, and employee training, pose additional problems in measurement. Regardless

---

[5] Richard O. Mason and E. Burton Swanson, "Measurement for Management Decision: A Perspective," *California Management Review*, Spring 1979, pp. 70–81.

of these measurement problems, performance must still be continuously evaluated if it is to contribute to managerial effectiveness. Thus, the search for accurate measures of performance is ongoing in virtually all modern organizations.

Comparing actual performance to standards

Once standards have been established and performance measured, the next step is to compare actual performance to established standards. This step is highly important to the total control process. For example, when employees know that their work will be evaluated, they tend to be more careful and exacting in their work. Unfortunately, there are too many instances where managers never get around to making such comparisons. As a result, they never really know whether performance is progressing as planned.

The comparison phase of a control system is shown in Figure 16–2 as part of a feedback loop. In this loop, the sensor is an information-gathering device that measures characteristics of the system. The comparer is a unit that compares information from the sensor against the standard that is stored in some type of memory unit. The activator is the decision-making unit of the loop that activates the appropriate component of the system, depending on what needs to be done and when it must be accomplished.

One of the values of automated control systems (cybernetics) is that comparisons are continuously taking place. The thermostat that regulates the temperature of an oven and the automatic frequency control on an FM radio are examples of control devices that constantly compare performance against predetermined standards.

An application of the automated feedback loop can be seen in the

FIGURE 16–2
Feedback loop

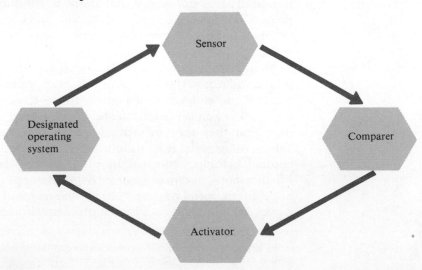

flow of oil through a pipeline. The amount of oil that is moved depends on time and the rate of flow. In order to maintain a predetermined rate of oil flow, a measuring device (sensor) monitors the rate of flow and sends a signal to a control mechanism for comparison. If a significant deviation from the predetermined rate of flow is noted, a mechanism (activator) adjusts the valve to change the rate of oil flow.

To utilize the feedback loop concept in a business system, three factors must be known: (1) the capacity of resources, (2) the volume of operations in the system, and (3) the rate of operating activities taking place within the system. Consider a production control department that has the responsibility for arranging production schedules so that orders will be filled to meet current market demand. By knowing work loads, the available capacity of resources, and the speed of operations, individual orders can be scheduled into the production process to achieve maximum efficiency. Here we see that management is involved in both planning and in comparing actual performance to desired standards.

Importance of timing   Maintaining a balance among resources requires rapid and accurate feedback. If this feedback is not present, comparisons of actual performance to standards are delayed. The result is information lag, the effects of which are similar to what happens when the control units are accidentally switched on an electric blanket for the occupants of a double bed. In this case, if one person gets too cold and turns up the thermostat, the other person will become warmer and may respond by turning the thermostat down. Thus, there is a continued disequilibrium and a significant time lag may develop before temperatures can be brought back into a desired range.

As related to timing, new controls may need to be established if certain control systems are not working effectively. If, for example, mistakes become more frequent in the credit department of a retail store, new work schedules might be established or additional training might be provided. With these changes, the original mistakes may be reduced to the point where they are no longer a major issue. However, other problems may then arise, such as higher training costs or increased employee dissatisfaction with new schedules and tighter controls.

Reducing time in reporting and comparing   Personal observation can sometimes help reduce reporting time, but it is limited by the inability of any person to observe all activities physically. Although a director of nursing can see what is going on while walking through the hospital or visiting with floor nurses, this type of observation does not generally lend itself to a high degree of precision. One way to overcome these limitations is to have employees keep their own records and submit periodic reports. However, this may result in longer reporting times unless computers, telephones, copying machines, or other electronic devices can be used in the reporting process.

The value of computers in reducing reporting times is illustrated by Litton Industries, Inc. The company headquarters receives monthly data from hundreds of profit centers by the eighth working day after the close of each month. Included in the information system are such reports as balance sheets, income statements, cash flows, accounts receivables, inventory levels, employment, debt, lines of credit, and use of capital appropriations. Each report from a profit center contains about 700 figures including product-line costs for labor, materials, overhead, marketing, and general accounting expenses. One very sensitive indicator of possible trouble is the daily comparison report that shows whether a division is using more, or less, cash than budgeted. In order to reduce the number of reports received, each executive office is equipped with a video screen connected to the computer so that executives can obtain and view selected control data.

Evaluating differences between actual performance and standards

Differences between standards and actual performance may be significant and meaningful, or quite unimportant. Determining the level of significance should be the responsibility of the manager in charge of the particular activity being measured. Just as a sales manager should be responsible for determining whether differences between budgeted and actual sales are meaningful, a shop supervisor should determine whether the quality of inputs into a given manufacturing process conforms to standard and what actions should be taken if there are deviations that fall beyond acceptable levels.

At times, a deviation may be so exceptional that it must be handled by someone at a higher level of authority. When this is the case, a manager reports the unusual or extraordinary deviation to a designated superior. Earlier, we referred to this concept as the *exception principle*. In reality, management by exception is the only practical approach for carrying out the control function effectively. Otherwise, top-level executives would find themselves involved in evaluating too many insignificant deviations from standards that could be handled by lower-level managers.

Taking corrective action

The last step in the control process is concerned with taking corrective action when necessary. Such action can result in revised plans, an elimination of defective materials, the training of ineffective employees, or the repair of faulty equipment. In any case, corrective actions can be grouped into two distinct categories: (1) corrections related to performance itself and (2) revisions of the standards against which performance is measured.

Correcting performance and/or plans Correcting actual performance refers to making adjustments in activities or programs in order to obtain desired results. Thus, when production falls behind schedule, corrective action might include the purchase of new equipment, a greater use of overtime, the implementation of a preventive maintenance program, or the purchase of some component parts from subcontractors.

Corrective action may also include revisions of plans. Standards that are appropriate during one period of time may not be adequate at a later date. Conditions change, and the most perceptive of managers can neither anticipate all consequences nor foresee all future events. Similarly, if corrective actions lead to changes in overall plans, it is necessary that corresponding changes be made in derivative plans. For example, if production volume is being reduced because of a decline in sales, other production plans such as those related to material purchases and employee recruitment must also be adjusted.

Additional considerations Other important considerations related to control focus on when corrective action should be taken and who should take it. Generally, corrections should be made as soon as possible after undesirable deviations from standards are noted. The completion time for corrective action will vary, depending on the nature of the action to be taken. While improving supervision and the motivation of employees may take a lot longer than adjusting a piece of equipment or clarifying orders, the longer one waits to make corrections, the less effective the action will be in directing performance toward desired goals.

When performance must be corrected, the manager responsible for results should have the authority to take corrective action. In this way, managers also keep in closer contact with their subordinates and reduce the overall volume of information flow.[6]

COST JUSTIFICATION AND CONTROL

A managerial guide to the selection of control points suggests that we include only those activities where the cost of establishing a control system is less than the benefits to be derived. Obviously, the amount to be spent on controlling must be judged accordingly.

The greater the degree to which preventive controls can be implemented, the less the total cost associated with either concurrent or postcontrols. As with precontrols, the cost of utilizing other types of controls is greatly dependent on initial planning. If, for example, preventive controls are effective in discouraging employee theft, then less money will need to be spent for postcontrols such as polygraph tests. In general, then, the costs associated with the establishment of a control system depend on the objectives to be accomplished, the courses of action to be followed in seeking objectives, and the attitudes of managers and other employees toward control.

Since organizations have multiple goals, they must develop control systems that interact with one another. In this case, each control system

[6] M. J. Jucius, B. A. Deitzer, and W. E. Schlender, *Elements of Managerial Action* (Homewood, Ill.: Richard D. Irwin, 1973), p. 145.

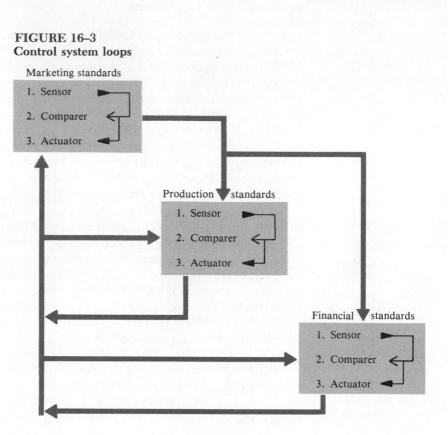

FIGURE 16–3
Control system loops

Marketing standards

1. Sensor
2. Comparer
3. Actuator

Production standards

1. Sensor
2. Comparer
3. Actuator

Financial standards

1. Sensor
2. Comparer
3. Actuator

must be looped to, and connected with, other systems. These interrelationships, as shown in Figure 16–3, indicate that a change in any part of an organization—for example, marketing, production, or finance—can have an impact on other organizational units. Consider the salesperson who may be unable to meet a stated quota because several large customers have been shut down due to strikes. The sales manager is informed of the situation and, in turn, contacts the head of the marketing department. Through this reporting procedure, the production manager is also informed that work schedules may have to be revised. Finally, the finance manager must be prepared to modify budgeted cash flows, expenses, and revenues as they relate to revised plans resulting from the total situation. Through this interactive approach, the entire control system is more fully integrated and the total costs of control can be reduced.

**ADDITIONAL
CONTROL
CONSIDERATIONS**

Operating the control process is a difficult task, and as an organization grows, control systems develop various weaknesses. Some of the reasons for weaknesses include:

Too much emphasis is placed on postcontrols, rather than on controlling activities before, or as, they take place.

Too much time is spent on identifying who is responsible for deviations from standard. Consequently, there is a delay before corrective action can be taken.

As an organization grows, control systems are often designed by staff units. These units may be given the authority to monitor various activities on a continuing basis in order to assist line managers in performing the control function. Many times, however, friction develops between line and staff managers and the system becomes an end in itself with each side forgetting the real purpose of control.[7]

Sometimes there is a tendency to expand control systems beyond key points. When this happens, costs tend to increase along with a volume of paperwork that is not really essential in the accomplishment of objectives.

Since the performance of staff specialists and technicians is hard to measure, evaluating such individuals may be difficult. Portions of this measurement stem from the fact that organizations and individuals have multiple objectives. In addition, there is the problem of decisions that can improve short-term profitability while having negative consequences in the long run.

In many cases, the performance of individuals working in teams cannot be measured separately. Informal control devices, however, can help members of the team identify those who are not doing their share. These techniques should be recognized as powerful forces within an organization's formal control system.

Even though performance is measured properly, the feedback of information may break down. In some instances, managers may not receive the appropriate information needed in time to decide whether or not corrective action is necessary.[8]

Establishing profit goals and measuring their level of attainment is not possible in all organizational units. Thus, measuring contributions to overall objectives is an extremely important factor for top management to consider in defining and measuring performance.[9]

SUMMARY

Control systems in any organization must be upgraded continuously. The feedback of information on actual performance needs to be rapid so that trouble spots can be noted and corrected quickly. A need to receive timely data emphasizes the fact that precontrols and concur-

[7] See Robert T. Golembiewski, *Organizing Men and Power* (Chicago: Rand McNally, 1967).

[8] See Harold Koontz and Robert W. Bradspies, "Managing through Feedforward Control," in *Emerging Concepts in Management*, eds. M. S. Wortman, Jr., and Fred Luthans (New York: Macmillan, 1975), pp. 158–68.

[9] Richard F. Vancil, "What Kind of Management Control Do You Need?" *Harvard Business Review*, (March–April, 1973), pp. 75–86.

rent controls are much more useful than postcontrols. Today, the state of technology permits preventive controls to play a significant role in many organizations. For example, computers and microelectronics can prevent the occurrences of some mistakes while providing immediate access to information on other activities to permit corrective action before deviations become too great.

Future control systems will definitely depend more on computers and other electronic equipment. Regardless of the level of technical sophistication, all control systems must include standards, means for reporting actual performance, systematic evaluations of performance to identify deviations, and provisions for taking corrective action.

KEY TERMS

Concurrent controls: Control systems that focus on activities as they are being performed, allowing deviations to be corrected before an activity has been completed.

Control process: Steps in the management control function that involve checking and comparing performance to established standards and initiating corrective action if necessary to achieve desired goals.

Feedback loop: The part of the control process that provides information on performance to managers as input to "control" decisions.

Exception principle: As related to control, a management concept suggesting that unusual or extraordinary deviations from standards should be reported to higher-level managers for appropriate action.

Postcontrols: Time phased control systems that utilize feedback through measuring, comparing, and noting the need for corrective action after a function or activity is completed.

Precontrols: Control systems that are preventive in nature and are designed to function prior to the performance of specific activities.

QUESTIONS

1. Why is control important to the total management process?
2. What steps are involved in controlling?
3. In what areas of an organization is control needed?
4. Distinguish among precontrols, concurrent controls, and postcontrols.
5. Why are planning and controlling related so closely?
6. Discuss two major problems associated with the measurement of actual performance against predetermined standards.
7. How are the following interrelated: sensor, comparer, activator, and feedback loop?
8. Why is reporting time important to the effectiveness of control? How can reporting times be reduced?
9. Why is the "exception principle" useful?

10. How can one determine whether or not a control system costs more than it is worth?

11. Corrective action can follow two basic courses. What are they?

12. What should be considered when determining who will be responsible for taking corrective action when performance is out of control?

13. What common problems can be expected when implementing a control system?

PROBLEMS

1. "Controlling is really quite simple. After all, managers have authority and with authority they have control over their subordinates." Do you agree with this statement? Explain your answer.

2. The yellow lines painted on the production floor, safety helmets to be put on before entering the plant, and the one-way turnstile allowing people to enter a discount store are examples of precontrol systems that attempt to prevent or keep deviations from happening. Does feedback in these systems tend to be as important as in concurrent controls? Cite some other examples of preventive controls that are used in McDonald's restaurants or at supermarkets.

3. Although the metric measurement by 10s is the most simple and coherent measure that has ever been devised, it is not in general use in the United States, Brunei, Burma, Liberia, and Yemen. Some of the history surrounding our fractions and conversion factors includes: *(a)* In building the Great Egyptian Pyramid of Cheops, the official *cubit* was used—the length of the arm from elbow to fingertip. *(b)* The *mile* was 1,000 double steps by a Roman legionary or 5,000 Roman feet. *(c)* Henry I established the *yard* as the distance from the tip of his royal nose to his fingertips. *(d)* King Edgar, in the 10th century, decreed the *inch* to be the span of the knuckle on his thumb. *(e)* The English standardized the *foot* in the statute books as 36 barleycorns "taken from the middle of the ear" and laid end to end. *(f)* The *six-foot fathom* equaled the span of a Viking's outstretched arms. *(g)* The *acre* was the amount of land plowed by a yoke of oxen in one day.

Could such unwieldy makeshift measures create problems in evaluating performance? From an international perspective, can the United States afford to follow any other alternative than metrication for measurement?

4. More statistics are collected about baseball players than is true for people in most other occupations. Detailed records are published on their times at bat, walks, hits, extra base hits, home runs, strikeouts, putouts, fielding chances, assists, errors, earned run averages, and so forth. Each time a player comes to bat, and almost every time that player handles a ball in the field, performance is observed and recorded.

a. Is such information useful to the team manager in evaluating the performance of players?

b. Can the question "Is A a better ball player than B?" be sufficiently answered by comparing the measured performance of the two players? What other factors do managers look at?

    c. Based on your answer to *b* above, what generalizations can you make about the control process?

    5. Consider the following questions: How much is a four-year-old Chrysler worth? What is one year's depreciation on a brick office building? How should the cost of a maintenance engineer be allocated to several operating departments? How much cash is in the bank?

    a. If you answer these questions in dollar terms, which ones can be measured most accurately?

    b. In general, are the techniques used in measuring business facts as accurate as the instruments used for measuring physical phenomena, such as temperature?

    c. Are there any business assets that cannot be measured accurately in dollars?

    6. The N&T Corporation holds the franchise for 17 fast-service hamburger units in a large midwestern city. Sales for last year were lower than anticipated, but they were spread over more customers than expected. Company profits were also lower than those projected for the year. A recent report shows that labor cost for counter help was 37 percent above budget, and management believes that this factor was the major cause for the low-profit figure.

    To reduce the labor costs for counter help, the company controller suggested that these employees be better disciplined, receive more training, and be subjected to tighter management controls. Mr. James, the operations manager, feels that these employees are as efficient as ever and suggests that the budget for labor costs be adjusted upward. Several of the unit managers see the problem as one resulting from an improper work flow for serving customers during peak periods of the day. With the current work flow, additional part-time employees are needed during these peak periods.

    The company president is quite aware of the fact that events did not go according to plan. However, he is at a loss to know what to do to correct the situation.

    a. What three corrective actions were suggested?

    b. Could part of the problem stem from an inadequate performance of one or more steps in the control process?

    c. How would you approach this problem?

SUGGESTED READINGS

Cammann, C., and D. A. Nadler. "Fit Control Systems to Your Managerial Style." *Harvard Business Review,* January–February 1976, pp. 65–72.

Churchman, C. West, and Philburn Ratoosh, eds. *Measurement: Definition and Theories.* Englewood Cliffs, N.J.: Prentice-Hall, 1967.

Forrester, Jay. *Industrial Dynamics.* Cambridge, Mass.: MIT Press, 1961.

Goetz, B. E. *Management Planning and Control.* New York: McGraw-Hill, 1949.

Lawler, E. E., and J. G. Rhode. *Information and Control in Organizations.* Pacific Palisades, Calif.: Goodyear, 1976.

Livingstone, J. L. "Management Controls and Organizational Performance," in *Dimensions in Modern Management,* edited by Patrick E. Connor. Boston: Houghton Mifflin, 1974.

McFarland, D. E. "Planning and Control," in *Supervisory Management: Tools and Techniques,* edited by M. G. Newport. St. Paul: West Publishing, 1976, pp. 57–69.

Mockler, R. J. "The Corporate Control Job: Breaking the Mold." *Business Horizons,* December 1970, pp. 73–77.

_____. *The Management Control Process.* New York: Appleton-Century-Crofts, 1972.

Newman, W. H. *Constructive Control.* Englewood Cliffs, N.J.: Prentice-Hall, 1975.

Ouchi, W. G. "The Relationship between Organization Structure and Organizational Control." *Administrative Science Quarterly,* March 1977, pp. 95–113.

Papathanasis, T. "Standards and the Firm." *Regional Business Review,* June 1980, pp. 34–38.

Strong, E. P., and R. D. Smith. *Management Control Models.* New York: Holt, Rinehart & Winston, 1968.

Thatcher, R. H. "Designing a Productivity Control Process." *Business Horizons,* December 1975, pp. 62–68.

Weaver, K. F. "How Soon Will We Measure in Metric?" *National Geographic,* August 1977, pp. 287–94.

17

APPLICATIONS
OF CONTROL

PURPOSE

In 1885, the five Ball brothers started the glass jar manufacturing company that bears their name. At that time, cost and financial controls were general rules of thumb that focused on maintaining high-quality products at low prices. Management decisions were based on personal judgment, experience, native shrewdness, and intuition. In fact, the Ball brothers might have been suspicious of anyone walking into their organization talking about systematic cost controls, break-even analysis, ratio analysis, rate of return on investment, or management audits.

Applications of control have changed dramatically over the years. Those of 1885 are no longer adequate for dealing with increased governmental regulations, a separation of ownership and management, the changing role of business in society, increased domestic and foreign competition, and a host of other factors. To be most responsive in a world of rapid change, managers must place added emphasis on the controlling function. The purpose of this chapter is to discuss major applications of control that reflect this growing emphasis.

OBJECTIVES

1. To emphasize the need for control that accompanies rapid organizational growth and change.

2. To present specific controls useful in evaluating marketing performance.

3. To discuss scheduling, order control, and quality control as specific applications of production control.

4. To show the importance of overall cost controls to organizational survival.

5. To examine break-even analysis, variable budgeting, comparative statements, financial ratios, and other specific financial controls.

Control techniques in all organizations are important managerial concerns. If a single area such as inventory turnover is of primary concern, techniques that monitor inventory levels will receive maximum attention. In other instances, major attention may be directed to quality, labor costs, or advertising expenditures. The specialized control techniques that result from this attention are as numerous as the organizations where they are applied. Obviously, then, this chapter can present only the more widely known techniques that assist in controlling performance in the major areas of marketing, production, finance, and personnel.

MARKETING CONTROLS

The business organization finds its alpha and omega in marketing since the business starts by identifying customer needs and ends with products or services to satisfy those needs.[1] In this respect, marketing is concerned with creating and satisfying consumer demand by facilitating exchanges. To be most successful in this role, the marketing function must match all products or services to consumer demand while identifying those which make the greatest contribution to profits. An evaluation of sales represents one method for determining the success of the marketing function in meeting these objectives.

Sales control

As a measure of consumer acceptance, sales probably represent the best single indicator of market performance. To monitor sales most effectively, however, various standards of performance must first be established. With such standards, realistic measurement, evaluation, and corrective action can then take place. While there are many specific techniques for achieving sales control, this discussion will consider only sales areas, market penetration, product mix, sales personnel, and types of customers.

Sales areas On some periodic basis, marketing managers must assess the performance of sales areas in terms of units sold and total dollar sales. In such assessments, each sales area (whether identified geographically, by product, or by customers) should be self-contained if the control process is to function effectively. By evaluating the data accumulated from daily or weekly sales reports, managers can quickly determine how each sales area is performing in relation to established goals.

It must also be noted that unforeseen changes in the business community (employment, competition), combined with changes in the composition of each sales area, can sometimes make standards unrealistic. Thus, there is a need to review the sales potential of each area on a continuous basis. If standards are found to be realistic, managers

---

[1] E. Jerome McCarthy, *Basic Marketing: A Managerial Approach*, 6th ed. (Homewood, Ill.: Richard D. Irwin, 1978), pp. 5–8.

can seek to improve sales performance by (1) hiring more sales staff, (2) developing greater enthusiasm among salespeople, (3) reassigning salespeople among the areas, (4) adjusting the level of sales compensation, (5) changing pricing policies, or (6) promoting more vigorously in areas of poor performance.

Market penetration   A further identification of goals for sales areas involves a determination of the portion of a potential geographic market that is to be sought by a company. This is referred to as *market penetration* or *share of the market* and is expressed as a percentage of company sales to total potential sales for a given area. As a control device, market penetration allows managers to determine whether a decline in sales is due to unforeseen events or to poor performance of the total marketing program.

When comparing actual market penetration to established standards, one sometimes notes that sales areas producing the highest volume do not have the highest market share. Thus, it is necessary to look beyond the figures on market penetration in conducting a thorough evaluation of each sales area. For example, how long has the company been in each area? What are the marketing costs for the various areas? Is the market share increasing or decreasing? Who are the chief competitors? What are the future plans in each area? These and other questions must be answered before any evaluation of a given sales area can be considered realistic.

Product mix   With new products appearing on the market each day, data about the performance of specific products have become increasingly necessary in sales control. Unless such sales data are available on some periodic basis, it is extremely difficult to spot shifts in consumer demand that may be taking place.

Control data by product, however, does not necessarily require that total sales be broken down for each individual product or product group. Since the acquisition of such data could cost more than the benefits derived from its use in the control process, one normally finds that only the highest profit earning products and/or products with the largest percentage of sales are considered. The procedure is to express sales of these products or product categories as a percentage of total sales for the year to date and for other selected years. In this manner, managers can easily spot any products that are falling behind in sales.

Sales personnel   In controlling sales, it is also necessary to consider the performance of sales personnel. Reports submitted periodically by salespeople are useful in this regard. When such reports include more than just dollar sales, they are a means for identifying the number of calls made, number of orders received, promotional work undertaken, potential customers contacted, miles traveled, extent of sales area covered, and an assessment of future business conditions and market potential for the area.

Summary forms that can be completed quickly by sales personnel are a definite aid when desired data are reported on a scheduled basis. While the types of reports and the amount of information requested will vary, some standardization of these forms is required in any given organization if they are to be of maximum value for control purposes.

Type of customer The percentage of sales by type of customer is also an important marketing control. In this case, wholesale and retail are two common categories in reporting sales by customers. If there are a large number of customers, the manager may need to develop a reporting system for only the most important ones. Where the number of important customers is relatively small, continuous and detailed information on such accounts is even more essential in determining whether business is being shifted to competitors. In short, customers that make the greatest contribution to profits must be included within the marketing control system.

Marketing cost controls

Controlling marketing costs is one of the best ways of measuring the efficiency of this function. By utilizing cost controls, managers may spot products and customers that contribute to sales volume while actually reducing the profit picture. In the short run, for example, total marketing costs do not have to be covered. Thus, weak products or customers may be carried temporarily when managers feel that it is wise to retain them. But since all costs must be covered in the long run, managers must be aware of the more profitable opportunities to which marketing efforts might be shifted. In this sense, marketing effectiveness implies that marketing strategies are directed toward an optimum achievement of established goals through the most efficient utilization of organizational resources.

The allocation of marketing costs by products, customers, channels of distribution, or territories is difficult and, in many cases, quite arbitrary. For example, when salespeople are involved with more than one product line, the assignment of marketing costs is especially difficult. Regardless of this difficulty, however, an analysis of marketing costs provides management with the data required in determining profit differentials among products.

PRODUCTION CONTROL

Whether religious, governmental, educational, or business, the production function is performed in all organizations.[2] In this sense, production refers to the physical creation of goods and the performance of services that may range from manufacturing hairpins to the auditing of accounts receivable for a hospital. Specifically, *production can be defined as the creation of utility to satisfy human needs.* One way

---

[2] Richard B. Chase and Nicholas J. Aquilano, *Production and Operations Management: A Life Cycle Approach* (Homewood, Ill.: Richard D. Irwin, 1981), pp. 5–10.

FIGURE 17–1
Systems view of the production function

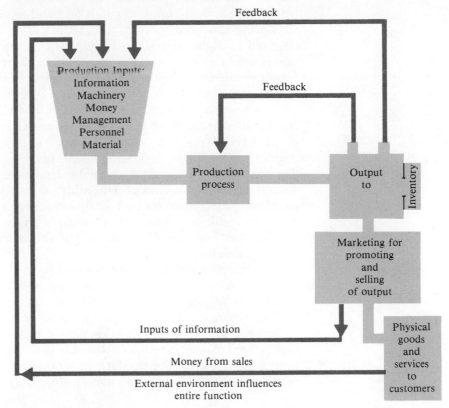

of viewing the entire production function is through the systems approach, as presented in Figure 17–1. *Inputs* of material, money, personnel, information, equipment, and facilities are brought together by management. By proper *processing* they are eventually transformed into a final product or service *(outputs)*.

Production controls are essential in maintaining a proper balance among the marketing, production, and finance functions. Production scheduling, order control, and quality control are three common production control techniques.

Production scheduling

The scheduling function can be viewed as an assignment of calendar and clock times for beginning and completing production activities. When operations are not going according to schedule, the production manager initiates corrective action to minimize any delays beyond established completion dates.

When a company manufactures for stock, production scheduling depends on the sales forecast, the availability of raw materials, and expected variations in sales volume. Since good production scheduling implies that the company does not "stock-out" of essential items and never has too many finished goods on hand, inventories must be built up during slow sales periods and orders filled from inventory when demand is high. Of course, keeping the warehouse full of finished goods would meet the goal of never being short of goods, but holding too large an inventory can be quite costly. Similarly, too few items in inventory can also result in lost sales.

In order to understand the production scheduling concept, consider the situation at the Neat-Trim Lawn Mower Company, a manufacturer of power mowers. The sale of mowers is highly seasonal, with the majority of company shipments taking place in April, May, and June. The marketing department estimates that sales for next year will be 48,000 mowers, to be shipped monthly, as shown in Figure 17–2. One problem facing management is determining a production schedule that will result in output levels sufficient to avoid stock-outs at peak periods, yet low enough to minimize the costs of carrying finished goods in inventory.

The sales budget does not necessarily represent the production schedule since maximum production capacity of the plant is limited to 7,000 units per month. The schedule, as developed in Figure 17–2, allows management to achieve its goals of having mowers available to meet spring demand while keeping the plant operating at a fairly stable level. Since inventories can be built up during the first four months of the year, the production schedule is more level than shipments. The result is that the average monthly inventory throughout

FIGURE 17–2
Expected sales and production schedule for next year, Neat-Trim Lawn Mower Company

Month	No. of mowers shipped	Accumulated shipments	Production	Accumulated production	Closing inventory
December	100	100	1,000	1,000	900
January	500	600	2,000	3,000	2,400
February	1,000	1,600	6,000	9,000	7,400
March	2,000	3,600	7,000	16,000	12,400
April	8,000	11,600	7,000	23,000	11,400
May	10,000	21,600	7,000	30,000	8,400
June	12,000	33,600	7,000	37,000	3,400
July	7,000	40,600	5,000	42,000	1,400
August	4,000	44,600	3,000	45,000	400
September	2,000	46,600	1,500	46,500	−100
October	1,000	47,600	1,100	47,600	0
November	400	48,000	400	48,000	0

the year is 4,000 units per month, which is equivalent to average monthly sales.

September shows a negative 100 units in closing inventory. This, of course, is not possible. It simply means that the production manager plans to be short 100 units in meeting current shipments. The assumption here is that sales will not be lost, even though the orders received in late September cannot be shipped until the first part of October.

If production during the year does not meet this time schedule, it is the responsibility of the production control manager to make any necessary adjustments. To a large extent, then, scheduling is involved with planning; but once schedules are implemented, they become standards for evaluating actual performance in the overall process of production control.

Job order control

Production scheduling is extremely important when companies produce for stock. Some firms, however, are custom producers and schedule output only after orders are received. Companies in the space industry and in airframe manufacturing are considered job-lot manufacturers since each job is planned and controlled individually. In such organizations, order scheduling is necessary in determining when individual parts must be completed and available for subassembly processes. By knowing the completion dates for all orders, the production manager can determine when items are behind schedule in order to initiate any corrective action that might be required. In this regard, computers are quite useful in calculating what must be done on a specific date in order to complete a job on time.

Another important consideration is to determine whether there are sufficient machines available to complete all required operations on time. Such determinations are normally made through the use of load charts that indicate whether machines are overscheduled or underscheduled. As discussed in an earlier chapter, one of the management control techniques that utilizes time as a common denominator for the scheduling of production equipment is called the Gantt Chart. Other scheduling techniques covered in Chapter 5 are PERT and the Critical Path Method.

Quality control

Beyond production scheduling, quality control is a major consideration of all organizations offering a product or service to customers. To most consumers, of course, quality is a relative matter in terms of the price they are willing to pay. For example, a person may buy a very inexpensive wristwatch with the knowledge that it will not be as accurate as one selling for a higher price. Even here, however, the customer still expects the best possible performance from the watch relative to its price.

Inspection and control   The inspection of products ensures their quality by comparing them to established standards—appearance, performance, items in a package, weight, and so forth. Such comparison may take the form of looking at the product, measuring it, or possibly testing it.

In oil refining, sample cases of oil are weighed periodically. If their weight is not the same as the predetermined standard weight, these cases are taken out of production and not placed in inventory. In addition, the equipment used in filling cans will be checked to see if it is out of adjustment. Inspection, therefore, goes beyond just removing nonstandard products from inventory. It also attempts to stop any further production of imperfect items.

Statistical quality control   Statistical quality control (SQC) was first introduced in 1924 and relates, in part, to the problem of how many items of a larger number should be inspected to determine a probability that the total number conforms to quality standards.[3] In many instances, it is impossible to test each item of a total group. For example, an entire truckload of wheat taken to the mill cannot be tested for moisture and foreign matter without incurring extremely high costs. Also, if testing destroys the product, sampling becomes a necessity. When automatic or semiautomatic equipment is involved in the manufacturing process, 100 percent inspection of parts may result in higher costs than no inspection at all. Thus, management may find that it is much more economical to inspect only samples. Without SQC, however, there is no assurance that a given sample size will be representative of an entire lot. Thus, managers must rely on this technique to determine the probability that a sample size will yield reliable results.

Normal curve distribution   In the production of identical products, the theory behind a sample is that the size of each individual item will vary to some degree. Even though some items will be smaller and some larger than others, most of the items will tend to fall around the average (mean size). In sampling it is assumed that the spread or dispersion of the measurements of individual items from the sample mean is about the same as for the entire population of items. Taking a large sample we find that the distribution of items would tend to approximate a normal or bell-shaped curve, as noted in Figure 17–3. The curve is actually the plotting of a frequency distribution in which the number, or frequency, of items is plotted on the vertical axis and the size of the items on the horizontal axis. It is possible, however, for the curve to be skewed to one side, and when this is the case, the frequency distribution is not normal and SQC cannot be utilized.

In Figure 17–3, the solid line in the center is the mean of the sample. The area to the right of the mean indicates that one half of the items is larger than the mean, and the area to the left of the mean represents

---

[3] W. A. Shewhart, *Economic Control of Quality on Manufactured Products* (Princeton: Van Nostrand Reinhold, 1931).

FIGURE 17–3
Normal curve distribution

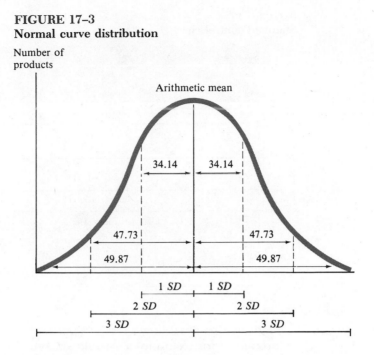

Number of
products

Arithmetic mean

34.14   34.14

47.73   47.73

49.87   49.87

1 *SD*   1 *SD*

2 *SD*   2 *SD*

3 *SD*   3 *SD*

the other half that is smaller than the mean. The standard deviation (SD) is also shown, which is a standard measurement of dispersion (the spread of individual items from the mean). As a standard, it represents a specific percentage of the items under the normal curve. For example, one standard deviation to the right of the mean represents 34.14 percent of the data and one standard deviation to the left of the mean also equals 34.14 percent of the data. Thus, one standard deviation to the left and one to the right of the mean equals approximately 68.28 percent of the data under the normal curve. For three standard deviations both to the left and right of the mean, approximately 99.74 percent of the data is under the normal curve. These relationships hold true as long as the curve is bell shaped, regardless of what values the mean and the standard deviation may assume.

The size of sample It is important to note that the size of a sample does not have to be extremely large, even in lots that are of considerable size. Large samples are, of course, more reliable than smaller ones, but they are not proportionately better. In SQC the objective is to achieve better quality control with a minimum of inspection costs. By increasing a sample size from 400 to 600, the sample is larger, but the increase in reliability is often so very small that it may not justify the additional cost of collecting and analyzing the additional items.[4]

---

[4] See James B. Dilworth, *Production and Operations Management* (New York: Random House, 1979), pp. 345–46.

FIGURE 17–4
Standard control chart

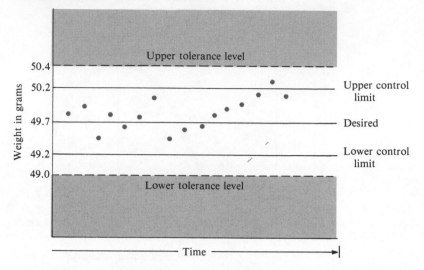

Many companies follow a straight percentage figure for various types of products. For example, a sample size could be 2 percent for parts from stamping machines, 5 percent for machine parts, and 10 percent for certain handmade items. Other companies follow specially prepared formulas to determine the sample size that should be taken in order to obtain a specific degree of reliability at a certain level of probability.[5] Another approach in sampling is to take small samples—5 to 25 observations—on a periodic basis. These results are then plotted on the control chart to observe their measured qualities.

Statistical quality control charts In order to facilitate the quality control process, control charts are developed as the final step in SQC. Figure 17–4 shows the upper and lower control limits for the filling of coffee jars by weight. The limits are established at plus and minus three standard deviations. When small samples are periodically taken, the average measurement of the individual items in the sample is plotted on the chart for the specific time period. Acceptable measures fall between the upper and lower control levels. By observing successive measurements, an overall pattern or trend of performance is indicated. In Figure 17–4, we see that the 15th observation is above the upper control limit. With this reading, the manager selects one of two alternative hypotheses:

Hypothesis A—The machine is still operating correctly, and the observation is just a rare chance event.

---

[5] For information on determining sample size, see Joseph G. Van Matre and Glenn H. Gilbreath, *Statistics for Business and Economics* (Plano, Tex.: Business Publications, 1980), pp. 244–54.

Hypothesis B—The machine filling the jars is out of control due to some assignable cause, such as a malfunction. Therefore, the process must be shut down to avoid waste.

If Hypothesis B is accepted, an investigation will take place immediately to find and correct whatever is wrong. This aspect of control is generally referred to as *management by exception*. Even if Hypothesis B is accepted, however, there is still a slight chance that nothing is wrong. Yet, it is important to recognize that the measures rose steadily from the 8th to the 15th periods. By the 13th or 14th period, one should have questioned if the process was really operating correctly, since the chances of getting an upward pattern for 6 consecutive observations randomly is two to the sixth power or 1 out of 64.

INVENTORY CONTROL

Production and marketing managers are constantly involved with inventory problems. In fact, many companies tie up more capital in inventories than in buildings or equipment. For example, inventories at the Bendix Corporation in 1980 were valued at $890 million while land, buildings, and equipment netted $706 million.[6] Thus, inventories not only represent a major dollar investment, but they are also costly to manage since some large firms may stock and keep records for 50,000 or more different items.

Primarily, managers are faced with two related inventory problems: (1) What quantity should be purchased when an order is placed? That is, what is the most economical quantity to order? (2) When should an order be placed (reorder point) in relation to existing inventory levels? Before discussing these issues, however, it is necessary to understand the costs associated with inventories.

Types of inventory costs

A major objective of inventory control is to minimize inventory costs. Basically, there are two costs that must be considered—*carrying costs* and *order costs*. Carrying costs are those incurred to maintain inventories and include such items as interest, taxes, obsolescence, deterioration, shrinkage, insurance, storage, handling, and depreciation. Total inventory carrying costs may range from 10 to 50 percent of inventory value per year with 15 to 25 percent being average. The significance of these costs can be seen by referring back to figures previously cited for the Bendix Corporation. Since that organization had 30 percent of its assets in inventories, a 25 percent carrying cost would be equivalent to a 7.5 percent return on total assets if all inventories could be eliminated.

Order costs include all costs from the selection of vendors to the final paper work that closes a transaction. Basically, they consist of salaries and supplies used in (1) preparing requisitions, (2) analyzing

---

[6] *Bendix Annual Report 1980* (Southfield, Mich.: The Bendix Corporation, 1980), p. 28.

FIGURE 17–5
Relationship between ordering and carrying costs

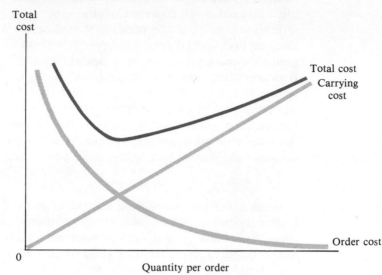

and selecting vendors, (3) writing purchase orders, (4) following up on orders, (5) receiving, inspecting, and storing materials, and (6) keeping proper inventory records and completing the final paper work.[7]

To minimize order costs, inventory kept on hand must be increased. Yet, by minimizing order costs, inventory carrying costs increase due to the larger average inventory that must be maintained. On the other hand, to hold down carrying costs requires more frequent ordering and results in higher ordering costs. An optimum course of action, then, is to find a balance between the two costs so that the total costs associated with inventory are at a minimum; see Figure 17–5.

Economic order quantity

Economic order quantity (EOQ) represents the size of order that minimizes total annual ordering costs and inventory carrying costs.[8] Two common approaches for determining the EOQ are (1) a tabular solution (iterative process) and (2) a mathematical formula.

Tabular solution to economic order quantity Assume that a plant manager uses 2,500 units of raw materials during the year costing $1 per unit. Order cost is $5 each time an order is placed, and the inventory carrying cost is 10 percent of the unit cost, or 10 cents per unit. By considering the costs associated with placing one order per year, two orders, then three, and so on, a manager can determine

---

[7] Elezer Naddor, *Inventory Systems* (New York: John Wiley and Sons, 1966), p. 35.
[8] For a more complete discussion of EOQ for beginning students, see R. I. Levin and C. A. Kirkpatrick, *Quantitative Approaches to Management* (New York: McGraw-Hill, 1978), chaps. 7–8.

the optimum size of order that will result in the lowest possible total inventory cost.

The cost data in Figure 17–6 indicate that five orders of 500 units each should be placed during the year since this is the point at which total inventory cost is at a minimum. The figure also shows that at five orders per year carrying costs and order costs are exactly equal. By increasing the number of orders, carrying costs go down, but ordering costs go up. When the two costs are equal, total inventory cost per year is at a minimum.

As concerns EOQ, we must also recognize that minimum inventory costs do not always provide the most realistic answer to the question of order quantities. In our illustration, a manager could order four, five, or six times a year with a negligible difference in cost. Thus, finding the space to store 500 items versus 416 is a more critical factor than the slight increase in total inventory cost. Or, if it is felt that the price of a product will increase, an order of 625 items may be more meaningful than the saving of $1.20 in total inventory cost. Consequently, when differences in total cost are not critical, deviations from the lowest possible cost are acceptable in light of subjective factors, such as those noted above, that cannot be built into the EOQ model.

Economic order quantity formula   The EOQ formula is a simple mathematical expression used to determine the minimum total incremental cost. The equation is given below:

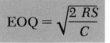

$$EOQ = \sqrt{\frac{2\,RS}{C}}$$

FIGURE 17–6
Tabular method in identifying the economic order quantity

Number of orders per year	Size of order	Average inventory*	Inventory carrying cost	Order cost	Total cost
1	2,500	1,250	$125.00	$ 5.00	$130.00
2	1,250	625	62.50	10.00	72.50
3	833	416	41.60	15.00	56.60
4	625	312	31.20	20.00	51.20
5	500	250	25.00	25.00	50.00
6	416	208	20.80	30.00	50.80
7	357	178	17.80	35.00	52.80

Note:
Annual usage = 2,500 units.
Order cost = $5 per order.
Inventory carrying cost = 10% or $.10 per unit per year.

* Average inventory is determined by dividing order quantity by two. On the average, only one-half of the order will be in stock from the time it is received until the receipt of another order.

460

FIGURE 17–7
Inventory level with constant usage and lead time (with safety stock)

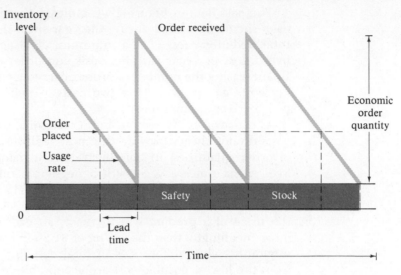

when R = annual requirement in units, S = order cost per order, and C = inventory carrying cost per unit per year.

Returning to the problem previously illustrated, we see that when R = 2,500 units, S = \$5, and C = \$.10, the EOQ can be determined quite rapidly:

$$EOQ = \sqrt{\frac{2(2,500)(\$5)}{\$.10}} = \sqrt{250,000} = 500 \text{ units}$$

Reorder points   Assuming a constant usage rate and a constant interval between the time goods are ordered and received (known as lead time), *the reorder point is the placing of a certain size order at a point in time that permits a shipment to arrive and replenish inventory before existing stocks dwindle to zero.* The reorder point is determined by using the following equation:

$$\frac{\text{Reorder}}{\text{point}} = \text{Usage rate } (U) \times \text{Lead time } (L) + \text{Safety stock } (S)$$

To illustrate the equation, assume a usage rate of 200 units per month, a lead time of 1.5 months, and a safety stock of 100 units.[9] The reorder point would be calculated as 400 units—(200 × 1.5 + 100). Realistically, however, usage rates and lead times vary due to changes in demand, strikes, power failures, and so forth. In emergency situations when shortages are likely to occur, many companies build in a buffer or safety stock, as shown in Figure 17–7.

---

[9] Usage rate and lead time must be expressed in the same time increment.

Even though reorder points can be calculated carefully with a knowledge of past practices combined with current and future performance data, stock-outs and excessive inventories can still occur. Generally, these problems are due to usage rates and lead times that do not conform to those usually observed. In any event, these factors represent added uncertainties with which managers must deal in controlling inventory costs.

OVERALL COST CONTROLS

The control of costs is as essential to the survival of an organization as a strong demand for its products or services. In fact, the control of costs is a good indication of how well an organization is being managed. By controlling overall costs, managers are able to gain an insight into the actual health of their operations.

Many small business misfortunes are not the result of an inability to produce or to market goods but a failure to monitor and evaluate costs. Thus, while purchasing, manufacturing, and selling are important, the control of costs is crucial in determining the success or failure of an organization. Two techniques helpful in this respect are break-even analysis and variable budgeting.

Break-even analysis

One of the most common approaches for portraying cost, volume, and profit relationships is to construct a break-even chart, such as that shown in Figure 17–8. The chart shows the volume or level of operation at which an organization breaks even. This is the point where total revenue is exactly equal to total cost.

FIGURE 17–8
Break-even chart

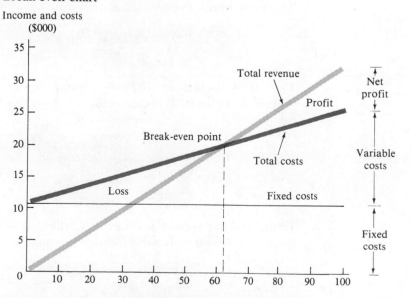

Income and costs
($000)

Potential sales volume (percent)

The five basic elements involved in understanding break-even analysis are revenues, costs, profit equation, break-even point, and contribution margin. Revenue from sales is shown in Figure 17–8 as a straight line through the origin. The line assumes that any quantity may be sold at the market price.

Costs for our purposes are classified into two major categories of fixed and variable. Total fixed costs (rent, utilities, insurance, interest, depreciation, management salaries) stay relatively the same regardless of sales volume. On the chart, fixed costs are shown as a horizontal straight line. Variable costs (cost of goods sold, commissions, delivery, supplies) increase directly with the level of sales or production. Therefore, at zero volume, total variable costs are zero and rise linearly as volume increases.

The basic relationship among costs, sales, and profits can be viewed in the profit equation:

$$\text{Profit } (P) = \text{Total revenue } (TR) - \text{Total variable costs } (TVC) - \text{Total fixed cost } (TFC)$$
$$\text{or } P = TR - (TVC + TFC) \tag{1}$$

The point at which total variable and fixed costs equal sales is called the break-even point (BEP). At the BEP, all costs are covered and profits are zero.

Since variable costs are always considered directly proportionate to sales, they represent a constant percentage of sales. Assume, for example, that variable costs represent 60 percent of sales. With sales of $100,000, variable costs are then $60,000 ($100,000 × .60 = $60,000). The basic break-even equation can now be written as follows:

$$\text{Sales at BEP} = \text{Variable cost as a percentage of sales} \times \text{Sales at the BEP} + TFC \tag{2}$$

Thus, if fixed costs are $40,000, variable costs are 60 percent of sales, and sales at the BEP is unknown (x), then the break-even point is as follows:

$$x = .60 \ (x) + \$40,000$$
$$1x - .60 \ (x) = \$ \ 40,000$$
$$.40 \ (x) = \$ \ 40,000$$
$$\text{Sales at BEP} = \$100,000$$

To find the break-even point in units, divide the $100,000 by the price, which is $10. Or, solve the following equation:

$$\text{BEP in units} = \frac{TFC}{\text{Price} - VC \text{ per unit}} \tag{3}$$

With the previous data, we find the BEP is as follows:

$$\frac{\$40,000}{\$10 - \$6} = \frac{\$40,000}{\$4} = 10,000 \text{ units}$$

The difference between revenue and variable costs is called contribution margin. For example, if an item sells for $20 and the variable cost per unit is 60 percent ($12), then the difference of $8 is a contribution toward covering fixed costs. When the margin is greater than the level of fixed costs, the additional amount represents profit.

The fixed cost line noted in Figure 17–8 does not change as sales increase. However, since variable costs do increase with sales volume, they are added to fixed costs to arrive at total costs. Thus, at 80 percent volume, total costs would include variable costs of $11,700 plus fixed costs of $11,000, totaling $22,700. The break-even point (BEP) is reached at $20,000 in sales and 61.5 percent of volume. If sales drop below this point a loss occurs, while sales above the BEP produce a profit.

While break-even analysis is an important tool for projecting cost and profit relationships, it is not without some limitations. It must be recognized, for example, that the break-even chart is a static type of analysis involving a fixed set of assumptions. In reality, cost relationships are not always linear. Fixed costs, for instance, may be characterized more accurately as a series of stair steps, rather than a straight horizontal line. Consequently, costs and revenues may shift in such a way that projections based only on past data can be misleading.

Under dynamic economic conditions, costs, sales, and volume relationships are also likely to change. Thus, to provide a better picture of these relationships, it is sometimes necessary to develop a separate break-even chart for each different set of conditions.

Variable budgeting   Since changes in environmental conditions are common, variable budgeting becomes an important managerial control technique. Such budgets provide greater accuracy in determining how costs will change if output varies from that which was planned. To understand this point, the concepts of marginal cost and the nonproportional relationship between profits and output must be examined.

Marginal cost concept   *The additional cost incurred from selling or producing an extra unit of output is called marginal cost.* Applications of marginalism to production and marketing can be seen quite easily: a plant manager is interested in the cost of producing additional units, while the marketing manager seeks to identify the costs associated with selling an additional product line, adding a new channel of distribution, or hiring a new salesperson.

The marginal cost of producing, servicing, or marketing one more unit of output is the increase in the variable portion of total costs. Thus, if it costs $280 to produce 10 units of a product and $290 to produce 11 units, the marginal cost is $10 for the 11th unit.

FIGURE 17–9
Variable budget data—Food Service Department, Havenwood Convalescence Center

Items	Low volume	High volume	Difference
Patient/care days	2,000	5,000	3,000
Labor and food costs			
Total	$6,250	$11,950	$5,700
Fixed costs			
Portion of total	2,450	2,450	—
Variable costs			
Portion of total	3,800	9,500	5,700
Marginal cost	$1.90	$1.90	—

Nonproportional relationship between profits and sales   When sales increase by $1,000, profits do not increase by an equal amount since a portion of each sales dollar must cover variable costs. To evaluate performance properly, the manager needs to know how much costs should increase when the volume of sales changes. This can be accomplished through the use of variable budgeting.

Developing a variable budget   Consider a situation at the Havenwood Convalescence Center where the administrator is evaluating the performance of the food service manager. One problem in evaluating this person's performance stems from the fact that monthly patient care days vary. Thus, without a sliding scale of costs for different levels of operation, the administrator has difficulty in determining the efficiency of the food service department.

To overcome this problem, the administrator developed labor and food cost figures for both low- and high-volume operations based on patient care days. The data assume that low-volume patient care days would not be below 2,000, and that 5,000 would represent a high volume. Cost figures for the two volumes are shown in Figure 17–9, and a graphic presentation of the data is noted in Figure 17–10.

Assume that the center provided 3,000 patient care days for the past month and that actual expenses in the food service department were $9,400. With the aid of a variable budget, the administrator can determine the efficiency of the department. Referring to Figure 17–10, we see that labor and food costs for 3,000 patient care days should be $8,150. The algebraic solution to the problem is: $2,450 (fixed costs) + 1.90 (marginal cost) × 3,000 (patient care days). Thus, actual expenses were $1,250 over budget. The administrator must now evaluate the variance and take corrective action as needed.

OVERALL FINANCIAL CONTROLS

Today, uncertainties in the business world have affected the nature of the stock market, accounting practices, and international monetary stability. As a result, the role of financial management in business orga-

FIGURE 17–10
Graphic presentation of a variable budget—Food Service Department, Havenwood Convalescence Center

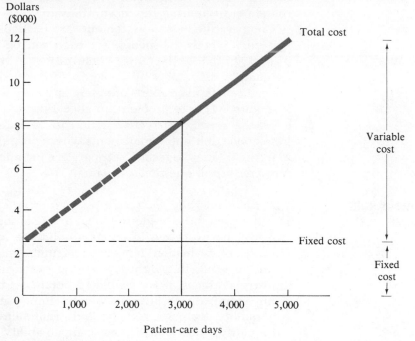

Source: Figure 17–9.

nizations has expanded to provide assistance in planning and controlling all operations of the business enterprise.[10]

Several techniques have been developed that help managers evaluate financial activities. Three of these overall financial control techniques are (1) comparative operating statements, (2) financial ratios, and (3) du Pont's system of return on investment.

Comparative statements

A common and valuable technique for maintaining overall financial control is provided through the use of comparative financial statements. Balance sheets and income statements represent the comparative statements utilized most often.

Balance sheet *The comparative balance sheet lists the assets, liabilities, and proprietorship of an organization for two or more dates.* Thus, the financial status of the organization can be compared over different operating periods allowing managers to identify those financial aspects of total operations that are contributing to, or detracting from, overall financial stability.

---

[10] See J. F. Weston and E. E. Brigham, *Essentials in Managerial Finance* (Hinsdale, Ill.: Dryden Press, 1979).

Income statement   The components of the income statement are revenues (sales), expenses, and net income. These components provide managers with categorized data so that controls can be applied to those areas requiring the most attention.

Comparative income statements are particularly useful for controlling units where the income for each can be computed in terms of its contribution to the entire organization. Furthermore, by including percentage differences in the comparative income statement, managers can isolate even more precisely any area where corrective action is required. Due to problems in allocating some overhead costs, however, the specific corrective action to be taken is not always clear. For service and staff departments where output is difficult to measure in terms of tangible results, comparative income statements for control purposes are of questionable value.

Financial ratio analysis

A financial ratio shows the relative value of one item to another. Data for such ratios are found in an organization's financial statements and may be expressed in either absolute terms or percentages. For purposes of evaluation, however, no single financial ratio is sufficient in and of itself. But, by using several ratios and comparing them to industry averages, it is possible to obtain a rather complete picture of an organization's financial health. Four categories of such ratios are liquidity, leverage, activity, and profitability.

Liquidity ratios   Ratios measuring an ability to pay short-term obligations are called liquidity ratios. Of these, the *current ratio* measures the extent to which short-term liabilities are covered by assets that can be turned into cash during the period through which these liabilities must be met.

$$\text{Current ratio} = \frac{\text{Current assets}}{\text{Current liabilities}}$$

Another liquidity check is the *acid-test* or quick ratio. This ratio indicates the ability to pay current liabilities without relying on the sale of inventories.

$$\text{Acid-test ratio} = \frac{\text{Current assets} - \text{Inventory}}{\text{Current liabilities}}$$

Leverage ratios   These ratios measure the extent to which an organization has been capitalized by debt. One such ratio that portrays the contribution of creditors to an organization's financing is the *debt ratio* that shows total debt to total assets.

$$\text{Debt ratio} = \frac{\text{Total debt}}{\text{Total assets}}$$

The *times-interest earned* ratio indicates the amount by which earnings can decline before the organization becomes unable to pay interest expenses. Income before taxes is calculated after interest charges are deducted from operating profit.

$$\text{Times-interest earned ratio} = \frac{\text{Income before taxes} + \text{Interest expense}}{\text{Interest expense}}$$

Activity ratios　These ratios help determine how efficiently an organization is using its resources in comparison to the level of sales. For example, the *inventory turnover* rate indicates how often inventory turns over or is replenished each year.

$$\text{Inventory turnover} = \frac{\text{Net sales}}{\text{Inventory}}$$

Fixed asset turnover is a ratio that measures the turnover of fixed assets to net sales and suggests how effectively an organization is using its fixed assets in relation to other similar organizations.

$$\text{Fixed asset turnover} = \frac{\text{Net sales}}{\text{Fixed assets}}$$

The *total assets turnover* ratio measures the effectiveness of an organization in using its assets to generate sales.

$$\text{Total assets turnover} = \frac{\text{Net sales}}{\text{Total assets}}$$

The *turnover of net worth* is an indicator of management's efficiency in using stockholders' equity.

$$\text{Turnover of net worth} = \frac{\text{Net sales}}{\text{Net worth (Stockholders' equity)}}$$

Finally, a measure in determining the effectiveness in using resources is provided by the turnover of *net working capital ratio*.

$$\text{Turnover of net working capital} = \frac{\text{Net sales}}{\text{Net working capital (Current assets} - \text{Current liabilities)}}$$

Profitability ratios　These ratios are truly overall financial control techniques since they reveal the returns generated on sales and invest-

468

ments. The *profit return on net sales* ratio is an expression of profit as a percentage of sales.

$$\text{Profit return on net sales} = \frac{\text{Net income after taxes}}{\text{Net sales}}$$

The *profit return on total assets* ratio is a measure of how well managers are using total assets in producing a profit. Thus, it is extremely significant to owners and creditors who provide assets to the organization.

$$\frac{\text{Profit return on total assets}}{\text{(Rate of return on investment)}} = \frac{\text{Net income after taxes}}{\text{Total assets}}$$

Profit return on net worth measures the proportion of net income in relation to funds invested by owners of the company. As such, it is a useful ratio to managers and investors as they evaluate other investment opportunities requiring the same amount of funds.

$$\text{Profit return on net worth} = \frac{\text{Net income after taxes}}{\text{Net worth}}$$

Du Pont system of return on investment
The du Pont system is based on the concept that the best measure of effort and performance for a manufacturing company with a large capital investment is the *rate of return on investment.*[11] This system brings together the various ratios discussed earlier and indicates their interrelationships in analyzing the profitability of assets.

Figure 17–11 shows that the percentage return on investment is determined by multiplying earnings as a percentage of sales by turnover of total assets (investment). In turn, the relationship between turnover and profit margins can be stated as an equation:

R (Return on investment) $= M$ (Margin on sales) $\times T$ (Asset turnover) where

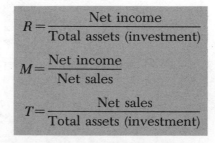

$$R = \frac{\text{Net income}}{\text{Total assets (investment)}}$$

$$M = \frac{\text{Net income}}{\text{Net sales}}$$

$$T = \frac{\text{Net sales}}{\text{Total assets (investment)}}$$

[11] The classic article concerning return on investment is found in C. A. Kline, Jr., and Howard L. Hessler, "The du Pont Chart System for Appraising Operating Performance," *NACA Bulletin*, August 1952, pp. 1595–1619.

FIGURE 17–11
The du Pont system of financial control showing the relationship of factors affecting return on investment

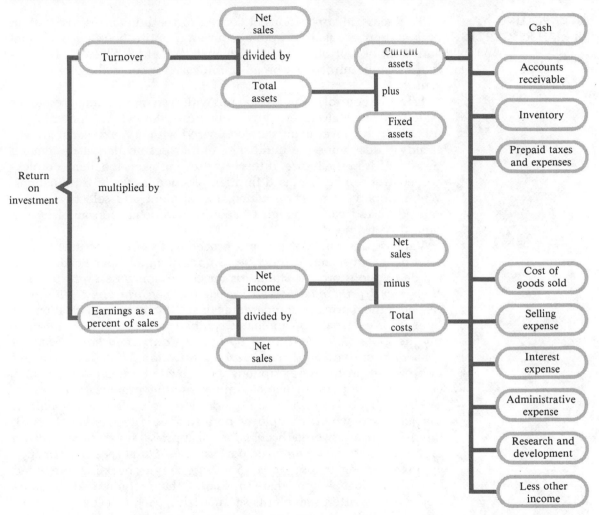

Return on investment *(R)* responds to changes in both *M* and *T.* If there has been no change in selling price, an improvement in sales turnover indicates that total assets are being used more effectively. Stated another way, the business is experiencing increased sales out of the same fixed and current assets.

With a constant selling price, an improvement in the gross profit margin reflects that costs in proportion to the sales dollar are being reduced. A manager can, therefore, improve return on investment by working existing investments harder or by reducing costs. Both of these changes can be influenced by management without a change in pricing policies or a larger capital budget for a given product or service.

CONTROLLING HUMAN RESOURCES

To discuss all applications of control to the human resources of an organization adequately would require an entire book on personnel administration or human resources management. Therefore, this section can only introduce a broad framework for controlling human resources.

Effective control in this area begins with systematic human resources planning. Through an employee inventory, known retirements and usual labor turnover figures are compared with organizational growth trends to determine the number of employees needed at designated time periods in the future. If this inventory projects too many employees, control can be exercised through planned layoffs or terminations. When employees must be added, recruitment and selection efforts can be started early enough to acquire additional personnel by the time they are needed.

Various personnel policies and procedures serve to control the recruitment and selection processes. In addition, job specifications and job descriptions provide standards for control purposes. *Job specifications identify the qualifications needed to perform given job duties.* As such, they provide standards against which the qualifications of internal or external job candidates can be compared in making selection decisions. *Job descriptions outline the duties, authority, and responsibilities of each job within an organization.* While usually stated in broad terms, these descriptions still provide minimal standards for controlling the performance of employees at all organizational levels.

Although job descriptions are standards for jobs, they do not address the question of whether employee performance is good or bad. Instead, this question is answered through formal appraisal systems that provide inputs for controlling employee performance. Numerous performance appraisal systems are used today. Some are simple checklists completed by each employee's immediate superior. Others require that the superior submit written statements summarizing each employee's performance in defined areas. Regardless of their format, however, all appraisal systems seek to provide information that goes beyond casual day-to-day observations. Through comparisons based on such information, steps can be taken to correct performance where needed. These steps may include additional training, transfer or demotion to another job, or even termination. Whatever the action, control is being exercised through corrective actions based on systematic evaluations of employee performance against established standards.

SUMMARY

Various applications of control are essential in our dynamic environment of change. Control techniques must be applied to such areas as marketing and production, while overall cost and financial controls are necessary to determine whether operations are progressing according to plan. Two overall cost controls that relate to both marketing and production are break-even analysis and variable budgeting.

Financial ratios are also important to management, but only when they are regarded as caution signals rather than absolute standards. Likewise, return on investment figures and techniques for measuring employee performance must be used with care. Above all, these and other control techniques must be selected to fit the specific needs of those organizational units where they are to be applied. Otherwise, they may be ineffective or even harmful to the total organization.

KEY TERMS

Activity ratios: Financial ratios that indicate how efficiently a company is using its resources in comparison to the level of sales.

Break-even analysis: An approach that examines cost, volume, and profit relationships to determine the break-even point where total revenue is equal to total costs.

Comparative financial statements: Balance sheets, income, or other financial statements that compare financial data over two or more operating periods.

Economic order quantity: The size of order that minimizes total annual ordering costs and inventory carrying costs.

Job description: An outline of the duties, authority, and responsibilities of each job in an organization.

Job specification: An identification and listing of the qualifications needed to perform given job duties.

Leverage ratios: Financial ratios that indicate the extent to which an organization is capitalized by debt.

Liquidity ratios: Financial ratios that indicate an organization's ability to pay short-term obligations.

Market share: The percentage of total potential sales for a given market area accounted for by the sales of one company.

Production: The creation of products or services having the utility to satisfy human needs.

Production scheduling: An assignment of calendar and clock times for beginning, processing, and completing production activites.

Profitability ratios: Financial ratios that reveal the returns generated on sales and investments.

Statistical quality control (SQC): A statistical approach for determining how many items of a larger number should be inspected to ensure that the total number conforms to quality standards.

---

1. Under what conditions might an organization justify offering a service to customers even though revenues do not cover the service's fair share of overhead expenses?

2. Why are standards or quotas important in controlling marketing activities?

3. What two major costs are associated with inventory control? How do they differ?

4. Under what conditions is statistical quality control useful to a manager?

5. How do lead times and safety stocks relate to the determination of reorder points?

6. What is meant by an economic order quantity?

7. Why is break-even analysis helpful to the practicing manager? What is the major limitation of break-even analysis?

8. Why is it important to distinguish between fixed and variable costs in break-even analysis?

9. What value do variable budgets have for management control purposes?

10. Discuss the use of comparative statements in overall financial control.

11. "Financial ratios are of little value in the absence of other information." Discuss.

12. Why are formal performance appraisals important in controlling human resources?

PROBLEMS

1. Actual Sales for the ZAM Corporation are given below:

Sales area	Sales
A	$45,000
B	30,000
C	95,000

Is the sales manager in Area A, B, or C doing the best job? Explain.

2. Charlene Jones was the assistant quality control manager for a cheese producing plant. Samples of cheese were periodically checked for texture and mellowness. A current control chart showed six straight sample measurements moving in an upward direction. In fact, a straight line would connect most of the six points. The last sample that was plotted was still within the upper control limit, but Jones was concerned over whether or not the production process was still operating correctly.

Required:

a. What two alternative hypotheses should Jones consider?

b. If you were Jones, what would you do?

c. What consequences could result from your decision?

3. Assume that inventory carrying cost is 20 percent per unit value per year, order cost per order is $10, and the average annual usage is 800 units. The price averages $8 per unit.

a. Determine the economic order quantity by using the tabular method.
b. Determine the EOQ by using the algebraic equation method.

4. Quality control managers often take the position that the production function exists to make the best product possible. As a marketing manager, what information would you present to react to this position.

5. As concerns economic order quantities and reorder points:

a. When might a company choose to order either a larger or smaller quantity than that specified by the EOQ formula?
b. When might an order be placed earlier or later than the time indicated by the reorder point?
c. Draw a graph showing the reorder point when the usage rate is 200 units per month, lead time is two months, and the safety stock is 100 units.

6.

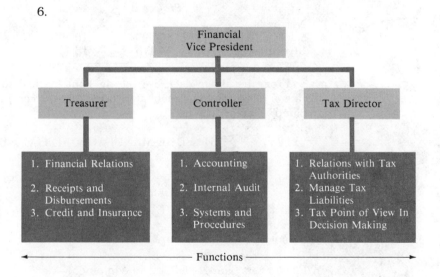

a. As revealed in the chart, what are some areas in which financial controls are applicable?
b. Discuss organizational activities in which the financial vice president would probably be involved.

7. As a departmental supervisor in an insurance company, Jane Rusher reached all objectives established for her research and statistics department during the past year. On Rusher's performance appraisal, her supervisor noted that she operated her department within the budget, objectives were successfully obtained, and reports and summary data were always turned in on time. At present, her supervisor is considering promoting Rusher to a higher managerial position.

a. As Rusher's supervisor should you be interested in any additional factors before you make a final decision about a promotion?
b. Is it possible that Rusher could be a flash in the pan?

8. If variable expenses equal 40 percent of sales and fixed expenses each month equal $72,000, at what level would sales be at the break-even point?

9. Utilizing the same cost structure as in problem 8 above, compute and show in tabular form the profit, or loss, for the sales figures of $100,000, $120,000, $150,000, and $180,000. Explain why profits do not go up by an equal amount when sales go from $150,000 to $180,000.

10. Company A has a profit margin of 5 percent on sales with a turnover of two for total assets. A much smaller company—B—has a profit margin of 4 percent but is turning over its assets four times. What is the rate of return for each company? Discuss the significance of your answers.

11. Data for the Kelsen Company (000 omitted) are:

Item	Projected	Actual
Net profit..........	$ 745	$ 750
Sales	10,000	10,500
Investment	14,175	15,750

From the above data, use the du Pont method to determine the actual rate of return on investment after taxes. Did the company do as well as anticipated? Why or why not?

12.
HAVDOE MANUFACTURING COMPANY
Balance Sheet
December 31, 1981

Assets

Cash	$ 60,437	
Accounts receivable	154,008	
Inventories	77,593	
Total current assets		$ 292,038
Fixed assets (land, building and equipment—net) ..		791,262
Total Assets...............................		$1,083,300

Liabilities and Stockholders' Equity

Current liabilities	$ 165,400
Long-term liabilities	159,000
Deferred income taxes	10,198
Minority interests	70,152
Stockholders' equity—Net	678,550
Total Liabilities and Stockholders' Equity ...	$1,083,300
Sales	$ 750,300
Interest charges................................	8,400
Net income before taxes (tax rate 46%)	167,574

a. Compute the financial ratios for this company.
b. What additional information is needed to make the ratios meaningful for control purposes.

c. Obtain the financial data to compute the ratios for a well-known manufacturing company, such as General Electric, and compare them to Havdoe Manufacturing Company.

SUGGESTED READINGS

Bell A. L.   "Flexible Budgets and Managerial Cost Pricing." *Management Accounting,* January 1977, pp. 34–37.

Chruden, H. J., and A. W. Sherman.   *Personnel Management: The Utilization of Human Resources.* Cincinnati: South-Western Publishing, 1980.

Danzig, S. M.   "What We Need to Know about Performance Appraisals." *Management Review,* February 1980, pp. 20–24.

Dewelt, R. L.   "Control: Key to Making Financial Strategy Work." *Management Review,* March 1977, pp. 19–22.

Dilworth, J. B.   *Production and Operations Management.* New York: Random House, 1979.

McCarthy, E. J.   *Basic Marketing: A Managerial Approach.* 6th ed. Homewood, Ill.: Richard D. Irwin, 1978.

Suver, J. D., and B. R. Neumann.   "Patient Mix and Break-Even Analysis." *Management Accounting,* January 1977, pp. 38–40.

Thacker, R. J., and L. Ellis.   *Management Accounting: Concepts and Applications.* Reston, Va.: Reston Publishing, 1981.

Van Matre, J. G., and G. H. Gilbreath.   *Statistics for Business and Economics.* Plano, Tex.: Business Publications, 1980.

Vickers, D.   "On the Economics of Break-Even." In *Contemporary Issues in Cost and Managerial Accounting,* edited by H. R. Anton et al. Boston: Houghton Mifflin, 1978, pp. 272–82.

Weston, J. F., and E. F. Brigham.   *Essentials of Managerial Finance.* Hinsdale, Ill.: Dryden Press, 1979.

18

AVOIDING DYSFUNCTIONAL CONTROLS

PURPOSE

About five years ago, some 1,000 persons applied for the position of police officer in Columbus, Ohio. Among others, one female failed the eye test given to all applicants and was not appointed to the police department. She filed a claim with the Department of Labor charging that the eye test was discriminatory against females. An investigation by the Department of Labor found that 10 percent of the male applicants had failed the eye test while 30 percent of the female applicants had failed. Based on these findings, the Department of Labor ordered the city of Columbus to stop using the eye test for selecting police officers until a test could be developed that would not discriminate between men and women.

Before the Department of Labor issued its cease and desist order, the city of Columbus gave the same eye test to another 1,300 persons. Of this group, more men than women failed the eye test, but when added to the first group, results for the 2,300 applicants showed that men and women failed the test in the same ratio. When this was pointed out to the Department of Labor, the matter was finally dropped. While it is not known how much the Department of Labor spent on its investigation of this case, the city of Columbus computed its costs at over $10,000

This is only one of many examples that could be cited to show how some controls cost more than they are worth. A look at the features of such negative, or dysfunctional, controls is provided by this chapter along with suggested guidelines for preventing their occurrence.

OBJECTIVES

1. To illustrate the negative results of too much control.

2. To relate management philosophies to control practices.

3. To show how dysfunctional controls can occur in an organization.

4. To present guidelines for avoiding dysfunctional controls.

5. To emphasize the importance of the human element in the control process.

Computerized control systems in the intensive cardiac care units of some hospitals monitor the vital signs of patients and regulate the medications that they receive. In another organizational setting, automation of the quality control process in various manufacturing companies leads to greater efficiency through a reduction of the costs associated with inspection and product waste. At the same time, automated control systems in these latter organizations have reduced the tedious mental concentration required in monitoring product quality through the inspection process.[1] While these advances are noteworthy, automation can never completely replace the human element in the controlling function. In fact, current and future control systems will continue to be only as good as the people who design and implement them.

Even with proper design, for example, controls can be adhered to so rigidly that their costs become greater than their benefits. As related to the human element, too much control can result in employee resentment, dissatisfaction, and antagonism. Employees may then seek ways to get around those controls that they dislike. They may report incorrect performance data, blame unwanted controls for lowered productivity, or try other things to beat the system. Such behavioral responses, combined with other negative results, are called dysfunctional consequences. In a broader context, *dysfunctional controls are those which produce undesirable results*. To understand better how controls can become dysfunctional, we begin by looking at the influence of managerial philosophies on the controlling function within organizations.

MANAGEMENT PHILOSOPHIES AND THE CONTROLLING FUNCTION

Just as management philosophies influence the nature of planning, organizing, and actuating, they play a major role in shaping control systems within an organization. In the early part of this century, for example, a dominant management philosophy was expressed through autocratic leadership. Control systems based on this philosophy were very confining and served to limit the actions of employees by restricting their authority and creativity at work. Due to their nature, these controls implied that employees lacked motivation, preferred to be led, and were indifferent to organizational needs and objectives.[2] In Figure 18–1, we see the impact of these behavioral assumptions on traditional accounting practices. Upon examination, it is obvious that these practices were designed to limit and restrain the authority of employees who were regarded as lazy, wasteful, and inefficient.

Today, many control systems still reflect behavioral assumptions that have been carried forward from the early days of industrialization. These systems include "tight" standards, quantitative measures of per-

---

[1] G. Bylinsky, "A New Industrial Revolution," *Fortune*, October 5, 1981, pp. 106–14.

[2] Douglas McGregor has characterized this set of assumptions as *Theory X*. See *The Human Side of Enterprise* (New York: McGraw-Hill, 1960).

FIGURE 18–1
Behavioral assumptions of "traditional" management accounting

---

Assumptions with respect to organization goals

A. The principal objective of business activity is profit maximization.
B. This principal objective can be segmented into subgoals to be distributed throughout the organization.
C. Goals are additive—what is good for the parts of the business is also good for the whole.

Assumptions with respect to the behavior of participants

A. Organization participants are motivated primarily by economic forces.
B. Work is essentially an unpleasant task that people will avoid whenever possible.
C. Human beings are ordinarily inefficient and wasteful.

Assumptions with respect to the behavior of management

A. The role of the business manager is to maximize the profits of the company.
B. In order to perform this role, management must control the tendencies of employees to be lazy, wasteful, and inefficient.
C. The essence of management control is authority. The ultimate authority of management stems from its ability to affect the economic reward structure.
D. There must be a balance between the authority a person has and his responsibility for performance.

Assumptions with respect to the role of management accounting

A. The primary function of management accounting is to aid management in the process of profit maximization.
B. The accounting system is a "goal-allocation" device that permits management to select its operating objectives and to divide and distribute them throughout the company, i.e., assign responsibilities for performance. This is commonly referred to as *planning*.
C. The accounting system is a control device that permits management to identify and to correct undesirable performance.
D. There is sufficient certainty, rationality, and knowledge within the system to permit an accurate comparison of responsibility for performance and the ultimate benefits and costs of that performance.
E. The accounting system is "neutral" in its evaluations—personal bias is eliminated by the objectivity of the system.

Source: Edwin H. Caplan, "Behavioral Assumptions of Management Accounting—Report of a Field Study," *The Accounting Review*, April 1968, p. 354. By permission of the publisher.

formance, and a frequent use of discipline to force employee compliance with standards. As might be expected, such controls also emphasize a short-run perspective, since they compare current output to established standards without considering patterns of performance over long periods of time.

By referring to Chapter 15, we see that the behavioral assumptions underlying other leadership styles lead to control systems different from those discussed above. Participative managers, for example, believe in the importance of actively involving subordinates in the controlling function to satisfy both individual and organizational needs. Leaders who show a maximum concern for people and a low concern for output will favor controls that are in line with the wishes of their subordinates. Likewise, the leadership styles of other managers will be reflected in the control systems for which they are responsible. More often than not, however, the controlling function in most organizations still has an autocratic flavor that approaches an overreliance on controls. Therefore, the remainder of this chapter is devoted to a discussion of the problems associated with such controls as well as methods for their prevention or elimination.

PROBLEMS RESULTING FROM AN OVERRELIANCE ON CONTROLS

Various problems may develop when managers rely too much on control systems. Some of these problems discussed by Jasinski over 20 years ago are still present in all types of organizations. They include:[3]

A waste of executive time.

Increased production and maintenance costs.

Low morale.

Impaired quality and irregular or inadequate output.

Labor recruitment problems.

Cynicism or dishonesty on the part of workers and supervisory personnel.

Interdepartmental friction.

While pointing out that an overreliance on controls usually comes from managerial efforts to counterbalance the likelihood of noncompliance by employees, McGregor cites the unintended results of control systems as (1) widespread antagonism, (2) resistance and noncompliance to controls, (3) unreliable performance information, (4) closer managerial supervision, and (5) high administrative costs.[4] By combining the problems identified by Jasinski and McGregor, we see that too much emphasis on controls may have several dysfunctional results. These are discussed in the following sections.

Higher costs due to lower output and quality

As concerns lower output and quality, Whyte relates that absolute control standards force employees to work at a comfortable pace, rather than at the rates desired by management.[5] If a worker, for instance,

---

[3] Frank J. Jasinski, "Use and Misuse of Efficiency Controls," *Harvard Business Review*, July–August 1956. Copyright © 1956 by the President and Fellows of Harvard College; all rights reserved.

[4] Douglas McGregor, *The Professional Manager.* Copyright © 1967, McGraw-Hill Book Company, p. 117. Used with permission of McGraw-Hill Book Company.

[5] William Foote Whyte, *Money and Motivation* (New York: Harper & Row, 1955), p. 234.

produced 150 units yesterday and only 100 today, there is a legitimate fear that the supervisor will want to know why the higher production level was not maintained. Consequently, the worker may decide that it is safer to produce 125 units per day on a regular basis; or if conditions are right, produce 150 and "bank" the extra 25 that can be pulled out for credit on a day when only 100 units are produced. To this extent, the control system ends up being no better than what employees desire it to be.

In order to make production records look better, quality is also likely to suffer. For example, one department manager is reported to have encouraged workers to get out as many units as possible to meet production standards, even if quality was below standard and the pieces had to be returned to the department for reworking at a later date.[6] This action resulted in higher output per work hour, but total production cost per item increased. In both of these examples, the problem is not with the skill of the worker, the basic design of the product, nor the necessity of control. Instead, there is evidence of a management failure to use appropriate qualitative and quantitative control systems to obtain proper feedback on performance levels. Thus, control systems that emphasize only the time it takes to produce an item, without considering quality and costs, will often hurt an organization in the long run.

Defensive behavior
Defensive behavior can result from control systems that provide only a part of the data required for effective control. Many employees tend to be defensive when their true performance is not recognized. One form of such behavior is to try to make performance look better than that which shows on the record. Employees may give excuses to explain why performance is lower than standard, or why it should be higher than reported. In any case, they develop excuses when legitimate reasons are not adequate to explain performance.

Chris Argyris notes that pressures for compliance with control standards can create even more serious behavioral problems.[7] Some unfavorable attitudes toward compliance with budgets can be seen in such behavioral patterns as conflict, dissatisfaction, tension, and frustration. Likert and Seashore suggest that these behavior patterns will eventually result in increased turnover and absenteeism, poorer labor relations, a more concerted effort to restrict production, and a lower quality of products and service.[8] Thus, tighter control systems may lead to

---

[6] Frank J. Jasinski, "Use and Misuse of Efficiency Controls," p. 106.

[7] Chris Argyris, *The Impact of Budgets on People* (New York: Controllership Institute Research Foundation, 1952); and "Human Problems with Budgets," *Harvard Business Review*, 1953, pp. 97–110.

[8] See Rensis Likert and Stanley E. Seashore, "Making Cost Controls Work," *Harvard Business Review*, 1963, pp. 96–108.

short-run increases in productivity; but when defensive behavior arises, long-term results may be much less desirable.

Ineffective achievement of goals

Ineffective goal achievement can also result when a single quantitative control measurement is overemphasized. We then have the problem of measurement orientation—that is, managers are more concerned with measurement than with the achievement of total goals. As an illustration, the interviewers in many state employment offices attempt to match job applicants to the job orders placed by prospective employers. The performance of each interviewer is then rated by the number of persons placed during a stated period of time. Consequently, applicants who are harder to place, such as the disadvantaged and handicapped, may not be given as much consideration as they deserve. In addition, federal funds allocated to state offices consider the number of placements. Thus, state administrators may focus attention on total numbers and fail to look at the qualitative aspects of minority, youth, or handicapped applicant placement.

Unreliable performance information

Basically, this problem is related to misrepresentations of performance data, such as time tickets or production reports, and to deviations from established control procedures. These actions may result when an individual or group finds it difficult, or impossible, to reach standards. Jasinski relates how top-level supervisors, anxious to equalize efficiency among departments, made paper transfers of personnel from low- to high-producing sections. "This move had a leveling result when the ratio of 'man-hours to time value per piece' in finished stores was computed."[9] Likert also suggests that if an exact level of performance is required, employees will see that management gets it, even to the extent of preparing and distributing phony performance figures.[10] Although false records may not result directly in added production costs, an acceptance of the practice by top management sets a poor example for managers at lower levels. In short, by giving dishonesty a sense of respectability, both managerial standards and professional ethics are eroded.

Low motivation and personnel dissatisfaction

Constant management pressure to increase output may simply cause workers to disregard efficiency ratings while resigning themselves to lower production levels. When this happens, top management may feel that the lowered production is due to poor supervision among middle managers and supervisors. These managers may, in turn, see the problem stemming from the workers themselves. Although any of these assumptions could be true, the real cause may be related to the overall development and administration of control systems. In many instances, management pressure may lead to temporary in-

[9] Frank J. Jasinski, "Use and Misuse of Efficiency Controls," p. 107.

[10] Rensis Likert, *New Patterns of Management* (New York: McGraw-Hill, 1961), pp. 208–9.

creases in output; however, dysfunctional consequences can eventually occur. They are seen as lower motivation, greater dishonesty, and a higher attrition rate among the better employees.

Personnel dissatisfaction can also lead to recruitment and training problems since the reputation of most organizations is known throughout the labor market. Consequently, when the labor market is tight, it may be extremely difficult for these organizations to attract qualified personnel. Furthermore, when wages for new and untrained employees are charged against a department's efficiency ratings, job opportunities for untrained applicants may suffer. Few department managers are eager to spend time training new workers when such efforts can detract from departmental efficiency ratings.

REASONS WHY DYSFUNCTIONAL CONSEQUENCES OCCUR

Since people are essential in achieving organizational goals, they become an important element in the control process. The systems that are used to evaluate individuals can have dysfunctional results simply because human behavior cannot be predicted with certainty.[11] It should also be noted that these approaches to control are open-loop systems since corrective actions do not automatically occur once unacceptable deviations are identified. In an open-loop control system, organizational members must decide what has gone wrong and select appropriate corrective actions. Since people directly influence how work is performed, the effectiveness of control devices depends on how well they can encourage positive human responses. In addition, as cited earlier, control procedures that are not behaviorally oriented may be perceived as a threat to individual security. As a result, people may attempt to eliminate the threat of such procedures by adopting negative behavior patterns.

Various conditions surrounding operational control systems can lead to dysfunctional results. Of these, the following deserve attention:[12]

1. Direct hierarchical pressure to reduce costs and increase productivity.
2. Negative feedback on performance.
3. Decline in trust and confidence in management.
4. Overreliance on quantitative measures of performance.

Direct hierarchical pressure

Research indicates that hostile employee reactions are often directed toward both control systems and management when control is exercised downward.[13] Consequently, increases in hierarchical pressure for greater productivity may bring about dysfunctional consequences.

---

[11] V. Bruce Irvine, "Budgeting: Functional Analysis and Behavioral Implications," in *A Contingency Approach to Management: Readings,* John W. Newstron et al. (New York: McGraw-Hill, 1975), pp. 425–30.

[12] McGregor, *The Professional Manager,* p. 119.

[13] Rensis Likert, *The Human Organization* (New York: McGraw-Hill, 1967), pp. 78–100.

Continued pressure, unless it is presented in a manner designed to gain support for various controls, will lead to dissatisfaction, a distortion of communications, and to a large degree, deterioration of the quality and accuracy of decision making.[14]

When imposed standards are not considered to be realistic, organizational members can become quite creative in getting around them. In fact, there are many documented examples of work groups that have deliberately restricted production.[15] Similarly, it is not uncommon to find workers on incentive pay restricting their output. More output, of course, means a larger paycheck, but workers sometimes feel threatened and think that higher levels of production will merely lead to increased standards. As a result, they adopt a comfortable work pace that falls somewhere below the established standards in their pay plan.

Negative feedback

Most people dislike negative feedback, and they have a limit for the amount of criticism they can accept. If feedback affects an individual's employment status or career plans, a great deal of anxiety may be exhibited due to pressures of the control system and a desire to improve performance.[16] Of course, feedback should be directed toward isolating differences between actual performance and standards so that appropriate corrective action can be taken. In traditional control systems, however, feedback is directed toward the individual, rather than the objectives to be achieved.

When organizational members understand and accept standards and procedures, they are more likely to react positively to feedback and a need for corrective action. Management's responsibility, therefore, is to provide an organizational environment, control systems, and leadership styles that will utilize, rather than antagonize, the energy and creativity of all employees.[17] When feedback procedures cause negative responses, very little, if any, improvement in productivity will be forthcoming.

Decline in trust and confidence in management

Where trust and confidence are lacking in management's ability to establish workable control systems, employees may also perceive threats to their security. When such threats are present, dysfunctional consequences in the form of negative behavior patterns may occur. A lack of trust may be due to such factors as (1) employees do not really know what is expected of them, (2) performance standards are not realistic, (3) certain staff managers are not viewed as having the authority to make control decisions, or (4) goals do not present a chal-

---

[14] Likert and Seashore, "Making Cost Controls Work," pp. 96–108.

[15] See F. J. Roethlisberger and J. J. Dickson, *Management and the Worker* (Cambridge, Mass.: Harvard University Press, 1938).

[16] Herbert H. Meyer, Emanual Kay, and J. R. P. French, Jr., "Split Roles in Performance Appraisal," *Harvard Business Review*, 1965, pp. 123–29.

[17] Raymond E. Miles and Roger C. Vergin, "Behavioral Properties of Variance Controls," *California Management Review*, Spring 1966, p. 59.

lenge to employees. Intensive studies at General Electric indicate that performance is not likely to improve unless performance goals are clearly established along with the plans for achieving them.[18]

Restoring employee trust requires that management establish realistic standards and procedures for measuring performance in such areas as quality, quantity, time, and costs. Furthermore, managers should motivate subordinates to improve by playing a supportive role. In fulfilling this role, managers must be concerned with assisting subordinates and in reaching agreement with them on how objectives are to be accomplished.

Overreliance on quantitative measures of performance

Managers who place too much reliance on control techniques that utilize absolute quantitative measures of performance are not generally concerned with the impact of controls on people. V. F. Ridgway relates various studies that show an undue reliance on quantitative measurements of performance can create false savings such as delayed repairs and neglected profit opportunities.[19] As discussed earlier, quantitative measures may create employee frustration and tension, particularly when suggestions are not offered as to how performance can be improved. Ridgway also shows that it does not matter whether these measures are single, multiple, or composite since all have undesirable consequences for overall organizational performance.

Efficiency controls that are based on the actual time taken to complete a task against a standard time may also produce many of the unsought consequences discussed earlier. Controls of this type give little room for measurement around an average (mean) level of performance. Performance is either at, or above, standard or it is below standard and requires corrective action. Most people, however, work within a range of performance. Thus, it should be unnecessary for management to search out causes and corrections for every variation in performance. Corrective action should be required only when feedback indicates that performance is beyond established control limits.

The reasons noted for dysfunctional controls suggest that an avoidance of negative consequences requires control systems to be technically sound, equitable, clearly understood, properly administered, and behaviorally oriented. The following section considers some important guidelines to follow in obtaining these conditions.

GUIDELINES FOR AVOIDING DYSFUNCTIONAL CONTROLS

Without question, effective control systems are important to any organization. In this sense, effective controls are those which prevent or minimize deviations between desired and actual performance without becoming ends in themselves and without producing human prob-

---

[18] Herbert Meyer et al., "Performance Appraisal," pp. 123–29.

[19] V. F. Ridgway, "Dysfunctional Consequences of Performance Measurement," *Administrative Science Quarterly*, 1956, pp. 240–47.

lems greater than their benefits. In this section, six guidelines for attaining more effective control systems are considered.[20]

Focus on the future

Controls must be forward looking since they are concerned with actions that take place in the future. Thus, if standards are to be realistic, they must also be geared to future expectations. This is especially true for preventive controls since managers must identify expectations in terms of where they intend to be at some point in the future.

Since they focus on the future, standards cannot be based solely on past performance. In some instances, the past may provide unacceptable and inequitable inputs for predicting future events such as employee turnover, machine breakdowns, and employee productivity. In fact, standards based only on past performance may reward poor results and, conversely, penalize good performance. Thus, forward-looking control systems must be based on a combination of past experience, present knowledge, and future expectations if they are to play a meaningful role in improving organizational performance.

Strive for flexibility

Regardless of whether forecasts are concerned with a single organization, industry, or the total economy, they must be subjected to continuous revision. Similarly, control systems must be flexible and adaptable if they are to aid management in realizing anticipated results.

Budgets, quotas, financial ratios, quality standards, position descriptions, and job specifications are examples of standards that are most meaningful only at a given point in time. As internal and external conditions change, control standards must be sufficiently flexible to meet any new needs that may arise. For instance, job descriptions that identify minimum standards of employee performance cannot be rigid and inflexible. Instead, where it is appropriate to do so, such standards should be changed to provide individuals with the initiative and freedom that help them grow and develop in their jobs. Likewise, if they are to meet changes in the labor market, job specifications that indicate the qualifications an individual should possess to fill a particular job must be flexible and adjustable.

Avoid obsolescence

Once a control system is implemented, it is difficult to eliminate even when it is no longer needed. As an illustration, the warehouse manager of a large mail-order firm consistently received both the projected minimum and maximum sizes for orders placed by merchandise managers. The maximum figure was, of course, useful in determining storage space requirements for the coming months. The minimum figures, however, were never used. When someone asked why the

---

[20] This section is based primarily on M. Gene Newport, *The Tools of Managing: Functions, Techniques, and Skills* (Reading, Mass.: Addison-Wesley, 1972), Chapter 7, pp. 104–10. © 1972, Addison-Wesley Publishing Company, Inc. Reprinted with permission.

minimums were submitted, the answer was, "because they have always been sent in the past." In this instance, obsolescence was not being avoided and the result was an ineffective use of time and money.

Another example of controls that do not contribute to goal achievement is found in the many reports and forms that often have little or no meaning to those who receive them. At times, even those individuals who have been promoted, or who have received other job changes, continue to receive data related to their old positions. Unfortunately, this problem is made greater by those who ask to continue receiving such reports, even though they may never take time to review them.

To make control systems more workable while eliminating their dysfunctional consequences, managers must also seek to learn how obsolete and inappropriate controls can be avoided. One method for acquiring such knowledge begins with an inventory of existing reports. The information yielded by these reports can then be compared to the types of information actually needed. Perhaps some reports can be eliminated, while others can be improved. In any event, this method helps managers understand that only certain data are helpful in measuring the most important aspects of actual performance.

Gain employee commitment

Since control systems are designed to prevent or to minimize deviations between desired and actual performance, they must be clearly understood by those who work within their framework. In addition, the environment of any control system must promote employee commitment to organizational goals, jobs, and performance standards. Some basic guidelines useful in gaining employee commitment can be summarized as (1) seek understanding, (2) promote participation, and (3) develop a supportive attitude.

Seek understanding   Standards should be easily applied and clearly understood. This requires that the standards themselves be stated in nontechnical language and that the methods used in their implementation be understood and accepted. If they are too complex, there is a much greater probability that they will be ineffective. Furthermore, they must be tailor-made if they are to adequately reflect the actual needs of the organizational environment in which they operate.

Promote participation   The potential benefits of employee involvement (participation) should also be considered in the establishment of control systems. At Texas Instruments, for example, teams of workers in certain departments set their own performance goals.[21] Through such participation, employees are actually involved in the control process. As a result, they can contribute creatively to the development of more effective approaches to goal accomplishment. This participation can even include suggestions for the elimination or revision of certain jobs. In general, participation in establishing performance goals

---

[21] Texas Instruments has advocated participative management since the 1960s.

helps create more meaningful standards as well as a willingness among subordinates to accept the authority of those responsible for developing and implementing control systems.

Even for managerial personnel, research indicates that imposed procedures and budgets have a negative impact on performance;[22] and again, the most widely recommended approach for overcoming such negativism includes a consideration of the feelings and ideas of those who will be covered by a given procedure or budget. In this case, the wisdom for having participation in the development of control systems is based on the assumption that most individuals strive for at least average levels of performance. In fact, individually determined standards often prove to be higher than those which management might have arbitrarily imposed. For example, salesmen who participate in establishing standards often recommend higher quotas than those which are determined by management alone.

At this point, it should be noted that participative approaches do not provide the only means for developing a workable control system. Some people do not desire to be involved in the control process. They may feel that they are hired to perform only a specified job and want no part of the control process, even when they are given the opportunity.[23] Such feelings seem to indicate a belief that management has the responsibility for exercising control in an organization. Yet, while these attitudes appear among certain individuals, one should not generalize by assuming that they are representative of all employees.

Develop a supportive attitude   Standards should be established in such a way that subordinates are not blamed for variations in performance that are beyond their control. It must be recognized that materials, machines, or other employees may be responsible for certain deviations. In addition, when poor performance does stem from the failure of an individual, management must develop a posture of supportive assistance. For example, Likert has suggested that higher levels of individual and group achievement are possible in the long run when supervisors:[24]

Exhibit confidence and trust in subordinates.

Understand and help them overcome problems in finding better ways of doing work.

Support subordinates in solving problems of their own.

Clearly, then, standards are not developed to discipline people for variations in performance nor do they exist to exert pressure on em-

---

[22] D. T. DeCoster and J. P. Fertakis, "Budget-Induced Pressure and Its Relationship to Supervisory Behavior," *Journal of Accounting Research*, 1968, pp. 237–46.

[23] See M. E. Wallace, "Behavioral Considerations in Budgeting," *Management Accounting*, 1966, pp. 3–8.

[24] Likert, *Human Organization*, pp. 156–88.

ployees. Instead, standards direct individuals toward higher levels of performance while helping them develop and use more of their potential.

Seek rapid feedback

In order to spot deviations from standards before or as they occur, rapid feedback is essential. In this respect, an important characteristic of good control is its ability to evaluate past performance, react to current conditions, and foresee future changes. When feedback of this type is available at the point of action, managers and subordinates are also able to evaluate and to correct their performance much more rapidly. Thus, where possible, self-initiated corrective action should be promoted, thereby saving the time of managers at higher levels of authority.

At present, computerized information systems can provide accurate and almost instantaneous feedback. As one example, retail establishments can maintain a perpetual inventory on all items in stock by linking cash registers to a computer. Before going to such systems, however, managers must consider all other possibilities that will provide rapid feedback while staying within the boundaries of a reasonable cost for the benefits received.

Recognize the human element

Most people like to know how their performance compares to established standards. They also prefer guidelines that let them know what is expected. However, they may resist controls that restrict individuality and growth.

To minimize resistance, subordinates must be convinced that management controls help them do the best job possible. Thus, full and complete information concerning the nature of and need for given controls must be communicated to employees before their installation. Once control systems are in force, managers must follow a well-established process for reviewing all standards on a periodic basis. In this way the standards that remain are clearly understood, viewed as equitable, and accepted as legitimate.

Without question, organizations cannot operate if they are geared to absolute and unchanging standards. Standards should be established in such a way that they take into account the normal variations in an individual's performance. Within a range of satisfactory performance, individuals can then establish their own performance goals.[25] As a result, self-control is promoted where individual employees evaluate deviations from standard and recommend the type of corrective action to be taken. This, in turn, may provide the worker with a sense of commitment, achievement, and recognition. Of course, to achieve

[25] See G. P. Lotham and J. J. Baldes, "The 'Practical Significance' of Locke's Theory of Goal Setting," in, *The Applied Psychology of Work Behavior: A Book of Readings,* ed., Dennis W. Organ (Plano, Tex.: Business Publications, 1978), pp. 285–90.

490

self-control it is also necessary to report deviations directly to those individuals responsible for the work. They must not be bypassed.

By following a supportive, problem-solving approach to control, management can create a climate where workers are (a) less inclined to blame poor performance on the inappropriateness of standards and (b) more willing to accept corrective action. In both instances, there is less fear of disciplinary action when mistakes are made. Thus, if control systems are truly to help individuals utilize more of their potential, the human element must receive full consideration in the design, implementation, and feedback stages of the process.

SUMMARY

Control systems are essential in preventing deviations between actual and planned performance. Yet, negative results may occur when control systems become ends in themselves. For example, requiring rigid conformity to standards, relying completely on quantitative performance measures, or pressuring for higher productivity by raising standards can all lead to dysfunctional consequences.

Managers must be continually aware of those elements of control systems that have an impact on the motivation of employees. In addition, for control procedures to become most effective, managers must develop and use them to generate cooperation, rather than resistance to change, among organizational members.

Several guidelines are available for avoiding dysfunctional controls. In turn, each of them deemphasizes the use of harsh and direct hierarchical pressure on subordinates. Effective communications, teamwork, and coordination depend on managers who are sensitive and responsive to environmental changes. Only in this manner can control systems be modified to keep pace with change.

Measurement and reporting practices must also be assessed regularly to ensure that resources are concentrated where the need for control is greatest. In addition, control systems should measure and evaluate external factors by comparing them to previous assumptions and forecasts. Similarly, control systems must take the human element into consideration.

To summarize, the architects of control must focus not only on improving the technical efficiency of measurement and reporting techniques but also on avoiding the dysfunctional consequences that can result from following traditional behavioral assumptions. If control systems are not oriented toward modern behavioral knowledge, they will eventually cause total organizational performance to suffer.

KEY TERMS

Dysfunctional controls: Controls that result in negative behavior, costs that are greater than savings, or other undesirable results.

Hierarchical pressure: As related to control, an arbitrary use of authority in imposing standards or gaining employee compliance in carrying out the controlling function.

Measurement orientation: An overemphasis on measurement causing managers to be more concerned with measures of performance than with the substance of the total control process.

Negative feedback: Feedback in the control process that concentrates solely on the mistakes of individuals rather than on objectives to be achieved.

Tight standards: Standards that limit deviations in quality or quantity to a very narrow range of tolerances.

QUESTIONS

1. "Any control system that does not consider the human element is probably doomed to failure." Why is this true?
2. Why are many control systems still very autocratic in character?
3. Define dysfunctional control. What things can cause a control system to become dysfunctional?
4. What types of problems can result from too much reliance on control systems?
5. How can periodic reviews of control systems help to keep them from becoming dysfunctional?
6. Why are considerations of the past, present, and future important in a review of control systems?
7. "Obsolete control systems are found in many organizations." Discuss.
8. Cite three things that managers can do to help gain employee support for control systems.
9. How can employee participation assist managers in the development and implementation of control systems? Are there possible dangers from too much participation in these processes?
10. Why is rapid feedback essential in developing effective control systems?
11. If one organization has controls that have proven effective, can another organization "borrow" them in an effort to avoid dysfunctional results?
12. Cite an organization with which you are familiar and describe any controls within the organization that you consider to be dysfunctional.

PROBLEMS

1. The administrator of a large hospital recently installed a new appraisal system to provide more detailed feedback on the performance of all nurses employed by the hospital. None of the members of the nursing staff were involved in either the design or implementation of the appraisal system. Consequently, none were familiar with the standards of performance that they would be expected to meet during the next year.

Approximately three months after the new appraisal system was installed, the director of nursing service met with the hospital administrator to present the following information: (1) the nursing staff was experiencing a lot of tension, and individual nurses were faced with what they considered to be role conflicts; (2) various units were suffering as a result of antagonism among some of the nurses; (3) distorted and blocked communications were occurring between nursing shifts; (4) strong informal groups were being formed; and (5) the authority structure of the nursing units was being challenged.

a. Why do you think these behavior patterns developed?
b. Can all of these behavior patterns be considered dysfunctional?
c. What net result could come from this behavior among members of the nursing staff?
d. What changes in the control system could be suggested to avoid dysfunctional results?

2. Like many drug stores, Rocky Creek Pharmacy is actually a mini-department store. Cosmetics, lawn furniture, fishing equipment, cameras, toys, tools, auto supplies, housewares, clothing, and a host of other items join drugs in the store's inventory. Self-service keeps the numbers of employees to a minimum but requires that most items other than prescription drugs be kept on open display. Therefore, possible shoplifting losses have concerned the pharmacist-owner, Mr. Shoals, since he opened the pharmacy six months ago.

A recent inventory listed several items with a total retail value of over $1,000 that could not be located in stock or on display. Immediately, Mr. Shoals suspected shoplifting and took steps to prevent further losses. Wide-angle mirrors were placed in several locations so that the pharmacist and checkout clerks could observe customers throughout the store. Shelves were moved to establish a traffic pattern that forced all customers to pass the checkout counter when leaving the store. Two closed-circuit TV cameras were installed to monitor the sales floor at all times, and a security guard was hired for eight hours every Saturday when customer traffic was at its highest level for the week. The total cost of equipment and architectural changes was over $5,000, and the security guard was to be paid $150 for working an eight-hour shift.

a. Is it likely that this new control system will be dysfunctional?
b. If faced with a similar situation, how would you proceed?

3. The Bank Pool Table Manufacturing Company recently hired a new controller. After a few weeks on the job, the controller observed that some of the skilled craftsmen who had been with the company for many years were exercising more freedom in their actions than was felt appropriate. They often left work early and spent 10 to 15 minutes longer for lunch than was officially allowed.

In a drive for stronger control systems, the controller devised a sign-in and sign-out sheet for workers to complete when they arrived for work and left in the evening. Also, all employees were to sign in and out for coffee breaks and lunch.

a. Do you feel that it will be easy to convince employees that there is a need for this added control system?
b. What reactions do you think will result from the new system? Are these reactions the same as those expected by the controller?

c. In this case, do the benefits of control outweigh the costs?

d. Do you feel the new control system is proper and necessary?

4. An economist for a labor union recently accused management of always (a) trying to measure the immeasurable, (b) using quantitative data to justify judgment and qualitative decisions, and (c) requiring employees to meet measurable standards, while failing to apply such standards to their own performance.

a. Are these criticisms justifiable?

b. What could management do to prevent such accusations?

5. A large auto parts wholesale house had previously installed a sophisticated inventory and flexible budget control system. Operations worked smoothly until this past year when changes in customer purchasing procedures began to emerge. Due to business conditions, retail establishments started shortening their order lead times and requiring last-minute changes in size and composition of orders. As a result, the wholesaler's warehouse operations have fluctuated between periods of overtime and layoffs with resulting increases in costs.

During this period, control systems were unable to help management spot problems and take corrective action. Yet both financial and nonfinancial reports indicated gross variances from operating plans and assumptions. Top management realized that previous budgets and performance assumptions were unrealistic and unattainable. Therefore, they disregarded all feedback information. The final result saw poor information lead to bad decisions, and the company is now contemplating bankruptcy.

a. What problems do you see in this company?

b. What recommendations for correcting present conditions would you suggest to the president?

6. Stock records for controlling the inventory of a large catalog sales company are currently kept in a large filing bin. All data for the files are obtained from shipping and receiving slips and are recorded on cards kept for each item in inventory. Due to the time delays in obtaining and recording shipping and receiving data, the files are often out of date by as much as one week. As a result, the company has experienced a widening gap between actual inventories and the amount of stock indicated by the inventory control system. Management suspects that employee theft accounts for some of this difference, but they cannot tell for sure. If you were responsible for maintaining the company's inventory control system, how would you approach this problem?

7. Since some control systems do not produce a net benefit for the organizations that use them, would organizational objectives be achieved more effectively if control systems were eliminated completely?

SUGGESTED READINGS

Benston, G. J. "The Role of the Firm's Accounting System for Motivation," in *Contemporary Issues in Cost and Managerial Accounting*, edited by H. R. Anton et al. Boston: Houghton Mifflin, 1978, pp. 47–58.

494

Brief, A. P., and R. J. Aldag. "The 'Self' in Work Organizations: A Conceptual Review." *The Academy of Management Review,* January 1981, pp. 75–88.

Cammann, D., and D. Nadler. "Fit Control Systems to Your Managerial Style." *Harvard Business Review,* January–February 1976, pp. 65–72.

Fagerberg, D., Jr. "Unmeasured Costs: A Checklist." *Management Accounting,* February 1974, pp. 29–32.

Flamholts, E. "Organizational Control Systems as a Managerial Tool." *California Management Review,* Winter 1979, pp. 50–59.

McFarland, W. B. *Manpower Cost and Performance Measurement.* New York: National Association of Accountants, 1977.

McMahon, J. T., and G. W. Peritt. "Toward a Contingency Theory of Organizational Control." *Academy of Management Journal,* December 1973, pp. 624–35.

Newman, W. H. *Constructive Control.* Englewood Cliffs, N.J.: Prentice-Hall, 1975.

Ouchi, W. G. "The Transmission of Control through Organization Hierarchy." *Academy of Management Journal,* June 1978, pp. 178–92.

Sihler, W. W. "Toward Better Management Control Systems." *California Management Review,* Winter 1971, pp. 33–39.

Vancil, R. F. "What Kind of Management Control Do You Need?" *Harvard Business Review,* March–April 1973, pp. 75–86.

Weiner, N. *The Human Use of Human Beings.* New York: Doubleday Anchor Books, 1954.

Central Phonograph Manufacturing Company

Dave Tool, assistant plant superintendent, presented a staff report to Mr. Jackson, the plant manager, dealing with plant coordination and control. A part of the report follows:

> What is coordination? Coordination is the fitting together of positions for the accomplishment of specific goals. This applies to management as well as to every job in the plant. It makes no difference if an organization is a manufacturing concern, a retail outlet, or a military establishment, coordination must exist throughout the entire structure.
>
> At Central Phonograph, managers feel that if jobs are well defined coordination will be forthcoming. However, for coordination to be achieved, jobs must not only be defined in terms of specific purposes, but their relationship to other activities must also be understood.
>
> What is control? Basically, the control function has four separate phases. First, operations are separated into units that will be evaluated. Secondly, standards are set up to determine what is to be done. Thirdly, techniques are devised to measure actual performance. And lastly, rules are established that determine whether corrective action is needed and what might be done in making adjustments at the right time and place. A satisfactory control system requires coordination if goals are to be efficiently achieved.
>
> At Central Phonograph the control process is an open-loop system. This means that one or more of the elements in the control process is missing, thus preventing feedback. In many open-loop systems, both the discriminator and the decision maker (the last phase of the control process) do not exist. Clearly, feedback must be present at all levels from workers to supervisors and on up to top management.

An incentive pay program developed by top management had caused David Tool to write his report. The plan is being implemented by supervisory personnel and pays an incentive for phonograph sets assembled beyond the minimum daily standard of 360 sets (45 per hour) per line. The incentive rate is equal to a fractional percentage of an employee's hourly base pay. In short, each set above 360 results in an incentive bonus equal to one forty-fifth of the hourly wage.

The layout of the production line is shown in Exhibit 1. Personnel on the chassis line assemble the circuitry and internal electronic compo-

EXHIBIT 1
Production line of central phonograph manufacturing company

CHASSIS LINE

Quality control
testing area

TRANSFER
POINT

FINALS LINE

Packing | Inspection | Production assembly (rear line) | Testing area | Production assembly (front line)

nents for insertion into the cabinet at the transfer point. After being placed in a cabinet, the set starts down the final line. The front line production assembly workers insert speakers, complete all wiring, and make the internal components functional. The set then enters the testing area where audio is inspected and adjustments are made. If adjustments cannot be made, the set is totally rejected.

After the rear-line assembly personnel supply the external components and finishing touches, the set is inspected for major defects, such as irregular voltage. Once a set passes inspection, it is rolled off the line for packaging. The quality control testing area acts as a completely separate operation. This unit selects and inspects at random 60 sets per day from the plant's two production lines.

Chassis line workers have their own quota and are included in the incentive program. Due to the nature of their assembly work, they are able to stockpile completed chassis, thereby operating independent of the finals line. In addition, personnel on the front and rear assembly lines are on incentive pay. However, testers and inspectors have been excluded from the incentive plan to prevent them from substituting speed for quality. Yet, it is this desire for quality that creates a problem.

Specifically, the front-line assemblers work at a speed that will earn their incentive pay, but the testers have no reason to work at the same speed. Consequently, they simply reject sets that they do not have time to check. As a result, the production line bogs down and the supervisor is faced with trying to motivate the testers to keep up with the assemblers' rate of production.

The problem has been diagnosed by top management as a failure by supervisors to understand and effectively apply the incentive program properly. Supervisors generally complain, however, that the incentive plan is neither satisfactory nor workable. In addition, they feel they are unable to communicate with top management about impending technical problems. Consequently, their time is spent trying to resolve these problems rather than with running their lines effectively. As a result, there has been a high turnover among supervisors due to both voluntary and involuntary separations.

Questions

1. Review Dave Tool's report. What do you feel he is trying to convey to Mr. Jackson?
2. How does the word *feedback* fit into the total picture at Central Phonograph.
3. What is the major control problem at this plant?
4. List some alternative solutions to the control problem.

General Pneumatics, Inc.

General Pneumatics was incorporated in 1965 and specializes in manufacturing pneumatic (air) blowers for use in industry, conservation, and pollution control. Several branch executives and other associates own large blocks of the corporation's stock. The president of General Pneumatics is Harold Goss who is also the major stockholder.

The product

General Pneumatics produces positive air rotary blowers. Its major customers are other industries and governmental agencies, with some business from trucking companies and fish hatcheries. The line of blowers manufactured is considered to be the "Cadillac" of the industry due to the company's high quality standards.

A supercharger designed for racing cars was once the corporation's primary product. From this product, the company developed four major lines that use the rotary blower principle:

1. Heavy-duty industrial blowers.
2. Gas meters.
3. Dry-air pumps.
4. Vacuum boosters.

The company has designed and engineered all of its products so as to remain competitive in each of the four lines. Its main competitors are producers of pneumatic conveyors and other manufacturers of pumps, air compressors, and vacuum systems.

The industry and its market

The pneumatic blower industry is relatively new, and potential customers rarely understand the advantages of a given product. For example, the use of pneumatics in a conveying system is new compared to conventional conveyor belts. In the trucking industry, pneumatic blowers create the pressure for unloading such items as cement and grain.

EXHIBIT 2
Organization chart, General Pneumatics, Inc.

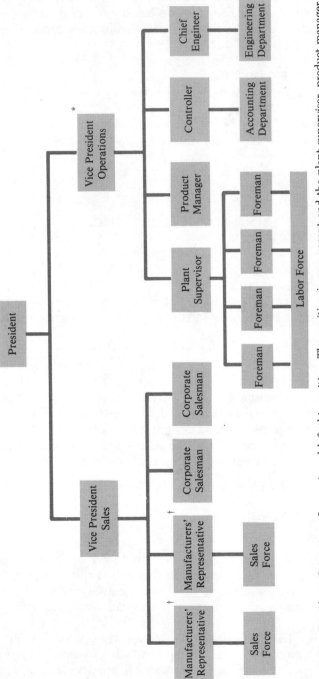

* Vice President, Operations, James Agred left this position. The position is now vacant and the plant supervisor, product manager, controller, and chief engineer report directly to the president.
† The manufacturers' representatives and sales force are not directly employed by the company but comprise an exclusive agency specializing in connecting buyers and sellers in industry. They work on a straight commission basis.

The Defense Department purchases industrial blowers for use as "deballasters" that take the place of pumps for removing water from submarines and ships. Fish hatcheries use pneumatic systems for circulating and enriching the oxygen content in the hatching tanks. Along the same line, the Army Corps of Engineers has explored the use of blowers for putting oxygen into large streams and lakes at certain times of the year when content is too low for fish to survive.

Sales and growth

With the exception of two salaried people in the sales department, General Pneumatics relies solely on a network of manufacturers' representatives for product distribution. These independent sales representatives work strictly on a commission basis and are not employed directly by the company. Exhibit 2 shows all sales personnel and their relationship to the total organization.

Exhibit 3 shows that sales increased gradually from $1.1 million in 1970 to $2.2 million in 1980. At the same time, however, General Pneumatics' share of the market decreased by 5 percent and profits declined.

In 1978, the company was unionized, and subsequently suffered a labor strike. A settlement in 1980 awarded the union a 9 percent wage increase across the board. This, along with the increased cost of raw materials, has caused total costs to soar at a tremendous rate. Thus, projections point to continuing losses for the future.

Organization

Since the company was formed, President Goss has retained centralized control over most activities. Authority relationships are classified basically as line and staff with little functional authority existing throughout the organization. The vice president of operations retired from the company in 1980 and that position remains vacant. In fact, the president feels that he has sufficient time for people in this area to report directly to him. All management personnel are regarded

EXHIBIT 3
Sales and profits, General Pneumatics, Inc.

Year	Sales	Net profit	Percent sales/profit
1970	$1,100,000	$132,000	12.0%
1971	1,300,000	163,000	12.5
1972	1,350,000	189,000	14.0
1973	1,500,000	195,000	13.0
1974	1,720,000	215,000	12.5
1975	1,800,000	243,000	13.5
1976	1,800,000	198,000	11.0
1977	1,850,000	212,000	11.5
1978	1,950,000	156,000	8.0
1979	2,100,000	105,000	5.0
1980	2,250,000	(33,000)	−1.5

as well qualified and ambitious. However, there is very little interaction among the different departments under the president.

Mr. Goss has realized for several years that the company's financial picture is getting worse, but he normally blames its poor performance on economic conditions. Recently, however, he called a meeting asking department heads for suggestions on how to get the company back on its feet. At the meeting, the following conversation took place:

President: We all realize that our company enjoys a good image in the industry. In addition, we are respected by our customers for manufacturing high quality products. Yet, our costs have risen to the point where it is becoming unprofitable for us to operate.

Controller: I think the whole problem lies in production. The employees are getting high wages, but they are not working very hard. Material costs are too high, and there seems to be a lot of waste.

Plant supervisor: My supervisors and I try our best to produce a quality product, but this requires a lot of time on each order. Our people work hard to put out a fine blower. I will agree, however, that there may be quite a bit of waste. Perhaps the Engineering Department hasn't shown us the very best way to make use of our materials.

Chief engineer: I didn't realize that any materials were wasted. I thought that all purchases and castings were made to minimize waste. You should talk to purchasing, I'm in charge of the engineering department.

Questions

1. What control problems are apparent at General Pneumatics?
2. What alternative courses of action are open to the president and which ones do you suggest he follow?
3. Justify the recommendations that you would offer to President Goss.

Janice Fry—Entrepreneur

Janice Fry left a small community in Illinois to try her luck in Los Angeles. Saving her money as a sales clerk in a large Los Angeles department store, she was able to buy an interest in a large dress shop that was seemingly successful. After about six months of operations, her associate unexpectedly left the business without any discussion with Ms. Fry about financial arrangements. Within four months after managing the business herself she realized that accounts payable exceeded the capacity of the shop to pay its bills. The balance sheet showed that current liabilities exceeded current assets by $75,000. Ms. Fry ceased operations and filed a bankruptcy petition for protection in U.S. District Court under Chapter 10 of the federal bankruptcy laws. In bankruptcy court, Ms. Fry stated:

> My associate left the business in a horrible state—bills were overdue that I did not even know existed. Suppliers called and asked when I

was going to pay bills that had been outstanding for several months. Some bills have been due for over a year. I had no idea I owed so much money. Cash is not available to pay off the suppliers, and the only way they will allow me to purchase new merchandise is to pay on some of my overdue accounts. In fact, any merchandise purchased must now be paid by cash in advance. My only alternative is to take bankruptcy.

Under Chapter 10 proceedings, the court appoints a trustee to oversee operations as the company attempts to restructure its financial condition while being protected from creditors. According to its bankruptcy filing, the shop was liable for "certain indebtedness" to five creditors that held a security interest for most of the significant assets of the shop.

The bankruptcy experience was disheartening, but Ms. Fry learned a great deal about people from it. Quite to her surprise, she learned that bankruptcy was not the end of the world and that business associates were quite understanding about her situation.

After the settlement, Ms. Fry sold fabrics and high quality curtain and drapery material. She was very effective as a salesperson, showing a high degree of aggressiveness and assertiveness. With the money she earned from her commissions, she invested in some new, microcomputer companies that had a high payoff in a short period of time. Several of the companies were taken over by larger electronic firms through mergers and direct purchases. Within a year, she had tripled her original investment.

The fabric shop for which she worked was a thriving innovative enterprise. The owner was presently negotiating to obtain a franchise from a national chain to sell dresses. Although the owner was in good health and enjoyed the business, Ms. Fry was effective in persuading the owner to sell the enterprise. Basically, Ms. Fry purchased the organization in anticipation that she would obtain the dress franchise and then expand by setting up a regional network of fabric/dress shops. Her intention was to open up several small stores throughout the Los Angeles area and then expand into San Francisco and the Seattle areas.

The dress franchise was not obtained because Ms. Fry was unwilling to pay the amount necessary to acquire franchise privileges. She felt the asking price was too high and that the purchasing, pricing, and merchandise return policy requirements would restrict the operational activities of the shop. Without the franchise, she still handled a quality line of dresses of all sizes, including a complete line of sportswear.

Although the business was earning a substantial profit, Ms. Fry reinvested only a small portion of the earnings back into the business. Coincidental to the shop's growth in profits, several large fabric stores were beginning to expand across the western part of the United States. The trend was toward multiple store operations with a centralized buying and warehouse arrangement.

Consequently, Ms. Fry felt that her business had ridden the crest of local sales and that the national chains would soon take over the fabric market. A buyer of the store was lined up, and Ms. Fry sold the entire operation.

For the past year now, Ms. Fry has been unemployed. Various business opportunities have not looked good to her since they did not meet her requirements for rapid growth. A business acquaintance of Ms. Fry has knowledge about a dress and bridal veil manufacturing company that is having financial trouble. The company can be bought quite reasonably, and with the proper development of a marketing strategy, it could earn a 20 percent return on investment. The company's poor performance is blamed on the late delivery of raw materials from suppliers that delayed production of garments. As a result, manufacturing expenses increased sharply. The idea presented to Ms. Fry was that once the company is acquired, through a partnership arrangement, a corporation would be established to purchase the building and equipment from the manufacturing company and then lease back the building and equipment to it. A friend who is an accountant and knowledgeable about financial acquistions felt that the proposed business deal is sound and the potential for success is good.

Ms. Fry, however, does not like the idea of having an associate since she still vividly remembers the early days of the dress shop. She feels she has a good knowledge of women's wear and how this line of product should be marketed. Nevertheless, she would like to have a free hand to manage the operation and make decisions without answering to a partner. The fabric business that she sold a year earlier has now expanded into a series of seven stores and is a major distributor of British and Italian sportswear for women.

Questions

1. What management concepts and functions do you think Janice Fry utilizes in her business ventures?
2. What control techniques should Ms. Fry use in making decisions?
3. If we consider Ms. Fry as a good example of an entrepreneur (a risk taker), how would you differentiate her role from the manager of a dress shop?
4. Based on what Janice Fry learned from the bankruptcy experience, should she enter into the new proposed partnership?

PART SIX

MANAGERIAL ADAPTATION

19

ORGANIZATIONAL GROWTH AND CHANGE

PURPOSE

Sears, Roebuck and Company is headquartered in the Sears Towers building in Chicago. A massive structure of 110 stories, the building is the tallest in the world. Like the building, Sears was the envy of many persons when the new headquarter's offices were occupied in 1973. At that time, the company had over 850 stores and more than 400,000 employees. Suppliers were sought out by an army of buyers and were usually convinced to provide their products at the lowest possible price. When combined with outstanding sales and profit figures, these factors stood as testimony to Sears' growth and success. Things have changed since 1973, however.

Sears is now a high-cost mass merchandiser. In fact, approximately 30 percent of its sales dollars goes for general and administrative expenses. As leading competitors, J. C. Penney and K mart devote some 5 to 7 percent less to the same expense categories. Along with shrinking profit margins and total merchandising profits, Sears has slipped elsewhere as shown by losses of over $8 million on credit card operations in just the first nine months of 1980. Contrasted with these negative performance results, Sears' insurance and real estate operations have done quite well. Retailing, however, is still the company's major emphasis (which accounts for over 65 percent of its total revenue). Accordingly, renewed progress is important in this side of the business if Sears is to maintain a strong growth position.

A multitude of problems accompany organizational growth, and certainly, Sears does not stand alone in this regard. Ford and General Motors are having their problems and those of Chrysler are even more widely known. Similarly, other companies have reached the top only to start slipping back down.

This chapter considers the meaning of organizational growth and provides examples of the growth process. Factors contributing to growth are also examined along with a discussion of the inevitability of change. Finally, the chapter presents organizational arrangements that often evolve from growth, development, and change.

OBJECTIVES

1. To discuss organizational growth as the ability of an organization to survive and prosper within its environment.

2. To provide examples of growth and adaptation through an examination of specific organizations.

3. To aid in developing an understanding of factors that influence organizational growth.

4. To illustrate the need for the management of change.

5. To present management development as an approach for meeting the challenges of organizational growth and change.

While president of General Motors, Alfred P. Sloan, Jr., stated: "To deliberately stop growing is to suffocate."[1] Sloan was telling us that managers must constantly strive for growth if their organizations are to survive in an ever-changing environment. Such organizational growth requires an awareness of the changing needs and goals of stockholders, employees, customers, the general public, and all other concerned groups. To achieve growth, therefore, managers must have a good understanding of the world in which they live.

The management of growth and change in an organization can be compared to a group of contractors building a house, office building, or apartment complex. Each contractor performs certain tasks, such as plumbing, wiring, painting, or roofing. All efforts, however, are guided by an overall architectural design and its accompanying specifications. Similarly, the growth of an organization is guided by an overall design (strategy). Individual managers are then able to blend various functions and activities together within the guidelines of this strategy and its accompanying policies.

ORGANIZATIONAL GROWTH

The exact meaning of organizational growth is not particularly clear in management literature. For instance, there is no agreement that an increase in sales or the number of employees necessarily means that growth has taken place. Increases in the sheer physical size of an organization may reflect a form of growth; however, we should be careful to recognize that size results from growth, rather than causing it.[2] With these points in mind, we begin to consider growth as it relates to the ability of an organization to survive and prosper within its environment.

As indicated, organizational growth expresses itself in many forms. The growth of a hospital can be evaluated through such measures as the number of beds, additions to the nursing staff, or the number of patients treated. Within business firms, a new product line, an expanded marketing area, or the creation of a research and development department may indicate that growth is occurring. In other cases, an organization may exhibit growth by simply maintaining its relative position in an environment of rapid change.

EXAMPLES OF ORGANIZATIONAL GROWTH

To emphasize the meanings of growth, K mart, Iowa Beef, Schlumberger, and Union Pacific are discussed as examples of how organizations grow in various ways.[3]

---

[1] Alfred P. Sloan, Jr., *My Years with General Motors* (Garden City, N.Y.: Doubleday, 1963).

[2] Joseph A. Litterer, *The Analysis of Organizations* (New York: John Wiley & Sons, 1972), p. 651.

[3] See "Where K mart Goes Next Now That It's No. 2," *Business Week*, June 2, 1980,

K mart

In 1960, the S. S. Kresge Company started branching out from its 5 cents and 10 cents variety store base by converting several units to Jupiter discount stores. This led to the opening of the first K mart in 1962. Fifteen years later, K mart accounted for over 95 percent of Kresge's sales, and the corporate name was changed to correspond with its continued progress as a national discount store chain.

K mart's early focus on low prices, value, and rapid inventory turnover has proven very successful for the Detroit-based company. Today, K mart Corporation has almost 2,000 stores in large and small cities across the country and is sandwiched between Sears and J. C. Penney as the nation's second largest retailer. This growth has led some analysts to predict that K mart will pass Sears in dollar sales volume by 1985. To accomplish this feat, K mart will have to deal successfully with a number of problems.

Faced with growing competition from regional discounters, such as Wal-Mart Stores and Caldor, Inc., K mart sees its ability to maintain a 20 percent annual growth rate becoming more limited. Therefore, a more modest growth rate of 12 percent has been targeted by the company's management and its accomplishment will require some careful decision making. The addition of several new stores each year has been a major factor in K mart's growth rate. Continuing this practice in the future will become more difficult, due to a saturation of major market areas. As another alternative, a slower growth rate can be accepted with more emphasis on productivity throughout the organization. Diversification is also a possiblity if the company can acquire other businesses with high growth potential.

K mart management seems uncertain of which alternative to choose. A small step toward diversification was taken in 1980 when the company acquired Furr's Cafeterias, Inc. At the same time, smaller market areas were being explored for the location of stores scaled down in size from those in larger urban areas. Such units will represent about one half of K mart's new stores in the future. Beyond these things, the company is also trying to change its image from one primarily attractive to blue-collar, low-income shoppers. Other problems are present in the latter course of action. By upgrading its merchandise, K mart moves away from some of the low-margin, high-volume items that have been so important to high inventory turnover. New store layouts to display such items are also required in some cases. In turn, this reduces sales per square foot of floor space and requires merchandising policies significantly different from those which have guided the company for two decades.

For these and other reasons, K mart is struggling to maintain its

pp. 109–14; "Iowa Beef: Moving in for a Kill by Automating Pork Processing," *Business Week*, July 14, 1980, pp. 100–102; "Schlumberger: The Star of the Oil Fields Tackles Semiconductors," *Business Week*, February 16, 1981, pp. 60–70; and "Back to Railroading for a New Era," *Business Week*, July 14, 1980, pp. 64–70.

market position. Whether the conservative management strategy that has been responsible for the company's success will be sufficient to maintain its future momentum remains to be seen.

Iowa Beef

About 15 years ago, Iowa Beef Processors, Inc., broke with tradition in the beef slaughtering industry. Rather than locating in large urban areas such as Chicago, Omaha, and Kansas City where cattle are transported for slaughter, Iowa Beef built packing plants in rural areas where the animals are raised. In addition to lower transportation costs, Iowa Beef's new plants enjoyed the advantages of highly automated meat-cutting and packaging processes as well as lower wage rates. The results pushed the company to the top of the beef packing industry in the United States with about 20 percent of the market. Iowa Beef is not content to rest on this accomplishment, however, and is shooting for one fourth of the market by 1984. Simultaneously, the company is building on its success in beef as it prepares to move into the pork industry.

As Iowa Beef enters the pork market, it will be faced with competition from Wilson Foods, Armour, Oscar Mayer, and other established companies against which it has competed successfully in the beef industry. Again, the company will build highly automated plants to go up against the older high-cost, labor-intensive plants of its rivals. Unlike its competitors, money to finance Iowa Beef's cash flow has been sufficient to cover some of its past expansion efforts, while a current ratio of 3 to 1 and a debt to equity ratio of 0.2 to 1 cause lenders to be very receptive to the company's proposals.

The timing for Iowa Beef's move into pork also seems to be well chosen. Between 1974 and 1978, the number of pork processing plants in the United States fell by 15 percent as older plants closed and smaller processors went out of business or were acquired by larger companies. Still, Iowa Beef will face new challenges from established companies in the pork industry. Most pork is processed into bacon, hot dogs, and cured hams that are sold under widely advertised brand names. Iowa Beef does not have a well-known brand in this market, and developing customer acceptance of new brands takes time and money. The company is not backing off, however. With plenty of cash, it is in a position either to buy an existing brand name or to develop a new one for its pork products. Another alternative is that of processing products for the labels of supermarkets or other packing companies. It is here that the company can benefit from the same strategy that made its beef operations so successful. Regardless of the strategy selected, the company will probably face increased competition in the future as new firms enter the beef and pork industries by following Iowa Beef's successful examples.

Schlumberger

The renewed search for oil throughout the world in recent years has created a booming business for service companies such as Schlumberger, Ltd. These companies provide a critical service to drilling contractors that involves a series of scientifically advanced measurements during the drilling process to help show how much oil and gas might be expected from the geological formations being tested. Although Schlumberger leads all competitors, the company is not content to rest on its success that accounts for 50 percent of the U.S. oil well logging business and an even larger percentage of foreign markets.

Building on its reputation as an innovator in the industry, Schlumberger is rapidly expanding into a new generation of computerized measurement devices. Already, it is apparent that this new technology will contribute greatly to sales figures that reached almost $5 billion in 1980. During the same year, earnings increased by an estimated 40 percent to approximately $940 million. With its excellent financial condition, Schlumberger also continues its commitment to research and development. As recently as 1979, for example, the company put 3.7 percent of sales into R&D, which was more than twice the oil industry average. This commitment, combined with a decentralization of authority to lower levels of management, has left an imprint on companies acquired by Schlumberger. The organization bought the French owned Compagnie des Compteurs in 1970. This manufacturer of gas, water, and electric meters was almost bankrupt after attempts to diversify into television, computers, and military electronics. After replacing several managers, pruning product lines, and reducing the number of employees, sales and earnings almost doubled in four years. The U.S. organization, Sangamo Electric Company, has also started moving ahead in market share since being acquired in 1975.

The results of one of Schlumberger's biggest gambles are not yet available. In 1979, the company acquired Fairchild Camera and Instrument Corporation for some $400 million. Fairchild had enjoyed a position of market leadership in the 1960s and was selected by Schlumberger to lead its entrance into the semiconductor business. Schlumberger's chairman, Jean Riboud, sees the company in the business of gathering and interpreting data. Semiconductors are important in this role, and their addition is being viewed as a refinement of Schlumberger's major thrust. This new market is far more competitive than the business now dominated by Schlumberger, but steps are already being taken to strengthen Fairchild's performance. The company's headquarters staff has been reduced by some 400 people in order to push more responsibility downward in the management ranks. The R&D budget for 1981 was increased by about 50 percent to more than $70 million, and the market appears to be gaining confidence in Fairchild's products. Whatever the results, it cannot be said that Schlumberger suffers from complacency.

Union Pacific Corporation

On May 10, 1869, a golden spike was driven at Promontory, Utah, to mark completion of the transcontinental railroad at the junction of Central Pacific and Union Pacific railroads. Since that time, Union

Pacific has remained a strong competitor in the industry. Less widely known by many people, however, is the fact that the organization has been joined by three other operating companies under the Union Pacific Corporation (UP) umbrella.

In the mid-1960s, the three top officers of UP saw that the company was overly dominated by the railroad. Their response was to create energy, natural resources, and land development strategies that have moved the company to a position where it enjoys some $5 billion in assets. In 1970, UP purchased the Champlin Petroleum Company for some $250 million. As a fully integrated company, Champlin is involved in the exploration, production, transportation, and marketing of petroleum products. By the end of 1980, Champlin had spent $500 million to improve its refinery operations and was UP's fastest growing operating company.

Rocky Mountain Energy Company is the second largest operating company in Union Pacific Corporation. The company carries out extensive mining operations and has coal reserves estimated to be the fourth largest in the United States. In addition, the organization mines uranium and other minerals from vast land holdings in states such as Wyoming. Joining Rocky Mountain and Champlin as the third operating company of UP is Upland Industries Corporation. As a land development and management subsidiary, Upland develops, sells, or leases industrial and commercial sites throughout the West. As a part of its administrative responsibilities, Upland manages over one million acres of land and some seven million acres of mineral rights carried forward from land grants made by Congress in 1862.

While the strategy that led to UP's diversification placed less reliance on its railroad business, the company is now turning its attention back to railroading. New profit and growth opportunities seem likely in the 1980s due to deregulation of the railroads and increasing fuel costs for the total transportation industry. A planned merger with the Missouri Pacific would add 11,500 miles of track throughout the southern Midwest. Another with Western Pacific would provide lines into northern California. Of these, the Missouri Pacific is particularly attractive since it serves a section of the Sunbelt that is growing rapidly.

Some observers of the Union Pacific and Missouri Pacific merger are skeptical. They point out that both companies are highly centralized and that their combined size may be too large to manage efficiently. This prediction may prove to be correct. Certainly, new challenges will be presented. Perhaps, however, Union Pacific's careful attention to long-range planning will see it through another significant change in corporate strategy.

**FACTORS
INFLUENCING
GROWTH**

Beyond the examples of organizational growth discussed above, we could cite many more. The extraordinary success of the Coca-Cola Company is known throughout the world. Franchise operations, such as Kentucky Fried Chicken, Holiday Inn, and McDonald's, are stories within themselves. Mergers and acquisitions have turned other companies into major industrial complexes within a few short years. As one illustration, an active acquisition program has made International Systems and Control Corporation (ISC) a rapidly growing multinational firm.

Changes in various environmental factors will always influence the growth patterns of these and all other organizations. Managers must be skilled, therefore, in identifying and evaluating environmental changes if they are to be successful in managing organizational growth. Some of the more important factors to be considered include:

1. External interfaces between the organization and general business conditions, population growth, competing organizations, social changes, technology, transportation, education, government, and the general public.
2. Organizational strategies, objectives, policies, plans, procedures, and methods.
3. Inputs into the organization in the form of human resources, materials, equipment, capital, technology, and management.
4. Processing factors related to marketing, production, finance, personnel, research and development, engineering, and purchasing.
5. Output considerations in terms of consumer demands and emerging needs for new products and services.

As change agents, managers must stay alert to these or other factors that can influence the growth of their respective organizations. Ultimately, of course, organizational adaptation to change may be required in various areas such as long-term objectives; employee attitudes, behavior, and performance; product lines; and organization structure. When women's skirts rose to the mini-length, for example, companies that moved rapidly into the production and sale of panty hose were able to increase their chances for future growth and profitability. Viewed in the light of this example, a growth enterprise is one that can adapt to internal and external changes innovatively without losing sight of the need for a long-term growth strategy.

THE MANAGEMENT OF CHANGE

Managers can be certain that change is a fact and will always occur. Warren Bennis has stated the following concerning the management of change:

> Our social institutions cannot withstand, let alone cope with the devastating rate of change without fundamental alterations in the way they negotiate their environments and the way they conduct the main operations of their enterprise.[4]

[4] Warren G. Bennis, *Organization Development: Its Nature, Origins, and Prospects* (Reading, Mass.: Addison-Wesley Publishing, 1969), p. 18. © 1969 Addison-Wesley. Reprinted with permission.

It is also apparent that a conscious management of change depends on the quantity and quality of information made available to organizational members. When internal and external forces affecting change go unrecognized due to a lack of information, organizational growth and survival are severely threatened.

J. M. Ewell of the Proctor & Gamble Company has stated that firms must find ways to anticipate the probable requirements of change in order to initiate their own adaptive changes in advance. If this is not done, managers will be forced to react to change, rather than positioning themselves to manage it. Clearly, the ability of any organization to adapt to change depends on managers who are creative in meeting new challenges and opportunities. Therefore, in organizations where environmental factors are relatively constant, management may actually choose to introduce changes periodically in order to combat complacency and to stimulate creativity.

To summarize, no organization is immune to the influences of change; consequently, the most successful managers of today and tomorrow will be those who can provide creative leadership in managing change. Growth strategies are particularly important in this regard since they provide a focal point for all organizational leaders. In the absence of such strategies, managers devote too much attention to pressures, constraints, and opportunities of the moment. Thus, when faced with great opportunities, these managers are not prepared to meet the challenges of change. As a result, their organizations are often left behind by competitors pursuing well-chosen growth strategies.[5]

ORGANIZATIONAL CHANGES AND GROWTH

Although a biological analogy is not always applicable, it is a convenient vehicle to use in considering organizational changes caused by growth. For example, the newborn child has all parts of its body as does the adult. Likewise, a new business must perform the same functions of sales, production, and finance as the mature enterprise. In adapting to a particular environment, a child develops into a mature adult with individual characteristics. An organization also reflects specific attributes as it adapts to its environment. With time, however, rather dramatic changes take place in the appearance of both adults and organizations. In the following sections, we will look at several organizational changes that are often associated with growth.

Specialists and generalists

As organizations grow larger, top-level managers tend to become generalists rather than specialists. This happens because the total number of demands on top management rapidly exceed the time available for dealing with them. A natural response is to delegate more special-

---

[5] See John D. Glover, *The Revolutionary Corporations* (Homewood, Ill.: Dow Jones-Irwin, 1980), pp. 388–89.

FIGURE 19–1
Typical long-run average cost curve

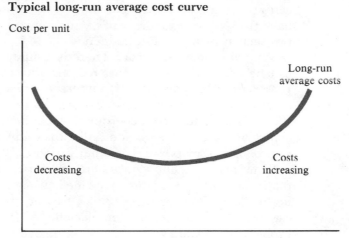

ized duties to subordinate line managers, or to create additional managerial staff positions to handle specific functional areas. Thus, we often see the development of entire departments in retail stores, manufacturing plants, hospitals, military units, or universities, each charged with coordinating specialized activities in their respective areas. Through proper combinations of specialists and generalists, organizations are in a better position to perceive and to adapt to those environmental changes that will influence their continued growth and success.

Economies of scale   As a firm increases its sales and production, economies of scale must be considered in making decisions about further expansion. The basic question related to economies of scale concerns whether or not the cost per unit of the product will decrease with increased organizational size. Traditional economic theory suggests that the long-run, U-shaped average cost curve represents increasing returns to scale at small levels of output and decreasing returns to scale after output passes a certain point. In most instances, the middle portion of the curve reflects situations where costs remain relatively constant. Figure 19–1 illustrates such a situation.

The long-run average cost curve shows that in some industries costs per unit decrease to a certain point as the size of an operation increases.[6] A decrease in costs could possibly be generated by a large machine that is more productive than a smaller one. For example, the large basic oxygen furnace in a steel mill is more productive than the smaller Bessemer blast furnace. Also, the quantity discounts and

[6] John Haldi and David Whitcomb, "Economics of Scale in Industrial Plants," *Readings in Managerial Economies,* ed. W. W. Haynes et al. (Plano, Tex.: Business Publications, 1973), pp. 219–31.

lower freight rates that are available through large-scale purchasing can reduce material costs per unit. In other cases, larger companies have the resources to hire staff personnel who can specialize in activities such as planning and budgeting.

Why diseconomies occur There is a limit to which costs per unit can be decreased. Traditional reasons why costs increase as output passes a certain point are (1) increased managerial expenses and (2) organizational ineffectiveness. Thus, as an organization grows in size, the costs associated with coordination, communication, planning, and controlling increase at a rate faster than any decreases experienced in production, marketing, or other expenses.

Some management scholars are critical of the view that long-run marginal costs increase due to the inefficiency of management. According to Peter Drucker, size is not a barrier to good management and can actually facilitate greater efficiency.[7] He also feels that various problems associated with growth can be overcome through decentralization—that is, delegating decision-making authority to smaller units within the organization. Although decentralization is a partial solution to diseconomies, the limits of manageable size will vary with the type of organization as well as the managerial techniques utilized within each organization.

Managerial efficiency and diseconomies of scale We are now faced with a perplexing situation. With continued increases in the size of an organization, could the long-run average cost curve actually become horizontal with proper managerial adjustments? Unfortunately, we have been unable to measure long-run costs effectively. Some statistical and engineering cost studies have shown the existence of a downward sloping curve that reaches a minimum and then becomes horizontal. Other studies, however, show an increase in costs at high levels of output.

Pragmatically, economies and diseconomies of scale vary with the type of firm being considered as well as with the industry in which it operates. In retailing, both large and small firms can enjoy certain advantages. On the other hand, automobile plants or steel mills reflect the cost advantages of a large size, with small firms being unable to compete effectively in these fields. Unfortunately, many managers have not yet moved beyond the trial and error method of determining an optimal scale of operations that permits their organizations to compete effectively. Part of the problem is due to (1) the difficulty in measuring long-run costs, (2) the varying nature of demand, and (3) the dynamic structure of factors affecting costs. In any event, all organizations should examine their long-run cost structure through appropriate models or an enumeration of projected results under alternative expansion plans.

---

[7] Peter F. Drucker, *The New Society* (New York: Harper & Row, 1962), pp. 225–27.

Changes in organizational structure

Since no two organizations are identical, an organizational design satisfactory for one may not be effective for another. The follow-the-leader approach is not a successful technique to use in designing an organization structure.[8] Instead, a contingency approach is far more realistic, given the dynamics of today's organizational environments. This approach implies that the structure chosen should be based on an analysis of the prevailing culture of the organization, its state of readiness for change, its technology, managerial expectations, and the organization's value system.[9] Through such analyses, the contingency approach places less emphasis on a mechanistic structure and more on a flexible design that will provide a meaningful interface with the external environment. The need for such flexibility is shown in the following sections that consider various changes in formally designed authority structures and their possible impact on managerial performance.

Modification of the pyramid Most organization charts reflect the pyramidal-shaped structure in which there are fewer people at higher levels than at the lower levels. However, this balanced pyramidal structure is not recognizable in all organizations. For example, an investigation of agencies in the federal government indicates that the true pyramidal structure is not always prevalent. Some agencies portray various modifications of the pyramid as the number of employees increases. When both line and staff positions increase rapidly during organizational growth, the change approaches that of a diamond-shaped structure.

The tendency toward a diamond-shaped structure, however, is not accepted by all researchers. Of particular interest is a study by Reinhard Bendix that compares the percentage of administrative personnel to all employees in German industry from 1907 to 1933.[10] He found that the highest percentage of administrative employees occurred in companies employing from 6 to 50 workers and that this percentage declined as the size of an organization increased. On the other hand, the highest percentage of technical staff members was observed in the largest organizations.

A classical study by Mason Haire also found that the ratio of superiors to subordinates declines sharply as an organization increases in size.[11] Haire also points out that when the number of employees increases beyond eight, the number of staff positions increases much more rap-

---

[8] See Jay W. Lorsch and Paul R. Lawrence, *Studies in Organization Design* (Homewood, Ill.: Richard D. Irwin and Dorsey Press, 1970).

[9] See Don Hellriegel and John W. Slocum, Jr., *Organizational Behavior: Contingency Views* (St. Paul: West Publishing, 1976).

[10] Reinhard Bendix, *Work and Authority in Industry* (New York: Harper & Row, 1963), pp. 212–22.

[11] Mason Haire, "Biological Models and Empirical Histories of the Growth of Organizations," *Modern Organizational Theory: A Symposium of the Foundation for Research on Human Behavior* (New York: John Wiley & Sons, 1959), pp. 272–306.

FIGURE 19–2
Predicted structural changes in organizations of the future

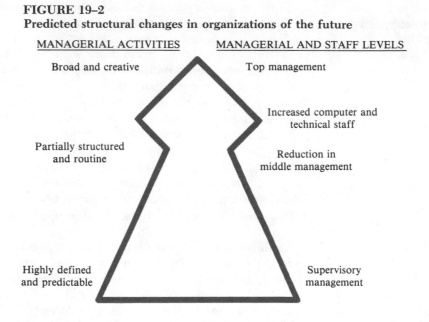

MANAGERIAL ACTIVITIES   MANAGERIAL AND STAFF LEVELS

Broad and creative   Top management

Increased computer and
technical staff

Partially structured   Reduction in
and routine   middle management

Highly defined   Supervisory
and predictable   management

idly than line positions. In support of the findings presented by both Haire and Bendix, a study of Veterans Administration hospitals shows that the largest hospitals have the smallest percentage of administrative personnel.[12]

Another facet of pyramidal modification is that the flat structure with wide spans of management may enhance satisfaction and productivity in small organizations. However, as an organization grows larger, the flat structure loses these advantages and may even become a liability.

Structural changes in the future   One set of predictions about the future design of large organizations suggests a structural form similar to a diamond balanced on top of a pyramid. As shown in Figure 19–2, the lower part of the diamond reflects our earlier discussion about the possible reduction of middle-management positions caused by the advancement of computer and information technology. The broadest part of the diamond indicates a greater number of highly trained staff personnel performing many of the planning activities traditionally associated with middle management.

Just how the variables of computer science and information technology will affect organizational design in the future is not clear. We can be sure, however, that the perfect pyramidal form is not a realistic picture of today's organizations, nor will it be in the future. For some

---

[12] T. H. Anderson and Seymour Warkov, "Organizational Size and Functional Complexity: A Study of Administration in Hospitals," in *Organizations: Structure and Behavior*, ed. J. A. Litterer (New York: John Wiley & Sons, 1967), pp. 317–21.

organizations, the pyramid may become flatter, showing fewer levels of management. In others, there may be relatively few observable changes.

Management development

During World War II, there was a tremendous drain on the supply of qualified managerial personnel. As a result, training and development activities were undertaken at a rapid pace. Training at that time focused on preventing or correcting technical deficiencies, while management development sought to prepare people for greater managerial responsibilities.[13] In both cases, however, the emphasis was on speed with most programs being of short duration.

Today, management education is viewed as a process that is never completed. Since employees differ from one another, the process is also one that must be individualized to a considerable extent. At the same time, however, individual needs must be balanced with those of the organization if the development process is to have maximum benefits for all concerned.

Areas covered by development In order for development to be tied to both individual and to organizational needs, it is important that key organizational problems and issues be identified. The areas covered by management development often include the following:

The "how-to" subjects where specific management techniques are taught. These areas might include guides to organizational development and design, statistical quality control, operations research, or approaches to business forecasting.

The development of problem-solving abilities. This area often stresses analyzing organizational problems and emphasizing the importance of recognizing and adapting to change.

The area of interpersonal relations where people become aware of their own behavior as a first step toward dealing with others more effectively.

Orientation sessions that discuss organizational objectives, policies, operations, and structure.

Whether stressing these areas, or others, development does not take place in a vacuum. It must be supported by top management and subjected to follow-up evaluations to determine whether learning is carrying over to job performance. A variety of methods and techniques must also be examined in order to tailor the development process to different management groups. Some of the more common methods and techniques are discussed below.

On-the-job development College graduates often state that an opportunity to participate in an on-the-job development program was

---

[13] Philip T. Crotty, "Development Programs for Mature Managers," *Business Horizons,* December 1974, pp. 80–86.

a major factor in their selection of one employer over others. In such programs, trainees receive coaching and individual instruction from supervisors while they are on the job. Thus, feedback on performance is rapid, making work experience a valuable part of the developmental process.

Job rotation   During the development process, trainees often desire more (1) facts about the organization, (2) experience in analyzing different types of problems, (3) opportunities to reveal their qualifications and skills in other positions within the organization, and (4) diversified preparation for future career opportunities. Job rotation assists trainees in fulfilling these goals.

Job rotation can be used at all organizational levels and involves the movement (rotation) of trainees through a planned series of positions before they are placed in a specific job. Throughout the process, three conditions must exist if job rotation is to be effective:

People within given departments must be willing to assist and coach trainees when necessary.

Trainees must have opportunities to conduct analyses and make decisions while being held accountable for results.

Trainees must remain in jobs long enough that the program does not become a shuffle system. If trainees move through several departments, staying only a short time in each, they cannot receive the feedback needed to assess their performance.

In-house programs   Conferences and seminars held on an organization's premises provide trainees with opportunities to broaden their outlook through an exchange of ideas with others. Conferences are especially valuable for introducing new programs, policies, or other significant changes. To be most successful, however, both conferences and seminars require active participation by all who are in attendance. This requirement, in turn, makes the program leader a key element in the total process.

External programs   Trade associations, professional groups, and universities offer various workshops, seminars, and courses that can contribute to the management development process. Some offerings stress specialized areas, such as distribution, advertising, personnel management, safety, leadership, communication, or the basic management functions of planning, organizing, and controlling. As with in-house programs, however, these must be viewed as only one part of the total developmental process; they cannot do the entire job by themselves.[14]

Teaching techniques   Various teaching techniques are available for use in either internal or external programs. While none will work with all groups, each can be quite beneficial when fitted to the subject

---

[14] "Just How Useful Are Courses?" *Industrial Management,* January 1977, pp. 17–18.

matter, instructor, participants, and any other relevant situational factor.

Case problems Cases serve to provide simulated problem situations. With information available in the case, participants must define problem causes, identify alternative solutions, evaluate and select an alternative, and suggest a framework for implementation. Thus, cases provide insight into various concepts while providing opportunities for gaining decision-making experience.

Business games Business games have been quite popular since the middle 1950s. They provide simulated situations in which trainees make decisions and carry out various management functions. Normally, participants are grouped into teams representing companies within an industry. Working with a simulated business environment, operating decisions are then made in areas of pricing, advertising, research and development, production, purchasing, and finance. Objectives to be achieved may include obtaining the highest rate of return on investments or establishing the highest stock price in the industry.

As a developmental exercise, games can help trainees broaden their perspectives of the entire organization, recognize interrelationships between inputs and outputs affecting a decision, improve problem-solving skills, and accept responsibility for decisions. However, games are not ends in themselves—they are merely one means for gaining a better understanding of management concepts and their application to business situations.

In-basket exercises This technique lets trainees play the role of a manager. Background materials on an organization's policies and procedures are given to participants, along with various letters, memos, and telephone messages that are placed in their "in-baskets." Within a stated period of time, each trainee must determine the problems to be solved, priorities for their solution, and specific courses of action to be taken.

The in-basket exercise is useful in that it gives trainees an idea of their effectiveness in decision making under simulated conditions. With proper feedback they gain insight into the behavior patterns utilized in the solution of different types of problems. Such information allows participants to determine whether another approach could have been employed with greater effectiveness.

When there is a correlation between parts of the in-basket exercise and criteria for management performance, the technique can be useful in making staffing decisions. For example, General Electric has utilized in-basket exercises in selecting individuals for promotion to managerial positions.

Sensitivity training As a developmental technique, sensitivity training attempts through unstructured small groups to make participants more sensitive and aware of themselves and their interrelationships with others. The technique assumes that goal achievement will be more effective if the emotional hangups among people are removed. Uncertainty exists, however, about the effectiveness of sensitivity training in improving job skills. Yet, advocates believe that an awareness of how humans relate to one another is now more important than technological processes in improving organizational effectiveness.[15]

Although different in nature, *transactional analysis* seeks objectives similar to those of sensitivity training.[16] Originally, the approach was developed as a method of psychotherapy and is normally used in a group setting. The objectives are to help people become more aware of (1) themselves, (2) how they transact with others, and (3) the structure of their own behavior. The payoff is not only better communication and understanding but also an opportunity for people to see themselves more clearly as a prelude to changing what they want to change and improving what they want to improve about themselves.

Behavior modification. A technique receiving attention in the training field today is behavior modification.[17] Founded on Thorndike's *law of effect* and B. F. Skinner's *operant analysis of positive reinforcement*, the technique proposes that job performance can be changed through positive reinforcements of desired behavior. Reinforcers, however, must be linked to occurrences of desired behavior if they are to be effective.

While it may be questionable to view behavior modification as a training technique, per se, it has a place in the day-to-day coaching and counseling interactions between superiors and subordinates. In this respect, it has the potential to become an important part of the total developmental process in all organizations.

Committees and change

A committee normally refers to a group of organizational members who are responsible for solving a specific problem or accomplishing a specific task. In this sense, committee activities involve group, rather than individual, decision making. Of course, there is always the question of whether a committee can actually make decisions or whether its responsibility must be vested in one individual. Certainly the answer to this question depends on the nature and purpose of a given committee; however, even committees that exist only to offer recommendations are involved in the decision-making process.

A committee as a formal entity is established by someone within an organization who has the authority to create, and subsequently, disband the group when its mission has been accomplished. Yet, to

---

[15] See Chapter 15 for an expanded discussion of sensitivity training as it relates to the development of leadership skills.

[16] See Eric Berne, *Games People Play* (New York: Grove Press, 1964); and Muriel James and Dorothy Jongeward, *Born to Win: Transactional Analysis with Gestalt Experiments* (Reading, Mass.: Addison-Wesley Publishing, 1971).

[17] Craig Eric Schneier, "Behavior Modification in Management: A Review and Critique," *Academy of Management Journal*, September 1974, pp. 528–48.

decide exactly when a committee should be created is difficult to determine. For some large organizations, the committee system is considered to be an important administrative device. In others, committees play a minor role within the total organizational structure. The use of committees, however, normally indicates that some organizational change has occurred and that management is adjusting the decision-making system to meet new environmental demands.

Work of a committee   Committees may undertake a myriad of activities, but one of the most common is to promote coordination by bringing together individuals from various parts of an organization. Through a sharing of ideas and experiences, members come to view interrelationships among organizational units quite differently than when they are considered in isolation.

It is also possible that better decisions come from a group where diverse inputs can be brought together for consideration. On the other hand, a great deal of managerial time can be consumed in committee meetings, thereby detracting from other important responsibilities. In addition, group decisions may represent compromises that satisfy all members, rather than innovative solutions. These limitations should be balanced against the benefits of group participation that can lead to a greater acceptance of decisions by individual members.

Some cautions in using committees   Without question, committees should not be used in certain situations. If, for example, managers do not want to accept full responsibility for a decision, they should not be permitted to hide behind the cloak of a committee. It is also inappropriate to use committees when accountabilities must be clearly defined. To illustrate, committee members may pass the buck when a decision turns out to be unsuccessful and top management wants to find out what went wrong. When time is of the essence for making a critically important decision, committees have additional limitations. Often, committee members are not available when emergencies arise and it takes time to arrange a suitable meeting time.

Another caution is not to place committees in a position where they must oversee the execution of policies. Many managers consider committees to be useful in formulating policy recommendations but highly ineffective in directing their implementation. In reality, a board of directors constitutes a committee; however, its major function is to formulate, rather than to execute, policies. Thus, while managers who are responsible for implementing policies may serve on the board, the board itself is strictly a policymaking body.

The plural executive   Although there are limitations, some committees are granted the authority to formulate and to administer policy. Committees of this type function as a plural executive and may serve under designations of "Office of the President" or "Executive Committee." In turn, these groups have both line and staff authority with major responsibilities in the areas of planning, coordination, and control. Generally, each member of the group has equal authority for making final decisions. As a planning and coordinating unit, the plural executive can be highly successful, but as an administrative group, it may be ineffective due to the spreading of responsibility and accountability among its members. When considered in total, these points indicate that committees, by themselves, cannot overcome organizational problems created by either change or poor management. Instead, like any other management technique, their use must be properly integrated within the organizational structure so that overall relationships are reflective of synergistic performance.

Change and human resources

More than ever before, managers operate in environments where there are no pat answers or standard procedures that can be followed to achieve organizational goals. With the growth of multinational corporations, advancing technology, and demands for a greater social awareness, a successful management style of just a few years ago may be completely out of step today.[18]

Throughout this chapter, we have pointed out how changes have impact on the human resources of an organization. Perhaps more than anything, change influences the attitudes and behavior of employees. It can disrupt established social relationships within organizations and is often perceived by employees as a threat to their security and well-being. Unfortunately, the impact of changes external to an organization cannot always be minimized. Changes introduced by management are a different matter, however.

A proper introduction of change is based on concepts and guidelines presented in several earlier chapters. It requires planning to determine where an organization wants to be after a given change is implemented. Decision making is essential since alternative approaches for introducing change must be identified and evaluated. Formal and informal authority relationships must be considered because resistance to change is often based on perceived threats to these relationships. Closely related to this consideration is the need to understand leadership, communication, and motivation.

The overall message of this discussion is that a consideration of the human element is all important in managing organizational change. Above all, changes necessitated by an organization's growth strategy must capitalize on its human resources if the efficiency sought through material resources is to be fully realized.

SUMMARY

Organizational growth and change is a fact of life in modern organizations. Growth in this case refers to the ability of an organization to survive and advance within its environment and may be expressed

---

[18] Gerard Tavernier, "Changing Climate for Future Managers," *International Management*, August 1976, pp. 11–12.

in many forms such as new product lines, expanded operations, increased assets, or an increase in the number of employees. The key to a company's growth rests with managers who are able to perceive environmental changes before they occur. Although astute managers desire stability and the least disruption to plans, they cannot wait until they are forced to adapt to environmental changes. To be accountable for performance, they must constantly search for new opportunities by anticipating problems through active programs of research and development.

With increasing size, an organization's dependence on computer personnel and other staff specialists often causes the traditional pyramidal structure to take on different configurations. There does not seem, at present, to be any one structural pattern common to all growth companies; however, two of the more usual forms are the diamond shape and the flattened pyramid. Future structural designs will continue to be influenced by organizational complexities, dynamics of growth, and the stability of external environmental conditions. Consequently, the major thrust will still be that of searching for organizational arrangements that utilize human resources most effectively.

KEY TERMS

Change agent: The person(s) in an organization who seek to diagnose problems and develop appropriate solutions so that given changes are introduced with minimal resistance from organizational members.

Economies of scale: Reductions in long-run average costs that accompany growth in output up to that point where costs begin to increase.

Growth enterprise: An organization that can adapt to internal and external changes innovatively without losing sight of the need for a long-term growth strategy.

Job rotation: The movement of trainees through a planned series of positions before they are placed in specific jobs.

On-the-job development: The coaching and day-to-day instruction received by employees as they carry out their assigned responsibilites.

Organizational growth: The ability of an organization to survive and to prosper within its environment.

Simulation training: The use of cases, business games, in-basket exercises, or other methods to simulate situations within which participants gain experience in performing management functions.

QUESTIONS

1. What is meant by organizational growth? Would an increase in the number of clients seeking counseling from a social services agency mean that the agency was growing?

2. List the factors that influence organizational growth.

3. Why might two similar organizations with essentially the same growth strategies experience markedly different rates of growth?

4. Discuss the statement, "Change is inevitable!"

5. Explain the organizational changes that require managers to move from specialist to generalist positions.

6. Discuss the meaning of economies of scale. Do all companies experience diseconomies of scale as they grow larger? Why?

7. Discuss characteristics of the following organizational structures: (a) pyramid, (b) diamond, (c) flat pyramid, (d) diamond balanced on top of a pyramid.

8. Why is management development so important in managing organizational growth and change?

9. Describe (a) on-the-job training, and (b) job rotation.

10. What are some of the possible advantages of using committees for decision-making purposes?

11. What is meant by the plural executive? What are advantages and disadvantages of such executive arrangements?

12. Why must managers consider human resources when organizational changes are being contemplated?

PROBLEMS

1. Valleydale Health Services, Inc., owns a large metropolitan hospital and provides management services for smaller hospitals throughout several states in the region where the corporation has its headquarters. The president of Valleydale recently stated: "Most successful organizations in America have demonstrated an unusual ability to grow. With contracts to provide management services for six additional hospitals next year, Valleydale is obviously a successful and growing corporation." How does this executive define growth? What other definitions of growth might be used?

2. The president of a recognized food brokerage company in Florida recently spoke to a group of management students at a local university. In his presentation, he stated:

> We had to start our company from scratch. It was our task to find out what forms of organization were suitable. This meant, above all, an organization that could adapt to rapid changes in the market. Any firm in the food business, no matter how large or how well established, is severely penalized when it cannot adapt to change.

What type of market changes might affect a food brokerage business? Why should the managers of such businesses be aware of these changes? Why is adaptation to change so important?

3. The Circle-D Doughnut Shop opened five years ago. Located in a small shopping center, the shop enjoyed monthly sales increases from both carryout business and special orders. The company was owned by three persons who held full-time jobs elsewhere in the community. Due to increasing demands

on their time, the owners decided to sell the business when sales reached a six-figure volume. This volume was reached two years ago.

After the business was sold, the new owner started responding to changes requested by customers. Pies and cakes were desired by some, while fresh bread was sought by others. The business soon changed from a doughnut shop to a full-time bakery. On year later, the business was bankrupt.

a. How can a business go bankrupt when it is responding to customer requests?
b. Would a growth strategy have helped this business expand while maintaining its ability to survive?

4. In 1930, the Waterman Company accounted for 90 percent of all fountain pen sales in the United States. With the introduction of ballpoints, however, fountain pen sales plummeted, and in 1958, the Waterman Company was sold to a European manufacturer for $1 million. By 1969, the company was losing money while producing virtually all pens marketed in France.

To get the company into a profit position, 9 of Waterman's 10 highest-ranking executives were fired, the payroll was trimmed from 1,200 to 715 employees, and the home-office staff was slashed from 200 to 55. In addition, management headquarters were moved to more modest offices, ink production was automated, and accounting procedures were computerized.

Today, Waterman is in the black with rapid gains in sales. Much of the company's success is due to its young chairman, Francine Gomez, and a young top-management team that has a median age of 31 years. Products have been redesigned to stress quality first and elegance second. Recently, the company introduced a refillable, high-quality, felt tip pen. Marketing plans are aimed at luxury gift shops and university campuses in the United States. A Latin American sales program is planned, and a contract has been signed with Japan's giant Mitsubishi Corporation that gives Waterman exclusive distribution rights for its products in Japan, South Korea, the Philippines, and Guam.

a. By the late 1960s, the growth of Waterman had come to a halt because the company had failed to recognize various internal and external environmental changes. What environmental changes seemed to have been overlooked?
b. Explain the firm's growth strategy and the organizational changes that were generated as the company became more aware of its environment?
c. To keep the company from reverting back to its position of the early 1960s, what advice would you give to the company's present management?

5. Of the 200 largest corporations of 1929, 75 were still among the top 200 in 1971. Another 25 fell from the top 200 but were still in the next 359. The remaining 100 from the top 200 of 1929 had disappeared by 1971.

a. Do these data imply that the 100 companies disappearing from among the nation's largest companies simply had not developed growth strategies to guide them through times of change?
b. What are some of the environmental factors that might account for the disappearance of so many large corporations in less than 50 years?

6. By considering the following organizational arrangements, describe the differences between A and B, A and C, and B and C. Base your discussion

on the relative number of managerial and nonmanagerial personnel in each of the arrangements.

7. Describe a committee on which you have served. What were the duties of the committee? What authority was given to the committee? Did the committee seem to make good decisions as a result of the group problem-solving process? Did your experience convince you that committees have an important place in the management of organizations?

8. Even in decentralized organizations, it is common practice to centralize the purchasing function. Stated advantages are that overall inventory levels can be reduced, while purchasing specialists can take advantage of price fluctuations. A major disadvantage of centralized purchasing is that the technical features of many products are not known by members of the purchasing department. To overcome this disadvantage, what type of organizational changes would you recommend? In your recommendation, seek to retain a coordination of purchasing without reducing the authority of operating managers.

9. Organization Development (OD) is an approach to bringing about an overall change in individual and group behavior to achieve organizational effectiveness. As a discipline, OD is involved with the skills, techniques, and models that can be used in changing interrelationships. With behavioral science knowledge, systematic behavioral changes are planned in an attempt to achieve goals more effectively. Some of the noted aspects of OD are team building, sensitivity training, and surveys to obtain data about employee attitudes and feelings (survey feedback). Such therapeutic attempts are designed to change values, beliefs, and attitudes of organizational members.

a. How effective do you feel OD has been in industry?
b. Do you feel that the overall goals of OD could be achieved by changing the structural design of the organization?
c. What are some structural changes you have studied (for example, MBO) that might be viable?

10. Honeywell, Inc., in 1971, was flush with cash from its leading position in the controls industry. With a decision to become a major contender in the computer market, Honeywell bought out General Electric's computer operations and increased research, manufacturing, and marketing of its own computers. Later Xerox's computer base was purchased. In 1977, Honeywell's computer business ranked last among the top five computer companies in pretax return on assets, at 1.4 percent, compared with Sperry Univac's 8.3 percent and IBM's 27.2 percent. In 1978, technical problems caused Honeywell to cancel its major new product entry in the large computer field.

To maintain a position, let alone achieve a growth position, the corporation will have to make major expenditures for the next generation of equipment that should emerge sometime in the 1980s. Honeywell's computer division has now taken a defensive, rather than an offensive, stance moving cautiously into new areas while at the same time avoiding the major risks that could give the company a competitive edge. The grand design to become a major contender on all fronts in the computer business seems destined to be altered.

a. Does the expansion of a product line imply growth?

b. To maintain its position in an industry of rapid technological changes, what types of factors will Honeywell face as it attempts to manage change?

SUGGESTED READINGS

Babb, H. W. and D. G. Kopp. "Applications of Behavior Modification in Organizations: A Review and Critique." *The Academy of Management Review,* April 1978, pp. 281–92.

Babcock, R. D. and W. B. Alton. "A Systematic Approach to Managing Corporate Change." *Management Review,* December 1979, pp. 24–27.

Beman, L. "Exxon's $600-Million Mistake," *Fortune,* October 19, 1981, pp. 68–91.

Burke, W. W. *Current Issues and Strategies in Organization Development.* New York: Human Sciences Press, 1977.

Glover, J. D. *The Revolutionary Corporations.* Homewood, Ill.: Dow Jones-Irwin, 1980.

Hobbs, J. M., and D. F. Heany. "Coupling Strategy to Operating Plans." *Harvard Business Review,* May–June 1977, pp. 119–26.

Kotter, J. P., and L. A. Schlesinger. "Choosing Strategies for Change." *Harvard Business Review,* March–April 1979, pp. 114–21.

Lundgren, D. C., and D. J. Knight. "Sequential Stages of Development in Sensitivity Training Groups." *The Journal of Applied Behavioral Science,* April–May–June 1978.

Porras, J. I., and P. O. Berg. "The Impact of Organization Development." *The Academy of Management Review,* April 1978, pp. 249–66.

Raia, A. P., and N. Margulies. "Organizational Change and Development." In *Organizational Behavior,* edited by S. Kerr. Columbus, Ohio: Grid Publishing, 1979.

Viola, R. H. *Organizations in a Changing Society: Administration and Human Values.* Philadelphia: W. B. Saunders, 1977.

20

MANAGEMENT AND THE INTERNATIONAL ENVIRONMENT

PURPOSE

In the bleak summer of 1940, the conquering German armies entered Paris. As they were making their triumphant procession up the Champs Elysees, a tank detached itself from the group and drove up a circular drive in front of National Cash Register's Paris office. The French manager of the office saw a German major climb out of the tank and proceed to the door. Clicking his heels as the French manager opened the door, the major bowed and presented his card, introducing himself as manager of National Cash Register's Berlin office. He stated that if his colleague needed his services at any time, he had only to call his unit. The officer then promptly returned to his tank to catch up with the passing parade and the pressing business of war.

This story, as noted by Edward McCreary in "The Escaping Corporations,"* highlights the nature of international management as it moves between countries, not being limited by national boundaries, political ideologies, and language differences. Similarly, this chapter points out that management is not just an American phenomenon, and that the way it is practiced varies among countries. Therefore, a contingency approach is necessary to assess situational differences that appear when management is viewed from an international perspective.

OBJECTIVES

1. To develop an understanding of the complexities of managing in an international environment.

2. To examine cultural factors as they affect the management process within transnational organizations.

3. To emphasize the need for planning in the transnational organization.

4. To discuss the problems associated with organizing and controlling international activities.

5. To stress the importance of human resources to success in international operations.

---

* In *International Business: An Introduction to the World of the Multinational Firm*, ed. R. D. Hays, C. K. Korth, and M. Roudiani (Englewood Cliffs, N. J.: Prentice-Hall, 1972), p. 39.

An important issue in international business is to determine whether management concepts are universally applicable or if they are suited only to given environmental situations. Undoubtedly, management techniques and styles do differ because of varying cultures and value systems. These differences, however, do not overshadow the fact that certain similarities also exist.[1] For example, Japanese companies operating in the United States find that developing proper employee attitudes, encouraging employee participation, and gaining product acceptance are as essential for organizational success in the United States as in Japan.[2]

INTERNATIONAL BUSINESS

From a managerial viewpoint, international business deals with the importing and exporting activities that cross national boundaries.[3] These activities include the movement of goods, services, capital, and technology. Beyond manufacturing and marketing, some of the more conspicuous fields of operation include transportation, petroleum, mining, hotels, engineering, banking, and finance. In addition, international business is distinguished from purely domestic activities because it involves operations (1) within different national sovereignties and over great geographical distances, (2) under differing economic conditions, (3) with people having different value systems and institutions, and (4) in markets varying in population and potential.

Foreign trade on an organized basis dates back to the emergence of the nation-state system and the merchants of Venice. Even prior to World War II, however, most business organizations did not consider the possibilities of investing in or establishing operations beyond their national boundaries. Even among firms that did so, most limited their activities to importing and/or exporting within specific geographic areas.

Since the end of World War II, a more international view of markets, resources, and production facilities has emerged. Several factors that have led to a more dominant role of international business in the world economy are:

An expanding world population desiring higher standards of living.

An increase in world demand and personal income.

Improved international laws to facilitate world trade.

Newer management techniques and business methods that assist companies operating in international markets.

---

[1] See Ezra F. Vogel, *Japan As Number One: Lessons for America* (Cambridge, Mass.: Harvard University Press, 1979).

[2] Hugh D. Menzies, "Can the Twain Meet at Mitsubishi," *Fortune,* January 26, 1981, p. 41.

[3] S. B. Prasad and Y. K. Shetty, *An Introduction to Multinational Management* (Englewood Cliffs, N.J.: Prentice-Hall, 1976), pp. 21–29.

Support from the more developed countries to assist emerging nations.

Based on these factors, the profitability of international business becomes more apparent. In the late 1950s, the Japanese saw an untapped market potential in the United States for selling motorcycles. A similar geocentric view by businesses in other countries has led to the establishment of multinational corporations throughout the world.

THE MULTINATIONAL CORPORATION

Multinational organizations came into prominence during the 1960s; however, earlier multinational corporations were the large oil and mining companies that appeared around the turn of the century—British Petroleum, International Nickel, and Anaconda. The first of the modern multinational firms is considered to be the giant Unilever organization, founded in 1929 by the Dutch organization Unie and Lever Brothers of Britain. Some of the reasons cited for its successful global operations include technical and managerial know-how, access to raw materials, attractiveness of markets, and financial incentives to invest. Prior to the Great Depression, Singer, National Cash Register, and the American auto and rubber giants were also added to the list.

Today, more than one half of the earnings of Colgate-Palmolive, Canon, Mitsubishi, National Cash Register, Singer, Exxon, and Coca-Cola, to mention only a few, come from foreign markets. In total, recent estimates place the business activities of overseas subsidiaries of multinational corporations at over $600 billion in terms of products and services—a figure that amounts to roughly one fourth of the total production in the non-Communist world. As a group, multinational firms produce about one half of the industrial output of the non-Communist world.[4]

A multinational corporation is often characterized as operating in at least six countries with foreign branches and/or subsidiaries accounting for at least 20 percent of its total assets, sales, or labor force. Using this criterion, it is estimated that there are more than 4,000 multinational corporations throughout the world.

Since multinational organizations are basically holding companies, they must conform with the requirements of the particular countries in which they operate. Their legal creation takes place within a specific country, but ownership portions are directly related to the control that the parent company can usually maintain. For example, Canadian companies usually want 100 percent ownership of international subsidiaries. The French desire only a minority interest, whereas German firms typically want 50–50 joint ventures. With 100 percent ownership, flexibility exists for assigning functions, establishing policies, and avoid-

[4] Raymond Vernon and L. T. Wells, Jr., *Managers in the International Economy* (Englewood Cliffs, N.J.: Prentice-Hall, 1981), p. 4.

ing arguments. However, national pride and a country's desire for economic independence can create opposition when foreign companies control a large portion of the country's national income. In Latin America, as an illustration, the desire for greater unity among countries has resulted in major expropriations of some U.S. holdings, as well as the passage of laws designed to force other companies to sell a majority interest to local investors. Currently, business organizations headquartered in the United States represent the world's largest overseas investors; however, Japan's Matsushita, France's Michelin, Canada's Massey-Ferguson, Switzerland's Nestlé, and Germany's Feberwerks Hoest are multinational corporations with large overseas investments.

COMPLEXITIES FACING INTERNATIONAL OPERATIONS

The rise of nationalism throughout the world has led to greater regulation of multinational firms. Pressures from local businesses and labor unions are forcing governments to discourage the inflow of foreign capital by adopting selective controls and stricter regulations on foreign investments.[5] In part, these actions are caused by a fear of economic control by the foreign capital investors. Also, there is a desire among nations to improve trade balances by encouraging investments in local export industries. Consequently, multinational firms are faced with the problem of reconciling their activities with the interests and desires of the nations in which they are investing. In fact, to help overcome the undesirable connotations often associated with multinational operations, the term *transnational* is being used.

Success and survival in international markets depend on sensitivity and adaptation to local circumstances while serving a genuine public need. Also, the international enterprise requires a contingency approach to managing worldwide operational units. Thus, their future success will require the use of sophisticated environmental analyses, flexible strategies, the employment of advanced technical skills, and the ability to produce open, positive employee attitudes toward other nationalities.

The risks involved in transnational operations are a major consideration in decision making.[6] Distance, time, reliability of data, and the variability of foreign environments are factors that combine to influence and modify the decisional processes employed in international operations. Accurate reports from competent staff personnel are also more difficult to obtain in many international operations than in most domestic situations.

---

[5] R. H. Mason, R. R. Miller, and D. R. Weigel, *International Business* (New York: John Wiley & Sons, 1981), pp. 386–412.

[6] Richard Capstick, "The Perils of Manufacturing Abroad," *International Management*, March 1978, pp. 43–46.

**THE INTERNATIONAL
ENVIRONMENT**

Since managers throughout the world do not operate under identical circumstances, a knowledge of specific environmental influences is important for successful international operations. This is especially true when the host country's goals change and result in a clash with the operations of international companies. By not recognizing environmental factors, therefore, a change in the environment can cause an efficient manager of a subsidiary to show poor performance. In short, management practices must reflect various environmental conditions that exist at a particular point in time and in a particular society. One way of viewing such environmental constraints is to consider them in terms of cultural variations.

**THE MEANING OF
CULTURE**

Culture has many different meanings and interpretations. From a social or anthropological standpoint, it refers to the *pattern of beliefs and behavior within a given society.* Culture reflects the learned behavioral traits shared by a society's members and is steeped in tradition and heritage.[7] Yet, cultures do not depend on heritage alone and, consequently, are constantly changing. However, cultures are not changing to the extent that they are unable to provide a coherent description of learned behavior patterns.

It is important to recognize that culture can influence personal ambitions and the need for achievement. For example, McClelland has found that societies placing a high value on individual and group achievement are more likely to reach advanced levels of economic prosperity, relative to their resources and technical knowledge, than countries where individuals show low-achievement motivation.[8] Japan and western Europe are notable examples in this respect since both emphasize the need for achievement. On the other hand, low levels of achievement may be associated with many Latin American countries where the traditional land aristocracy does little physical work. To do otherwise would result in a loss of status. Also, the profit objective may be given a low priority in a hierarchy of goals, particularly when more importance is attached to advancing the prestige of the owner or keeping the business within the family. Thus, objectives, authority relationships, styles of leadership, the extensive use of controls, and the way employees are rewarded are elements of culture that influence the need for a contingency approach to international management.

**ELEMENTS OF
CULTURE**

A list of specific elements among various cultures can be quite extensive. An understanding of at least the major ones is important in deter-

---

[7] For an interesting discussion of the impact of the Japanese culture on business, see Sugioku Sekio, "Big Economic Power with Isolated Culture," *Japan Quarterly,* January–March 1977, pp. 38–43.

[8] David C. McClelland, *The Achieving Society* (Princeton, N.J.: D. Van Nostrand, 1961).

mining how they may affect the practice of management in different societies. We will consider seven cultural dimensions that impose constraints and limits on management. These include technology, language, aesthetics, education, religion, social organization, and political life.

Technology

Technology influences productivity, the jobs people perform, interpersonal relations, and the structure of organizations. It consists of *a body of knowledge (state of the art) concerned with techniques, equipment, and processes developed throughout the ages.* While there is an abundance of technological capacity in some countries and a virtual absence in others, individuals in a given social system determine its levels of fulfillment. In some societies, we can find people using picks and shovels to build roads while in other societies bulldozers and earthmoving equipment are used.

Significant changes are occurring in our own social systems as a result of energy shortages, electronic advancement, medical improvements, and computerization. We can only speculate on the social changes that may be forthcoming, especially as technology advances in the less-developed nations. Based on current trends, however, it is evident that technology will continue to affect international management, and a company's technological superiority in international operations provides a major explanation for its direct foreign investment. This may suggest why transnational organizations are likely to grow faster than domestic firms operating within specific industries. Along these lines, French oil exploration firms working in Mexico have proven to be much more successful than Mexican oil-drilling companies.

Managers in the international sphere must also determine how the levels of technology in foreign markets might affect their sources of raw materials, energy, transportation, communication, and production processes.[9] At the same time, these managers are faced with making changes in their activities that will allow them to function effectively as new economic systems and technologies emerge.

Language

Language expresses itself as an important dimension of culture in patterns of communication among individuals. In Latin America, for example, plant grievance procedures are handled basically by governmental representatives, rather than through a union-management arrangement. This is due, in part, to the reluctance of workers to express differences face to face with their superiors and a preference of communicating through a third party.

The extensiveness of vocabularies also reflects cultural differences in language. Some languages require a series of words to express a particular concept. The term *white collar worker* requires three words

---

[9] See Mason, Miller, and Weigel, *International Business,* pp. 234–68.

in English, while the one word *empleado* is sufficient in Spanish. Whyte indicates that the concept of leadership cannot be translated easily into Spanish.[10] The verbs *lead* (which suggests voluntarism) and *command* (which suggests coercion) are both represented in Spanish by a single verb *manbar.* Exxon Corporation learned that its former name, Enco, had unfortunate connotations or sounds in some languages. In Japanese, for example, Enco means *stalled car.* Thus, selecting the two *x*s in Exxon was unique because the combination is uncommon, appearing only in the Maltese language and in some proper English names.

Without question, when the communication process is confronted with the language barrier, misunderstanding often occurs. Furthermore, language barriers are more extensive in countries, such as Switzerland, Belgium, Canada, India, and many African nations, where more than one language is spoken. For international management, then, language is a critical factor since it is the key to communicating within local cultures around the world.

Aesthetics

Aesthetics refers to *attitudes toward beauty and good taste.* Maintaining a sensitivity to a country's aesthetic values is extremely important to organizational success. To avoid aesthetic mistakes, managers must consider in depth such factors as design, color, and brand names.

Another important aesthetic factor concerns the conduct of business among managers. For North American business people, getting down to the issues at hand is an acceptable practice. In Japan, however, casual conversation precedes business matters and reflects one's sincerity and personal character. Likewise, Japanese executives rarely reject any proposal flatly since a reaction of this type is considered impolite and threatening to group harmony. In Latin American cultures, the priorities attached to work and pleasure are also quite different from those in the United States. The slower pace of life in business is quite a contrast to the long hours and heavy schedules characteristic of American executives.

Education

An organization is no better than its people. In addition, the quality of the educational system within a country is important in determining the level of its managerial competence. Many societies, however, provide training basically in law, philosophy, and political science, with little emphasis on business since it is not always considered to be a prestigious career. As a result, intellectual talent is channeled away from managerial positions in business organizations.

When managers are trained in technical specialities, businesses function differently than when people are trained in management. In many

---

[10] William F. Whyte, *Organizational Behavior: Theory and Application* (Homewood, Ill.: Richard D. Irwin, 1969), pp. 719–42. © 1969 by Richard D. Irwin, Inc.

of the Communist nations, individuals with engineering degrees are often placed in managerial positions, regardless of their knowledge of management, economics, industrial technology, or the behavioral sciences. To improve organizational effectiveness, however, many of these nations will need to develop management training centers that focus on management education. Recognizing this fact, Saudi Arabia is emphasizing business administration in the College of Petroleum and Minerals in Dhahrau and in other new universities being built.

Religion

Managers must also be aware of religious differences if they are to understand the beliefs and attitudes that help explain why workers behave as they do. For example, the caste system in the Hindu religion prescribes the specific occupation and social role for each of its members. In addition, Hindu teachings suggest that acquisition and achievement are not to be sought since they are the major causes for suffering in one's daily life.

Knowledge of the Moslem religion also provides insights into human behavior patterns. As an illustration, during the month of Ramadan, Moslems are required to fast from sunrise to sunset. During this period, worker output falls off sharply since Moslems may spend a large part of their normal sleeping hours consuming food. In addition, Moslems are prohibited from drinking alcohol or eating pork, and the role of women is viewed differently than in the United States.

Some Christian beliefs are also quite different from those of other major religions throughout the world. Among these beliefs, many Christians view work not only as a means of getting ahead but also as a positive moral value. Max Weber, the German sociologist, called this view the Protestant Work Ethic.[11] Leaders of the Protestant Reformation emphasized the importance of the individual and the work of individuals as evidence and assurance of salvation. This view led many of the early capitalists, such as Rockefeller, Carnegie, and Jay Gould, to believe that achievement and eventual salvation resulted from hard work, initiative, thrift, and the accumulation of wealth.

An additional consideration related to the work ethic concerns attitudes toward rational risk taking. Societies that equate large risks with opportunities for accumulating further wealth will be more open to managerial risk-taking practices than those who view a reasonable risk as unsafe. In other societies, managerial efficiency is influenced by religious attitudes toward the use of the scientific method. For example, in some of the less-developed countries, animistic religions practice spirit worship and witchcraft. In these instances, knowledge is not based on a predictive, rationalistic view of the world, but on taboos, mysticism, and fatalism that severely restrict a scientific approach to management.

---

[11] Max Weber, *The Protestant Ethic and the Spirit of Capitalism,* trans. Talcott Parson (Glencoe, Ill.: Free Press, 1948).

Social organizations

The social structure of family units and other groups must always be considered in understanding a given culture. Generally, the family unit is the most primary social grouping. In the Hindu family, a new bride lives within the groom's family circle. The oldest male has chief authority, while older women have authority over the younger women. The entire family thinks and acts as a unified body; thus, each person supports the "joint family" and the group supports each individual. These and other types of extended family relationships strongly influence the work environment.

In some Latin American countries, the manager who gives special treatment to a relative is considered to be fulfilling an obligation. This type of behavior is not considered unfair as it might be in the United States. Another element of social relations is the incidence of legal confrontation. While lawsuits jam the U.S. court system, Japan is the world's most nonlitigious society. The United States has some 500,000 lawyers, but there are only 11,000 lawyers serving 117 million Japanese. By being aware of these and other social relationships, managers are better prepared to predict the behavior of others, especially as they respond to organizational authority and participate within group activities.

Political environment

Political factors often exert the most direct influence on international operations. Clearly, a firm's industrial relations system is closely intertwined with the political institutions of a country. Similarly, supply and demand relationships are affected by governmental policies. Examples include U.S. price supports, import quotas, and financial regulations by the Export-Import Bank and the Federal Reserve System that affect a foreign country's exports and imports.

Some governments follow a political philosophy that includes ownership of business operations, while others only regulate economic activity. Of course, governmental ownership gives management a different role from that found under private ownership. In the socialistic countries of eastern Europe, for example, the heads of governmental agencies possess the primary authority for the overall direction of economic activity and industrial operations. Managers of these countries' industrial enterprises generally have limited authority in strategy planning.

The political stability of a country's government can also affect managerial success. For instance, the Brazilian-Bolivian natural gas pipeline that was recently completed was considered impractical for many years because Bolivian governments were notoriously unstable. Brazilians feared that agreements negotiated with one political regime might be nullified by the next. When political situations are this unstable, long-range planning is bounded by even more uncertainty.

In many instances, the political ideologies of various countries may differ from those held by the management of international firms. When this occurs, managers may try to change a country's political environment; however, such attempts by American multinational firms in Latin American countries have often brought criticism to these enterprises. In fact, the establishment of the United Nations Commission on Multinational Corporations was a direct consequence of International Telephone and Telegraph's attempt to intervene in a Chilean election.

Legal environment

The legal parameters facing international business managers are based on a country's political environment, contract laws, patents, labor legislation, and tax laws. Notably, there is no comprehensive international law nor court system, and legal systems throughout the world are not identical. Middle Eastern countries do business under religious law, while countries in other parts of the world operate under either the Anglo-Saxon legal code (common law), or the Napoleonic Code (civil law). Japan, for example, follows the Napoleonic Code.

Domestic laws concerning ownership arrangements, tariffs, export licenses, antitrust rulings, joint ventures, and marketing agreements represent important considerations for managers of international organizations. In addition, treaties, conventions, and other agreements between two or more countries can be viewed as a part of an organization's legal environment. Some of the many international agreements include the Friendship, Commerce, and Navigation treaties between the United States and other countries; the International Monetary Fund Agreement; the General Agreement on Tariffs and Trade (GATT); and the International Convention for the Protection of Industrial Property. The complexity in the legal environment, combined with other cultural factors, suggests that the elements of culture have a major impact on management practices and performance in international operations.

INTERNATIONAL PLANNING

The uncertainties of international activities, growing environmental pressures, and increased competition are forcing international companies to place more emphasis on planning. While required in all organizations, planning is vitally important for the coordination of global activities. The increased complexity of international planning, as compared to that at the domestic level, is shown in Figure 20–1.

By its very nature, global planning must consider environmental factors, foreign market opportunities, and alternative strategies for those specific foreign countries where operations are conducted. To illustrate:

> Back in the 1950s, a motorcycle in America was a big 1,200-cc Harley Davidson that thugs, police, and nostalgia buffs drove around. It was the only American-made motorcycle, selling about 10,000 bikes per year. Even in 1979, only about 50,000 Harleys were sold out of more than 1,000,000 motorcycles marketed in the United States; 91 percent of them were Japanese.

FIGURE 20–1
Complexity of environmental factors in domestic and worldwide markets

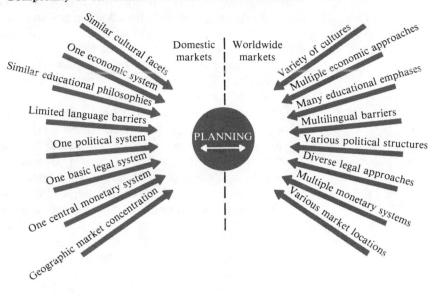

In the late 1950s, Mr. Soichiro Honda envisioned a mass-produced, mass-marketed motorcycle in the United States. An analysis of all the variables suggested that it could be done. The great breakthrough was in 1962 when Honda ran an advertisement proclaiming, "You meet the nicest people on a Honda." Even more revolutionary was that 5 of the 11 people in the advertisement were female. There was no competition in the United States for the Honda 90-cc bike; thus, the door was opened for Honda to sell over 400,000 units in 1979. Honda analyzed the U.S. market as to what would appeal to Americans and was not bound to the notion that they would not accept motorcycles. Geared for the long-term expansion of the market, Honda gave Americans a bike size they could handle and an image with which they could live. Clearly, Honda's plan was one that was well thought out and more daring than any U.S. manufacturer was willing to undertake.

As with all planning, that on an international basis can be divided into long- and short-range time frames. Long-range planning assists managers in determining market potential, a desired rate of return, and social responsiveness that should be assumed in guiding the use of corporate resources. Short-range planning refers to the development of specific organizational goals, along with the courses of action needed to meet such goals. Generally, short-term plans spell out the approaches and techniques to implement a strategy. As such, they often include a schedule of events and activities, assignment of authority and responsibility, and detailed budget allocations. If, for example, an international firm's five-year plan calls for achieving a certain market share within several Latin American countries, short-range plans would be linked to this objective. In doing so, the short-range plans would specify the products to be introduced; the timing of production schedules; and the marketing activities involved in pricing, promoting, and distributing the products. While most short-term plans usually span a one-year operating period, the length of time is not all that essential. Of more importance is the idea that specific plans are part of the overall international strategy of a firm. To conclude, planning on an international scale consists of several steps:

1. An analysis of international environments (both current and future) is required in order to determine worldwide strategies, objectives, and policies. For example, in redefining Westinghouse's international strategy in 1980, executives looked at more than 140 international markets and singled out 17 countries where business looked especially promising from political, economic, and commercial viewpoints.

2. Company strengths and weaknesses are weighted against those of competitors in order to isolate differential advantages.

3. A uniform information system is developed to communicate plans to subsidiaries and to ensure that all planning efforts are totally integrated.

4. The overall package is approved by top management prior to the allocation of resources among various divisions.

ORGANIZING MULTINATIONAL FIRMS

Once the decision is made to invest abroad, an organization structure must be devised that will contribute to the firm's profits. In order to be effective, the structure of an organization must be compatible with its goals, technology, and external environment. Yet, the variety of languages, laws, tax regulations, and political loyalties of various countries complicate the organizing function. Similarly, organizational effectiveness depends on informational flows that become more difficult to maintain as geographically dispersed decision centers are established. Nonetheless, any international organization requires a worldwide communication system for transmitting information throughout the management hierarchy.

When a company first enters foreign markets, it normally appoints an export manager. As sales increase, the organization may then establish an export department. With continued growth, an international division may be created with responsibilities for various foreign facilities, such as branch/subsidiary offices, warehouses, and production plants. Although international corporations use a variety of organizational structures, the purpose of organizing remains the same; namely, to integrate separate national operations into a coordinated unit.

The need for an international division becomes most evident when operations require a single unit to make decisions concerning specialized international operations. The main functions of such a division are to identify international business opportunities, direct and control

FIGURE 20–2
International division of a multinational corporation

foreign operations, and provide a coordinating link between corporate headquarters and other organizational units. Figure 20–2 depicts one approach for organizing an international division. In this instance, international operations are centralized in a single, semiautonomous unit with its own profit responsibilities. The managers in countries A and B have some degree of autonomy for providing a wide range of specialized activities and information. However, the actual amount of autonomy depends on the company's products, the manager's international expertise, and the communication time required between divisional levels and foreign subsidiaries.

At present, many international companies have moved beyond the international division structure to a worldwide or global organizational design. This design has two characteristics: (1) a decentralization of decision-making authority among subdivisions and (2) a centralization of strategic planning and control to take advantage of opportunities wherever they may exist. The global design concept necessitates a cosmopolitan management philosophy and a top-management team that thinks in terms of worldwide commitments. In the process, management makes few distinctions between domestic and foreign business. Thus, the global approach to organizing provides a structure to optimize corporate performance on a worldwide basis.

FIGURE 20–3
Product-line structure

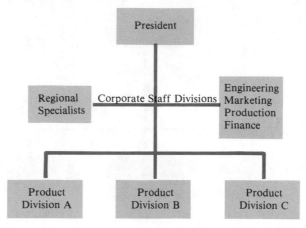

Regardless of whether the international division or the global structure is followed, decisions on how activities will be grouped must still be made. Numerous approaches for grouping activities are available; however, all of them could be classified as product, geographic, or functional groupings.

Product-line structure

As illustrated in Figure 20–3, companies that follow the product-line structure assign functional and operational responsibilities for a line or group of products to a single unit. It is popular with companies having a diversified range of products going into a variety of end-use markets. Thus, management responsibilities are worldwide, although there may be regional departmentation within a product division. The major advantages of this type of structure are (1) coordination is facilitated within a specific product group and (2) communication problems are reduced.

A number of U.S. companies, such as Sperry Rand and Clark Equipment Company, employ the product-line structure. Clark, for example, has product managers at different geographic locations who report to general managers in their particular product line. In turn, these managers report to product divisional managers located in the United States. Fiat, an Italian multinational company, also has product divisions, each with its own administration, personnel, purchasing, production programming, quality control, and sales organization. In this manner, each product group thinks of its markets on a worldwide basis.

Geographic structure

The geographic structure, shown in Figure 20–4, groups all functional and operational responsibilities into specific geographical areas. It is a popular choice of companies with low product diversity. The area managers possess decentralized decision-making authority and coordinate virtually all of the operations within their territories. As

FIGURE 20–4
Geographic organization structure

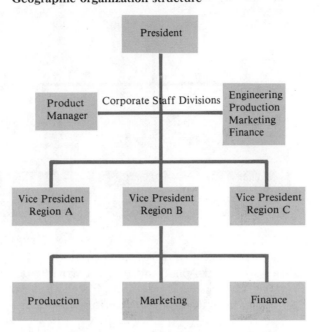

in other structures, however, top management generally retains the authority for worldwide strategy planning and control.

The geographical structure also produces an awareness of the political, social, and business opportunities that prevail within a given market, thereby facilitating responses to environmental forces and the idiosyncracies of various markets. International Telephone and Telegraph and Charles Pfizer Corporation, a large pharmaceutical company, are examples of U.S. corporations that organize their international operations on a geographic basis. IBM also uses this structure, although foreign operations are handled through its separate IBM World Trade Corporation.

The major problem with the geographic design concerns the communication of specific knowledge to various geographic territories. One way to handle this problem is to establish a product manager position with staff authority, as noted in Figure 20–4. A major responsibility of the product manager then becomes that of facilitating the transfer of information throughout all geographic regions. Such an arrangement is similar to General Electric's International Group that has four area managers who are responsible for providing operating assistance to product managers in their geographic areas.

Functional structure   In the functional design, worldwide responsibilities for marketing, production, finance, and other functions are assigned to managers in corporate headquarters who report directly to the chief executive.

FIGURE 20–5
Functional organization structure

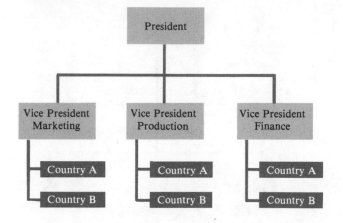

As shown in Figure 20–5, all functional vice presidents have direct line authority to plan and control worldwide operations within their functional areas. In production, for example, the manager would have authority over foreign production subsidiaries, as well as worldwide responsibilities for quality control, research and development, and product design. Similarly, the marketing vice president has global responsibilities for sales, distribution, and other marketing activities.

A major advantage of the functional structure rests in its ability to provide a coordination of policies for each functional area. This is especially true as long as the company has a limited product line and only minor variations in regional operations. In these instances, a duplication of effort is largely avoided and functional controls are easily implemented.

The disadvantage of the functional structure is that it violates the concept that multinational corporations should choose an organizational structure that maximizes decentralization while still centralizing activities that are interdependent. Functional departmentation may result in (1) a lack of direct representation of geographic areas and/or product lines and (2) some loss of coordination among functions below the top-management level. For example, the separation between sales and production activities may result in each functional unit making different forecasts of future trends in various geographic areas.

The extractive industry is representative of companies utilizing the functional structure. However, the functional structure is more dominant among European organizations, allowing a relatively small group of the executives to exercise centralized control over an entire organization.

Selecting the best structure

Due to variations in the factors that influence the choice of an organizational structure, successful international companies within the same industry may use different organizational designs. In this sense, there is no one perfect structure since responding to rapid changes in foreign markets, product strategy, and competition require that an organization's design be flexible.

Inflexible patterns that cannot be modified easily will surely result in communication gaps and segregated decision making. Furthermore, as found in domestic companies, there is always a blending of various organizational forms. Rarely does an international organization have a "pure" product, geographic, or functional design. The most effective structures normally have some elements of each in order to minimize the problems associated with any one particular grouping. The Westinghouse organization, for example, is structured on a product basis, having 37 operating business units. The international hierarchy, however, is organized on geographical lines. Thus, a plant manager of a circuit-breaker factory in Brazil reports to the managers who oversee all business units in that country, and to the stateside business unit manager who is responsible for electrical transmission and distribution equipment. This is a matrix-type system, and most successful multinational companies employ some sort of matrix design.[12]

Centralization and organizational design

Within international companies, a major concern is the degree to which management decision making should be centralized. Of course, the relative importance and size of an organization's international operations are major factors affecting the degree of centralization practiced. Generally, the more importance attached to international operations and the greater the probability that the actions of one subsidiary will affect the results of others, the greater the likelihood that centralization will exist. For example, Nestlé, the world's largest food company, is seeking to increase U.S. business to 30 percent of the corporate total by centralizing its U.S. operations.[13] The intent is to have each unit report to a U.S. and Canadian zone manager. Yet, even here, a given subsidiary may possess significant authority to make certain major decisions.

Management's task in these situations is to sort out the kinds of decisions that need to be centralized and those that should be delegated to local subsidiaries. In General Motors, decisions on various job enrichment and motivational programs are made by individual plant managers in the 29 countries where GM now manufactures products. Establishing objectives and overall policies, however, are centralized. This is due to (1) the potential worldwide range of resources and opportunities, (2) the interdependence of coordinating diversified production and finance operations, and (3) environmental uncertainties. Thus, by centralizing such areas as research and development and finance, an

---

[12] Hugh D. Menzies "Westinghouse Takes Aim at the World," *Fortune*, January 14, 1980, pp. 48–53.

[13] "Nestlé: Centralizing to Win a Bigger Payoff from the U.S.," *Business Week*, February 2, 1981, pp. 56–58.

organization is more likely to function on a truly international basis, as opposed to a collection of autonomous national units. It must be remembered, though, that a centralization of important decisions is not without its costs. One cost is that it does little to improve the motivation of subsidiary managers and, secondly, extensive communication is required that is both costly and time consuming.

Cultural patterns also influence decisions concerning the degree to which authority is centralized. Most foreign firms having subsidiaries in the United States exercise centralized control over financial matters. As in the case of Italian and Scandinavian subsidiaries, however, marketing, production, and research and development may be virtually independent. On the other hand, German and British subsidiaries have limited authority in all of these areas.

One way to establish a balance between centralization and decentralization is through the development of a regional management center or a "halfway house."[14] A regional center permits a decentralization of authority while at the same time maintains a close relationship between subsidiaries and corporate headquarters. Further, such centers assist in coordinating local activities while providing a communication link with top management.

CONTROLLING INTERNATIONAL OPERATIONS

Most of the control concepts discussed in earlier chapters are applicable to international management. However, special control problems do arise. For example, the inevitable friction that develops between people and control systems is magnified in international operations. Because of cultural differences, the control process is not utilized in many foreign countries to the same degree as it is in the United States. Quality control, performance appraisals, and cost controls may have little meaning in some countries. In this respect, differing environmental conditions, the availability of local management talent, communication gaps, and the geographical dispersion of subsidiaries are international factors that combine to make the control process unique.

Establishing standards

A determination of standards for international operations must not only consider overall corporate needs but also conditions at the local level. In arriving at realistic standards, foreign managers must be brought into the planning process. As citizens of the country in which they work, these managers often try harder to achieve goals that they have helped determine, and participation helps minimize a certain amount of intercultural conflict.

Measuring performance

Measuring the performance of international operations can also produce problems that may not be experienced by domestic organizations.

---

[14] Thomas H. Bates, "Management and the Multinational Business Environment," *California Management Review*, Spring 1972, p. 39.

For instance, there is the question of determining whether profits should be calculated in local currency or currency of the home country. The inflation and deflation of currencies are problems that may cause the parent company to measure performance differently than local managers. Similarly, local variations in accounting practices can result in financial reports not being comparable from one country to another.

International operations can also result in reports that are written in different languages. Most international companies, however, have adopted their own official company language. English and French are two of the most common company languages, even for Swedish, Dutch, and Swiss firms. Thus, a company language, as well as a common currency and accounting system, are essential in comparing and measuring the performance of various subsidiaries.

Reports must also use standard units of measurement. Oddly enough, the United States is the only major trading country clinging to English weights and measures. Special metric studies indicate that U.S. trade balances suffer extensively each year because it has not switched to the metric system. Without question, the use of common international standards of measurement serves to unify markets for all products. They make it possible for substantial cost savings and a greater consistency of operations in both production and marketing.

Another major problem in measuring the performance of international operations is that information systems can become clogged with irrelevant data when long distances exist between subsidiaries and the parent company. This makes it imperative that information systems be designed to minimize and streamline those reports considered essential for control purposes.

Profit centers

Sophisticated information systems are now making centralized control more feasible. Even when control can be centralized, information may still arrive too late for preventive action to be taken. One way to deal with this problem is to treat foreign subsidiaries as profit centers.

Profit centers serve to handle many control problems by permitting local managers to make adjustments that correct deviations from standards. In this way, a knowledge of local conditions and speed in decision making are maximized. To be effective, however, local managers must feel that they are part of the total international organization while having a degree of autonomy that lets them control local activities.

INTERNATIONAL MANAGEMENT AND HUMAN RESOURCES

The quality of an organization's management is probably one of the most important determinants of success in international business. Yet, different social and cultural environments make it difficult to measure the efficiency of managers. Legal, political, economic, sociological, and educational variables influence managerial decisions and, in turn, determine managerial effectiveness.

Managerial selection

In the United States alone, thousands of managers and professional personnel are selected annually to represent American companies abroad. Determining who is to be selected for such assignments is important to the success of an international organization. Although the selection process does not differ in principle from that used for domestic managers, the matching of environmental variables to the characteristics of individuals is of the utmost importance.[15]

Several studies have reported that technical and managerial qualifications, social adaptability, feelings toward non-Americans, and a spouse's attitudes are all important in selecting international managers. In reality, however, the qualifications of a candidate, environmental factors, and the importance of foreign operations to corporate success are the criteria used when selecting individuals for specific assignments.[16] Personal characteristics of an individual may be recognized as important in some environments, while past performance may be the determining factor in others. If special qualifications are to be developed, management training could be useful. For many U.S. corporations, training normally includes some kind of cultural sensitivity orientation about the country to which executives are being assigned.[17]

Host country nationals as managers

Many multinational firms operating in foreign countries do not reserve important managerial jobs for host country managers. This is particularly true for most Japanese and European organizations. For example, it is highly unlikely that the president of Mitsubishi International Corporation (MIC)—the American subsidiary of Japan's Mitsubishi Corporation—will ever be an American. MIC has a heavy reliance on Japanese managers, although there is some effort now to hire Americans so that it will not be in conflict with U.S. equal employment opportunity laws. Even at Nestlé, only one American-born employee has risen quickly through the ranks.

Some international companies follow a policy of filling all executive positions in foreign operations with local nationals. This practice overcomes the objections of local citizens who may feel that foreigners are directing economic development within their country. It also puts into management positions those people who know the national language, customs, markets, and behavior patterns.

A problem occurs, however, when hiring and promotional opportunities are restricted by a limited supply of managerial talent. In such

---

[15] Edwin L. Miller, "The International Selection Decision: A Study of Some Dimensions of Managerial Behavior in the Selection Decision Process," *Academy of Management Journal*, June 1973, pp. 239–52.

[16] See "Bayer's Formula for Product Innovation," *International Management*, February 1978, pp. 18–22.

[17] Cecil G. Howard, "The Returning Overseas Executive: Cultural Shock in Reverse," *Human Resource Management*, Summer 1974, pp. 22–26.

cases, an organization has no choice other than that of supplementing available talent with "outside" managers. Probably the most appropriate strategy for an international company would be one of staffing operations at all levels in the organization with truly international managers. Clearly, it increases the number of candidates available for selection and increases the chances of finding qualified managers.

SUMMARY

The success of international operations depends largely on an ability to anticipate and to adjust to changes in internal and external environments. To this extent, organizational flexibility requires innovative management and can be considered as part of a company's overall strategy for international survival.

Due to their massive size, some international corporations have lost their organizational flexibility. This in itself emphasizes that managers of such organizations must become more aware of their role as change agents. Important to this role is the ability to stop doing those things that are traditional and unproductive. Certainly, long-run effectiveness is reflected in an ability to react confidently and rationally to the multiple opportunities that face international companies.

At no time in the past has it been more important for international organizations to understand the world in which they operate. The problems surrounding food supplies, energy, medical care, and transportation provide some indication of resource imbalances that point to a need for interdependence among all nations. In this respect, multinational firms will undoubtedly play an important part in creating and maintaining an international economic and political balance. This, of course, will not be an easy job since these companies will probably face increased competition and less stability in the decades ahead. Consequently, they will be required to work more closely with host countries while understanding their demands for tighter international controls and regulations.

KEY TERMS

Culture: Learned patterns of beliefs and behavior within a particular society.

Direct foreign investment: International investment in the equity (ownership) of an enterprise with the intent of exercising some management control and responsibility.

Elements of culture: Factors that influence the management of an operating branch/subsidiary, including elements of the material culture (technology and economics); social institutions (social organizations, education, and political structures); aesthetics (art, folklore, music, drama, and dance); language; and religion.

International business: Both public and private business activity affecting the economic well-being, political status, convictions, skills, or knowledge of persons or institutions of more than one nation, territory, or colony.

International management: Management practices in part can be transferred from one culture to another; however, adaptations in some aspects of these practices are required, depending on the degree to which the operating subsidiary considers local cultures; local acceptance of corporate managerial values; and the nature of the operating entities in terms of marketing, industrial relations, public relations, finance and accounting, production, quality control, and strategic planning.

Joint venture: Joint ownership of an operation in which at least one of the partners is foreign-based with the foreign company taking a major share, a minority share, or an equal share in ownership.

Legal organization of foreign operations: The legal form taken by a corporation operating in many countries depends on the laws of the countries and the laws of the home country from which foreign investments are made.

Multinational corporation: A business organization that is headquartered in one nation but has its operations spread over many countries, following the strategy of acquiring and allocating resources without regard to national boundaries except when they affect either cost or return.

Technology: A body of knowledge concerned with techniques, equipment, and processes developed throughout the ages.

Transnational organization: A term sometimes used synonymously with multinational organizations because of the negative connotations often associated with the latter; however, a distinction may be added that ownership and management of transnational companies are by persons of different nationalities.

QUESTIONS

1. How does international business differ from that which is purely domestic?
2. Discuss the general nature of the multinational enterprise.
3. Why is the management of a multinational company more complex than for a domestic enterprise?
4. What elements of culture should the international manager consider when making decisions?
5. Discuss how different cultural elements can affect managerial efficiency.
6. Do you believe that an effective manager in one country can be just as effective in another?
7. Distinguish between the difficulties associated with international planning and purely domestic planning.
8. List the organizational structures that evolve with the growth of a company involved in international business.

9. Is there one best organization structure for all multinational organizations? Why?

10. Why is a centralized structure for all multinational organizations considered to be important at the present time?

PROBLEMS

1. During the past few years, Japan has become one of the world's three great industrial powers, and by 1985, it is anticipated that the Japanese will have the highest standard of living of any country in the world. Although many factors have contributed to Japan's phenomenal growth, key elements must definitely include its management practices. Several characteristics of Japanese business organizations are quite different from those found in the United States or western Europe.

Decision making One major difference is the use of joint decision making or decisions by consensus. Major decisions are debated throughout an organization. When plans are initiated, they are carried out in the name of the administrative unit, rather than the person initiating the plan. Since this system disperses the decision-making process, the locus of authority is also dispersed. In order to obtain lateral and vertical approval of plans, emphasis is placed on defining problems, rather than on answers. When consensus can first be obtained on the need for a decision, the answer is often much more agreeable to the persons involved. The use of this approach involves a great amount of time; therefore, it is too cumbersome to be effective in making all decisions. It is quite applicable, however, to major decisional matters.

Employment Employment practices in Japanese industries tend to reflect two major characteristics: (1) managerial paternalism in dealing with subordinates and (2) the belief in a long employment commitment to one company. Except in a severe economic crisis or bankruptcy, most Japanese employees have a guaranteed job once they are hired. With a guaranteed job, workers can then look forward to security and steadily rising incomes. Consequently, employees are generally willing to accept changes in technology and management practices while working toward greater productivity.

Once a person is employed, promotions and wages are generally based on seniority and attitudes, rather than on performance. In other words, pay is independent from how well one is doing a job. Since workers are neither rewarded for performance nor penalized for nonperformance, there is no such thing as performance appraisal. Because of seniority, a floor sweeper may make more money than a highly skilled electrician who has been on the job for a shorter period of time. In addition, hiring from the outside to fill upper-level positions is practically unknown.

The paternalistic feature of Japanese companies consists of low-rent housing for employees, as well as free transportation and cultural programs. Due to the benefits of paternalism, most young managers and professionals consider it unthinkable to ask for a transfer. Similarly, few quit to take jobs with other companies, except with permission from their present employer.

Training and management development Japanese managers emphasize continuous personal training as a regular part of each employee's job. Furthermore, training is extended to other jobs in the plant so that workers not only perfect their own specialties but become reasonably proficient in all jobs at their level. Consequently, employees can be transferred to other jobs when necessary.

Managers are also quite concerned about the development of their subordinate managers. In fact, managers are expected to help their colleagues look good, rather than to stand out through their own individual brilliance or aggressiveness. Peter Drucker refers to this type of care and feeding of young managers as being comparable to the "godfather" concept.

a. Compare and contrast these Japanese practices of management with those followed in the United States.
b. As Japan continues to advance economically, are some of its management practices likely to change?
c. What factors contribute to managerial differences between Japan and the United States?
d. What Japanese practices might prove beneficial to U.S. managers? Do you feel that they could be easily initiated in American companies?

2. Multinational companies operating in a developing nation are often wealthier than the country itself. For example, the annual sales figure for General Motors is more than $28 billion and exceeds the gross national product of all but 14 or 15 countries in the world. Since the interests of wealthy companies may clearly transcend national boundaries and adversely affect the culture of a particular nation, is it justifiable for such organizations to be operating in developing countries?

3. The International Distribution Corporation attributes over one third of its sales to markets outside of the United States. Recently, the company brought its international and domestic managers together for a long-range planning conference at the offices of its Brazilian subsidiary. By having the meeting at this location, corporate executives felt that more managers from other foreign subsidiaries would attend. In fact, of the 63 top executives present, 28 were from European, Latin American, Far Eastern, and African operating units.

Prior to the meeting, top corporate executives had set an annual sales target of $1 billion by the end of the five-year planning period. Operating managers were encouraged to outline sales projections, operating objectives, and problems anticipated during the five-year period. Special resource people were available to supply information in such areas as population, demography, technology, and political environments. By the end of the conference, overall corporate strategies had been established, along with the objectives, policies, and programs essential for their attainment.

a. Do you think that such a planning approach leads to the development of meaningful long- and short-range plans?
b. Were the following steps of the planning process utilized at the planning session?
   (1) The establishment of targets by corporate executives.
   (2) A review and agreement between operating units and corporate headquarters on desirable goals for each unit to achieve.
   (3) A forecast of sales in all territories in response to corporate targets.
   (4) The development of strategies, schedules, and programs for each area of operation.

4. The international manager is often referred to as an agent of cultural change. What does this mean? What are the consequences if the role is not fulfilled satisfactorily?

5. In 1973, Libya took over a 51 percent interest in the holdings of multinational oil companies, such as Exxon, Royal Dutch Shell, Mobil, Texaco, and Standard Oil of California. Furthermore, the government gradually usurped the day-to-day managerial operations of these companies by appointing two members of a three-person executive board for each organization. The Libyans nationalized the companies only on the basis of the so-called net book value of the initial investment less profits. No payment was provided for the millions of barrels of oil still in the ground. Even though the companies theoretically retain 49 percent ownership, they have to pay full government tariff on each exported barrel of oil.

a. What kinds of environmental pressures can cause developing countries to nationalize foreign industries?
b. Can the management of these firms do anything to prevent such events?
c. Does the nationalization of companies affect managerial performance?

6. Nationalization, unreliable business partners, untrained or incompetent labor, inadequate and inaccurate market surveys, and ill-conceived government regulations are factors that can restrict a multinational enterprise from setting up manufacturing facilities abroad. Why then, do so many companies manufacture overseas? What steps can be taken to overcome some of these problems?

7. Professor Herbert Grünewald is chairman of the board of management of the multinational German firm Bayer A.G. In response to a question about why the firm does not have a foreigner heading a division or serving on the management board, he stated that in the long run the president of the U.S. operation should be an American. He noted, however, that employees in foreign divisions should be nationals from that country. Apparently there are no rules concerning the nationality of Bayer managers since several managers of foreign nationality are in the parent company. The firm has a policy of filling top-management positions from inside, requiring at least 15 to 20 years of work experience with the company. The implication is that a foreigner would have to work in the parent company to obtain a feeling of "the spirit and understanding of the firm." All top-level managers are required to learn German.

a. Do you feel that the promotion policy reflects a global attitude?
b. Is the policy of not filling positions from outside the company sound?

8. A British company agreed to transfer its technology to a Turkish partner in order to make electric motors in Turkey. Components were bought, labor recruited and trained, and the motors built. However, no one would buy the motors because they did not conform to Turkish safety rules. Neither the British company nor its Turkish partner had thought to check. What does this have to say to the manager involved in international trade?

SUGGESTED READINGS

Alpander, G. "Multinational Corporations: Homebase-Affiliate Relations." *California Management Review,* Spring 1978, pp. 47–56.

Bradway, M. K. "Styles of Mideastern Managers." *California Management Review,* Spring 1980, pp. 51–58.

Carson-Parker, J. "Stop Worrying about the Canadian Invasion. *Fortune,* October 19, 1981, pp. 192–200.

Clutterbuck, D. "Soviet Workers Appraise Their Managers." *International Management,* December 1977, pp. 51–54.

Fay, N., and H. Godon. "Worker Participation: Contrasts in Three Countries." *Harvard Business Review,* May–June 1976, pp. 71–83.

Gladwin, T. N. "Environmental Policy Trends Facing Multinationals." *California Management Review,* Winter 1977, pp. 81–93.

Lammers, C. J., and D. J. Hickson, eds. *Organizations Alike and Unalike: International and Inter-Institutional Studies in the Sociology of Organizations.* London: Routledge and Kegan Paul, 1979.

Negandhi, A. R., and D. Robey. "Understanding Organizational Behavior in Multinational and Multicultural Settings." *Human Resource Management,* Spring 1977, pp. 16–23.

Ozawa, T. "Japanese World of Work: An Interpretive Survey." *MSU Business Topics,* Spring 1980, pp. 45–55.

————. "Japan's Industrial Groups." *MSU Business Topics,* Autumn 1980, pp. 33–41.

Pascale, R. T. "Zen and the Art of Management." *Harvard Business Review,* March–April 1978, pp. 153–62.

Prahalad, C. K. "Strategic Choices in Diversified MNC." *Harvard Business Review,* July–August 1976, pp. 67–78.

Robinson, R. D. *International Business Management: A Guide to Decision Making.* Hinsdale, Ill.: Dryden Press, 1978, chaps. 4, 5, and 8.

Salmans, S. "Paternalism with a Difference." *International Management,* March 1978, pp. 40–42.

Schollhammer, H. "Ethics in an International Business Context." *MSU Business Topics,* Spring 1977, pp. 54–63.

Stupford, J. "The German Multinationals and Foreign Direct Investment in the United States." *Management International Review,* 1980–81, pp. 7–15.

Tanaka, H. "The Japanese Method of Preparing Today's Graduate to Become Tomorrow's Manager." *Personnel Journal,* February 1980, pp. 109–12.

"What Can The Japanese Teach U.S. Management?" *World Business Weekly,* January 19, 1981, pp. 10–12.

Whit, J. D. "Multinationals in Latin America: An Accent on Control." *Management Accounting,* February 1977, pp. 49–51.

Zeira, Y. "Overlooked Personnel Problems of Multinational Corporations." *Columbia Journal of World Business,* Summer 1975, pp. 99–103.

Zey-Ferrell, M. *Dimensions of Organizations: Environment, Context, Structure, Process, and Performance.* Santa Monica, Calif: Goodyear, 1979.

Instant Furniture: Part II

Sixteen years ago Rudy Nesbit recognized the opportunity of moving away from the traditional furniture store approach to one that would have a distinct competitive edge. His intent was to imitate the carryout convenience of supermarket shopping by building a cavernous warehouse-showroom combination building near a rail siding with a "carton-and-crates atmosphere" of low overhead and low prices.

Nesbit followed up on his idea and built a warehouse-showroom, stocking it with furniture and merchandise for immediate pickup. Thus, in an industry where delivery is normally slow because conventional furniture stores do not stock merchandise in quantity, Nesbit's customers were hauling home their own purchases the same day they bought them. The strategy was to produce high-volume sales on relatively low gross and net profit margins.

This marketing concept was parlayed from two stores with sales of $21 million after 1 year of operation to 55 stores in just 10 years with sales of $38 million. Due to an economic recession about the 10th year of operation, Nesbit suffered his first financial loss of $142,000. Also, the rapid growth of the company led to a lack of central controls over inventory, advertising, purchasing, and other functions. Specifically, the company had increased its inventory level to over $80 million and all 55 stores were being operated as though they were fragmented, independently-managed units.

Realizing that 55 stores were possibly more than he could effectively manage, particularly during a recession, Nesbit hired P. G. Ness to professionally manage the company. Ness came on board as president and chief executive officer with several years of experience as a regional vice president with a large national retailer.

The Ness approach

During the past five years with Ness as president, there has been a gradual shift to emphasize conservative growth and higher gross margins. Budget fare merchandise is now being replaced with more expensive furniture inside the showrooms, and overall gross margins have risen from 40.3 percent of sales to 44.1 percent. Ness is also changing store locations and styles. As an illustration, three nonprofitable Chicago outlets were closed, although they represented 3 percent of the company's total sales. Ness suggests that growth is not being abandoned since the goal through the 1980s is to open an average of six new stores per year. But, instead of building the typical 170,000–180,000-square-foot unit, the desire is to have 64,000-square-foot stores located in smaller metropolitan markets. These "satellite" stores would be established to serve as showrooms for warehouse stores approximately 25 miles away. With 74 stores, a majority of the 13 directors of the board believes that Ness has taken a 15-year-old concept and kept it up to date on a spectacularly successful basis.

Being a strong-willed CEO, Ness does not permit anyone even to imply that the discounting concept has been abandoned. Rather, it has been supplemented with furnishings and stores that can better serve a new rising segment of furniture buyers—the maturing baby-boom generation. This group now includes affluent homeowners with "more of a desire and ability to buy the good life." Ness predicts that within five years, sales will total $1 billion without sacrificing margins.

The Nesbit position

Rudy Nesbit, who is chairperson of the board of directors, still owns 25 percent of the company's stock but by no means controls the board. He is not at all pleased with Ness and the company's new marketing strategy; however, he has insufficient votes to unseat the president. Nesbit feels that Ness must be relieved and the original Nesbit strategy reinstated since the furniture field is "wide open and ready for the taking." The chairperson's position is that continued increases in energy costs are expected to reduce mobility and consequently to shift spending on homes. Currently, the organization's sales represent only 3 percent of a $20 billion industry, but that is sufficient to make the company second only to Sears, Roebuck and Company among all furniture competitors.

The company is expected to announce another year-to-year decline for its second quarter, and earnings are predicted to be down by 25 percent. On the other hand, the president has managed to increase earnings per share at an average annual rate of 48 percent, even though sales have gone up just 14 percent per year.

Rudy Nesbit suggests that a $1 billion sales level could be reached within two years if original discounting tactics are used to make new appeals to price-conscious buyers. In an attempt to take the company back from the president, Nesbit has tried two alternatives. One has been to collaborate with a group of investors, personally offering to buy the corporation for $27.00 per share. The board rejected the price as too low. The other maneuver was an attempt to discredit Ness with allegations of "nest-feathering." Part of the allegation is based on the fact that Ness was able to negotiate an annual salary contract with the board for $425,000 plus benefits worth approximately $196,000. Nesbit has sued the president, charging excessive salaries and benefits and a waste of assets through such actions as the purchase of a $1.6 million company jet.

Questions:

1. Explain the difference between the marketing strategies of Nesbit and Ness.
2. What organizational changes occurred within the Nesbit chain to bring about the desire of Nesbit to hire Ness?
3. Should growth and change within an organization be viewed with a sense of peace and tranquility, implying that all efforts can be totally coordinated?
4. Do you agree more completely with Nesbit's arguments or those of Ness? Why? What managerial actions would you take to implement the position of the person with whom you agree?

Ryan Machine and Bearing Company

The Ryan Machine and Bearing Company, located in Pittsburgh, Pennsylvania, produces as its major product a tubular, self-sealed roller bearing that is used in various types of industrial equipment. During the early years of the company, operations were seldom profitable due to the founder, E. J. Ryan, who persisted in creating new inventions, rather than concentating on managing the organization. Thus, after several years of repeated losses, the major stockholders of the company decided that they were no longer willing to put up additional funds to support Ryan's hobbies.

Eilon Norstrom, a major stockholder who served as production manager, agreed to purchase $20,000 of additional stock if he was given complete control as president of the organization. With Norstrom as president, the financial picture changed within six months: from a deficit of $12,000 to a $10,000 profit.

During the next 10 years, Norstrom provided the managerial leadership for the company and profits continued to increase. Last year's operations showed a profit of over $400,000. Financially, the company is in excellent condition, having a low debt to equity ratio and a strong liquidity position. The rate of return has consistently been twice as high as the industry average, and Norstrom now values the company's total assets in excess of $20 million.

History of the firm's growth

Within a few years after Norstrom became president, small tractors and riding lawn mowers were introduced on the market. At first, the small tractor business was something of a novelty and orders for tractor bearings were relatively small. During the early years of Norstrom's presidency, however, he made numerous trips to tractor manufacturers in order to acquaint them with the Ryan bearing. Whenever he heard of companies considering the manufacture of small tractors or riding lawn mowers, he would help their engineers design Ryan bearings into the tractor or mower. Consequently, Ryans's bearings became very popular in this industry.

The sale of bearings ultimately expanded to the point where the company was faced with the problem of increasing production rapidly in order to satisfy the new market. To keep orders flowing, a new building was constructed and new production equipment was installed. In addition, Norstrom now devotes his efforts almost exclusively to consulting with potential buyers on their engineering problems.

An offer to buy Ryan

Based on Norstrom's personal relationships and engineering advice, Ryan bearings were used almost exclusively by several large equipment manufacturers. In fact, two of the company's customers purchased about 60 percent of the total bearings produced. One day, as Norstrom was working on a design change with an engineer from one of these customers, the president of the organization asked Norstrom to have lunch with him at his club. During the luncheon, Norstrom was asked if he would sell the Ryan Company. Mr. Norstrom stated that he would take the matter up with the board of directors and contact him later. In a report to the board, Norstrom made the following points:

1. All of the board members have helped in building the business to its present position and all are proud of their accomplishments.
2. The company is dependent on a limited number of buyers for its products that are basically roller bearings. A change in customer relationships could result in a major shift in the marketing structure of the organization.
3. Due to technological advancements, the bearings produced by Ryan could gradually be replaced by another product. Also, changes in the design of tractors and mowers could result in decreased demand. Such changes would require dramatic reorganization of the company. In fact, it could mean a really new and different business.
4. At the present time, sales are high and profits are exceptionally good. With a continued increase in market demand for small tractors and riding lawn mowers, the growth of the organization seems strong, but not assured.
5. The company has not entered into new product research and design to any significant degree. Ryan is more of a speciality manufacturer, rather than a producer appealing to a broad market.
6. The purchase of the company would be made in the form of cash and stock in the corporation purchasing Ryan.

The board members listened intently to Norstrom's report; however, they did not take a position one way or the other on the issue.

The following evening, Norstrom, who is 55 years old, told his wife about the firm offering to buy Ryan Machine and Bearing Company and about his report to the board. He then related to his wife how he had devoted most of his life to developing the company into a large organization with substantial profits. Dividends from the company, however, had never been large and he stated that maybe this would be the time to turn the company into a sizable profit for himself and other stockholders.

Questions

1. How would you evaluate the management insight of Norstrom as concerns the future of Ryan?
2. Is Norstrom's desire to make a profit on the sale of the company short-sighted in terms of his future financial position?
3. If the market for the tubular bearing changes due to advanced technology, would the present managerial role of Norstrom have to change significantly?
4. What actions could the board take and what course should it follow?

Inter-Continental Hotel

The Republic of Zaire is located in West Africa. Jacques Carpentier, manager of the partially completed Inter-Continental Hotel, located in Zaire's capitol of Kinshasa, has stated that the interior of the country is fabulously rich and underdeveloped. He feels that the economy of the country is stable and that the government is relatively friendly to the United States.

Large manufacturers from the United States have been developing affiliations with Zaire. Goodyear, for example, is constructing a $16 million factory to produce tires. Both Ford and General Motors are known to be negotiating for permission to build assembly plants, and Kaiser and Alcoa are waiting for the government to build a World Bank-financed dam that will enable them to take advantage of cheap energy for producing aluminum ingots. At the mouth of the Congo River, Gulf Oil hit a gusher with its first test hole and Union Carbide is prospecting for exotic metal ores in the eastern section of the country.

Inter-Continental Hotel is part of the Inter-Continental Hotel chain, a multinational resort enterprise. When the hotel officially opens, it will have 260 rooms at a cost of $7.5 million. Surrounded by embassies and villas, it will be the first hotel in downtown Kinshasa to offer guests comfortable beds, air conditioning, dependable flush toilets, and a reliable telephone system.

At the present time, construction of the hotel is running several months behind schedule and about 10 percent over budget. One of the reasons for the delay in construction is that most of the building materials have to be imported. The only Atlantic Ocean port, Matadi, is generally backed up with goods awaiting delivery on the rickety, poorly maintained rail line to Kinshasa. One illustration of how delays can occur concerned a Farrell Lines ship that could not find a vacant dock spur. Consequently, the ship dumped some 60 crates of critical materials at Luanda in neighboring Angola, then a Portuguese territory with which Zaire has no diplomatic relations. Eventually, the shipment was reloaded and sent to Matadi, but it arrived six months late and damage was so extensive that many of the contents were useless.

Another reason for the construction delay concerns the way business is done in Zaire. One of the local customs is referred to as *matabish,* translated as *bribe.* Management executives of Inter-Continental vowed that they would not resort to bribery in order to open the hotel on time. However, bribes are so common in Zaire that police officers charge motorists with violating nonexistent laws so that they can create situations where a bribe will be offered.

Several incidents have occurred that reflect the attempted use of bribes on executives of the hotel. As an illustration, critical furnishings and building materials were flown into the N'Djili airport three months ago and are presently stored in customs offices. The items would be released quickly if the hotel executives would resort to *matabish.* In another incident, government officials informed the Inter-Continental Hotel that at least one half of its funds would have to be placed in the Banque de Kinshasa, which is controlled by leading government officials. Furthermore, it was communicated that the Banque de Kinshasa would be the only bank permitted to have offices in the new hotel after its completion.

Governmental pressure is also seen in the innumerable letters received by the hotel from top ministry and party leaders who demand that the hotel hire relatives or friends. The manager of Inter-Continental is not certain how he will handle these letters that are filling up his file drawers. Some of the signatures on the letters are illegible, and there are cases where lower-ranking officials have stolen letterhead stationery to write over their superiors' signatures.

Questions

1. How should Carpentier react to the pressure being exerted by governmental officals?
2. Should Jacques Carpentier and other management personnel resort to bribery to get the hotel built on time?
3. Recognizing that socially acceptable practices differ from culture to culture, should U.S. companies expect to do things their own way when operating in a foreign country?

Appendix A
Classical Principles of Management

1. Frederick W. Taylor's four principles of management that provide the basis for scientific management are given below:

    a. Each element of work is to be analyzed scientifically instead of by rule of thumb.

    b. Workers are scientifically selected, trained, and developed for positions for which they are best suited, rather than letting them select their own work and utilize their own methods in performing jobs.

    c. Cooperation is encouraged between managers who plan the work and those who perform the work to ensure that all work is done in accordance with developed scientific principles.

    d. Responsibility for the work is shared and assumed appropriately between those who plan the work and those who perform it.

Another principle of management noted by F. W. Taylor is as follows:

> The Exception Principle—The manager should receive only condensed, summarized, and comparative reports including both the especially good and the especially bad exceptions.[1]

2. Henri Fayol states that principles of management are not rigid since the same principle may not be applied twice in identical conditions. The application of principles is an art, and they must be capable of adaptation. The principles Fayol most often referred to are:[2]

    a. *Division of work*—specialization of labor produces more and better work with the same effort.

---

[1] All of the above are from Frederick W. Taylor, "Shop Management," pp. 126–27; and "The Principles of Scientific Management," pp. 36–37, in *Scientific Management* (New York: Harper & Row, 1947). Copyright 1947 by Harper & Row, Publishers, Inc.

[2] Henri Fayol, *General and Industrial Management* (London: sir Isaac Pitman and Sons, 1949), pp. 19–42.

b. *Authority and responsibility*—wherever authority is exercised, responsibility arises.

c. *Discipline*—obedience should be observed in accordance with the standing agreements between the firm and its employees; and it is essential for the smooth running of business, for without it no enterprise could prosper.

d. *Unity of command*—for any action, an employee should receive orders from only one superior.

e. *Unity of direction*—for a group of activities having the same objective, there should be only one head and one set of plans.

f. *Subordination of individual interest to general interest*—the interest of one employee or group should not prevail over that of the total organization.

g. *Remuneration of personnel*—the price granted for services rendered should be fair and afford satisfaction to both personnel and the firm.

h. *Centralization*—the degree of initiative left to managers varies depending upon top managers, subordinates, and business conditions.

i. *Scalar chain*—the line of authority of superiors ranging from the ultimate authority to the lowest ranks.

j. *Order*—once the jobs for essential, smooth running of the business have been decided upon and those people to fill such jobs have been selected, each employee occupies that job wherein she or he can render the most service.

k. *Equity*—for the personnel to be encouraged to fulfill their duties with devotion and loyalty there must be equity based on kindliness and justice in all employee dealings.

l. *Stability of tenure of personnel*—the more stable the managerial personnel of an organization, the more prosperous will be the organization.

m. *Initiative*—the ability to think through and execute a plan is a powerful motivator of human behavior.

n. *Esprit de corps*—harmony, union among the personnel of an organization, is a source of great strength in that organization.

3. J. D. Mooney suggests three most noteworthy principles:[3]

a. *Coordination*—is the orderly arrangement of group effort to provide unity of action in the pursuit of a common purpose.

b. *Scalar*—refers to a series of graded duties according to degrees of authority and corresponding responsibility.

c. *Functionalism*—in every organization there must be functions that (1) determine objectives, (2) move to attain objectives,

---

[3] James D. Mooney, *The Principles of Organization* (New York: Harper and Row, Publishers, © 1947).

and (3) make interpretive decisions in accordance with those rules of procedure that have been predetermined.

4. Lyndall Urwick in his book, *The Elements of Administration*, 1943, suggests several principles of administration that are, to a large extent, a synthesis of ideas by Fayol, Taylor, Mooney, and Mary Parker Follett. Three of the principles Urwick has explicitly stated are:[4]
   a. *Investigation*—all scientific procedure of activities is based on investigation (research) into the facts.
   b. *Objective*—it is a necessary activity to have a complete and clear statement of the objective of the activity.
   c. *Span of control*—no superior can supervise directly the work of more than five or, at the most, six subordinates whose work interlocks.

5. A. V. Graicunas used mathematics to support the concept of a narrow span of control. His formula, however, is not necessarily applicable to all situations since the variable of motivation and the nature of tasks may override the need for coordination and control.[5]

Appendix B
Illustrations of Management Science Models

The management science models presented in this section are simplified versions that can be studied without an extensive background in mathematics or even the aid of a hand calculator. The objective is to provide an understanding of the nature of each model, how it operates, and its practical application in solving management problems.

PROBABILITY DECISION MODEL

The probability model is a composite of various input variables that affect the outcome of a decision. One set of variables (the alternative solutions to the problem) is controllable and can be changed at the discretion of the manager. Another set of variables that directly affects the outcome of various alternative courses of action cannot be controlled by the decision maker. This group of variables includes environ-

---

[4] Lyndall Urwick, *The Elements of Administration* (New York: Harper and Row, Publishers, © 1943), pp. 19–26.

[5] A. V. Graicunas, "Relationship in Organization," in *Papers on the Science of Administration*, ed. Luther Gulick and Lyndall Urwick (New York: Institute of Public Administration, 1937), pp. 181–88.

mental forces, such as the prime rate of interest and general economic conditions. The probability decision model provides a framework to study these two sets of variables systematically and quantitatively. Understanding this model is the first step in studying other management science techniques. For problems that are applicable to the probability decision framework, the following terms are important in setting up the model:

Alternative—An alternative course of action selected by the decision maker. Alternatives are under the control of the decision maker and are designated by the symbol A_i.

State of nature—A variable outside the influence of the decision maker that directly affects the attainment of an objective, regardless of the alternative chosen. States of nature, such as weather conditions or stages of the business cycle, are uncontrollable variables and are represented as S_j.

Competitive action—A specific course of action taken by competitors. A competitive action is an uncontrollable variable and is designated by the symbol C_j.

Payoff matrix—A two-dimensional arrangement of figures representing the conditional payoff of various strategies under different states of nature or competitive actions. The values in the matrix are for a specified period of time or decision horizon.

Figure B–1 represents a payoff matrix with three alternatives, three states of nature, and the payoff value for each cell. The purpose of the matrix is to show the payoff value of various alternatives under different states of nature. It indicates that the decision maker knows the payoff for each alternative under each state of nature. However, since there are three possible states of nature, the decision maker is not certain which one will actually exist at given points in time. As noted in Chapter 3, such uncertainty is often due to imperfect knowledge of future conditions and/or a lack of sufficient data related to the problem.

FIGURE B–1
Payoff matrix (payoff in percentage return on investment)

Alternatives	States of nature		
	S_1 War and inflation	S_2 Peace and recession	S_3 Peace and stagnation
A_1 speculative stocks	20	4	−2
A_2 mutual funds	10	6	2
A_3 savings deposits	6	6	6

The approach assists managers in interrelating potential strategies with various states of nature or competitive actions. Furthermore, it provides a means for solving complex problems having a large number of variables. By using the model, managers are also better equipped to recognize the "how" and "why" of decisions. As a result, they are more capable of selecting sound courses of action from among available alternatives.

Applications of decision theory under different situations

Basically, managers are faced with four kinds of decision situations: (1) certainty, (2) risk, (3) uncertainty, and (4) conflict. In each of these situations, the payoff matrix is essentially the same as that used in the probability model.

Decision making under certainty Under conditions of certainty there is only one state of nature to face. For example, the decision maker is certain (100 percent) that there will be peace as opposed to war, or that the weather will be sunny and warm over the weekend. Referring back to Figure B–1, if conditions of certainty exist for the state of nature S_3, the decision matrix would be:

Alternative	S_3
A_1	−2
A_2	2
A_3	6

With one state of nature and an objective of obtaining the maximum outcome, the manager will select the alternative with the highest payoff—in this case, A_3.

While the existence of a single state of nature simplifies decision making, certainty in our daily lives is more illusory than factual. The rapidity of change in a complex society seldom permits variables in a problem situation to be stated with complete assurance. If certainty is assumed, it surely would be for a very brief time horizon. More realistically, managers deal with probabilistic occurrences of various states of nature, such as the number of Christmas trees that might be sold during the yuletide season.

Decision making under risk In decision making under conditions of risk, managers are faced with multiple states of nature. However, information concerning each state of nature is probabilistic, and not certain. The probability that a given state of nature will occur is based on the manager's research, experience, and other information.[1] Person-

---

[1] The probable outcome is known because one accepts the idea that probabilities are related to the frequency of events that have occurred over long periods of time. For example, in tossing a coin, one does not know exactly (100 percent certainty, or a probability of 1.0) whether it will come up heads or tails. However, over the long run with a large number of similar coin tosses, it can be assumed that the probability of

FIGURE B–2
Net profit payoff values for two strategies at various projected sales volumes (in thousands of $)

Alternatives	States of nature (projected sales volume)			
	S_1 $100,000	S_2 $250,000	S_3 $500,000	S_4 $750,000
New suburban store (A_1)	−3	11	23	34
Expansion of downtown store (A_2)	7	12	22	33

nel managers, for example, might determine the probability of a certain employee turnover rate, absenteeism figures, or safety record. Likewise, a credit manager might determine the probability of having 20 percent of accounts receivable overdue.

Using the assumed probability of each state of nature and the associated payoffs, the decision maker can determine the expected monetary value for each alternative strategy. The *expected monetary value (EMV)* of an alternative is the summation of the probabilities of various states of nature multiplied by the particular payoffs.[2]

To illustrate decision making under risk and the use of *EMV*, consider the decision to locate a store in a new suburban shopping mall or to expand an existing downtown store to make it more appealing to customers. Expressed as net profit, the conditional values of the two alternatives are presented in Figure B–2 and represent the payoffs associated with different sales volumes (states of nature).

As noted in the matrix, an expansion of the downtown store produces better payoffs when the lower sales volumes of S_1 and S_2 are considered. The construction of a new suburban store would be a better decision if sales in the $500,000 and $750,000 ranges are determined to be more realistic. The problem, then, is to select the strategy that provides

---

heads is 0.5 and the probability of tails is 0.5. In cases where there is no past experience, subjective probability may be used. In these instances, stated probabilities are no more than a belief in the likelihood of certain events happening.

[2] For any alternative, the expected monetary value is as follows:

$$EMV = \sum_{i=1}^{n} x_i P(x_i)$$

when x_i is the conditional value or payoff of each outcome, $P(x_i)$ is the probability associated with the particular value, and

$$\sum_{i=1}^{n}$$

refers to the sum of the individual $P(x_i)$ events when

$$P_1 = P_2 + \cdots P_n = 1.0$$

the greatest profit. However, without knowledge of the probability of occurrence for each state of nature, it is difficult to arrive at a logical solution. One way to determine a probability for the different sales volumes is to obtain information about retail store expansion programs by type of business, size of trading area, and competitive conditions. For this illustration, assume that the following probabilities have been determined through a combination of research and personal experience:

State of nature—sales volume	Probability that state of nature will occur
S_1 \$100,000	0.20
S_2 250,000	0.30
S_3 500,000	0.35
S_4 750,000	0.15
	1.00 or 100%

By multiplying the probability of each state of nature by the associated payoffs of each strategy (shown in Figure B–2), the EMV for A_1 and A_2 can be determined. The expected monetary value for the new suburban store (A_1) is:

$$EMV(A_1) = (-3)\,0.20 + (11)\,0.30 + (23)\,0.35 + (34)\,0.15$$
$$= 15.85 \text{ thousand dollars, or } \$15,850$$

The expected monetary value for the expansion of the downtown store (A_2) is:

$$EMV(A_2) = (7)\,0.20 + (12)\,0.30 + (22)\,0.35 + (33)\,0.15$$
$$= 17.65 \text{ thousand dollars, or } \$17,650$$

Therefore, since the EMV for A_2 is larger than the EMV for A_1, an expansion of the downtown store is the best strategy for obtaining the highest net profit. Accepting this strategy implies, of course, that the total utility to be derived from the decision is closely equivalent to the expected monetary value.

By deciding on A_2, it should be realized that the EMV of \$17,650 is not an assured profit level. Only one state of nature can occur at any point in time. As little as \$7,000, or as much as \$33,000, could be obtained. The EMV means that on the average over a long period of time A_2 would produce a profit of \$17,650. A decision to expand the downtown store means that the manager is willing to play the percentages.

Suppose that the decision maker, however, is not happy with playing the percentages involved in making a decision under risk. If the manager is willing to pay a marketing research company to obtain some additional information, he or she would have a situation of determining the *value of perfect information.* For purposes of simplicity, assume the research company is able to tell the manager with certainty which state of nature will occur (a situation of perfect information). Thus, the manager would be able to make a decision with complete certainty.

If the company stated a fee of $400 to provide the additional (perfect) information, the manager must then decide the value of this information. To do this the manager computes the expected value with perfect information by selecting the best alternative under each state of nature. The average (expected) value is given below:

$$(7)\ 0.20 + (12)\ 0.30 + (23)\ 0.35 + (34)\ 0.15 = \$18,150$$

By comparing the value of perfect information with the highest value, the manager presently knows, under risk, the expected value of perfect information *(EVPI)* is $18,150 − $17,650, or $500. Since the research company is charging $400 for the prediction, the manager can gain, on the average, $100 by obtaining the additional information. The implication here is that the information is 100 percent reliable, and the decision-making situation is placed under conditions of certainty.

Decision making under uncertainty With no historical data from which to infer probabilistic occurrences of the states of nature, managers are faced with making decisions under conditions of uncertainty. In this instance, the decision maker has less information than under conditions of risk because of the difficulty of assessing the probability of each state of nature. Four different approaches to decision making under such conditions are presented below. They include the decision philosophies of (1) optimism, (2) pessimism, (3) least regret, and (4) insufficient reasoning.

Maximizing the maximum payoff—If a decision maker is completely optimistic about the probable occurrence of certain events, it would be natural to select the strategy providing the maximum payoff. For example, assume that the payoff matrix shown in Figure B–3 was developed by a home builder for determining the number of new houses to build during the next five years under various market rates of interest.

Looking at the payoffs for each alternative, we see that the maximums are 12, 18, and 22 for A_1, A_2, and A_3, respectively.[3] With an optimistic attitude, the builder would select A_3 in order to maximize the maximum payoff. This approach is referred to as the *maximax* decision criterion. In other words, with an optimistic philosophy about the occurrence of payoffs, and with no knowledge of the probable

---

[3] In this example, the maximum payoffs for all three alternatives existed under the same state of nature. With a different set of variables, the maximum payoff for A_1 could be under S_2; A_2 could be under S_3; and A_3 could be under S_1.

FIGURE B–3
Payoff matrix for home builder (net profit in thousands of dollars)

Alternatives (number of houses to build)	States of nature (prime interest rate)			
	S_1 8%	S_2 10%	S_3 12%	S 14%
$A_1$10	12	9	8	6
$A_2$20	18	16	13	4
$A_3$30	22	18	11	1

existence of a given interest rate, the builder would select the alternative providing the maximum payoff under the various states of nature.

If the builder, however, felt some uncertainty about seeking the largest possible payoff, the largest and smallest payoffs for each strategy could be taken and probabilities assigned to them in relationship to some level of optimism. If an optimistic probability of .7 were assigned to the highest payoff of an alternative, a .3 probability would be assigned to the smallest payoff of that same alternative. The calculations for this modification of the maximax criterion are given below:

$$EMV\,A_1 = 0.7\,(12) + 0.3\,(6) = 10.2$$
$$EMV\,A_2 = 0.7\,(18) + 0.3\,(4) = 13.8$$
$$EMV\,A_3 = 0.7\,(22) + 0.3\,(1) = 15.7$$

The results show that the builder would still select A_3 (build 30 houses), since this strategy has the highest expected monetary value *(EMV)* of the three alternatives.

Maximizing the minimum payoff—Since high-interest rates have been experienced for the past few years, the builder might have the attitude that the future looks bleak. Thus, a feeling of pessimism would prevail. In order to be as rational as possible with this attitude, the builder would attempt to maximize the minimum payoffs for each alternative and would then select the maximum one (best of the worst). Referring back to Figure B–3, we see that the minimum payoffs for each alternative are as follows:

Alternatives	Minimum payoff
A_1	6
A_2	4
A_3	1

In selecting the maximum payoff, the builder would choose A_1, which is to build only 10 homes since this strategy provides the best results from the list of the minimum payoffs. This approach is referred to as *maximin* decision criterion.

Minimizing the maximum regret—An interesting decisional approach that could be followed by the builder is to determine how much regret might be experienced relative to the payoff of a given strategy under a particular state of nature. Referring back to Figure B–3, we see that the prime interest rate might turn out to be 8 percent with the builder following A_3. If so, there would be no regret since other alternatives would not produce a higher payoff. But, if the builder was following A_1, and the interest was actually 8 percent, there would be a \$10,000 regret (\$22,000 − \$12,000 = \$10,000) since A_3 would have provided \$10,000 more profit. For further clarification in calculating the regrets (opportunity losses), if the actual state of nature was 14 percent (S_4) and the builder selected A_1, there would be no regret. In this instance, \$6,000 is the highest profit attainable when the rate of interest is 14 percent. However, if A_3 was selected rather than A_1, the builder would experience \$5,000 of regret or opportunity loss for not having selected A_1 (\$6,000 highest payoff value minus \$1,000). The following matrix represents the various regrets (in thousands):

Alternatives	States of nature			
	S_1	S_2	S_3	S_4
A_1	10	9	5	0
A_2	4	2	0	2
A_3	0	0	2	5

The next step is to select the largest (maximum) regret for each alternative. These are given below:

$$A_1 = 10$$
$$A_2 = 4$$
$$A_3 = 5$$

Logically, the builder would then select the alternative that would provide the minimum amount of regret—that is A_2. By selecting A_2, the builder is guaranteed not to have a regret larger than \$4,000, regardless of which state of nature will occur. By minimizing the maximum regret, this approach is referred to as *minimax* decision criterion.

Insufficient reasoning—Even though decision making under uncertainty implies that managers do not have enough experience to arrive at probabilities of occurrence, they may take the position that one state of nature is just as likely to occur as another. In other words, there is no reason to believe that the probability of one state of nature is any different from that of all others. Thus, equal probabilities are assigned to each state of nature. This philosophy is referred to as the doctrine of insufficient reasoning.[4]

Referring again to Figure B–3, our home builder following this criterion would assign a one-fourth probability to each state of nature since there are four of them. The *EMV* for each alternative is then calculated as follows:

$$EMV A_1 = \tfrac{1}{4}(12 + 9 + 8 + 6) = 8.75$$
$$EMV A_2 = \tfrac{1}{4}(18 + 16 + 13 + 4) = 12.75$$
$$EMV A_3 = \tfrac{1}{4}(22 + 18 + 11 + 1) = 13.00$$

In this instance, A_3 would be selected since it has the highest expected monetary value.

Using the four approaches to decision making under uncertainty, alternative A_3 was selected by the optimistic maximax; alternative A_1 by the pessimistic maximin; alternative A_2 by minimizing maximum regret (minimax); and alternative A_3 by following subjective reasoning. In each case, the criterion chosen determined the ultimate selection of an alternative for a given set of variables. Consequently, determining an alternative to follow depends upon the decision criterion used by a manager.

More specifically, the choice of criteria depends on (1) the specific situation facing the decision maker, (2) personal attitudes of optimism or pessimism, and (3) the economic and financial conditions of the organization. In reality, there is no "one best" criterion to follow. An important point to remember in choosing a criterion is to select one that does not disregard useful, available information. Thus, if information about the probable occurrence of states of nature becomes available, it should be used in the decision process, even though the probabilities may be determined subjectively. Of course, the personalities of managers always have a great deal to do with understanding why certain decisions are made in lieu of other alternative courses of action.

Decision making under conflict Another interesting decision model utilizing the payoff matrix is game theory. In this model, competitive strategies are controlled by an adverse intellect or interest. Thus, decisions are made under conflict. Depending on the number of intellects (opponents), some games are extremely complex. When only two persons are involved, the game can be handled in a manner similar to that for decision making under uncertainty. Solving a two-

---

[4] In this instance, the decision maker does not have any reason to believe that one state of nature may be more likely to occur than another.

person game is referred to as a finite-zero-sum game where only one person can win. This means that A's course of action is I's state of nature. Thus, what I gains, A loses.

Games have had wider appeal in military situations than in business management decisions. From a military standpoint, let us hypothetically consider a rescue mission of American hostages in a foreign embassy who are being held by insurgents. The success of the mission is measured in terms of getting all of the hostages released without harm. Suppose that the Americans have only two strategies available if they decide to undertake a military action:

A^1—move in a covert military force that makes its way incognito through the countryside to the American Embassy for a surprise rescue attempt.

A_2—attempt to secretly land a major military force that would overtly fight its way to the embassy, capturing the ground and holding it.

The insurgents, let us suppose, also have two strategies:

I_1—to restrict communications and release conflicting reports so that the Americans are uncertain as to the whereabouts and the condition of the hostages.

I_2—to be fully, militarily prepared for battle, even if this meant entering into a long-term military engagement.

The payoff matrix for both sides could be represented as follows:

Insurgents	Americans	
	A_1	A_2
I_1	2	1
I_2	4	2

In reading the matrix, the 2 in cell $I_1 A_1$ means that if the insurgents followed strategy I_1 and the Americans chose A_1, the gain for the insurgents would be the value of 2 with an equivalent loss for the Americans. In decision making under conflict, opponents know the possible payoffs for each side. Thus, what the insurgents gain in either strategy, I_1 or I_2, the Americans will lose.

In arriving at a solution, the insurgents would logically follow the maximin criterion. The minimum gains for the two insurgent strategies are given below:

$$I_1 = 1$$
$$I_2 = 2$$

To maximize the minimum gains, the insurgents would choose strategy I_2. The Americans would want to follow a minimax criterion in order to minimize the worst or maximum loss. The maximum loss for each alternative is as follows:

$$A_1 = 4$$
$$A_2 = 2$$

Thus, the Americans would logically follow A_2 as the course of action that would minimize their worst possible loss.

By utilizing the competitive game model, we see that the insurgents should follow I_2 with the Americans selecting A_2. Since these are the most rational approaches for both (if a battle can ever be considered rational), there is complete conflict. What one side gains, the other loses. If the Americans select A_2, the insurgents could not improve their position by selecting any strategy other than I_2. Likewise, since the Americans believe that the insurgents will select I_2, they must follow A_2. Strategy A_1 would result in an equal loss if the insurgents followed I_1. In this situation, there is no need for espionage or spying since each of the opponents knows the actual payoff. However, if the insurgents had information indicating that the Americans would not follow A_2, they should consider the probability of another strategy being followed. Since the Americans stand to lose regardless, and the game ball is in their court, the most logical decision would be not to enter into any type of military confrontation.

This simple illustration of game theory does not fit situations where both opponents can gain, or where there are more than two competitors. Yet, it does provide a framework within which managers can reach more efficient decisions and has some possible uses in business situations. For example, the zero-sum game can be applied where two competitors are vying for a larger share of the market, when two managers are seeking the same promotion or assignment, or when two departments are seeking a larger share of fixed funds.

LINEAR PROGRAMMING

Linear programming (LP) is one of the best-known operations research models being applied to many business-related problems. Developed primarily at the RAND Corporation, LP can be used in situations where a firm seeks to maximize profits or minimize costs while operating within the constraints of capital equipment, physical facilities, labor, raw materials, and management. Basically, the model is used to determine an optimal allocation of limited resources within the organization.

Applications of the model in business include:

1. Mixing proportions of product ingredients in order to minimize costs.
2. Assigning components of the business, such as personnel and machines.

3. Allocating the use of resources so that the output quantities maximize profits.
4. Distributing output so as to minimize transportation costs.
5. Scheduling output to balance demand, production, and inventory levels.

The LP model assumes linearity (a straight-line relationship in which one unit on the X axis represents a certain number of units on the Y axis). Time is not considered. Thus, if operating conditions change, a decision that was viable for an earlier period may no longer be applicable. Consequently, over any long period of time, the planning attributes of the model are severely restricted since past conditions never remain the same (certainty).

To illustrate a use of the model, assume that a manufacturer of novelty articles has excess plant capacity and is considering the production of one or two independent products, A and B. It is possible to produce and sell only product A, only B, or any combination of the two that would be consistent with production capacities and requirements in machining, painting, and assembling. The problem is to find the combination of products A and B that should be produced to cover fixed costs and to obtain a maximum contribution to profits.

The production requirements are noted in the following data:

Production centers	Product A (hours required/unit)	Product B (hours required/unit)	Capacity available (hours)
Machining	8	4	96
Painting	4	8	120
Assembly	5	0	45
Contribution per unit	$6/unit	$4/unit	

Based upon the above data, an apparent question arises: Why not produce all of product A since it provides the highest contribution per unit? Of course, this alternative is possible. However, by manufacturing some combination of the two products, the total contribution might be even higher. This relationship can be stated as follows: Total contribution is a function of the contribution per unit for both A and B times the number of products produced and sold. Thus,

Total contribution = f (contribution per unit for A and B, and the number of A and B produced)

or

$$\text{Total contribution} = \$6 \ (A) + \$4 \ (B)$$

The first step in arriving at a solution to the problem of maximizing total contribution is to develop a model of the situation—that is, to set up mathematical expressions of the production center constraints. Equations for the problem are given below:

Machining/unit:	$8A + 4B \leq 96$
Painting/unit:	$4A + 8B \leq 120$
Assemblying/unit:	$5A + 0B \leq 45$

These algebraic expressions denote that the combination of products A and B must be equal to or be less than the available capacity for each process. Production of A and B, however, cannot be less than zero: $A \geq 0$ and $B \geq 0$.

The best way to illustrate these expressions is to graph them, as shown in Figure B–4. The Y axis of the figure represents the number of units of A and the X axis represents the number of units of B. If A is set equal to zero, the production level of B would be represented

FIGURE B–4
Linear programming: graphic solution

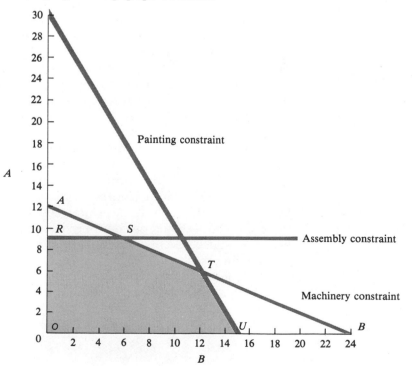

someplace along the X axis for each of the constraints. Likewise, if B is set equal to zero, the production level of A would be represented someplace on the Y axis for each constraint.

Considering only the machining constraint, assume that no B products are produced. The question can then be asked, "How many units of A can be machined if it takes 8 hours to do one of them?" The answer is that 12 As could be machined with 96 hours of available machining time. This point is then plotted on the graph as A. By turning the situation around and machining all of B and none of A, we find that 24 Bs could be produced. These two points are then connected with a straight line that represents a condition of equality for the machine equation. In other words, any point on the machinery constraint line represents the machining of a certain number of A and B products within the capacity requirements of the 96 hours of machining time available. For example, 8 Bs and 8 As could be produced and still be within the 96 hours restriction: 8 Bs (4 hours) + 8 As (8 hours) = 96 hours of machinery time. Thus, every point along the machinery line results in an equality condition.

In a similar manner we can handle each of the other two constraint expressions. For example, the painting constraint is represented by 30 As and 0 Bs, or 15 Bs and 0 As. Note that the assembly constraint is represented as a straight horizontal line intersecting the Y axis at 9 units. Since no assembly time is required in the production of B, assemblying is not a constraint in B's production.

The area of the graph that is bounded by the X and Y axes and the constraint lines is the feasible area in which production can take place. Any point outside this area would reflect negative activities. To illustrate, consider the question, "Why not produce 30 As?" There is, of course, sufficient painting capacity to produce 30 As; however, since it takes 8 hours to machine 1 A and there are only 96 hours available, the best that can be done is to machine 12 As. But since product A also requires 5 hours of assemblying time and there are only 45 hours of assembly time available, a maximum of 9 units of A can be produced in the specific period of time.

The feasible area, therefore, is the one that is represented by the area *ORSTU*. The letters represent the points within the area where lines intersect. It is only at these intersections that alternative combinations of A and B should be considered. At any other point, total contribution would be increasing or decreasing to a termination point at the next intersection.

In establishing the combination of products A and B that will provide the greatest contribution, the location of the points in the feasible area must be determined. Three points have already been established:

O (zero *A*, zero *B*),   *R* (9*A*, zero *B*), and   *U* (zero *A*, 15*B*)

Points S and T must also be located if area $ORSTU$ is to be delineated properly. One way of doing this is to read their location from the graph in Figure B–4.

Another more accurate method is to solve simultaneously the equations of the two lines that intersect to form the particular point. The equations to be solved for point S are:

$$5A + 0B = 45 \qquad (1)$$
$$8A + 4B = 96 \qquad (2)$$

Since we know that A in equation (1) is equal to 9, we can substitute 9 for A in equation (2) and solve for B:

$$8\,(9) + 4B = 96$$
$$72 + 4B = 96$$
$$4B = 24$$
$$B = 6$$

Thus, point S is $9A$ and $6B$.

The equations to be solved for point T are:

$$8A + 4B = 96 \qquad (3)$$
$$4A + 8B = 120 \qquad (4)$$

The two unknown linear equations may be solved simultaneously by using the addition and subtraction method. The first step is to multiply equation (3) by -2:

$$-2\,(8A + 4B = 96) = -16A - 8B = -192$$
$$4A + 8B = 120$$
$$-12A = -72$$
$$A = 6$$

Now substitute 6 for A in equation (4):

$$4\,(6) + 8B = 120$$
$$24 + 8B = 120$$
$$8B = 96$$
$$B = 12$$

Thus, point T is $6A$ and $12B$.

By calculating the contribution of the product mixes at points R, S, T, and U, the point that yields the greatest contribution can be determined. Referring to Figure B–5, the greatest contribution ($84) is at point T, the combination of producing 6 As and 12 Bs.

An algebraic solution to linear programming problems of this type

FIGURE B–5
Total contribution for various product mixes

Point	Units of A	×	Contri- bution ($)	+	Units of B	×	Contri- bution ($)	=	Total contri- bution ($)
O	0		6		0		4		0
R	9		6		0		4		54
S......	9		6		6		4		78
T	6		6		12		4		84
U	0		6		15		4		60

is also possible. At this point we will not examine the algebraic method; however, it is quite useful when two, three, or more possible product dimensions are involved.

The graphical approach works best when only two products are considered, therefore necessitating only a two-dimensional surface. When there is a large number of products and processing centers, even the algebraic solution becomes impractical due to the sheer magnitude of the problem. In such cases, the linear programming model is still valid, but the solution method changes. A computing algorithm referred to as the simplex method is used to solve more complicated problems. This is a mathematical procedure involving a series of iterations, the last giving the best solution.[5]

In summary, linear programming is one of the best-known management tools to solve allocation-type problems. Although the example used to illustrate LP is fairly simple, it does present the basic parts and functioning of the model. The important point to realize at this time is that management science has moved decision making from pure guesswork and hunch to a systematic way of solving complex problems having innumerable alternatives.

TRANSPORTATION METHOD

Another example of linear programming is the transportation method. This method is valuable when managers are involved with the movement of specific quantities of goods from several shipping points. To illustrate, consider the Everfit Shoe Company that has two regional warehouses and two manufacturing plants. The capacity of Plant A is 100 units and 200 units for Plant B. One of the warehouses located in St. Louis has a demand of 175 units, while the Chicago warehouse requires 125 units. At present, the company ships shoes from plants to warehouses as shown in the distribution matrix in Figure B–6. The figure in the upper left corner of each major cell in the

---

[5] The simplex method technique was originated by G. E. Dantzig, University of California, Berkley.

FIGURE B–6
Original distribution matrix of a transportation problem, Everfit Shoe Company

Plant	St. Louis warehouse		Chicago warehouse		Plant capacities in units
A	$0.90	100	$1.00	0	100
B	$0.75	75	$1.20	125	200
Warehouse requirements		175		125	300

matrix represents the shipping cost per unit from the factory to the warehouse. Thus, the cost to ship 1 unit from Plant A to St. Louis is $0.90.

To minimize transportation costs, a systematic approach is essential in arriving at the most economical shipping pattern. The first step in systematically determining the least expensive transportation plan is to examine, one at a time, each empty cell in the matrix. Since there is only one empty cell (A–Chicago) in this problem, the question may be asked, "Would it be cheaper to ship some goods from Plant A to Chicago, rather than shipping all production to St. Louis?"

If, for example, 1 unit was shipped from Plant A to Chicago, costing an additional $1.00, 1 less unit would have to be shipped to St. Louis in order to maintain the capacity balance of Plant A. Shipping 1 less unit to St. Louis would save the company $0.90; however, warehouse requirements there would be short by 1 unit. To satisfy the demand of 175 units, 1 additional unit must be shipped from Plant B, which will add $0.75 to shipping costs. Consequently, to keep Plant B's capacity in balance, 1 less unit must be shipped to Chicago, thus saving $1.20. By adding additional shipping charges and subtracting out savings, the manager can determine whether a different shipping pattern would reduce overall dollar costs.

A procedure to follow in calculating potential transportation savings is:

1. Start with an empty cell. If the movement of only one unit is considered, put a plus in front of the transportation cost since additional costs would be incurred.
2. Make only right or left turns, do not move diagonally, and move only to cells where a distribution already exists.

3. Once the next full cell is reached, put a minus in front of the transportation cost and then alternate from plus to minus until reaching the empty cell where the process started.
4. Add up the transportation costs considering the plus and minus designation. In the above example we have the following:

To:	A–Chicago	+$1.00
From:	A–St. Louis	− 0.90
To:	B–St. Louis	+ 0.75
From:	B–Chicago	− 1.20
		−$0.35

The interpretation of the −$0.35 is that money could be saved if some goods were shipped to Chicago from Plant A. The next decision is to determine how many units should be moved into cell A–Chicago. An easy rule to follow in making this decision is to move no more than the smallest distribution value in the cells with negatives. Thus, 100 units would be moved into A–St. Louis, 100 units subtracted from A–St. Louis, 100 added to B–St. Louis, and 100 subtracted from B–Chicago. The new matrix appears in Figure B–7.

Is the best distribution now available, or is there another pattern that would be less expensive? To answer this question, we must go through the same movement of goods from empty to full cells in the matrix. This movement is shown below:

To:	A–St. Louis	+$0.90
From:	B–St. Louis	− 0.75
To:	B–Chicago	+ 1.20
From:	A–Chicago	− 1.00
		+$0.35

FIGURE B–7
Revised matrix of transportation problem, Everfit Shoe Company

Plant	St. Louis warehouse		Chicago warehouse		Plant capacities in units
A	$0.90		$1.00		
		0		100	100
B	$0.75		$1.20		
		175		25	200
Requirements in units		175		125	300

FIGURE B–8
Transportation costs of two distribution patterns, Everfit Shoe Company

Plants-warehouses	Transportation cost per unit	Original transportation cost		Revised transportation cost	
		Units	Total transportation cost	Units	Total transportation cost
A–St. Louis.....	$ .90	100	$ 90.00	0	$ 0
A–Chicago	1.00	0	0	100	100.00
B–St. Louis.....	.75	75	56.25	175	131.25
B–Chicago	1.20	125	150.00	25	30.00
			$296.25		$261.25

The +$0.35 indicates that any movement of goods into cell A–St. Louis would result in a higher transportation cost. In fact, there is no other possible distribution of goods between plants and warehouses that would further minimize costs.

The total transportation costs of the distributions in Figures B–6 and B–7 are presented in Figure B–8, which shows a savings of $35 by changing the distribution pattern ($296.25 − $261.25 = $35.00).

The illustration above is simple, utilizing only one empty cell. For a firm such as Genesco, Inc., with as many as 17 manufacturing facilities and thousands of retail shoe outlets, the matrix would be quite large with several empty cells. Regardless of the matrix size, the cost savings of each empty cell is considered. The selection of the cell for the actual redistribution should be the one that has the largest potential cost saving. For example, if there were four empty cells and the new cost for each pattern were +$0.30, −$0.20, −$0.50, and −$0.10, the cell with a −$0.50 would be selected and the goods redistributed to this cell. After the physical redistribution, the empty cells would be checked again to determine whether any additional cost savings would be forthcoming by developing a new distribution pattern. This type of reiteration is continued until all empty cells indicate positive values.

With the use of a computer, a great deal of time can be saved in solving large and complex transportation problems. The use of this model has reduced distribution costs for many firms. Its application is almost unlimited in the areas of production, marketing, and finance. When managers are attempting to find a combination (plan) that will result in maximum efficiency within the constraints of the resources, it is an excellent operations research technique to follow.

Finally, it should be noted that the linear programming models described above are prescriptive (normative). This means that they obtain optimal solutions by seeking the maximization or minimization of a particular objective. They give the one best answer from among various alternatives in terms of given variables and their interrelationships.

SIMULATION

Simulation is a descriptive operations research model that shows how decision-making systems work in a particular situation. It differs from prescriptive linear programming models in that it does not select the best possible alternative, although it can display various alternatives by experimenting with the variables.

When a problem cannot be expressed by a standard mathematical model because of the complexity of the situation, it may be possible to construct a simulation model representing the real world system. Some management problems are so complex that mathematical models, such as linear programming, cannot be used since the exact relationships among variables are not known, or because managers cannot arrive at a satisfactory measure of optimality. When this is true, the use of simulation permits managers to try out several different alternatives while observing how they perform within the total system. Applications of simulation in management can be seen in the areas of inventories, reordering, merchandising, adding a new checkout counter in a supermarket, developing a schedule for the operation of a barge line, and so forth.

Simulation has been especially helpful in solving problems dealing with physical facilities and their capacities. For example, steel companies have simulated entire plant operations to observe how various alternative methods could reduce the effects of bottlenecks. In mining, manufacturing, and petroleum production, there are many reported uses of simulation.

In general, simulation permits a manager to evaluate the performance of a proposed system before it is actually installed. For example, a manager could ask the question, "If I increase maintenance expenses by 10 percent, what will happen to labor and material costs per unit?" By using a simulation model, the manager can alter the variables to determine the output change that might take place.

One famous model in this area was developed by RAND Corporation to simulate various military air transportation systems. In this simulation model, variables can be systematically changed, and after an extended number of trials, researchers can arrive at answers that are satisfactory or preferable under different sets of conditions. In other words, various performances and outcomes are determined by considering possible alternatives under different states of nature. In this respect, a simulation model represents an experimental approach for arriving at a satisfactory answer, rather than an optimal solution.

The trial and error approach of simulation models is useful in training future managers. In business schools, for example, management games are used where students are asked to make decisions that affect a company's financial statements. Variables in the game are generally expressed as a series of descriptive equations about the company and are based on experimental or empirical data.

Monte Carlo simulation

The Monte Carlo technique is one of the most interesting applications of simulation. The heart of the technique is the use of variables having probabilistic (stochastic) relationships. Since relationships are built on probability, a random selection of values is used to simulate the natural ordering of events. Thus, the model is not treated as being prescriptive in arriving at optimal values.

Monte Carlo has many applications, such as determining the level of inventory to carry in stock. Another application is that of determining the number of loading docks that a wholesale distributor should have when the arrival of trucks and their unloading times are quite irregular. Monte Carlo can help in arriving at a solution to these problems by testing proposed policies or rules based on the random collection of sample data.

Consider the case of Evertrue, Inc. This firm often receives 80 to 120 additional orders in January, February, and March to manufacture a seasonal product. Additional equipment must be leased to take on this additional business and a three-month notice of intent is required to lease the equipment. To complete a single order, one full workday of machine time is needed. If the order is not processed the day it is received, shipping schedules cannot be met. The rental for each machine is $750 a month, and the profit is $50 for each order processed and shipped on time.

The problem facing the managers of Evertrue, Inc., is how to determine the number of machines to rent in order to maximize profits. If the company has 60 working days during the three-month period, and if the average number of orders in the past has been 100, then an average of 1.7 orders per day would justify renting two machines. This, however, may not be the best number of machines to rent since the receipt of orders is irregular and the loss of some orders is not taken into consideration. The Monte Carlo technique, therefore, can be used to simulate the arrival of orders.

Based on past experience, the probability distribution of orders per day is determined as follows:

Orders per day	Probability of occurrence
0	0.20
1	0.40
2	0.25
3	0.10
4	0.05
	1.00

The first step in determining the number of machines to rent is to assign a range of two-digit numbers to correspond to the probability

FIGURE B–9
Assignment of the range for determining the orders per day based on the probability of occurrence

Order per day	Probability of occurrence	Range
0	0.20	00–19
1	0.40	20–59
2	0.25	60–84
3	0.10	85–94
4	0.05	95–99

distribution noted above. The five probabilities of occurrence with the assigned range of numbers is shown in Figure B–9.

The next step is to simulate the daily order rate by using a table of random numbers, or by putting 100 two-digit numbered balls in a bowl so that any one number is as likely to be drawn out of the bowl as any other number. If the first ball drawn is 87, we would simulate the number of orders for the day by consulting Figure B–9. Since the number 87 falls in the 85–94 range, the number of orders for the day would be three.

As noted in Figure B–10, step three is to simulate a 30-day working period that shows the number of orders to be received. Thus, 41 orders would be lost without renting any machines; 16 lost if only one machine is rented; 6 orders lost if two machines are rented; and only 1 sale lost if three machines are rented. Considering the rental cost of each machine at $750 per month and the potential loss of profits of $50 for each order not filled for the 30-day period, costs and profit losses would be minimized by renting one machine, as shown in Figure B–11. An interesting point to recognize is that costs can be minimized by not filling all orders. In other words by renting only one machine, some orders will be lost, but the result is still a higher total profit.

It is possible to stimulate another 30 days to compute the entire 60-day period under consideration. However, a more practical approach is to repeat the 30-day simulated period several times in order to arrive at a frequency distribution. This permits a determination of the number of machines that most frequently produces the smallest lost profits. The implication here is that the simulation will indicate the one alternative that is clearly dominant.

The Monte Carlo problem presented here is by no means complex. Other possible techniques might have provided the same answer. There are, however, situations where the variables become so complex, numerous, and interrelated that simulation is the only satisfactory method for determining the outcome values. The complexity of the sample problem would be increased, for example, if we added the

FIGURE B–10
Simulated daily order arrivals for Evertrue, Inc.

Day	Random number	Number of orders	Lost orders per number of machines rented			
			0	1	2	3
1	87	3	3	2	1	
2	51	1	1			
3	85	3	3	2	1	
4	36	1	1			
5	15	0	0			
6	31	1	1			
7	53	1	1			
8	22	1	1			
9	02	0	0			
10	42	1	1			
11	33	1	1			
12	51	1	1			
13	14	0	0			
14	20	1	1			
15	21	1	1			
16	01	0	0			
17	70	2	2	1		
18	30	1	1			
19	86	3	3	2	1	
20	27	1	1			
21	70	2	2	1		
22	57	1	1			
23	09	0	0			
24	99	4	4	3	2	1
25	81	2	2	1		
26	45	1	1			
27	63	2	2	1		
28	61	2	2	1		
29	94	3	3	2	1	
30	53	1	1			
Totals			41	16	6	1

maintenance cost of machinery. This would be particularly true if the cost would vary by frequency of use over time, or if some rented machines differed in failure rates. In such situations, additional numbers would be randomly selected to represent the natural occurence of these events.

In business, most simulation models utilizing the Monte Carlo technique are computer oriented since many trials can be completed in short periods of time. With a computer, the variables can also be changed easily to determine different outcomes. In any case, the attempt is to arrive at a satisfactory decision through a model that replicates a real system.

FIGURE B–11
Expense and lost profits related to the number of machines rented for
Evertrue, Inc.

	Number of machines rented			
	0	*1*	*2*	*3*
Machine rental expense, $25 per day	$ 0	$ 750	$1,500	$2,250
Profits given up due to lost orders	2,050	800	300	50
Totals................	$2,050	$1,550	$1,800	$2,300

PROBLEMS

1. If managers could predict the future with certainty, most decisions would be quite different from those that are actually made. Explain this statement in terms of production levels, the pricing of goods and services, stock market prices, and business failures.

2. The number of tire chains sold by a service station during the winter depends on the severity of weather conditions. Describe what would represent the alternatives and states of nature to the service station manager.

3. You have been given the chance to play a game in which you will receive 15 cents each time a fair coin comes up heads after it is tossed. Using expected monetary value, should you play the game if it cost you 10 cents per toss? Why?

4. Suppose you have the choice of making two investments of $100 each. Investment X yields 6 percent and the return on investment Y is 8 percent.

Required:

a. If the yields are certain and you are motivated to obtain the largest possible return, which choice would you make?
b. Assume the investments are risky, such that the probability of a return on X is 80 percent (0.80) and for Y, 50 percent (0.50). If you were motivated to obtain the largest possible return which choice would you make?

5. The purchasing manager of an auto supply house finds that 20 percent of a specific purchased part is defective. Each returned part is estimated to cost $1.25 in handling, transportation, and clerical expense.

Required:

a. What is the expected return cost per part purchased?
b. Would having this information be valuable to the managers of the company? (Explain).

6. The Able Company is considering the opening of a new sales route. The cost of servicing this route will be $3,000 per month, which includes wages to sales staff, transportation costs, and expense accounts. Able's president contemplates an expected gross profit of $20,000 per month if the route is

successful. In the past, new routes for the company have been successful about one out of eight times and at least 10 months of sustained sales effort have been required to determine the success or failure of a route. Calculate the expected value of the new route and indicate your advice to the president.

7. Funland Carnival Company must decide if it should stay in its present location for another two weeks or move to a new area. Various weather conditions determine the states of nature. The matrix and the probability of occurrence for each state of nature is shown below:

Alternatives	States of nature		
	S_1 (hot) (0.10)	S_2 (mild) (0.50)	S_3 (rainy) (0.40)
A_1	$-4,000	$3,000	$ 4,000
A_2	1,000	6,000	-2,000
A_3	-3,000	4,000	3,000

Required:

a. Prepare a table of expected monetary values and indicate the alternative that optimizes profits under conditions of risk.
b. What is the expected value of perfect information *(EVPI)?*

8. The merchandise manager for the Price Is Right Discount Store is planning to order fall sport coats for the men's department. Orders must be placed in lots of 25. Since demand is anticipated to be 50, 75, or 100, the alternatives considered are those of stocking 50, 75, or 100 sport coats. With this information, the following payoff matrix was determined:

Strategies (sport coats purchased)	States of nature (demand)		
	S_1	S_2	S_3
$A_1 = 50$	$1,500	$1,500	$1,500
$A_2 = 75$	1,000	2,250	2,250
$A_3 = 100$	500	1,750	3,000

Required:

a. Which strategy would be chosen using maximax criterion?
b. Which strategy would be chosen using maximin criterion?
c. Which strategy would be chosen using minimax criterion?
d. Which strategy would be chosen using insufficient reasoning criterion?

9. The Linear Manufacturing Company can produce parts X and Y, each requiring the use of two machines. When machine I is used, 4 minutes are needed to make part X and 4 minutes are needed to make part Y. For machine II, the comparable times are 2 minutes for part X and 6 minutes for part Y. During each working hour, 36 minutes of machine I time are available for scheduling and 42 minutes of machine II time may be used. This information is shown below in matrix format.

Machine	Minutes required to make parts		Machine minutes available each hour
	X	Y	
I	4	4	36
II	2	6	42

Required:

a. Illustrate graphically the area of feasible solutions in determining the optimum production quantities of parts X and Y.
b. If the contribution margin for part X is $8 and $12 for part Y, what product mix would optimize the total contribution margin?
c. Solve algebraically the point of intersection of the two constraints.

10. Materials are produced daily by the Zeb Paving Company at sites Y and Z for daily use at construction locations I and II. The following information is available:

Production site	Daily truck load production
Y..............	10
Z	20

Construction location	Truck load usage requirement
I	15
II	15

Cost of transportation per truck load:

From	To	
	I	II
Y	$12	$ 8
Z	8	10

Required:

Allocate the production at sites Y and Z to the usage requirements at locations I and II in order to minimize total transportation costs. What is the minimum transportation cost?

Appendix C
Using Time Series in Forecasting

Forecasting by time series analysis assumes that identified numerical relationships will persist in the future. As an integral part of the analysis, a trend line reflects the smooth progression of a particular phenomenon taking place over time. The time series data in Figure C–1 are represented by a straight line that assumes that past incremental changes will continue to occur until some point in the future. However, trend

FIGURE C–1
Trend line developed from hypothetical data plotted as a scatter diagram

Units (000)

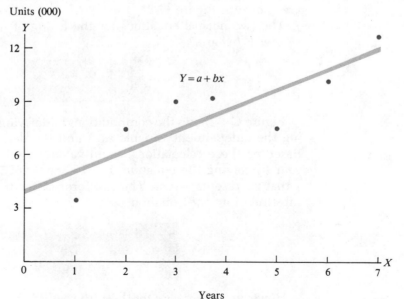

$Y = a + bx$

Years

The Y value is the amount of output, or dependent variable, that changes as x (represented as the time variable) changes. The a is a constant referred to as the Y intercept when $x = 0$ years, while b is the slope of the trend line that represents the rate of change of Y with each increase in x. In other words, for every one unit increase in x, there will be an increase in Y by a certain amount. When referring to a straight-line trend, the Y variable always increases by a constant amount with each one unit increase in x.

lines give insights into the future only if the associated variables continue to operate in the same way.

TREND ANALYSIS   A trend line may either be curved or straight. When it is drawn by visual inspection, the data by time frames is first plotted on graph paper (referred to as a scatter diagram) as seen in Figure C–1. Then a line is drawn so that there is equal deviation on both sides of the line. The scatter diagram is most useful in helping to determine if the line more nearly approximates a straight line or a curve. If arithmetic graph paper is used for the scatter diagram, it is best to work with straight lines, rather than with trend curves. Thus, when a change in the trend is indicated, a new line is drawn.

For a more precise method of determining trend, a mathematical approach called the *least square regression* method can be used. When the trend line is straight, it is represented by the equation: $Y = a + bx$. It can be used for both short-term forecasting (using quarterly data for at least the last five quarters) and for long-term forecasting data (using at least one recent business cycle that has prosperity and depressionary years well balanced).

As a forecasting method, the least squares regression technique can be demonstrated by using the tons of steel products shipped by a major steel company. These data and the derived straight-line trend are shown in Figure C–2.

The two normal equations for the fitting of the straight-line trend ($Y = a + bx$) are:

$$\Sigma Y = Na + \Sigma Xb \tag{1}$$
$$\Sigma XY = \Sigma Xa + \Sigma X^2 b \tag{2}$$

Figure C–3 shows the computations in deriving the trend line, treating the independent variable as X and the dependent variable as Y. Based on these calculations, trend values may be computed for each year by solving the equation $Y = 16.386 + .525(x)$ for each value of x that represents a year. Thus, to forecast for the 15th year, one can substitute into the equation:

$$Y = 16.386 + .525 (15) \text{ or}$$
$$Y = 16.386 + 7.875$$
$$Y = 24.261 \text{ for the 15th year}$$

However, the forecast for the 15th year is in no way a precise forecast for the period. This may be illustrated by going back to Figure C–3. In calculating the trend line, the last two years of 1979 (year 12) and 1980 (year 13) were omitted from computations. In this manner, one can determine how well the trend will forecast any periods that are

FIGURE C–2
Straight-line trend fitted to steel products shipped by a steel company

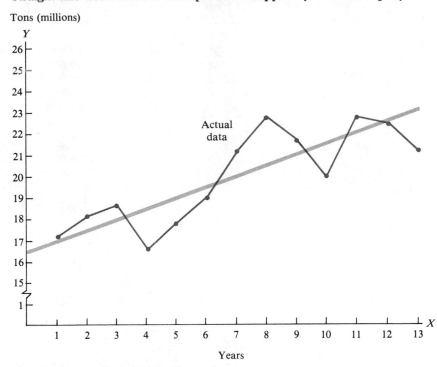

Tons (millions)

omitted. It is quite evident in Figure C–2 that the trend forecasted the actual quite well in 1979. For 1980, however, the trend by itself would not have provided a reliable forecast.

Trend projections, therefore, do not apply to a given year, but to an average year based on designated past years. For yearly actual data, very few points fall exactly on the line. Consequently, for a more precise forecast, data must be adjusted for the business cycle.[1] For instance, if a manager believes that general business conditions will be down 10 percent, then the forecast should be revised downward to reflect possible effects of the business cycle. In arriving at the impact of cyclical influences, managers have several approaches available to them. These include the use of various business cycle indicators, such as stock market prices, retail sales, manufacturers' new orders for durable goods, and so forth. Information about cyclical changes is also available from various sources published by governmental and private organizations.[2]

---

[1] For trend equations that are subject to changes in scale, yearly data may be changed to quarterly or monthly totals with some simple mathematical adjustment. See Samuel B. Richard, *Statistical Analysis* (New York: Ronald Press, 1964), p. 375.

[2] Norbert L. Enrick, *Market and Sales Forecasting* (San Francisco: Chandler Publishing, 1969). pp. 88–113.

FIGURE C–3
Solving the least squares regression function for a straight-line trend

Year N	X	Y	X(Y)	X^2
1968	1	17.0	17.0	1
1969	2	18.1	36.2	4
1970	3	18.7	56.1	9
1971	4	16.8	67.2	16
1972	5	17.8	89.0	25
1973	6	18.9	113.4	36
1974	7	21.2	148.4	49
1975	8	22.5	180.0	64
1976	9	21.6	194.4	81
1977	10	19.8	198.0	100
1978	11	22.5	247.5	121
Total	66	214.9	1347.2	506

1. The normal equations for fitting of the straight line are:

$$\Sigma Y = Na + \Sigma Xb \qquad (1)$$
$$\Sigma XY = \Sigma Xa + \Sigma X^2 b \qquad (2)$$

2. Substituting into the equations, we see that the function is:

$$214.9 = 11a = 66b \qquad (3)$$
$$1347.2 = 66a = 506b \qquad (4)$$

3. Solving the two equations simultaneously by multiplying equation (3) by six and subtracting (3) from (4) results in:

$$-1289.4 = -66a + 396b \qquad (5)$$
$$\underline{1347.2 = \quad 66a + 506b}$$
$$57.8 = \qquad\quad 110b \qquad (6)$$
$$b = .525$$

4. Substituting into (3) above, we get:

$$214.9 = 11a + (66 \times .525)$$
$$180.25 = 11a$$
$$a = 16.386$$

SEASONAL FLUCTUATION ADJUSTMENTS

An important adjustment to data reported on less than a yearly basis is that of *seasonality*. Seasonal phenomena are periodic since they recur within a uniform period of time. When data are in quarterly or monthly series, for example, they may be used to develop indexes showing seasonal variation. A popular technique used to arrive at a seasonal index is the "centered 12-month moving average." Briefly, the technique involves a comparison of actual monthly observations to an average of 12 months that is independent of seasonal variation. By developing ratios of the observations to the averages, a basis is established for the seasonal indexes. When the index is multiplied by the trend forecast, a more precise forecast is determined. This process is referred to as *synthesis*.

COMPONENTS OF THE FORECAST MODEL

The use of time series analysis in forecasting is mainly a mathematical approach. As a multiplicative model, it is so designed that it describes a vast number of forces according to their effects on certain phenomena. The model may be represented as $Y = T \times S \times C \times R$, where

$Y =$ Time series, the observed actual phenomenon
$T =$ Secular trend
$S =$ Seasonal variation
$C =$ Business cycle
$R =$ Residual variation, that is, anything that cannot be accounted for by T, S, and C.

As noted earlier, when the components are put together they produce the observed series of business data over a period of time. The data can be adjusted for seasonal variation by dividing by the seasonal index:

$$\frac{Y}{S} \quad \text{or} \quad \frac{T \times S \times C \times R}{S} = T \times C \times R$$

By dividing the data by trend values $\frac{(Y/S)}{(T)}$, the model is further adjusted to the following equation:

$$\frac{\frac{T \times S \times C \times R}{S}}{T} \quad \text{or} \quad \frac{T \times S \times C \times R}{S \times T} = C \times R$$

After dividing by seasonal and trend, cyclical and residual effects are expressed as percentages and have no unit value, such as units of production or dollar sales.

When both trend and seasonal variation have been taken out of time series, the data may be graphed as a straight horizontal line (100 percent) if no variations existed in C (business cycle) and R (residual factors). This is generally not the case; thus, variations in the data reflect the influence of the business cycle. Residual factors must also be read into the data and they are reflected as unusual events that have occurred, such as strikes, riots, natural phenomena, and so forth. There is no way to account for these factors mathematically.

A major problem in working with cyclical and residual factors is the lack of periodicity. This means that such factors are recurring but not on a periodic basis. For example, the noted 40-month business cycle with its 27-month upswing and 13-month downswing did not fit the U.S. experience from 1961 to 1980.

SLOAN AND JASON WHOLESALERS—AN EXAMPLE IN FORECASTING

Sloan and Jason Wholesalers sell a major line of mens' and womens' nonfashion, soft goods along with high-quality seasonal fashionable-type items. In order to plan operations for next year in terms of personnel requirements, working capital, and purchases, the president of the company decided that a forecast of sales for the succeeding year would have to be made. Based on the past three years of actual sales, Jason developed the following trend equation for the middle of 1979:

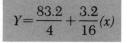

$$Y = \frac{83.2}{4} + \frac{3.2}{16}(x)$$

By using the "centered 12-month moving average" method, Sloan arrived at a seasonal index that he felt was adequate for explaining the seasonal variations of the company:

First quarter......................	60
Second quarter	100
Third quarter.....................	100
Fourth quarter	140

Multiplying the trend values times the seasonal index, a projection of "normal" was determined for the coming year, as noted in Figure C–4. Also shown in the figure is the pattern of cyclical influences that is determined by dividing actual sales by "normal" sales. Utilizing this calculation, it is assumed that the cyclical percentages are primarily a result of the business cycle, rather than irratic and random residual

FIGURE C–4
Forecasting procedure used by Sloan-Jason Wholesalers (in $100,000s)

Year and quarter	Actual sales	Trend values	Normal sales (season × trend)	Cyclical pattern (actual as a percent of normal)
1978				
1	12.0	19.7	11.8	101.7%
2	20.7	19.9	19.9	104.0
3	21.5	20.1	20.1	107.0
4	30.8	20.3	28.4	108.5
1979				
1	14.3	20.5	12.3	116.3
2	25.0	20.7	20.7	120.8
3	25.4	20.9	20.9	121.5
4	35.0	21.1	29.5	118.6
1980				
1	14.0	21.3	12.8	109.4
2	22.0	21.5	21.5	102.3
3	21.0	21.7	21.7	96.8
4	28.0	21.9	30.7	91.2

FIGURE C–5
Sales forecast by quarters, Sloan-Jason Wholesalers 1981 (in $100,000s)

(1)	(2)	(3)	(4)
			Final projection
	Trend	Normal	(trend × seasonal
Quarter	values	(trend × seasonal)	× cyclical)
1	22.1	13.3	$12.17
2	22.3	22.3	20.63
3	22.5	22.5	21.26
4	22.7	32.4	31.59
Total yearly estimated sales	—	—	$85.65

Source: Figure C–4.

factors. The cyclical pattern, therefore, means that if actual sales are higher than normal sales for a particular quarter, the reason can be attributed to the prosperity reflected in general business conditions.

In an executive staff meeting, the president, sales manager, and company controller agreed that the downswing in the business cycle would bottom in 1980 and that in 1981 a gradual upswing would begin. Their feelings were based on the slower decline in the business cycle index and on articles in current publications and trade association journals. For the entire year of 1981, company sales were expected to be only about 94 percent of normal sales, based on the assumption that sales by quarters (1 through 4) will be 91.5 percent, 92.5 percent, 94.5 percent, and 97.5 percent of normal. The yearly forecast is shown in Figure C–5. It is derived by multiplying the cyclical index for each quarter times the quarterly "normal" values (column 3) and then adding the derived values for the four quarters.

VALUE OF THE FORECAST

With their 1981 sales projection of $8,565,000, executives of Sloan-Jason Company are in a position to do a more effective job in planning future operations. Purchases can be planned to meet customer demands without delays while holding inventories to manageable levels throughout the year.[3] By anticipating quarterly sales, customer demands can be met from current inventories, thereby reducing the threat of excess inventories that might have to be held or sold at considerably reduced prices. Finally, personnel requirements can be determined more accurately and cash requirements can be arranged prior to need.

[3] Chapter 17 discusses the role of management planning and inventory control by looking at the cost associated with inventory and the importance of projecting annual inventory needs.

INDEX

This book has been set CAP, in 10 and 9 point Gael, leaded 2 points. Part numbers are 36 point Avant Garde Book; chapter numbers are 54 point Avant Garde Book. Part and chapter titles are 24 point Avant Garde Book. The size of the type page is 36 by 48 picas.